THE UNITED STATES AND ITS NEIGHBORS

THE UNITED

SERIES AUTHORS

Val E. Arnsdorf, Professor,
  College of Education, University of Delaware,
  Newark, Delaware
Herbert J. Bass, Professor of History,
  Temple University, Philadelphia, Pennsylvania
Carolyn S. Brown, Late Principal,
  Robertson Academy School, Nashville,
  Tennessee
Richard C. Brown, Former Professor of History,
  State University of New York College at Buffalo
Patricia T. Caro, Assistant Professor of Geography,
  University of Oregon, Eugene, Oregon
Kenneth S. Cooper, Professor of History, Emeritus,
  George Peabody College for Teachers, Vanderbilt
  University, Nashville, Tennessee
Gary S. Elbow, Professor of Geography,
  Texas Tech University, Lubbock, Texas
Alvis T. Harthen, Professor of Early Childhood
  Education,
  West Georgia College, Carrollton, Georgia
Timothy M. Helmus, Social Studies Instructor,
  City Middle and High School, Grand Rapids,
  Michigan
Bobbie P. Hyder, Elementary Education
  Coordinator,
  Madison County School System, Hunstville,
  Alabama

Theodore Kaltsounis, Professor and Associate
  Dean,
  College of Education, University of Washington,
  Seattle, Washington
Richard H. Loftin, Former Director of Curriculum
  and Staff Development,
  Aldine Independent School District, Houston,
  Texas
Clyde P. Patton, Professor of Geography,
  University of Oregon, Eugene, Oregon
Norman J. G. Pounds, Former University Professor
  of Geography,
  Indiana University, Bloomington, Indiana
Arlene C. Rengert, Associate Professor of
  Geography,
  West Chester University, West Chester,
  Pennsylvania
Robert N. Saveland, Professor of Social Science
  Education,
  University of Georgia, Athens, Georgia
Edgar A. Toppin, Professor of History and Dean of
  the Graduate School,
  Virginia State University, Petersburg, Virginia

GRADE-LEVEL CONTRIBUTORS

Vivian L. Brown, Teacher,
  Silver Spur Elementary School, Rancho Palos Verdes,
  California
Viola Gonzalez, Teacher,
  Ryan Elementary School, Laredo, Texas
Lucy Hatch, Basic Skills Consultant,
  Region 14 Education Service Center, Abilene, Texas
Geoffrey Kashdan, Principal,
  New Jersey Regional Day School at Morris for
    Handicapped Children, Morristown, New Jersey
William Lentino, Fifth Grade Teacher,
  Lloyd Harbor Elementary School, Huntington, New York
Ray Ringley, Teacher,
  Coeburn Middle School, Coeburn, Virginia

Chapters 1 and 14 by Stan Christodlous, Executive Editor,
  Social Studies, Silver Burdett Company

STATES AND ITS NEIGHBORS

TIMOTHY M. HELMUS

Classroom Teacher, City Middle and High School, Grand Rapids, Michigan

VAL E. ARNSDORF Professor, College of Education,
University of Delaware, Newark, Delaware

EDGAR A. TOPPIN Professor of History and Dean of the Graduate School,
Virginia State University, Petersburg, Virginia

NORMAN J. G. POUNDS Former University Professor, Geography,
Indiana University, Bloomington, Indiana

SILVER BURDETT & GINN **MORRISTOWN, NJ** • **NEEDHAM, MA**

Atlanta, GA • Cincinnati, OH • Dallas, TX • Menlo Park, CA • Northfield, IL

CONTENTS

ATLAS

GRAPHS

DIAGRAMS

TABLES

TIME LINES

SPECIAL INTEREST MATERIALS

END-OF-CHAPTER SKILLS DEVELOPMENT

A LETTER TO YOU FROM THE AUTHORS

Dear Student:

We hope you will enjoy using this book that we have written for you. It is all about the countries of North and South America, especially your country, the United States.

You will learn about the first Americans who lived here, the explorers who came here, and the people from other lands who settled here. You will also learn the wonderful story of the birth and growth of a new nation—the United States of America. And you will see how the United States became a world leader.

In this book we have divided the United States into seven geographic regions. You will learn many interesting facts about these different parts of the country. In addition to the written material in The United States and Its Neighbors, there are maps, charts, tables, and many pictures to help you.

We hope you will come to appreciate the beauty and variety of the land and the people in your country and in the rest of the Western Hemisphere. We hope you will also learn that what people have done in the past affects us today, and that what we do today will affect the future.

Most of all, we hope that this will be an exciting year for you.

Sincerely,

Timothy M. Helmus

Dal Ansdorf

Edgar Allan Toppin

Norman J. G. Pounds

Tools for Learning About Your Country

CHAPTER

1 Reading Maps

Where Is It?

┌─VOCABULARY─────────────────┐
│ hemisphere   longitude   │
│ North Pole   Arctic Circle   │
│ Equator   Antarctic Circle   │
│ South Pole   Tropic of Cancer   │
│ continent   Tropic of Capricorn│
│ compass rose   meridian   │
│ latitude   Prime Meridian   │
└────────────────────────────┘

Our nation: a big, beautiful land   We live in one of the biggest countries in the world, the United States of America. We live in one of the most beautiful countries on earth, also. Few other nations have as many different and interesting kinds of people and places as ours. Poets and songwriters have written about the great size and beauty and the rich history of our land. You have probably sung this song many times.

O beautiful for spacious skies,
For amber waves of grain,
For purple mountain majesties
Above the fruited plain!
America! America! God shed His grace on
    thee
And crown thy good with brotherhood
From sea to shining sea!

O beautiful for patriot dream
That sees beyond the years
Thine alabaster cities gleam,
Undimmed by human tears!
America! America! God shed His grace on
    thee

And crown thy good with brotherhood
From sea to shining sea!

Do you remember this song? Do you know what its words mean? The song is "America, the Beautiful." Its words were written in 1893 by an American teacher who was also a fine poet. Her name was Katharine Lee Bates. As you read this book, you will learn a great deal about what the poet meant when she wrote the words. You will learn about our people, our land, and our history.

Hemispheres   Let's begin our study of the United States by imagining that you and your family are planning a trip. You are going far away. What do you need to know in order to make your plans?

First, you will want to know just where you're going. Suppose your parents have said that you will be going to Yellowstone National Park. Unless you live near the park, have been there before, or have learned about national parks in school, you probably do not know where Yellowstone is. How might your parents go about telling you where it is?

They might begin by telling you that it is in the Northern Hemisphere (hem′ ə sfir). (See the Key to Pronunciation, page 476.) A **hemisphere** is one half of the earth's surface. (Words in heavy type are in the Glossary, pages 486–495.) The Northern Hemisphere includes all of the surface of

This photograph shows the rugged beauty of Yellowstone National Park.

the earth that lies between the **North Pole** and the **Equator**.

The North Pole is the most northern place in the world. North is the direction toward the North Pole. The North Pole is at the opposite end of the earth from the **South Pole.** The South Pole is the most southern place in the world. South is the direction toward the South Pole.

Halfway between the North Pole and the South Pole is the line called the Equator. The Equator circles the whole earth. Mapmakers use this line to divide the earth into the Northern Hemisphere and the Southern Hemisphere. You will learn more about the Equator a little later. Look at the maps at the top of page 5. These maps show the Northern Hemisphere and the Southern Hemisphere. Find Yellowstone National Park in the Northern Hemisphere.

There is another way to divide the earth into halves. It can be divided into a Western Hemisphere and an Eastern Hemisphere. Look at the maps at the bottom of page 5. In which of these two hemispheres do you find Yellowstone National Park?

When you face north, east is the direction to your right. West is to your left. East and west are opposite each other just as north and south are opposite each other.

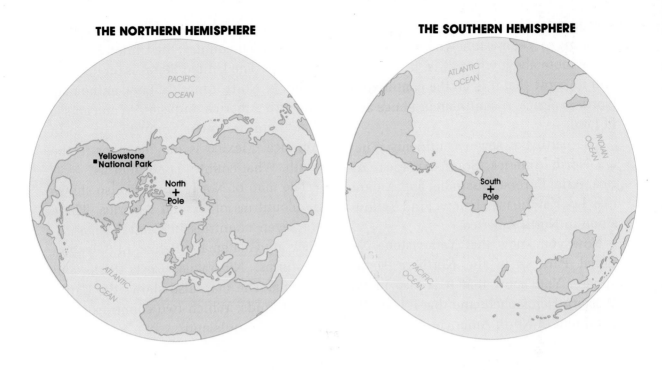

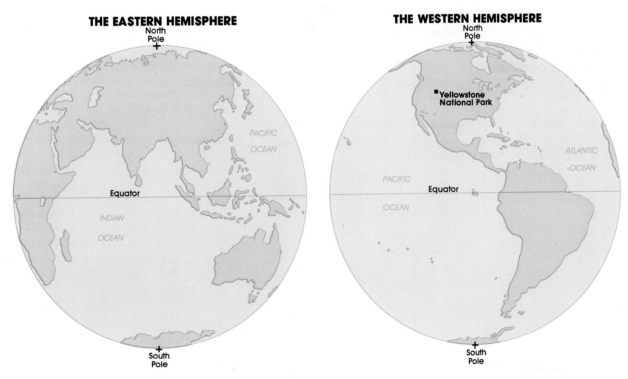

Dividing the earth at the Equator gives you the Northern Hemisphere and the Southern Hemisphere. Dividing the earth in half along a line passing through the North and South Poles results in the Eastern Hemisphere and the Western Hemisphere.

Continents   Of course, if you are traveling to Yellowstone you will have to know more about where it is. It will help you to know that it is on the **continent** of North America. A continent is a huge area of land.

The earth has seven continents. They are North America, South America, Africa, Asia, Europe, Australia, and Antarctica. Look at the map below. Find Yellowstone in North America.

Now you know that Yellowstone National Park is in the Northern Hemisphere. You know that it is also in the Western Hemisphere and that it is on the continent of North America.

Countries   Yellowstone National Park is also in our country, the United States of America. The United States is on the continent of North America. Look at the map of North America on page 7. You can see that there are other countries in North America. Mexico is our neighbor to the south. What country is north of us?

The map of North America also shows the countries of Central America. There are seven countries in Central America. They are Guatemala, Belize, El Salvador, Honduras, Nicaragua, Costa Rica, and Panama. The map also shows the Caribbean Islands. Which two countries share one Caribbean Island?

Find the four major oceans of the world on this map. What are their names? Sometimes people think of Europe and Asia as one continent. They call it Eurasia.

THE EARTH'S CONTINENTS

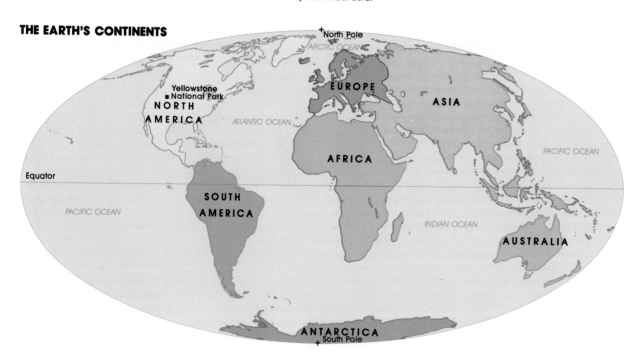

The map on page 7 shows countries and capital cities of North America. The islands of the Caribbean Sea are part of North America, but there isn't enough room on the map to label all the countries and capitals there. What is the capital of Mexico?

6

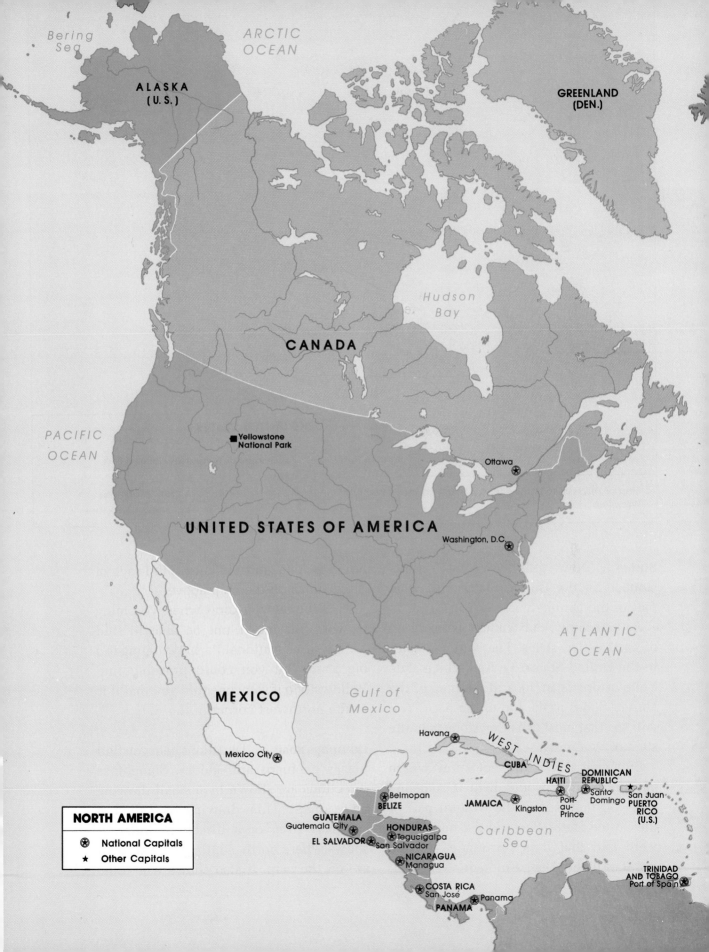

Bering
Sea

ARCTIC
OCEAN

ALASKA
(U. S.)

GREENLAND
(DEN.)

Hudson
Bay

CANADA

PACIFIC
OCEAN

Yellowstone
National Park

Ottawa
✪

UNITED STATES OF AMERICA

Washington, D.C.
✪

ATLANTIC
OCEAN

MEXICO

Gulf of
Mexico

Havana
✪

WEST INDIES

Mexico City ✪

CUBA

DOMINICAN
REPUBLIC

HAITI

Belmopan
✪

BELIZE

GUATEMALA
Guatemala City ✪

EL SALVADOR

HONDURAS
✪ Tegucigalpa
San Salvador ✪

JAMAICA
✪
Kingston

Port-
au-
Prince
✪

Santo
Domingo
✪

San Juan ★
PUERTO
RICO
(U.S.)

Caribbean
Sea

NICARAGUA
✪
Managua

COSTA RICA
✪ San José

Panama ✪

TRINIDAD
AND TOBAGO
Port of Spain

PANAMA

NORTH AMERICA

✪	National Capitals
★	Other Capitals

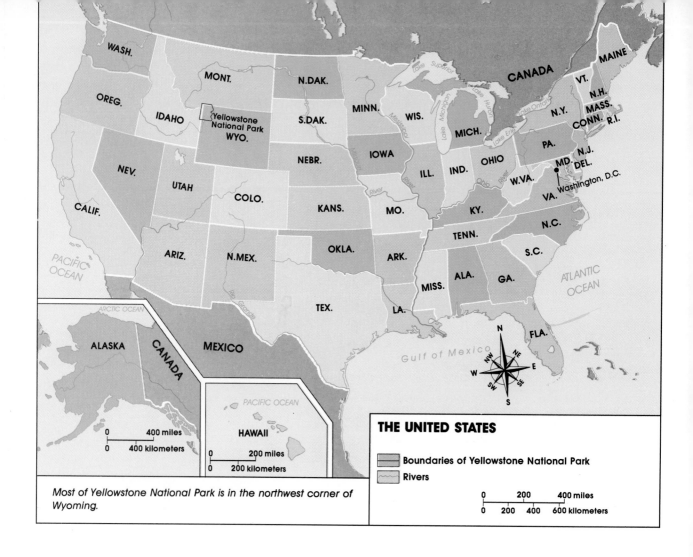

Most of Yellowstone National Park is in the northwest corner of Wyoming.

States   Now you know that Yellowstone is in the United States. But what part of the United States is it in?

As you know, our country is made up of parts called states. There are 50 states in the United States. To find which state Yellowstone is in, look at the map of the United States at the top of the page. You will see that most of Yellowstone is in the state of Wyoming.

But what if you did not know where Wyoming is? It would help if someone told you that it is in the western part of the United States. It would also help if you were told that it is surrounded by the states of Idaho, Utah, Colorado, Nebraska,

South Dakota, and Montana. Find each of these states on the map above.

Even though you know where Wyoming is, you still might not be able to find Yellowstone National Park. Wyoming is a big state. But you could probably find Yellowstone if someone told you that it is in the northwest corner of the state.

Compass rose   Directions help you find places on maps and globes. Sometimes directions are shown by a small drawing on a map. This drawing is called a **compass rose,** or a direction finder. It shows where north, south, east, and west are on the map. It also shows where the in-between directions are. It shows you how to find northwest (NW), northeast (NE), southwest (SW), and southeast (SE). On the map on page 8 find Yellowstone National Park in the northwest corner of Wyoming.

Latitude   A more exact way to tell you where to find a place is to give you its **latitude** and **longitude.** Look at the map on this page. The lines drawn on this map are called lines of latitude. You can see that these lines stretch east and west.

You have already learned the name of a very important line of latitude. It is the Equator. You know that the Equator is halfway between the North Pole and the South Pole. The lines of latitude north of the Equator are called lines of north latitude. The lines south of the Equator are called lines of south latitude.

The Equator itself is numbered 0. All other lines of latitude measure distances north or south of the Equator. These distances are measured in degrees. The sign for degrees is °. So the Equator is always marked 0° and is read "zero degrees." Find the Equator on the map on this page. Now find the line marked 15°N. This is read "15 degrees north." How do you read 15°S? 30°N? 30°S?

There are other lines of latitude that have names. Two of them are the **Arctic Circle** and the **Antarctic Circle.** The Arctic Circle is at 66½° north. The Antarctic Circle is at 66½° south. The other two named lines are the **Tropic of Cancer** and the **Tropic of Capricorn.** The Tropic of Cancer is at 23½° north. The Tropic of Capricorn is at 23½° south. Find these four lines on the map.

THE IN-BETWEEN DIRECTIONS

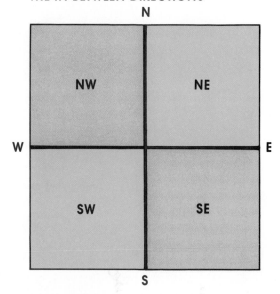

The letters NW stand for northwest. What does NE stand for? SE? SW? What are the 5 named lines of latitude on the map below?

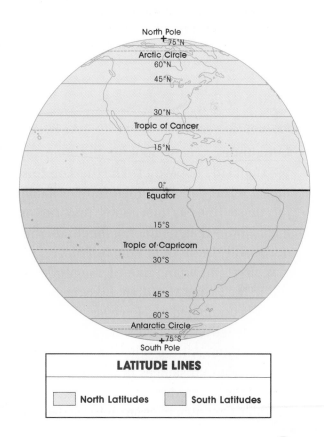

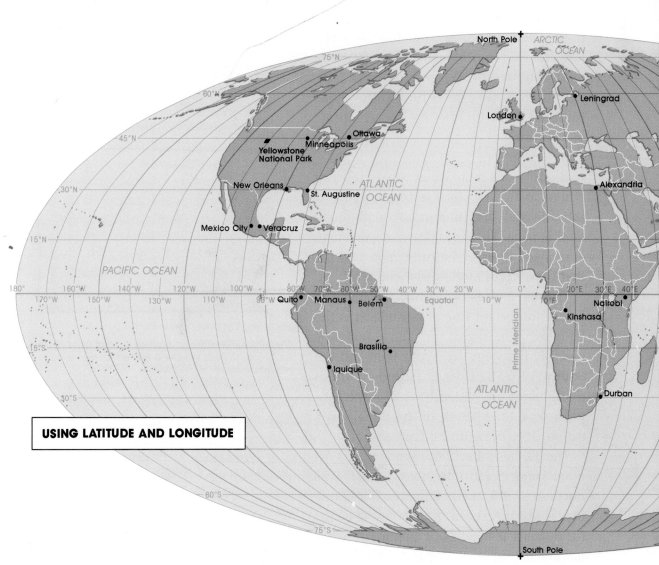

Map labels:
North Pole · ARCTIC OCEAN · Leningrad · 75°N · 60°N · London · Ottawa · 45°N · Minneapolis · Yellowstone National Park · Alexandria · 30°N · New Orleans · St. Augustine · ATLANTIC OCEAN · Mexico City · Veracruz · 15°N · PACIFIC OCEAN · 180° · 160°W · 170°W · 150°W · 140°W · 130°W · 120°W · 110°W · 100°W · 90°W · 80°W · 70°W · 60°W · 50°W · 40°W · 30°W · 20°W · 10°W · 0° · 10°E · 20°E · 30°E · 40°E · Quito · Manaus · Belém · Equator · Nairobi · Kinshasa · Prime Meridian · 15°S · Brasília · Iquique · Durban · 30°S · ATLANTIC OCEAN · 60°S · 75°S · South Pole

USING LATITUDE AND LONGITUDE

Longitude Now look at the map on the right side of page 11. The lines on this map are lines of longitude. Another name for these lines is **meridians** (mə rid′ ē ənz). Notice that the lines of longitude run north and south, from Pole to Pole.

A very important line of longitude is called the **Prime Meridian.** Like the Equator, it is numbered 0°. However, the Equator is 0° latitude. The Prime Meridian is 0° longitude. All the other lines of longitude measure distances in degrees east or west of the Prime Meridian. This line passes through Greenwich (gren′ ich), a part of

London, England. Half of all lines of longitude are west of Greenwich. The others are east of Greenwich.

Using latitude and longitude Now you know something about lines of latitude and longitude. Let us see how they can help you locate Yellowstone.

A good way to tell you how to find Yellowstone is to say that it is at 45° north latitude and 110° west longitude. Look at the map above. This map of the world shows both lines of longitude and lines of latitude. Put one finger on the line marked

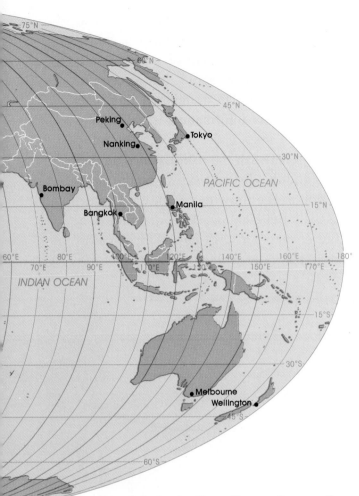

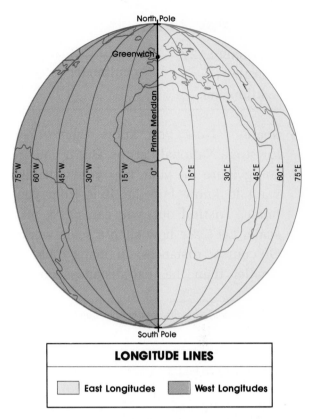

LONGITUDE LINES

	East Longitudes		West Longitudes

The Prime Meridian divides the world into east longitudes and west longitudes. Find the latitude and longitude of each city shown on the world map.

45° north latitude. Put a finger of your other hand on the line marked 110° west longitude. Now move your fingers toward each other on these lines. The place where these two lines meet is Yellowstone National Park.

In telling someone where Yellowstone National Park is, you could say, "It is in the northwest corner of the state of Wyoming. Wyoming is in the United States. The United States is on the continent of North America. North America is in the Western Hemisphere." But you can see how much more exact it is to say that Yellowstone National Park can be found at 45° north latitude and 110° west longitude.

Find Yellowstone in the Gazetteer, pages 476–485. Notice how the latitude and longitude is given. This form is used for most of the places listed.

You can find any place in the world on a map if you know its latitude and longitude. Almost all globes and maps have these lines marked to help you locate places quickly and easily.

CHECKUP
1. In which hemispheres is Yellowstone found?
2. On which continent is the United States found?
3. In which state is Yellowstone found?
4. Which lines measure distances north and south of the Equator?
5. Which lines measure distances east and west of the Prime Meridian?

11

How Far Is It?

┌─VOCABULARY──────────────────┐
│ scale   centimeter │
│ kilometer   │
└───────────────────────────────┘

Scale Now you know where Yellowstone National Park is. But if you are going there on your trip you will also want to know how far it is from your home. To find out, you can use a map **scale.** Let's see how such a scale works. Of course, distances on maps must be smaller than the real distances on the earth. So a certain number of inches on a map stand for a certain number of miles on the earth. On a map of a very small area, 1 inch can stand for a certain number of feet. The numbered line that gives you this information is called the scale. The map scale tells you the relationship between the real distance on the earth and the distance shown on the map.

Look at the drawing of a Little League baseball field below. This drawing is a kind of map. On this map, 1 inch stands for 50 feet. The scale at the bottom of the

The scale tells you the relationship between the real distance on the earth and the distance shown on the map.

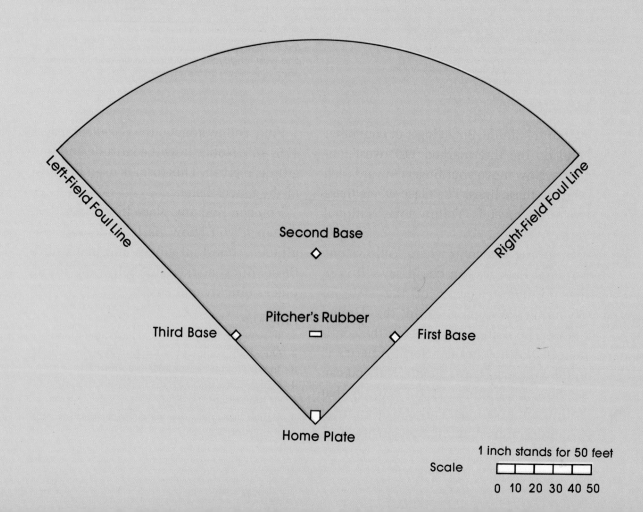

LITTLE LEAGUE FIELD

Left-Field Foul Line

Right-Field Foul Line

Second Base

Pitcher's Rubber

Third Base

First Base

Home Plate

1 inch stands for 50 feet

Scale

0 10 20 30 40 50

THE METRIC SYSTEM OF MEASUREMENT

In the section below, you will read that one kilometer (km) and a little more than half a mile are about the same distance. A kilometer is a unit of measure in the metric system.

This system is used for measuring distance. It is also used for measuring such things as weight, capacity, and heat. The metric system is in use or being introduced in all the major countries of the world except the United States. Someday the United States will probably "go metric" also.

To prepare you for this change, we have used both U.S. and metric measurements in this book. When a U.S. measurement appears in this book, it is followed in parentheses ( ) by the metric measurement that is about equal to it. Inches are changed to centimeters (cm), feet and yards to meters (m), miles to kilometers (km), and acres to hectares (ha). Pounds are changed to kilograms (kg), and quarts to liters (L). Degrees Fahrenheit (°F) are changed to degrees Celsius (°C).

map tells you that. Place a ruler along the right-field foul line. You will see that it is 4 inches from home plate to the end of the right-field foul line.

Remember, each inch on the map stands for 50 feet on a real baseball field. To find out how far it is from home plate to the end of the right-field foul line, you multiply 4 by 50. By doing this you will see that on a real Little League baseball field, home plate is 200 feet from the end of the right-field foul line.

Miles and kilometers On pages 14–15 is a map of the United States. Look at the map scale. Notice that this map scale gives distances in **kilometers** (kil′ ə mē tərz) as well as in miles. Kilometers are a measure of distance in the *metric system*. A kilometer (km) is a little more than half a mile. You can find out more about the metric system above.

On this map 1 inch stands for 200 miles. The map scale also tells you that 2 **centimeters** (cm) stand for 250 kilometers. Find Yellowstone on the map. Now

find Washington, D.C., our nation's capital. Lay a ruler between Washington, D.C., and Yellowstone National Park. You will see that the distance on the map is about 8½ inches. You know that the scale on this map is 200 miles to an inch. So by multiplying 8½ by 200, you find that it is 1,700 miles from Washington, D.C., to Yellowstone National Park.

Find your state on the map on pages 14–15. Then find your community. No map can show every city and town in the United States. Don't be surprised if yours is not on the map. Just find on the map the city you think is nearest to where you live. Using what you know about scale, find out how many miles it is to Yellowstone. How many kilometers is it?

CHECKUP

1. What part of a map helps you find out how far one place is from another?
2. How long is a kilometer?
3. Kilometers and centimeters are units of measure in what system?

THE UNITED STATES OF AMERICA

Key
- ⊛ Rivers
- ⊛ National Capital
- ⊛ State Capitals
- • Other Cities
- ▬ Boundaries of Yellowstone National Park

0   100   200 miles
0   100   200   300 kilometers

15

The Language of Maps

Map key and symbols   Look at the map of Yellowstone National Park on page 17. Find the map **key.** As you probably know, the map key is one of the most important parts of any map. This part of a map is called the key because it unlocks the map's secrets for you. It also tells you about all the **symbols** used on the map.

Maps use symbols, or signs, to show where places are and to tell you something about them. Sometimes letters are used as symbols. Sometimes small pictures are used. All the symbols stand for

Old Faithful is a geyser. It shoots steamy water into the air once every hour.

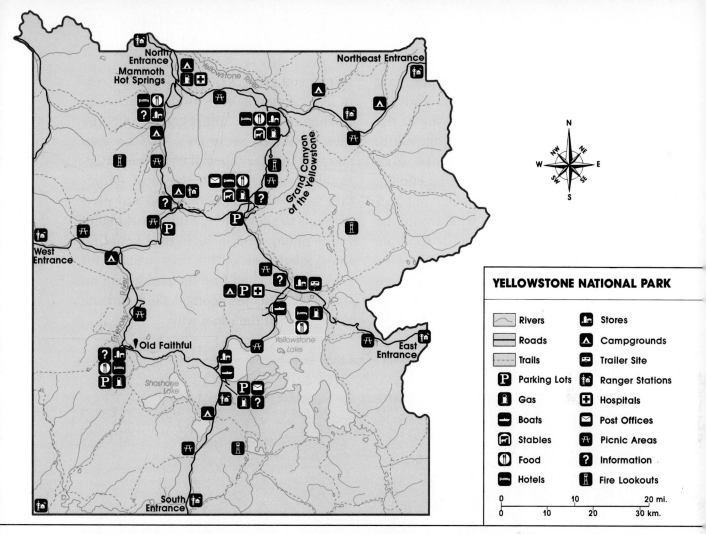

YELLOWSTONE NATIONAL PARK

Symbol	Meaning	Symbol	Meaning
	Rivers		Stores
	Roads		Campgrounds
	Trails		Trailer Site
P	Parking Lots		Ranger Stations
	Gas		Hospitals
	Boats		Post Offices
	Stables		Picnic Areas
	Food	?	Information
	Hotels		Fire Lookouts

0   10   20 mi.

0   10   20   30 km.

Yellowstone National Park was the first national park in our nation. It was made a national park in 1872.

real things and places. The map key tells you just what real things and places the symbols stand for. For example, a cross is one symbol in the key on the map of Yellowstone National Park above. If you were to go to each place marked on the map with a cross, you would find a real hospital. What symbol would you look for if you wanted to find a picnic area? What symbol would you look for if you wanted to find a parking lot? A ranger station?

Labels   Quite often map symbols do not tell you everything you might want to know. If you want to find Yellowstone Lake on the map above, the key will not help you. There is no symbol for lake in the key. You will have to look at the lakes on the map and find the one labeled "Yellowstone Lake." On page 16 is a picture of Old Faithful. Look on the map above to find the label that shows where Old Faithful is.

The map key shows you the symbol for rivers. But the key does not tell you the names of the rivers in Yellowstone National Park. To find a certain river you have to look for its label on the map. Find the Firehole River on the map.

Drawing a map   In this chapter, you have seen many maps. As you know, a map is a special kind of drawing of the earth's surface. It shows what the earth, or part of the earth, looks like from straight overhead. If you were far enough out in space, you could see about one half of the earth's surface. But what would the earth look like if you were only a couple of thousand feet (600 m) above it?

The photograph on page 19 was taken from about 1,500 feet (460 m) above the earth's surface. The map on page 19 shows you what a **cartographer** (kär tog′ rə fər), or mapmaker, can do with such a photograph. The photograph and the map show the same area. But the map shows it in a very special way. The cartographer has picked out the most important features of the photograph and used symbols to show them. Find a parking lot in the photograph. Look in the key to find the symbol used on the map to stand for parking lots. Then find the parking lot on the map. Find the football field and the water tank in the same way.

This is one of the cartographers who made the maps in this book. He is working on the map shown on page 19.

FROM PHOTOGRAPH TO MAP

0   100   200 Feet
0   50 Meters

Legend		
Houses	Running Track	Baseball Diamonds
Roads	Tennis Courts	School Buildings
Woods	Football Field	School Grounds
Water Tank	Soccer Field	Other Land
Parking Lots	Basketball Court	

N NW NE E W SW SE S

Road map symbols   Many people in the United States travel by car. In 1982 there were about 107 million cars in this country. If you go to Yellowstone National Park, there is a good chance that you will go by car. Suppose someone handed you a road map and said, "What roads will you take?" Could you read the map? If not, you should learn, because road maps can help you in many ways.

If you go to Yellowstone you may want to take the widest road you can find. Wide highways have many lanes for cars to travel on. Highways with many lanes are sometimes called *expressways*. Cars can move along on them without having to stop for traffic lights. *Interstate highways* are expressways. Interstate highways are roads that connect two or more states. Some of these big highways run through many states.

Look at the map key on page 21. Then on the map find Routes 16, 34, 80, and 85. Which is wider, Route 16 or Route 85? Route 80 or Route 34? What symbols in the map key and on the map helped you answer? You can see how important it is to understand the symbols on a road map.

This map also uses symbols to show the size of cities. Find Casper on the map. It is on Route 220. Notice that the symbol used to show Casper is a larger yellow dot. By looking at the key you will see that this means that Casper has a **population** of between 25,000 and 60,000. In other words, between 25,000 and 60,000 people live in the city of Casper.

Remember, symbols stand for real things and places. What other information can the symbols on this map give you?

This camper is traveling on a road in Grand Teton National Park in Wyoming. Find this park on the map on page 21. Which road might the camper be using?

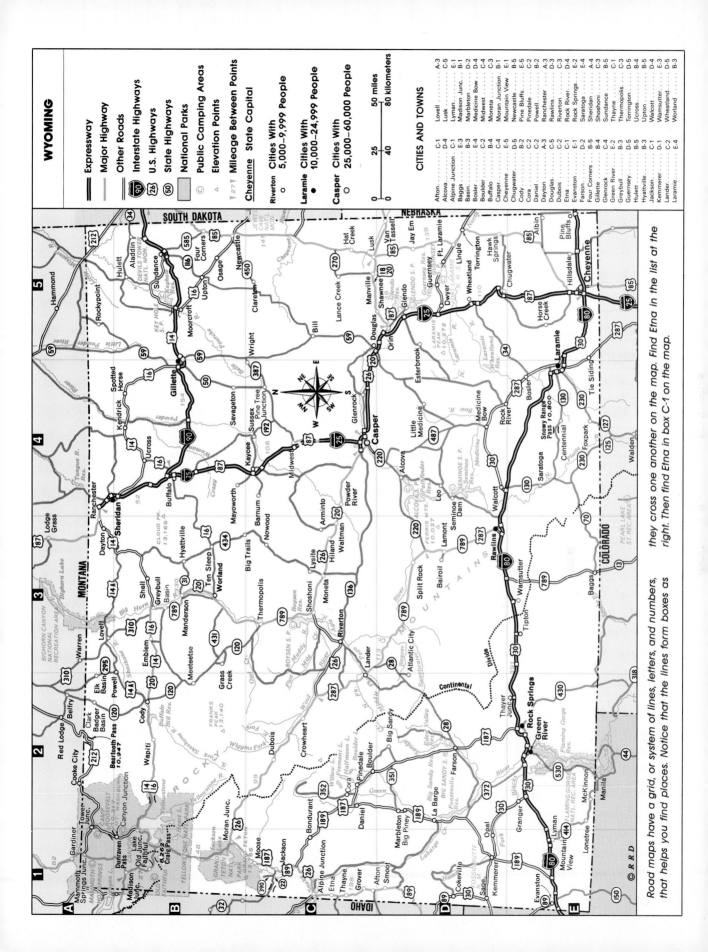

WYOMING

▬▬▬	Expressway
▬▬▬	Major Highway
▬▬▬	Other Roads
🛡90	Interstate Highways
⬤26	U.S. Highways
⬤50	State Highways
	National Parks
Ⓒ	Public Camping Areas
▲	Elevation Points
▼27▼	Mileage Between Points
Cheyenne	State Capital

Riverton ○ Cities With 5,000–9,999 People

Laramie ⬤ Cities With 10,000–24,999 People

Casper ⬤ Cities With 25,000–60,000 People

0	25	50 miles
0	40	80 kilometers

CITIES AND TOWNS

Afton	C-1
Alcova	D-4
Alpine Junction	C-1
Baggs	E-3
Basin	B-3
Bosler	D-4
Boulder	C-2
Buffalo	B-4
Casper	C-4
Cheyenne	D-5
Chugwater	D-5
Cody	B-2
Cora	C-2
Daniel	C-2
Dayton	A-3
Douglas	C-5
Dubois	C-2
Etna	C-1
Evanston	E-1
Farson	D-2
Four Corners	A-4
Gillette	B-4
Glenrock	C-4
Green River	E-2
Greybull	B-3
Guernsey	D-5
Hulett	B-5
Hyattville	B-3
Jackson	C-1
Kemmerer	D-1
Lander	C-2
Laramie	E-4
Lovell	A-3
Lusk	C-5
Lyman	E-1
Madison Junc.	B-1
Marbleton	D-2
Medicine Bow	D-4
Midwest	C-4
Moneta	C-3
Moran Junction	B-1
Mountain View	E-1
Newcastle	B-5
Pine Bluffs	D-5
Pinedale	C-2
Powell	A-3
Ranchester	A-3
Rawlins	D-3
Riverton	C-3
Rock River	D-4
Rock Springs	E-2
Saratoga	D-4
Sheridan	A-4
Shoshoni	C-3
Sundance	B-5
Thayne	C-1
Thermopolis	B-3
Torrington	D-5
Ucross	B-4
Walcott	D-4
Wamsutter	E-3
Wheatland	D-5
Worland	B-3

Road maps have a grid, or system of lines, letters, and numbers, that helps you find places. Notice that the lines form boxes as they cross one another on the map. Find Etna in the list at the right. Then find Etna in box C-1 on the map.

© R R D

Mileage Chart	Boston	Chicago	Dallas	Denver	Kansas City	Los Angeles	Miami	Montreal	New Orleans	New York	St. Louis	San Francisco	Seattle	Washington, D.C.
Chicago	990		960	995	510	2120	1370	850	945	790	285	2195	2020	705
Dallas	1805	960		780	495	1425	1370	1780	505	1565	650	1785	2165	1375
Denver	1990	995	780		600	1170	2135	1900	1295	1760	875	1270	1385	1645
Kansas City	1420	510	495	600		1610	1530	1320	830	1185	255	1890	1925	1050
Los Angeles	3085	2120	1425	1170	1610		2820	2985	1920	2765	1820	390	1180	2725
Miami	1565	1370	1370	2135	1530	2820		1680	870	1300	1265	3160	3425	1115
Montreal	310	850	1780	1900	1320	2985	1680		1665	370	1100	3060	2800	585
New Orleans	1550	945	505	1295	830	1920	870	1665		1320	710	2295	2695	1115
New York	215	790	1565	1760	1185	2765	1300	370	1320		950	2930	2825	220
St. Louis	1160	285	650	875	255	1820	1265	1100	710	950		2140	2175	805
San Francisco	3190	2195	1785	1270	1890	390	3160	3060	2295	2930	2140		825	2875
Seattle	2950	2020	2165	1385	1925	1180	3425	2800	2695	2825	2175	825		2845
Washington, D.C.	445	705	1375	1645	1050	2725	1115	585	1115	220	805	2875	2845	
Yellowstone N.P.	2410	1385	1310	575	1135	1105	2560	2125	1860	2135	1380	985	785	2065

How far is it from Miami to New York?

Road distances   Earlier you learned how to use a map scale to find out how far one point is from another. However, when you are going by car, just measuring the distance on a map may not work. The roads you take might not go in a straight line. You need another way to tell how far you have to drive.

Often road maps have **mileage charts.** Such a chart is shown above. It tells the number of *road miles* between one place and another.

Suppose you want to find the distance between Los Angeles, California, and Yellowstone. Find *Yellowstone* on the left side of the chart. Put a finger on *Yellowstone*. Now find *Los Angeles* at the top of the chart. Put a finger of your other hand on *Los Angeles*. Move both fingers, one across and one down, until they meet. They should meet at 1,105. That is the number of road miles between Los Angeles and Yellowstone. How far would you have to drive from Dallas, Texas, to Yellowstone?

CHECKUP

1. What do map symbols tell you?
2. What does *population* mean?
3. When you read a road map, why might you need a mileage chart in addition to a map scale?

Mass Transit

┌─VOCABULARY─────────────────┐
│ mass transit   schedule │
│ subway   express │
└────────────────────────────┘

Other ways to go   So far you have been learning about traveling by automobile. And many people do drive around our country. But there are other ways to visit the different parts of the United States. People can go by train, bus, or plane. The name for all these ways of travel is **mass transit.** *Mass* means "a great amount." *Transit* means "the moving of people or things from one place to another." Mass transit is a way of moving a great many people at the same time. You might use mass transit to go to and from school. Perhaps your parents use it to get to and from work. Mass transit gives people a way of going places without having to use an automobile.

Trains   There are about 335,000 miles (540,000 km) of railroad track in the United States. Our country is tied together by railroad lines that reach from the Pacific Ocean to the Atlantic Ocean and from Mexico to Canada. You can travel thousands of miles across the country by train.

Of course, many trains go only short distances. Some of these trains connect large cities like San Francisco, California, or New York City with smaller communities nearby.

Subways   Trains also help people get around in some of our country's large cities. Often these trains run under the ground. Then they are called **subways.** New York City; San Francisco; Chicago, Illinois; Philadelphia, Pennsylvania; Boston, Massachusetts; and Washington, D.C., all have subways.

This is part of the Metro system in Washington, D.C. Metro trains run above ground and underground.

People can take a bus and see their country. This bus is in Glacier National Park in Montana.

Buses   Buses, like trains, connect all parts of our country. People can visit almost every part of the United States by bus. As in a train, they can sit back in comfortable seats. They can watch our country's beautiful scenery pass by their windows.

Like trains, buses are helpful when traveling within a city. Most big cities have bus systems that take people from one part of their city to another.

Planes   People who want to get somewhere very quickly often fly. All of our big cities and many smaller cities and towns have airports.

Many airplanes that fly from city to city in the United States are huge. They carry about 375 people. They fly about 560 miles (900 km) an hour. Most planes fly so high that they are above the clouds. All you can see from the windows are white clouds below and blue sky above.

Schedules   When you want to take a train, bus, or plane, it is helpful to read a **schedule.** A schedule tells you when a train, bus, or plane leaves one place and arrives at another. Why is it important to know these facts?

The schedule shown on page 25 tells you about buses that go into and out of New York City. You will see that the numbers in red are for the **express** service. Express buses are those that make the fewest stops to pick people up or let them off. They take less time to get from one place to another than other buses.

If you left Hackettstown at 6:30 on an express bus, you would be in New York City by 8:00. The ride would take an hour and a half. However, if you left Hackettstown at 7:25 on a nonexpress bus, you would get into New York City at 9:20. That ride would take 1 hour and 55 minutes. It would take 25 minutes longer than the ride on the express bus.

Look at the schedule again. If you left Netcong at 2:10, what time would you be in New York City? Would you have been riding on an express or a nonexpress bus?

CHECKUP

1. Name three kinds of mass transit.
2. What is a subway?
3. What do schedules tell you?

LEAVE — MON. through FRI. — Westbound from N.Y.C. — ARRIVE

NEW YORK (LEAVE)	MT. VIEW CIRCLE	PINE BROOK	LINCOLN PARK	BOONTON	MT. LAKES RT. 46 & BLVD.	DENVILLE	ROCKAWAY	DOVER	MINE HILL KENVIL	SPARTA	LAKE HOPATCONG	NETCONG	MT. OLIVE BUDD LAKE	HACKETTSTOWN (ARRIVE)
7:00	7:25	7:35	—	—	7:45	7:50	7:55	8:00	—	—	—	—	—	—
7:30 / 7:45	7:55 / 8:10	8:20	8:05	8:20	8:30	8:30	8:35	8:40	—	—	8:45	8:50	9:00	—
8:00	8:25	8:35	—	—	8:45	8:50	8:55	9:00	—	—	—	—	—	—
8:30 / 8:45	8:55 / 9:25	9:05	—	9:20	9:45	9:30	(VIA RT. 80) 9:55 / 10:00	9:00	—	10:00	—	—	—	—
9:30	9:55 / 10:25	10:05 / 10:35	10:20	10:20	10:45	10:30 / 10:50	10:35 / 10:55	10:40 / 11:00	—	—	—	—	—	—
10:30 / 11:00	10:55 / 11:25	11:35	11:20	11:20	11:45	11:30 / 11:50	11:35 / 11:55	11:40 / 12:00	—	—	—	—	—	—
11:30 / 12:00	11:55 / 12:25	12:25	12:05	12:20	12:45	12:30 / 12:50	12:35 / 12:55	12:40 / 1:00	1:05	—	1:35	1:20	1:30	6:50
12:30 / 1:00	12:55 / 1:25	1:05 / 1:35	1:20	1:20	1:45	1:30 / 1:50	1:35 / 1:55	1:40 / 2:00	—	—	—	—	—	—
1:30	1:55 / 2:25	2:05 / 2:35	2:20	2:20	2:45	2:30 / 2:50	2:35 / 2:55	2:40 / 3:00	—	—	—	—	—	—
2:30 / 3:00	2:55 / 3:25	3:35	3:05	3:20	3:45	3:30 / 3:50	3:35 / 3:55	3:40 / 4:00	—	—	—	—	—	—
3:30 / 4:00	3:55 / 4:25	4:05 / 4:35	—	4:20	4:45	4:50	4:35 / 4:55	4:40	—	—	—	—	—	—
4:30 / 4:50	4:45 / 5:15	4:55 / 5:25	5:05	5:20	5:35	5:10 / 5:40	5:15 / 5:45	5:00 / 5:20	—	—	—	—	—	—
5:00 / 5:15	5:25	5:35	—	5:50	(EXPRESS) 6:15	5:40 / 6:00	6:05	5:40 / 5:50	(VIA RT. 80)	6:35	6:20	6:30	6:40	—
5:20 / 5:30	6:00 / 5:55	6:05	6:10	—	—	6:35 / 6:20	6:40 / 6:25	6:45 / 6:30	8:05	—	6:50	6:55	—	—
5:35 / 5:40	6:10 / 6:20	6:20 / 6:35	—	6:45	6:45	6:45 / 6:50	6:50 / 6:55	6:55 / 7:00	—	7:25	—	—	—	—
5:50 / 6:00	6:25 / 6:40	6:50 / 7:00	7:05	7:05	7:10	7:15 / 7:15	7:20 / 7:25	7:25	—	—	—	—	—	—
6:10 / 6:30	6:55 / 7:10	7:20 / 7:35	—	7:20	7:45	7:30 / 7:35	7:35 / 7:40	7:40 / 7:45	8:05	—	8:15	8:20	8:25	—
6:55 / 7:00	7:25 / 7:55	8:05 / 8:35	—	8:20	8:45	7:50 / 8:30	8:00 / 8:40	8:00 / 8:40	—	—	—	—	—	—
7:30 / 8:00	8:25 / 8:55	9:05 / 9:35	—	9:20	9:45	8:50 / 9:30	8:55 / 9:35	9:40	10:05	—	10:15	10:20	10:25	—
8:30 / 9:30	9:55 / 10:55	10:05 / 11:05	—	10:20 / 11:20	—	10:30 / 11:30	10:35 / 12:35	10:40 / 11:40	—	—	—	—	—	—
11:30 / 1:00	11:55 / 1:25	12:05 / 1:35	—	12:20 / 1:50	—	12:30 / 2:00	12:35 / 2:05	12:40 / 2:10	—	—	—	—	—	—

RUSH HOUR — NUMBERED CODE: 46, 1, 80, 99, 22, 46, 32, 10, 1-8, 46

LEAVE — MON. through FRI. — Eastbound to N.Y.C. — ARRIVE

HACKETTSTOWN	MT. OLIVE BUDD LAKE	NETCONG	LAKE HOPATCONG	SPARTA	MINE HILL KENVIL	DOVER	ROCKAWAY	DENVILLE	MT. LAKES RT. 46 & BLVD.	BOONTON	LINCOLN PARK	PINE BROOK (ARRIVE)	MT. VIEW CIRCLE (ARRIVE)	NEW YORK (ARRIVE)
—	—	—	—	—	—	5:30	5:40	5:45	—	—	—	6:00	6:10	6:40
—	—	—	—	—	—	5:45 / 6:00 / 6:15	5:55 / 6:10 / 6:25	6:00 / 6:15 / 6:30	5:48 / 6:33 / 6:58	6:10 / 6:25	6:40	6:25 / 6:45	6:35 / 6:50 / 6:55	7:05 / 7:20 / 7:25
—	6:45	6:50	6:55	6:25	—	6:30	6:40	6:45	—	6:35 / 6:55	—	7:00 / 7:25	7:10 / 7:35	7:20 / 7:45
—	—	—	—	—	—	6:45	6:55	7:00	—	—	7:30	7:30	7:40	7:45 / 8:00 / 8:05
—	—	—	—	—	—	7:00	7:10 (EXPRESS) 7:18	7:15	—	7:15	—	—	7:40	8:10 / 8:10
6:30	—	—	6:55	6:55	—	7:15 / 7:30 / 8:00 / 8:30	7:25 / 7:40 / 8:10 / 8:40	7:30 / 8:15 / 8:45	7:33 / 8:48	7:25 / 7:55 / 8:25	—	7:40 / 8:40 / 9:00	7:50 / 8:20 / 8:50 / 9:10	8:00 / 8:25 / 8:50 / 9:20 / 9:40
—	—	9:40	9:45	10:00	9:55	9:00 / 9:30 / 10:00 / 10:30	9:10 / 9:40 / 10:10 / 10:40	9:15 / 9:45 / 10:15 / 10:45	9:48 / 10:48	9:25 / 10:25	10:40	9:40 / 10:00 / 11:00	9:50 / 10:50 / 11:10	10:20 / 10:40 / 11:20 / 11:40
—	—	—	—	—	—	11:00 / 11:30 / 12:30	11:10 / 11:40 / 12:10 / 12:40	11:15 / 11:45 / 12:15 / 12:45	11:48 / 12:48	11:25 / 12:25	1:40	11:40 / 12:00 / 12:40	11:50 / 12:10 / 12:50	12:20 / 12:40 / 1:20
—	2:05	2:10	2:15	7:30	—	1:00 / 2:00 / 2:30 / 3:00	1:10 / 1:40 / 2:10 / 2:40 / 3:10	1:15 / 1:45 / 2:15 / 2:45 / 3:15	1:48 / 2:48	1:25 / 2:25 / 3:25	4:10	2:00 / 2:40 / 3:00 / 3:40	1:50 / 2:10 / 2:50 / 3:10 / 3:50	1:40 / 2:20 / 2:50 / 3:20 / 3:40
—	—	—	—	—	—	3:30 / 4:00 / 4:30	3:40 / 4:10 / 4:40	3:15 / 3:45 / 4:15 / 4:45	4:48	3:55 / 4:25	—	4:40	4:20 / 4:50	3:50 / 4:20 / 4:50
—	—	—	—	—	—	5:00 / 6:00 / 7:00	5:10 / 6:10 / 7:10	5:15 / 6:15 / 7:15 / 7:50	7:53	5:25 / 6:25 / 7:25	—	5:40 / 6:40 / 7:40 / 8:05	5:50 / 6:50 / 7:20 / 8:15	5:40 / 6:20 / 7:20 / 8:20 / 8:45
7:25	7:35	7:40	7:45	—	7:55	8:00 / 10:00	8:10 / 9:10 / 10:10	8:15 / 9:15 / 10:15	—	8:25 / 9:25 / 10:25	—	8:40 / 9:40 / 10:40	8:50 / 9:50 / 10:50	8:20 / 9:20 / 10:20 / 11:20
—	9:35	9:40	9:45	—	9:55	11:00 / 11:30	11:40	11:45	—	11:55	—	12:10	12:20	11:20 / 12:50

When would you be in New York City if you left Denville at 6:45 in the morning?

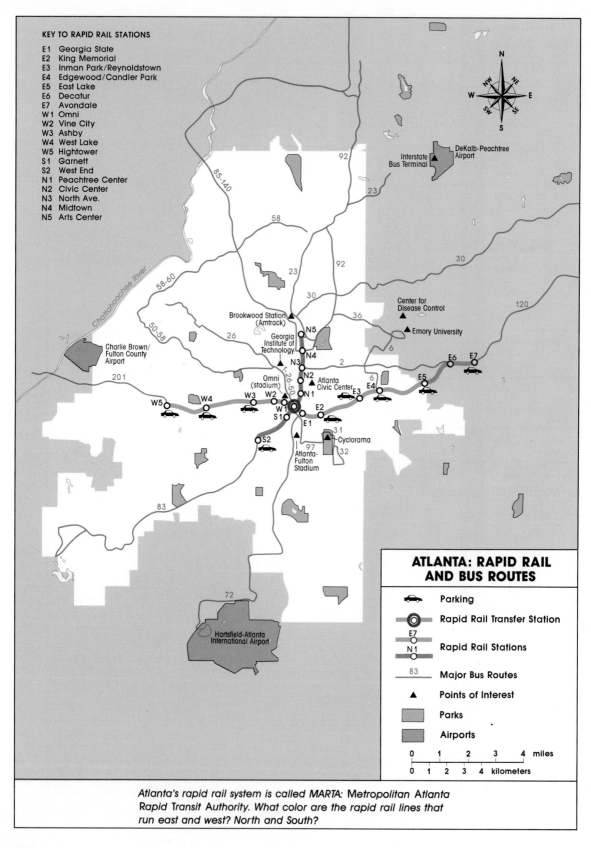

KEY TO RAPID RAIL STATIONS

E1 Georgia State
E2 King Memorial
E3 Inman Park/Reynoldstown
E4 Edgewood/Candler Park
E5 East Lake
E6 Decatur
E7 Avondale
W1 Omni
W2 Vine City
W3 Ashby
W4 West Lake
W5 Hightower
S1 Garnett
S2 West End
N1 Peachtree Center
N2 Civic Center
N3 North Ave.
N4 Midtown
N5 Arts Center

ATLANTA: RAPID RAIL AND BUS ROUTES

Parking

Rapid Rail Transfer Station

E7
Rapid Rail Stations
N1

83 Major Bus Routes

▲ Points of Interest

Parks

Airports

0 1 2 3 4 miles

0 1 2 3 4 kilometers

Atlanta's rapid rail system is called MARTA: Metropolitan Atlanta Rapid Transit Authority. What color are the rapid rail lines that run east and west? North and South?

Maps Are Important

┌─VOCABULARY──────────────────┐
│ resort   event   │
└─────────────────────────────┘

Living with maps   By this time, you should have a good idea about how important maps are for planning a trip. Yellowstone National Park is just one of the thousands of places in our country you might visit. And of course there are places in other countries that you might visit one day. If you can read a map, chances are you will not get lost. You might even find some other interesting places to visit that you didn't know about before.

There are many other times when you will find it helpful to read maps. It is not possible to show you all the maps that you might use in your life. It would take more pages than there are in this book to do that. However, there will be many times when a map will be useful. Here are some of them.

1. To find your way on the subway in New York City, Washington, D.C., San Francisco, or Atlanta
2. To find your seat at a football game at the Louisiana Superdome in New Orleans, or at Three Rivers Stadium in Pittsburgh, Pennsylvania
3. To find your seat at a basketball game at the Spectrum in Philadelphia or at the Boston Garden in Boston
4. To find the animals that you are most interested in at the zoo in St. Louis, Missouri, or in San Diego, California
5. To find the ride you want to go on at Walt Disney World in Orlando, Florida, or at Great Adventure in Jackson, New Jersey
6. To pick the ski trail you want to try at a ski **resort** in Aspen, Colorado; Stowe, Vermont; or Lake Placid, New York
7. To find the theater you are looking for at the Lincoln Center for the Performing Arts in New York City
8. To plan a tour of Colonial Williamsburg in Virginia

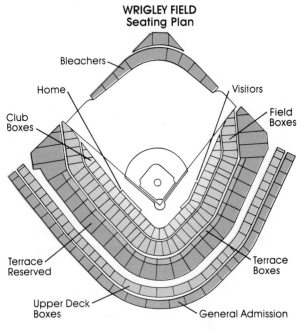

WRIGLEY FIELD Seating Plan

Bleachers

Home

Visitors

Club Boxes

Field Boxes

Terrace Reserved

Terrace Boxes

Upper Deck Boxes

General Admission

A seating plan is a kind of map.

Textbook maps   Maps are important to the study of our country. Many of the facts about our country's history and geography will be shown on the maps in this book. The **events** and places you will be reading about will become more interesting and will mean more to you when you look carefully at the maps in this book.

CHECKUP

1. Give three examples of when you might use a map.
2. Why are maps important to the study of our country's history?

KEY FACTS

1. A hemisphere is half the earth.

2. The seven continents of the earth are North America, South America, Asia, Europe, Africa, Australia, and Antarctica.

3. The most exact way of locating places on the earth is to use latitude and longitude.

4. A map scale gives the relationship between distance on the map and distance on the earth.

5. Maps use symbols, labels, and colors.

6. There are many kinds of mass transit in the United States.

VOCABULARY QUIZ

Write the letter of the term next to the number of its description. Use a separate sheet of paper.

a. Equator
b. hemisphere
c. Prime Meridian
d. latitude
e. mileage chart
f. kilometer
g. schedule
h. longitude
i. compass rose
j. subway

1. This line of longitude is labeled 0° and goes through Greenwich, England.

2. This chart tells you when a bus (or any other kind of mass transit) leaves and arrives.

3. These lines go from the North Pole to the South Pole.

4. This drawing tells you the directions on a map.

5. This line of latitude is halfway between the North Pole and the South Pole.

6. This chart tells you the distances between cities.

7. These lines measure distances north and south of the Equator.

8. This kind of mass transit travels underground.

9. This word means "half the earth."

10. This is the name given to a unit of measure in the metric system.

REVIEW QUESTIONS

1. What are the four hemispheres?

2. In which two hemispheres is the United States found?

3. How would you describe the North Pole and the South Pole?

4. What is a continent?

5. On which continent is the United States found?

6. What does a map scale tell you?

7. What does a map key tell you?

8. What is mass transit?

9. Name three kinds of mass transit.

10. Give two examples of times when you might want to use a map.

ACTIVITIES

1. Get a road map of your state. Plan a trip from your home to a place you would like to visit. On paper, list the routes you would take and any places you would like to visit along the way. How far would you have to travel? What would you take with you on the trip?

2. Trace a map of the United States. Label each state. Use several different colors for the different states.

3. Find a map of your state in an atlas. What is the latitude and longitude of your community?

4. Trace a map of the world. Label the continents and the oceans. Use a different color for each continent.

I/SKILLS DEVELOPMENT

OUTLINING

MAKING AN OUTLINE

One way of reviewing, summarizing, or organizing what you have learned is to make an outline. An outline shows the important ideas in an orderly way. Below is the beginning of an outline of Unit 1.

I. Reading Maps
   A. Where Is It?
      1. Our nation: a big, beautiful land
         a. "America, the Beautiful"
         b. Katharine Lee Bates
      2. Hemispheres
         a. Hemisphere: half the earth
         b. North Pole: most northern place

In the above outline, the title of Chapter 1 is Roman numeral **I.** Notice that Chapter 1 is divided into five main sections, the first of which is *Where Is It?* This heading becomes capital letter **A** in the outline. The headings of the other four sections would be letters **B, C, D,** and **E.**

Each main section is in turn divided into smaller parts. There are nine such parts in the first main section of Chapter 1. We have shown only the first two of those headings: *Our nation: a big, beautiful land* and *Hemispheres.* They appear in the outline beside the Arabic numerals **1** and **2.** Lowercase letters are used to show some of the information found under those headings.

SKILLS PRACTICE

Look through Unit 1 of your text to answer these questions about the outline.
1. What information should be listed as lowercase letter **c** under *Hemispheres?*
2. What should appear as Arabic numeral **3?**
3. What should appear as capital letter **B?**
4. What should appear as Roman numeral **II?**

ORGANIZING IDEAS

Outlines are also used to organize ideas for reports. Suppose you want to report on your state's geography. The first question to ask is, What broad topics do I want to cover? You might choose *Land, Climate, People, Agriculture, Industry,* and *Cities. Land* would be Roman numeral **I;** *Climate,* **II;** *People,* **III;** and so forth.

Each of those broad topics can be divided into smaller topics. For example, under *Land,* you could write about *Lakes, Mountains,* and *Plains.* Each of these would be shown as a capital letter in your outline.

Next you would break each smaller topic into even smaller parts. Under *Lakes,* you might discuss *Uses of Lakes, Names of Lakes,* and *Locations of Lakes.* You would give each of those topics an Arabic numeral.

You could divide the topic *Uses of Lakes* into still smaller topics. These topics would be shown by lowercase letters. Then the beginning of your outline would look like this.

I. Land
   A. Lakes
      1. Uses of Lakes
         a. Fishing
         b. Swimming
         c. Drinking water

SKILLS PRACTICE

To get some practice in outlining, either complete this outline using some of the headings suggested above, or make an outline for a report of your own.

CHAPTER

2 Our History

What Is History?

VOCABULARY

chronological   factories
  order   swamp
transportation

The story of a family Suppose your teacher gives you the task of writing about your family. You are to find out about your family as far back as you can. What would you write? Where would you begin? Would you write everything there is to say about your family? Would you tell about the bad things as well as the good? How would you decide what to write?

You might begin by writing about some important things that happened in your family even before you were born. These events may have been passed down to you in stories told by your parents or grandparents.

You could tell about important people in your family. You might tell about your great-great-great-grandmother Annie, who once held Abraham Lincoln's horse. Perhaps you could tell about your great-grandfather Carlos, who was the first member of your family to live in the United States. Maybe you could tell about your great-great-uncle Tony, who had the first car in town.

You could tell about important events, like the time your parents were teenagers and went to hear President John F. Kennedy make a speech. Or maybe you could write about the fireworks your older brother or sister saw when this country celebrated its two hundredth birthday.

You could write about yourself, of course. You could give the date of your birth. You could share other important points in your life. You might tell about the prize you once won for swimming. You might write about the time you had to stay in the hospital with a broken leg. Maybe you could tell about the summer you drove to Yellowstone National Park.

You might end your story by telling what you are doing right now. This would bring your family's story up to the present day.

The story you write about your family would be your family's *history.* Families have a history. So do countries. The history of a country tells the story of how the country was born and how it grew. It tells about people and events that were important in the life of the country.

History is a telling of what happened in the past. History is often told in **chronological** (kron ə loj′ ə kəl) **order.** That means events are told in the order in which they happened. You would be likely to write in chronological order when writing your family's history. The history of countries may also be written in chronological order.

A special Fourth of July celebration takes place in New York Harbor in 1976.

People affect history   People make history happen. History is the story of great people. History is the story of great leaders, such as George Washington. It is the story of inventors, such as Thomas Edison. It is the story of freedom workers, such as Martin Luther King, Jr. It is the story of brave people, such as Amelia Earhart.

But history is not only about well-known people. When people vote, they are making history. Their votes decide who will lead the country. When large numbers of people move from one place to another, they make history. This happened about 130 years ago in the United States when people moved west.

People cause events to happen. You cannot tell a family's history without telling about the people in the family. And you cannot tell a country's history without telling about its people.

Mount Rushmore honors four Presidents. Can you tell who they are?

Someday this mountain will look like the statue of Chief Crazy Horse.

Events affect history   People make events happen. If your team wins a game, that is an event. But who made the event happen? People, of course. Sometimes people make events happen that cause other people to make other events happen. So you might say that events themselves make history happen. Suppose you wanted to watch a favorite television show last night. But your parents said that before you could watch the show you had to do your homework. Your parents made something happen. They made sure you would do your homework. Doing your homework was an event. That event made it possible for something else to happen. It made it possible for you to watch television. That was another event.

One event leads to another. Events are connected to each other. Events cause other events to happen. Can you think of an event in your life that caused something else to happen? Of course, it still takes people to make things happen.

Geography affects history   The third thing that affects history is geography. Geography is a study of the earth. When you study geography you learn about the different forms that the earth's surface takes. You study the different kinds of weather all over the world. You learn about the waters of the earth. You study plants and animals. And you study where people live on the earth and what they do. What might all this have to do with things that happened in the past? What does it have to do with history?

Imagine that it is about 150 years ago. It is 1840. You are a farmer looking for a good place to farm. What kind of place would you want to live in? You would try to choose a place with a lot of flat land, good soil, and the right amount of rain. You would want a place where it is warm long enough for you to raise good crops.

You would also try very hard to find a place near a river. A river would give you good **transportation.**   Transportation means moving people and things from one place to another. A riverboat would be a good way to get farm products to market.

Suppose you wish to work in a city. You would find that most early cities and towns are near a river. The river makes it easier to get things and people to and from the city. The river makes a good place to build **factories.** A factory is a building where goods are made by machines. The moving water in the river could be used to run the machines in the factories. The first factories in the United States were built next to rivers.

The rushing water supplied power for this mill.

How did Francis Marion use his knowledge of geography against the British?

The flat land, good soil, rainfall, and warm weather the farmer would have looked for are all part of geography. So are the rivers that were so important to both the farmer and city worker of 1840. You can see that geography had a lot to do with what people did and where they lived.

The history of our country is full of examples that show how geography affected what happened in the past. Geography helped the Americans during the Revolutionary War. One famous leader of that time was Francis Marion. He was called the "Swamp Fox." This was because he knew the wet, muddy **swamp** lands of what is now the state of South Carolina.

Marion made daring raids on the British soldiers. He would hide among the thick trees and bushes of the swamps. The British could not follow him without getting lost. He was able to escape capture because he knew geography. Marion and many others used geography to affect American history.

Geography is just as important right now. Later in this book you will learn more about geography and how it affects the people of this country.

CHECKUP

1. What is history?
2. In what order is history generally told?
3. What three things affect history?

How Do We Learn About the Past?

┌─VOCABULARY─────────────────┐
│ **oral history**   **artifact** │
│ **archaeologist**   **historian** │
└────────────────────────────┘

Oral history   You might wonder how it is possible to find out so much about the past. Think again about trying to write your family history. Where might you get information about your family? One of the best ways might be to ask older family members. They can tell you stories from long before you were born. They can tell you about life when they were young.

This is called **oral history,** or spoken history. People who take part in an event can tell about it. Or it can be passed down through your family from parent to child. In some places in the world, this is the only kind of history people have.

Written records   But there are events that happened so long ago that no one who was there is still living. Suppose nothing was passed down orally. How would you find out about these events? You would have to find written records. Letters, family Bibles, newspapers of the time, diaries, and business records are examples of written records.

One way to learn about history is to ask older people what they remember.

Pictures   Pictures or paintings can also tell you much about the past. They can show what life was like in earlier times. The picture on this page shows you what life was like in an American city more than a hundred years before you were born. The picture was made by an artist in the mid-1800s. What do you see in this picture that is different from what you might see in an American city today?

Archaeologists   Often we want to find out about things that happened before written records were kept. Or we might wish to find out about things for which the records have been lost or destroyed. What do we do then?

In such cases **archaeologists** (är kē ol′ ə jists) can help. Archaeologists are people who study plant and animal remains, ruins of buildings, and other **artifacts,** or objects. These things left by people who lived long ago may be found buried in the ground. Archaeologists dig in places where they think people once lived. They must be very careful so that no clues are lost. Each thing is important. Each bone, pot, or tool helps to tell a story about people from the past.

Finding out about the past in this way is like trying to solve a giant jigsaw puzzle with only a few of the pieces. However, trained archaeologists can tell us a great deal from a few objects. Whole groups have had their story told in this way.

Suppose archaeologists found some stone arrowheads when they were digging where people lived hundreds of years ago. Would that tell you something about how these people got their food?

Many times findings of archaeologists are used together with written records and oral history. This gives us a more complete history.

This is the corner of Clark Street and Water Street in Chicago around the middle of the 1800s. Notice the ships' masts in the background at right.

Plastic sheets and old tires protect an archaeological dig from the weather.

Historians   If you wrote your family history, you would be doing the job of a **historian.** Historians are people who work at understanding and writing about the past. Doing this kind of work is like being a detective. Historians have to go back and find clues. They must try to put the clues together in a way that makes sense. They use oral history. They use the things that archaeologists have discovered. They also use written records and pictures. In our country historians have many written records. This makes it possible for us to know a great deal about the past of the United States.

It would be hard for you to write about everything that ever happened in your family history. It would also be hard to write a history about everything that happened in the United States. The job of the historian is to choose only those happenings that are very important. The authors of this book have done that. They will tell you what our country was like years ago.

CHECKUP

1. What is the difference between oral history and written records?
2. How do pictures help us learn about the past?
3. What does an archaeologist do?

37

Why Study United States History?

──VOCABULARY──
| Native Americans | citizen |

Understanding the present There are many reasons why people should study the history of their country. Think back to your family history. Your family history is about *you*. When you learn about the past of your family, you understand more about yourself.

United States history is about you, too. It is a big part of your own story. To understand the past of your country helps you to understand more about how you live today. It helps you see why you do the things you do.

You are in this school now because long ago Americans decided that all young people had the right to learn. You and your family are free to belong to any religious group you want. This is because long before you or your parents were born, great Americans fought for your right to this freedom.

You have many such freedoms. You live in a free country. Why is that? It is because Americans who have lived before you have been willing to work for and defend that freedom.

Do you like to go to the movies? Do you enjoy talking to a friend on the telephone? Do you think it's fun to fly in a plane? You can enjoy all these things and many more because of Americans who lived before you. They worked hard on inventions that

Marines are raising the American flag after the battle of Iwo Jima in 1945.

The United States has been called a melting pot of people because Americans have come from all parts of the world.

changed the world. Imagine what your life would be like without these things. The past makes it possible for you to live the way you do. Studying history helps you to understand life today.

You are part of United States history right now. People in years to come may look back at your life today to understand how people lived. You may even be written about in future history books. You are like a bridge between the past and the future. Things that have happened in the past have important meaning for your life today. Things that happen now may be important for the future.

Learning from the past Studying United States history is important because it really is a family history. You could think of the United States as one enormous family. In this family are men and women and children of all ages, religions, skin colors, and languages. Everybody in this "family" came from other lands. Some, like the **Native Americans,** who are also called American Indians, came long before anyone else. Other members of the family have come to the United States much more recently.

We are proud of the good things the people of our American family have done.

39

Americans from Northern states fought Americans from Southern states in the Civil War.

We want to learn about these people and what they did. We want to try to be like the many fine Americans who lived before us.

Sometimes, as you know, families are not happy. They go through bad times. Brothers and sisters fight. They are cruel to each other. When these things happen families try to learn from their mistakes. They try not to repeat them.

This is part of United States history, also. Once we had slavery in this country. Some members of the American family treated other Americans cruelly. We had a war in which one part of the great American family fought against another part.

All families and countries have these sad times. But the United States has always had people who wanted to learn from the past. They wanted to make life better. And United States history shows that things are getting better. We still have problems. We are not perfect. But we are trying. We want to learn from our mistakes and avoid them in the future. We study history to do just that.

40

Good citizenship   There is another very good reason for studying United States history. You live in this country. You are a **citizen** of the United States. That means you are a member of this nation. It is necessary for you to be a good citizen.

Suppose you tried to put together a model airplane without reading the instructions first. What might happen? The airplane probably would not fly very well. It might not fly at all. It might even fall apart very quickly.

Some day you are going to have to help run the affairs of the United States. It will be up to you to see that things stick together and run smoothly. To do this well you must understand how this country was put together in the first place. History tells you that. An understanding of history helps you play your part as a citizen of the United States.

CHECKUP

1. What does history have to do with your being in school today?
2. How can learning about mistakes made in the past help us in the future?
3. Why is it important to learn how this country was put together?

Taking part in school government helps train you to be a good citizen.

KEY FACTS

1. History tells of what happened in the past.
2. People, events and geography all affect history.
3. We learn about the past through oral history, written records, pictures, and artifacts.
4. We must study United States history in order to understand the present, to learn from the past, and to be good citizens.

VOCABULARY QUIZ

Use the vocabulary listed here to fill in the correct words in this story. Write your answers on a separate sheet of paper.

oral history
artifacts
Native Americans
historian
citizen
history
chronological order
geography
archaeologist
transportation

"Hello! I am a person who works hard at understanding and writing about the past. I am a (1) _____. What happened in the past is called (2) ____. When I write about the past, I write about events in the order in which they happened. This is called (3) _____.

"Sometimes when I write about the past, I have to study old objects, called (4) _____. These objects are found by an (5) _____, a person who studies remains and ruins from people of long ago. Some of these people, the (6) _____, were the first to come to America.

"The study of the past is important for any member of this country who wants to be a good (7) ____. Study of the past includes many things. It involves a study of the earth, called (8) _____. It involves understanding (9) _____, or the different ways of moving people and goods from place to place. Sometimes you even get to hear about the past from people who lived it. This is one form of (10) _____. Studying the past is very interesting."

REVIEW QUESTIONS

1. Describe one thing you might do during a day at work if you were a historian; a geographer; an archaeologist.
2. In what four ways do historians learn about the past?
3. Why is it important for you to study United States history?

ACTIVITIES

1. Become a historian and write your family's history. In telling your story, make use of as many of the following tools as possible: oral history from older family members, pictures, written records, and objects.
2. What kind of artifacts would be most helpful to future archaeologists who wanted to study about life today? Draw pictures of ten of these artifacts. You could use pictures cut from magazines instead of drawing if you like. Or you could make a list of these artifacts. Be ready to explain why you chose as you did.
3. Many inventions from the past help you in your life today. Design or build an invention that would be helpful for people in the future. Be prepared to tell how it would work and what problem it would solve.

2 / SKILLS DEVELOPMENT

USING TIME LINES

ORGANIZING INFORMATION

Making a time line is one way to organize information in history. It helps you put things in the order in which they happened. Events that happened longest ago are farthest left on most time lines. Events that happened closer to the present are farther right.

Look carefully at the time line on this page. It is divided into two parts, B.C. and A.D. The letters B.C. mean "before Christ." The year 10,000 B.C. would be 10,000 years *before* the birth of Jesus. What would 20,000 B.C. mean? 30,000 B.C.? Which came first in history— 20,000 B.C. or 30,000 B.C.?

The letters A.D. refer to the Latin words *anno Domini*. That means "in the year of our Lord." A.D. 1000 means 1,000 years *after* the birth of Jesus. What would A.D. 2000 mean? You can see that there is much less time in A.D. than B.C. Most of American history has happened since A.D. 1492. What happened in A.D. 1492?

RULES FOR TIME LINES

Two rules apply when finding the number of years between events.
1. To find the number of years between two B.C. events or two A.D. events, *subtract*.
Examples: The amount of time between 30,000 B.C. and 20,000 B.C. is 10,000 years. The amount of time between A.D. 1000 and A.D. 1492 is 492 years.
2. To find the number of years between a B.C. event and an A.D. event, *add*.
Example: The amount of time between 10,000 B.C. and A.D. 1000 is 11,000 years.

SKILLS PRACTICE

Use the time line on this page to answer the following questions. Write on a separate sheet of paper.
1. What came first, A.D. or B.C.?
2. Which covers more time, A.D. or B.C.?
3. Except for Native American history, does American history take place in B.C. or A.D.?
4. The events that happened longest ago are on the ___ side of the time line.
5. The events that happened nearest the present are on the ___ side of the time line.
6. Which came first, 40,000 B.C. or 10,000 B.C.?
7. Which came nearest the present, 10,000 B.C. or A.D. 1000?
8. How many years between 40,000 B.C. and 20,000 B.C.?
9. How many years between A.D. 1492 and the present?
10. How many years between 40,000 B.C. and A.D. 1492?

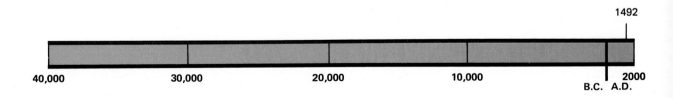

1492

40,000   30,000   20,000   10,000   2000
                                                    B.C. A.D.

I/UNIT REVIEW

1. A hemisphere is half the earth. — *Name the four hemispheres. Be ready to locate them on a globe.*

2. The earth has seven continents. — *Name them. Be ready to label all seven on an outline map of the world.*

3. There are five named lines of latitude: the Arctic Circle, the Antarctic Circle, the Tropic of Cancer, the Tropic of Capricorn, and the Equator. — *Be ready to label these five lines, as well as the North Pole and the South Pole, on an outline map of the world.*

4. All lines of longitude are measured east and west of longitude 0°, which goes through Greenwich, England. — *What is the name given to 0° longitude?*

5. Latitude and longitude help us locate places on the earth. — *Explain how you can find the city of San Diego, California, using latitude and longitude. What is San Diego's latitude and longitude?*

6. The four cardinal directions are north, south, east, and west. — *What are the four in-between directions?*

7. Maps use scale, colors and other symbols, and labels. — *Make a map of your classroom. Include a scale, and use labels and colors and other symbols. Make a key to explain the colors and other symbols.*

8. There are many kinds of mass transit in the United States. — *Name at least three kinds.*

9. People, events, and geography affect history. — *Give an example of how each — a person, an event, and geography — has affected history.*

10. We learn about the past through oral history, written records, and artifacts. — *From which of these sources, do you think, have we learned most of the history of the United States?*

11. We must study United States history to understand the present, to learn from the past, and to be good citizens. — *What kinds of things do good citizens do? Make a montage, picture, or cartoon showing people being good citizens.*

An Age of Adventure

3 The First Americans

Native Americans

┌─VOCABULARY─────────────────┐
strait	mound
tribe	culture
descendant	custom
└──────────────────────────────┘

How did they get here?   Native Americans were the very first Americans. They were here long before any other people. Where did they come from? How did they get here? How did they spread out through all of North and South America?

Look at the map on page 48. Find a place where only a narrow stretch of water separates the continent of Asia from North America. This small body of water is called the Bering (ber' ing) Strait. A **strait** is a narrow waterway that connects two large bodies of water.

Once, thousands and thousands of years ago, the Bering Strait was dry land. The first Americans probably crossed over from Asia to America on this narrow strip of land. These people from Asia were hunters. They needed animals for their food. They needed animal skins for their clothes. They needed the bones of animals to make their spears. These Asian hunters depended on animals in order to live. Most likely they followed herds of animals from Asia across the narrow land bridge that is now the Bering Strait. They discovered America by walking to it!

No one is really sure how long ago this happened. There is proof that human beings lived in North America over 12,000 years ago. Other people say the first Americans arrived as long ago as 70,000 years. And, of course, these early people did not all arrive at the same time. Small groups of Asian hunters came to America over a period of many hundreds of years.

Spreading out   These earliest Americans did not just stay in one place. For a time they would live where hunting was good. If the animals moved on, the hunters would follow them. If the animals became scarce, the hunters moved on, looking for new supplies.

Sometimes, after many years, a group might get too large. It was hard to find food for everyone. So a part of that group would move to another place. Sometimes a group, or **tribe,** would move to avoid war with another group.

This kind of moving from place to place went on for many years. At last almost all parts of North and South America were settled by these earliest Americans and their **descendants.** There were hundreds of tribes in the Americas by 1492. That was the year Christopher Columbus arrived in America from Europe and called the people he found here Indians.

Perhaps the people who became the first Americans looked like this.

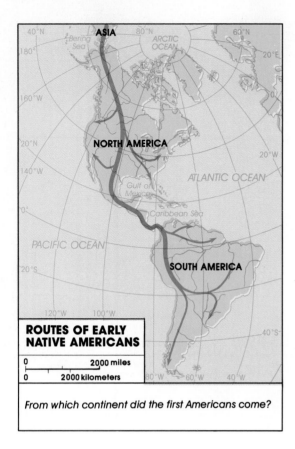

**ROUTES OF EARLY
NATIVE AMERICANS**

0   2000 miles
0   2000 kilometers

From which continent did the first Americans come?

hunters even kept tame dogs. Archaeologists think these dogs might have been used to carry loads or to help in the hunt.

Mound Builders   Beginning about 3,000 years ago, some Native Americans built huge piles of earth called **mounds.** Many different groups of Mound Builders built these piles all through the middle and eastern parts of what is now the United States.

The mounds were different shapes. Some were round. Some were square. Some had wide bases and smaller, flat tops. Some were made in the shape of animals like turtles or snakes. Many of these piles of earth were used as burial places for great leaders.

Archaeologists have learned a great deal by digging in these mounds. Sharp stone axes found inside the mounds told that these Native Americans could cut down

Digging for history   By digging where they believe that people once lived, archaeologists have discovered a number of things about early people in America.

They found spearpoints near the bones of animals. From these finds they could tell that the First Americans hunted big animals. From the bones they knew that some of these animals looked like giant buffalo, some were very large elephant-like beasts, and some were huge cats like tigers. All these animals died out long ago.

Besides the spearpoints, archaeologists found sharp arrowheads made of stone. They found well-made tools of bone as well as stone. They discovered that the first Americans used fire to cook their meat. They found out that these early

Animals such as this mammoth were hunted by the Native Americans.

This mound is in Ohio. What animal does it represent?

trees and make things from wood. Stone arrowheads and knives proved that they killed animals for food. Stone scraping tools and bone needles showed that they knew how to clean animal skins and sew them into clothing. Farm tools such as hoes showed that they knew how to grow food.

Also in the mounds were found fine pieces of artwork, such as small stone figures, beautiful pots, and masks made of wood and shell. These things meant that the Mound Builders were very skilled craftworkers. Archaeologists found things in the mounds that came from far away. This meant that the builders were travelers and traders.

Our debt to the first Americans
Americans today owe a great deal to the first Americans. Over half of our states and many of our cities, rivers, and streets still have Native American names. Words such as *skunk, canoe, chipmunk, moccasin,* and *succotash* all come from American Indian languages. In fact, nearly 500 Indian words are part of everyday English.

Many foods, such as potatoes, corn, peanuts, turkey, tomatoes, cocoa, beans, and squash were borrowed by later settlers from the Native Americans. It was from the Indians that other Americans learned how to use rubber. Indians taught them how to travel over snowy land on snowshoes and on the water in canoes.

You may at some time have slept in a hammock. You may have raced down a snowy hill on a toboggan. It was the Native Americans who first taught other people to use these things.

49

Several healing medicines used for fevers and other sickness were also borrowed from the Native Americans. In fact, without the help of the Native Americans many more of the early European settlers might have died.

Many cultures   What was life like for these Native Americans who lived here when the first European settlers began to arrive? What did they eat? What did they wear? What was their daily life like?

These questions are not easy to answer. They are hard because there were so many Native American tribes and **cultures.** The culture of a people means their way of life. Native Americans did not all live in the same way. They had different **customs**, or special ways of doing things. They wore different kinds of clothes. They spoke different languages. What was true for one group might not have been true for another.

We must look at more than one group and more than one way of life in order to get some idea of what Native Americans were like long ago. We will start by looking at some Native American groups who lived in what was to become the United States. These groups were here when the first settlers began to arrive from Europe and Africa.

CHECKUP

1. How did the first Americans get to America?
2. Why did they spread out throughout the Americas?
3. How do we know that the earliest Americans were hunters?
4. List five things that have been borrowed from the Native Americans.

Iroquois, Sioux, and Pueblo

┌─**VOCABULARY**─────────────
│ longhouse   tepee
│ league   desert
└──────────────────────────

The Iroquois: people of the Eastern Woodlands   The picture on this page shows you what much of the eastern part of America looked like when the Eastern Woodland people lived there. It was a land of trees and lakes and rivers. It was a good land for hunting and fishing. The summers were warm enough and there was enough rain for people to grow some of their food.

In this rich land lived many Indian groups. One of the largest and most important was the Iroquois (ir′ ə kwoi). The Iroquois lived in the northeastern part of the Eastern Woodlands area.

Let us find out a little about what life was like for an Iroquois boy long long ago.

The Eastern Woodland peoples lived in an area that looked much like this.

Lacrosse, a Native American game, is a popular sport in many schools today.

An Iroquois boy   Two Rivers was excited. But he did not want anyone to know. An Iroquois warrior should never show his feelings. That would be a sign of weakness.

For all of his 12 years Two Rivers had prepared to be a warrior. He practiced long-distance running on the trails around his home. Some of his older friends were great runners. They could cover a hundred miles (160 km) in a day! Two Rivers had also taken part in the game of lacrosse. In this tough game, teams had to try to get a ball into a goal using webbed sticks. Many players got hurt. The game was not for the weak or cowardly.

Two Rivers had practiced using weapons, also. He was quite good with a tomahawk and bow and arrows. He had learned to move quietly through the woods in his soft deerskin moccasins.

Running the gauntlet   Why was Two Rivers excited? Iroquois warriors had just come back from battle. They had brought back many captives. Two Rivers was sad that some brave Iroquois had been killed. But heroes of battle would receive great honors both in this life and the next, he believed.

Now the captives were being put to a test. This was the Iroquois way of replacing their dead warriors. The Iroquois wanted only the best of the captives. To prove he was worth keeping alive, the captive had to run the gauntlet. This

51

meant running and dodging between two rows of women and children holding sticks, whips, or clubs. They tried to hit the captive. If he ran through bravely and without getting badly hurt, he was made a member of the tribe. If he did not run the gauntlet well, he was killed.

The longhouse Later in the day Two Rivers returned with his family to the **longhouse.** The longhouse was his home. There were over 100 such houses in Two Rivers's village. The longhouse was about 80 feet (24 m) long and 18 feet (5½ m) wide. It was made of poles covered with the bark of trees. There were four fires on the floor down the middle of the house. One family lived in a small section on each side of the fire. Each family had a raised sleeping platform. A family also had a shelf for its belongings. At one end of the longhouse was a large meeting room.

Food When Two Rivers and his family got home it was time for the evening meal. Two Rivers always ate well. The men fished and hunted in the rich streams and forests. They also cleared the land for farming. But it was the job of the women to plant the "Three Sisters"— corn, beans, and squash. Each family had its own field. The village also had fields on which to raise food for festivals and for visitors.

Iroquois government After eating, Two Rivers's grandfather told a story. It was Two Rivers's favorite story. He always listened to it carefully. One day he could tell his own children. It was the story of the great leader, Hiawatha.

The Iroquois nation was really five different tribes. These tribes often fought each other until the time of Hiawatha. Hiawatha believed in peace. He went to all five tribes. He convinced them to live in

What material was used to build a longhouse?

peace. These five tribes were called the Iroquois League. A **league** is a group of people joined together for a common purpose.

There were 50 sachems (sā' chəmz), or leaders, in the league. Each year they held a peace council.

"What a great honor it is to be a sachem!" thought Two Rivers. Such a leader has to understand his people very well. He has to be honest and work hard. If he does not do a good job, the women of the tribe will replace him.

Women could not be sachems. But the women chose these leaders. The women were the real rulers of the tribe. Besides choosing the government leaders, the women also chose the religious leaders. They chose the Pine Trees, too. These were a group of warriors who decided when the Iroquois League would fight. Two Rivers could not know that many years later a great American leader, Benjamin Franklin, would point to the union of the Iroquois tribes as a model for the 13 colonies to follow. Before he fell asleep, Two Rivers's head was full of the things he had seen and thought about this day. He hoped that when he grew up he would be a Pine Tree or a sachem. He wanted to bring honor to his family.

The Sioux: people of the Plains   A young person who belonged to one of the Sioux (sü) tribes lived a very different kind of life from that of Two Rivers. The Sioux were Plains Indians.

This land was not the rich, forested country of the Eastern Woodlands. The Sioux and many other tribes lived on

The animal we call the buffalo is actually the American bison, not a buffalo at all.

wide, open land, covered with short, tough grass. It was not easy land to farm. The ground was hard, and often dry. There were few trees to give the Sioux wood and bark for building. But these Native Americans had something very important. They had the buffalo.

Buffalo   Great herds of buffalo roamed the grasslands where the Sioux lived. These animals gave the people almost everything they needed in order to live.

The Sioux ate fresh buffalo meat. What could not be eaten right away was dried in the sun and saved to eat later. The thick hairy hides of the buffalo were used for warm robes and blankets. The skins without the hair were used to make shoes, shirts, leggings, and dresses. The women sewed several hides together to make coverings for their homes. Not a single part of the buffalo was wasted. Even the hooves and stomach were used. Hooves were boiled and made into glue. Stomachs were used for cooking pots.

The hunt   Life for the Sioux, as well as for other Plains tribes, depended on the buffalo. So hunting was the most important job in their lives.

It was a dangerous job to hunt buffalo on foot with bow and arrows. Sometimes the hunters tried to kill the animals by driving them over cliffs. In the winter the hunters tried to drive them into deep snow or into icy lakes where the animals found it hard to move. But this was a risky way to get food. And it didn't always work.

Horses   Later on, people from Europe came to these grassy lands. And with them came the horse. The horse made a great difference in the life of the Native Americans.

With a horse a hunter could move faster than any angry buffalo. He could shoot it with his bow and arrows more easily. It became much easier and less dangerous for the Sioux hunters to bring down these great beasts on which their people depended.

Tepees   When scouts signaled that buffalo were nearby, the men quickly dashed off. The women had to pick up camp, homes and all, and follow.

Each Sioux family lived in a buffalo-skin tent. These tents were called **tepees**. These tent homes weighed very little. They could easily be taken apart, carried to a new camp, and quickly set up again.

The tepees were good homes. They were waterproof and they kept out the wind. Fires burning inside kept them warm. The smoke was let out by little flaps in the buffalo-skin covering. These

A tepee is made of skins and poles.
How is it different from the longhouse?

homes were very different from Two Rivers's longhouse. But they fit the life of the Sioux very well indeed.

War   Sioux men, like the Iroquois, were expected to be good warriors. As boys, they too had to be good runners. They had to wrestle. They were taught to swim in the ice-cold water. They had to learn to do without food for a long time. They had to learn to take a great deal of pain without complaining.

All this training was to make them good fighters. War was just as important to the Sioux as hunting. The great heroes of the Sioux were the bravest warriors.

The Pueblo: people of the Southwest   The Native Americans we call the Pueblo (pweb′ lō) lived in still different ways from those of the Eastern Woodland and Plains tribes. *Pueblo* is the Spanish word for "village." Pueblo is the name for the people as well as for a town or a building in which they lived. The picture on this page shows the remains of a Pueblo village.

The land where the Pueblo people lived is very dry. It is so dry that some of it might be called **desert** land. There are few trees and it is often very hot.

Now let us look at one exciting event in the life of a Pueblo girl.

Pueblos were often built into the sides of cliffs as protection from enemies and the weather.

A Pueblo girl   "Run! Run! The Navajo are coming!" Tuma was washing her hair in a little stream. But she ran home as quickly as she could. The Navajo were another tribe who lived nearby. They tried to raid Pueblo villages in search of food and other supplies. The peace-loving Pueblo people did not like to fight. But they could not allow their food to be stolen. They would fight for their food.

"Hurry, Tuma," cried Yonga, her older brother. Tuma scrambled up the ladder. Yonga pulled it up after them.

Tuma's building was like an apartment house. One room was stacked on top of another. More than 300 families lived in this tall pueblo made of stone and clay. The only way to get from one floor to another was by ladder. Under attack, all the ladders were pulled up. It became very hard for an enemy to reach the people inside.

Tuma climbed down through the roof and through the homes of many families. At last she reached the room she shared with her family. Meanwhile the men of the village hurried to the roof to defend their home.

Farming   Tuma thought back to all the work the men had done to grow the corn that the Navajo wanted so badly. They built fences so that soil would not blow away. They dug ditches to bring water to the fields from a nearby stream. They were careful not to plant the seed too early in the growing season. They offered many prayers for a good crop.

The women and girls did not help plant the corn. But they spent hours grinding it into cornmeal. They made many different foods from the corn. Much of their time was also spent making clay pots for the corn. Plain pots were used for cooking the corn. Beautifully painted pots were used for storing the corn.

Everyone in a Pueblo village depended on this important food. They all worked and prayed for it. They would not let the Navajo take it away from them.

Pueblo religion   Tuma hugged her kachina (kä chē′ nə) doll as she listened to sounds of fighting from the roof. The Pueblo people believed that kachinas were good spirits who protected them and their crops. Boys and girls alike had dolls made to look like the different kachina spirits. That way children could learn to know the different kachina masks worn by dancers at religious festivals.

The Pueblo held many religious ceremonies each year. There was much sing-ing and dancing at these ceremonies. Each song and dance was a prayer to bring rain and to make the corn grow tall.

Homes   Tuma looked around her home. It was a good home. Thick walls kept it cool in the hottest summer. A cooking fire burned brightly in the firepit. When she grew up she would receive this home from her mother's family. When she married, her husband would come to her home to live.

"The women have their homes; the men have their kivas (kē′ vəz)," she thought. Kivas were underground rooms. The Pueblo men used them for religious ceremonies. But in the winter, the men gathered in kivas to tell stories, weave blankets, and teach the younger boys.

A sharp bang frightened Tuma! It was Yonga. He had dropped his club in returning from the roof. He was out of breath but happy.

"The Navajo have gone away," he said. "They used tree trunks to climb our pueblo. But we drove them away . . . this time."

Tuma gave her kachina doll a hug. She was happy too. She knew why the Navajo had been driven away. She must remember to thank the good spirit who protected her people.

Dolls helped children recognize the kachina spirits.

CHECKUP

1. What were the homes of the Iroquois, Sioux, and Pueblo peoples called? What were they like? How did the area in which each group lived influence the kind of housing in which they lived?
2. Which people got their food by hunting, fishing, and farming? Which got their food mostly by hunting? By farming?

Mayas, Aztecs, and Incas

VOCABULARY

civilization	causeway
pyramid	canal
human sacrifice	terrace
empire	

Great civilizations   About 8,000 years ago somewhere in Middle America, a great discovery was made. People learned how to plant and grow corn.

Before this discovery people had to hunt animals or gather wild plants for their food. Everybody had to help in the search for food. They had very little time for anything else. But when people learned to grow their own food, many ways of life began to change. People had time to do other things. Cities, trade, government, writing, art, and science developed. These can all be called marks of a **civilization.**

Civilizations grew up in Middle and South America. Most early Native Americans lived in these places. You are going to learn about two early Middle American cultures and one early South American culture.

Mayan farming   The Mayas (mä′ yəz) were one group of Native Americans whose ways of life were changed by the new way of getting food. The Mayas lived in Central America and in the southern parts of what is now Mexico. On the map on page 58 find the lands of the Mayas.

The Mayas had good soil for growing crops. They raised squash, beans, sweet potatoes, chili peppers, and corn.

After a while Mayan farmers became able to raise more food than they needed for themselves. This meant that while most Mayas continued to farm, not everyone had to be a farmer. Some people could do other kinds of work.

Mayan cities   The Mayas became very good at many new jobs. Some learned to weave beautiful cloth. Others became fine builders. Some learned to be artists. Some became traders.

Because of all these new skills and many others, it became possible to build cities. There were Mayan cities more than 1,600 years ago. They were beautiful cities. They had huge **pyramids** made of earth and stone, with fine temples at the top. There were wide courtyards and palaces with many rooms.

Religious festivals were held in the cities. So were market days when all kinds of goods were for sale. Traders traveled to faraway places to bring back goods for the city markets.

The temples built on top of the pyramids were the scenes of important Mayan religious ceremonies.

Mayan priests   While each city had one main ruler, the priests were also very important in the life of the Mayas. They did much more than lead the people in worship. They helped govern the cities. Many of the things that people did were directed by the priests. The builders and craftworkers were under the priests' orders. Roads and many important buildings were built under their orders.

The priests were also scientists. They studied the stars. They learned to tell by the stars when the rainy seasons would come. How did this help the farmers?

The priests invented a system of arithmetic and a calendar. They also worked out a way to write their language. This made it possible for them to keep records of Mayan history.

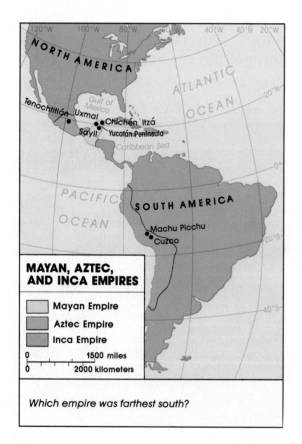

MAYAN, AZTEC, AND INCA EMPIRES

Mayan Empire
Aztec Empire
Inca Empire

0   1500 miles
0   2000 kilometers

Which empire was farthest south?

Aztecs: a warlike people   The Aztecs (az′ teks) and Mayas were alike in many ways. The Aztecs lived in what is now Mexico. Their homes, clothes, arts, science, farming, foods, and writing were almost the same as the Mayas'.

The religion of each group called for **human sacrifice.** Both groups killed people as offerings to their gods. But the Aztecs made many more such sacrifices to their gods than the Mayas did. Unlike the Mayas, the Aztecs went to war often to get enough prisoners to sacrifice.

Every Aztec boy was trained for war. The Aztec warriors defeated many other groups of Native Americans. The Aztecs built a huge **empire** by taking the lands of the people they defeated in battle. Find the Aztec empire on the map. This great country was very carefully governed and it lasted for at least 300 years.

Tenochtitlán   The great Aztec city of Tenochtitlán (tā näch tē tlän′) was one of the largest cities in the world only 400 years ago. Up to 300,000 people may have lived there at one time. Tenochtitlán was the center of Aztec government and trade.

Tenochtitlán was built on an island in the middle of a lake. **Causeways,** or land bridges, were made by building earth up above the water in narrow strips. Goods and people could move along these land bridges to get from the city to the mainland. Wooden bridges were added to the land bridges. These could be moved away, leaving empty spaces in the land bridges. This made it hard for enemies to enter the city.

Tenochtitlán was always busy. It was always full of people. All roads led to the

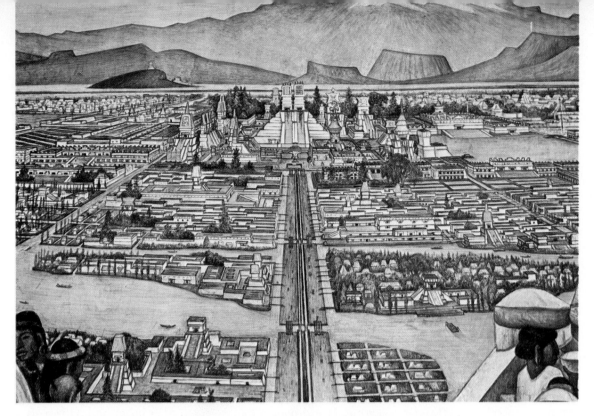

A modern Mexican artist, using old maps and drawings as sources, painted this mural of Tenochtitlán.

center of the city. There were also **canals,** or waterways dug out for boats. These also led to the center of the city. In the city center, on top of large pyramids, were temples for each of the Aztec gods.

The Inca empire   Over 500 years ago the empire of the Incas stretched along the western mountains of South America. This huge land took in all of what is now the country of Peru and parts of present-day Chile, Ecuador, and Bolivia. On the map on page 58, find the land of the Incas.

In 1450 this empire, 3,000 miles (4,800 km) long, held over 4 million people. The tribes conquered by the great Inca armies were treated well. Some tribes even asked to be made part of the Inca empire. The Incas protected them. In return, they allowed the Incas to rule them.

The Incas were great builders. They were able to build fine roads over the steep mountains. They could build bridges across the deep valleys. These roads helped the Inca government keep in touch with everything that was going on.

The rulers and rich people among the Incas lived in great stone palaces. They ate from gold plates. They wore beautiful jewelry made by Inca artists. A great many people waited on them and worked for them.

But most Incas were not rich. They lived in small mud, stone, or reed houses. Their main food was potatoes. They also ate corn, beans, squash, and tomatoes. They raised guinea (gin′ ē) pigs for meat. The llama was very important to the Incas. They used its wool to make clothes. They used it to carry loads. They even ate llama meat.

59

Getting It Straight: The Americas

The terms *North America, South America, Central America, Middle America,* and *Latin America* can be confusing. The Western Hemisphere, our half of the globe, really has only two continents, or large masses of land. These are North and South America.

North America means everything north of South America (see map 1). This includes Panama and the small countries northwest of Panama, the islands in the Caribbean Sea, Mexico, the United States, and Canada. *South America* means only the large continent south of the entire area of North America (see map 2).

Sometimes it is helpful to refer to certain regions in this area. *Central America* (see map 3) really means only the narrow part of North America connecting the larger part of North America with South America. It includes Guatemala, Belize, El Salvador, Honduras, Nicaragua, Costa Rica, and Panama. *Middle America* (see map 4) is the whole area south of the United States and north of South America. It also includes the islands in the Caribbean Sea.

Latin America is a helpful term we use to identify part of the Americas by language. Latin America means all the countries south of the United States. Many of the people in these countries speak a language based on the old Latin language. Often this language is Spanish.

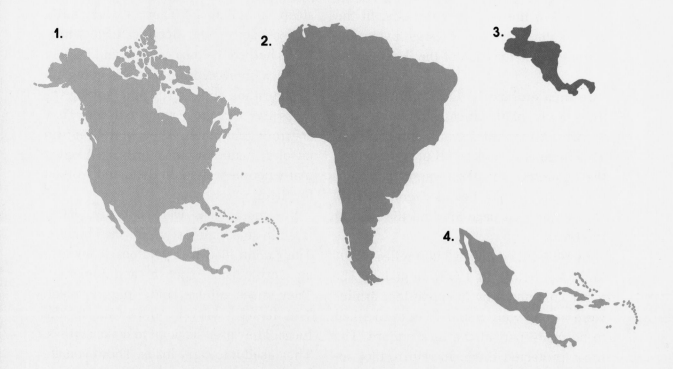

1.

2.

3.

4.

60

Inca farming   Most Incas were farmers. They learned to grow crops on the steep sides of the mountains as well as in the valleys. They cut **terraces**, or rows of wide steps, into the mountainsides to plant their crops. Stone walls kept the soil from washing away during heavy rains.

The government owned all the land. The people were allowed to farm it. But in return they had to give part of their crop to the government. The government stored some of this food in special buildings. Then when times were hard and crops were poor, the people had food to eat.

Inca religion   The Incas had many gods. One of the most important was the sun god. The Incas even called their land the Kingdom of the Sun.

The Incas, like the Mayas and the Aztecs, believed their gods wanted sacrifices. But the Incas generally sacrificed animals instead of people.

The priests had an important place in the lives of the Incas. These religious leaders were also the doctors. They took care of the people who became sick. Some of them became so skilled that they were even able to operate on people's heads!

Inca education   Most Inca children did not go to school. They learned by working with their parents every day. But some of the children of rich people did go to school. The boys were sent to the capital city of Cuzco to learn to become government workers. They studied history, war, religion, and language.

They did not learn to write. The Incas

This llama made of silver shows the skill of the Inca artists.

did not have writing. But they did have a way of remembering things and of counting by using knotted strings of different lengths and colors.

Some 10-year-old girls were also picked to go to a special school. Here they learned how to work in the emperor's palace. They learned how to be the wives of rich and important men.

Inca arts and crafts   The Incas were fine artists and craftworkers. They made beautiful pottery. They made jewelry, tools, and many other things out of different metals. They wove fine cloth from wool and cotton.

The Incas were famous for their stonework. They could build stone walls that fit tightly together without cement. Some of these walls have stood for hundreds of years.

CHECKUP

1. What are the marks of a civilization? Which of them were found among the Mayas? Aztecs? Incas?
2. Why was it possible for Mayas to develop skills other than farming?

61

KEY FACTS

1. Native Americans came to America long before any other groups.

2. Americans have learned a great deal from Native Americans.

3. To understand what early Native Americans were like you must study many different tribes, because each tribe is different.

4. A civilization is marked by cities, farming, trade, government, writing, art, and science.

5. Many Native American groups had very advanced civilizations.

VOCABULARY QUIZ

Write **T** if the statement is true and **F** if it is false. If the statement is false, change the underlined term to make the statement true.

1. The first Americans came to America by crossing what is now a <u>causeway</u>.

2. A <u>civilization</u> is marked by government, science, and art.

3. Another name for a group of Native Americans is a <u>crowd</u>.

4. Huge piles of earth in which archaeologists have found clues about how some Native Americans lived are called <u>terraces</u>.

5. <u>Human sacrifice</u> is the practice of killing people and offering them to the gods.

6. A large land area ruled by one leader or group is called <u>a longhouse</u>.

7. A <u>desert</u> is a dry, often hot, land with few trees.

8. Native Americans had many <u>cultures,</u> or ways of life.

9. Waterways dug out for boats are called <u>canals</u>.

10. A group of people joined together for a common purpose is a <u>sachem</u>.

REVIEW QUESTIONS

1. What is the importance of a "land bridge" in the coming of the first people to the Americas?

2. What do you think was the greatest accomplishment of the Iroquois? The Sioux? The Pueblo?

3. Prove that the Mayas, Aztecs, and Incas had great civilizations by naming at least three of the marks of civilization for each.

ACTIVITIES

1. Native Americans had to develop written languages. They did this by making pictures or symbols for their words. Some of these written languages still have not been entirely solved.

Make your own secret code by giving each letter in the alphabet a symbol. For example: "A" could be #. Write a note and share it with a friend or the whole class. See if they can solve the code or if they need help from you.

2. Draw a picture of something you found interesting in the chapter. Here are some suggestions: "Running the Gauntlet," "A Game of Lacrosse," "Buffalo Hunting," "A Religious Ceremony," "Human Sacrifice."

3. You learned in this chapter that there are over 500 Native American words in the English language. Make a list of words you know or think are of Native American origin. Look in a dictionary to check those words you are not sure of. Also check your spelling.

Now make a picture dictionary. First put the words in alphabetical order. Illustrate each work with a picture you have drawn or cut from an old magazine. Write a definition for each word and its picture. Make your work as neat and attractive as possible.

READING FOR CONCLUSIONS

A CHIPPEWA STORY

All religions tell the story of creation. Native Americans have many songs and stories that tell about how the world began.

The Chippewa (chip′ ə wä) are a tribe of Native Americans. Once they lived in the forests around what is now called Lake Superior. There are many stories in the Chippewa religion that tell of the beginnings of the people. The story that follows tells how man and woman came to be.

The Great Manitou was a ruling spirit. Long long ago he took the form of a giant bird. This giant bird had an egg in its nest. The Great Snake found the nest. The egg looked good to eat. As the Snake came near, the egg moved. The Manitou heard the egg move. He took a big rock in his claws and killed the Great Snake. But he also broke open the egg.

A man came out of the broken egg. The man could not move far. He had a large rock on his feet. The Manitou wanted to teach the man many things. Soon the man learned how to make tools and to hunt. He learned how to make clothing and grow food. At last he learned enough. One day he awoke to find a woman beside him.

The Manitou removed the rock from his feet. The two people ran away. These people were Native Americans. They were the first people to live on earth.

DRAWING CONCLUSIONS

To "draw conclusions" means to take information and use it in a new way. A story does not have to say something clearly. Because of the way the story is written, however, you can draw conclusions that certain things are true.

SKILLS PRACTICE

Some of the following statements are correct conclusions from the story. Some are not. Write **T** if the conclusion is true and **F** if it is false. Use a separate sheet of paper.

1. The Great Manitou and the Great Snake were enemies.

2. The Chippewa believed that all birds are gods.

3. The Great Manitou built a nest of straw.

4. The man could not move because his feet were pinned by a rock.

5. The Chippewa believed humans came from godlike animals.

6. The Great Manitou would not let the man go free until he had learned to take care of himself.

7. The Chippewa were descended from the two people who ran away.

8. The skills of hunting and farming came to the Chippewa from the Great Manitou.

Early Explorers

VOCABULARY

explore

What is an explorer? Have you ever gone exploring? Perhaps you have hiked deep into a wood, deeper than you had ever been before. You might have discovered trees or flowers or insects there that were new to you. Maybe you found a stream you didn't know about. You probably brought back a leaf or a plant to show your parents or friends. Or perhaps you moved to another home and went for a walk around your new neighborhood. You might have found streets and buildings you had never seen before and people you had never met. You probably told your family what you had seen.

If you have ever done anything like these things, you were exploring. To **explore** means to search for new things or places. It means making discoveries.

A great age There was a time in the history of Europe when there were many great explorers. They were daring people who voyaged to unknown lands. They made wonderful discoveries. They brought back plants and treasures and even people that no one at home had ever seen before. They brought back information that people at home had never heard about before. Some of these daring adventurers found their way to America. We often call the time of the great explorers the Age of Exploration.

Who was first? We know that people came to America from Asia many thousands of years ago. These were the Native Americans. But who were the first people to come to America *after* the Native Americans? Who were the first explorers to discover America?

Many claims have been made that different groups from Africa, Asia, or Europe were the first to arrive in America. But no real proof has been found for any of these claims except one.

The Vikings The Vikings (vī′ kingz) were a bold and brave sailing people. They came from the countries we now call Norway, Denmark, and Sweden. Find these northern European countries on the Atlas map on pages 466–467. Some of these daring people had left their home country and settled on the small northern island of Iceland. Others had gone still farther west. They had made settlements on the large island of Greenland. Find Iceland and Greenland on the map on pages 466–467. Stories about these settlements made many hundreds of years ago became part of Viking oral history.

This is what the Santa Maria, Christopher Columbus's flagship, might have looked like on the evening of October 11, 1492.

Oct. 1892

Leif Ericson   The Vikings also passed down stories about a great explorer named Leif (lāv) Ericson. The stories told that in the year 1000 Leif Ericson had sailed west across the North Atlantic from a Viking settlement in Greenland to a new and unknown land. He named the new land Vinland. The stories also said that after Leif's discovery, other groups of Vikings settled in this new land. They built stone houses. They planted crops and raised cattle.

But old stories alone are not proof that something really happened. If there had been settlements, they had disappeared. Certainly no other European settlers had followed the Vikings to the new land. However, about 25 years ago, archaeologists discovered the remains of some old stone buildings on the island of Newfoundland. Look at the map on page 470. Find Newfoundland along the eastern coast of Canada. You can see that it is not very far from Greenland.

The archaeologists could prove that the oldest stone buildings they found had

Danish Sea Scouts built this replica of a Viking ship. Imagine crossing an ocean in such a ship!

During which years did most of the exploration of North America take place?

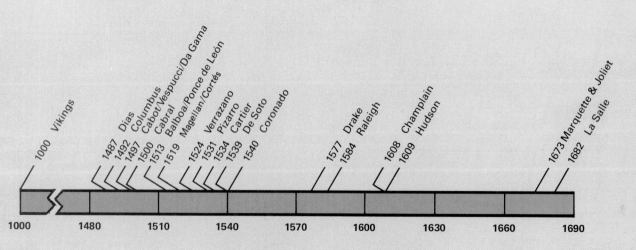

been built by the Vikings. They were able to tell that these buildings had been built about A.D. 1000. Many Viking artifacts were also discovered nearby. Now there was real proof that the Vikings had come to North America as early as the year 1000.

A forgotten discovery   The Vikings were probably the first Europeans in America. But they had no idea that Vinland was part of a whole new world. And they found nothing valuable to take back home with them. After a very few years their settlements died out. As far as the rest of Europe was concerned, the Vikings' great discovery went almost unnoticed. Only in the old Viking tales was Leif Ericson's adventure remembered. Nearly 500 years later another discovery would cause much more excitement.

CHECKUP

1. What does an explorer do?
2. What proof has been found that the Vikings came to America about 1,000 years ago?

Christopher Columbus

──VOCABULARY──
colony

Land ho!   "¡Tierra! ¡Tierra!" The cry of the lookout drove the sleep from the eyes of the sailors. A cheer went up. It was early morning, October 12, 1492. The land sighted was a small island southeast of what is now the state of Florida. The cheering sailors were part of the crew of the Spanish sailing ship the *Santa Maria*. Perhaps no one on board the *Santa Maria* was happier than the captain, Christopher Columbus.

A boy who wanted to be a sailor   Columbus had been born in 1451, the son of a wool weaver in the busy Italian seaport of Genoa on the Mediterranean Sea. Genoa was one of the busiest trading ports in Europe. Christopher loved the sea. As a boy he had spent many happy hours watching the tall sailing ships come and go in Genoa's harbor.

The harbor of Genoa looked like this when Christopher Columbus was a boy.

More than anything else young Christopher wanted to go to sea. And while he was still a teenager, Christopher Columbus became a sailor. He spent many years sailing to foreign lands. He was a brave sailor and a good one. He learned much about the seas and about the ships that sailed on them. And after a while Christopher Columbus became a captain.

Trade routes   At that time every important country in Europe wanted to find an all-water route to India, the Spice Islands, and China—all the lands that people then called the Indies. From these far-off places came jewels, ivory, and silks. The spices, such as nutmeg, cinnamon, cloves, and pepper, were almost as valuable as jewels. They covered the bad taste of unrefrigerated, slightly spoiled foods.

The young Columbus had watched these precious goods being taken off the ships in Genoa's harbor. But they had not made their whole journey by ship. A large part of their trip had been overland on the backs of camels or other pack animals. The trade routes across deserts, over mountains, and through valleys were long and hard. They were also very dangerous. Robbers lay in wait for the richly laden animal trains. Even the parts of the journeys made by ship were risky. Pirates often attacked these treasure ships, robbing, burning, and killing.

Most people talked about the possibility of sailing around the southern tip of Africa and then northward across the Indian Ocean to India. From there ships could sail to the Spice Islands. They might even sail on to China.

A different idea   Captain Christopher Columbus was as much interested as anyone else in finding a new route to the Indies. He knew if he could find such a route he would become rich and famous. Besides, it would be such a great adventure! And Columbus had a new idea. He believed, as did many people of the time, that the world was round. "If that is true," thought Columbus, "why not sail west to get to the East?"

Portugal   It is one thing to have a good idea. It is another and sometimes harder thing to make that idea work. Voyages cost a great deal of money. Where would Columbus get enough money to try out his idea?

He decided to go to the king of Portugal for help. He asked the king for three ships. And he asked for the title of admiral. He wanted to keep some of the gold and other riches he believed he would find for himself. And he wanted to rule any new lands he might discover. The king of Portugal refused to agree to Columbus's demands. He felt that Columbus was asking too much.

There was another reason that the king refused Columbus. Columbus had said that Asia was only 2,400 miles (3,860 km) west of Europe. The king's geographers believed that this distance was not correct. It was too short. They believed that it was really about four times as far to Asia. It just was not possible, they felt, to make such a long voyage.

The king's geographers were much more nearly correct than Columbus about the distance between Europe and Asia. Of course neither they nor Columbus knew that the huge continents of the Americas lay between Europe and Asia.

Columbus was not the kind of person who gives up easily. This was part of what made him a great man. He wanted riches for himself and his family. He was also sure that God wanted him to make this voyage. If Portugal would not help him, he would try Spain!

Ferdinand and Isabella   King Ferdinand and Queen Isabella of Spain were very interested in Columbus's idea. But Spain was at war. Wars are very expensive. Spain had no money to pay for such a costly voyage. Columbus would have to wait.

While he was waiting, Portuguese explorers were sailing farther and farther down the coast of Africa. Finally, in 1488, Bartholomeu Dias, a Portuguese sea captain, rounded the southern tip of Africa. While he did not sail on to India, a

Columbus, about to set sail on his first voyage, says good-bye to Ferdinand and Isabella.

new trade route to the Indies was ready to open. And Columbus still had not been able to test his idea. At last he decided to leave Spain early in 1492.

While on the road home, Columbus was stopped by a messenger from the palace. King Ferdinand and Queen Isabella had finally decided to help him. Spain still had very little money to spare, but Columbus must sail!

A dream comes true   Columbus's dream was going to come true. He went about the work of getting ships and crews together. In August of 1492, Columbus set sail. He had 90 sailors in three ships, the *Niña*, the *Pinta*, and the *Santa Maria*. The ships stopped at the Canary Islands for supplies. Find the Canary Islands on the map on page 71. Then in September Columbus and his sailors set out into the vast Atlantic Ocean.

After they had been out of sight of land for a month, the sailors began to get frightened. No one had ventured out this far upon the "Sea of Darkness" before. They were afraid that if they went any farther, they would never be able to return home safely. The sailors talked of taking over the ships and turning back to Spain. Columbus reminded them of the gold they would surely get if they completed the voyage. But still the sailors threatened to take over and turn the ships back.

Just as it seemed they would go no farther, they saw branches and leaves in the water. This was a sure sign that land was near. Then on October 12, 1492, the welcome call was heard that land had been sighted.

Later that morning Columbus went on shore and claimed the land he had found for King Ferdinand and Queen Isabella of Spain. He named the small island San Salvador. *San Salvador* means "Holy Savior" in Spanish.

Columbus's mistake   San Salvador is one of a group of islands we call the Bahamas. Look at the map on page 71. Find these islands off the southern tip of Florida. Columbus made a mistake. He was sure that he had reached the East Indies, islands very close to Asia. He even called the friendly people he found on the island "Indians," after the term *Indies*. The islands became known as the West Indies. Columbus never knew that he had discovered the Americas.

With the help of the Native Americans, Columbus explored some of the other islands. He sailed along the coast of a larger island we call Cuba. And as he sailed farther east he found still another island. He named this smaller island Hispaniola. You can find these islands on the map on page 71. Columbus found white beaches, beautiful forests, and colorful birds and flowers. He saw people smoking tobacco, something no European had ever seen. He saw corn growing in the fields. Nowhere in Europe did people grow corn. But he found very little gold and no silks or spices. Still Columbus believed that he had reached the outposts of Asia and that all the riches of the Indies were almost within his grasp.

After a long, stormy journey, Columbus arrived back in Spain in March 1493. He was received as a great hero by King Ferdinand and Queen Isabella. He had not brought home much gold. But he had proved that brave sailors could cross the huge unknown sea and return home safely. And he had claimed new lands for Spain. Besides, everyone was sure that on future voyages to the new lands Columbus would find all the riches of the East to bring back to Spain.

Other voyages   Columbus made three other voyages to what we now know was a new world to Europeans. You can follow each voyage on the map on page 71. On his second trip he started the **colony** of Isabela. A colony is land that is settled far from the country that governs it. It was on the third trip that he first set foot on the American mainland in what is now Venezuela. Columbus's fourth voyage was started in 1502. He wanted to find a water passage through these unknown lands. But he could not find a passage that was not there.

Columbus thought he was landing on an island off the coast of Asia.

70

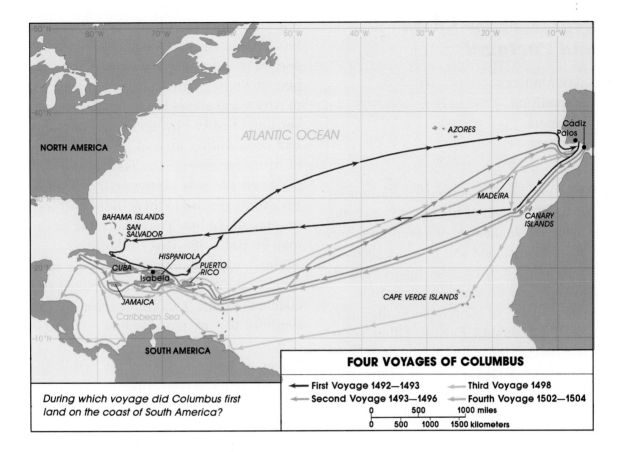

FOUR VOYAGES OF COLUMBUS

← First Voyage 1492—1493 ← Third Voyage 1498
← Second Voyage 1493—1496 ← Fourth Voyage 1502—1504

0   500   1000 miles
0   500   1000   1500 kilometers

During which voyage did Columbus first land on the coast of South America?

On this last voyage Columbus stayed on the island we now call Jamaica for a whole year. In order to get food, Columbus played a trick on the people who lived on the island. He told them to bring him food or his God would take away the light in the night sky. They did not believe him. But before long it became very dark and the moon was gone from the sky. Soon people with food were coming from all over. They begged Columbus to put back the light. What do you think happened? Have you ever seen an eclipse of the moon?

The contributions of Columbus   In 1506, two years after he returned from his last voyage, Columbus died. He was poor and disgraced. He had never found the gold he expected. He had not found a new route to Asia.

It is true that Columbus made mistakes. But he was a man of great courage and skill. And he made one of the greatest discoveries in history. He is the explorer who opened the Americas to Europe. And his discovery was not forgotten, like that of the Vikings. More and more people learned of Columbus's great discovery. It was not very long before hundreds and then thousands of people followed where he had led.

CHECKUP

1. What was Columbus's new idea?
2. What was the date of Columbus's discovery of America?
3. Why was Columbus's discovery more important than that of the Vikings?

71

Explorers for Spain and Portugal

VOCABULARY
- expedition
- isthmus
- armada

"First come, first served" Columbus was the first man of his time to reach the Americas. He claimed the land he found for King Ferdinand and Queen Isabella of Spain. Only 4 years later Spain built its first lasting settlement on Hispaniola.

The news of Columbus's discovery spread throughout Europe. Other countries became interested in the new lands beyond the Atlantic. Many explorers and settlers came after Columbus. They claimed land for the countries that sent them. Generally the first country to have explorers and settlers in an area would be able to control it and profit from it. The rule for claiming American lands seems to have been "First come, first served."

A claim for Portugal In 1500 a Portuguese sailor, Pedro Cabral (kä bräl'), was trying to sail around Africa to Asia. He somehow got off course and landed on the coast of what we now call Brazil in South America. Cabral claimed this land for Portugal. Find the area he claimed for Portugal on the map on page 74. Another explorer sailing for Portugal also landed on that coast. Find the route of Amerigo Vespucci (ve spü' chē) on the map.

Portugal was not as interested in the Americas at that time as were other European countries. Three years earlier another Portuguese sailor, Vasco da Gama, had become the first to sail around Africa and on to India. The trade route from Lisbon in Portugal around the southern tip of Africa and across the Indian Ocean had become a reality. Portuguese trading ships had been sailing up and down the coast of Africa for some years. Traders and sailors knew the area pretty well. So Da Gama's route seemed to them the easiest way to get to the Indies. Trace this route on the map on pages 466–467 in the Atlas.

Brazil was to remain Portugal's only claim in the Americas. Spain explored and claimed almost everything else in the southern part of the Americas.

Ponce de León One of the first Spanish explorers was Juan Ponce de León (wän pons də lē' ən). He had sailed with Columbus on his second voyage. Ponce de León lived in the West Indies for many years. He went on several **expeditions** in search of gold. An expedition is a journey for a certain purpose. Ponce de León's purpose was to look for gold. In 1508 he did find some gold on the island we now know as Puerto Rico. And he claimed that land for Spain.

Ponce de León had heard stories about a wonderful fountain whose waters could make people young again. In 1513 he sailed off to find this Fountain of Youth. Of course Ponce de León never found this magic fountain. But he did find a beautiful warm land filled with flowers. He named this land Florida and claimed it for Spain. It was here that the first Spanish settlement in mainland North America, St. Augustine, was started. Find St. Augustine on the map on page 74.

Balboa   Also in 1513 another Spaniard, Vasco Núñez de Balboa (vas′ kō nü′ nyās də bal bō′ ə), was leading an expedition in Central America. He, too, was looking for gold. But he was also looking for a water passage through the land. Such a passage, many Europeans felt, would allow ships to continue sailing westward to Asia. Balboa was leading his group through the Isthmus of Panama. An **isthmus** (is′ məs) is a narrow strip of land connecting two larger pieces of land. It has water on both sides. Find the Isthmus of Panama on the map on page 74.

Climbing a high mountain after a hard journey through thick wet forests, Balboa saw a huge body of water before him. He called this body of water the South Sea and claimed for Spain all the land that its waters touched. Balboa had discovered the Pacific Ocean.

Magellan   Ferdinand Magellan (mə jel′ ən) is thought by many people to be the greatest sailor in the history of the world. In 1519 Magellan sailed southwest from Spain. He, like so many others, was looking for a new water route to the Indies.

When he reached South America, he sailed south along the coast. You can trace his route on the map on pages 466–467 in the Atlas. At the tip of South America he discovered the water passage that led through the land to the west. Today we call this passage the Strait of Magellan.

It took Magellan a long time to sail through this narrow, rough waterway. But when he did, he became the first European to sail on the great ocean that Balboa had named the South Sea. Magellan found this ocean so calm that he called it *Pacific*, meaning "peaceful."

Magellan had great difficulty getting his ships through the strait at the tip of South America.

South America was the last land Magellan and his crew would see for 14 weeks. They ran out of food and water as they sailed across this vast, calm ocean. They became so hungry they were eating shoe leather, rats, and sawdust. Many of the sailors were dying.

At last they reached the island of Guam. Here they were able to rest and get fresh water and food. Magellan and his crew then sailed for the Philippine Islands. Here Magellan was killed in a battle between two groups of islanders. But his men continued the journey westward

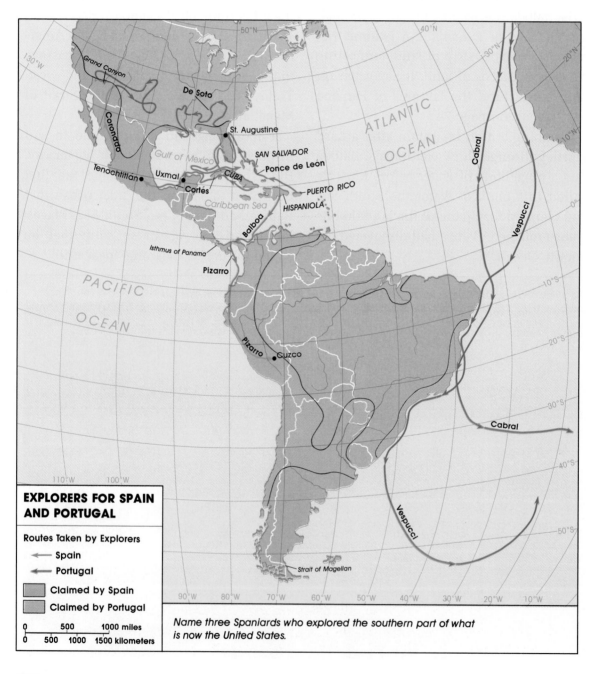

EXPLORERS FOR SPAIN AND PORTUGAL

Routes Taken by Explorers

⟵ Spain

⟵ Portugal

▨ Claimed by Spain

▨ Claimed by Portugal

0   500   1000 miles

0   500   1000   1500 kilometers

Name three Spaniards who explored the southern part of what is now the United States.

until they reached the Spice Islands. They bought some precious spices and rested again. Then they set sail for Africa. They sailed west around the tip of Africa and up the coast. They finally limped into their home port in Spain in 1522, exhausted and ill. Trace the voyage from the Strait of Magellan back to Spain on the Atlas map on pages 466–467.

Five ships and 240 men had left Spain in 1519. One ship and 17 men returned in 1522. The price had been great. But human beings had sailed all the way around the world for the first time! The huge size of the world was understood for the first time. For the first time and for all time it had been proven that the East could be reached by sailing west.

Cortés   Hernando Cortés (kôr tez′) had been in the Caribbean area since he was 19. He had helped conquer Cuba for Spain and had become very rich. But he wanted still more! Reports of the great riches of the Aztec empire in the land we call Mexico had reached Cuba. In 1519 Cortes left Cuba and set out for Mexico. With him he brought a small army of well-armed Spanish soldiers.

Cortés found that the Aztecs possessed gold and silver even beyond his dreams. And these Native Americans, although very brave, were no match for the Spanish soldiers with their horses, guns, and swords. By 1521 the Spaniards had conquered the Aztecs. They tore down the beautiful Aztec capital city of Tenochtitlán and made the proud Aztecs slaves. Turn back to page 59 to see what Tenochtitlán looked like. The great Aztec empire now belonged to Spain.

Pizarro   Ten years later the bold Spanish explorer Francisco Pizarro (pə zär′ ō) sailed from Central America to the rich empire of the Incas on the west coast of South America.

In order to gain control of this empire, Pizarro and his soldiers killed thousands of unarmed Incas. He took the Inca ruler captive. And after taking all his gold, Pizarro had him put to death. Pizarro soon won the whole huge Inca empire for Spain.

De Soto   Spain had almost complete control of Latin America by 1540. But Spanish explorers also made claims in the southern part of what is now the United States.

Hernando de Soto was one of these explorers. In 1539 he began a search for gold that took him from Florida and across the Southeast. He never did find gold. But he did discover what the American Indians called the Mississippi, the "Father of Waters." Why, do you think, was it given this name?

Coronado   Francisco Coronado was another Spanish explorer. In 1540 he left Mexico and went searching for the "Seven Cities of Gold" in the southwestern part of what is now the United States. He had heard about these cities from a black explorer named Estevánico (ās tā vä′ nē kō).

For about two years, Coronado and Estevánico, along with many Spanish soldiers, searched in vain for these cities of gold, which did not really exist. However, some of Coronado's men were the first Europeans to see the Grand Canyon in what is now the state of Arizona. And

75

In his search for gold, Coronado traveled as far north as what is now Kansas.

Coronado was able to claim the wide lands of the American Southwest for Spain.

Spanish leadership ends   Spain had taken the lead in exploring, conquering, and settling the Americas. By 1580 thousands of Spanish people were living in the Americas. Gold and silver from the Americas were pouring into the Spanish treasury. Spain led the world in wealth and power.

However, in 1588 the Spanish sent an **armada** (är mä′ də), or group of armed ships, to raid England. The English were able to crush this Spanish fleet. With this defeat, Spain began to decline as a world power. Spanish growth in America slowed. The French, Dutch, and English would soon be starting permanent settlements in America.

CHECKUP

1. How was Portugal able to claim Brazil? Why did Portugal claim only Brazil?
2. What was the major accomplishment of each of the following Spanish explorers: Ponce de León, Balboa, Magellan, Cortés, Pizarro, De Soto, and Coronado?
3. At what point did Spanish growth in America decline?

French, Dutch, and English in America

┌─VOCABULARY──────────────┐
Northwest
   Passage

missionary
└─────────────────────────┘

Northwest Passage   France, England, and the Netherlands, or Holland, which was the country of the Dutch people, had long been looking for a way to get around or through North America by water. They still wanted a short route to Asia and the Indies. Many brave explorers tried and failed to find such a **Northwest Passage.** But because of their journeys they were able to give their home countries much valuable information about the new lands. And as a result of their searches they were able to claim these new lands for their countries.

Verrazano   French beginnings in the Americas were small and slow. French fishing boats had been working off the coast of Canada since 1504. But no explorers came from France until Giovanni Verrazano (văr rə zä′ nō) sailed for North America in 1524.

Verrazano had been hired by French merchants to find a Northwest Passage. He did not succeed in this. But he did explore the northeast coast of what is now the United States. Trace Verrazano's route on the map on page 78. He discovered New York Bay and entered the mouth of the Hudson River. He sailed up the coast as far as what is now Newfoundland in Canada before he returned to France.

One of the first maps of the North American coast was made from the rough drawings Verrazano had done during this voyage.

Cartier   In 1534 a fine French sailor named Jacques Cartier (zhäk kär tyā′) made the first of several voyages to North America. He too was looking for a Northwest Passage. He was not able to find this water route through the continent. But he discovered the Gulf of St. Lawrence and the great St. Lawrence River in Canada. He sailed westward up this mighty river and claimed it for France. The land that is now called Canada became known as New France.

You can follow Cartier's route on the map on page 78.

Champlain   French fur companies began sending explorers and traders to Canada. The Native Americans were happy to trade furs for metal tools. The French got along well with the Indians. They did not try to conquer them as the Spanish had done in Mexico and Peru.

In 1603 one of the French fur companies sent Samuel de Champlain (sham plān′) to New France. For over 30 years Champlain explored North America, trading for furs and searching for a Northwest Passage.

He explored the coast of what is now New England. He also explored northeastern Canada all the way to the Great Lakes area. Everywhere he went he drew maps and made pictures of the places he saw and the people he met. He also wrote long reports about them and sent much information back to France.

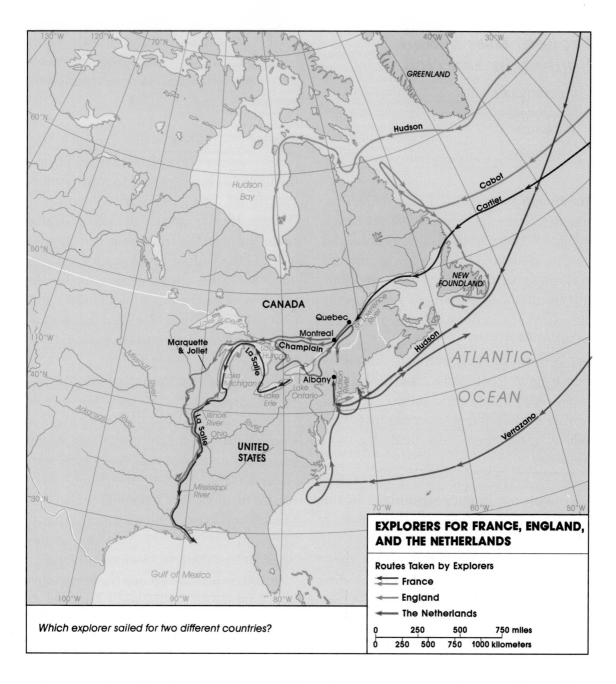

Which explorer sailed for two different countries?

EXPLORERS FOR FRANCE, ENGLAND, AND THE NETHERLANDS

Routes Taken by Explorers
- France
- England
- The Netherlands

0   250   500   750 miles
0 250 500 750 1000 kilometers

In 1608 Champlain founded the city of Quebec. Find Quebec on the map on this page. Quebec was the first lasting settlement in New France. It started as a small trading post on the St. Lawrence River. Now it is one of the leading cities in Canada. French is still spoken by the people who live in this lovely old city.

Marquette and Joliet   Many **missionaries** also came to North America from France. A missionary is a person sent to teach religion and provide help for people who need it. One of the French missionaries was Father Jacques Marquette (mär ket'). He wanted to teach Christianity to the American Indians.

Champlain discovered this lake, which was later named after him.

It was from these Native Americans that Father Marquette first heard stories of a "great water" that led to an even greater water. Father Marquette thought that these waters must certainly be part of the Northwest Passage. And in 1673 he set off to find the passage. With him was a French fur trader named Louis Joliet (zhô lyé) and several others.

They paddled south along the shores of Lake Michigan and eventually found the broad Mississippi River. They saw that the river flowed north and south, not east and west. It could not be the Northwest Passage after all. However, Marquette and Joliet followed the Mississippi River as far as the mouth of the Arkansas River before turning back.

You can follow the route of Marquette and Joliet on the map on page 78.

La Salle   In 1682 another Frenchman, Robert de La Salle, became the first European to travel the whole length of the Mississippi River to the Gulf of Mexico. He added greatly to French lands in North America by claiming all the land along the river for France. La Salle named the whole Mississippi Valley *Louisiana* for King Louis XIV of France.

Henry Hudson   Henry Hudson, an Englishman, made four trips to America looking for the Northwest Passage. He explored much of the eastern coast of North America while sailing for the Dutch in 1609. In his small ship, the *Half Moon*, Hudson was the first European to sail up the Hudson River. Find the Hudson River on the map on page 78. Follow the river northward to where the city of Albany now stands. This is the point Hudson reached before turning back.

Of course the Hudson River was not the great Northwest Passage. But Hudson was able to claim much of the beautiful land along the Hudson for the Dutch. It was good land with rich soil and many fur-bearing animals. The land that Henry Hudson claimed for the Dutch came to be known as New Netherland when a settlement was started there.

79

One of the first Dutch settlements in North America was built on an island at the mouth of the Hudson River. The Dutch named this settlement New Amsterdam, for a city in Holland. This small Dutch fur-trading settlement would eventually become New York City.

In 1610 Henry Hudson was hired by England to look for the Northwest Passage. This time he sailed farther north than he had gone before. He discovered the huge Hudson Bay in Canada. Hudson and his crew spent the long, cold winter there. This bay is so large that it is little wonder Hudson thought it might be the Pacific Ocean. Hudson Bay did not, of course, prove to be part of the Northwest Passage to the East. But England was able to claim a large part of Canada because of Henry Hudson's voyage.

While exploring for the Dutch in his ship, the Half Moon, *Henry Hudson sailed up the river later named for him.*

Cabot   Henry Hudson was not the first explorer to be sent to the Americas by England. An Italian called John Cabot believed, as Columbus did, that he could reach the Indies and all the wealth of the East by sailing westward. In the spring of 1497 Cabot was sent by England to test this idea.

Cabot's voyage across the cold and stormy North Atlantic was a rough one in his small ship. But on June 24 he became the first known European to set foot on North America since Leif Ericson. The land he discovered was an island off the eastern coast of Canada.

He found no spices or jewels or gold. He had not reached the Indies any more than Columbus had. But his voyage gave England its first claim to much of North America.

Drake   From the time of Cabot to the time of Sir Francis Drake, England did very little exploring in the Americas. Drake was an explorer, a sea captain, and a great adventurer. His looting of Spanish treasure ships as they returned from America brought great wealth to England.

In December of 1577 England sent Drake on a voyage of exploration to the Americas. On December 12 he left Plymouth, England, on a journey that was to take him around the world.

One of the things Drake wanted to do was to find the western outlet of the Northwest Passage into the Pacific Ocean. He sailed through the Strait of Magellan and up the Pacific coasts of both South America and North America. He claimed land along the northern coast of what is now California for England. Some historians believe that he claimed land for England as far north as the southern coast of Oregon.

Drake sailed back to England by traveling westward across the Pacific and Indian oceans, around the southern tip of Africa, and northward along the coast of Africa. He reached his home port of Plymouth in September of 1580. He was the first person from England to sail around the world. Turn to the map on pages 466–467 in the Atlas and trace Drake's route around the world.

Raleigh and Roanoke   Just a few years after Drake's famous voyage, another Englishman, Sir Walter Raleigh, started a colony in North America. Raleigh called the new land Virginia. For many years this name was used to describe a huge piece of land. It stretched from our present-day state of Pennsylvania to what we now call North Carolina.

Raleigh's group settled on Roanoke Island off the coast of North Carolina in 1585. But the colony was a failure. The people found life too hard. Many of them became sick. Within a year the settlers returned to England.

However, Raleigh decided to try again in 1587. This time his ships carried 117 men, women, and children. This new group also settled on Roanoke (rō′ ə nōk) Island. Soon after they arrived a baby was born. She was named Virginia Dare. Virginia Dare was the first English baby to be born in the Americas.

Because England was at war with Spain, Raleigh was not able to get supplies to Roanoke for 3 years. When the supply ships finally arrived, the colony had disappeared. The sailors found empty buildings, but not a single person remained. The sailors also found the word *Croatoan* (krō ə tō′ ən) carved into a tree. This was the name of a friendly group of American Indians who lived on an island about 100 miles (160 km) from Roanoke.

No one ever found out what happened to the English people of Roanoke. To this day that early settlement is known as the "Lost Colony of Roanoke."

The name of an Indian tribe carved on a tree was the only trace of the settlers on Roanoke Island.

CHECKUP

1. What were most of the explorers from France, Holland, and England looking for in the Americas?
2. Why was Canada once known as New France?
3. On what basis could the Dutch claim the area around what is now New York City?
4. Who was the first English person to sail around the world?

81

4/CHAPTER REVIEW

KEY FACTS

1. The Vikings were probably the first Europeans to discover America.

2. Christopher Columbus's discoveries made the rest of Europe aware of the Americas.

3. Explorers from Spain, Portugal, France, England, and the Netherlands made claims for their countries in the Americas. Usually claims were made on the basis of which country got explorers and settlers to an area first.

4. The Spanish had a huge empire in the southern part of the Americas long before lasting French and English colonies were begun to the north.

VOCABULARY QUIZ

Match these terms with the definitions. Use a separate sheet of paper.

a. explore	**f.** Northwest Passage
b. Vikings	**g.** Quebec
c. colony	**h.** St. Augustine
d. isthmus	**i.** armada
e. strait	**j.** expedition

1. The first Europeans to reach America

2. The first Spanish settlement in North America

3. A journey for a certain purpose

4. Many explorers looked for this

5. To search for new things or places

6. A narrow strip of land connecting two larger pieces of land

7. The first French settlement in North America

8. A narrow water passage connecting large bodies of water

9. A place far from the country that rules it.

10. A group of armed ships

REVIEW QUESTIONS

1. Why was Columbus's discovery of America so important?

2. Why did Spain have the greatest and earliest claims to lands in the Americas?

3. What are the differences between Spanish and French treatment of Native Americans?

4. What seem to be some of the difficulties in starting a settlement or a colony?

ACTIVITIES

1. Use an encyclopedia or some other library book to answer these questions.

(a) What did Ponce de León do in the Americas besides discovering Florida?

(b) Why was Balboa in the Americas?

(c) How did Estevánico get to the Americas?

(d) Where is Father Marquette buried?

(e) Why was Sir Francis Drake in the area of the Roanoke colony in 1586?

2. Find out as much as you can about one of the early explorers or settlers mentioned in this chapter. Read a book or look him or her up in the encyclopedia. Present the person you studied to the class by pretending you are that person. Tell about your life. Answer questions about your life as though you are that person.

3. Make a chart of famous explorers. Tell what country each explored for and the areas he explored. Include the following explorers: Leif Ericson, Christopher Columbus, John Cabot, Hernando de Soto, Juan Ponce de León, Jacques Cartier, Robert de La Salle, and Francis Drake.

4/SKILLS DEVELOPMENT

USING THE LIBRARY

A SOURCE OF INFORMATION

In reading this chapter you have learned about the people who explored North and South America. Perhaps you would like to know more about them. Or maybe you would like to know more about the kinds of ships on which they sailed. Do you know what instruments they used to sail such great distances on unknown seas? Do you know about other, more modern explorers? Who discovered the North Pole? The South Pole? Are people still exploring today?

The answers to these questions can be found in books in your school or public library. A great deal of material is available in the library. It is divided into several sections.

REFERENCE SECTION

First is the reference section. Here you will find encyclopedias, almanacs, atlases, dictionaries, and other books of general information. Start with an encyclopedia if you do not know very much about a topic.

You will also find the *Reader's Guide to Periodical Literature* in the reference section of most libraries. This guide tells you whether any magazine articles have been written about your topic. Many libraries have magazines of general interest. For a report on exploration, magazines such as *National Geographic*, *Smithsonian*, and *Natural History* may help.

CARD CATALOG

Admiral of the Ocean Sea is a book about Christopher Columbus written by Samuel Eliot Morison. You can find out whether your library has this book by looking in the card catalog. You could look under the author—Morison, Samuel Eliot. Or you could look for the title—*Admiral of the Ocean Sea*. You could also look under the name of the subject—Columbus. Looking at a subject name is a good way to see how many books the library has on that topic.

VERTICAL FILE

Many libraries also have collections of pictures, illustrations, and maps. A library may also have files of pamphlets and articles cut from newspapers. These are all kept in the vertical file. They are usually stored alphabetically by subject.

SKILLS PRACTICE

Let's see how good you are at using the library. Pick a topic listed below or one of your own choice. Using the books and articles you find in the library, do enough research to write a short essay on your topic. Be sure to list, at the end of your essay, the library resources you used.

Roald Amundsen
Robert E. Peary/Matthew A. Hensen
Richard E. Byrd
Henry Morton Stanley
Roy Chapman Andrews
John W. Powell
Robert Gray
Robert F. Scott
Edwin E. Aldrin
James Cook
Explorers' Club
Navigation Instruments
Ships
Northwest Passage

CHAPTER
5 Colonization

The First Colonies

VOCABULARY

London Company	burgess
journal	House of Burgesses
peninsula	pilgrim
indentured servant	Separatist
representative	Mayflower Compact

The London Company Other people shared Sir Walter Raleigh's dream of an English colony in Virginia. But they had learned from Raleigh's experience that starting a colony was too costly for one person. So a number of these people got together and formed the **London Company.** That way they could share the costs. Of course they also had to share any earnings. In 1607 Jamestown, Virginia, the first lasting English settlement in America, was founded by the London Company.

A settler's journal What was it like to be part of this new adventure? Suppose one of the first settlers had kept a **journal.** Parts of it might look like this:

20 December 1606 Great Excitement! Today 120 men sail from London in three ships, *Susan Constant, Godspeed,* and *Discovery.* We are to find gold and farm the land of Virginia.

26 April 1607 After 18 weeks at sea, land at last! It will feel so good to step on firm ground again! Sixteen of our number died on the long voyage. . . .

14 May 1607 Today our leaders, Captain Christopher Newport and Captain John Smith, chose a small **peninsula** for the settlement. We named it Jamestown in honor of the king. With water on three sides, Jamestown will be easy to defend against enemies. But I worry that it is too low and swampy. There is no freshwater spring. It may not be healthful to live here.

26 May 1607 Problems already! The "gentlemen" among us refuse to help with the work. They want only to search for gold. It's lucky everyone does not feel that way. We had just finished building our shelters when we were raided by Indians. I do not care to think what might have happened to us without the shelters.

Already we are running out of food and supplies. Captain Newport will sail to England soon to get more.

25 December 1607 I cannot remember a more unhappy Christmas! Only 53 of us are still alive. Disease and hunger are our worst enemies. If Captain Smith had not obtained food from Chief Powhatan, we might all be dead.

A struggle to survive You can see from the journal that life at Jamestown was not easy. However, the colony struggled on. Shortly after New Year's Day in 1608, Captain Newport returned with supplies and more settlers, two of whom

Logs were laid across the sawhorses and sawed into usable lengths. Skilled workers became important members of the Jamestown settlement.

were women. Captain Smith made a strict new rule: "No work, no food." Everyone had to work in the fields. For a while it seemed as though things were going well. But then Captain Smith was hurt and had to return home. Without his leadership, the settlers went back to their old ways.

By the fall of 1609, almost 500 people had come to Jamestown. But by June of 1610, the old enemies—sickness and hunger—had taken all but 60 of the settlers. These few survivors decided to leave Jamestown. Just as they set sail, they met a ship carrying supplies and 300 new settlers. The Jamestown group decided to join the new settlers.

Indentured servants   Many people wanted to come to the colony but they were too poor to pay the fare on the ship. So they came as **indentured servants.** Someone in the colony would agree to pay the fare of the poor person who in turn would agree to work without pay for a certain length of time—sometimes as long as 7 years. The master would have to give the servant food, clothing, and a place to live. When the time of service was up, the person was free. Both men and women came to America as indentured servants. This way of getting enough people to settle and work in the new land was used throughout the English colonies.

Tobacco   After several more years of hard work, the Jamestown settlement began to hold its own. In 1611 each settler was given land. In return a part of the crops was given to the London Company. Soon the colonists began growing tobacco, which proved to be very well suited to the area. In no time, ships loaded with tobacco to sell to England were sailing from Jamestown. Tobacco was used for money. It was even planted in the streets of the town. Some settlers became very wealthy, even though King James I at first tried to stop the tobacco trade. He said smoking was "hateful to the nose, harmful to the brain, dangerous to the lungs. . . ." Many people today would agree with him. Do you?

How many years were there between the settlement of the first English colony and the last?

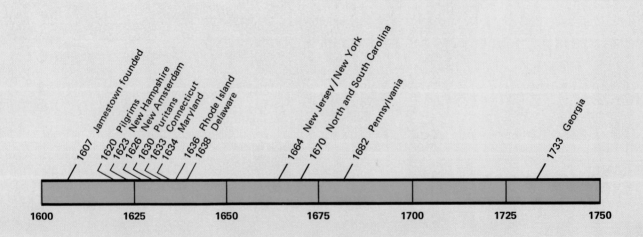

POPULATION OF JAMESTOWN, 1619–1624		
Year	Number of people arriving	Total population
1619	—	1,000
1620	100 (est.)	866
1621	1,051	843
1624	4,000	1,277

Success at last In 1619 the colonists were given the right to make their own laws. They voted for **representatives** called **burgesses.** They met as the **House of Burgesses.** Also in that year the first Africans were brought to Jamestown. They were put to work on the farms as indentured servants to pay their fare from Africa.

Let's look once more at the journal before we leave Jamestown:

> **25 December 1619** This is my thirteenth Christmas in Jamestown. When I think back over the years, I am sad. So many people have lost their lives here. We still have lots of sickness, and the natives are a constant threat.

Yet this has been my best year ever! My tobacco crop was excellent. I own my own farm and am thought to be quite rich. [Each settler was given 100 acres in 1616. All the crops grown on that land belonged to the settler.] And I got married! A shipload of women was brought to Jamestown by the London Company. They could choose a husband from the 1,000 men here. Each husband had to pay for his wife's passage. It is good to have a home at last!

As you can see from the journal, Jamestown was going well. Many good things had happened. The people had land and family life. They were free to choose their own representatives for their own government. The English had one successful colony in America. Another would soon be started.

The Pilgrims In 1620 another group of people came to America. These were the Pilgrims. A **pilgrim** is a person who travels for religious reasons. The story of the Pilgrims begins in England. There they were called **Separatists** because they

The House of Burgesses met here in the Capitol Building at Williamsburg.

had broken away from the English church. Because of this some of them were put in prison or watched closely. Others lost their jobs or had to leave their homes. Things got so bad in England that the Separatists decided to move to the Netherlands. Here, they heard, they could worship as they pleased.

The Separatists found religious freedom in the Netherlands. But they did not feel at home. They were country people in the city, strangers in a strange land. They did not like having their children grow up learning a different language and way of life. Many decided to move again, this time to Virginia.

The *Mayflower* In September 1620, about 100 people set sail for Virginia on a small ship called the *Mayflower*. Most of the travelers were Separatists. Others came for different reasons. None of the Pilgrims knew what they would find when they got to this new land.

After about 2 months the Pilgrims finally saw land. They were off the coast of what is now Massachusetts, far to the north of Virginia. They fell to their knees and thanked God for their safe arrival. Only one person had died in crossing.

Since they were so far from Virginia, the Pilgrims realized that they would need to make their own laws. So before they left the *Mayflower*, they made a compact, or agreement, with each other. They agreed to make laws as needed for the colony's good. They agreed to obey these laws. The paper, signed by the men of the new colony, was called the **Mayflower Compact.**

The Mayflower *was only 90 feet (27 m) long—there was very little room for passengers and crew.*

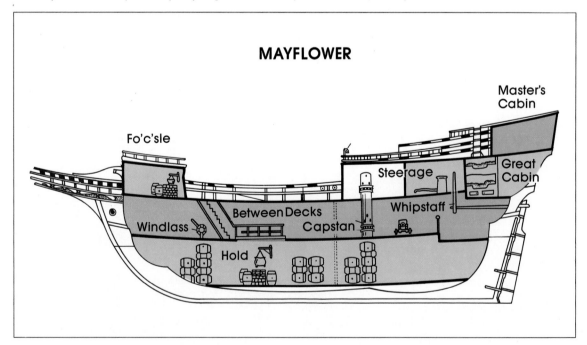

MAYFLOWER

Master's Cabin

Fo'c'sle

Steerage

Great Cabin

Whipstaff

Between Decks

Windlass

Capstan

Hold

The first year   After a few weeks of exploring, the little group finally chose an area to make their home. Here were a good harbor, fresh water, and a cleared field. They first went ashore on December 16, 1620. They called the area where they settled Plimoth Plantation.

Soon they were building houses and settling in. It was winter, and their clothing was not warm enough. They were alone, and they feared wild animals and what they called "wild men." Yet they trusted God for their help. By the end of 2 or 3 months half of the group had died. Disease and the cold were too much for them. At times there were only six or seven people well enough to care for the rest.

Squanto   In the spring of 1621, a Native American named Samoset came to visit the Pilgrims. He made it possible for them to meet Squanto, who spoke English well. Squanto had been taken to England some years before. When he returned, he found his entire tribe was dead from disease. Samoset also brought together the Pilgrims and Massasoit (mas ə soit'), the chief of the Wampanoags (wom' pä nōgz). The Native Americans and the Pilgrims agreed not to hurt one another or steal from one another. They would live together in peace. They would help each other in case of attack.

Squanto stayed on with the Pilgrims. They felt he was a special help sent from God. He showed them where to fish. He taught them how to plant corn. Fish heads and tails were put in the ground with the corn seed. This helped the corn grow. He also acted as a guide.

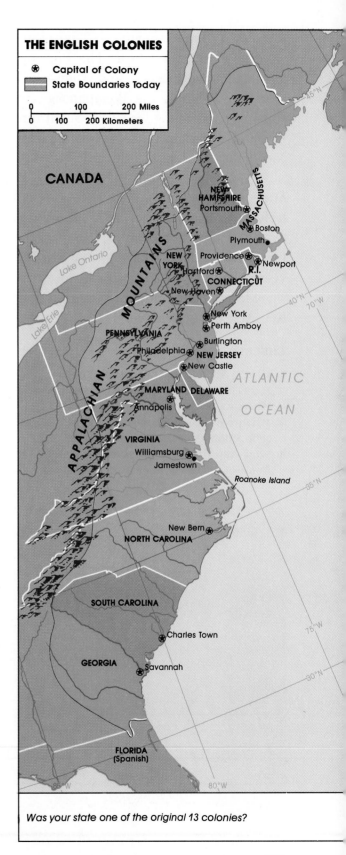

Was your state one of the original 13 colonies?

The first Thanksgiving The crops were good that first year. The Pilgrims decided to give thanks to God. They asked their new friends, the Wampanoags, to come to a feast. The Indians brought turkey and deer meat. They celebrated together for three days in the fall of 1621.

After 1621 The Plymouth Colony lasted because the Pilgrims were willing to put up with hardships. No one returned to England after that first terrible year. They stayed and worked together. They farmed and traded. They had a new life. And they were free.

CHECKUP

1. What were the first two lasting English settlements in North America? When was each begun? Where was each located?
2. Who were each of the following people: Captain John Smith, the Pilgrims, and Squanto?
3. Why were the Mayflower Compact and the House of Burgesses important?

New England Colonies

┌─VOCABULARY──────────────┐
Puritan	democracy
common	apprentice
town meeting	
└──────────────────────────┘

Massachusetts Bay Colony Ten years after the Pilgrims started the Plymouth Colony, English **Puritans** started coming to America. Like the Pilgrims, the Puritans wanted to worship in their own way. But they didn't want to leave the Church of England. Instead they wanted to "purify" it, or change it. The Puritans in England were treated just as badly as the Pilgrims. That was one reason they left England for America. They also came because they felt they could make a better living for themselves in America. The colony the Puritans started was the Massachusetts Bay Colony. Its chief city was Boston. Massachusetts Bay became the

John Winthrop led a group of Puritan settlers ashore to start a new colony.

most powerful New England colony. The Plymouth Colony founded by the Pilgrims became part of Massachusetts Bay Colony in 1691. Maine was a part of Massachusetts until 1820 when it became a state.

New Hampshire and Connecticut People moved from the Massachusetts Bay Colony into New Hampshire and Connecticut. New Hampshire remained a part of Massachusetts until 1679. The broad river valleys of Connecticut with their rich soil were good for farming. There were fine harbors on the coast. Fishing and shipping soon became important ways to make a living.

Rhode Island The Puritans of Massachusetts Bay Colony felt that everyone had to believe as they did. People who held other beliefs were punished.

This puzzled and angered Roger Williams. Williams was a minister in the Massachusetts Bay Colony. He taught that all people had the right to their own religious beliefs. He wondered how a colony such as Massachusetts Bay could punish people for holding different beliefs. Had it not been founded by people seeking religious freedom?

The Puritans felt Roger Williams had to be punished for his new ideas. He would be sent back to England. But Williams did not want this. He escaped with several followers and lived with Native Americans for a time. In 1636 Williams started a town that would later become the capital of Rhode Island. He named the town *Providence*, because he believed that God had "provided" the place.

Anne Hutchinson defied the church leaders of the Massachusetts Bay Colony and was banished.

Another of the first settlers of Rhode Island was Anne Hutchinson. She was sent out of the Massachusetts Bay Colony for her religious beliefs. Because of people like Anne Hutchinson and Roger Williams, Rhode Island became known as a place in which people could believe as they pleased without fear of punishment. Their ideas about freedom of religion are still basic in the United States.

New England towns The early colonists found that the rocky soil and hilly land of New England were not good for large farms. But most families could grow enough food for themselves and their animals. The settlers also found rapidly moving rivers and a coastline with many harbors. Fishing, shipping, and trading soon became more important ways to make a living than farming.

Towns quickly sprang up along the rivers and on the coast of New England. The largest of these was Boston, on Massachusetts Bay.

At the center of most New England towns was the green, or **common.** The common land was owned by all the people in the town. Here they could put their animals to graze. At the edge of the common stood the most important building in the town—the meeting house, or church.

The meeting house was used for the **town meeting.** Not everyone who lived in the town could take part in the town meeting. Only those men who owned property could discuss and vote on town business. Women and people who did not own land did not have a voice in running the town. The town meeting is, nevertheless, one of the earliest forms of **democracy** in America. *Democracy* means "rule, or government, by the people."

Church was very important to the people of New England. No work could be done on Sunday. Worship services often lasted 3 hours or more. There were morning and evening services. The minister of the church was one of the most important people in the town.

Schooling and apprenticeship   By law, every Puritan town of a certain size had to have a school. Let us follow a young boy of Boston and see what his education was like. This boy's name was Paul. His first school was a dame school, which met in the house of a townswoman. There were both boys and girls in the dame school. Here Paul was taught to read and write, to do a little arithmetic, and to mind his manners. If he did well, he was sometimes given a little cake. Children who did poorly had to wear the dunce cap. Those who misbehaved were beaten.

This meeting house in Cohasset, Massachusetts, has been in use for over 200 years.

When he was 8, Paul went to another school. Here he improved his reading and writing. He went on with his arithmetic. This school was usually for boys only. Girls, it was thought, did not need a good education.

At age 13 Paul became an **apprentice.** This means he became the pupil of a master craftworker in order to learn a trade. Many boys had to leave home to become apprentices. But Paul was lucky. He would learn how to be a silversmith from his own father. By the time he was 18 he was as good as his father.

As a teenager, Paul learned to ring the church bells. This way he could earn extra money. From high in the church tower Paul could look over Boston. He could see what a busy, crowded town it was. He could look over the harbor and see how important ships were to this port city. Almost everyone who lived in Boston was connected with shipping or fishing in some way.

Paul would have a great deal more to do in this city of Boston when he grew up. It would be helpful for him to know the city well. For Paul, the silverworker from old Boston, was also Paul Revere, Patriot. He would play a big part in the colonies' struggle for independence. You will learn about that in the next chapter.

This is a famous portrait by Copley of Paul Revere, the silversmith.

CHECKUP

1. What was the difference between the Pilgrims and the Puritans? What colony did each group start?
2. Why was New England not really good for farming, but good for fishing, shipping, and trading?
3. How was the town meeting a form of democracy? In what way was it not democratic?
4. What did a child learn in a dame school?

The Southern Colonies

VOCABULARY

naval stores	indigo
debt	Middle Passage
plantation	spiritual

Virginia   You have learned that the first of the 13 colonies to be settled was Virginia. It always had more people than any other southern colony. By 1760 it was the largest colony in America.

The other four southern colonies were Maryland, North and South Carolina, and Georgia. Can you find all five southern colonies on the map on page 89?

Lord Baltimore and his grandson are shown here with a map of the Maryland colony.

Maryland   Cecilius (sə sēl′ yəs) Calvert, Lord Baltimore, was a friend of King Charles I. Calvert was a Catholic. It was hard for Catholics to practice their religion in England at that time. King Charles listened to his friend's plea for a colony in America. It was to be a haven for Catholics.

Many Catholics settled in Maryland. In a short time people other than Catholics also came to Maryland. A law had been passed that allowed freedom of religion to any Christian. Maryland soon became a prosperous colony. The settlers grew many crops. The most important was tobacco. Many of these crops were sent back to England to be sold.

The Carolinas   King Charles II gave eight of his friends land in North America. They called the colony *Carolina* in honor of the king. (*Charles* is *Carol* in Latin.) The northern part of the colony was settled by people moving south from Virginia. They lived on small farms and grew enough food to feed their families. There were forests of pine trees. Ship masts, pitch, tar, and turpentine can be made from pine trees. These goods, called **naval stores** because they were used by the navy, were sent to England. The climate in the southern part of the colony was better for growing crops such as rice and **indigo.** A blue dye is made from the indigo plant. There were many good harbors in this part of the colony. Founded in 1670, Charles Town (now Charleston), was the major port from which these crops were shipped. In 1729 the king bought the colony back from his friends and divided it into two colonies—North and South Carolina.

Georgia   The last of the original 13 colonies was begun by James Oglethorpe. He felt sorry for British people who owed money and had been put in jail until they could pay their **debts.** As long as they were in jail, how could they earn money to pay the debts?

Oglethorpe went to King George II and asked to start a colony. Some of its settlers would be people from debtors' prisons. King George II feared that the Spanish in Florida would try to take over his North American colonies. He wanted a colony between South Carolina and Florida for protection. He allowed Oglethorpe to settle this region. It was named Georgia in the king's honor.

Oglethorpe and 114 settlers started their colony at Savannah in 1733. Not too many debtors ever came. But those who did could thank James Oglethorpe for a fresh start.

Life on a southern plantation   The South was very different from New England. There were not as many large towns. There was a great deal of flatland with rich soil. Many people in the South became farmers.

Many of the southern farms were **plantations.** Often on these large farms only one main crop was grown. The main crops at this time were tobacco, rice, and indigo. Most plantations were built along the banks of rivers. Crops could be loaded on the ships that would take them to England to be sold. The drawing below gives you an idea of what a plantation looked like.

The center of the plantation was the big house set in the middle of green grass, flower beds, and vegetable gardens. There would be several smaller buildings around the big house. There was usually a kitchen building, for it was too hot to cook inside the main house. There were barns for the horses. There might also be a separate school building. The sons and daughters of plantation owners were educated at home. There was often a tutor for the boys. Girls were usually taught to read and write by their mothers. Some girls, however, received just as good an education as the boys.

Set off at a distance from the big house were the slave quarters. There were small houses. They had dirt floors and few windows. There was very little furniture. Sometimes the houses had small vegetable gardens.

Nearly everything the people on a large plantation needed could be grown or made there.

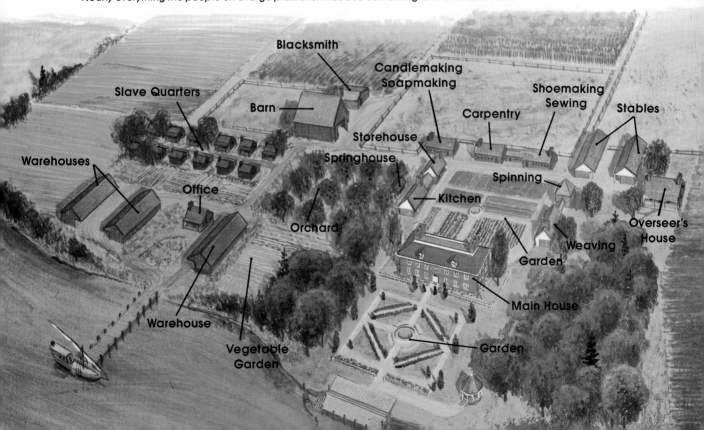

Only the very wealthy lived on plantations. Most people in Virginia were small farmers. They had few slaves, if any. They raised most of their own food and traded very little.

Many other people lived in small towns or villages. Williamsburg was the capital of Virginia. This is where the House of Burgesses met.

COLONIAL POPULATION BY RACE (selected colonies and years)

Colony	Black	White	Total
Virginia (1756)	120,156	173,316	293,472
North Carolina (1756)	19,000	60,000	79,000
South Carolina (1765)	90,000	40,000	130,000
Georgia (1766)	8,000	10,000	18,000
Maryland (1750)	40,000	100,000	140,000
New York (1771)	19,883	148,124	168,007
New Jersey (1745)	4,606	56,797	61,403
Massachusetts (1764)	5,235	218,950	224,185
Rhode Island (1749)	3,079	28,439	31,518
Connecticut (1756)	3,587	128,212	131,799

Slavery in the colonies By 1760 the English were the largest group of people in the American colonies. The second largest group were Africans. The English came freely. At first many Africans came freely or as indentured servants, but after 1650 nearly all came as slaves.

Perhaps the cruelest part of the slave trade was the **Middle Passage.** This was what the trip from Africa to America on the slave ship was called. Slave ships were very overcrowded. Traders felt they could make more money by filling the ships. Slaves were squeezed in and chained together. Some were laid on rough boards. There was not room for exercise. The smell was terrible. The people were covered with filth.

Living like this caused much illness and death. Many slaves wished they could die. Often they tried to jump overboard. If caught they would be savagely whipped.

Most of these slaves were separated from their families. The ship and the way

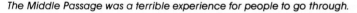

The Middle Passage was a terrible experience for people to go through.

Slaves worked long, hard hours, especially those who worked in the fields.

of life were new to them. They did not know where they were being taken. The Middle Passage showed how cruel humans could be to each other. It was a taste of the life in slavery to come.

There were slaves in every one of the 13 colonies by 1760. Because plantations were so large and needed so many workers, there were far more slaves in the southern colonies than in the middle colonies or New England. Yet only one out of four southerners owned slaves.

Life as a slave   The worst thing about slavery was the lack of freedom. Food, clothing, and shelter all came from the master. Slaves had no legal rights. They could not be taught to read and write in most colonies. They could not own property. They could not even marry legally.

Slavery was for the most part constant hard work. Most slaves worked in the fields. Slaves said they worked from "can-see" (dawn) until "can't-see" (dusk). After field work there were other chores, such as mending roads and fences. It was usually late in the day before they could eat their first hot meal of the day. This kind of hard work went on 6 days a week, every week of the year.

Other slaves worked as servants in the big house. They often had easier lives than the field slaves. But they, too, worked all day, 6 days a week. House servants had to cook, clean, weave, sew, mend, and nurse. Slaves were also skilled craftworkers, such as carpenters, masons, blacksmiths, potters, and silversmiths.

Slaves usually ate the same plain food day after day. Pork and cornmeal were most common. Clothes were old and patched. Shoes were provided only in winter. You have already read a description of the slave quarters on a plantation. Sometimes these quarters were little more than shacks that did not keep out the rain and cold.

Some owners treated their slaves well. Kindness worked the best in keeping the loyalty of slaves. Unfortunately many owners used force and punishment. Beatings, whippings, torture, less food, and threats of being sold away from family members were all used to make slaves obey. Because there were so many slaves in the South, owners feared the slaves would harm them. Many slaves tried to run away. Some tried to fight back.

Most slaves were very religious. Their belief in a better life after death helped many live with hope. Their **spirituals,** or religious songs, are often sung today.

These slaves helped get the United States started. They helped build the country with their labor. But as we shall see, the treatment of blacks as slaves led to many problems.

CHECKUP

1. Name the five southern colonies. Which was the first to be settled? The last?
2. Which was the largest group of people to come to the colonies? Second largest?
3. Why did the South have so many more slaves than other parts of the country?

The Middle Colonies

VOCABULARY
Quaker

Why "middle" colonies? Turn to the map on page 89. Find the colonies of New York, Pennsylvania, New Jersey, and Delaware. These are called the "middle colonies." Notice they are between the New England and southern colonies. Does this give you a clue as to how the middle colonies got their name?

The middle colonies were a mixture of New England and southern colonies. They were like New England in that people worked in shipping, lumbering, and fishing. They were like the southern colonies because there were also large farms.

Pennsylvania William Penn received land in America as payment for a debt owed by the king to Penn's father. He called the new land *Pennsylvania,* which means "Penn's woods." He wanted to start a colony on this land where people of any religion would be free to worship as they pleased.

William Penn belonged to a religious group called **Quakers.** Because of their love for all people, Quakers called themselves simply "Friends." Quakers believed God had made all men and women equal. They refused to take part in war. During the 1600's they were being jailed and even killed in England. This was because their beliefs were different from those of the Church of England.

Beginning in 1682, Quakers and others quickly settled Penn's colony. In 2 years

Philadelphia has been a busy port since the eighteenth century.

there were 8,000 colonists in Pennsylvania. The Native Americans and Penn made a treaty of friendship very quickly. He paid them for their land. Because of this, the two groups got along well.

Philadelphia, the largest city in Pennsylvania, was on its way to becoming the leading city in the colonies. It was already very busy. It was the chief port for newcomers to America. It was a center of trade for the many small farms that dotted the countryside of the middle colonies. Many groups of people with different jobs and different religions lived together peacefully here. Philadelphia had public libraries, a fire department, and the first hospital in America. The city had some well-lighted, paved streets, as well as police protection. There were three newspapers, a college, and discussion groups to talk about problems. Philadelphia became the most advanced city in America.

New York Henry Hudson claimed much of North America for the Dutch in 1609. The area he claimed was named New Netherland. Early Dutch settlers traded furs with the Native Americans.

In 1625 the Dutch began settling New York City, which they called New Amsterdam. Peter Minuit (min' yü it), their leader, bought Manhattan Island, part of New York City, from the Native Americans for goods worth $24.00.

In 1664 the Netherlands and England were at war. The king of England decided to take over New Netherland. He gave his brother, the Duke of York, four warships to capture it.

The leader of New Netherland was Peter Stuyvesant (stī′ və sənt). He was not well-liked by the Dutch settlers. When the English warships came, the Dutch would not fight under Stuyvesant. New Netherland was taken by the English without a shot being fired! It was renamed New York.

The Dutch had a lasting influence on New York. Brooklyn and Yonkers are Dutch names. Three Presidents of the United States, Martin Van Buren and Theodore and Franklin Roosevelt, had Dutch ancestors in New York.

New Jersey   The Duke of York gave a large part of his huge colony to two friends, George Carteret and John Berkeley. Carteret had defended the island of Jersey in the English Channel during a war. So the area was called New Jersey. Some Dutch people had already settled there, near the Hudson River. There were also some Swedish settlers near the mouth of the Delaware River. Find these rivers on the map on page 311.

Land in New Jersey was sold for low prices so that people would come there to live. There was also religious freedom. By 1702 there were so many new settlers in New Jersey that it was decided to separate it from New York. It became a colony with its own government.

Delaware   The first European settlement in Delaware was made by Swedes. They called the colony New Sweden. These early settlers made a very important contribution to life in the colonies. In Sweden, where they came from, people lived in houses made of logs rather than planks or boards. They built the same

Notice the fort, the windmill, and the gallows—all part of the colony of New Amsterdam. Why, do you think, was each important to the colony?

kinds of houses in New Sweden. Other settlers liked these easy-to-build houses and copied them.

In time New Sweden became part of the New Netherland colony and then part of New York. The Pennsylvania colony wanted a way to reach the Atlantic Ocean. William Penn bought Delaware from the Duke of York. In 1704 it finally became a separate colony.

CHECKUP

1. What colonies were known as the middle colonies? Why?
2. Who started Pennsylvania? Why was there total religious freedom there?
3. Why was Philadelphia a leading city of the time?
4. What colonies started out as New Netherland and New Sweden?
5. With what colony are Carteret and Berkeley connected?

THE ENGLISH COLONIES

Colony	Place and date of first settlement	Founders	Facts
Virginia	Jamestown, 1607	English	Founded to make profit for company and to improve settlers' fortunes.
Massachusetts	Plymouth, 1620	English	Established so that settlers could live according to their religious beliefs
New Hampshire	Dover, 1623	People from Massachusetts	Settlers sought greater opportunity.
New York	Fort Orange (Albany), 1624	Dutch	Dutch set up trading posts. English seized colony, 1664.
Connecticut	Windsor, 1633	People from Massachusetts	Settlers sought land and religious freedom.
Maryland	St. Mary's City, 1634	English	Founded by Cecilius Calvert, Lord Baltimore, as a refuge for Catholics.
Rhode Island	Providence, 1636	People from Massachusetts	Founder Roger Williams sought religious freedom.
Delaware	Fort Christina (Wilmington), 1638	Swedes	Small Swedish towns, taken over by Pennsylvania after 1681.
New Jersey	Pavonia (Jersey City), about 1640	Dutch	Early Dutch settlements. Land granted to Englishmen John Berkeley and George Carteret, 1664.
Pennsylvania	Tinicum Island, 1643	Swedes, English	Early small Swedish colony. William Penn founded English colony as refuge for Quakers and others.
North Carolina	Albemarle County, about 1653	People from Virginia	Eight men given area later divided into North and South Carolina.
South Carolina	Charles Town (Charleston), 1670	English	(See above.)
Georgia	Savannah, 1733	English	Founded by James Oglethorpe as refuge for debtors and others.

5/CHAPTER REVIEW

KEY FACTS

1. The first English colonies were started at Jamestown, Virginia, in 1607, and Plymouth, Massachusetts, in 1620.

2. Thirteen colonies in three areas, New England, the middle colonies, and the southern colonies, had been started by 1760. Each area had its own characteristics and way of life.

3. Geography played an important part in where the first settlements were located and in the types of jobs colonists in different parts of America had.

4. Black Americans were forced to come to America as slaves almost from the beginning. A large part of the southern way of life depended on their labor.

VOCABULARY QUIZ

Match these terms with the definitions. Use a separate sheet of paper.

a. peninsula   **f.** democracy
b. burgesses   **g.** town meeting
c. pilgrim   **h.** apprentice
d. Mayflower Compact   **i.** plantation
e. Puritans   **j.** slavery

1. Representatives who made laws in Virginia
2. Rule by the people
3. Settlers of Massachusetts Bay Colony
4. A large farm
5. A person learning a trade from a master craftworker
6. Being treated as less than human
7. Land with water on three sides
8. Agreement made by Plymouth settlers to govern themselves
9. A gathering to vote on matters of concern to all
10. A person who travels for religious reasons

REVIEW QUESTIONS

1. In what ways were the people of Jamestown and the Pilgrims helped by the Native Americans?

2. Why is the Mayflower Compact important to United States history?

3. In what way did geography help New Englanders decide what jobs to do?

4. Why were the middle colonies called by that name?

5. Explain the statement, "The South was built on the backs of blacks."

ACTIVITIES

1. Make your own map and map key of the original 13 colonies. The map should give the name and location of each of the colonies. Identify the colonies by group—New England, Middle, Southern—in the key. Use the map on page 89 as a guide, but think of your own key.

2. Benjamin Franklin, who lived in Philadelphia, was one of the first of many people to work with electricity. It has become very important to all of us. Make a poster or scrapbook on one of the following themes: "Uses of Electricity," "Life Without Electricity," or "How I Can Save Electricity."

3. Write and act out a two-person play on one of the following ideas or one of your own.

(a) Captain John Smith explaining why the "No work, no food" rule was important

(b) Penn making a treaty with the Native Americans

(c) An apprentice looking for a master craftworker to learn from

(d) Slaves talking about their life on a southern plantation

INTERPRETING PROVERBS

FRANKLIN AND HIS ALMANAC

Benjamin Franklin earned lasting fame as the publisher of *Poor Richard's Almanac*. This small book with a paper cover was put out yearly from 1733 to 1758. People in all the colonies read it. The almanac had information about holidays, weather, tides, quarters of the moon, jokes, and much more.

Perhaps *Poor Richard's Almanac* is best remembered for the many wise sayings or proverbs Franklin put in it. Some sayings were about good manners. Others were about the value of hard work or saving money. Most of the important parts of daily living were the subjects of these proverbs. Franklin's ideas were stated clearly and often in a funny way. They were easy to remember. People were always repeating them to each other. Here are some of these sayings.

Fish and visitors smell in three days.

God helps those that help themselves.

A small leak will sink a great ship.

A word to the wise is enough.

Early to bed and early to rise
makes a man healthy, wealthy, and
wise.

A penny saved is a penny earned.

When the well is dry, you know the worth of water.

He that goes a borrowing goes a sorrowing.

SKILLS PRACTICE

Show that you understand the meaning of Franklin's sayings by writing them in your own words. Then choose one saying and write a story to show that the saying is true.

What do the proverbs around the border of the painting mean?

103

2/UNIT REVIEW

1. Native Americans arrived in the Americas long before any other settlers. — *What is one theory about the way they came?*

2. There were many different Native American cultures throughout North and South America. — *Can you name a Native American group that used to live or still lives in your area?*

3. Native Americans made many contributions to the way of life in the United States. — *What foods have you eaten recently that were developed by Native Americans? What are some Native American words that have become part of the English language?*

4. Explorers had to be very brave. — *Compare an early explorer, such as Columbus, with modern explorers, such as the astronauts.*

5. Many European countries sent explorers to the Americas. — *On an outline map of North and South America, show the claims made by various nations.*

6. Each group of settlers that came here helped the country to grow and develop into what it is today. — *Cut out pictures of many different Americans. Use old newspapers and magazines. Paste your pictures on a large piece of cardboard or around an empty cereal box. Cover the whole surface. Title your montage "Americans All."*

7. Early settlers came for many different reasons: desire for riches, religious freedom, a chance to make a new life, or because they were forced to. —*Name at least one group of settlers that fits each reason.*

8. Thirteen English colonies were located along the Atlantic coast. They have been divided into New England, southern, and middle colonies. — *Name the New England colonies, the southern colonies, and the middle colonies. Tell who settled each colony.*

A New and Growing Nation

CHAPTER
6 Birth of a Nation

Bad Feelings Grow Between Britain and the Colonies

VOCABULARY

independence

revolution

Parliament

massacre

Committees of Correspondence

Boston Tea Party

Continental Congress

The French and Indian War   In 1763 Britain and the colonies ended a 7-year war with the French and Indians. As a result of this war France was driven out of North America. Britain would now rule Canada and other lands that had belonged to France. This brought peace to the American colonies. The colonists no longer had to fear attacks from Canada. The Americans were happy to be a part of Britain in 1763. Yet a dozen years later, these same people would be fighting the British for **independence,** or freedom from Great Britain's rule. This war was called the War for Independence, the American Revolution, or the Revolutionary War. A **revolution** changes one type of government or way of thinking and replaces it with another. In this chapter, you will learn about the American Revolution and the changes it brought about.

"No taxation without representation!" The British lawmaking body was and still is called **Parliament.** The colonists were not members. The British Parliament started passing laws to tax the colonies. Britain thought the colonists should pay their share of the cost of the French and Indian War. The taxes would also help pay for keeping British soldiers in America. The soldiers would serve along the borders of the colonies to protect the settlers from Indian attacks. It seemed fair to the British that the colonists share these costs too. They put taxes on legal papers and everyday items such as glass, paint, and tea.

The colonists got very upset about these taxes. Their own colonial assemblies had not voted for them. They did not welcome Parliament's tax laws. Their motto became, "No taxation without representation." People would not buy anything British. Colonial assemblies would not collect the taxes. Perhaps the most excitement was caused by groups called the Sons of Liberty. They destroyed tax collectors' homes and drove some tax people out of town.

Trouble in Boston   British soldiers in America became special targets of the colonists' anger. They were constant reminders of British control.

This famous painting is called "The Spirit of '76." Can you tell why?

In March 1770, a crowd gathered near some British soldiers in Boston. The crowd waved sticks, threw snowballs and stones, and yelled at them.

After some time the soldiers feared for their safety and fired into the crowd. Five people died. Among them was Crispus Attucks, a freedom-loving runaway slave. Colonial leaders called this sad event a **massacre.** A massacre is a killing of many people who cannot defend themselves very well.

Committees of Correspondence Things quieted down for a few years. In 1770 most of the hated taxes were ended. Parliament and the king felt that collecting the taxes was too much trouble. But what had happened in Boston was only a sample of what was to come.

In order to keep contact between colonies, leaders started groups called **Committees of Correspondence.** They kept in touch by writing letters. In these days before telephone, radio, and television, this was the best way to get news from one colony to another. Many leaders, such as Samuel Adams, Thomas Jefferson, and Patrick Henry, were members of these committees.

Boston Tea Party George III, the king of Great Britain, said that there had to be a tax on something to prove that the British had the right to tax. So there was still a small tax on tea. The colonists remained firm. They would not pay any tax passed by Parliament. Colonial women refused to buy or serve tea.

British merchants were not selling much tea. So Parliament passed a law that greatly lowered its price. Boatloads of tea were sent to America. Since it was cheaper than ever, the British thought that surely the colonists would buy tea now!

They were wrong. Tea was burned. Tea was left to rot. Ships loaded with it were not allowed in ports. In Boston the Sons of Liberty dressed up as Indians. Late at

In what year did the Constitution become the law of the land?

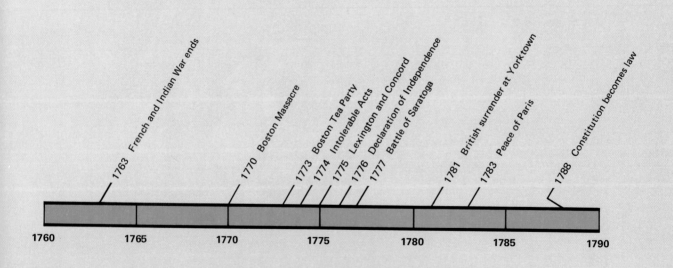

The Boston Tea Party took place the night of December 16, 1773.

night they went to Boston Harbor and threw more than 300 chests of tea into the water. This action was called the **Boston Tea Party.**

The Intolerable Acts   The British were very angry! Within a few months, they passed what the colonists called the Intolerable Acts. *Intolerable* means "unbearable." These acts were meant to punish the people of Boston. The port of Boston was closed. No self-government was allowed in Massachusetts. British troops had to be housed and fed by the Massachusetts colonists.

The Committees of Correspondence acted quickly—letters were sent telling what was happening in Boston. Other colonies sent help and supplies. People wondered if their colony would be the next to feel the anger of Great Britain. The colonies agreed to meet together in late summer of 1774.

First Continental Congress   The first meeting of the group of representatives from the colonies was called the **Continental Congress.** It was held in Philadelphia on September 5, 1774. Efforts were made to keep peace with Great Britain. Parliament was asked to agree that the colonists had the same rights as citizens who lived in Britain. The colonists decided to meet again the next spring.

But events were almost out of control already. King George III was too stubborn to give in. He said that the king and Parliament would rule the colonies! Before the Congress met again, the first shots of the American Revolution had been fired.

CHECKUP

1. What were the results of the French and Indian War?
2. How did Britain try to get the colonies to pay for keeping soldiers in America?
3. What did the colonists mean by the slogan "No taxation without representation"?

The Move To Independence

VOCABULARY

Minuteman
preamble

Declaration of Independence

"The British are coming!" It was early morning, April 19, 1775. Captain John Parker was getting tired. He was waiting with a group of **Minutemen.** These farmers and other citizens were ready to fight "with a minute's warning." They had been up since midnight.

Paul Revere had galloped through Lexington warning everyone that the British soldiers were on their way from Boston. The British wanted to capture colonial leaders John Hancock and Samuel Adams, who were in Lexington. They also wanted to get the military supplies that were stored in Concord.

Now it was nearly dawn. Parker paced the floor of the tavern in which he was waiting. Many men had gone home. Would the British come? What would he do if they did come?

Suddenly a rider broke the morning silence. "The British are coming! They are nearly here!" The men sprang to action. There was shouting and beating of drums. About 70 citizens of Lexington followed Captain Parker to the grassy area in the center of town called the green. The British marched up. They found themselves facing a group of proud colonists who refused to go home when told to do so.

Parker said, "Don't fire unless fired upon, but if they mean to have a war, let it begin here." A shot was fired, but whether by a British soldier or a Minuteman, no one knows. Other shots fol-

The midnight ride of Paul Revere is a popular story in American history.

lowed. Eight colonists were killed and ten wounded. Only one British soldier was wounded. The War for Independence had begun.

"... the shot heard round the world" The British went on to Concord. They destroyed military supplies and fought with another group of Minutemen at Concord Bridge. Adams and Hancock were not captured. The British then started back to Boston. It seemed that Minutemen were behind every tree and rock on the way. The Minutemen fired at the British as they marched past. Almost one third of the British soldiers were killed or wounded on the return trip to Boston. Find Lexington and Concord on the map on page 115.

Second Continental Congress The representatives from the colonies met again on May 10, 1775. Perhaps at no time in our history has a finer group ever met together. Samuel Adams, John Adams, John Hancock, John Jay, Patrick Henry, Thomas Jefferson, George Washington, and Benjamin Franklin were only a few of the outstanding people who gathered in Philadelphia. They would lead the country through the war.

The Continental Congress soon got news of armed fights. Ethan Allen and the Green Mountain Boys captured Fort Ticonderoga in New York (see map on page 115). In June of 1775 the Battle of Bunker Hill was fought in Boston (see map on page 115). The British won the hill, but lost over a thousand men. Peter Salem, a freed slave, was given credit for killing the British leader. The Americans

New Yorkers pull down the statue of George III on the Bowling Green after they get news of the signing of the Declaration of Independence. There is a park there today.

learned that they could fight the British successfully. But the colonies were still not ready to declare independence.

George Washington The Second Continental Congress picked Washington as Commander in Chief of the Continental army. George Washington was a tall, quiet man. He was well-known for being wise and kind. Washington was raised on a large Virginia plantation. As a 16-year-old boy he explored lands in western Virginia. Later he gained experience as a soldier and became well-known in the French and Indian War.

After that war Washington married and settled down to a life as a farmer and land owner. He became one of the richest men in the colonies. He was a member of the Virginia House of Burgesses for 15 years. He was elected to both the First and Second Continental Congresses. Washington did not want war. But he saw no other way. He would prove to be an outstanding leader.

111

John Adams (left), Thomas Jefferson (center), Benjamin Franklin (right), Roger Sherman (left rear), and Robert Livingston (right rear) present the Declaration to the Congress.

Independence comes at last Loyalty to Britain and the king was still very strong in the colonies as late as 1775. Many people still thought of themselves as subjects of the king. War was a very serious matter. But the Continental army had been formed and battles were being fought. Britain was doing nothing to try to keep the peace. A booklet called *Common Sense* was getting more people to favor independence. The author was Thomas Paine, an Englishman who came to live in Philadelphia in 1774. In *Common Sense* Paine gave good reasons why the colonists should be free from "the royal brute of England."

Finally, in June of 1776, a committee was chosen to write a declaration of independence. Thomas Jefferson wrote the draft of the declaration based on the committee's suggestions. On July 4, 1776, after two days of discussion, Congress passed the **Declaration of Independence.** Church bells rang all over Philadelphia to make independence known.

John Hancock, the president of the Continental Congress, was the first to sign. According to legend he wrote his name in large letters, "so the king of England could read it without his glasses." When Hancock mentioned the need for complete agreement on the

Declaration, Ben Franklin commented, "We must all hang together or we shall all hang separately." This remark showed the great risk each of the signers was taking.

The Declaration of Independence gave reasons for fighting the American Revolution. It has served as a guide to freedom-loving people throughout the world.

There are four parts to the Declaration of Independence. They are the **Preamble,** or introduction; a Statement of Rights, telling what rights all people should have; a list of wrongs done by King George III, and a Statement of Independence. The following summary gives some of the ideas that Jefferson put into the Declaration.

THE DECLARATION OF INDEPENDENCE

IN CONGRESS, JULY 4, 1776
All 13 of the United States of America agree on this Declaration

The Preamble   Sometimes in history people have to free themselves from control by other people. They have to make their place with the nations of the world, in keeping with the laws of nature and the laws of God. When people do this, it is only right that they give their reasons.

A Statement of Rights   We believe these truths: People are created equal. God gives people certain rights that cannot be taken away. Among these are the right to life, the right to liberty, and the right to try to be happy.

Government should help people keep these rights. Governments get their power from the people they govern.

When government does not protect people's rights, the people must change the government or get rid of it. They then must start a new government based on these rights. It is only wise that a change in government

not be made lightly. It is such a serious matter that most people throughout history would rather suffer than change governments. However, when people's rights are taken away over and over again, it is their right and duty to get rid of the old government and start a new one.

List of George III's Wrongs   This is what has happened in the colonies. Therefore the people have to start a new government. The king of Great Britain has a history of trying to take away freedoms. These facts are presented to the world.

A Statement of Independence   In spite of all these things, we have tried to get along. We have not been helped. George III has proved he cannot rule a free people. The British people have been no better. We have warned them, reminded them, and asked them to consider our freedom. They have turned a deaf ear to us.

Therefore, we in Congress, representatives of the good people of these colonies, with God as our Judge, declare the following:

That these colonies are now free states and they have the right to be free states.

That these states have no connection at all with Great Britain.

That because they are free states, they have the right to make war and peace, make friends, trade, and do everything free states can do.

In support of this Declaration, with God's protection, we pledge to each other our lives, our wealth, and our honor.

CHECKUP

1. Why are the events at Lexington and Concord important?
2. Who took a midnight ride? Captured Fort Ticonderoga? Was made Commander in Chief of the Continental army? Was a hero at Bunker Hill? Wrote *Common Sense*? Wrote the Declaration of Independence?
3. On what date was the Declaration of Independence passed by the Continental Congress? Name the four major parts of the Declaration.

WAR!

VOCABULARY

militia	Hessian
Loyalist	privateer
Patriot	

Outlook bad   Most of Washington's army thought they could go home after independence was declared. John Adams knew better. He said, "We shall have a long and bloody war to go through." The war would go on for 5 hard years. The peace treaty was not signed until 1783, 2 years after the War for Independence had ended.

The new United States of America faced a tough challenge in 1776. Britain had the best navy in the world. The United States had no navy. Britain had a well-trained army and also hired soldiers from other countries. In the beginning most of the United States Army was made up of state **militia,** such as the Minutemen of Massachusetts. These men agreed to serve in the army for a period of time. When that time was up, they went home. As the war went on, a small, full-time regular army was built up. British soldiers were well supplied. George Washington had to beg Congress for proper food, clothing, and weapons for his troops.

The United States had a population of less than 3 million people. Of that number perhaps 500,000 were **Loyalists.** Loyalists were people who still supported Britain and George III. Many fought in the king's army. Also, about one third of the

The winter of 1777–1778 spent at Valley Forge was one of the most difficult of the war.

114

Americans took no side. They really did not care who won. The remaining people were **Patriots,** however, who gave their best for the cause of liberty.

War in the Northeast   In late 1776 General George Washington had to take a chance. His army was in poor shape. Many soldiers had been killed, captured, or had simply left for home. British soldiers had taken New York City. If British General Howe had pushed a bit harder in New York, Washington could have lost his entire army.

On Christmas night, 1776, Washington sent soldiers across the ice-blocked Delaware River. They were to attack the **Hessians** who were celebrating Christmas in Trenton, New Jersey. Hessians were German soldiers hired to fight for the British. The plan worked! The Hessians were totally surprised. Almost 1,000 prisoners were taken.

In 1777 much fighting took place in Pennsylvania. When the British captured Philadelphia, the Continental Congress had to leave the city. But the turning point of the war was the battle of Saratoga in New York. The British under General "Gentleman Johnny" Burgoyne were badly defeated. About 5,000 British soldiers surrendered to the American army led by General Horatio Gates.

This great American victory brought France into the war. The French had not forgotten the loss of the North American colonies to the British in 1763. But France wanted some sign that the colonists could win against the British. The battle of Saratoga showed the French that the colonists had a good chance of winning their

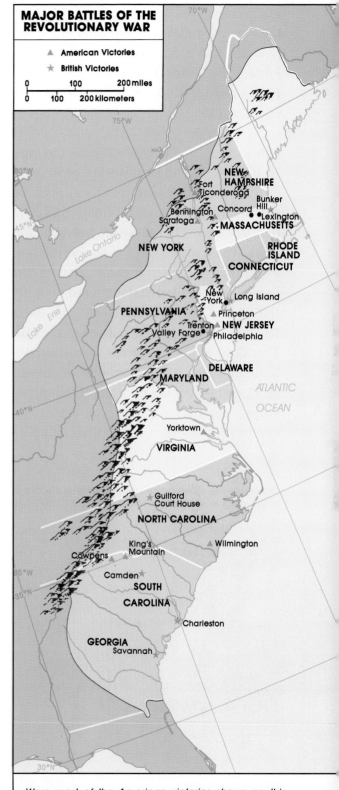

Were most of the American victories shown on this map in the North or in the South?

independence. This was especially true if the Patriots could get help from European powers. Later Spain and Holland also joined the Patriots against the British. Find the sites of these battles on the map on page 115.

War at sea   The United States did very well at sea, fighting the world's most powerful navy. One reason was because of the **privateers.** These were small privately owned ships. They were armed with cannons. The owners were given permission by Congress to attack the British in the name of the United States government. By the end of the war the 2,000 privateers had sunk or captured 600 enemy ships. The Continental Congress also started a national navy. It, together with the navies of 11 states, numbered no more than 100 ships. Yet they managed to destroy or capture twice that many British ships.

This engraving shows cavalrymen fighting at the battle of Cowpens in South Carolina on January 17, 1781.

The greatest American naval officer was John Paul Jones. He was daring. He attacked ships off the British coast. In a famous battle, Jones's ship, the *Bonhomme Richard* fought the British ship *Serapis.* At one point in the battle Jones's ship was sinking. When asked to give up, Jones answered, "I have not yet begun to fight!" He went on to win.

Battles in the South   After the battle of Saratoga, the major land battles were fought in the South. For a time the British were very successful. They controlled most of Georgia. Americans suffered their greatest defeat of the war at Charleston, South Carolina.

But Americans would not give up. People like Francis Marion, the "Swamp Fox," made constant daring raids on the British. Washington put General Nathanael Greene in charge of the army in the South. The Americans began to win some battles.

The British general, Lord Cornwallis, tried hard to capture Greene's army. He was unable to do so and marched his army north to Yorktown, Virginia. Look at the map on page 115. Notice that Yorktown is on a peninsula. Can you see how Cornwallis and his army could be trapped there?

Washington raced his army south from New York. He used the French army and navy to complete the trap of the British. The British could not win against such a combination of fighting forces. There was nowhere they could retreat to. Cornwallis had to surrender at Yorktown on October 19, 1781. This was the last big battle of the war. With Cornwallis's surrender, the British were ready to make peace.

Why the Americans won   The Americans won the war in spite of great odds against them. But some things favored the Patriots. They were fighting for their homes and families. They knew the land. Their sources of supplies and new soldiers were nearby.

Perhaps the greatest strength of the United States was its people. While not everyone was for the war, those who favored it were willing to die for what they believed. The people's courage and belief in freedom started our country.

The leadership of the United States was outstanding. George Washington was a wise and respected general. His skill held things together when all seemed lost. And he was helped by a number of other able leaders—Samuel Adams, John Adams, Benjamin Franklin, Robert Morris, John Hancock. The list of names could be a long one.

Many great leaders came from foreign countries. They believed in the ideas for which the Americans were fighting. Marquis de Lafayette came from France. He became one of Washington's most trusted aides. Thaddeus Kosciusko (thad′ ē əs kos ē us′ kō) from Poland helped build important defenses such as the fort at West Point. Another Pole, Casimir (kaz′ i mēr) Pulaski, bravely fought in the South. He was killed leading the charge at Savannah, Georgia. Baron de Kalb, a German, served well and died of wounds he got in battle. In the hard winter at Valley Forge, Baron von Steuben (stü′ ban) of Prussia taught the soldiers how to drill. These soldiers proved to be the equal of the British.

Toward the end of the war a young British officer wrote that even if all the American men were defeated, the British would still have to beat the women. His remark was correct. Women played an important part in the American victory. Some women ran farms and businesses while the men in their families went off to fight in the war. Others marched with their husbands. They worked in army camps. They served as nurses. They made clothing and gunpowder.

Some women fought. One such woman was Mary (Molly) Hays. She carried pitchers of water to her husband and others during a battle on a very hot day. Because of this soldiers called her Molly Pitcher. When her husband was wounded, she took his place and helped fire his cannon.

Deborah Sampson Gannett took a male name and joined the army. She fought for 18 months and was wounded. After the war Paul Revere helped her receive money for her service to the country.

Molly Pitcher earned her reputation as a hero of the Revolution at the battle of Monmouth. This battle took place in June 1778.

Women served as spies. Deborah Champion carried important information to George Washington. She rode for two days on horseback. General Howe chose Lydia Darragh's Philadelphia home for a headquarters. She secretly listened to his staff meetings. She then sent her son to Washington's camp with important news about the British plans. This information once saved the American army from a surprise attack.

Signing a treaty   Americans played many different roles in the struggle for freedom. Benjamin Franklin spent the war in France. His efforts gained vital French help. He was in Paris to sign the peace treaty in 1783. Joining Franklin were John Adams, John Jay, and Henry Laurens.

The treaty said three things:

The United States was an independent nation bounded by the Mississippi River, the Great Lakes and Canada, and Florida.

The United States would have fishing rights off Canada's coast.

All war debts had to be paid by both sides.

The new states had met their goal. They were free and independent. But they were not yet united.

CHECKUP

1. Name at least three things that were against the Americans at the beginning of the Revolutionary War.
2. Why was the battle of Saratoga so important?
3. When, where, and how did the Revolutionary War come to a virtual end?
4. Give at least three reasons why Americans were able to win the war.

The Constitution of the United States

VOCABULARY

Articles of Confederation	executive branch
Constitution	judicial branch
republic	amendment
federal	Bill of Rights
separation of powers	census
legislative branch	ratify

Articles of Confederation   With independence came many problems. The United States were joined together under one government by the **Articles of Confederation.** The articles listed the powers of the central government and the powers of the states. There was a national Congress made up of representatives from each state. But Congress had almost no power at all. The 13 states acted like 13 separate little nations. There were many times when states would not cooperate with the central government. They were too busy quarreling with each other. The United States was in danger of failing.

A Constitutional Convention   In May 1787, a meeting began in Philadelphia to change the Articles of Confederation. Representatives from all the states except Rhode Island were present. It was soon decided that a whole new **constitution** had to be written. A constitution is a set of laws by which a country is governed.

This meeting became known as the Constitutional Convention. George Washington was chosen president of the convention. Adding his wisdom was 81-year-old Benjamin Franklin. A new group of first-rate leaders were at this meeting. Among these leaders were James Madison and Gouverneur Morris. Madison made a careful written record of the meetings. Morris headed a committee that drew up the Constitution. He put the final touches on it. The people who attended the convention did their job very well. The Constitution has lasted to the present.

A new plan of government   What kind of government would be best for the United States? The delegates all agreed that the new government should continue to be a **republic.** This means that the people would elect representatives to manage their country.

Other things were not so easy to decide. The delegates knew they wanted a **federal** government. In such a government the power is divided between the national and the state governments. But how much power should go to the states? And how much to the national government?

They solved this problem by writing just which powers the national government would have. It would collect taxes and borrow money. It would control trade with foreign countries and between states. The national government would print or coin money. It alone could declare war. All other powers were left to the states. Matters within a state would be settled by that state.

Separation of powers   The members of the Constitutional Convention wanted a government that would protect the people's rights, not take them away. So they divided the government's power into three parts, or branches. This is called **separation of powers**.

The **legislative branch** was the Congress. Its major job was to make laws. The **executive branch** was the President and his helpers. It was their job to carry out the laws the Congress passed. The **judicial branch** was the courts. They had to decide the meaning of the laws.

The people who came together at the Constitutional Convention knew they had an important job to do. Can you find Benjamin Franklin in this picture?

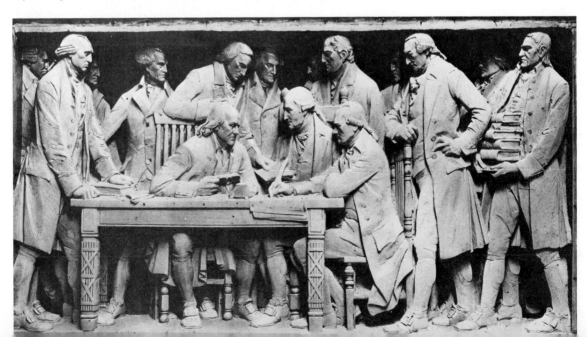

Each branch had some power over the other two. No one branch would be allowed more power than the others.

Congress   A big debate at the convention was over the matter of who would control Congress. Large states wanted representatives to Congress based on the number of people in the state. Small states wanted an equal vote with the larger states. This problem was solved by giving Congress two parts. Regardless of size each state would send two representatives to the Senate, one part of Congress. States with more people would send more delegates to the House of Representatives, the other part of Congress. In order for a law to be passed, it had to go through both parts of Congress.

Changing the Constitution   The new Constitution included a way to make changes, called **amendments.** If things did not work out, or if the United States grew or changed, the Constitution could be amended without being entirely changed. This was to prove helpful very soon.

Bill of Rights   Nine state governments had to approve the Constitution before it could become the law of the land. Many states refused to do so unless the Constitution listed people's rights as well as the rights of the government. They argued that important freedoms must be written down. Once the states were promised that this would happen, the Constitution would become law.

James Madison saw to it that these freedoms were written down. Madison

This man is using his right to speak freely.

had been very active at the Constitutional Convention. After the convention he worked hard to explain the Constitution to the people. Once the new government was started, Madison wrote many amendments that would make rights like freedom of the press, speech, and worship part of the Constitution. Ten of these amendments were passed by the states. These first ten amendments to the Constitution are known as the **Bill of Rights.**

CHECKUP

1. Why was the United States government in danger of failing when the Articles of Confederation were the law of the land?
2. What were the roles of George Washington, James Madison, and Gouverneur Morris at the Constitutional Convention?
3. What powers did the new Constitution give to the national government? To the states?
4. Why were powers divided among three branches of government?
5. Why was Congress divided into two parts?
6. Why was it necessary to add a Bill of Rights to the Constitution?

A SUMMARY OF THE CONSTITUTION OF THE UNITED STATES

PREAMBLE

Reasons for Constitution   The people of the United States made this Constitution and put it into practice for the following reasons: (1) to have a better government than under the Articles of Confederation, (2) to give everyone fair treatment, (3) to keep peace within the country, (4) to defend the country from enemies, (5) to live comfortably and well, and (6) to keep people free both now and in the future.

ARTICLE I—LEGISLATIVE BRANCH

Description (Section 1)   The legislative branch of government, or Congress, makes all the laws. It has two parts, or houses, the Senate and the House of Representatives.

House of Representatives (Section 2)   Members of the House of Representatives serve a 2-year term. They are elected by the people. Representatives must be at least 25 years old, citizens of the United States for at least 7 years, and citizens of the state they represent.

The number of representatives from each state depends on that state's population. In order to decide on the number of representatives from each state, the government must count the people every 10 years. This is called a **census.**

The Senate (Section 3)   The Senate is made up of two senators from each state. Senators have a 6-year term. Senators must be at least 30 years old, citizens of the United States for at least 9 years, and citizens of the state they represent.

The Vice-President of the United States is in charge of the Senate, but may only vote in case of a tie.

Rules (Sections 4–7)   Instructions on how to operate both the House and the Senate are covered. Behavior of members, record keeping, pay, and how a bill becomes a law are covered.

Duties (Sections 8–10)   The exact jobs of Congress are listed. Congress makes all money and trade laws. Congress decides how people can become citizens of the United States and can declare war if necessary. Powers Congress and the states do *not* have are also listed.

ARTICLE II—EXECUTIVE BRANCH

Description (Section 1)   The executive branch is made up of the President of the United States and those who help carry out laws passed by Congress. The President manages the government. A President and Vice-President are elected to a 4-year term.

A President must have been born in the United States, must be at least 35 years old, and must have lived in the United States for at least 14 years.

Duties (Sections 2–4)   Some of the President's jobs include carrying out the laws made by Congress, responsibility for all the armed forces, pardoning crimes, and reporting to Congress at least once a year on what the nation is doing. The President makes treaties and appoints government leaders; the Senate must give its approval.

If the President does wrong, he may be removed from office.

ARTICLE III—JUDICIAL BRANCH

Description (Section 1)   The judicial branch of government is the federal court system. The Supreme Court is the nation's highest court. It has the final say in all matters of law. Judges are appointed, not elected to office.

Duties (Section 2)   The federal courts have a say in all cases that are not entirely within a state.

Treason (Section 3)   The crime of treason, trying to overthrow the government, is explained.

ARTICLE IV—THE STATES

Rules about the states (Sections 1–4)   All states must accept acts, records, and laws of other states. A citizen of one state must be given the same rights as the citizens of another state he or she may be in. The governor of one state may send an accused criminal from another state back to that state for trial.

New states may be added to the United States. The United States government will protect all states from enemies.

ARTICLE V—AMENDMENTS

Making changes   The Constitution may be amended, or changed.

ARTICLE VI—HIGHEST LAW

Above all others   The Constitution of the United States is the highest law in the land. State laws must be under this law. All national and state lawmakers and offices must support the Constitution.

ARTICLE VII—PASSING THE CONSTITUTION

Ratification   This Constitution becomes law when 9 of the 13 states **ratify** it, or approve it.

AMENDMENTS

Amendment I   Congress may not make rules to change freedom of religion, freedom of speech, freedom of the press, or the right of people to come together in a peaceful way or to send petitions to their government.

Amendment II   The people have the right to keep and bear arms.

Amendment III   During peacetime, the government cannot make citizens put up soldiers in their homes.

Amendment IV   People or their homes may not be searched unreasonably.

Amendment V   Persons accused of serious crimes have the right to a jury trial. They may not be forced to give evidence against themselves. Their lives, freedom, and property may not be taken from them unfairly. If the government takes a person's property for public use, it must pay the owner for it.

Amendment VI   Persons accused of serious crimes have the right to a speedy and public trial. They must be told what they are accused of. They have the right to have a lawyer. They have the right to see and question those who accuse them.

Amendment VII   In most cases, there must be a right to a jury trial.

Amendment VIII   Punishment may not be cruel and unusual.

Amendments IX and X If the Constitution does not give a certain right to the United States government, and also does not forbid a state government to have that right, then the states and the people have it.

Amendment XI The power of the judicial branch is limited to certain kinds of cases.

Amendment XII Electors vote for President and Vice-President separately.

Amendment XIII Slavery may not exist in the United States.

Amendment XIV People born in the United States or naturalized here are United States citizens. They are also citizens of the states they live in.

States may not make laws that limit the rights of citizens of the United States. They may not take away a person's life or freedom or property unfairly. They must treat all people equally under the law.

Amendment XV No citizen may be denied the right to vote because of race.

Amendment XVI Congress is allowed to pass an income tax law.

Amendment XVII United States senators are elected by the people.

Amendment XVIII Liquor may no longer be manufactured or sold in the United States.

Amendment XIX No citizen may be denied the right to vote because of sex.

Amendment XX Presidents start their new terms on January 20; Congress starts its new term on January 3.

The Constitution is on display at the National Archives Building in Washington, D.C.

Amendment XXI The eighteenth amendment to this Constitution is repealed, or taken back.

Amendment XXII Presidents are limited to two terms in office.

Amendment XXIII Residents of Washington, D.C., have the right to vote for President.

Amendment XXIV Citizens need not pay a tax in order to vote for President, senators, or members of Congress.

Amendment XXV In case the President becomes too ill to carry on the job, the Vice-President will take over as Acting President until the President is better.

Amendment XXVI No citizen who is 18 years of age or older may be denied the right to vote because of age.

KEY FACTS

1. The Revolutionary War was fought because the colonists felt Great Britain was taking away their freedoms.

2. The war started in Lexington, Massachusetts, in 1775 and came to a virtual end at Yorktown, Virginia, in 1781.

3. The Declaration of Independence, signed on July 4, 1776, gave the reasons why the colonists thought they had the right to set up a new government.

4. The United States won the Revolution because of devoted people who fought hard for an idea, because of brilliant leadership, and because the Americans were fighting at home.

5. The type of government created by the Constitution of the United States has lasted to the present without major changes.

VOCABULARY QUIZ

Write **T** if the statement is true and **F** if it is false. If the statement is false, change the underlined term to make the statement true.

1. The Boston Massacre was a protest against tax on tea.

2. The Continental Congress made laws for the British.

3. A revolution replaces one type of government or way of thinking with another.

4. Minutemen were colonists who were ready to fight the British on a minute's notice.

5. A Loyalist was a foreign soldier hired by the British.

6. The United States was first governed by the Constitution.

7. A republic has power divided between the state and national governments.

8. The legislative branch of government makes the laws.

9. The executive branch of government decides the meaning of laws.

10. Changes in the Constitution are called separation of powers.

REVIEW QUESTIONS

1. How did a strong desire for freedom lead the colonists to fight the Revolutionary War?

2. Why is the Declaration of Independence such an important writing?

3. What do you think was the most important battle of the Revolutionary War? Explain.

4. Why is the war discussed in this chapter called both the Revolutionary War and the War for Independence?

5. What were the results of the Revolutionary War?

6. Which amendment ended slavery? Guaranteed freedom of speech and press? Allowed both men and women to vote? Repealed another amendment?

ACTIVITIES

1. Research and recreate one of the battles of the American Revolution. You might make a three-dimensional board and use toy soldiers, do a storyboard, make a drawing, or even act out a famous battle scene. Lexington, Concord, Bunker Hill, Trenton, or the surrender at Yorktown are very exciting possibilities.

2. Write a constitution for your class. Give reasons for writing it, and spell out all the rules necessary for your class to get along well together.

3. Find or draw pictures that show life without one of the rights listed in the Bill of Rights. For example, what would life be like without freedom of religion?

READING A DIAGRAM

SEPARATION OF POWERS

You read on pages 119 and 120 how, in order to protect the rights of the people, the Constitution divided power among the three branches of government. Each branch was also given some power over the other two. This check, or control, on the powers of each branch kept the balance of power equal among the three branches.

SKILLS PRACTICE

Use the chart on this page to do this activity. For each power listed below, write **E** for executive branch, **J** for judicial branch, and **L** for legislative branch, according to which branch has that power. Use a separate sheet of paper.

1. Passes laws.
2. Can veto bills.
3. Interprets laws.
4. Grants pardons.
5. Interprets treaties.
6. Approves treaties.
7. May impeach the President.
8. Recommends legislation.
9. Sees that laws are enforced.
10. Creates federal courts.

In each of the following cases, choose the act (**A** or **B**) that *checks* the stated power.
1. The President appoints justices.
   A. The Supreme Court approves the appointments.
   B. Congress approves the appointments.
2. The Supreme Court declares that a law is unconstitutional.
   A. Congress may propose a constitutional amendment.
   B. The President passes a new law.

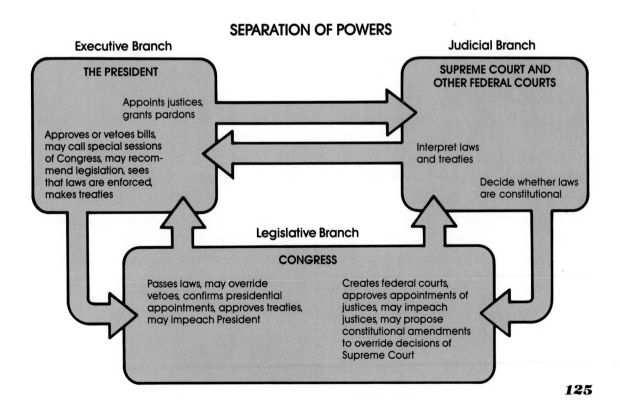

SEPARATION OF POWERS

Executive Branch

THE PRESIDENT

Appoints justices, grants pardons

Approves or vetoes bills, may call special sessions of Congress, may recommend legislation, sees that laws are enforced, makes treaties

Judicial Branch

SUPREME COURT AND OTHER FEDERAL COURTS

Interpret laws and treaties

Decide whether laws are constitutional

Legislative Branch

CONGRESS

Passes laws, may override vetoes, confirms presidential appointments, approves treaties, may impeach President

Creates federal courts, approves appointments of justices, may impeach justices, may propose constitutional amendments to override decisions of Supreme Court

125

Our First President

---VOCABULARY---

inauguration	term
oath	District of Columbia
secretary	
Cabinet	White House
Chief Justice	
Union	

Everyone's choice   Thomas Jefferson said, "He was, indeed, in every sense of the words a wise, a good, and a great man." Abigail Adams felt ". . . no other man could rule over this great people and unite them into one mighty empire." One of his officers ("Light-Horse Harry" Lee) said he was "First in war, first in peace, and first in the hearts of his countrymen." And Phillis Wheatley, the poet, wrote "Fam'd for thy valour, for thy virtues more,/Hear every tongue thy guardian aid implore!"

All of these statements were made about George Washington. You can see how well-loved and respected he was. Washington was trusted and admired. He was the only choice for the honor of being the first President of the United States.

Washington did not want to be President. He wanted to live at his beautiful home, Mount Vernon. But he put his love for his country ahead of his own wishes.

Inauguration day   April 30, 1789, was Inauguration Day for the young nation's first President. An **inauguration** is the ceremony that puts someone in office. Washington traveled from Mount Vernon to New York City by coach and on horseback. New York City was the nation's first capital. In every city and town along the way people came out to cheer him and wish him well. There were parades, fireworks, dinners, and balls.

A huge crowd came to the inauguration. They watched Washington place his left hand on an open Bible, raise his right hand, and take the **oath** of office. An oath is a promise. The oath the President takes is written in the Constitution. Washington promised to do his best to keep, protect, and defend the Constitution. He ended the oath with the words, "So help me God." Most Presidents since then have added these words.

The Constitution listed the powers and duties of the President. Washington knew what he had to do. But the Constitution did not tell him *how* to carry out his duties. This Washington had to decide. He was a wise and thoughtful man. Many of Washington's acts as President have served as examples to the Presidents that have followed him. See how many you find as you read about President Washington in this chapter.

Washington passed through Trenton, New Jersey, on the way to his inauguration in New York City.

Starting a government The new government was started with a Constitution, a Congress, a President, and little else. The states had been used to going their own way under the Articles of Confederation. Both Washington and the Congress knew that the new government would have to show its strength quickly. With Washington's leadership the new government went to work.

The job of President was too big for one person alone. Congress formed three departments to help Washington. These departments went to work on three of the biggest problems facing the new nation.

The State Department would work on relations with other nations. The War Department would build a national navy and army. The War Department is now called the Department of Defense. The Treasury Department would handle the nation's money problems.

Washington chose able leaders for each of these departments. Each leader would be called a **secretary.** Thomas Jefferson be-came secretary of state; Henry Knox, secretary of war; and Alexander Hamilton, secretary of the treasury.

Each of these men advised the President. Final decisions were made by the President, however. This group of advisors became known as the **Cabinet.** Future Presidents would all have a Cabinet.

The Constitution called for a third branch of government—a Supreme Court. All questions about the Constitution and federal law would be settled by this court. Washington appointed John Jay as head of the Supreme Court. He was called the **Chief Justice**.

The government grew stronger In 1791 Congress passed a tax law in order to raise money for the new government. Some people thought they would rather fight than pay these taxes. Washington formed an army to stop them. The new government could not have its laws disobeyed. Washington showed future Presidents how to be a strong leader.

In what year did George Washington begin to serve as President of the United States?

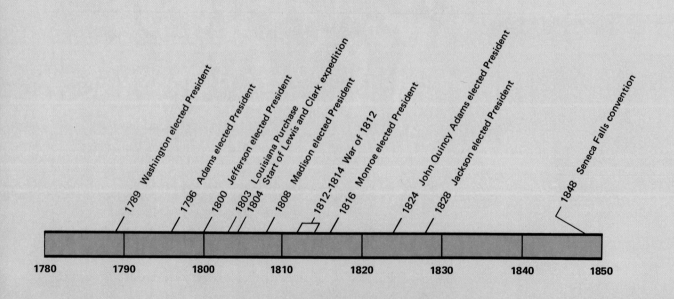

1789 Washington elected President
1796 Adams elected President
1800 Jefferson elected President
1803 Louisiana Purchase
1804 Start of Lewis and Clark expedition
1808 Madison elected President
1812–1814 War of 1812
1816 Monroe elected President
1824 John Quincy Adams elected President
1828 Jackson elected President
1848 Seneca Falls convention

1780   1790   1800   1810   1820   1830   1840   1850

Interesting Notes About the Presidents

Three Presidents held national public office after their terms ended: John Quincy Adams served as a representative for 17 years; Andrew Johnson represented Tennessee in the Senate; and William Howard Taft was Chief Justice of the Supreme Court from 1921 to 1930.

Woodrow Wilson was the first President to hold regular press conferences and the first President to speak over the radio.

Franklin D. Roosevelt was the first President to appear on television.

The first President to travel to a foreign country was Theodore Roosevelt.

Eight Presidents died in office: William Henry Harrison, Zachary Taylor, Abraham Lincoln, James Garfield, William McKinley, Warren Harding, Franklin Roosevelt, and John Kennedy.

Three Presidents died on the Fourth of July: John Adams and Thomas Jefferson in 1826; James Monroe in 1831.

Ulysses Grant, Dwight Eisenhower and Jimmy Carter were graduates of United States military academies; Eisenhower and Grant from West Point and Carter from Annapolis.

The first President to be inaugurated in Washington, D.C., was Thomas Jefferson. Only one child of a President was born in the White House. That was Esther Cleveland, the daughter of Grover Cleveland, in 1893.

William Henry Harrison made the longest inaugural speech, and caught cold and died one month later. As a result John Tyler became the first President to take office on the death of the previous President.

There have been three sets of presidential relatives: John Adams and John Quincy Adams (father and son); William Henry Harrison and Benjamin Harrison (grandfather and grandson); Theodore Roosevelt and Franklin D. Roosevelt (cousins).

The nation also grew and expanded while Washington was President. Three new states—Vermont, Kentucky, and Tennessee—entered the **Union.** When people or groups such as states join together, they form a union. The United States is a union of 50 states.

Washington steps down   Washington could have been President for life. But he did not feel this was right. He had devoted most of his life to helping his country. Now, however, he was 65 years old and had served two **terms,** or 4-year periods, as President. With the exception of Franklin Roosevelt, every President has followed Washington's two-term tradition. In 1951, a constitutional amendment limited all future Presidents to two terms.

" 'Tis well."   Washington spent his last years managing his large farm at Mount Vernon. But he remained active for his country. The nation's new capital was being built near his home. The capital was going to be the **District of Columbia.** The district was not part of any state. In time the city would be named in Washington's honor. Washington, D.C., was a planned city. The chief designer was Pierre L'Enfant (pyār län fänt), from France. Benjamin Banneker was appointed by President Washington to make a survey of the land. Banneker was the first black person to get a presidential appointment to work for the government.

Then on a wet, snowy day in December of 1799, Washington caught a cold while riding around Mount Vernon. He became seriously ill and died two days later.

Washington's last words, " 'Tis well," are good words by which to remember him. He had been Commander in Chief during the Revolution, president of the Constitutional Convention, and first President of the United States. He had done well.

Some rooms on the main floor of the White House are open to the public at stated hours.

The President Travels

Once during his time in office, George Washington decided to tour the South. Men to handle the horses and a personal servant went with him on this 3-month tour. The President slept in inns along the way. The innkeepers had no idea he was coming. For almost 2 months his government could not keep track of where he was.

In the summer of 1979 President Carter took a 37-minute train ride from Washington, D.C., to Baltimore, Maryland. Mrs. Carter was with him. There were many guards. Communications experts were along to keep Carter in touch with his government. A train filled with Secret Service people went ahead of the President's train to check the tracks. Three helicopters watched the progress from above. Reporters also came along.

Can you imagine the President today being away from Washington for 3 months? Think about the many changes that have taken place since President Washington took his trip. There were no reporters with Washington. There was no radio or television to let all the people in the country know what the President was doing that day. There were no telephones and telegraphs. And there were no trains, planes, or helicopters.

These two trips show how the presidency has grown in size and importance since Washington's time.

A growing presidency Washington had two people on his personal staff. When they went on vacation, Washington wrote his own letters. Today the President has over 500 people working just for him.

Washington had three Cabinet advisors. Today there are 13. Under Washington, all three branches of the federal government employed only 350 people. Today almost 3 million people work for just the executive branch of the government.

Washington was paid $25,000 a year. He had to pay all his expenses from that. Today the President receives $200,000 per year. He also receives money to pay for transportation, staff, and entertainment. This totals in the millions of dollars.

Washington lived in a small house in Philadelphia, which was the nation's capital from 1790 to 1800. He had to buy furniture with his own money. Today the President lives in the **White House,** a 132-room mansion. It is beautifully furnished at governmental expense.

Why, do you think, have these great changes been made? The presidency has grown with the United States. There are many more people today than in 1790. They demand many more services. Our government must be able to meet the changing needs of the American people.

CHECKUP

1. Why was Washington "the only choice" for President in 1789?
2. Name at least three things that Washington did that set an example for future Presidents.
3. What three departments made up Washington's Cabinet? Who was the first secretary of each?
4. Name three differences between Washington's presidency and the modern presidency.

Thomas Jefferson, A Remarkable Man

Jefferson designed the building shown here.

A man of many talents He was a lawyer. He wrote the Declaration of Independence. He was the representative of the United States at the court of the king of France. A person who does this kind of work is called a **diplomat.** He was the first secretary of state, second Vice-President, and third President of the United States. While he was President, the size of the country doubled.

He came from Virginia. He served that state as governor and congressman. As an **architect** he drew the plans for many buildings in Virginia. Some of these buildings are the state capitol, buildings at the University of Virginia, and his beautiful home, Monticello (mänt ə sel' ō).

At the same time, he was also a fine violinist and composer. He studied Native American languages. He knew Greek, Latin, and Hebrew. He could speak French and Italian.

His work as scientist and inventor should not be forgotten. He did practical things such as improving farming methods by inventing a new type of plow. He experimented with different seeds. He developed the swivel chair and the "dumbwaiter," a gadget that brought food from one floor to another. His home is filled with inventions like this.

In his later life he was very proud of his work in education. He started the University of Virginia.

HERE WAS BURIED
THOMAS JEFFERSON
AUTHOR OF THE
DECLARATION
OF
AMERICAN INDEPENDENCE
OF THE
STATUTE OF VIRGINIA
FOR
RELIGIOUS FREEDOM
AND FATHER OF THE
UNIVERSITY OF VIRGINIA

Jefferson died July 4, 1826. He was buried at Monticello.

The picture above shows part of Jefferson's tombstone. Jefferson chose the words that are on it. They name those acts in his life of which he was most proud. Thomas Jefferson was truly one of the most talented Americans who ever lived.

132

The Louisiana Purchase   Jefferson's greatest accomplishment as President was the Louisiana Purchase. At this time, Louisiana included just about all the land from the Mississippi River to the Rocky Mountains. (See the map on page 135.)

The Mississippi River was a highway for those Americans who lived west of the Appalachian Mountains. They took their goods downriver to the port of New Orleans, near the mouth of the Mississippi. Find those places on the map. New Orleans was not part of the United States. It belonged to France, which had received the city and the rest of what we call the Louisiana Territory from Spain in 1800.

Americans living in the West were afraid that France would not allow them to use the port of New Orleans for trade. This was because Napoleon, the ruler of France, wanted to start another French empire in America. Jefferson sent James Monroe to join Robert Livingston in France. They were to try to buy New Orleans from the French for $10 million.

A revolution in Haiti helps the United States   Haiti was a French colony in the Caribbean Sea. Find Haiti on the inset map on page 466 in the Atlas. Napoleon needed a strong naval base in Haiti if he wanted a French empire in America. But a former slave, Toussaint L'Ouverture (tü sän' lü ver tür'), led the people of Haiti in a successful fight for freedom at this time. Without Haiti, Louisiana lost some of its appeal for Napoleon. It also looked as though France would soon be fighting Great Britain. If so, France would be unable to defend Louisiana. The soldiers would be needed in Europe. "So why not sell the entire Louisiana Territory to the United States?" thought Napoleon.

Livingston had been dealing with the French for some time. He was surprised when he was asked, "What will you give for the whole of Louisiana?" The entire Louisiana Territory was bought for $15 million, or about 3 cents per acre (1 cent per hectare). By this act the United States doubled in size. There would be room to grow and expand.

Lewis and Clark   President Jefferson wanted to know more about the Louisiana Territory. He wished to find out about the Native Americans, the animals, the minerals, the climate, and the type of land. To make such an exploration, Jefferson chose Meriwether Lewis, his personal secretary, and William Clark, Lewis's

New Orleans is still one of the busiest seaports in the United States.

close friend. They were to try to find a route all the way to the Pacific Ocean.

Lewis and Clark kept day-by-day records of their journey, or expedition. The following is based on their records. It will give an idea of what they saw and did.

May 14, 1804   We are now ready to begin our journey. We will leave from St. Louis and follow the Missouri River (see map). We have gathered about 45 men together. Most are regular army soldiers, but there are a few others. York, Clark's black servant, is along. We are also taking supplies and many small gifts to trade with Indians.

June 16   Hunting is excellent. We got two deer and two bear today. But the mosquitoes and other bugs are a real bother.

July 4   We celebrated Independence Day by firing guns. We named Fourth of July Creek and Independence Creek in honor of the day. One of our number was bitten by a rattlesnake.

August 23   We can tell we are getting farther west—we killed our first buffalo today. The Indians are all very friendly so far.

April 7, 1805   We have spent the winter among the Mandan Indians. We have had a good time sharing with them and learning from each other.

We have had the good fortune of taking on a new guide. He is a French Canadian named Toussaint Charbonneau (tü′ sän shär bô nō′). He brings his wife, Sacagawea (sak ə gə wē′ ə), with him. She is a young woman of the Shoshoni tribe. She was raised in the western lands. She will guide us in the Rocky Mountains.

July 22   We have been traveling over 2 months. Sacagawea recognizes the area we are now in. She was captured from here as a little girl. We have been in sight of the Rocky Mountains for weeks. We believe that no white people have ever been here before.

August 17   When we met the Shoshoni (shə shō′ nē) people, Sacagawea recognized some friends. Imagine everyone's surprise when we found that the chief was her long-lost brother!

October 16   Today we had our first bites of tasty salmon from the Columbia River. We will follow this river to the Pacific.

Sacagawea guided Lewis and Clark through the Pacific Northwest. She is pictured here with the two explorers at Three Forks, Montana.

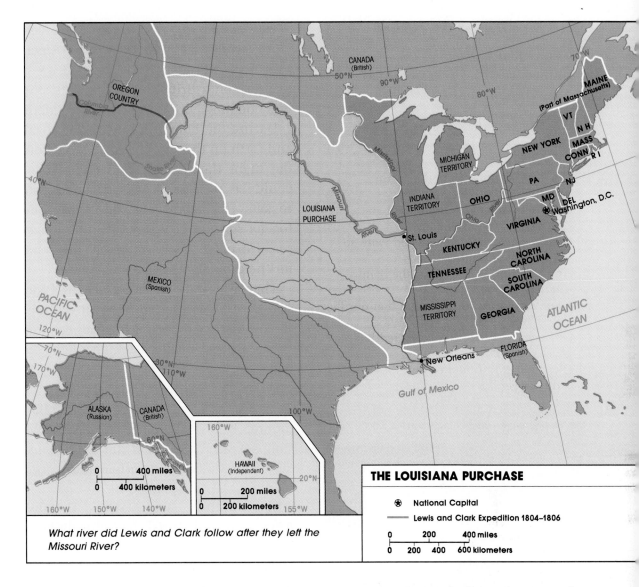

What river did Lewis and Clark follow after they left the Missouri River?

THE LOUISIANA PURCHASE

✷ National Capital

—— Lewis and Clark Expedition 1804–1806

0   200   400 miles
0 200 400 600 kilometers

November 7 We are so excited! We can hear the roar of waves crashing on shore. We have finally reached the great Pacific Ocean!

Results Lewis and Clark built a fort and spent the winter on the shores of the Pacific. In the spring they started the trip home, finally reaching St. Louis in September 1806.

President Jefferson received an excellent report of their journey. He learned a great deal about the geography of the new territory. He learned about the animals, trees, and plants there. The work of Lewis and Clark gave the United States a claim to the Oregon Country. In 1846 this area became part of the United States.

CHECKUP

1. List at least five of Thomas Jefferson's talents or accomplishments.
2. What was the importance of the Louisiana Purchase?
3. What were two results of the Lewis and Clark journey?

135

Our National Anthem

Oh, say! can you see, by the dawn's early
    light,
What so proudly we hailed at the
    twilight's last gleaming,
Whose broad stripes and bright stars,
    through the perilous fight,
O'er the ramparts we watched were so
    gallantly streaming?
And the rockets' red glare, the bombs
    bursting in air,
Gave proof through the night that our flag
    was still there.
Oh, say, does that Star-Spangled Banner
    yet wave
O'er the land of the free and the home of
    the brave?

The "Star-Spangled Banner" now is in the Smithsonian.

"The Star-Spangled Banner" These words were written in 1814 by an American named Francis Scott Key. He was a prisoner on a British warship. This ship was bombing Fort McHenry in Baltimore.

During the bombing Key walked back and forth on the ship's deck. Throughout the night the flag of the United States could be seen as it was lit up by the rockets and bombs. But the smoke and fog got so thick that Key could no longer see. He must have wondered, "Has the fort held out? Is the flag still flying?"

Then, "by the dawn's early light," Key saw the torn and tattered flag. It was still there! Wishing to record his feelings, Key wrote a poem on the back of a letter he was carrying.

When Key was freed the next day, the poem was printed and passed around Baltimore. It was soon set to music. The song spread rapidly, but did not become our country's national **anthem** until 1931.

Why another war with Britain? Americans and British had already been at war for 2 years when the firing on Fort McHenry took place. What were the causes of this war, the War of 1812?

Americans were angry about British conduct on the sea. Britain, always in need of sailors, was stopping American ships and taking sailors. The British said they were taking only runaway British sailors. But many American citizens were also taken. People felt this had to be ended. Britain had also passed laws that interfered with American trade. Many Americans felt that Britain should be shown once and for all that our country was free from British control.

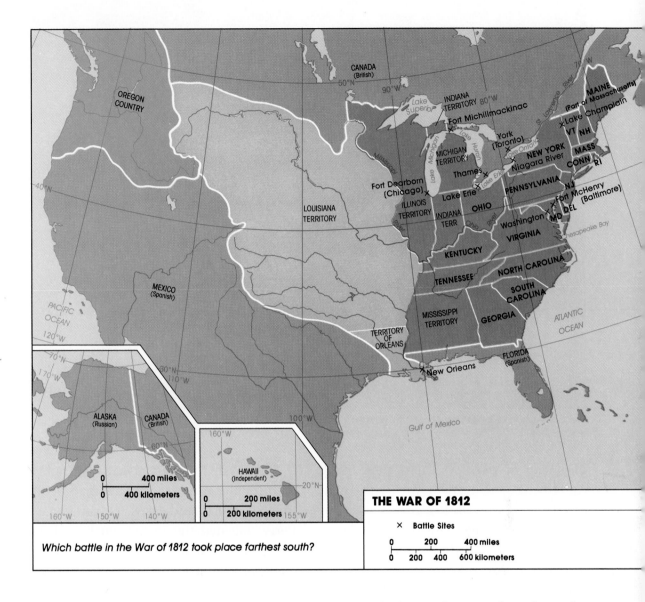

CANADA
(British)

OREGON
COUNTRY

INDIANA
TERRITORY

Fort Michilimackinac ×

MICHIGAN
TERRITORY

York
(Toronto) ×

NEW YORK

MAINE
(Part of Massachusetts)

VT NH

MASS

CONN RI

Fort Dearborn
(Chicago) ×

Thames ×

Niagara River

PENNSYLVANIA

NJ

Fort McHenry
(Baltimore)

ILLINOIS
TERRITORY

Lake Erie

OHIO

INDIANA
TERR

MD DEL

LOUISIANA
TERRITORY

Washington ×

VIRGINIA

Chesapeake Bay

KENTUCKY

MEXICO
(Spanish)

TENNESSEE

NORTH CAROLINA

SOUTH
CAROLINA

MISSISSIPPI
TERRITORY

GEORGIA

ATLANTIC
OCEAN

PACIFIC
OCEAN

TERRITORY
OF
ORLEANS

FLORIDA
(Spanish)

New Orleans ×

Gulf of Mexico

ALASKA
(Russian)

CANADA
(British)

HAWAII
(Independent)

0   400 miles
0   400 kilometers

0   200 miles
0   200 kilometers

Which battle in the War of 1812 took place farthest south?

THE WAR OF 1812

×   Battle Sites

0   200   400 miles
0   200   400   600 kilometers

Relations between the United States and Great Britain had not been good since the Revolution. Also the British and Canadians were urging Indians to fight settlers. Many Indian groups were already angry with the settlers for taking their land and breaking promises. Americans were angry with the British for causing more trouble. Tecumseh (tə kum′ sə), a great Indian leader, united the tribes to fight the settlers. He later joined the British and was killed in the War of 1812.

Rising feelings of national pride in the United States were another reason for the war. Some Americans felt that Canada rightfully belonged to the United States. Henry Clay and many other leaders in Congress favored fighting Britain. These new leaders were known as the **War Hawks.** There were some Americans, however, especially those from New England and the Middle Atlantic states who were against the war. Strong feelings nearly split the country.

The Constitution *is the oldest American warship afloat today. It can be seen in Boston Harbor.*

The War of 1812   There were many Americans who wanted war with Great Britain, but the United States was not ready to fight one. The American navy was small. The British had the largest navy in the world. There was only a small American army. West Point had just begun to train officers. The British, even though they were also fighting a war in Europe, were able to send well-trained troops to fight in America.

The navy provided the high points of the war for the Americans. The wooden warship *Constitution* gained lasting fame by defeating a British ship. It was said that British cannon shots bounced right off the sides of the *Constitution*. Because of this, the ship was given the nickname **Old Ironsides.**

The war on the ocean usually did not go well for the Americans. They had better luck on the inland lakes. Oliver Hazard Perry defeated the British on Lake Erie. His report of victory, "We have met the enemy and they are ours," is still a proud part of American naval history. The Americans stopped a British raiding party coming from Canada at the battle of Lake Champlain.

Burning of Washington   In 1814 the British marched into Washington, D.C. The President, James Madison, was with the troops who were trying to defend the city. His wife, Dolley, was left to manage the White House. She stayed in Washington until the last possible minute. She gathered important papers and a few

138

White House treasures for safekeeping. She refused to leave until a famous portrait of George Washington was in safe hands. Dolley Madison finally fled only 2 hours before the British arrived. At the White House the British soldiers ate a hot meal that had been prepared for the President and his Cabinet!

The British burned just about every public building in Washington. They then went on to Baltimore. There British warships in the harbor unsuccessfully bombarded Fort McHenry.

A peace treaty is signed   There were many Americans who had opposed the War of 1812 from the start. As time wore on both sides grew eager for it to end. Finally, in December 1814, a peace treaty was signed. None of the problems that were reasons for the war were settled by the treaty. However, it was agreed as part of the treaty to work out future problems peaceably.

This is the portrait saved by Dolley Madison.

The peace treaty had been signed in Europe. It took many weeks for the news to get back to the United States. So the biggest battle of the war was fought 2 weeks after the peace treaty was signed. Two thousand British were killed or wounded at the battle of New Orleans. The Americans lost 13 men and 58 were wounded. The victory gave the Americans great confidence, but lives were lost in a needless battle.

Second war for independence   The peace treaty itself changed very little. However, there were positive results from the war. Two military leaders in this war were later to become Presidents. Andrew Jackson, "the Hero of New Orleans," was elected in 1828. And William Henry Harrison was elected in 1840 because of the battles he fought on the frontier.

In addition to new leaders, the war gave the people of the United States a new way to look at themselves. They were proud of their ability to fight a great power. Europe now respected the United States more. Our country was free to go its own way. The War of 1812 is often called "the Second War for American Independence." After the War of 1812 Americans were much more united. New states were added. The young nation was sure of itself.

In 1816 James Monroe was elected President. Things went so smoothly that this time is called the **Era of Good Feelings.**

CHECKUP
1. What caused the War of 1812?
2. Tell one fact each about Old Ironsides, Oliver Perry, and the battle of New Orleans.

Jacksonian Democracy

"Victory for the common man" Glass and china were smashed. Noses were bloodied. People fainted.

A riot? No. Another British raid on Washington? No. About 4 months earlier Andrew Jackson had been elected President. For weeks thousands of people had been coming to Washington, D.C., to see his inauguration. Jackson was their hero. His victory was seen as a "victory for the common man."

After Jackson was sworn into office, the crowd followed him to the White House. They jammed themselves in to get food and drink. Most of all they wanted to get closer to their hero. Muddy boots ruined expensive carpets and chairs as people pushed and shoved to see Andrew Jackson.

People cheered Jackson on the way to his inauguration.

Jackson welcomed them at first. But the crushing force of the crowd soon caused him to leave by the back door. He spent his first night as President in a hotel. But he would truly be a President "of the people."

"Old Hickory" To understand this deep love for Andrew Jackson, you have to understand who Jackson was and where he came from. Andrew Jackson was a fighter. At age 13 he was already fighting the Revolutionary War in the Carolinas. He and his brother were captured by the British and taken to a prison camp. When ordered to clean a British officer's boots, Andy refused. The angry officer slashed Andy with a sword. Andy's brother was also badly cut.

The boys' wounds went untreated. Both caught smallpox. Andy's brother died. Andy was sick for months and carried scars for life. Perhaps Jackson lived because of his fierce temper and stubborn nature.

Jackson had moved to Tennessee as a young man. He was just the kind of man the people of Tennessee liked. Westerners had to be tough, and Jackson was tough. His soldiers later called him "Old Hickory," because hickory wood was the toughest thing they knew.

A man of the people Jackson served the people of Tennessee as a lawyer, judge, congressman, and senator. But he won his greatest fame as a soldier. Both before and after the War of 1812, Jackson fought in the wars against the Creeks of Alabama and Georgia and the Seminoles in Florida. Because of his activity in Florida, the

United States was able to take control of that area from Spain.

The people loved this bold, take-charge, fiery fighter. Jackson believed in people. He felt that common people could run the government. This idea has come to be called **Jacksonian democracy.** These people elected Andrew Jackson as their President in 1828. He gave them their first chance to really have a part in government.

Not everyone benefited while Andrew Jackson was President. Women, blacks, and Native Americans were not able to take part in government. In fact, in some cases, the government worked against them.

Trail of Tears The Cherokee nation serves as an example of what happened to many Native American tribes and people in Jackson's time. The Cherokees had a great deal of land in Georgia and Alabama. The Cherokees were farmers. They had roads and lived in houses. They had a written language and a weekly newspaper. Their government was democratic. But many whites felt that the Cherokees were in the way. White settlers wanted their land.

The land was promised to the Cherokee nation by treaty. Missionaries, Congressman Henry Clay, and the Supreme Court all said that the Cherokees had

The Trail of Tears led Cherokees west after they had been forced from their homes. How do you think they felt as they traveled to reservations across the Mississippi?

rights to their claims. Even so, the Cherokees were thrown off their land. They were told to go to Oklahoma. With soldiers watching them, they had little choice but to obey.

This journey lasted several months. Disease, hunger, and cold brought death to many. Over 4,000 Cherokees were buried along the **Trail of Tears**, which stretched from Georgia to Oklahoma.

Andrew Jackson said that this removal was necessary. Without it, he said, the Cherokees all would have been killed by white settlers looking for more land.

The rise of women Jackson did a great deal to make people feel a part of government. But as we have just seen, Jackson was not ready to give equality to Native Americans. A slaveholder all his life, Jackson did not believe in equality for blacks either.

Yet in Jackson's time, some people were starting to oppose slavery. These people were called **abolitionists.** Among the abolitionists were the Grimké sisters. They had been brought up on a southern plantation, but they were against slavery. They wanted equal rights for all humans. In 1838, Angelina Grimké became the first woman ever to speak to a lawmaking group. She spoke to the Massachusetts legislature about equal rights for women and blacks. She tied the two issues together quite easily. She felt that freedom was being denied to large groups of Americans. She thought lawmakers and all people should worry about this.

Women today have benefited from the women's rights movement. Shown here are (left) Gray Panther leader Maggie Kuhn and (right) Supreme Court Justice Sandra Day O'Connor. Gray Panthers work for equal rights for older people.

Seneca Falls   Another link between the two issues occurred when women were not allowed to speak at the World Anti-Slavery Conference in London in 1840. At that point, two abolitionists, Lucretia Mott and Elizabeth Cady Stanton, decided to start a women's rights group.

Eight years later, in Seneca Falls, New York, Mott and Stanton called a meeting on women's rights. At the **Seneca Falls convention**, a set of goals was agreed upon. Women should have the same rights as men. Women should have free speech. Women should have the chance for equal education. Women should have the right to vote.

Women went to work quickly to meet these goals. But it was a hard job. One early speaker, Lucy Stone, was treated rudely and had things thrown at her. Once in the winter she was sprayed with icy water. She simply pulled her shawl tighter and went on talking. Stone became the "star" speaker of the movement at this time and won many followers.

A team of fighters for women's rights soon developed. In 1851 Elizabeth Cady Stanton met Susan B. Anthony. The two liked each other at once. Stanton was the thinker and the writer. Anthony was the organizer and the person of action. By 1860 they had won some basic rights for women in the state of New York. Other and larger gains would follow as they worked together over the next 40 years.

Another early worker for human rights was a former slave, Sojourner Truth. In 1851 she made a stirring speech to the women's rights convention in Akron, Ohio. As men tried to shout her down, she went to the platform and said,

Sojourner Truth worked for human rights for all people.

"That man over there says that women need to be helped into carriages and lifted over ditches, and to have the best place wherever. Nobody ever helps me into carriages or over mud puddles, or gives me any best place. And ain't I a woman? Look at me! I have ploughed and planted and gathered into barns and no man could head [do better than] me. And ain't I a woman? I could work as much and eat as much as a man—when I could get it—and bear the lash [whip] as well.

And ain't I a woman? I have borne thirteen children and seen most all sold off to slavery, and when I cried out with my mother's grief, none but Jesus heard me. And ain't I a woman? . . ."

CHECKUP

1. Why was Andrew Jackson's election called a "victory for the common man?"
2. What three groups were left out of this victory?
3. Why were the Cherokees removed from their lands in the early 1800s?
4. What roles did Elizabeth Cady Stanton and Susan B. Anthony play in the early women's rights movement?

7/ CHAPTER REVIEW

KEY FACTS

1. The first President of the United States, George Washington, helped to define the powers and duties of the President.

2. The Louisiana Purchase doubled the size of the United States.

3. There was no clear victory for either side at the end of the war with Great Britain in 1812. But Americans had more pride in their country and were much more united after the war.

4. With the election of Andrew Jackson as President in 1828, more and more people took part in government. Yet women, blacks, and Native Americans were not included in this participation.

VOCABULARY QUIZ

Fill in the blanks with the correct word or words. Write on a separate sheet of paper.

1. The capital of the United States is _____.

2. The leader of the Supreme Court is the _____.

3. The President's advisors make up the _____.

4. A formal ceremony to put someone in office is called an _____.

5. With the _____ the United States doubled in size.

6. People in Congress who favored the War of 1812 were called _____.

7. "The Star-Spangled Banner" became our national _____ in 1931.

8. The path taken by many Cherokees to Oklahoma was called the _____.

9. A person who wanted to end slavery was called an _____.

10. The first convention of the women's rights movement was at _____.

REVIEW QUESTIONS

1. What was one great accomplishment of President Washington? President Jefferson? President Jackson?

2. Name at least two results of the War of 1812.

3. Give evidence from the time of Andrew Jackson that not all Americans were enjoying equality.

ACTIVITIES

1. You may wish to find out more about Washington, D.C. Use an encyclopedia to learn more about some of the following:

a. Why was this place chosen for the capital of the United States?

b. What was life like there in 1800?

c. How were streets named?

d. Read about some famous government buildings—the Capitol, White House, Library of Congress, Supreme Court Building.

e. Find out about some tourist attractions—the Washington Monument, Jefferson Memorial, Lincoln Memorial, Ford's Theatre, Bureau of Engraving and Printing.

f. Read about some of its famous museums—the Smithsonian Institution, the National Gallery of Art, or the Museum of African Art.

g. Learn about some famous nearby attractions—Arlington National Cemetery, Mount Vernon, Marine Corps War Memorial.

h. What type of government does Washington, D.C., have?

2. Johnny Appleseed, Daniel Boone, Davy Crockett, Mike Fink, and Jean Laffite were real people. Try to find out at least one true story and at least one tall tale from the life of one of these people. Tell or act out your stories to the class.

STATING A POINT OF VIEW

SACAGAWEA

In this chapter you read parts of the journals kept by Lewis and Clark as they explored the Louisiana Purchase territory. One person who was very important to them on this journey was a Native American woman named Sacagawea. Turn to page 134 and reread what Lewis and Clark wrote about her. Now read the short biography below.

Sacagawea was a Shoshoni. No one knows exactly when or where she was born. It is thought that she was born around 1787 in either western Montana or eastern Idaho. As a young teenager she was captured by a slave-hunting party of Indians from the area around North Dakota. They sold her to a French Canadian trapper who married her when she was about 18 years old.

Sacagawea and her husband joined the Lewis and Clark expedition shortly after their marriage. Sacagawea gave birth to a son in February 1805, during the time the expedition wintered with the Mandan Indians. The baby was named Jean Baptiste.

In April, Lewis and Clark and all the members of the group started out again. Sacagawea and the baby went, too. In May a river that feeds into the Platte was explored and named the Sacagawea River. In June, Sacagawea became sick with a bad fever and stomach pains. At the same time, the baby was having trouble with his teeth. Captain Lewis gave them both medicine.

In August, the expedition made its first contact with Sacagawea's people. They were given horses by Sacagawea's brother and they eventually continued their journey. Sacagawea and her husband and baby went on with Lewis and Clark to the coast, wintered on the shores of the Pacific, and began the return journey.

When Lewis and Clark went on to Washington, D.C., Sacagawea and her family stayed in the North Dakota area. They never saw Meriwether Lewis again. It is thought, however, that in 1809 they met William Clark in St. Louis and turned Jean Baptiste over to him to be educated.

There is a mystery connected with the death of Sacagawea. Some sources say she died at Fort Lisa, near present-day Omaha, Nebraska, on December 20, 1812. However, in 1875 an old woman living among the Wind River Shoshoni in Wyoming claimed she was Sacagawea. This woman died in 1884. If she was Sacagawea, she was then nearly 100 years old.

SKILLS PRACTICE

The journals kept by Lewis and Clark told about the expedition from their points of view. What do you think Sacagawea would have written if she had kept a journal? What would have been her feelings about joining the expedition, about returning to her homeland, about seeing her brother again? Use the information in this book as source material, and write a journal of the Lewis and Clark expedition from the point of view of Sacagawea.

CHAPTER
8 A Nation Changes

A Changing Way of Life

VOCABULARY

turnpike	interchangeable parts
canal	mass production
textile	
Industrial Revolution	telegraph
cotton gin	immigrant

Heading west   Americans had been heading west even before the War for Independence. One of the first great western adventurers was Daniel Boone. He led a group of people to Kentucky. They used a trail that had been used for many years by Native Americans. This trail became the famous Wilderness Road. Find this road on the map on page 159.

Boone made his trips west on foot. But transportation would soon be much improved. Many roads, canals, steamboats, and railroads were built in the early 1800s. And better transportation changed the United States.

Roads   Most roads were built by private companies that charged money for use of the roads. They came to be known as **turnpikes.** This was because a pole, or pike, was set across the road. After people paid their money, the pike was turned so that people could pass.

The early roads were nothing like the modern, hard surfaced roads you know today. Early roads were covered with stone and gravel. In spring they turned to mud. Often traffic was held up by sheep or cattle going to market. But the roads were like today's roads in one way. They cost a lot to build and use.

Canals   While roads were a great help, people soon demanded cheaper forms of transportation to the West. A great time of **canal** building began in 1825. A canal is a waterway dug across land. Rivers and lakes had always been used for transportation in the United States. Canals were dug to join major rivers and lakes. They made transportation of people and goods easier and cheaper.

Perhaps the greatest of the early canals was the Erie Canal. It was begun at the urging of Governor DeWitt Clinton of New York. The Erie Canal connected Buffalo and Lake Erie with Albany on the Hudson River. Goods were then shipped downriver to New York City. Cities grew up around the canal. But most important, the cost of shipping fell. What had once cost $100 a ton ($90.70 per t) to ship overland now cost $10 a ton ($9.07 per t) by canal. Trade between East and West prospered. And more people headed west.

Pioneers moved west in wagon trains. Other methods of transportation, such as canals, opened the settled areas to industry and commerce.

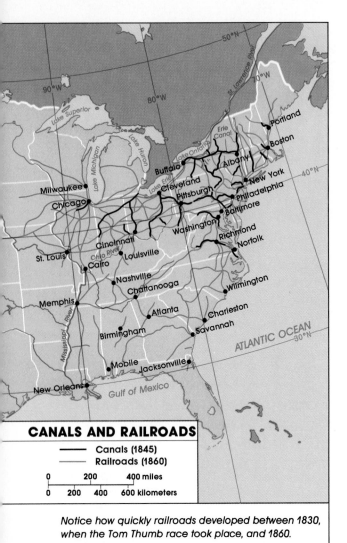

CANALS AND RAILROADS

—— Canals (1845)
—— Railroads (1860)

0   200   400 miles
0 200 400 600 kilometers

Notice how quickly railroads developed between 1830, when the Tom Thumb race took place, and 1860.

In what year was the first telegraph message sent?

Steamboats   An English invention, the steam engine, helped improve American transportation in the United States. In 1787 John Fitch demonstrated the first steam-powered boat in America. In 1807 Robert Fulton's ship the *Clermont* became the first steamboat to provide regular service.

Steamboats were seen on the Mississippi River by 1820. Twenty years later most of the goods being shipped on that river were sent by steamboat.

Railroads   In 1804 an Englishman put a steam engine on a locomotive. The locomotive pulled a train along a track. This seemed like a good idea to some people in the United States.

In 1830 Peter Cooper's early locomotive, the *Tom Thumb*, ran a famous race with a horse. Cooper had been challenged by a stagecoach owner to see which of the two was faster. The *Tom Thumb* would have won, but it had an engine problem. One of the first locomotives in the United States had been beaten by a horse!

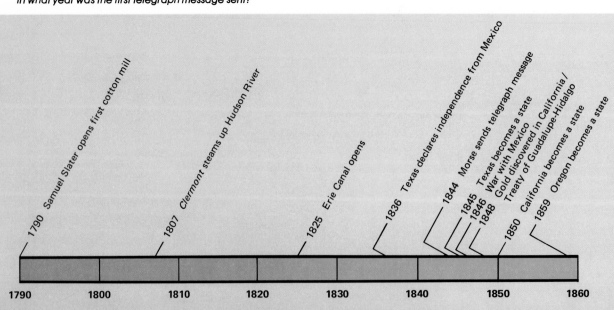

1790 Samuel Slater opens first cotton mill

1807 *Clermont* steams up Hudson River

1825 Erie Canal opens

1836 Texas declares independence from Mexico

1844 Morse sends telegraph message

1845 Texas becomes a state

1846 War with Mexico

1848 Gold discovered in California / Treaty of Guadalupe-Hidalgo

1850 California becomes a state

1859 Oregon becomes a state

1790   1800   1810   1820   1830   1840   1850   1860

Most people were impressed by the railroad. It grew rapidly. By 1860, about 30,000 miles (32,000 km) of railroad tracks linked many parts of the East with the Mississippi River.

Results of improved transportation
The effects of these improvements in transportation were amazing. A trip from New York to Chicago took 6 weeks in 1800. The same trip in 1860 took less than 2 days. New areas of the West were opened up because travel to these areas was made much easier. Trade flowed more quickly and cheaply between the factories of the East and the farms of the West. Many towns were started along the trading routes to the Midwest. Improved transportation helped the nation to grow and prosper.

The rise of industry   The United States was changing in the early 1800s. In 1800 there were 15 farmers to every city dweller. By 1850 there were only five farmers to every nonfarmer. More and more people were working in factories.

This change started in 1789 when young Samuel Slater arrived from England. Slater came with secret knowledge about England's cloth-making, or **textile,** industry. Information about the machines used to make cloth was not supposed to leave England. England wanted to keep the textile business for itself. Nevertheless, Slater built machines and set up the first American textile factory in Rhode Island. He did this all from memorized plans. Soon other factories were built. The rapid building of many factories became known as the **Industrial Revolution.**

Working long hours among machines could be dangerous, especially for young children.

One interesting feature of the Industrial Revolution was the beginning of several towns like Lowell, Massachusetts. The factories of Lowell attracted many young women. They were given a room, food, and about $2 a week for working 12- to 13-hour days, 6 days a week. Girls as young as 10 years worked these hours. People in the early 1800s were used to working long hours on the farms. They did not think it strange to work long hours in factories, too.

The Lowell girls lived by strict rules. They were required to go to church. They had to remain clean and honest. They could not stay out past 10 o'clock at night. In spite of the long days, the girls still found time to study and attend lectures.

This Industrial Revolution and changes in transportation aided each other. The better transportation became, the more goods were shipped. The easier and cheaper it was to buy these goods, the more people wanted factory products. So many factories were built to make what people wanted. And the greater the number of factories, the more goods there were to ship.

Important contributions to industry
Two very important contributions to the growth of industry in the United States were made by Eli Whitney. One was an invention; the other was an idea.

The invention was the **cotton gin.** This machine allowed a worker to pick the seeds out of a boll of cotton quickly and easily. When this was done by hand, a very good worker could clean only a few pounds of cotton a day. It was possible to clean 50 pounds (23 kg) of cotton a day using the cotton gin. Now textile factories in the North could count on a steady supply of cotton from the South. The cotton gin was a very important invention.

But even more important was Whitney's idea about **interchangeable parts.** Eli Whitney owned a factory that made guns. Guns were once made by craftworkers called gunsmiths. The gunsmith would make the whole gun—all the parts—and put it together. This would take time and no two guns from the same

worker would be the same. And if part of the gun broke, a new part would have to be made for it. Whitney knew that guns could not be made like this in a factory. It was too slow and would cost too much money. Factories had to be used for **mass production**—making large numbers of the same product. If all the parts in one gun were just like all the parts in another gun of the same type, then even an unskilled worker, someone who wasn't a gunsmith, could put the weapon together quickly. This was the idea of interchangeable parts. This became basic for most manufacturing industries. Today automobiles, radios, refrigerators, and many other products are all built on this idea.

More inventions New inventions brought great changes. Two inventions in the 1830s especially helped farmers. These were the reaper, invented by Cyrus McCormick, and the steel plow, invented by John Deere. These inventions came just at the time the West was being opened up for farming. They saved hours of work in preparing the fields and in harvesting, or reaping, the crops.

A third invention greatly changed communication. In 1844 Samuel Morse sent the first **telegraph** message from Baltimore, Maryland, to Washington, D.C. He used a code to send his message by wire. This code is now called the Morse code. As the crowd watched, Morse tapped out the message, "What hath God wrought?" The age of instant communication had begun. Now Americans would be drawn closer together not only by better transportation, but also by rapid communication.

The reaper made great changes in the lives of farmers.

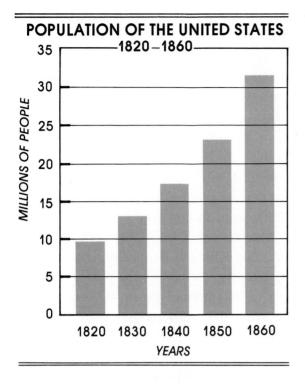

POPULATION OF THE UNITED STATES
1820–1860

MILLIONS OF PEOPLE

YEARS

Study these graphs carefully. What connection can you see between the increase in the number of immigrants and the increase in population? What effect do you think this had on the expansion of the United States?

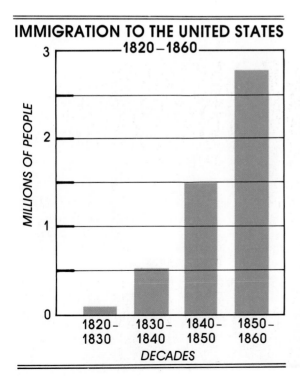

IMMIGRATION TO THE UNITED STATES
1820–1860

MILLIONS OF PEOPLE

DECADES

Immigration   The United States was an exciting place to be. There were new jobs, new land, and new opportunities here because of the Industrial Revolution and changes in transportation. Many people in other parts of the world wanted a new chance in life. Beginning in the 1830s, **immigrants** came to the United States by the thousands. Immigrants are people who leave one country to come into and settle in another.

Almost all of these immigrants came from northern Europe, mostly from England, Scotland, Ireland, and Germany. People had many different reasons for coming to the United States. Hardships in Europe, chances for work on farms and in factories in this country, and a desire for greater freedom were their chief reasons for leaving their old homes and traveling so far.

Unfortunately, there were so many immigrants coming so rapidly that many Americans did not welcome them. They were seen as outsiders who did things differently. There was ill-feeling between immigrants and lifelong Americans. Still the immigrants came. Their hard work and belief in democracy helped shape the United States.

CHECKUP

1. Name four improvements in transportation in the early 1800s.
2. List at least three results of improved transportation.
3. How did the Industrial Revolution begin in the United States?
4. Name three inventions that helped the United States grow in the 1800s.
5. Why did so many immigrants come to the United States in the early 1800s?

The Lone Star Republic

Americans in the Southwest   In 1820 the vast southwestern part of what is now the United States belonged to Mexico. By 1860 the entire Southwest was controlled by the United States. How did this come about?

Both Presidents Adams and Jackson had tried to buy Texas from Mexico. They were refused. But Mexico did invite people from the United States to settle in Texas. In 1823 Stephen Austin was allowed to bring 300 families into Texas. They were given a large amount of land. By 1830 United States citizens in Texas numbered over 20,000. There were four Americans from the United States for every Mexican there.

Desire for independence   The Mexicans were losing power in Texas. The Mexican government did not like what was happening there. In 1830 no more immigration to Texas from the United States was allowed. But this law was disobeyed by people hungry for land. They moved to Texas as fast as ever!

Mexico got a new president, General Antonio López de Santa Anna (san' tə an' ə), in 1834. He wanted the power in Mexico to be centered in the government in Mexico City. He took away much of the self-government that the people in Texas had enjoyed until that time. The Americans and some Mexicans in Texas reacted quickly. They set up a government and formed an army. The army captured the town of San Antonio.

The battle for the Alamo is an important part of the history of Texas.

"Remember the Alamo!" Of course Mexico did not want to lose Texas. General Santa Anna and an army of 4,000 soldiers moved to crush the revolt. A battle took place at an old Spanish mission in San Antonio. The mission was called the **Alamo.** Davy Crockett, the frontier hero, and Jim Bowie, inventor of the Bowie knife, were among the 187 defenders of the Alamo. Santa Anna began the attack on February 23, 1836. It was March 6 before the Alamo fell to the Mexicans. None of the defenders were still alive.

A few weeks later a battle was fought at San Jacinto (jə sint′ ō). With the shout "Remember the Alamo!" to spur them on, the Texans under Sam Houston defeated the Mexican army. Santa Anna was captured.

After Texas became a state, Sam Houston served as a United States senator and later as governor of the state.

The independence that the Texans had declared had become a fact. Texas was a free nation. It remained independent of both Mexico and the United States for 10 years. It was called the **Lone Star Republic,** because its flag had only one star. Samuel Houston became its president.

Texas becomes a state Many Americans badly wanted the United States to control all the territory from the Atlantic Ocean to the Pacific Ocean. They wanted the southern border to extend at least to the Rio Grande (see map, page 157). This area included Texas. Most of the Americans living in Texas wanted to become part of the United States. Finally, in 1845, Texas became our twenty-eighth state.

War with Mexico Making Texas a state did not help relations between our country and Mexico. Neither did our desire to spread from the Atlantic to the Pacific. The two countries could not agree on the southern boundary of Texas. And the United States wanted to buy from Mexico the land between Texas and the Pacific Ocean. The President of the United States at the time, James K. Polk, sent troops to the Mexican border. The Mexicans were angry at this show of force. They sent troops north. Trouble was certain to start between the two angry armies. A small American force was attacked, and all the soldiers were killed, wounded, or taken prisoner. President Polk asked Congress to declare war on Mexico, which it did in May 1846.

Treaty of Guadalupe Hidalgo The war with Mexico went well for the United

States. It lasted less than 2 years and during this time the United States did not lose a major battle. The American heroes of this war were General Zachary Taylor and General Winfield Scott. Other army officers, such as Robert E. Lee and Ulysses S. Grant, gained military experience that they would use not too many years later in the Civil War.

The Treaty of Guadalupe Hidalgo (gwäd′ əl üp hi dal′ gō) ended the war. Mexico recognized the Rio Grande as the southern boundary of Texas. Mexico also **ceded,** or gave, to the United States the land labeled "Mexican Cession" on the map on page 157. Compare this map with the map of the United States in the Atlas on pages 468–469. Which states were part of the Mexican Cession? In 1853, the United States paid Mexico $10 million for the piece of land labeled "Gadsden Purchase" on the map on page 157. This land is now the southern parts of New Mexico and Arizona.

A Mexican heritage   In Chapter 4 you read about the Spanish explorers of the southwestern part of what was to become the United States. The first permanent Spanish Mexican settlement north of the Rio Grande was made in 1598. The colony was started by Don Juan de Oñate. (ō nyä′ tā). He was born in Mexico of a Spanish family. De Oñate's wife was a granddaughter of Cortés and a great-granddaughter of Montezuma, the last Aztec emperor. De Oñate was the first colonizer. By 1630 there were 25 settlements and missions scattered throughout what the Spanish were calling New Mexico. Santa Fe, the most important settlement,

This was the Palace of the Governor when Santa Fe was part of Mexico. It is the oldest public building still standing in North America.

was started in 1609. This was only 2 years after the British started their first colony in Virginia.

The Spanish Mexican settlers brought many changes into New Mexico. Missionaries converted many Native Americans to Christianity. New ways of farming were introduced. Great cattle ranches were started. The cowboy, or *vaquero* (vä kär′ ō), became a common sight. And so too did the Indian on horseback. Two very important parts of the legend of the American West—the cowboy and the Indian—were given their start when the first settlers brought horses into the American Southwest. Spanish **architecture,** or style of building, can still be seen in the area.

Our country still has a large Mexican American population. A number of Mexican Americans, past and present, have influenced the history of the United States. Father Eusebio Kino (ā ü sā′ byō kē′ nō) was known as "the Padre on Horseback."

He started a group of missions in what is now southern Arizona and spent 25 years exploring the southwestern part of the country. He was also a mapmaker and was the first white person to prove that California was not an island. José (hō sā') Navarro fought for Texan independence, first from Spain and then from Mexico. He helped write the constitution of the state of Texas. The signature of Romana Banuelos (bän wā' lōs) appeared on all the paper money printed in this country between 1971 and 1974. She was the treasurer of the United States during this time. Cesar Chavez started the United Farm Workers of America to help farm workers get better wages.

CHECKUP

1. How did defeat at the Alamo help Texans win their war with Mexico?
2. Why did the United States go to war with Mexico?
3. What land did the United States gain by the Treaty of Guadalupe Hidalgo?
4. What was the Gadsden Purchase?

California

Early settlement   California was settled by the sword and the cross. In 1769, Gaspar de Portolá (pôr tō lä') led a military force north from Baja, or Lower, California to a spot near present-day San Diego. Here he built a **presidio,** or military fort. In 1770 he built another presidio at Monterrey. Six years later settlers and soldiers established another presidio near what is now known as San Francisco.

In time five of these forts were built. The presidios protected the settlers. They also served to hold this part of the Spanish empire from the English. The English claimed land on the west coast of North America because of the voyages of Sir Francis Drake (see Chapter 4).

Five missionaries went with Portolá on his military expedition. They were led by

The missions were an important part of life in Spanish California.

Father Junípero Serra (ser' rä). Father Serra spent the next 15 years building missions up and down the coast. The first was at San Diego. In time, there were 21 missions between San Diego and San Francisco. The missions were about 30 miles (50 km)—a day's march—apart.

The missions were run by priests who trained Indians to do the farming and building. The soil was good and the climate warm. The missions did well. By the early 1800s they had over 30,000 head of livestock and were harvesting more than 30,000 bushels (1,000,000 L) of grain and vegetables each year. Mission workshops made pots, dishes, furniture, and cloth. The California missions, presidios, and pueblos (small villages) were far away from the government in Mexico and even farther away from the king in Spain. The population stayed small and self-supporting. The culture was part Spanish and part Indian.

The Bear Flag Republic   In 1846 most of the population of California was Native American, Mexican, and Spanish. There were fewer than 1,000 United States citizens living there.

Yet these few people wanted California to be part of the United States. They joined a revolt against the Mexican government and helped form the Republic of California. It was also called the Bear Flag Republic, because the flag showed a bear. Mexico was too busy fighting the United States to do anything about the revolt. United States troops were in California when the war ended. The republic became a United States territory as part of the Treaty of Guadalupe Hidalgo.

California gold fever   In 1849 San Francisco grew from a small, sleepy village to a busy town of 25,000. The population of California went from 15,000 to over 100,000.

People moved to California any way they could. They took boats around the tip of

Life in the mining camps was not easy for the men and women who came to California to find fortunes. People who provided services, such as cooking, often became richer than those who looked for gold.

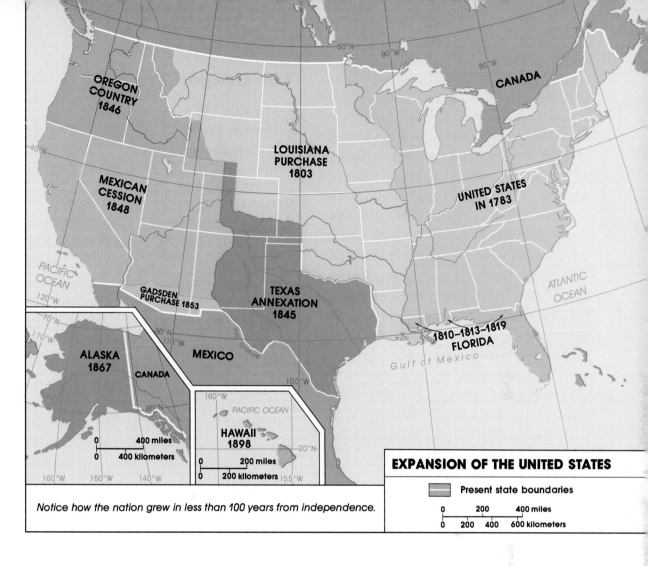

Notice how the nation grew in less than 100 years from independence.

EXPANSION OF THE UNITED STATES

Present state boundaries

South America. They took covered wagons across dangerous trails. The most important thing in life was getting to California. Why do you think so many people wanted to move to California?

That question can be answered in one word: "Gold!" In January 1848, James Marshall was working at a sawmill near Sacramento for his boss, John Sutter. Suddenly something caught his eye. It had glittered in the small stream beneath his feet. He picked up the small lump. It felt heavy. Could it be gold?

It was gold! Marshall told John Sutter and the two agreed it should be kept secret. But the word got out and spread rapidly. "Gold! Gold at Sutter's Mill!" The words were whispered and repeated over and over. Soon there was a report in the newspaper.

People caught gold fever. It seemed as though the whole world wanted to move to California and "get rich quick." People on their way to Oregon turned to California instead. People traveled overland by wagon train. Some made long ocean voyages around South America or cut through the jungles of Panama. States back East lost hundreds of citizens to the gold rush. Word spread throughout the world. South Americans, Australians, Chinese, and Europeans all hurried to California.

157

Gold by the wheelbarrowful in California! You could kick it around! Instant wealth just by bending over and picking it up! This was not true, but the thought of gold made people willing to believe anything. Thousands of miners followed a tale of a lake that had a gold bottom. The slightest rumor of a new discovery caused people to move. Enough people were getting rich to keep the dreams alive.

Perhaps the surest way to get rich was to sell supplies to the miners. Hundreds became wealthy by charging high prices for their goods. Flour was $40.00 a barrel. Picks and shovels were $10.00 each. Tin pans for gold washing were $30.00. So were butcher knives. Eggs were $10.00 a dozen. This **inflation,** or rise in prices, was caused by the large amounts of money and small amounts of goods available on which to spend it.

California becomes a state   California was a rough place to be during the early years of the gold rush. There was little law and order. There was an urgent need for government. In 1850 Californians elected a governor. They chose a legislature to make laws. Later in 1850, California became the thirty-first state.

The excitement over gold died down in a few years. But California has not stopped growing. Today more people live in California than in any other state.

CHECKUP

1. How did Portolá, Serra, and Marshall each contribute to the development of California?
2. What was the Bear Flag Republic?
3. What is inflation?
4. When did California become a state?

The Oregon Trail

VOCABULARY

Oregon Trail
mountain men
pioneer

Oregon fever   The Southwest was not the only place of growth and activity in the 1840s. People from all over the East caught "Oregon fever." They had heard reports of the beautiful land and plentiful game found in the Oregon Country. The **Oregon Trail** was made up of hopes and dreams of men and women who wanted to start new lives in Oregon. With everything they owned in covered wagons, people took on the challenges and dangers of the rugged 2,000-mile (3,200 km) journey west. "Oregon or Bust" was the slogan of the day. Thousands moved to Oregon. Many died trying.

Jim Beckwourth spent his later years running a ranch and trading post near the mountain pass he discovered.

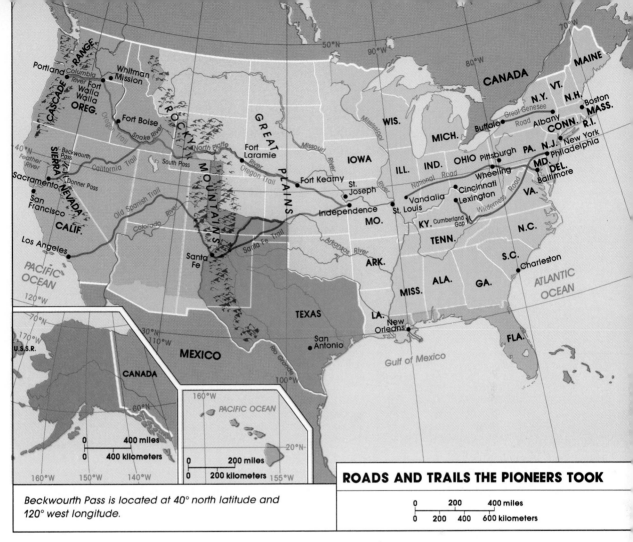

ROADS AND TRAILS THE PIONEERS TOOK

Beckwourth Pass is located at 40° north latitude and 120° west longitude.

Mountain men What kind of people went to Oregon? First there were the **mountain men.** These men went west to get beaver fur. In the nineteenth century, men's hats were made of beaver fur and so there was much demand for it. Mountain men had to be rough and tough in order to survive. They had to go deep into the mountains to trap the animals. Most mountain men got along well with the Native Americans. Kit Carson spent part of his life as a mountain man. Another famous mountain man was Jim Beckwourth. Beckwourth found and explored a pass through the Sierra Nevada. Find this pass on the map on this page. Because they came to know the land so well, the moun-

tain men served as guides for the pioneers headed to Oregon.

Pioneers Several trading posts were started. Mountain men used them to get supplies. Indians traded furs for manufactured goods such as blankets and iron pots. American churches soon sent missionaries to the area. One such missionary, Narcissa Whitman, was the first white woman from the East to settle west of the Rockies. She came as a young bride in 1836 along with her husband, Dr. Marcus Whitman.

The courage of the **pioneers** who followed the mountain men and the missionaries to Oregon is remarkable. Dis-

Rules of the Road

Why do Americans drive on the right side of the road? The reason dates back to the days of the Conestogas.

These wagons were used to carry goods on the early roads. They were sturdy. Teams of four to six oxen or horses pulled them. The people who drove the wagons rode what was called the left wheelhorse. This was the animal closest to the wagon on the left side. In order to have a clear view of what was ahead, the driver would keep the animals and wagon to the right side of the road or the trail.

The Conestoga wagons were used to carry people and their household goods to the West. Driving on the right side of the road became a habit. Eventually it became the law throughout the United States.

ease, starvation, flooding streams, or deserts with no water were some of the problems they faced. Not wishing to see their land taken, Native Americans constantly threatened attack. Still, between 1841 and 1845 about 5,000 people made the trip to the Oregon Country.

John Sager The legend of John Sager symbolizes the courage and determination of the people who went to Oregon. Thirteen-year-old John joined a wagon train to Oregon in the summer of 1844 with his parents, younger brother, and five younger sisters. Sager's father had the dream of helping settle the Oregon Country for the United States. Sadly, both parents died when they were about 500 miles (800 km) from where they wanted to settle. Kit Carson helped the children for a time before he went back East to lead another wagon train. When other members of young Sager's wagon train decided to go to California rather than to Oregon, John decided to take the family to Oregon. He wanted to fulfill his father's dream.

Of course, the adults would not have let him take small children and a baby through dangerous territory. So he left a note saying he had gone back East with Kit Carson. Then he set out for Oregon.

Travel was difficult. The rugged country was very hot during the day and cold at night. After traveling 300 miles (480 km) in several weeks, the Sagers straggled into Fort Boise in Idaho. Their clothes were ragged. They were dirty and hungry and the baby was very sick. Yet when John found that he could get no help for the

The beauty and richness of the land drew the pioneers to Oregon.

baby here, he decided they would leave again the next day. He was told there would be help at the Whitman mission, 200 miles (320 km) away. Fresh horses and Native American guides were sent along to help them.

Within a few days the guides left with the horses, leaving John and the children alone. The strain on John was terrible. The children often said they would go no farther. John yelled at them and did everything he could to keep them moving toward the Oregon dream.

Getting through the mountains was hard. The oldest sister had broken her leg. This made travel slower. They kept on. Oregon! The oxen were starving and had to be left behind. They kept on. Oregon! Feet were nearly frozen, sores went unhealed, hunger was constant.

Then, finally, after weeks of struggle, a beautiful sight—Oregon! The Whitman mission! Narcissa Whitman took the baby and began caring for her. Dr. Whitman helped the other children. They were invited to stay. Their father's dream came true. They were in Oregon together!

The Sager story is based on fact. However, some people think the children stayed with a wagon train all the way to the Whitman mission. Whatever the truth, the story gives you a good idea of the hardships the pioneers faced.

CHECKUP

1. What is meant by the phrases "Oregon fever" and "Oregon or Bust"?
2. What three groups of people went to Oregon?
3. Choose three words that describe John Sager. Explain why you chose those words.

8/CHAPTER REVIEW

KEY FACTS

1. Due to the development of roads, canals, steamboats, and railroads, transportation became faster and cheaper in the early 1800s.

2. America was changing in the early 1800s due to the rise of industry, new inventions, and immigration to this country.

3. Between 1845 and 1853 America gained from Mexico a great deal of land in the Southwest.

4. Mexican Americans have made and are making great contributions to the United States.

5. Hoping for a better life, pioneers flocked to Oregon in the 1840s.

6. The discovery of gold in California in 1848 caused thousands of people from all over the world to rush to that area in hopes of getting rich quick.

VOCABULARY QUIZ

On a separate sheet of paper write **T** if the statement is true and **F** if it is false.

1. Many of our clothes are made of textiles.

2. The Lone Star Republic is the first name given to Texas.

3. The Industrial Revolution is a name for a time when a lot of factory workers fought each other.

4. Inflation occurs when prices go down.

5. Many people followed the Oregon Trail west to California and Oregon.

6. A type of road you have to pay money to use is called a turnpike.

7. Someone who comes from one country to live in another country is an immigrant.

8. On the telegraph you can talk to another person.

9. Architecture is the style of a building.

10. Jim Beckwourth and Kit Carson were pioneers in the Oregon Country.

REVIEW QUESTIONS

1. Of all the changes and improvements in transportation in the early 1800s, which do you think was the most important? Explain.

2. How did the Industrial Revolution and changes in transportation help each other?

3. Name at least three events that led to the independence of Texas in 1836.

4. What territory did the United States gain as a result of the 1848 war with Mexico?

ACTIVITIES

1. The following headlines could have been found in newspapers of the 1800s. Arrange them in the order in which they happened. Write a brief news story about each one.

PIONEERS CATCH "OREGON FEVER"

HORSE FASTER THAN LOCOMOTIVE

TEXANS WIN AT SAN JACINTO: "REMEMBER THE ALAMO!" THEY CRY

ERIE CANAL OPENED

GOLD IN CALIFORNIA: GET RICH QUICK

2. Debate with another pupil on one of the following topics or one of your own:

a. Railroads were more important than canals to the growth of our country.

b. The United States got land from Mexico in a proper way.

c. The steel plow was a more helpful invention than the telegraph.

d. Immigrants to the United States have helped the country grow.

READING FOR SEQUENCE

GOLD!

Read the following story carefully. Notice especially the order, or sequence, of events.

The discovery of gold in California started the most famous gold rush in American history. So many people hurried to the area for gold that California became a state within a year. But the California gold rush was not the first in America. About 20 years earlier, Georgia had had the first gold rush in the history of our country. Even before that, the Spaniards had searched hungrily for gold in areas that were to become the United States.

Nor was California's gold rush the last. Ten years later thousands of people flocked to Colorado to "get rich quick." Just before the close of the nineteenth century, Alaska had a large gold rush. Even today, whenever the price of gold rises, many people can be found panning for gold in the streams of many of these western areas. They even find tiny amounts once in a while. The dream of sudden wealth has not died.

SKILLS PRACTICE

Place the following statements in the order in which they happened. Write on a separate sheet of paper.
1. California becomes a state.
2. There is a gold rush in Georgia.
3. Spaniards search for gold.
4. Gold is discovered in Alaska.
5. There is a gold rush in California.
6. People look for gold in Colorado.

Copy the time line on this page. There are six markers on the time line. The first has been filled out for you. Put the items from your list on the time line in the correct order. You may, if you wish, use a history book and an encyclopedia to find dates for these events and add them in the proper places on the time line.

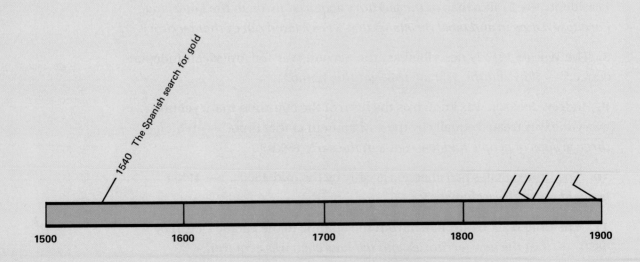

3/UNIT REVIEW

1. The American Revolution was fought because the colonists felt they had lost their rights as British subjects. — *What does the phrase "No taxation without representation" mean?*

2. The Declaration of Independence states ideas of freedom and equality and provides reasons for fighting the Revolution. — *Name the four major parts of the Declaration of Independence.*

3. Americans won the Revolutionary War because of outstanding leadership, help from people in foreign countries, and the strength of the American people. — *Make a chart titled "Heroes of the American Revolution." Include leaders, foreign helpers, and the ordinary men and women who became heroes.*

4. The Constitution of the United States makes our government a republic divided into three branches on the federal level. — *Make a chart showing the three branches and how each is a separate part of the power of the government.*

5. The Bill of Rights protects our basic freedoms as Americans. — *Which one of these first ten amendments to the Constitution would you least like to give up or do without? Explain your answer.*

6. The presidency has grown enormously since George Washington became our first President. — *Make a scrapbook of newspaper and magazine articles that tell about the work done by the President and staff during a week.*

7. The United States nearly doubled in size while Thomas Jefferson was President. — *Draw a map of the territory acquired through the Louisiana Purchase. Draw in and label the states that were carved out of that territory.*

8. The War of 1812 is described as "the Second War for American Independence." — *Why did the War of 1812 get this name?*

9. Andrew Jackson was known as the hero of the common man, yet not everyone was treated equally by the government at that time. — *Which three groups of people had few rights in the early 1800s?*

10. The United States had changed greatly by the mid-1800s. — *What brought about these changes?*

11. The United States stretched from the Atlantic to the Pacific Ocean by 1850. — *List the new territories and tell how each was acquired.*

The United States Comes of Age

9 A Nation Divides and Reunites

Slavery

┌─ VOCABULARY ──────────────────┐
| free state | sectionalism |
| Underground Railroad | secede |
└───────────────────────────────┘

Differences In the early 1800s differences arose among three sections of the United States: the Northeast, Southeast, and West. These three sections had developed in different ways. In all three, farming was the chief means of making a living. But in the Northeast, farms were smaller, factories and trade were important, and those in business were the leading citizens. In the Southeast, farms were larger. Cotton, tobacco, and sugar were the main crops. The leading citizens were the great planters who owned 100 or more slaves. The West had large farms that grew corn and wheat, but milling, meat-packing, and other industries were growing more important.

The sections disagreed on what was best for the country, but for a long time they found ways to settle their arguments. No one section could control Congress. Until the 1840s, West and Southeast generally worked together as people in the West shipped their goods to market down the Mississippi River. From the 1840s on-ward, West and Northeast tended to unite as canals and railroads linked them in trade and travel. (See map on page 148.)

Slavery The most troublesome issue among the sections was slavery. Originally all 13 American colonies had slavery. After the War for Independence, slavery slowly came to an end in the Northern states where slave labor, as part of the work force, was not important. These became known as **free states.** Slavery was needed in the South, where slaves were a main part of the work force. They were one third of the population. Slaves were owned for life by their masters. They were forced to work without pay, receiving only food, clothing, and housing.

You read in Chapter 5 about the hardships of slaves. Poor food, poor housing, very hard work, and often cruelty were all part of a slave's life. Slaves were able to bear these hardships because of the strong support they gave each other. Many slave owners tried to break up slave families to make it easier to control slaves. But the strong family ties that blacks had when they were free in Africa carried over in the United States. The love and care that slave parents, children, brothers, sisters, and other relatives gave one another helped them pull through a rough time.

One of the most important battles of the Civil War was the one fought at Gettysburg. The battle lasted 3 days. This painting shows a moment during the third day.

Resistance grows   Many slaves fought against slavery. Some fought openly, even though that meant almost certain death. This was the punishment set by law for any slave who raised a hand against a master.

Others fought back in milder but safer ways. They broke their tools on purpose but said it was an accident. Slaves pretended not to know the difference and cut down crops and left weeds standing. They dropped sand or stones into machinery to break it. They set fire to haystacks, barns, and crops in the fields. Some slaves did as little work as possible, slowing down whenever the master or his helpers turned their backs.

Slaves also ran away. Some hid nearby while fellow slaves sneaked food to them. After some weeks, such runaways often were caught or gave up. Their punish-

ment was a severe whipping. Some runaways tried to escape to freedom in the North. They would travel along side roads by night and hide during the day from slave patrols and slave catchers.

There were also revolts in which people were killed. Probably the best known of these was the revolt led by Nat Turner in 1831. He was a slave in Virginia. Before the revolt was finished, over 160 people, white and black, had died. Turner himself was captured, tried, and hanged.

The abolitionists   In 1831, William Lloyd Garrison, editor of a new Boston newspaper, *The Liberator*, called for ending, or abolishing, slavery at once. People who supported this idea called themselves abolitionists. Abolitionists held large meetings to win support for their cause. They sent papers to the South say-

When did the Civil War begin? The war ended with Lee's surrender. When was that?

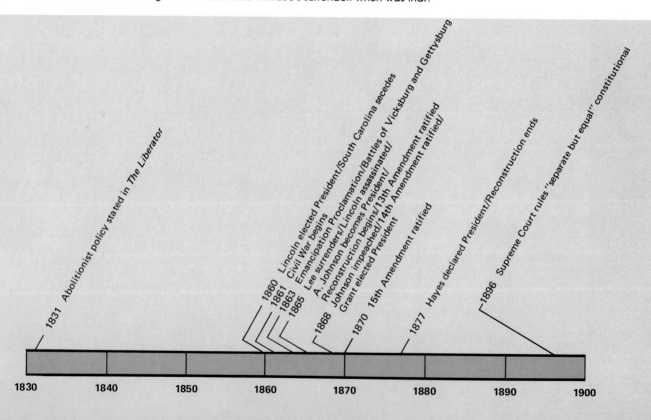

1831 Abolitionist policy stated in *The Liberator*
1860 Lincoln elected President/South Carolina secedes
1861 Civil War begins
1863 Emancipation Proclamation/Battles of Vicksburg and Gettysburg
1865 Lee surrenders/Lincoln assassinated/A. Johnson becomes President/13th Amendment ratified/Reconstruction begins/14th Amendment ratified
1868 Johnson impeached/Grant elected President
1870 15th Amendment ratified
1877 Hayes declared President/Reconstruction ends
1896 Supreme Court rules "separate but equal" constitutional

1830   1840   1850   1860   1870   1880   1890   1900

ing that slavery was evil. They asked Congress to do away with slavery, without payment to owners.

Many of the leading abolitionists were whites, like Garrison or the Grimké sisters, about whom you read in Chapter 7. Free blacks and runaway slaves also joined the movement. They were active as officers, speakers, and givers of money. Blacks were free if their parents were free, or if their masters set them free. Sometimes relatives and friends bought their freedom. In 1860 about 8 to 10 percent of blacks living in the United States were free. There were more free blacks living in the South than in the North.

Frederick Douglass was the most famous black abolitionist. He was born a slave on a large plantation in Maryland. He was taught to read and write by the wife of his owner. He said that the slave who frees his or her mind by learning to read and to think as a free person is no longer a slave even though still in chains. Douglass escaped to the North. He was skilled in shipbuilding but had a hard time finding a job. He started to speak before small groups about his life as a slave. In time he became an outstanding speaker at large abolitionist meetings. Douglass was a major leader of blacks in the United States from the late 1840s to his death in 1895.

Liberia   Not everyone who wanted to see an end to slavery thought that it was something that should happen all at once. Some groups, such as the Quakers, put forth other plans. Some of these plans called for ending slavery slowly and paying the owners for the freed slaves. The freed blacks would then be sent back to Africa to live in colonies of their own.

The American Colonization Society was started in 1822. Over 12,000 blacks were returned to Africa by this group. The colony was called Liberia (for *liberty*) and the capital, Monrovia, was named in honor of President James Monroe. Liberia became an independent country in 1847. Find Liberia on the Atlas map on page 466.

Underground Railroad   Many slaves escaped on the **Underground Railroad.** On this railroad, a "conductor" was a person guiding slaves, called "passengers," who were escaping from the South to the North. The "trains" traveled only at night. The slaves hid in "stations," which were homes and barns, during the day. The "tracks" were the routes followed to the North. The "terminals" were Northern cities, such as Cincinnati or Philadelphia. Here abolitionists helped slave passengers get jobs and start living as free people. Some slaves went even farther north. They left the United States to settle in Canada. Some of them returned after the start of the Civil War. The Underground Railroad was most active in the years between 1830 and 1860. There are no records of how many slaves were helped to escape to freedom during this time.

Harriet Tubman, a conductor on the railroad, was one of the bravest women in American history. She was an escaped slave who returned to the South 19 times to lead 300 slaves to freedom. Rewards of more than $40,000 were posted for her capture, dead or alive. She boasted that she never lost a passenger and that her

These slaves have come closer to freedom as they reach an Indiana station on the Underground Railroad.

train never jumped the tracks. She never let a slave who got tired on the long and dangerous journey turn back.

Abraham Lincoln   Slavery was ended by a man who did not like slavery but who opposed the abolitionists, Abraham Lincoln. He was born in the slave state of Kentucky. His family was poor. They did not have either the money or the wish to buy a slave. When he was 8, the family moved across the Ohio River to the state of Indiana, later settling in Illinois. Neither of these was a slave state. Lincoln had less than a year of formal schooling. He read every book he could borrow. He read and reread the family Bible. On trips carrying goods down the Mississippi River to New

Orleans, he saw slavery. He did not like what he saw. He said slavery was "monstrous injustice."

Lincoln became known for his honesty and wit. He was a good speaker. He served four terms in the Illinois state legislature. Meanwhile, he studied law books and became a lawyer in the state capital, Springfield. He later served one term in the United States House of Representatives. Lincoln felt that while slavery was wrong, the government did not have the right to stop slavery where it already existed. What the government could do, and should do, according to Lincoln, was to stop slavery in the territories. When these areas became states, they would be free states. There would be no slavery.

Abraham Lincoln became President of a divided nation.

The states in the Deep South would not accept Lincoln as President. His victory was looked upon as an insult and a danger. Before the election, Southerners had said that if Lincoln won they would leave the Union. They would **secede.** Now that Lincoln was elected, they would act on that threat.

CHECKUP

1. How was farming different in the sections of the United States in the early 1800s?
2. In what part of the country did most slaves live?
3. What was the Underground Railroad?
4. What did Lincoln feel should happen to slavery in the territories?

A Civil War

┌─VOCABULARY──────────────────┐
blockade   **emancipate**
proclamation
└─────────────────────────────┘

Election of 1860   At the start of this chapter you read about **sectionalism,** how the country was divided into three main areas. The election of 1860 shows that by that time there were really only two sections. They were the North and the South—those states that were against slavery and those that were for it. The question of slavery was tied to another question as well. Did the government in Washington, D.C., have the right to tell the states what they could or could not do?

In the election of 1860 Lincoln did not win in a single slave state. The candidate who was in favor of slavery throughout the United States did not win in a single free state. This showed how clearly the country was divided.

Secession   South Carolina left the Union the month after Lincoln's election. By February 1861, six more states had seceded. At a meeting in Montgomery, Alabama, they formed the Confederate States of America (C.S.A.) and chose Jefferson Davis of Mississippi as their President. Like Lincoln, Davis had been born in Kentucky, but Davis's family moved to Mississippi, a slave state. He graduated from West Point and later became a wealthy cotton planter. He was also a congressman, secretary of war, and United States senator. He left the Senate when Mississippi seceded.

War began on April 12, 1861. The Confederates attacked Fort Sumter at Charleston, South Carolina. Northerners rushed to fight for the Union. Southerners were

171

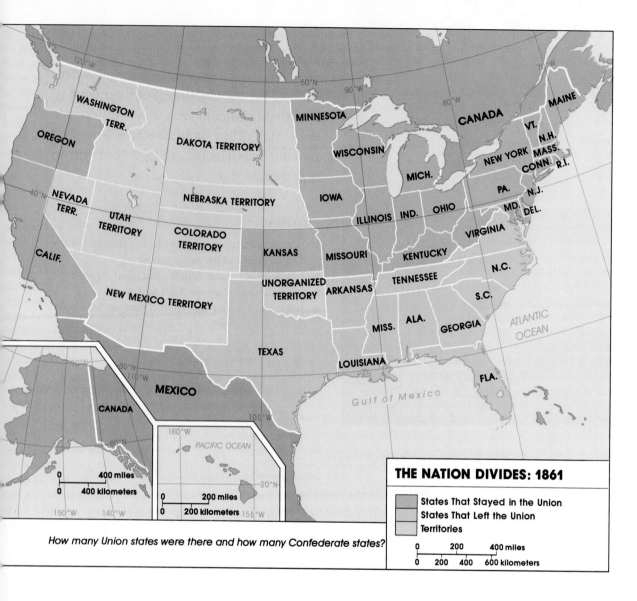

THE NATION DIVIDES: 1861

- States That Stayed in the Union
- States That Left the Union
- Territories

How many Union states were there and how many Confederate states?

surprised that Northerners cared enough about keeping the nation together to fight to do so. After Sumter, four more slave states joined the Confederacy; the other four stayed in the Union. The map above shows how the country was divided.

Unequal fight?   The Union had far more states, people, money, factories, resources, railroads, and ships. The Confederacy did at the start have better generals and more men used to outdoor life.

Southerners graduating from West Point stayed in the army because fewer jobs could be found in the South. When the war began, Southern generals were in charge of five of the nation's six military districts. Also, the Confederacy's 3,500,000 slaves did so much of the work that more of the 5,500,000 whites could fight. The Union had to beat Confederate armies and take over the Confederate states to force them back into the United States. Confederates wanted only to depart from the

Union in peace. They had only to keep the war going until the Union side grew tired of it and stopped fighting, leaving them and their slaves alone. Also, Confederates had an easier time because they were fighting on their own familiar land, while Union troops had to fight on Southern soil.

When the war began, President Lincoln ordered the Union navy to **blockade,** or stop, shipping from Confederate ports. At first he did not have enough ships. More ships were built and the blockade became more nearly complete. Confederates found it harder and harder to ship their cotton and other goods for sale overseas or to bring in needed supplies.

Two great generals   Robert E. Lee ranked with Lincoln as one of the greatest men of his day. Lee was born into one of America's most famous families. His father, "Light Horse Harry" Lee, served with General George Washington. Harry Lee later became governor of Virginia. Other relatives were congressmen, governors, and signers of the Declaration of Independence. Robert E. Lee graduated from West Point and married Martha Washington's granddaughter. He served in the Mexican War, and was a top Union officer when the war began. Lee disliked slavery. He had freed the few slaves he inherited. Lincoln asked him to be field commander of all the Union armies, but he said he could not. Lee went with his state when Virginia seceded. He held minor commands and served as an aide to President Jefferson Davis until June 1, 1862, when he took over one of the Confederate armies. Lee became General-in-Chief of all the Con-

federate armies 2 months before the war ended.

The general who led the Union forces to victory was Ulysses S. Grant. He grew up on a farm in Ohio and also graduated from West Point. He became lonely while serving on army posts in the West away from his wife and children. He left the army. When the Civil War began, the Union needed men with West Point training. Grant went back into the army. He soon became one of the best generals in the West.

Early battles   The Confederates won the first big battle of the war. This was at Bull Run in northern Virginia in July 1861. The Union's Army of the Potomac rushed to do battle before the 3-month volunteers who signed up after Sumter returned home. A large crowd came out from Washington to watch. Their picnic mood turned to fear when the Union army, after fighting hard all day, suddenly began to lose. The soldiers ran the 25 miles (40 km) back to Washington, dropping their guns and packs on the way.

Clara Barton fought infection and disease to save the lives of many wounded soldiers.

The battle of Petersburg was actually a siege of the city that lasted for 10 months in 1864–1865. It finally ended in a very costly Union victory.

They trampled over the people who had come out to see them.

After Bull Run, George B. McClellan became commander of the Army of the Potomac. McClellan organized, equipped, and trained his soldiers brilliantly. His men drilled and paraded perfectly, but McClellan was slow to fight. President Lincoln said McClellan had the "slows." He did everything except the most important thing, attack.

McClellan did not obey Lincoln's demands for action for months. President Lincoln was going to replace him when finally he began to move his army south. He planned to capture Richmond, Virginia, the Confederate capital. Find Richmond on the map on page 175. See how close it is to Washington, D.C. For 4 months McClellan moved his army around this part of Virginia, barely avoiding total defeat. He was finally forced to retreat to Washington by General Lee.

Lee's greatest victory against the Union forces came in May 1863, at Chancellorsville, Virginia. The Union general had 130,000 men to Lee's 60,000. Lee's victory was amazing. It gave the Southern troops and their leaders new confidence.

Emancipation Proclamation Blacks tried to join the Union army. They were told, "Keep out of this; this is a white man's war." President Lincoln said that the war was to "save the Union," not to end slavery. After a year he changed his mind: "Things had gone on from bad to worse, until I felt that we must change our tactics, or lose the game. I now determined [decided] upon the adoption of the Emancipation Policy."

The President secretly wrote a **proclamation,** an order, that would **emancipate,** set free, the slaves and let them join the Union army. He believed that black soldiers would help win the war: "Keep

[them] and you can save the Union. Throw [them] away and the Union goes also." His Cabinet asked him to wait for a victory before announcing this new policy so that it would not look as if the government needed blacks to save the Union.

Lincoln waited 3 months until a Union army won an important victory. This was the battle of Antietam (an tē′ təm) in September 1862. Lincoln's Emancipation Proclamation of January 1, 1863, declared the slaves in all Confederate areas to be "then, thenceforward, and forever free."

Black soldiers

About 180,000 blacks joined the Union army. Forty thousand were free blacks from the North. The rest were Southern blacks, mostly slaves who ran away from their owners. Until mid-1864, blacks were paid less than white Union soldiers. One black regiment took no pay until all were paid equally. One sergeant was tried and shot after he and his men laid down their guns because of unequal pay.

Twenty-one black soldiers and sailors were among the many who won the Medal of Honor for bravery. The first black man to win the medal was Sergeant William Carney of Massachusetts. He was hit by many bullets in the attack on Fort Wagner, Charleston, South Carolina, but kept the flag flying. Blacks made a difference in the last 2 years of the war.

**THE CIVIL WAR:
Some Major Battles**

× Battle Sites

0   100   200 miles

0   100   200   300 kilometers

Many of the battles of the Civil War were fought in Virginia.

These men are part of a guard detail of a black regiment stationed near Washington, D.C. The regiment fought in the Carolinas later in the war.

The Monitor and the Merrimac

In March 1862, the Confederates tried to break the blockade. Sailors on Union ships blocking Virginia's Hampton Roads ports saw a strange looking vessel move boldly toward them. Union guns fired at it but the shells simply bounced off. It was the Confederate ironclad warship, the *Virginia,* better known by its old name, the *Merrimac.* The Confederates had taken the *Merrimac,* an old Union ship, and turned it into an ironclad vessel by putting iron all along its sides. On the front they put extra slabs of metal to make a battering ram. They renamed the ship the C.S.S. *Virginia.*

The *Virginia* steamed to the attack against the wooden ships of the Union navy. Two were destroyed. It seemed that a way had been found to break the blockade.

These hopes were dashed the next day when the *Virginia* returned to the attack. This time the Confederate sailors were surprised to see a strange object in the water. It was a comical sight. It did not look like any ship ever seen. It looked like a box sitting on a raft. It lay flat in the water with guns poking out from a circular turret rising from its center. It was the U.S.S. *Monitor.* The newly built *Monitor* was on its trial run from the shipyard at New York. It arrived off the Virginia coast just in time to defend the blockade fleet.

The famous duel between the *Monitor* and the *Merrimac* (*Virginia*)—the first in the world between ironclads—lasted all day on March 9, 1862. Neither ship could harm the other, but the *Monitor* stopped the *Virginia* from sinking any more Union ships.

In May, the Confederates sank the *Virginia* to keep the ship from the invading Union army. Later that year, the *Monitor* went down in a storm off Cape Hatteras, North Carolina.

Two important battles   The two most important battles of the Civil War were Vicksburg in the West and Gettysburg in the East. They can be called turning points. Victory began to follow the Union armies.

Vicksburg was a Confederate stronghold on the Mississippi River. Find it on the map on page 175. This battle was General Grant's greatest success. His plan was simple. His army would cut off all supplies from Vicksburg. It took 6 weeks before the people in the city and the army gave up. During this time people were so hungry they ate anything, even shoe leather. Vicksburg surrendered on July 4, 1863.

At nearly the same time—July 1 to 3—but hundreds of miles away, the battle of Gettysburg was taking place. General Lee decided to try again to invade the North, but he failed. Both sides lost many men. Lee returned to Virginia with what was left of his army. He would not try again to invade the North.

The war ends   Grant and Lee never fought each other until the last year of the war. Lee was in the East and Grant was in the West. In 1864, however, Grant was put

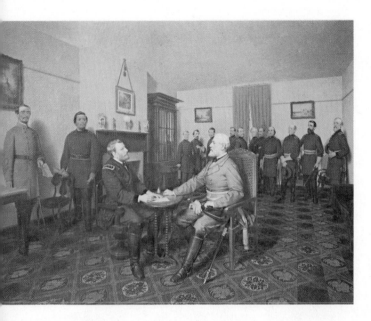

General Grant (left) and General Lee (right) discuss the terms of surrender as they sit in the parlor of a house in the village of Appomattox Court House.

in charge of all the Union armies. Grant's plan to win the war was to attack Lee daily. He would pin him down while other Union forces closed in on Lee from other directions. Many of Grant's men were killed or wounded. In the end, however, Lee was forced to retreat. Lee moved westward. Grant followed, finally catching up with him at Appomattox Court House, Virginia. Lee surrendered on April 9, 1865.

The Civil War ended 4 years after it began. The United States was one nation again. Slavery was about to be ended throughout the land.

CHECKUP
1. How many states were there in the Confederate States of America?
2. At the time of the Civil War, who was President of the United States? Of the Confederate States?
3. Who was the most outstanding Confederate general? Union general?

Reconstruction

—VOCABULARY—

Reconstruction	impeach
Freedman's Bureau	carpetbagger
refugee	scalawag
sharecropping	poll tax
crop lien	grandfather clause

Lincoln dies   Less than a week after the war ended, Abraham Lincoln was dead. He was shot by John Wilkes Booth, an actor. Booth was angry over the South's defeat. When Lincoln died Vice-President Andrew Johnson became President. He was a Democrat, a Southerner, and a former slave owner. He had been nominated in 1864 to bring wider support for Lincoln and the Republicans in that election.

President Lincoln's leadership was greatly needed during **Reconstruction.** This is the name given to the dozen years after the Civil War, 1865 to 1877. It was during this time that two big questions would have to be answered. Under what conditions would the former Confederate states be given back all their rights and powers? How would real freedom be given to the millions of freed slaves?

After the war   Four years of fighting had left much of the South's railroads, factories, and bridges torn up. Several cities, such as Atlanta, Georgia, and Columbia, South Carolina, had been burned. Many people had been driven from their homes. Some areas had very little food. Others with more than enough had no way to ship food to places in need.

By the end of the war, fire and artillery shells had destroyed most of the city of Richmond, Virginia, which had been the Confederate capital.

Near the end of the war Congress set up the **Freedmen's Bureau.** It helped the poor and the homeless. It gave food, blankets, and housing to freedmen, persons just set free from slavery, and to **refugees,** whites and blacks who fled from their homes because of the fighting. It also set up schools for black children.

Since the South was mainly a farming region and the soil was not hurt by war, rebuilding would not be hard. All that was needed were seeds, tools, and workers. However, it took money to buy seeds and tools and to pay workers. Confederate money printed during the war was worthless. Freeing the slaves left landowners, especially planters, without their workers. Freed workers, unlike slaves, had to be paid. But landowners had no money to hire anyone. Planters and other

large landowners could sell or rent land to the newly freed blacks and to landless whites. These blacks and whites, however, had no money to buy or rent land.

Sharecropping New ways—**sharecropping** and **crop lien**—were found to solve these problems. In sharecropping, farmers, black and white, paid for the use of the land by giving the owner of the land a part of the crop. It was usually a fourth to a half. Storekeepers sold seeds, tools, supplies, and other needs to landowners and sharecroppers on credit. In return, they got a lien, or first claim, on the crop. The storekeepers sold the crops and took what was owed them. Any money left was shared by the landowners and farmers. The Freedmen's Bureau protected blacks who could not read or write from unfair sharecropping and lien agreements.

Some freed blacks tested freedom by wandering and not working. In slavery they had been forced to work all day and could not move about. Most wandering was to find relatives, separated when slaves were sold, or to get back to homeplaces from which they and their masters had fled when battles were fought nearby. Most soon settled down and were ready to work. Many whites, used to free labor from slaves, were not willing, even when they had the money, to pay freed blacks a fair wage. Blacks were unwilling to work for sums so small that they could not feed themselves and their families.

Constitutional amendments From 1865 to 1870, three constitutional amendments changed life for blacks. The Thirteenth Amendment, ratified late in 1865, ended all slavery everywhere in the United States. The Fourteenth Amendment made blacks citizens of the United States, equal in rights and status to any other citizen. The Fifteenth Amendment gave blacks everywhere in the United States the right to vote.

Black Codes The South had lost the war, but many Southerners thought that the wishes of the winners, the North, did not matter. The states returning to the Union elected former Confederate generals, congressmen, and Cabinet members, as well as the vice-president of the Confederacy, to represent them in the United States Congress. Southern states passed Black Codes. These codes gave freed blacks

rights to sue, marry, speak in court, and own property. Other parts of the codes seemed like a return to slavery.

Black youngsters without parents were put under guardians, often their former masters. They would teach the children a trade but also would have full control over them. Black men without jobs were arrested, fined, and jailed. They would have to work a year without wages to repay any employer who paid the fine. When that year ended, the sheriff could start all over again by arresting the man for being without a job.

Johnson and the Radical Republicans The President and Congress could not agree on how to treat the former Confederate states. The leader of the Radical Republicans was Thaddeus Stevens. He was a congressman from Pennsylvania. The Radicals wanted to punish the South. President Johnson wanted to follow Lincoln's plan to let the Southern states return "with malice toward none."

Congress would not allow the former Confederate leaders to take their seats in the House of Representatives and the Senate. Congress passed laws to protect the rights of blacks and to continue the Freedmen's Bureau. Congress also passed laws that put all the former Confederate states except Tennessee under military rule. To be allowed back into the Union, the states had to ratify the Fourteenth Amendment. This was the amendment that made blacks citizens. Tennessee had already ratified this amendment.

When President Johnson tried to block Congress's program, the House of Representatives **impeached** him. To impeach is to charge an officeholder with wrong-doing while in office. The impeachment charges against the President were not fair. They did show, however, how strong the feelings were against him.

Impeachment   Under the Constitution, the House of Representatives impeaches, but the Senate holds the trial to see whether the officeholder is guilty and should be removed from office. There were 54 senators then. A vote of 36 to 18 was needed to find the President guilty. Thirty-five senators voted guilty. The other 19 senators voted not guilty. By the narrow margin of one vote, Johnson stayed in office. He is the only President ever to have been impeached.

Andrew Johnson accepts the notice that the House of Representatives has voted to impeach him and that the Senate will be sitting in judgment of him.

Carpetbaggers and scalawags   Carpetbaggers were Northern whites who moved to the South after the war. Most of them were soldiers and officers who had learned during the war that the South had good soil and a pleasant climate. Some were business people who wanted to invest in rebuilding the South. These soldiers, officers, and business people made the South their home. There were other people seeking to make money from the South's troubles. The name *carpetbagger*—given to all Northerners coming South after the Civil War—arose because this last group supposedly entered the South with all their belongings in a carpetbag suitcase.

Scalawags were Southern whites who joined the new state governments that had been set up during Reconstruction. Many Southerners believed that these governments had been forced upon them. The people called scalawags believed that the South would be better off by helping than by fighting these governments. Many scalawags had been respected before, but many lost friends and standing by aiding these governments.

Blacks in office   Most black voters in the South could not read or write. However, most of the blacks they elected to office, especially higher posts, were educated. The two black men elected to the United States Senate, Hiram Revels and Blanche K. Bruce, were born in the South but went to Knox and Oberlin colleges in the North. South Carolina State Supreme Court Justice Jonathan J. Wright was a free black who had graduated from the University of Pennsylvania. Jonathan

The central figures in this picture are (left to right) Blanche Bruce, Frederick Douglass, and Hiram Revels. Can you tell what part of black history each corner scene shows?

Gibbs, who became Florida's state superintendent of education, was a graduate of Dartmouth College. Francis Cardozo, state treasurer and state secretary in his home state of South Carolina, had graduated from the University of Glasgow in Scotland.

There were black lieutenant governors in Louisiana, Mississippi, and South Carolina. P.B.S. Pinchback served 43 days as acting governor of Louisiana when the governor left office a month and half before his term was over.

Twenty blacks served in the United States House of Representatives from 1870 to 1901. One of them, Robert Small of South Carolina, was elected to five terms in Congress. He had been a war hero.

Waste and debt   While Reconstruction governments controlled the South, some state funds were wasted or stolen. Partly as a result of this, the amount of money owed by these states went up greatly. The states were left with debts that took years to pay off.

All the blame for misuse of state funds should not be placed on Reconstruction governments. There was waste and stealing nationwide at all levels of government.

181

Benefits Some good did result from Reconstruction governments. They began the public school systems in their states. Among these states, only North Carolina already had a sound system of public schools in operation before Reconstruction. Also, these governments had roads, canals, and railroads built. They sold bonds for such projects and for helping businesses, especially from the North, to set up in the South. Bringing in industry improved the South's way of life. It gave farm workers a chance to work in better-paying factory jobs.

In addition, the South became more democratic during the Reconstruction period. More people took part in government than ever before. Up to then, the South had been run by the planters and other people who were rich or successful. The poorer classes, white and black, generally had been left out and had little to say. Under Reconstruction rule, they too had a voice in public affairs.

Building and running school systems also added to the cost of government and state debt. Building more roads, hospitals, state colleges, and mental institutions to serve the people also added to the cost. Thus there was a rise in state spending and a rise in debt. But the Reconstruction governments did much for the people. They did far more than was done before the war, when little attention was paid to the needs of poor people.

Southern reaction Many Southerners could not see any good in the actions of these Reconstruction state governments. They felt that they had not chosen these governments. The federal government in Washington was forcing Reconstruction on them. These Southerners became more and more angry. Sometimes this anger turned to violence.

Secret societies such as the Ku Klux Klan were formed. The Klan started in Tennessee in 1866. Members wore hoods. The Klan was against everyone and everything connected with Reconstruction. They beat and killed blacks. They burned schools and churches. They attacked people who had come to run the Freedmen's Bureaus and to teach in schools. They frightened people to try to keep them from voting or holding office. The Klan grew more violent as the Reconstruction governments grew stronger.

The Klan officially broke up in 1871. Its actions drew so much attention that federal laws were passed. Federal officers began taking steps against it.

The hoods hid the faces of the Klan members so that they could not be identified by their victims. The rest of the costume was supposed to further frighten people.

1876 election   The 1876 presidential election ended without a clear winner. The Democrat, Governor Samuel Tilden of New York, had 184 of the 185 electoral votes needed to win. The Republican, Governor Rutherford Hayes of Ohio, had only 165 votes. There were 20 other votes that both sides claimed. Of these 20, 19 came from the last three states still under Reconstruction governments, Florida, Louisiana, and South Carolina. A commission set up to settle the argument gave all 20 votes to Hayes. He won 185 to 184. Democrats and Southerners agreed to accept this decision on three conditions: (1) that Hayes put a Southerner in his Cabinet; (2) that federal troops be removed from the South; (3) that Congress give help for building a transcontinental railroad by the southern route (New Orleans to Los Angeles). This agreement is the Compromise of 1877. After Hayes became President in March 1877, he took the federal soldiers out of the South and the last Reconstruction governments fell.

Losing what had been won   From 1890 to 1901 Southern states took steps to stop most blacks from voting. All voters had to pay a **poll tax.** Many blacks were too poor. All voters had to take a test to show they could read and understand the state constitution. Often, well-educated blacks were told they had failed, but whites with little education were told they passed. The **grandfather clause** let a white who failed the literacy test vote as long as he, his father, or his grandfather had voted before January 1, 1867. Most blacks had not been able to vote before March 1867.

Blacks also lost the right to use public places, such as trains, streetcars, hotels, theaters, and restaurants, freely. Southern states passed many laws to separate the races in such places. The United States Supreme Court ruled in 1896 that laws ordering "separate but equal" treatment did not take away civil rights given to blacks in the Fourteenth Amendment. However, the separate places were almost never equal. Not until the civil rights movement of the 1950s and 1960s did blacks get back the rights lost between 1890 and 1910.

Reconstruction ends   The nation was reunited. The North and South stopped arguing in the 1890s over rights for blacks. The Republicans no longer needed the votes of black Republicans in the South because new western states backed the Republican party. Republicans no longer feared a Democratic party takeover because Southern Democrats supported business interests. The Republicans therefore allowed Southern Democrats to do as they wished in dealing with blacks. The Civil War, 1861–1865, had made clear that one part of the country could not pull out and form another country. The 1890s saw an end to much of the bitterness left by that war. The United States of America was firmly one nation indivisible.

CHECKUP

1. What did the Thirteenth Amendment do? The Fourteenth? The Fifteenth?
2. Who was the only President ever impeached?
3. Who were carpetbaggers? Who were scalawags?
4. Name one good thing Reconstruction governments did.

KEY FACTS

1. Slavery was one of the main differences between the South and the rest of the nation.

2. With the election of Abraham Lincoln as President, the Southern states left the Union and formed a new nation.

3. In the Civil War, the Union side was more powerful but the Confederacy started with better generals, was fighting on its own ground, and merely had to hold on till the North grew tired of the war.

4. The Emancipation Proclamation freed slaves in Confederate areas. After the war the Thirteenth Amendment ended slavery everywhere in the United States.

5. The Fourteenth and Fifteenth Amendments made blacks citizens and gave black men the right to vote.

6. Reconstruction governments wasted some money but also began the public school systems in almost all Southern states.

7. Blacks lost many of their rights between 1890 and 1910.

VOCABULARY QUIZ

Choose the word or words from the list that best complete each of the sentences below. Write on a separate sheet of paper.

sharecropping
Underground Railroad
impeach
Freedmen's Bureau
emancipate
secede

blockade
poll tax
scalawags
carpetbaggers
free states

1. To free slaves is to _____ them.

2. Before the 1860s the United States had slave states and _____.

3. Eleven Southern states decided to _____ after the election of 1860.

4. A _____ keeps ships from entering or leaving a port.

5. Many slaves escaped on the _____ _____.

6. The _____ was started to help the former slaves.

7. Paying for use of the land by giving the owner of the land part of the crop was known as _____.

8. The _____ and the grandfather clause were used to keep blacks from voting.

9. Northerners who came to the South after the war were called _____.

10. To _____ is to charge an officeholder with wrongdoing while in office.

REVIEW QUESTIONS

1. What were the main differences between the different parts of the country in the 1830s and 1840s?

2. Compare the Union and Confederate states. What did each have to do to win?

3. How did the Thirteenth, Fourteenth, and Fifteenth Amendments help the freed slaves?

4. Choose three positive acts by Reconstruction governments. Explain your choices.

ACTIVITIES

1. There were many exciting battles during the Civil War. Choose one and write a report describing the battle. You may find it helpful to use maps to show troop movements.

2. Take the role of one of the following: an abolitionist, a Southern farmer without slaves, a slave owner, a free black living in the North, a plantation slave. Pretend it is early 1860 before the election. Write a letter, newspaper article, or speech telling what you feel is going to happen or what should happen.

USING CONTEXT CLUES

A SIMPLE SPEECH

On November 19, 1863, President Lincoln gave a speech in Pennsylvania, at the site of the battle of Gettysburg. People had gathered at the battlefield to dedicate part of it to those who had been killed in the battle.

Lincoln's Gettysburg Address is still remembered as one of the best speeches ever given. It was short and simple. People could understand it. It was very moving.

SKILLS PRACTICE

Read the speech. As you read it, notice in it the words listed below. Try to define the words as they seem to be used. Write your answers on a separate sheet of paper. Check your definitions in a dictionary. How close were you to the correct meaning of these words?

score	consecrate
continent	hallow
conceived	detract
dedicated	devotion
proposition	vain
created	perish
engaged	earth
fitting and proper	

THE GETTYSBURG ADDRESS

Four score and seven years ago our fathers brought forth, upon this continent, a new nation, conceived in Liberty, and dedicated to the proposition that all men are created equal.

Now we are engaged in a great civil war, testing whether that nation, or any nation, so conceived, and so dedicated, can long endure. We are met here on a great battlefield of that war. We have come to dedicate a portion of it as a final resting place for those who here gave their lives that that nation might live. It is altogether fitting and proper that we should do this.

But in a larger sense we can not dedicate—we can not consecrate—we can not hallow this ground. The brave men, living and dead, who struggled here, have consecrated it far above our poor power to add or detract. The world will little note, nor long remember, what we say here, but can never forget what they did here. It is for us, the living, rather to be dedicated here to the unfinished work which they have, thus far, so nobly carried on. It is rather for us to be here dedicated to the great task remaining before us—that from these honored dead we take increased devotion to that cause for which they here gave the last full measure of devotion—that we here highly resolve that these dead shall not have died in vain; that this nation shall have a new birth of freedom; and that this government of the people, by the people, for the people, shall not perish from the earth.

CHAPTER 10 The Nation Expands

Westward Movement

VOCABULARY

survey	land grant
dry farming	homestead
bonanza	recall
open-range grazing	initiative
	referendum

Westward to the mountains You read in Chapter 8 how brave pioneers have moved westward from the earliest times in our country's history. Daniel Boone, Kit Carson, and Jim Beckwourth led settlers into new areas. The Civil War slowed this movement for a while. But the end of the war saw more and more people, many of them displaced Southerners, moving west. The West was seen as a place where a person could make a new life. The country of the Native Americans and the mountain men was being settled by miners, ranchers, and farmers.

The Great American Desert Trees were important to the pioneers. Before they could plant crops, they had to cut down forests. It was hard work. The trees made logs, lumber, and firewood. Trees were used to build forts, houses, and fences. Wood was used to cook meals and to heat homes. Farmers could easily turn the soft, rich earth because tree roots had kept the soil loose and moist. Tree branches had shaded the soil from the baking sun.

But as pioneers went farther west, especially beyond the Mississippi River, there were fewer trees. Since they did not know how to live without trees, pioneers at first passed by the grassy, treeless prairie and plains. The prairie grass was about 4 to 10 inches (10–25 cm) high, but the grass on the Great Plains was not so high. The sun-baked soil had a hard crust that a wooden plow could not break through.

In 1806, Captain Zebulon Pike explored the plains. He called the region the Great American Desert. In the 1820s, Major Stephen Long was sent to **survey,** or measure, this area. He said it was "almost wholly unfit for farming." But today this "desert" that stretches from western Iowa to the Rocky Mountains (see map, page 191) is a rich farm region. You will read more about it in Chapter 19.

Learning how to live on the Great Plains The pioneers learned to cope with the prairies and plains. Instead of wooden plows, they used iron plows that could break through the foot or two (30–60 cm) of grass roots and dried earth to the rich soil beneath. They used substitutes for wood. Wire fences were used in place of wooden fences. Corncobs and grass stalks were used for firewood. Pioneers lived in dugouts, which were cut into the

The expansion of the railroads made it easier for people and goods to move west.

Even though their sod house was warm in winter and cool in summer, this pioneer family was probably eager to give it up for something more permanent.

ground or into the sides of small hills. Sod was also used to build houses. Sod is the hard top layer of soil of the prairies and plains. This soil is held together by the roots of grass and other plants. Sod was plowed up in long strips and then sliced into bricks about 1 foot square (0.1 sq m). The bricks were set out in the sun to dry and harden and then used to build homes. Thick grass was used for the roof.

A hard life   Can you imagine how hard it was to live in dugouts and sod houses? When it rained, mud oozed from the walls and dripped from the roof, and the floor became a puddle. Dust was everywhere in dry times. Dirt fell from the roof and walls onto the beds, chairs, tables, dishes, and food. Gophers, snakes, and other creatures burrowed through the walls into the rooms. No wonder some families could not take it and moved back East.

Dry farming   Those who stayed were rewarded when great crops of wheat and corn finally came in. Settlers had to use **dry farming** on the plains because little rain fell. In dry farming, land is plowed in curves rather than straight lines. This holds rainfall until it can soak into the

In what year did the railroads meet at Promontory Point?

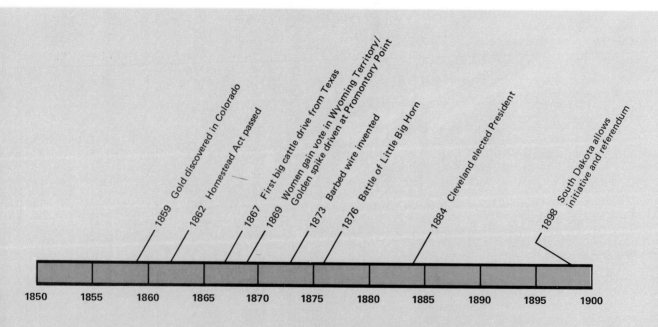

1859 Gold discovered in Colorado
1862 Homestead Act passed
1867 First big cattle drive from Texas
1869 Women gain vote in Wyoming Territory/Golden spike driven at Promontory Point
1873 Barbed wire invented
1876 Battle of Little Big Horn
1884 Cleveland elected President
1898 South Dakota allows initiative and referendum

1850 1855 1860 1865 1870 1875 1880 1885 1890 1895 1900

ground. Also, the settlers allowed the land to lie idle every other year to build up moisture. They began to plant grain from Europe's steppes, which are lands like the Great Plains, instead of the kinds of grain they had brought with them from the East, where rainfall was heavier.

The fifty-niners   Many other pioneers were pushing onward while farmers were learning to live on the prairies and plains. Leading the way westward were mountain men, who trapped fur-bearing animals and traded with Indians for furs. Next were miners prospecting for gold. The gold rush of 1849 filled California with people long before the rest of the Far West was settled.

Gold was discovered in Colorado in 1858. The gold rush the next year sent "fifty-niners" from the East pouring into Colorado saying "Pikes Peak or Bust." Many went bust.

Bonanzas and boom towns   Twelve different silver **bonanzas,** rich veins of ore, were found between 1859 and 1873. The biggest mining discovery of all was the Comstock Lode in Nevada in 1859. At first prospectors thought it was a gold mine but soon learned it had far more silver. Like towns near other bonanzas, Virginia City, Nevada, boomed. By 1876 it had 23,000 people, fine homes, an opera house, and theaters. A young reporter who used the name Mark Twain worked for the city's newspaper in the early 1860s.

Good times did not last for the boom towns. When the mines gave out, the towns ran down. This happened to Deadwood in

Virginia City was a boom town when this photograph was taken. Today it is a quiet village.

South Dakota. The boom town grew with the discovery of gold in the Black Hills in 1874. Among Deadwood's colorful citizens were Calamity Jane and Wild Bill Hickok. They were famous on the frontier. Hickok was killed in a Deadwood saloon. You can visit a cemetery in Deadwood and see his grave.

Martha (Calamity) Jane Canary was a native of Missouri who grew up in mining camps and boom towns. She became an expert with a pistol and an excellent horsewoman. She wore men's clothing at a time when women just didn't do that. She settled in Deadwood during the gold rush. A few years later she nursed victims of a smallpox outbreak. Calamity Jane married and moved away but much later returned to Deadwood. She died there in 1903 and is buried near Hickok.

The long drive   The third group that moved west, after the mountain men and miners, were cattle ranchers. To ship their cattle to markets, the ranchers had to get them to a railroad. The nearest rail depot for the ranchers of western Texas was Abilene, Kansas. It was a thousand miles (1,600 km) away. Cattle ranchers began walking their herds to Kansas. The first major drive was in 1867. During the next 20 years, some 6,000,000 cattle reached market by the long drive along such trails as the Chisholm Trail to Abilene. Other trails went to Dodge City, Kansas, and St. Louis, Missouri.

The longhorn cattle roamed freely in **open-range grazing.** Each animal was marked by the brand of its owner. In twice-a-year roundups the cattle were driven into corrals. They were separated according to the brands stamped on them. Young calves were given the same brands as their mothers. A calf separated from its mother or whose mother had died was called a stray, or maverick. The mavericks were divided up according to how many cattle a rancher had in the roundup. For example, a rancher who owned 15 percent of the cattle got 15 percent of the mavericks.

Cowboys   At roundup and long-drive times, cowboys lived in the open for days on end. They were far from the ranch bunkhouse. They were fed from the chuck wagon. The wrangler handled their horses. They were led by a top hand, the ranch foreman. The high time of the cowboy was from the 1860s to the 1880s. There were some 40,000 working cowboys at this time; 5,000 of them were black. American cowboys learned a lot from Mexican vaqueros, who were among the world's most skilled cowboys.

The open range ends   When sheep ranchers came west, cattle ranchers fought them. Sheep cropped closely, leaving little grass for cattle. The groups joined to fight off homesteaders, or farmers. The barbed wire fences of the farmers cut up the open range. Also, rapid spread of animal diseases made it necessary to keep herds apart. Many cattle died in the harsh winters from 1885 to 1887. Fewer cowboys were needed.

Horse and rider had to be highly skilled to handle the nearly wild cattle during the roundups.

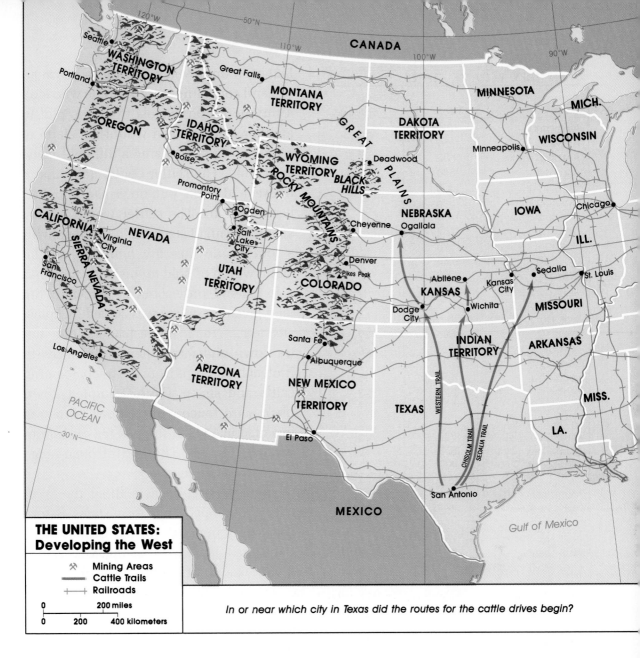

THE UNITED STATES:
Developing the West

⚒ Mining Areas
━━ Cattle Trails
╫╫ Railroads

| 0 | | 200 miles | |
| 0 | 200 | | 400 kilometers |

In or near which city in Texas did the routes for the cattle drives begin?

Homesteaders   The Homestead Act of 1862 encouraged farmers to move westward. This law gave 160 acres (65 ha) of land free to anyone who settled on the land for 5 years and improved it by planting crops and building a house. The hardships of prairies and plains kept many people from taking full advantage of the plan. Also, the best land was given to railroads and to **land-grant** colleges. These were colleges set up in the territories to teach farming. Moreover, 160 acres (65 ha) was too small an area on which to profitably use the new, expensive farm machinery.

Some homesteaders gave up and sold their **homesteads** to land companies. These companies held the land until more people moved to the area. Prices rose enough to make a big profit in selling the land. Some land companies also got homesteads by cheating. A person filing a claim would have to swear that the land

WHEN THEY BECAME STATES

State	Year	Order of admission*
Alabama	1819	22
Alaska	1959	49
Arizona	1912	48
Arkansas	1836	25
California	1850	31
Colorado	1876	38
Connecticut	1788	5
Delaware	1787	1
Florida	1845	27
Georgia	1788	4
Hawaii	1959	50
Idaho	1890	43
Illinois	1818	21
Indiana	1816	19
Iowa	1846	29
Kansas	1861	34
Kentucky	1792	15
Louisiana	1812	18
Maine	1820	23
Maryland	1788	7
Massachusetts	1788	6
Michigan	1837	26
Minnesota	1858	32
Mississippi	1817	20
Missouri	1821	24
Montana	1889	41
Nebraska	1867	37
Nevada	1864	36
New Hampshire	1788	9
New Jersey	1787	3
New Mexico	1912	47
New York	1788	11
North Carolina	1789	12
North Dakota	1889	39
Ohio	1803	17
Oklahoma	1907	46
Oregon	1859	33
Pennsylvania	1787	2
Rhode Island	1790	13
South Carolina	1788	8
South Dakota	1889	40
Tennessee	1796	16
Texas	1845	28
Utah	1896	45
Vermont	1791	14
Virginia	1788	10
Washington	1889	42
West Virginia	1863	35
Wisconsin	1848	30
Wyoming	1890	44

*For first 13, year of ratification of the Constitution.

had been improved by putting a house on it. Land companies hired people who took a tiny house on wheels from one plot to another. Each person would lay claim to a number of sites, using a different name each time. The settler could claim that a house had been put on a site and had been slept in. The settler would merely spend one night sleeping in the open with a foot inside the tiny house. Then the claim would be sold to the land company.

In the end, only about 14 percent of the land given away free was settled by home-steaders. When homesteaders did settle down and farm, they built fences to protect their crops from the freely roaming cattle and sheep. Cattle trampled down plain wire fences. But barbed wire was invented in 1873. It stopped the cattle from coming through. The end of open-range grazing was in sight.

Homesteading farmers filled the West with enough people to form states. Before 1821, only one state in the Union, Louisiana, had land west of the Mississippi River. The chart on this page shows the order in which the states entered the Union. How many states were there in 1865? Which state entered the Union 100 years after the signing of the Declaration of Independence? By what year were there 48 states? In what year did the United States reach its present number of states?

Western reforms Westerners often seemed more willing than easterners to try new ways. Women first gained full voting rights in Wyoming Territory in 1869 and the first three states to let women vote freely were Wyoming in 1890,

This picture, which appeared in a magazine in 1870, shows women in Wyoming voting for the first time.

Colorado in 1893, and Idaho in 1896. The first states with the **recall** were western states. Recall lets voters remove a person from office before that person's term is over. When about 25 percent of the voters sign petitions asking that a person be removed, the office is said to be empty. A special election is held. South Dakota in 1898 and Oregon in 1902 were the first states to use the **initiative** and **referendum.** Initiative allows voters to introduce a bill they would like to see become a law. Referendum allows people to vote on a law instead of leaving it to elected representatives.

CHECKUP

1. How were the prairies and the Great Plains different from areas back East? How did metal plows, wire, dugouts, sod houses, and dry farming help settlers in treeless areas?
2. What group of settlers did the Comstock Lode attract to the West?
3. Why did open-range grazing end?
4. Explain *recall; initiative; referendum.*

The Transcontinental Railroads and the Indian Wars

VOCABULARY

transcontinental
reservation

Bureau of Indian Affairs

Iron horse   The coming of the "Iron Horse"—the name Native Americans gave to railroads—helped destroy the way of life of the Plains Indians. The railroads made it possible for millions of people to move to and fill up the West.

Railroads began operating in the East in the 1830s. They crossed the Appalachian Mountains in the early 1850s, and reached Chicago before 1860. Rail lines from Chicago reached the Mississippi in 1854. The river was bridged 2 years later. Earlier, in 1852, a short rail line began operating on the west side of the river, near St. Louis.

The gold rush filled up California, making it the thirty-first state in 1850. But more than a thousand miles (1,600 km) of unsettled country separated California from the nearest states: Texas, Arkansas, Missouri, and Iowa. A rail link was needed to tie California to the rest of the nation.

Federal aid   Most eastern railroads were built without federal aid. But the distance to California was so great that business could not build such a railroad unaided. Federal land grants had been given in 1851 to help build an eastern railroad, the Illinois Central, running from Chicago toward the Gulf of Mexico. In 1862, during the Civil War, Congress chartered the first **transcontinental** railroad. The transcontinental railroad would connect the two sides of the continent—the East, or Atlantic, Coast and the West, or Pacific, Coast. The Union Pacific Railroad was to build westward from Omaha, Nebraska, toward Utah to meet the Central Pacific Railroad building eastward from Sacramento, California.

The federal government gave the railroads 1-mile-long (1.6 km) sections of land on alternating sides of the railroad track, running as far back as 10 miles (16 km). Also the government lent the railroads $16,000 for each mile built on level land, $32,000 for each hilly mile, and $48,000 for each mile over mountainous areas.

The golden spike Thousands of Chinese workers built the Central Pacific. Thousands of Irish and blacks worked on the Union Pacific. Many died in the effort. The two roads met at Promontory Point, near Ogden, Utah, on May 10, 1869. Find Promontory Point on the map on page 191. A golden spike was driven into the last rail to show that the first transcontinental railroad was complete. A person could now travel from California to New York on the railroad.

Soon other transcontinental railroads were built. The Atchison, Topeka, and Santa Fe connected Kansas City to Los Angeles in 1881. The Southern Pacific com-

What, do you think, were the feelings of the people who took part in or watched the ceremony when the golden spike was driven to join the two sets of tracks? Promontory Point is at 41° north latitude and 112° west longitude.

bined with the Texas Pacific in 1882 to provide a line from New Orleans to Los Angeles. The Northern Pacific, completed in 1883, connected Duluth, Minnesota, with Portland, Oregon. The Great Northern ran from Minneapolis—St. Paul, Minnesota, to Seattle, Washington, when it was completed in 1893.

Taming the West   The transcontinental railroads finished the conquest of the West. Both coasts, Atlantic and Pacific, were tied firmly together. Railroads brought more settlers to the West. Pioneers had learned new ways to cope with prairie and plains. They were turning what some thought to be a desert into rich farming and grazing country. Unfortunately, the rights of Native Americans to the land were trampled on. Backed by the armed might and power of the United States, settlers ignored the claims of the Native Americans as first occupants of the land.

Two views of the land   The settlers moving westward suffered many hardships. They were willing to leave behind the life they knew because there was hope of beginning a better life in the West. That better life included owning land. Each family looked forward to having its own place to settle after the long trip west.

Native Americans looked at the land and all of nature as gifts to be shared. The land was to be cared for and treated with respect. Land belonged to the whole tribe. Crops were used for the good of all. Land was not divided up into farms and ranches for the sole ownership and use of

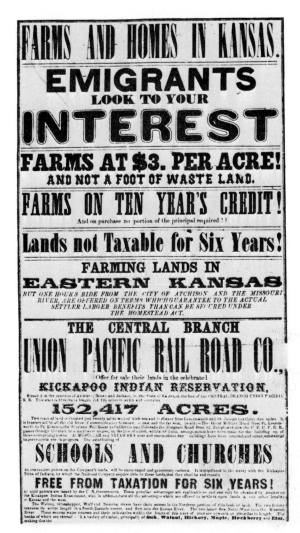

Immigrants, city people, and farmers were all drawn to the West by promises such as those on this poster.

the family that claimed or bought it. Animals were hunted for food and skins, not just for sport.

These two views about the land led to trouble between the settlers moving westward and the Native Americans already living in the West. Each group believed its view of the land was right. Each group expected the government to protect its rights to the land. There were many attempts to settle the differences between the settlers and Native Americans peacefully. Many of these attempts failed.

The land is taken   A famous writer, Helen Hunt Jackson, wrote a book in 1887 about relations with the Indians and titled it *A Century of Dishonor*.

Before the Civil War, most of the tribes living east of the Mississippi River had been driven off their land. They had been sent to live on territory set aside for them in the West. This new land was to be theirs, "as long as the rivers shall run and the grass shall grow." That promise was not kept. Instead, as waves of settlers pushed westward in search of furs, gold, grazing ground, and farms, the Indians' new land was also taken from them.

Broken promises   In many treaties the Native Americans were promised supplies and other help for giving up their land. Very little was ever delivered. In many treaties they were promised protection on the lands left to them. Yet settlers kept moving into the new tribal lands set aside for Native Americans.

Some tribes were simply cheated out of their land. Sometimes they were not told what the treaty they signed really said. Sometimes the terms and boundaries were changed after the treaty was agreed to and signed. In other cases, when the real chiefs refused to sell tribal lands, minor chiefs with no power to bargain for the whole tribe would be forced or bribed to sell the land.

Warfare   Some tribes of Native Americans were gentle people who greeted the settlers warmly and tried hard to stay friendly and peaceful. Other tribes had many fierce warriors eager and ready to fight for the land they claimed as their own. The warfare between the settlers and the Native Americans became bitter and brutal. Both settlers and Native Americans suffered.

In 1870 a peaceful village of Piegan (pē′gan) Blackfeet was attacked without warning. Only one United States soldier died, but 174 Piegan were killed, including about 90 women and 50 children. Cheyenne Chief Black Kettle, who lived through an earlier attack, was killed in 1868 in still another massacre, this one led by George A. Custer in Indian Territory (now Oklahoma).

Custer's last stand   Custer was a West Point graduate from Ohio who became the Union army's youngest general, at the age of 23. After the Civil War, he returned to his permanent rank of captain and later advanced to lieutenant colonel, commanding the Seventh Cavalry Regiment. Custer had a low opinion of the Native American. He described the Native American as "savage in every sense of the word; not worse, perhaps, than his white brother would be [if he were] similarly born and bred, but one whose cruel and ferocious nature far exceeds that of any wild beast of the desert." At the battle of Little Bighorn on June 25, 1876, Custer and about 250 of his soldiers were killed by Sioux warriors. They were led by Crazy Horse and Sitting Bull.

A losing cause   Despite some victories such as Little Bighorn, Native Americans were doomed to defeat. The odds against them were too heavy. More and more settlers pushed westward. The pressure for land was too great. As Sitting Bull, the great Sioux chief, said in 1889, "They want

Sitting Bull (left) and Chief Joseph (right) were two great leaders of their people. Each fought for freedom, but both died on Indian reservations.

us to give up more of our tribal land. This is not the first time or the last time. They will try to gain possession of the last piece of ground we possess."

"Fight no more forever" Chief Joseph and the Nez Percé (nez′ pərs′) learned how little hope they had. A few unimportant chiefs signed a treaty with the United States government in 1863 giving up Nez Percé lands in the Wallowa Valley of Oregon. None of those who signed were among the Nez Percé living in that valley. The major tribal chiefs protested. A government commission agreed that the treaty was false and that the Nez Percé could stay on the land. More settlers crowded westward, looking eagerly at Nez Percé holdings. The decision was turned around. In 1877 the Nez Percé were ordered to pack up and move to other, poorer lands.

Chief Joseph refused at first, but he was put in prison until he gave in. As the Nez Percé were preparing to leave, some young braves stole away. They killed four white men in revenge for the murder of some braves. Fearing punishment, the tribe fled. They traveled over 1,200 miles (1,930 km) in winter weather in an effort to shake off the pursuing troops led by General Oliver Howard and Colonel Nelson Miles. When they were caught and had to surrender, Chief Joseph said:

I am tired of fighting. Our chiefs are dead. . . . It is cold and we have no blankets. The little children are freezing to death. . . . Hear me, my chiefs. I am tired; my heart is sick and sad. From where the sun now stands, I will fight no more forever.

197

The buffalo herds   The tribes living on the Great Plains—such as the Arapaho, Blackfeet, Cheyenne, Comanche, and Sioux—needed the buffalo herds for food, fuel, and skins. But in the course of building the transcontinental railroads, these bison were destroyed. Hunters were paid to kill off the great herds of some 13,000,000 bison. Without the buffalo, many tribes became very poor. By 1900 the Native American population had dropped to only a quarter of a million.

The Indian Bureau   Many whites felt that Native Americans were standing in the way of settlers trying to conquer the American wilderness. There were some whites, however, who treated them fairly, honestly, and kindly. One such person was Major Edward Wynkoop. He was a friend of Black Kettle and his band of peaceful Cheyenne.

Wynkoop treated Native Americans decently when he was an army officer. He continued to do so when he became an Indian agent. As an agent he worked for the **Bureau of Indian Affairs.** This was the federal agency that had the duties of controlling Native Americans and looking out for their interests. Some agents, like Wynkoop, helped the Native Americans. But many agents cheated them of their supplies and lands. The federal government would pay for blankets, meat, grain, ammunition, and other supplies. The dishonest agents stole most of the best goods, leaving the Indians only a small part of what they needed.

In 1869 President Ulysses Grant appointed a Native American, Ely Parker, to head the Bureau. Parker was an Iroquois and a civil engineer educated at Rensselaer (ren' sə lir) Polytechnic Institute in New York. He served under General Grant in the war, becoming his military secretary. Parker tried to reform the Indian Bureau and get rid of dishonest agents. He was not successful. He resigned in 1871.

The Dawes Act   Until 1887, the United States dealt with Native Americans as tribes, buying their lands and resettling them on land reserved (set aside) for them. On the **reservation** as off, decisions were made by the elders and chiefs for the whole tribe. Some reformers wanted to change this. They wanted individual Native Americans to own land, make decisions for themselves, and more easily fit into the white American way of doing things. These were the aims of the Dawes Act, passed in 1887. It divided tribal land among the members. They were to become farmers. They would be educated to live like other Americans. After 25 years, United States citizenship was to be granted to Native Americans.

The reformers meant well, but the act was more harmful than helpful. Few members of the tribes wanted to farm. Many sold their lands. They lived on the money until it ran out, and then had to depend on federal aid. Because of this, an act postponing citizenship for Native Americans was passed in 1906. It was not until 1924 that Indians were made citizens of the United States. In 1934 the Wheeler-Howard Act returned land ownership to the tribes as a whole. They have done better under this arrangement. The Native American population is now over 1,400,000.

Native Americans on the reservations —being almost completely dependent on the government for food, clothing, and shelter, forced to give up old customs and traditions, not having the freedom to hunt and roam —found life very difficult.

The West changes The untamed wilderness loved and respected by the Native Americans was taken from them to build western ranches, farms, factories, railroads, dams, and cities. The Native Americans fought for the land. They lost and were forced to live on reservations. New states were formed and added to the Union, completing the 48 mainland states.

To the settlers and the nation this was progress. But Native Americans might wonder about that.

CHECKUP

1. What is a transcontinental railroad? Why was such a railroad needed?
2. How and why did the federal government aid in the building of the transcontinental railroads?
3. How did the railroad affect the Native American?

199

10/CHAPTER REVIEW

KEY FACTS

1. Miners, ranchers, and farmers followed the mountain men to settle the West.

2. Settling the prairies and the Great Plains was a challenge to the pioneers.

3. The coming of the homesteader and the railroad meant an end to open-range grazing and the long drive.

4. The Native Americans could not stop the westward movement of the settlers.

VOCABULARY QUIZ

On a separate sheet of paper write **T** if the statement is true or **F** if it is false. If the statement is false, rewrite it so that it gives the correct definition for the underlined word.

1. A sod house is built largely of soil cut into bricks.

2. Fifty-niners went west to Colorado looking for bonanzas.

3. Ranchers sent their cattle to market on the long drive.

4. Open-range grazing meant that cattle roamed freely.

5. Homesteader is another name for *rancher*.

6. Recall allows voters to introduce a bill they would like to see become a law.

7. The transcontinental railroad connected the East and West coasts of the United States.

8. Native Americans believed strongly that land belonged to the person who had paid or fought for it.

9. The Bureau of Indian Affairs was formed to take care of and protect the interests of the Native Americans.

10. A reservation was land set aside for the resettlement of Native Americans.

REVIEW QUESTIONS

1. What changes did the pioneers who settled on the Great Plains have to make in the way they lived?

2. What turned Virginia City, Nevada, into a boom town?

3. What was the high time of the cowboy? About how many working cowboys were there at that time?

4. What did the Homestead Act do?

5. How did a homesteader file a claim?

6. How did the federal government help build the transcontinental railroads?

7. How did the Native American and the settler differ in their views on land?

8. What did the federal government do to and for Native Americans?

ACTIVITIES

1. Put yourself in the place of a young person moving west with his or her family around 1870. Keep a diary. Describe what you see and what your life is like as you and your family settle on the Great Plains.

2. Draw a diagram on poster board of how a sod house is constructed. You may have to use an encyclopedia to get more information on the subject.

3. You learned in this chapter how the American cowboy was greatly influenced by the Mexican vaquero. A great many Spanish words were taken over by the cowboys. The word *ranch*, for example, comes from the Spanish word *rancho*, meaning "camp" or "small farm." Make a list of all the words you can think of that are connected with cowboys or cowboy life. Look in the dictionary to find how many of these words have Spanish origins.

10/SKILLS DEVELOPMENT

RECOGNIZING ATTITUDES AND EMOTIONS

SYMPATHETIC OR UNSYMPATHETIC

You have just finished reading about the relations between the Native Americans and the settlers as the westward movement took place. The two groups had very different attitudes toward the land. They did not agree about how it should be used and who it belonged to. These differing attitudes affected how they felt about each other.

The statements that follow show how some people of the 1800s felt about Native Americans. Some of these statements are exact quotes. Others have been rewritten to make them easier to understand.

SKILLS PRACTICE

Read each statement. Decide whether the statement is sympathetic or unsympathetic to the attitudes and emotions of the Native American. On a separate sheet of paper write the numbers of the statements. Write **S** if the statement is sympathetic or **U** if it is unsympathetic.

1. They were the first to live on the land we now own. They have been driven from place to place. Many, if not most, of our Indian wars have had their beginnings in broken promises and acts of injustice.

2. The more we can kill this year, the less will have to be killed in the next war. They will all have to be killed or kept on as a type of pauper.

3. "The white man has been the chief obstacle in the way of Indian civilization."

4. It does not make a farmer out of an Indian to give him a piece of land. There are hundreds of thousands of white men who cannot be turned into farmers by any such gift.

5. "I have never in my life seen a good Indian (and I have seen thousands) except when I have seen a dead Indian."

6. The United States should give up the idea of a transcontinental railroad and give the Indians a department in the Cabinet to look out for their rights.

SKILLS PRACTICE

Those statements were made by the following people, respectively.

1. President Rutherford B. Hayes

2. William T. Sherman, Civil War general

3. Ely Parker, Bureau of Indian Affairs

4. Congressional Committee on Indian Affairs

5. James M. Cavanaugh, a settler in Montana

6. Wendell Phillips, an abolitionist

Select one of the six statements given above. Pretend you are the person making that statement. Write an essay explaining how you would solve the following problem: Native Americans wanted to hold their land and continue in their ways. Some people wanted to take their land and have the Native Americans adopt a different way of life.

11 A Modern Nation Emerges

The Continuing Agricultural Revolution

VOCABULARY

combine	Grange
agricultural	Populist party
subsistence farmer	income tax
commercial farmer	secret ballot

An economic revolution How do Americans earn their living? What kind of work do they do? We were a nation of farmers during the first three centuries of this country's history. In 1850 most Americans lived on farms. In the 1980s only about 3 out of every 100 Americans were living on a farm. Yet the United States today is one of the biggest producers of farm goods in the world. How is it possible for so few farmers to grow so much? This revolution in farming came with the use of machinery and science.

Farm machinery Before the Civil War, farmers used more hand labor than machinery. But widespread use of farm machinery, such as the reaper you read about in Chapter 8, began in the 1860s. Many farmhands were in the armies during the Civil War. Yet farmers had to grow more than before to feed both the large armies and the citizens at home.

Such farm machinery as threshers, binders, rotary plows, and disc harrows became widely used. Later the combined harvester-thresher, or **combine** (kom′ bīn), replaced separate machines such as the reaper, harvester, and thresher. The farm machines were at first pulled by horses. Later they were pulled by tractors or became self-powered with gasoline engines.

Science in farming Science also helped farmers grow larger crops. As you read in the last chapter, Congress set up land-grant colleges to help farmers. Scientists at these **agricultural** colleges experimented to find better ways to farm. Teachers at the colleges taught these better methods of farming. Also at this time, Congress set up the Bureau of Agriculture. It became the Department of Agriculture in 1889. It, too, carried out scientific research to improve farming. The department spread this knowledge to farmers.

Farming as a business Before the Civil War, most small farmers in the South and most farmers in the North and West were **subsistence farmers.** They grew enough different crops to take care of the basic needs of the family: food and

These two pictures show the changes that have taken place in large-scale farming. One gasoline-powered engine can do the work of 33 mules in far less time.

clothing. Since farming was done mainly by hand, a farm family and sometimes one or two hired laborers raised many different things on the farm. A farmer might raise potatoes, beans, corn, tomatoes, chickens, hogs, cows, and sheep. The farmer did not have to spend a lot to raise the crops since most of the work was hand or animal labor done with hoes and plows.

Farm machinery forced midwestern grain farmers to become **commercial farmers.** To make best use of the machines, they had to buy much more land. To earn the money to pay for the land and machines, they had to raise moneymaking crops. They had to grow just one or two crops. Farmers had to get enough money from these crops to buy all their family and farm needs. They had to depend on markets that were far away.

Most farmers could no longer take their crops to market themselves. They sold to dealers who would ship the farm goods to market and sell them. There was often a big difference between the price the farmers got and the prices the dealers got at the market. Farmers often had to borrow money to buy more land or machines. If prices dropped or the weather was bad, farmers would go deeper into debt. And prices did drop after the Civil War. Farmers grew even more crops. Prices kept going down. Yet people who bought the loaves of bread were not paying that much less. "Who is making all the money?" the farmers asked. Part of the answer, they felt, was the railroads and the bankers. One or two farmers alone could not fight these big businesses. Farmers would have to organize into large groups.

In what year was the Grange organized? The telephone invented?

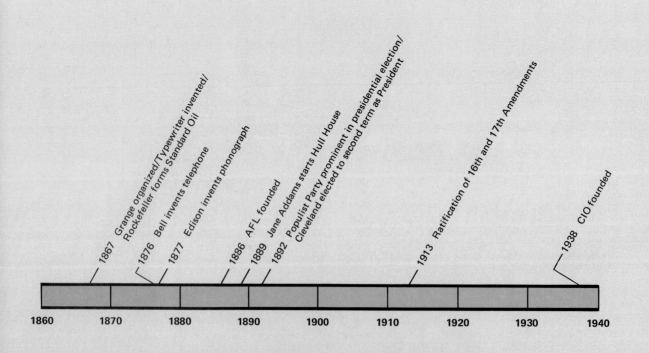

The Grange was both a social and a political group.

The Grange   The first major farmers' group was the **Grange.** It was organized to get better farm prices. It was also a way for farm families to get together and enjoy themselves. In time the Grange moved into politics. Grangers were able to get several states to pass laws that controlled the rates that railroads could charge. The Supreme Court said states could not make laws that affected transportation in other states. Such laws would have to be made by Congress and apply to all the states. In 1887 Congress finally passed the Interstate Commerce Act. This helped the farmers.

The Populist party   There have always been two major parties in politics in the United States. Since 1860 these parties have been the Republican and Democratic parties. Sometimes a third party appears. One of the most important of these third parties was the **Populist party.** *Populist* means "people." The party was started in 1892. The membership was made up largely of farmers and working people. They felt that the government did not think their problems were very important. They wanted to make the government aware of how they felt.

In the election of 1892 the Populist party suggested a number of changes. These changes seemed very revolutionary at the time. People who were against the Populists said such changes would destroy the American way of life. But as you can see from the following list, these changes did, in time, become law.

Populists wanted (1) an **income tax** that would rise as the amount of money a person had rose; (2) election of United States senators directly by the people; (3) the **secret ballot**—so no one could know how a person voted; and (4) a shorter working day for labor. The Constitution had to be changed because of two of these Populist ideas. Read about the Sixteenth and Seventeenth Amendments on page 123. Which Populist ideas became part of the Constitution of the United States?

CHECKUP

1. What is the difference between subsistence and commercial farming?
2. Why did the Civil War help the growth of large-scale farming?
3. Name two Populist party ideas that have become the law.

205

A Revolution in Industry

VOCABULARY

capital   patent
competition   monopoly
communicate   union

Industry expands   A revolution took place in industry as well as in farming. In the Industrial Revolution, factory machines driven by waterpower—and eventually by steam power—replaced handwork, simple machines, and home crafts. As you read in Chapter 8, the revolution began with the textile mills started in New England by Samuel Slater. Other industries grew. The Civil War speeded up the growth of industry. It pushed the United States toward becoming the world's greatest industrial nation.

The United States changed as people moved from farms to cities and from hand labor to factory machines. There was an increase in the output of goods.

Causes of industrial growth   What made these changes possible? The United States was blessed with a large supply of the natural resources needed to become an industrial power, such as coal and iron ore. Americans had the **capital,** or saved-up wealth, to invest in developing power machines and factories. There was a large labor force. Inventions greatly changed ways of doing things. Bold, daring, and sometimes ruthless business leaders put together the resources, capital, labor, and inventions to build the United States into an industrial giant. As a result, the nation grew in ways hardly imagined 100 years earlier.

Steelmaking is one of our most important industries.

Giant industries appeared. These were huge businesses that had nearly all the power and made great fortunes for their owners. One reason for the growth of these companies was the desire to do away with **competition.** There is competition when there are many companies in an industry. Sometimes competition is a waste. It makes more sense to have just a few telephone companies rather than hundreds or thousands of them—all different—scattered across the country. Competition is also good. It keeps prices down. It also forces companies to be efficient. But in the years following the Civil War, a few business giants came to control the major industries. It was not until the beginning of this century that laws began to control the industrial giants.

This was a telephone exchange in 1907. Most operators by this time were women.

Inventions The most important changes in American life during the Industrial Revolution came about because of inventions. The typewriter, telephone, electric light, phonograph, and automobile all brought changes in American life during the first 30 years after the Civil War. Some American inventors, like Alexander Graham Bell and Thomas Alva Edison, became world famous for their inventions. Edison is often said to be the greatest inventor who ever lived.

Four inventions greatly speeded up the way we **communicate** with, or make things known to, each other. These were the typewriter in 1868, the telephone in 1876, the linotype for printed matter in 1884, and wireless telegraphy in 1895.

The table on this page lists many American inventors and some of their inventions. Imagine what your life would be like without these inventions. (The screw propeller was used for ships; the vacuum tube for radio and television.)

IMPORTANT INVENTIONS

Invention	Inventor(s)
Lightning rod (1752)	Benjamin Franklin
First workable steamboat (1787)	John Fitch
Cotton gin (1793)	Eli Whitney
Cast-iron plow (1819)	Jethro Wood
Screw propeller (1826)	John Ericsson
Revolver (1835)	Samuel Colt
Steel plow (1837)	John Deere
Morse code (1840)	Samuel Morse
Sewing machine (1846)	Elias Howe
Refrigeration (1851)	John Gorrie
Safety elevator (1852)	Elisha Otis
Typewriter (1868)	Christopher Sholes
	Samuel Soulé
	Carlos Glidden
Railroad air brake (1868)	George Westinghouse
Barbed wire (1873)	Joseph Glidden
Telephone (1876)	Alexander Graham Bell
Submarine (1881)	John Holland
Linotype (1884)	Ottmar Mergenthaler
Shorthand (1888)	John Gregg
Adding machine (1888)	William Burroughs
Machine gun (1890)	John M. Browning
Airplane (1903)	Wright Brothers
Vacuum tube (1907)	Lee DeForest
Stoplight (1923)	Garrett Morgan
Computer (1930)	Vannevar Bush
Instant camera (1937)	Edwin Land
Transistor (1947)	John Bardeen
	Walter Brattain
	William Shockley

Two Great Inventors

Two Americans, above many others, certainly deserve the title "Genius of Invention." They are Thomas Alva Edison and George Washington Carver.

The pleasure of listening to recorded music is the result of Edison's invention of the phonograph in 1877. This alone would give him a place among the world's great inventors. But he also invented or improved upon the electric light, the mimeograph machine, the stock ticker, the typewriter, and a type of telephone transmitter. Another of his inventions has also brought entertainment to millions. In 1889 he developed the kinetoscope. This machine made pictures seem to move. *The Great Train Robbery,* made in the Edison studio, was the first movie that told a story. Edison held over one thousand **patents.** A patent is a right given by the government to an inventor to be the only one to use, make, or sell his or her invention.

George Washington Carver did not take out patents on his inventions. He wanted as many people as possible to make use of his ideas. Carver made things from plants. He found more than 300 uses for the peanut. Face cream, coffee, shoe polish, and ice cream are only a few of the peanut-based products he developed. He did the same for sweet potatoes and soybeans. His work freed many southern farmers from having to depend on just one crop. During World War I he invented dehydrated foods. Dehydration takes the water out of food. Eggs, milk, and potatoes in powdered form are easy to ship and to store. Thomas Edison and Henry Ford wanted Carver to work for them. However, he stayed in his laboratory at Tuskegee Institute in Alabama.

Business leaders   Natural resources, capital, workers, and inventions were the base of the Industrial Revolution in the United States. Hardworking business people put them all together to form the giant businesses.

Three men stand out more than any others: Andrew Carnegie in steel; John D. Rockefeller in oil; John P. Morgan in banking.

Andrew Carnegie   Carnegie was born in Scotland in 1835. His family came to the United States when he was a boy. In Scotland they had been very poor. They hoped to find a better life here. Carnegie went to work full time even though he was only 12 years old. During the Civil War he put money into the iron ore business. After the war he became interested in the steel industry. It was here that he made his great fortune.

Carnegie built very up-to-date steel mills. He hired skilled workers. His mills turned out large numbers of steel rails for the growing railroads. Carnegie wanted as little competition as possible. He began to drive other steel mill owners out of business. By 1892, Carnegie ruled a giant steel empire. Less than 10 years later, he decided he had had enough of big business and sold his company to J. P. Morgan. Morgan used the Carnegie Company to put together an even larger steel company. This was the United States Steel Corporation.

Carnegie did feel that his money should be used for the good of the people. He spent the rest of his life giving away much of his fortune.

Andrew Carnegie

John D. Rockefeller   Rockefeller was born in western New York but he grew up in Cleveland, Ohio. He worked as a clerk and bookkeeper. He was noted for his careful handling of money. After oil was discovered at Titusville, Pennsylvania, in 1859, Rockefeller entered the oil industry. He joined an inventor who found a better way to refine oil. Rockefeller formed Standard Oil Company in 1867.

Under Rockefeller's leadership, Standard Oil drove out just about all competing firms. By 1877 Rockefeller controlled 95 percent of all the oil refineries in the United States. This was almost a complete **monopoly** (sole control) of the entire oil business in the country. Standard Oil made petroleum products for lighting and heating and for gasoline engines. In 1911, the Supreme Court ordered Standard Oil broken up into different competing companies. Many of today's oil companies were once part of Standard Oil, which by itself is still the nation's leading oil company. It is also one of the largest of all corporations in the world.

In 1911 Rockefeller, who lived to be nearly 98, turned over the business to his son. He devoted much of his billion-dollar fortune to good works.

John D. Rockefeller

John P. Morgan   J. P. Morgan was born into a wealthy family in Connecticut. His father, Junius S. Morgan, was an American who founded a banking house in London, England. The younger Morgan was educated in Boston, Switzerland, and Germany. After working in his father's bank in London he entered banking and railroad businesses in the United States.

John Pierpont Morgan

Morgan's firm became one of the leading banking houses in the world. He controlled vast amounts of money. He believed in putting businesses together into larger, more efficient units. He organized many great corporations, such as United States Steel, International Harvester, and the Southern Railroad.

Morgan collected great works of art. You can see them today in such places as the Metropolitan Museum and Pierpont Morgan Library in New York City.

Controlling big business Many Americans did not agree with Morgan about combining businesses into giant corporations. They felt that companies competing with each other would offer lower prices, better quality, and better service.

The state and federal governments tried to control business combinations that lessened competition. Congress set up the Interstate Commerce Commission to regulate railroads. This was the first federal attempt to control American business. In 1890 Congress passed the Sherman Antitrust Act. This law was used to break up big business that tried to do away with competition.

Labor The giant industries of the United States could not have grown without a large work force. Working conditions usually were not good. People worked long hours. Children often worked the same hours as men and women. There was very little concern about worker safety. Many people were killed in factory or mine accidents. Others were crippled for life. Workers could not do much about these conditions. They lost their jobs if they complained. Many workers felt that they had to act together in groups. Only in this way would they be powerful enough to make the owners of mines and factories listen to them. They would have to form **unions.**

There were many small unions started in the United States. None was really successful. In many cases, the membership was too small to have any power.

In 1886 Samuel Gompers founded the American Federation of Labor (AFL). This union worked for better wages, shorter working hours, and safer working conditions for its members. The members of this union were the skilled craftworkers.

This is a Labor Day parade in New York City in 1909. The women in the wagons are members of the International Ladies Garment Workers Union. The average pay for a garment worker at that time was $4.00 for an 80-hour workweek.

Another important and successful labor union was the Congress of Industrial Organizations (CIO). This group was started in 1938. Most of the members of this union were workers in an industry rather than a craft. They could be unskilled as well as skilled. The CIO drew its members from industries such as the automobile and steel industries. By 1945 there were 6 million members in the CIO. The two groups—the AFL and the CIO—became one large union in 1955. The membership today is about 17 million.

The average worker in the United States today enjoys a high standard of living. There are strict laws to see that working places are safe and clean. Child labor laws limit the amount of work a child may do. These laws also limit the kinds of work children may do. Labor unions and the concern of most Americans for the way people live have brought about these changes.

CHECKUP

1. Name one invention and tell why you think it was important.
2. With what industry or business was each of the following men connected: Andrew Carnegie, John D. Rockefeller, J. P. Morgan?
3. What are the AFL and CIO?

211

Welcome to Our Shores!

Land of immigrants The United States is a land of **immigrants**—people born in other countries. More people have come here than to any other country. The original 13 colonies were settled mainly by people from England, Ireland, and Scotland.

Fewer than one million immigrants came here in the 50 years from 1790 to 1840. In the next 80 years, more than 35 million immigrants came.

Why they came Most people came because they believed that the United States was a land of opportunity—a land where they and their children would have a new start in life and a good chance to succeed.

Those who had come first, wrote back to tell of the vast land. They wrote of chances to get ahead or even get rich. What made the United States still more attractive were the bad conditions in their own countries. To live, many had to **emigrate,** to leave their native lands.

American citizens There are two kinds of American citizens. One is native-born. The other is **naturalized.** The native-born person is born in the United States or to parents who are American citizens. Naturalized citizens are people who were born in a foreign country and were citizens of that country. They come to the United States. They give up their foreign citizenship and state that they would like to become American citizens. After 5 years they take an oath of allegiance to the United States and become naturalized citizens. They have nearly all the rights and duties of native-born citizens.

The Statue of Liberty has been a welcome sign to immigrants since 1886.

New citizens are pledging allegiance to the United States.

Changes in immigration About 17 million immigrants came to the United States from 1840 to 1900. About 18 million more entered between 1900 and 1920.

From 1840 to the 1870s, the great bulk of immigration was from northern and western Europe, from such places as Great Britain, Germany, and Scandinavia. Most of these people settled on farms and homesteads in the western part of the United States. Many Irish did settle in cities such as Boston and New York. Some Germans settled in western cities such as Cincinnati, St. Louis, and Milwaukee.

More and more people came from southern and eastern Europe in the period from 1880 to 1920. Mostly they were from Italy, from Austria-Hungary and other parts of the Austro-Hungarian empire, from Russia and Poland, and from Greece. These new immigrants were lured here to work in factories and mines. Recruiters traveled all over Europe looking for people who would work for low pay in growing American industries.

These immigrants settled in cities for the most part. They tended to settle together in sections of the city where they could live among people from home. This kept their customs and native languages alive. They drew comfort from living near and taking care of one another. Such neighborhoods where people of similar ethnic, racial, or religious backgrounds live are often called **ghettoes.** Big cities such as New York and Chicago had large immigrant neighborhoods, or ghettoes.

Closing the door The United States generally welcomed immigrants with open arms. The United States was used to many different people living here from colonial times onward. "Give me your tired, your poor, your huddled masses yearning to breathe free, the wretched refuse of your teeming shore" are the words of welcome in Emma Lazarus's poem inscribed on the Statue of Liberty.

Immigrants have given a great deal to this country. I.M. Pei (right), who was born in China, is the architect who designed this wing of the National Gallery of Art in Washington, D.C. (left).

Some Americans did not feel comfortable with these new immigrants. Their ways of living seemed so foreign and strange. Movements grew to close the doors of the United States and not let people come in as freely as before.

From 1776 until 1882, there were no laws dealing with immigration. All could come here to live and work. In 1882 a law stopped Chinese laborers from entering. That year there was also a law that banned criminals. Insane people, very poor people, and those who were sick were also banned. A law in 1917 kept out people who could not read. Under this law, all immigrants 16 years or older had to prove that they could read 30 to 80 words in English or any other language.

During the 1920s, immigration was limited still more. Only about 350,000 immigrants a year were allowed into the United States. By 1929 only 150,000 could enter each year. This number was divided among the countries of the world. Each country got a **quota**—a set number of people who could come to the United States.

Immigrants from northern and western Europe were favored. Asians were kept out completely. Later laws changed this. Today immigrants may come from any country. There are, however, very strong rules about the number who may enter each year.

CHECKUP

1. What was one reason why many immigrants came to the United States?
2. What is a quota? A ghetto?
3. Name two ways to become a citizen.

Growth of the Cities

┌─**VOCABULARY**─────────────────┐

rural	sanitation
urban	zoning
suburb	reform
tenement	social work

Country to city   After the Civil War there was a shift of the population of the United States. The country was changing from a **rural** to an **urban** nation.

Urban areas are city areas. These range from towns of at least 2,500 people to large cities of more than 1,000,000. A city has both an inner-city area and the **suburbs** around it. Suburbs are small towns just beyond a city. Rural areas are country areas, either farm or nonfarm. Of the 54,000,000 people in rural areas in 1950, for example, only 23,000,000 lived on farms. The other 31,000,000 people lived in villages and other nonfarm places.

In 1850, 85 percent of Americans lived in the country, mostly on farms. Only 15 percent lived in cities. See the chart on this page. By 1880, 72 percent of Americans were rural and 28 percent were urban. This change was mainly a result of three things. First, more and more of the immigrants coming here after 1870 were settling in cities. Second, machinery replaced some farm labor. So people moved from farms to urban places. Third, the building of factories in and near cities caused many country people to move to cities for the new jobs.

Cities get larger   In 1790 only 28,000 people lived in Philadelphia. It was the second largest city in the United States. By 1850 Philadelphia had a population of over 100,000. However, at that time it was only the fourth largest city.

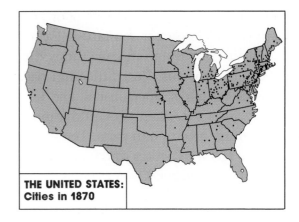

THE UNITED STATES: Cities in 1870

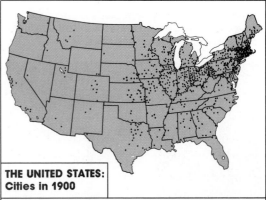

THE UNITED STATES: Cities in 1900

The number of cities more than doubled in 30 years. In what parts of the United States did most of the new cities appear? What caused this growth?

The cities grew rapidly during the period from 1850 to 1900 with little planning. This caused problems. **Tenement** houses were built quickly for the many people moving to the city. They had little

RURAL AND URBAN POPULATION, UNITED STATES, 1850–1980					
Year	Total	Urban	Percent	Rural	Percent
1850	23,192,000	3,544,000	15%	19,648,000	85%
1880	50,156,000	14,130,000	28%	36,026,000	72%
1900	75,995,000	30,160,000	40%	45,835,000	60%
1920	105,710,000	54,158,000	51%	51,552,000	49%
1950	150,697,000	96,468,000	64%	54,229,000	36%
1970	203,212,000	149,325,000	72%	53,887,000	28%
1980	226,505,000	166,965,000	74%	59,539,000	26%

air or light. The plumbing was poor and there was little proper **sanitation**. Factories dirtied the water and air. Cities did little to control this. Very little land was set aside for parks, open spaces, and recreation areas. And there was little **zoning,** or dividing the city into parts. The result was that factories, stores, and homes were all jumbled together. Overcrowded housing, lack of recreation, and boredom led to more family problems and crime.

Making city life better Efforts were made to **reform** cities, to change them for the better. One way was to build parks, to keep open spaces. Frederick Law Olmsted built Central Park in New York City in 1858. He also designed and built parks in other cities in the United States. He made up a name for his work—landscape architecture. He made American cities more beautiful and livable with the parks he built.

People crowded into the cities. Housing could not keep up with the numbers. Often whole families lived in one room. On the Lower East Side in New York City at the turn of the century over 5,000 people lived on one block.

Some cities value their old buildings. Quincy Market in Boston is a good example of how an old market area has been made useful once again.

Laws were passed to improve housing and sanitation. Buildings had to have a certain number of windows for better light and better air circulation. Sewers and waste disposal plants were built. Pigs no longer roamed in New York City to clean up the garbage in the streets.

In 1889 Jane Addams began Hull House in Chicago. It was the most famous settlement house in the United States. A settlement house provides services for the people who live in a crowded city neighborhood. At Hull House, workers ran a nursery for young children of working mothers. They taught English to recent immigrants. They helped people get jobs, aided them when they got in trouble. Hull House gave people in the neighborhood a place to come to play games from checkers to basketball. Milk and other foods were provided for poor families. Another famous settlement house was the Henry Street Settlement House in New York City.

Settlement workers like Jane Addams were doing **social work**—helping people. The new profession of social work came from their efforts. Addams won the Nobel Peace Prize in 1931.

A changing nation   The United States was changing in many ways. There was the change from an agricultural to an industrial way of life. There was the change from country to city living. The changes came very fast in the years from 1850 to 1900. Problems arose because of this. Americans went about the business of solving the problems and making the changes as they had always done, with energy and confidence.

CHECKUP

1. In 1850, what percent of Americans lived in rural areas? In urban areas? In 1970, what was the percent of rural people? Urban?
2. How does zoning help city growth?
3. What good did settlement houses do?

KEY FACTS

1. Improved farm machinery and scientific developments in crops and livestock changed farming in the United States.

2. A seemingly endless supply of raw materials, a growing population, new inventions, and leadership that believed in unlimited growth turned the United States into an industrial giant.

3. More people have come to the United States to live than to any other country.

4. As the United States has changed from a rural to an urban nation, the growth of most cities has not been planned, which has resulted in many problems.

VOCABULARY QUIZ

On a separate sheet of paper write the word or phrase that best completes each sentence.

1. Most farmers in the United States before the Civil War were (**a**) commercial farmers, (**b**) subsistence farmers.

2. *Populist* means (**a**) people, (**b**) well-liked.

3. Capital is (**a**) saved-up wealth, (**b**) natural resources.

4. The telephone and telegraph are inventions in (**a**) transportation, (**b**) communication.

5. Sole control of an industry is an example of (**a**) monopoly, (**b**) competition.

6. People coming together for a common purpose form a (**a**) ghetto, (**b**) union.

7. Naturalized citizens are born in (**a**) the United States, (**b**) a foreign country.

8. A quota is (**a**) a set number of people, (**b**) an immigrant.

9. Suburbs are (**a**) country villages, (**b**) small towns just outside a city.

10. Social work is (**a**) helping people, (**b**) planning a city.

REVIEW QUESTIONS

1. What two things brought about a change in farming after the Civil War?

2. How did inventions help American industry grow?

3. Why did working people want to form labor unions?

4. Where did most immigrants come from before 1880? Between 1880 and 1920?

5. In what year did the census show that more Americans lived in cities than in the country?

6. Give two reasons why zoning and city planning are important.

ACTIVITIES

1. Write a report on George Washington Carver, Luther Burbank, or some other agricultural scientist. Emphasize how the person's work has aided the commercial farmer.

2. Make a catalog of farm machines. Describe what each is used for.

3. Learn about the life of a famous immigrant to the United States. Make a report to the class.

4. Plan an ideal city. Draw a picture of what you think it would look like.

INTERPRETING A CARTOON

VEHICLE PRODUCTION IN THE 1940S

This cartoon was drawn in the late 1940s. Passenger cars were not manufactured during World War II. The factories were turning out tanks, trucks, and other war vehicles. In 1946, after the war ended, 2 million passenger cars were produced.

SKILLS PRACTICE

Study the cartoon carefully and answer these questions.

1. How many new cars were to be produced by 1948?

2. How do you know that the cartoon is about the United States?

3. Who or what does the figure in the cartoon represent?

4. What feeling or emotion do you think he is showing?

5. What is the cartoonist's message?

In 1982 American automobile makers produced about 6 million cars. About 2 million foreign cars were sold here.

Draw a cartoon of your own on this same theme.

4/UNIT REVIEW

1. Some Southern states seceded after the 1860 election fearing that President-elect Lincoln would try to abolish slavery. — *Was Lincoln really a threat to slavery? Would he have tried to end slavery in the South?*

2. The Union side had more people, ships, factories, and money than the Confederate side, yet the Union had a struggle to win the Civil War. — *Why was the war so hard to win? How did emancipation help win the war?*

3. Black voting and carpetbag governments began in the South in 1867, two years after the war ended; the carpetbag governments stayed in power an average of only four years and did some good things such as starting public school systems. — *Why, do you think, are these governments criticized so harshly as poor and corrupt?*

4. As Americans crossed the Mississippi and moved westward, the main groups of pioneers were trappers, miners, cattle ranchers, sheepherders, and farmers. — *What did each group contribute? Why did ranchers and sheepherders fight each other and then unite to fight the homestead farmers? Why did open-range grazing come to an end?*

5. The transcontinental railroads helped to open up the West to more settlers, but at the same time aided in the destruction of the way of life of the Native Americans. — *How did the railroads play a role in both of these developments? How were the Native Americans treated unjustly?*

6. The use of machinery and science made big changes in agriculture. More farmers became commercial farmers. — *What problems did farmers have as commercial farmers? What solutions did they develop?*

7. Inventions played an important role in a revolution in industry that made great changes in life and labor in the United States. — *Name the three inventions that you think had the greatest effect on American life. How did they change the United States? How did workers respond to the rise of big business in American life?*

8. The United States has been blessed with the contributions of immigrants. — *Select any nation and try to find up to five persons from that land who have contributed to the United States. Tell what they did.*

9. Cities in the United States grew so rapidly with so little planning in the period after the Civil War that many problems arose in regard to crowding, government, health, housing, play areas, and sanitation. — *In what ways did cities start to change from the 1890s onward?*

The United States in the Twentieth Century

Expanding Beyond Our Shores

VOCABULARY

| foreign policy | public opinion |
| annexation | protectorate |

Foreign policy before 1890 The people of the United States were busy at home. There were the western parts of the country to be settled. The population was growing. Industry was developing. All growth brought problems with it. National affairs seemed more important than foreign affairs.

What were the relationships to foreign countries, or the **foreign policy,** of the United States in the early history of our country? There were two wars with other countries—the War of 1812 with Great Britain and the Mexican War (1846–1848). You read about these wars in Chapters 7 and 8. During most of the 1800s, however, our foreign policy was to stay out of European affairs. We also wanted to discourage the countries of Europe from interfering in the affairs of the Western Hemisphere.

Expansion into the Pacific By the end of the Civil War the United States began to look more seriously at territory beyond its borders. Alaska was purchased from Russia in 1867. In the same year the flag of the United States was raised over the Midway Islands in the Pacific. By 1899 we also controlled the Samoan Islands. Find these places on the map on page 227.

Why were Americans so interested in expanding into the Pacific area? One important reason was trade. Merchants from the United States, especially from New England, were trading with China as early as the 1780s. The whaling ships were very active in the Pacific in the 1820s and 1830s. All these ships needed places where they could stop to get fresh water and food. And when steam replaced the sail, the ships needed places where they could take on more coal. It would be better, thought the merchants and sea captains, if these places were under American control. Then we could always be sure of getting the goods we need. The United States Navy could also use these places as naval bases. That way our ships could fight well in many parts of the world. By 1898 the United States had a very good navy.

Hawaii Another reason why Americans became interested in places in the Pacific was the desire to spread our way of life to other people. Missionaries went to the Pacific islands to bring Christianity to the people who lived there. This is the

President Theodore Roosevelt sent the United States fleet on a goodwill trip around the world in 1907. It showed foreign powers the strength of this country.

way Americans came to the Hawaiian Islands. The missionaries were the first permanent American settlers. As you will read later in Chapter 21, the soil of Hawaii is very good for growing sugarcane. Soon Americans were starting large sugar plantations. In time they began to grow pineapples, too.

Hawaii was a kingdom, under the control of native rulers. But Americans owned a good deal of the land and had influence. In 1893 the Americans organized a revolt against the Hawaiian queen. They set up a new government and asked to become part of the United States. Congress was in favor of this. President Grover Cleveland did not approve of the way the new government came into being. He would not agree to the **annexation,** or taking, of Hawaii. In 1894 Hawaii declared itself an independent republic. Which states that you studied earlier were also republics before they became part of the United States? (See Chapter 8.)

When the Spanish-American War started in 1898, Hawaii became important to the United States. Part of that war took place in the Philippine Islands. Hawaii was a halfway point. Troops and supplies could be sent from there. Interest in making Hawaii part of the United States grew. Congress and the President acted. In 1898, Hawaii became a United States territory. Find the Hawaiian Islands on the map on page 227.

"Remember the *Maine*!"   Turn to the world map on pages 466–467 in the Atlas. Find Cuba. It is an island not far from the southern tip of Florida. Now find the Philippine Islands in the Pacific Ocean. These two places, so far apart, were scenes of fighting during the Spanish-American War.

The war started in Cuba. Cuba had been ruled by Spain since the time of Columbus. Many Americans had long been against this rule. Newspapers stirred up feelings by writing about the unjust and

In what year did the Spanish-American War start? Who was President at that time?

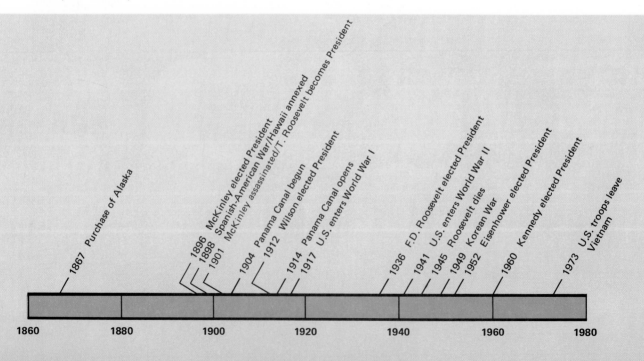

United States troops were not prepared to fight in a tropical climate. These soldiers fighting near Santiago, Cuba, are wearing woolen uniforms.

cruel treatment of the Cubans by Spanish rulers. Some of these stories were true, but many were not. Revolution and riot between Cubans and the Spanish were common.

The United States battleship *Maine* was sent to Cuba to protect Americans who lived there during this time of unrest. On February 15, 1898, the *Maine* was blown up in the harbor of Havana, Cuba. The blast killed 260 Americans.

No one knows for sure who blew up the *Maine*. But Americans blamed Spain for the tragedy. American **public opinion,** that is, the feelings of most of the people, demanded war with Spain. By the end of April 1898, the Spanish-American War had begun. Its rallying cry was "Remember the *Maine!*"

Fighting in the Philippines Commodore George Dewey was in charge of the United States fleet in the Pacific. He had orders to attack the Philippine Islands, which belonged to Spain, if war broke out. Dewey sailed into the harbor of Manila at night. There were 10 very old Spanish ships in the harbor. Nearly 400 Spanish sailors were killed or wounded. Only one American died. Manila is on the Philippine island of Luzon. See the map on page 473.

Emilio Aguinaldo is a hero in Philippine history. His major interest was independence for his country. He lived to see the creation of the Republic of the Philippines.

When American troops got to the Philippines they were joined by Filipino freedom fighters. These were people who wanted freedom from Spanish rule. Their leader was Emilio Aguinaldo (ā mē′ lyō ä gē näl′ dō). The Spanish soldiers were soon defeated by American and Filipino forces.

Fighting in Cuba   The United States was not ready for this war. The troops that landed in Cuba in June wore heavy woolen uniforms. The food supplies were not protected from the heat and rain. A New York regiment known as the Rough Riders had to leave their horses in Florida because there was not room for them on the ship. The second in command of the Rough Riders was a young man from New York named Theodore Roosevelt. He had gathered together the cowboys, college athletes, and other adventure seekers who made up the regiment.

The Rough Riders were part of the most famous battle of the war. This was the charge up San Juan Hill. The Americans lost many men in this battle but the hill was captured.

Results of the war   The Spanish-American War was over in 4 months. Far more Americans were killed by sickness than in battle. As a result of the war the United States gained the former Spanish territories of Guam, Puerto Rico, and the Philippine Islands.

A military government was set up in Cuba. Its purpose was to help the Cubans set up a government of their own. In 1901 the United States withdrew as a military government in Cuba. But Cuba was not completely independent. It was a **protectorate** of the United States. This meant that the United States would continue to get involved in Cuban affairs if we thought they needed help. The United States ended this policy toward Cuba in 1934.

Even though the war was over, fighting did not end in the Philippine Islands. The Filipinos, under Aguinaldo, did not want to exchange Spanish control for American control. They wanted independence. And they fought for it. Aguinaldo was captured and this put an end to the fighting but not to the independence movement. As time passed, many Americans began to agree that the Philippines should be prepared for self-government and should become independent. This happened after World War II.

The Spanish-American War made the rest of the world take a good look at the United States. This country had defeated a European power. We had gained new

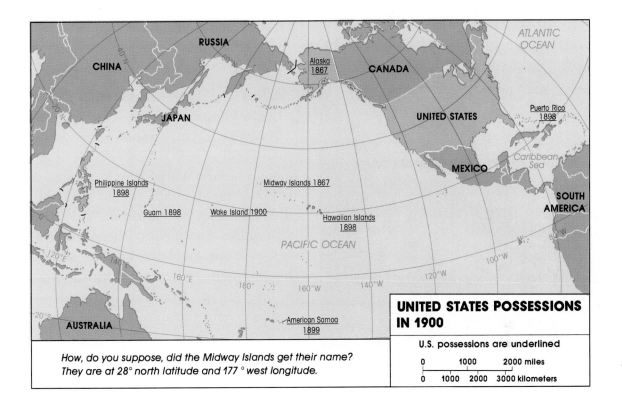

UNITED STATES POSSESSIONS IN 1900

U.S. possessions are underlined

0   1000   2000 miles
0   1000   2000   3000 kilometers

How, do you suppose, did the Midway Islands get their name? They are at 28° north latitude and 177° west longitude.

land in the Pacific Ocean and the Caribbean Sea. The war did not make the United States a great power. It just made the rest of the world realize that we already were one.

Panama Canal   Study the map on this page. Find all the overseas possessions of the United States in 1900. See how many there are in the Pacific Ocean. How was the United States going to protect these islands? Of course, the navy was the answer. But what would happen if most of the ships were in the Atlantic and something happened in Hawaii? It would take weeks and weeks for the ships to move down and around the South American continent. It became very clear that a faster way had to be found. The idea of building a canal, a waterway, across Panama, was

not a new one. The California gold rush showed the need for a canal across the isthmus. (Do you remember what an isthmus is? If not, look in the Glossary, pages 486–495.) Look at the map on pages 466–467 in the Atlas. Much time would be saved if a ship going from New York to San Francisco did not have to go all the way around South America.

A French company had started to build a canal across Panama. But work had been stopped by disease and a lack of money. The United States government offered to take over the task if the government of Panama would give the United States control of a zone 10 miles (16 km) wide along the canal.

Work began on the canal in 1904. Colonel George Goethals (gō′ thəlz) directed the work. President Roosevelt's orders "to

The waters of the Atlantic and Pacific oceans merged after the explosion shown here. This was part of the ceremonies connected with opening the Panama Canal in 1914.

make the dirt fly" were closely followed. It cost over $375 million to build the Panama Canal and took over 10 years. But when the first ship went through in 1914, everyone thought the money and time had been well spent.

The Canal Zone was under complete United States control until 1978. At that time this country ratified a new treaty with Panama. Under its terms the government of Panama took over the Canal Zone. It will take control of the Panama Canal in 2000.

CHECKUP

1. What is one reason why the United States wanted territory in the Pacific Ocean?
2. What territory did the United States gain as a result of the Spanish-American War?
3. Why was it important to build the Panama Canal?

The World Wars

┌─VOCABULARY─────────────────────┐
neutral   dictatorship
Allies   persecution
Central Powers   Axis
armistice   ration
└────────────────────────────────┘

Europe before World War I   Most of the countries of Europe around 1900 were ruled by kings or emperors. They had large armies and navies. These powerful nations were divided into two groups. Great Britain, France, and Russia were in one group. Germany and Austria-Hungary were the major powers in the other group. These countries kept building their armies and navies. They became larger and larger. This was dangerous. Anything could start these countries fighting with each other and soon all of Europe would be in a war. This is what happened in 1914 when World War I started in Europe.

The United States before World War I The United States was not very interested in what was going on in Europe. Americans were more concerned with what was happening in the Western Hemisphere and within the United States itself. Woodrow Wilson was President when the war began in Europe. He asked the American people not to take sides, to stay **neutral.** Most Americans were neutral. They did not think that the United States should take part in this European war.

The United States in World War I   As the years passed and the war in Europe went on, the United States found it harder and harder not to take sides. Most Americans favored the **Allies**—Great Britain, France, and Russia. German submarines were sinking British ships. Sometimes Americans were passengers on these ships and American lives were lost. The most famous of these incidents was the sinking of the *Lusitania* in 1915. There were 128 Americans among the 1,200 people who were killed. Strong feeling against the **Central Powers**—Germany, Austria-Hungary, and the Ottoman Empire (Turkey)—grew. But still people did not want American soldiers to fight in Europe. One of the reasons President Wilson was reelected in 1916 was because "he kept us out of war."

By 1917, however, Germany had started up submarine warfare again, and more American lives were lost. The United States decided at last to enter World War I on the side of the Allies. President Wilson asked Congress to declare war to make the world "safe for democracy."

The United States was not really ready for war. But lessons had been learned from the Civil War and the Spanish-American War. All young men had to sign up for the armed forces. Those who had special jobs, such as farmers, or those who were studying to be doctors did not have to join. Those young men who did go into the armed forces were sent overseas with the proper supplies. Money for the war was raised by the sale of Liberty Bonds. Farmers worked overtime to raise more crops. People at home had "wheatless Mondays" and "meatless Tuesdays" so that more food could go to the soldiers. Gasoline use was limited. Pleasure and business travel on railroads was also limited. Trains were used to move troops and supplies. People at home made sacrifices to help the soldiers in Europe.

The United States did not enter World War I until 1917. American troops, such as those shown here, made a big difference to the Allied cause.

Women went to Europe as nurses and with the Red Cross. They replaced the men who had worked on farms and in factories. They worked in groups that made warm scarves, socks, and gloves for the soldiers who had to face the cold European winter. They kept their families fed on the wheatless and meatless days. Women were very active in the war effort during this time.

The Allies were helped enormously by the presence of the American soldiers. By May 1918 American soldiers were pouring into France at the rate of 10,000 a day. Americans took part in several big battles. They fought in the second battle of the Marne River, at Château-Thierry (sha tō tye rē'), and at Saint-Mihiel (san mē yel'). The Central Powers were in retreat.

In November 1918, the Germans asked for an **armistice,** an end to the fighting. At eleven o'clock in the morning on November 11, 1918, fighting in World War I stopped.

Woodrow Wilson understood how tragic war is. He wanted World War I to be a "war to end all war." He thought no one should be a winner or a loser. Punishment would only cause a future war, he thought. But many people could not easily rid themselves of the feelings of hatred stirred up by the war. They had lost a great deal. Look at the chart on this page. See how many lives were lost. In the peace settlement, therefore, Germany was forced to give up land to the victorious Allies. Germany also had to pay the victors for part of the cost of the war. In just 20 years, German feelings about "getting even" would result in an even bigger and more tragic war.

COMBAT CASUALTIES OF WORLD WAR I	
United States	49,000
Italy	460,000
Great Britain	1 million
Austria	1.2 million
France	1.4 million
Russia	1.7 million
Germany	1.8 million

The League of Nations Woodrow Wilson had another idea on how to avoid war. This was the League of Nations. Instead of fighting, countries could meet together and talk about their problems. The powers of Europe accepted the idea. But the President could not convince the United States Congress of the importance of the League. Wilson lost his health in the bitter fight to see his dream come true. But Congress voted against joining the League of Nations. And without one of the most powerful nations in the world, the League was doomed to failure.

Another war World events in the 1930s seemed to be bringing another war closer and closer. **Dictatorships,** or harsh rule by one person or group, were appearing. Several countries were beginning to prepare for war. They hoped to gain more land through war. Japan invaded China. Italy invaded Ethiopia. Find these countries on the world map in the Atlas, pages 466–467. But Germany became the greatest threat to the world under the powerful leadership of Adolf Hitler.

Hitler wanted to restore the pride of the German people. The peace treaty ending World War I made them pay heavily. Many Germans saw war as the only way

The Nazis collected and burned books by Jewish authors and other books that contained what they thought were dangerous ideas. They wanted to control the minds of the people.

of gaining back their national honor. Hitler blamed Germany's defeat in World War I on the Jews. Many Germans believed him. Even before the war started, a steady **persecution** of the Jews within Germany began. When people are persecuted they are made to suffer for their beliefs. The persecution continued as Germany conquered other European countries. The result was the horrible death of six million Jews.

Hitler built an army and marched on neighboring countries. The League of Nations did nothing as Hitler disobeyed the terms of the World War I treaty. Finally England and France declared war on Germany. By mid-1941, the Allies, led by Britain, France, Russia, and China were at war with the **Axis** powers, chiefly Germany, Italy, and Japan. The Axis powers controlled much of Europe at this time and were victorious in the Pacific.

Pearl Harbor   Most Americans did not want to enter war again. The United States did supply a great deal of war materials to the Allies for several years. But war was avoided until December 7, 1941. President Franklin Roosevelt called this day "a date which will live in infamy." On that day Japan, hoping to gain control of the Pacific Ocean, made a surprise attack on United States forces at Pearl Harbor, Hawaii. On December 8, 1941, Congress declared war.

United States industry rose to the challenges of wartime production. An enormous number of planes, tanks, and ships were produced. No other country ever made such a large amount of war materials in such a short time.

This oil painting is called "Women with Masks." It shows women in a defense plant during World War II. Women played an important part in defense operations.

Billions of dollars worth of weapons and other military equipment were made in factories across the United States. Millions of Americans were involved in war work.

The United States was lucky to have such outstanding military leaders as Dwight D. Eisenhower, Douglas MacArthur, and Chester Nimitz. Eisenhower led all Allied troops to victory in Europe. A brilliant plan called *island hopping* led to victory in the Pacific. MacArthur was commander of the Allied forces in the southern Pacific. Nimitz was in charge of the naval and marine forces.

Over 15 million American men and women served in the armed forces in World War II. Well over a million were killed, wounded, or missing in action. But they and their allies fought boldly and bravely, and the Axis powers were defeated. The war ended first in Europe in the spring of 1945. Franklin Roosevelt had died suddenly, just weeks before the European victory. Hitler killed himself before being captured.

It would be the task of Roosevelt's Vice-President, Harry Truman, to end the war in the Pacific. The Japanese refused to agree to a surrender. Then Harry Truman made one of the most difficult decisions any leader in history has had to make.

The United States, with the help of many scientists who had escaped Hitler's Germany, had developed a terrible weapon of destruction—the atomic bomb. Should it be used to save American lives and end the war more rapidly?

Truman's answer was "Yes!" On August 6, 1945, a plane dropped the first atomic bomb over Hiroshima (hir ə shē′ mə), Japan. Three days later a second Japanese city —Nagasaki (näg ə säk′ ē)—was hit. More than a quarter of a million people were killed or injured. The cities were destroyed. Five days later the Pacific war was over.

The war at home   The American people made sacrifices in this war also. The use of many goods, such as gasoline, sugar, and meat, was **rationed,** or limited. Millions of people went to work building needed war equipment. Many people spent part of their income to buy war bonds. War bonds raised money to pay for the war.

About 6 million women went to work during the war. Over 2 million women worked in the nation's defense plants. Women also served in the armed forces.

Japanese Americans were not treated well during World War II. Other Americans feared them. After the attack on Pearl Harbor they were taken from their homes and brought to camps. They lived under very crowded conditions in the camps. They were kept under guard. Many sons and daughters of Japanese Americans fought honorably for the United States. No Japanese American was ever found guilty of spying. But their story shows how war brings out people's fears, suspicions, and anger.

Results   World War II was the most destructive war in history. More than 55 million people died. The cost is impossible to measure. It is just too large! Cities were destroyed. People were moved from their homelands.

It is hard to understand in the face of this enormous tragedy that some good things happened also. Many valuable inventions, such as sulfa drugs, resulted. Americans made friends in Europe and Japan after the war by helping to prevent starvation and to rebuild homes, cities, and countries.

233

The Japanese signed surrender terms on September 2, 1945, on board the battleship Missouri in Tokyo Bay.

Another result of the war was the organization of the United Nations. This group of world nations would work together for peace and human rights. In an age of atomic bombs, war had to be avoided if at all possible. The United States would play an active role in the United Nations. The headquarters are even in New York City.

The Soviet Union and the United States became the two leading world powers. The differences between these two countries would influence United States foreign policy for years to come.

CHECKUP

1. How did the United States get into World War I?
2. What were the causes of World War II?
3. What was the difference in United States involvement in the League of Nations and in the United Nations?

The Cold War

--- VOCABULARY ---

communism	Peace Corps
cold war	isolated
NATO	

Changing sides   The United States and the Soviet Union did not remain friends after World War II ended. The Soviet Union has a Communist government. People who live under **communism** have less freedom than people in democracies. One goal of communism, as stated by many of its leaders, is to spread the idea to as many countries as possible.

Many countries in Eastern Europe became Communist with Russian support after the war. What went on in these countries became a secret from the Western countries, including the United States. Winston Churchill, the British leader, said that the Soviet Union was "pulling down an iron curtain." The United States and other Western nations began to actively encourage democratic governments, especially in those parts of Asia and Africa that were just becoming independent. Communists were also active in these countries. The United States sent large amounts of food and military supplies to countries around the world to stop the spread of communism.

The competition between the Western nations and the Communist countries led by the Soviet Union became known as the **cold war.** A cold war has no battles, no tanks, no bombs. There is no destruction. A cold war is a war of words. The United Nations has often served as a major battleground in the cold war.

The Soviet Union has been successful many times in gaining new followers. It was a great shock to many Americans when Cuba became Communist in 1959. Cuba is only 90 miles (145 km) from Florida. Find Cuba on the map on page 470.

NATO Relations between the iron curtain countries and the Western democracies did not get better as the 1940s came to an end. The United States joined the countries of Western Europe in a military treaty and formed the North Atlantic Treaty Organization—**NATO.** The first members of NATO were the United States, Canada, Great Britain, France, Norway, Denmark, Iceland, Belgium, the Netherlands, Luxembourg, Portugal, and Italy. Later other countries joined, making 16 members in all. Find the NATO countries on the map below. These countries promised to help one another in case of attack by the Soviet Union. They formed an armed force made up of soldiers from each country. Dwight D. Eisenhower became the first commander of the NATO forces.

The Soviet Union and other European Communist countries formed a similar

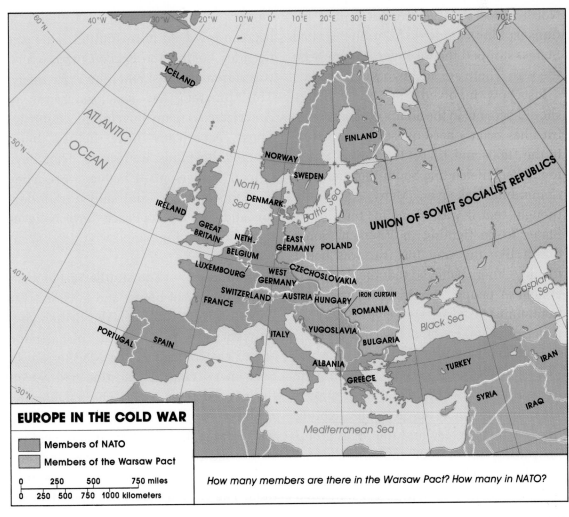

EUROPE IN THE COLD WAR

Members of NATO

Members of the Warsaw Pact

| 0 | 250 | 500 | 750 miles |
| 0 | 250 500 750 | 1000 kilometers |

How many members are there in the Warsaw Pact? How many in NATO?

group in 1955. They are known as the Warsaw Pact countries. The map on page 235 shows which they are. The Warsaw Pact membership is made up of all the Communist countries of Europe except Albania and Yugoslavia.

Small hot wars   World War II did not end all fighting all over the world. China became a Communist nation soon after World War II. Korea had been divided into two parts after the war. North Korea was a Communist country. China backed North Korea in an attempt to make all Korea one Communist country. The Soviet Union also sent weapons and supplies to North Korea. A large force of United Nations soldiers, mostly from the United States, stopped the takeover. No one won the war. There are still two Koreas today.

Just how involved the United States should become in the affairs of other countries has been a hard question to answer. In the 1960s and 1970s, the United States found itself defending South Vietnam from Communist takeover. Many Americans thought that it was wrong for the United States to be fighting in Vietnam. Some didn't like the way the war was being fought. Others believed that the South Vietnamese people should be fighting the Communist takeover themselves. Still other Americans believed that the United States should send guns and planes, but not troops. In the late 1960s the Vietnam War came close to splitting the American people into two camps, one group for fighting the war to a victory and the other group for getting out of Vietnam as quickly as possible. The last American soldiers finally left South Vietnam in 1973. In 1975

the country fell to North Vietnam. Today there is only one Vietnam and it is under Communist rule.

Recently, the United States has become involved in the strife in Middle America. We have sent aid and military advisors to El Salvador and Nicaragua, two Central American countries torn by civil war. In October 1983, American forces, with the help of troops from six Caribbean countries, removed Communist revolutionaries from power in Grenada. Grenada is a tiny island nation in the Caribbean.

Peace Corps   If people have enough to eat, live in good housing, and have clothes to wear, they are less likely to become involved in revolution. This was the idea behind the **Peace Corps,** which was started by President John F. Kennedy. This program has sent thousands of Americans to many developing countries. These Americans have helped build schools, hospitals, and roads. They have helped farmers plant better crops. They have taught school and helped train doctors and nurses. The Peace Corps believes in people helping people.

Peacemaker   The Middle East has had a long history of unrest and tension. War broke out in 1948 when the British government gave up its control of Palestine at the eastern end of the Mediterranean Sea. Jews living in Palestine had set up the new State of Israel. The neighboring Arab countries did not like it and went to war against Israel. The United Nations succeeded in stopping that war, but several other wars have been fought there since then. The United States has played an ac-

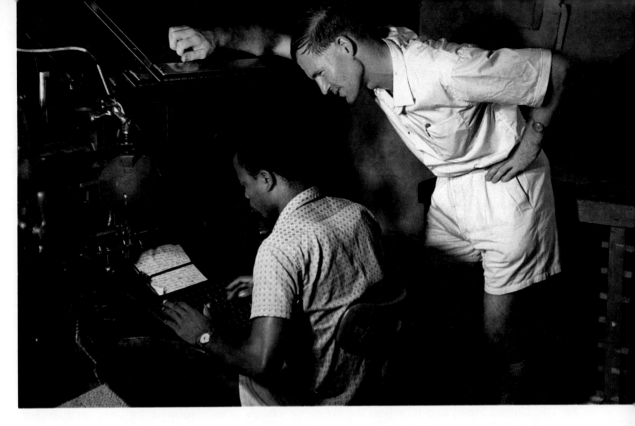

This Peace Corps volunteer is teaching a Nigerian student how to operate a linotype machine.

tive part in trying to keep peace in the region. Only time will tell whether lasting peace will come to this part of the world.

In 1972 President Richard Nixon visited China. There had been no diplomatic relations between the two countries since 1949. This trip helped improve relations between the United States and China.

Relations with the Soviet Union are sometimes good and sometimes bad. Among the good things have been agreements not to test atomic weapons above the ground, where they could cause dangerous fallout, or airborne waste materials. There is more trade now between the two countries. In 1975 Russian and American spaceships joined in space.

However, the Soviet Union still tries to spread communism to more countries. In 1979 the Soviet Union invaded Afghani-stan. Find Afghanistan on the map on pages 466–467. In protest against the Russian takeover, the United States led a boycott of the 1980 Summer Olympic Games held in the Soviet Union. The Soviets, in turn, led a boycott of the 1984 Summer Olympics in Los Angeles.

The United States has changed its foreign policy since 1900. We are no longer **isolated,** or standing apart, from what happens in the rest of the world. We know we have to work with the other countries of the world if we want peace.

CHECKUP

1. When did the cold war start?
2. Whom did the United States support in the wars in Korea and Vietnam?
3. What is NATO?
4. What is the Warsaw Pact?

KEY FACTS

1. During the nineteenth century the United States gradually acquired overseas territories.

2. The Spanish-American War added to United States overseas possessions and led to recognition of the United States as a world power.

3. The United States did not want to become involved in a European war but eventually joined the Allies in World War I.

4. The failure of the League of Nations, harsh treatment of Germany after World War I, and Japanese expansion in Asia all led to World War II.

5. The United States and its allies, the Western democracies, oppose the Soviet Union and its allies, the Eastern Communist countries, in the cold war.

VOCABULARY QUIZ

On a separate sheet of paper, write the word or phrase that best completes each sentence.

1. The feeling of most of the people about a subject is called (**a**) majority rule, (**b**) public opinion, (**c**) voting, (**d**) campaigning.

2. A country that has been a protectorate of the United States is (**a**) Great Britain, (**b**) Soviet Union, (**c**) France, (**d**) Cuba.

3. A narrow strip of land between two large bodies of water is called (**a**) a canal, (**b**) an island, (**c**) a waterway, (**d**) an isthmus.

4. In World War I Great Britain, France, and Russia were known as the (**a**) League of Nations, (**b**) Allies, (**c**) Central Powers, (**d**) Rough Riders.

5. If a country is neutral it (**a**) has a Communist government, (**b**) has territory in many parts of the world, (**c**) does not want to take sides in war, (**d**) is a member of NATO.

6. An armistice is (**a**) an end to fighting, (**b**) a declaration of war, (**c**) a collection of guns, (**d**) a group of countries.

7. The Axis Powers in World War II were (**a**) Russia, China, and Japan, (**b**) Germany, Italy, and Great Britain, (**c**) France, Russia, and Great Britain, (**d**) Germany, Italy, and Japan.

8. The group founded after World War II so that countries may talk over their problems is the (**a**) United Nations, (**b**) Central Powers, (**c**) League of Nations, (**d**) Allies.

9. Fighting with words, not bombs or guns, is called (**a**) a treaty, (**b**) a reform, (**c**) a cold war, (**d**) an armistice.

10. A group formed to help people help themselves is (**a**) NATO, (**b**) the Central Powers, (**c**) the Peace Corps, (**d**) the Warsaw Pact.

REVIEW QUESTIONS

1. What are two reasons why the United States wanted territory in the Pacific Ocean?

2. Why did President Wilson think the League of Nations was necessary?

3. What is the United Nations? NATO? The Peace Corps?

4. Name two "hot" wars that have taken place since World War II.

ACTIVITIES

1. Write a report on the history of either Hawaii or Alaska. For the one you choose, tell what life was like before the place became part of the United States and how it came to be part of the United States.

2. Write a report about one of the following men: Theodore Roosevelt, Woodrow Wilson, Emilio Aguinaldo, George Dewey, John Pershing, Dwight Eisenhower, or Douglas MacArthur. You may use an encyclopedia as well as biographies for your source material.

READING A TABLE

SKILLS PRACTICE

Sometimes it is easier to present many facts in table form. The table below tells about land that belongs or belonged to the United States. Such land is called an overseas territory or possession. Use the information in the table to answer these questions.

1. In what area were most of the territories or possessions located?
2. What two possessions have become states?
3. In what year did the United States acquire Hawaii, Guam, and Puerto Rico?
4. What did the United States acquire in 1903?
5. Which is the smallest possession?
6. Which United States possession has the smallest population?
7. Where are the Virgin Islands?
8. What is the present status of the Philippine Islands?
9. Which is larger in size, Alaska or Hawaii?
10. Which of the two has more people?

UNITED STATES OVERSEAS TERRITORIES AND POSSESSIONS

Name	Location	Size	Population	Acquired	Present status
Alaska	Pacific	586,400 sq mi (1,518,766 sq km)	479,000	1867	State (1959)
Midway Islands	Pacific	2 sq mi (5 sq km)	2,300	1867	Possession
Hawaii	Pacific	6,424 sq mi (16,638 sq km)	1,023,000	1898	State (1959)
Guam	Pacific	212 sq mi (549 sq km)	106,000	1898	Territory
Philippines	Pacific	115,707 sq mi (300,000 sq km)	50,310,000	1898	Independent (1946)
Puerto Rico	Caribbean	3,435 sq mi (8,897 sq km)	3,197,000	1898	Commonwealth
Wake Island	Pacific	3 sq mi (8 sq km)	300	1899	Possession
American Samoa	Pacific	76 sq mi (197 sq km)	32,000	1899	Territory
Canal Zone	Panama	647 sq mi (1,676 sq km)	42,000	1903	U.S./Panama control
Virgin Islands	Caribbean	133 sq mi (344 sq km)	96,000	1916	Territory
Northern Mariana Islands	Pacific	184 sq mi (477 sq km)	16,860	1947	Commonwealth (1982)
Marshall and Caroline islands	Pacific	533 sq mi (1,380 sq km)	116,555	1947	U.S. Trust Territory of the Pacific Islands (U.N.)

CHAPTER

13 A Time of Rapid Change

The United States Since 1900

Bicentennial   On July 4, 1976, the United States had a birthday party. As a country, we celebrated our **bicentennial,** or two-hundredth anniversary. People from all 50 states celebrated by remembering our past. It was a celebration that helped us understand the many good things that have taken place in American history. It gave us continued pride in our country and the things for which it stands. But it was also a time to take an honest look at our country's problems.

The United States was a greatly different place in 1976 than it was in 1876, when the country celebrated its one-hundredth birthday. A new United States, a modern United States, was born during this country's second hundred years.

In Chapter 12 you studied how the United States' role in world affairs really grew during this time. In this chapter you will see how new ideas, inventions, and laws have made changes within the United States. People and events have come together to change the way our country thinks and acts.

Theodore Roosevelt   Theodore (Teddy) Roosevelt was an early leader of this new, modern United States. Roosevelt was born into a wealthy, upper-class Dutch family in New York. As a boy Teddy was weak and sickly. He suffered from a disease that made it hard to breathe. He also had poor eyesight and other problems. But through hard work and determination he built a strong and healthy body. He was able to enjoy rugged sports such as boxing, swimming, hiking, and hunting.

In his early life he was a **naturalist** (a person who studies nature), a legislator, a rancher in the West, a historian, New York City police commissioner, and assistant secretary of the navy. He quit this last job to become a colonel in the Spanish-American War. He was part of a group called the Rough Riders. He returned from the war a national hero. Soon he was elected governor of New York. This led to his election as Vice-President during William McKinley's second term. But 6 months later, McKinley

In the mid-1900s, the United States turned its attention to space. At right are the space shuttle Challenger *and* Kathy Sullivan, *the first American woman to walk in space.*

was assassinated. At age 42, Theodore Roosevelt was the youngest person ever to take the office of President of the United States.

Roosevelt and reform   As President, Roosevelt worked hard to improve the standing of the United States in international affairs. He also worked hard to make this country a better place to live.

Roosevelt was greatly influenced by a group of writers he called **muckrakers.** These people wrote about wrongdoing in business and politics. Roosevelt hated injustice. Poor working conditions and mistreatment of Americans made him very angry. He was joined by many men and women who wanted to make things better.

Roosevelt moved to control business more closely. Then some of the worst wrongdoings could not occur. A major triumph was the passage of the Pure Food and Drug Act. This law called for some government control over the contents of food items. It ended practices like leaving shredded bones in cans of meat. Certain drugs could be sold only with a doctor's prescription. These reforms were small but important beginnings.

Roosevelt, the naturalist, also developed a program of **conservation.** Conservation is saving important natural resources. The United States Forest Service was started. Millions of acres of forestland were set aside as national land in the West. New national parks, game preserves, and wild-bird refuges were established. In Chapter 1 you read about Yellowstone, which was our first national park.

These kinds of government activities were rare before Roosevelt's time. The two Presidents who followed Roosevelt—William Howard Taft and Woodrow Wilson—continued the reforms he began. These reforms are still continued today.

When was the first airplane flight? When did Americans first land on the moon? When did women get the vote?

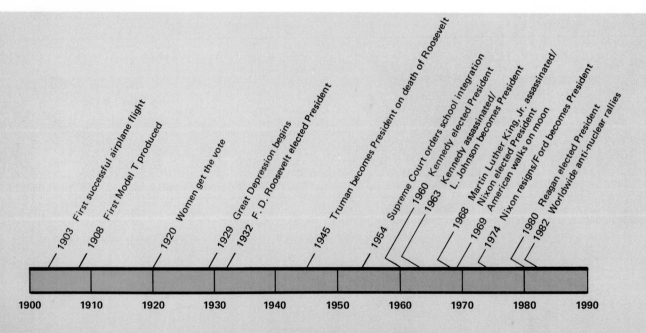

These hikers in California's Yosemite National Park are using a map to identify the landforms around them. They are at a spot called Glacier Point.

New discoveries   Many things that we take for granted today were unknown 100 years ago. These things would change the nation and the world. Among them were inventions that would lead to radio and to television. In 1903 the first movie that told a story, "The Great Train Robbery," appeared. **Synthetic** fibers made from chemicals were first produced in 1935. A giant industry was to grow from the discovery of oil near Spindletop, Texas, in 1901.

Transportation was changed in two ways. On December 17, 1903, on the windy beaches of Kitty Hawk, North Carolina, Orville Wright flew a "heavier than air" machine for 12 seconds. Later that day his brother, Wilbur, made a 59-second flight. Many people refused to believe a flight had really happened. It was too amazing! Humans could not fly! But they could fly, thanks to these two hard-

working bicycle shop owners from Dayton, Ohio. Not even the Wrights could have dreamed of the many ways **aviation** would change our country. Can you think of some of the ways aviation has improved the United States?

The automobile   In the same year that the Wright brothers made their flights, a young man in Detroit, Michigan—Henry Ford—was starting out in the automobile business. He was not the first person to build an automobile. Many Europeans and Americans were ahead of him. But all of these early cars were expensive. Only the rich could have them.

In 1908 Ford decided to build a lightweight, practical, cheap car that most people could afford. The car would be the Model T. To hold down costs, the Model T would be the only model built by the Ford Motor Company. As Ford said, "Any customer can have a car painted any color that he wants so long as it is black."

Ford combined ideas borrowed from others with ideas of his own. He used Eli Whitney's idea of interchangeable parts. In 1913 he applied the idea of the **assembly line.** Each worker does one small part of the job while the product rolls past.

The Ford Model T cost $895 in 1908, still too expensive for most people, but $600 less than any other car on the market. As more people bought it and as the assembly line was started, the price steadily dropped. By 1925 a new "Tin Lizzie," as the Model T was nicknamed, cost only $260. A total of 15 million of these cars were sold before they were replaced by the Model A late in 1927.

Building Model T automobiles on assembly lines and keeping the design simple made it possible for the Ford Motor Company to make cars that people could afford to buy.

And the United States changed as never before! In the early 1900s, roads were poor and almost impossible to drive on after rain or snow turned them to mud. Cars were open and dirty to ride in. Gas stations were few and far between. Speed limits were set at 6 to 10 miles (10–16 km) per hour to protect horses. These conditions changed as more people bought cars. A new freedom developed. It was easier to travel longer distances. The suburbs were born. New businesses sprang up. The United States was on wheels.

The Great Depression Newspaper headlines of the 1930s might have read: *Millions Out of Work! Fortunes Lost Overnight! People Lose Homes—Live in Piano Crates and Junked Cars! Thousands of Americans Starving!*

After a long period of wealth and well-being, the United States was entering the Great Depression. What causes a **depres-**

sion? In the 1930s the Depression came about because too many people were spending more money than they had. Their **income,** or money earned, did not keep up with the money they spent. They borrowed money from banks that they could not repay. Often people took their savings from banks. Soon many banks had to close because they had no more money. Over 4,000 banks closed between 1929 and 1932.

Without money, people could not buy new things. If businesses could not sell goods, they would close. And if businesses closed, people lost jobs. By 1933, one out of four American workers had lost his or her job. Poor farming methods and dry weather had turned much of the farmland in the Great Plains to dust. Find the Great Plains on the map on page 263. Thousands of farming families were forced to move from the **Dust Bowl,** as this area came to be called.

Many thousands of acres of farmland on the Great Plains were turned to dust by poor farming practices and many years of very little rain. Scenes such as this one were not unusual; many farms were buried under the dust.

During the Great Depression thousands of people were left with no money, no homes, no food. The country was in bad shape. "Brother, Can You Spare a Dime?" was a popular song of the time. The American people hoped that new leadership would solve this terrible problem. Franklin Delano Roosevelt was elected President in 1932.

FDR   Franklin Delano Roosevelt was called FDR by the newspaper people. Roosevelt was born into a wealthy family in New York in 1882. He was a distant cousin of Theodore Roosevelt. Shortly after graduation from law school, FDR became involved in politics. He became a state senator for New York in 1910. From 1913 through World War I he was assistant secretary of the navy. He ran unsuccessfully for Vice-President in 1920.

Tragedy struck in 1921. He became a victim of polio. He could not move his legs. Many thought his career was over. But Roosevelt gamely fought back. He exercised hard to regain his strength. Although he would always need help to walk, his recovery was successful. Out of this experience Roosevelt started the Warm Springs Foundation, a place in Georgia to help other polio victims.

Roosevelt soon returned to national politics. In 1928 he was elected governor of New York. In 1932, he defeated Herbert Hoover for the office of President.

The New Deal   Roosevelt had been elected because many voters felt he could lead them out of the Great Depression. The first task he had was to give the nation faith in itself again. "The only thing we have to fear is fear itself," declared the warm, confident voice of the new President. Often during his time in office, Roosevelt explained his programs and tried to make people feel better through a series of "fireside chats." These radio broadcasts reached millions of people.

Roosevelt saw the government as the solution to the country's problems. He caused the government to create jobs and grant other types of aid to people. This was known as a **New Deal** for the American people. Soon millions went back to work for the federal government on jobs such as forestry projects and the building of dams, parks, sewers, schools, airports, roads, and public buildings. Artists, writers, singers, and dancers were aided by money from the government. Farmers were given more help. The labor union movement was encouraged to grow.

Roosevelt's efforts were well thought of by most people. He was reelected three times, in 1936, 1940, and 1944. He is the only person ever to have been elected to more than two terms as President.

By 1940, the Depression was easing, but it was not over. Large numbers of Americans still did not have work. It would take another world war to put Americans back to work.

The postwar nation   The United States came out of World War II as the most powerful nation in the world. Two of its war heroes succeeded Harry Truman as President—Dwight Eisenhower in 1953 and John Kennedy in 1961. The country faced a promising future!

But the United States faced some very painful times as well. **Assassination** took the lives of John F. Kennedy, his brother Robert, and Dr. Martin Luther King, Jr. The war in Vietnam bitterly divided our nation. President Richard Nixon and several aides had to resign because of illegal acts carried out to get Nixon reelected. Americans were held hostage by a foreign country. Energy was in short supply. Air, land, and water became dirtier. Prices went higher.

Americans are concerned about these problems. Many people are willing to make sacrifices to control high prices. *Sacrifice* means "the giving up of one thing for the sake of another." Steps have been taken to make our environment safer and healthier. Energy is being conserved. We have shown that no American, not even a President, is above our laws.

Space holds a promise for the future. Neil Armstrong was the first person to step on the moon, in 1969. As he did, he said, "That's one small step for a man, one giant leap for mankind." In one way, he expressed the desire of this country to do things for the good of all people all over the world.

A decade of change   The 1980s will surely prove to be another period of change. Ronald Reagan was first elected President in 1980. He was faced with a number of serious problems. Inflation continued to be a problem. Unemployment was another problem. The need to keep a strong army and navy was felt as war kept breaking out in the Mideast. Helping to keep world peace would not be an easy task for the President. When Reagan was reelected in 1984, he faced many of the same problems.

The 1980 census showed that the United States was continuing to change. People were still moving to the western and southern parts of the country. State representation in Congress changed between 1970 and 1980. Some states lost represen-

These people are members of the Gray Panthers, a human rights group that works for the rights of older people. Their signs support various causes.

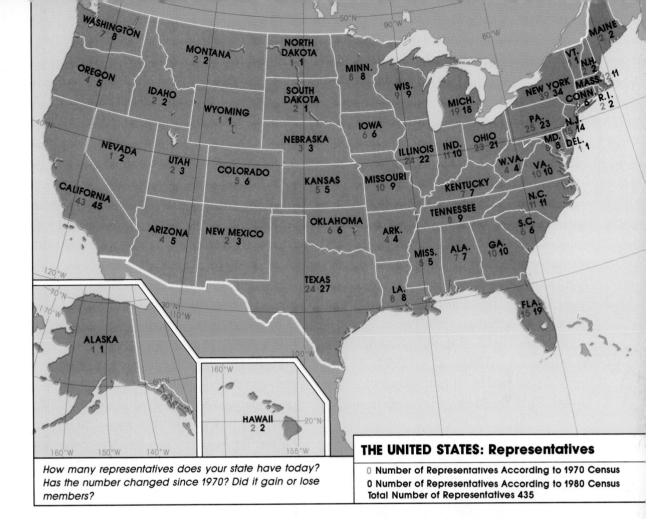

WASHINGTON 7 8

OREGON 4 5

MONTANA 2 2

IDAHO 2 2

WYOMING 1 1

NEVADA 1 2

UTAH 2 3

CALIFORNIA 43 45

ARIZONA 4 5

NEW MEXICO 2 3

NORTH DAKOTA 1 1

SOUTH DAKOTA 2 1

MINN. 8 8

WIS. 9 9

MICH. 19 18

IOWA 6 6

NEBRASKA 3 3

COLORADO 5 6

KANSAS 5 5

OKLAHOMA 6 6

TEXAS 24 27

MISSOURI 10 9

ILLINOIS 24 22

IND. 11 10

OHIO 23 21

KENTUCKY 7 7

TENNESSEE 8 9

ARK. 4 4

MISS. 5 5

ALA. 7 7

GA. 10 10

LA. 8 8

FLA. 15 19

S.C. 6 6

N.C. 11 11

VA. 10 10

W.VA. 4 4

PA. 25 23

N.J. 15 14

MD. 8 8

DEL. 1 1

NEW YORK 39 34

MASS. 12 11

CONN. 6 6

R.I. 2 2

VT. 1 1

N.H. 2 2

MAINE 2 2

ALASKA 1 1

HAWAII 2 2

How many representatives does your state have today? Has the number changed since 1970? Did it gain or lose members?

THE UNITED STATES: Representatives

0 Number of Representatives According to 1970 Census
0 Number of Representatives According to 1980 Census
Total Number of Representatives 435

tatives because their population became smaller. Other states gained. There were other changes in the population, too. In the future there will be more older people than young people in this country. There will also be more women than men. Isn't it interesting to think what the United States will be like in the years to come?

CHECKUP

1. What changes did Theodore Roosevelt bring to the United States?
2. What new ideas and discoveries changed the country in the early 1900s?
3. What caused the Great Depression?
4. What things did Franklin Roosevelt do to try to end the Depression?

The Struggle for Human Rights

VOCABULARY

human rights   boycott
sit-in

Human rights   Perhaps the great struggle for **human rights** since World War II best shows the pain and the promise of the United States. It is a painful thing when not all people are treated fairly and equally. But it is very promising when millions of Americans of all races join together to try to build a country that lives up to the promises of the Declaration of Independence and the Constitution.

247

In 1954 the Supreme Court of the United States declared that public schools had to serve both black and white students equally. Through the brave efforts of many students, some as young as you are, educational opportunities grew.

A leader in the human rights movement was Dr. Martin Luther King, Jr., a preacher with a mission in life. "I have a dream," spoke Dr. King stirringly. That dream was for the complete equality of all Americans. King was patient. He worked through the legal system. He challenged unjust laws, but always acted peacefully.

Dr. King gained nationwide fame in Montgomery, Alabama, in 1955. At that time blacks had to sit in the back of public buses. But one day a quiet woman named

Martin Luther King, Jr., walks children to school on the first day of integrated classes in Mississippi in 1966.

Rosa Parks decided to sit in the "whites only" part of the bus. She was arrested. Dr. King led a **boycott** of Montgomery buses to protest her arrest. People who supported Dr. King would not use the buses until anyone could sit wherever she or he pleased. The boycott worked.

King's ideas were used widely. **Sit-ins** were held in which people refused to leave "whites only" lunch counters until they were served. Protest marches were staged. Many people, including King himself, were beaten and thrown in jail. Many people came to support laws and rights that would help blacks.

During the presidency of Lyndon Johnson, great progress was made. In 1964 a law was passed that gave blacks the right to use all businesses that serve the public. Equal chances for jobs were also promised by this law. Johnson's "War on Poverty" provided help for poor Americans of all races. Robert C. Weaver was appointed as secretary of housing and urban development, becoming the first black Cabinet member in 1966. A year later, Thurgood Marshall became the first black Supreme Court justice. The black middle class continued to grow.

Still there are wide differences in the way many black and white Americans live. Riots in our large cities in the 1960s made this point clear. King's assassination pointed out the hatred that still exists. But millions of lives are greatly improved because of the leadership of Dr. King.

Equality for all   Many other groups also demanded better treatment under the law. Native Americans demanded that treaties be honored. Some tribes received hunting and fishing rights that had been promised them. Farm workers, many of whom are Mexican Americans, gained rights under the leadership of Cesar Chavez. Our government recognized that many Japanese-American citizens were treated badly during World War II.

You read in Chapter 7 how, in 1848, American women came together for the first time to demand rights equal to those of men. The movement grew. Some states passed laws that gave women more control over their own lives. Wyoming gave women the vote in 1869. Women's colleges were started. Slowly, very slowly, women began to enter the professions. Elizabeth Blackwell was, in 1849, the first woman to graduate from medical school.

An amendment to the Constitution that would give women the right to vote was first proposed to Congress in 1878. It did not receive enough votes to pass. The amendment came before Congress nearly every year after that. Each time it was defeated. Finally in 1919—success! The Nineteenth Amendment giving all female citizens the right to vote was passed by Congress and became part of the Constitution of the United States in 1920.

Today 38 percent of American women hold full-time jobs. In 1970 only 18 percent worked full-time outside the home. Women are doing jobs today that once were thought suited only for men. There are women coal miners and telephone linepersons. Women are engineers and scientists. They are running big industries. Some women are still being paid less for doing the same work as men. There is still a way to go in the struggle for equal rights for women.

Decisions made by government leaders throughout the United States affect human rights. Above is Toney Anaya, who became governor of New Mexico in 1982.

This movement toward equality is a process that has been carried on throughout history. It will not end until *all* Americans can say for themselves the words carved on Dr. King's tombstone: "Free at last, free at last, thank God Almighty, I'm free at last."

Promise for the future Americans must realize what a wonderful place this is to live. We have goods and wealth beyond the dreams of much of the world. We have ways to be heard when we disagree with one another and the government. We have freedom. We have sharp minds and fresh ideas. We have people willing to work hard for themselves and for others. It is our responsibility to continue to build our country and fulfill the dreams of the brave men and women who have gone before us.

CHECKUP

1. What decision did the Supreme Court make in 1954 that affected human rights?
2. What was Martin Luther King, Jr.'s contribution to the struggle for human rights?
3. In what year did women citizens of the United States get the right to vote?

KEY FACTS

1. New ideas, inventions, and laws have greatly changed our nation since 1900.

2. Theodore Roosevelt is an example of the new American leadership that helped the country progress in its second hundred years.

3. Franklin Delano Roosevelt used the power of government to lift the United States out of the depression of the 1930s.

4. Americans have successfully survived the pain of assassination and scandal in the 1960s and 1970s and are constantly taking steps to make the United States better.

5. Due to the efforts of Dr. Martin Luther King and others, the goal of equal rights for all Americans is much closer to reality.

VOCABULARY QUIZ

Fill in the missing words or phrases in the following paragraphs. Write your answers on a separate sheet of paper.

The United States celebrated its (1) _____ , its two hundredth birthday, in 1976. The country had changed a great deal in that time.

Once people made most of the things they needed at home. Then the (2) _____ revolution took place. Goods manufactured in factories took the place of goods made at home. Industries grew. One of the most important was the automobile industry. (3) _____ designed a car he called the Model T. The car was made on an (4) _____ line. When things do not go well for businesses, and workers do not have jobs or money to buy goods, the country goes into a (5) _____ . (6) _____ was President during such a time in the 1930s. (7) _____ is another problem. It affects the value of money.

People today are very interested in the environment. Theodore Roosevelt was interested in (8) _____ , saving natural resources. While he was President the (9) _____ was started. People are also interested in human welfare. Freedom and equality for all are (10) _____ .

REVIEW QUESTIONS

1. Why was a national forest system started?

2. Who were the muckrakers? What did they do?

3. How does an assembly line work?

4. Why was the Model T such a popular car?

5. How did New Deal policies help people during the Depression?

6. What was Dr. Martin Luther King's part in the battle for human rights?

ACTIVITIES

1. There are national parks of one kind or another all over the United States. Find out the name of a park near where you live. Investigate what the park offers. Plan a trip to the park. Describe what can be done there.

2. The idea behind the Model T was to design a car that could be built cheaply and in great numbers so that many people could afford to buy one. Do you think this was a good idea? What do you think the automobile of the future will look like? Will it run on gasoline? Design a car of the future. You can draw a picture, write a description, or do both.

3. The first person to step on the moon was an American. Make a list of the Americans who have flown in space. Tell what each did. Begin your list with Alan B. Shepard.

READING A MAP: THE 1984 PRESIDENTIAL ELECTION

ELECTORAL VOTES

In 1984 Ronald Reagan was reelected President of the United States. When people vote for President they do not vote directly for the candidate. They vote for electors. These electors are pledged to vote for one or the other of the candidates. Their votes are called electoral votes. In order to be elected President, a candidate must have more than half of the 538 electoral votes. The person with the most votes in each state gets all that state's electoral votes.

SKILLS PRACTICE

The questions below are based on the map and the information on this page.

1. Which two states have the most electoral votes?

2. How many *states* did Walter Mondale win in the 1984 election?

3. How many electoral votes did he get?

4. How many *states* did President Reagan win?

5. How many electoral votes did President Reagan get?

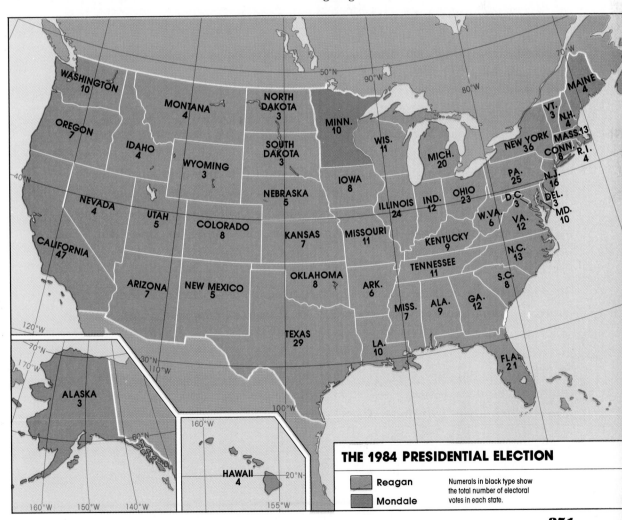

THE 1984 PRESIDENTIAL ELECTION

Reagan
Mondale

Numerals in black type show the total number of electoral votes in each state.

5/UNIT REVIEW

1. The United States began to expand beyond its shores in the nineteenth century. — *List the territories acquired by 1900 and tell how or why each was acquired. Which of these are still part of the United States?*

2. The United States has fought in two world wars. — *What caused World War I and World War II? How did the United States get involved in each?*

3. Woodrow Wilson's dream of a League of Nations after World War I came true with the creation of the United Nations after World War II. — *Find more information about the League of Nations and the United Nations in an encyclopedia. Why did the United States join one but not the other?*

4. Since World War II the United States has been more involved in world affairs than ever before in its history. — *Give at least three examples of United States involvement in world affairs since 1945.*

5. The years around 1900 are often called the "birth of modern America." — *Why is this so?*

6. Theodore Roosevelt had strong ideas about the role of government. — *How did his activities in conservation and controlling big business show this?*

7. New inventions, such as the automobile and the airplane, changed the way of life in the United States. — *Imagine life without one of these important inventions. Write a story about how your life would be different without automobiles, or airplanes, or synthetic fabrics, or any other invention you think is important.*

8. The Great Depression occurred in the period between the two world wars. — *What causes a depression? Do you think it can happen again? Explain.*

9. The movement for human rights and equality is a process that has gone on throughout our history. — *Which groups have made the largest gains in the area of human rights in the last 35 years?*

The United States: A Land of Great Variety

CHAPTER

14 Geography of the United States

Tools of Geography

┌─VOCABULARY──────────────────────┐
│ region   population │
│ political map   density   │
│ boundary   │
└─────────────────────────────────┘

The study of geography In the first chapter of this book you learned about reading maps. You also learned that being able to read maps will help you find out about the geography of our great country.

But what does learning geography really mean? Of course it means more than reading maps. Maps are just one of the tools we use to study geography. When we study geography, we learn about the earth's physical features. Mountains, plains, rivers, forests, and islands are just a few of the physical features found in our country.

When we study the geography of a place, we also learn something about its climate. If you know the climate of a place, you have a good idea of how hot or cold that place is at any time of the year. You also know the parts of the year in which rain or snow is expected.

The study of natural resources, such as oil, coal, and iron, is a part of geography. Geography also deals with cities and industries. But most of all, geography is the study of how people use the earth.

The United States: one nation, many regions Because our country is so big, you could not possibly study all of its geography at once. It helps to divide the country into parts, or **regions.** Then you can study one part at a time. In the next seven chapters of this book, you will be learning about the different parts of the United States—one at a time.

We could divide the United States in many different ways in order to study it. We could divide it into dry lands and wetlands, or highlands and lowlands. Or we could divide it into parts with many people and parts with few people. These are all perfectly good ways to divide the United States into regions.

Your book uses still another way of dividing the country. The map on page 255 shows the regions you will be studying this year. They are the New England, Middle Atlantic, Southeast, North Central, South Central, Mountain West, and Pacific regions.

Find your state on the map. In which of these seven parts is your state?

Maps Before studying the regions of the United States, let's learn something about the states that make up the whole country. One way of doing this is to look at maps.

The map shows the regions you will study. The picture shows DeSoto Falls at the upper end of Alabama's Little River Canyon, one of the deepest canyons east of the Rockies.

THE UNITED STATES: Regions

WASH.

MONT.

N.DAK.

CANADA

NEW MAINE
ENGLAND

OREG.

IDAHO

MINN.

WIS.

VT. N.H.

PACIFIC

WYO.

S.DAK.

MICH.

N.Y.
MASS.
CONN. R.I.

MOUNTAIN
WEST

NORTH CENTRAL

MIDDLE

NEV.

UTAH

NEBR.

IOWA

ILL. IND. OHIO

PA. ATLANTIC
N.J.

W.VA.

MD. DEL.

CALIF.

COLO.

KANS.

MO.

KY.

VA.

Washington, D.C.

ARIZ.

N.MEX.

OKLA.

ARK.

TENN.

N.C.

SOUTHEAST

S.C.

SOUTH
CENTRAL

MISS.

ALA.

GA.

ATLANTIC
OCEAN

PACIFIC
OCEAN

TEX.

LA.

FLA.

ARCTIC OCEAN

U.S.S.R.

ALASKA

MEXICO

Gulf of Mexico

CANADA

PACIFIC

PACIFIC OCEAN

PACIFIC

HAWAII

0	400 miles
0	400 kilometers

0	200 miles
0	200 kilometers

THE UNITED STATES: Regions

0	200	400 miles
0	200 400	600 kilometers

You have already learned about some of the facts that maps can tell you. When you found Yellowstone National Park at 45° north latitude and 110° west longitude, you used the map on pages 14–15. That map told you the name of each state. It showed you where each state is and gave you an idea of its size.

Turn to the map on pages 14–15 again. A map like this is called a **political map.** This one shows you the different states in our country. Another political map might show you the different countries in the world. In other words, a political map shows you the names and **boundaries,** or borders, of different countries or states. A boundary is a line that separates one state or country from another.

Find the boundaries of your own state on the map. Name the states that share these lines. Find the boundary between the United States and Canada. Do you see the boundary between the United States and Mexico?

A political map might also show you where the cities of a state or country are. How does the map key on page 15 help you find some important cities in the United States? The key also helps you find the state capitals. A state capital is the city in which the government of the state meets. Do you know the capital city of your state? Find it on the map. Can you find the capital of our country? How does the map key help you find it?

Tables   The map on pages 14–15 is a good tool for learning some facts about the United States. But as you know, there are other ways in which you can find information. The rows and columns of the table on page 257 give you, in another form, some of the same facts shown on the map. A table is a fast and handy way to learn what you want to know.

The table on page 257 gives you the area, or size, of each state. The table also gives you the rank in area of each state. Which is our biggest state? Our smallest? Is your state one of these two? If not, what is the rank of your state? What is the area of your state? You can see that it is easier and faster to find certain facts in a table than on a map.

For example, you can tell by looking at the map on pages 14–15 that Nevada is bigger than Delaware. However, the map can't tell you exactly how big each of those states is. For that kind of information, the table on page 257 is more useful.

Graphs   A third way to show the size of some of our states is to use a graph. A graph is any one of several different kinds of drawings. You have already used graphs in this book. Some graphs, like the one on page 281, use symbols to give information. Some, like those on pages 258 and 271, use lines or bars. One kind of graph is shaped like a pie divided into parts. There is a pie graph on page 357. What does it show?

A bar graph makes it easy to compare facts. Look at the top graph on page 258. It uses bars to show the sizes of our five largest and five smallest states. In this case, the graph gives you an idea of the great differences in sizes.

No one way of learning facts is better than another. You will need to be able to use maps, tables, and graphs to learn about the geography of the United States.

AREA AND POPULATION OF THE FIFTY STATES

State	Area in sq mi	Area in sq km	Rank in area	Population (in thousands)	Rank in population
Alabama	51,705	133,915	29	3,990	22
Alaska	591,004	1,530,700	1	500	50
Arizona	114,000	295,260	6	3,053	28
Arkansas	53,187	137,754	27	2,349	33
California	158,706	411,049	3	25,186	1
Colorado	104,091	269,595	8	3,178	26
Connecticut	5,018	12,997	48	3,154	27
Delaware	2,044	5,295	49	613	47
Florida	58,664	151,939	22	10,976	6
Georgia	58,910	152,576	21	5,837	11
Hawaii	6,471	16,759	47	1,039	39
Idaho	83,564	216,432	13	1,001	40
Illinois	56,345	145,934	24	11,511	5
Indiana	36,185	93,720	38	5,498	14
Iowa	56,275	145,753	25	2,910	29
Kansas	82,277	213,098	14	2,438	32
Kentucky	40,409	104,660	37	3,723	23
Louisiana	47,752	123,677	31	4,462	18
Maine	33,265	86,156	39	1,156	38
Maryland	10,460	27,092	42	4,349	19
Massachusetts	8,284	21,456	45	5,798	12
Michigan	58,527	151,586	23	9,075	8
Minnesota	84,402	218,601	12	4,162	21
Mississippi	47,689	123,515	32	2,598	31
Missouri	69,697	180,516	19	5,008	15
Montana	147,046	380,848	4	824	44
Nebraska	77,355	200,350	15	1,606	36
Nevada	110,561	286,352	7	911	43
New Hampshire	9,297	24,032	44	977	41
New Jersey	7,787	20,169	46	7,515	9
New Mexico	121,593	314,925	5	1,424	37
New York	49,108	127,189	30	17,735	2
North Carolina	52,669	136,413	28	6,165	10
North Dakota	70,702	183,119	17	686	46
Ohio	41,330	107,044	35	10,752	7
Oklahoma	69,956	181,186	18	3,298	25
Oregon	97,073	251,419	10	2,674	30
Pennsylvania	45,308	117,348	33	11,901	4
Rhode Island	1,212	3,140	50	962	42
South Carolina	31,113	80,582	40	3,300	24
South Dakota	77,116	199,730	16	706	45
Tennessee	42,144	109,152	34	4,717	17
Texas	266,807	691,030	2	15,989	3
Utah	84,899	219,889	11	1,652	35
Vermont	9,614	24,900	43	530	48
Virginia	40,767	105,586	36	5,636	13
Washington	68,139	176,479	20	4,349	19
West Virginia	24,231	62,759	41	1,952	34
Wisconsin	56,153	145,436	26	4,766	16
Wyoming	97,809	253,326	9	511	49
Washington, D.C.	69	178	X	623	X
United States	3,618,770	9,372,614	X	236,158	X

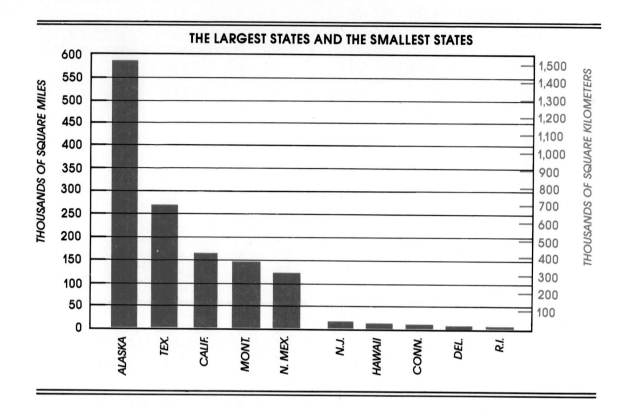

THE LARGEST STATES AND THE SMALLEST STATES

Which state is the largest in area? Which has the highest population density?

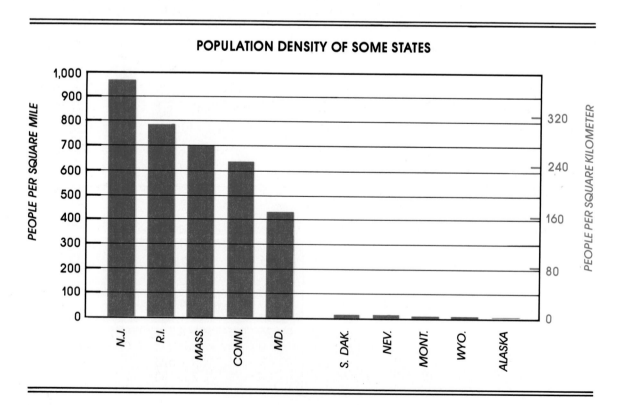

POPULATION DENSITY OF SOME STATES

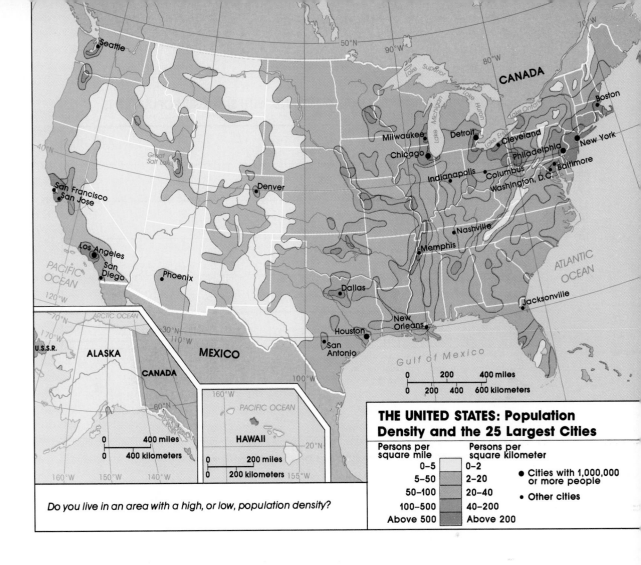

THE UNITED STATES: Population Density and the 25 Largest Cities

Persons per square mile	Persons per square kilometer
0–5	0–2
5–50	2–20
50–100	20–40
100–500	40–200
Above 500	Above 200

● Cities with 1,000,000 or more people

● Other cities

Do you live in an area with a high, or low, population density?

Using the tools of geography to learn about people The study of people is one of the most important parts of geography. There are more than 235 million people in the United States. Where do they all live? The map above shows you. It is called a population density map.

When we speak of **population density,** we are referring to the number of people per square mile or square kilometer in a certain area, such as a state or country. Of course, each square mile or kilometer in that area won't have exactly the same number of people. Population density means the average number of people per square mile or kilometer. The higher the average number of people to the square mile or kilometer, the higher the population density.

The map above shows you the population densities of the United States. It also shows you the 25 largest cities in the United States. Six of these cities have at least 1 million people living in them. They are New York, Los Angeles, Chicago, Houston, Philadelphia, and Detroit.

Population density, like size, can be shown on a graph. Look at the lower graph on page 258. It shows the population densities of ten of our states. Compare this graph with the top graph. You can see that some of our large states,

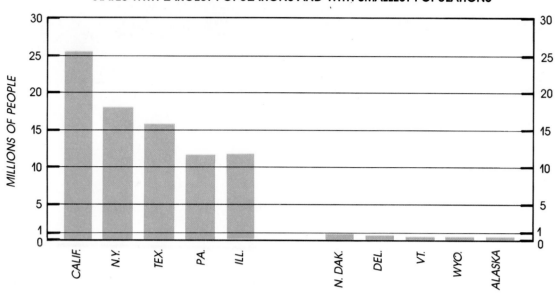

Which state has the largest population? Which state has the smallest population?

such as Alaska and Montana, have very low population densities. On the other hand, some of the small states, such as New Jersey, Connecticut, and Rhode Island, have very high population densities.

Remember, population density is the average number of people per square mile or kilometer. It is not the total number of people in a state. The graph above shows the total number of people in ten states: the five with the most people and the five with the fewest. If you look again at the table on page 257, you can find the total number of people in every state.

The map on page 259, the graphs on pages 258 and 260, and the table on page 257 together give you a very good idea of where Americans live.

Los Angeles is one of our nation's largest cities.

CHECKUP

1. What kind of information is usually given on a political map?
2. Which are the five largest and the five smallest states in our nation?
3. Which are the five most populated and the five least populated states in our nation?
4. What is population density?

Landforms of the United States

The varied land   The surface of the earth is not the same all over. Some of the earth's surface is high, and some is low. Some of the earth's surface is land. A great deal more of the earth's surface is water. Some parts of the earth's surface are easier for people to live on than others. Some parts have many people. Some have very few.

Look at the map on page 263. This is a **relief map,** or **physical map.** It shows you the kinds of land surfaces, or **landforms,** the United States has. It tells you how high or low the land is. It also names the largest rivers and lakes.

Do you remember the words from "America, the Beautiful," which you read at the very beginning of your book?

> For purple mountain majesties
> Above the fruited plain!

Those words tell you something about two very important landforms.

Plains   Some of the many millions of people in the United States live on our country's **plains.** A plain is a wide area of flat or gently rolling land.

Combines harvest wheat on the Great Plains in western Texas.

The peak of Mount McKinley is covered with snow all year round.

The largest plain in the United States is in the middle of the nation. This is the Central Plains. Look again at the relief map on page 263. Find the Great Plains on the western edge of the Central Plains. See how the Great Plains stretches north and south from the Canadian border to the Mexican border, a distance of more than 1,000 miles (1,600 km). You will be learning more about the Great Plains when you study the North Central states.

A plain that is bordered by a large body of water is called a **coastal plain.** The Atlantic Coastal Plain and the Gulf Coastal Plain are two large coastal plains in the United States. Find them on the map.

Plateaus   Another landform is called a **plateau.** A plateau is a large, high area of land. It generally rises steeply from the land around it, at least on one side. The top, or surface, of a plateau is usually flat and level, like a plain.

The Colorado Plateau is a large plateau in the region called the Mountain West. Find it on the map on page 263. Is it higher or lower than the coastal plains? Than the Great Plains? How did the map key help you answer?

Mountains   Some Americans live on or near high, steep lands called **mountains.** A mountain is a part of the earth's surface that rises sharply from the land around it. A mountain has a broad base and narrows to a small peak at the top. A group of mountains is called a chain or a range.

The highest mountains in the United States are in Alaska. Among them is Mount McKinley, the highest point in the United States. It is 20,320 feet (6,190 m) high. Find this towering mountain on the map on page 263.

The longest mountain chain in the United States is the Rocky Mountains. Like the Great Plains, these mountains stretch from Canada to within a few hundred miles of Mexico. The Rocky Mountains are very high. Some peaks rise more than 14,000 feet (4,300 m). Find the Rockies on the same map.

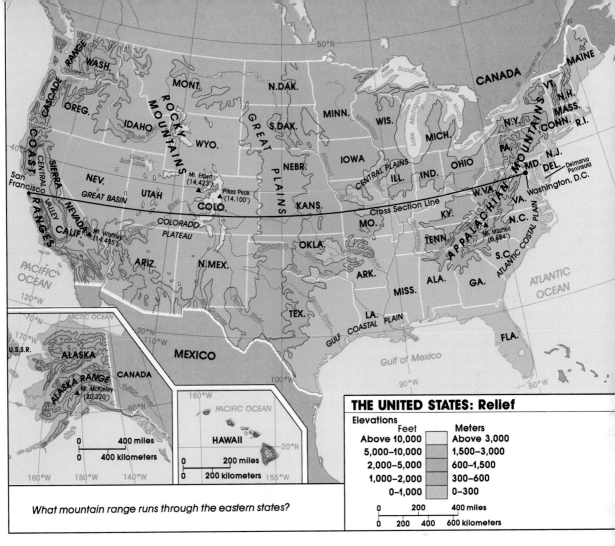

THE UNITED STATES: Relief

Elevations

Feet		Meters
Above 10,000		Above 3,000
5,000–10,000		1,500–3,000
2,000–5,000		600–1,500
1,000–2,000		300–600
0–1,000		0–300

0   200   400 miles

0   200   400   600 kilometers

What mountain range runs through the eastern states?

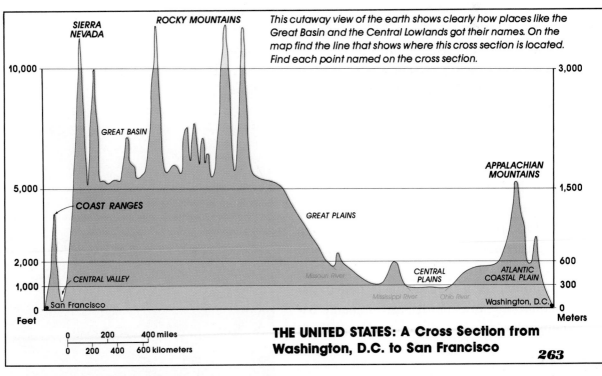

This cutaway view of the earth shows clearly how places like the Great Basin and the Central Lowlands got their names. On the map find the line that shows where this cross section is located. Find each point named on the cross section.

THE UNITED STATES: A Cross Section from Washington, D.C. to San Francisco

0   200   400 miles

0   200   400   600 kilometers

These islands are in a lake in the Tongass National Forest in southeastern Alaska.

Islands and peninsulas Many people in our country live on **islands.** An island is a body of land completely surrounded by water. Turn to the map of the United States on pages 468–469. You can see that several states have islands off their shores. One state, Hawaii, is made up entirely of islands. The Hawaiian Islands are in the Pacific Ocean. More than 1 million people live on another island. It is a small island called Manhattan. Manhattan Island is in New York City.

In some states, people live on land called a **peninsula.** A peninsula is a piece of land almost surrounded by water. Most of one state—Florida—is a peninsula. Find the peninsula of Florida on the map on pages 468–469. What bodies of water touch this piece of land?

Another large peninsula is called the Delmarva Peninsula. It has this name because it is made up of parts of three different states. The *Del* stands for Delaware. The *mar* stands for Maryland. And the *va* stands for Virginia. The Delmarva Peninsula is on the east coast of the United States. See whether you can find it on the map on page 263.

This peninsula is on the coast of Washington.

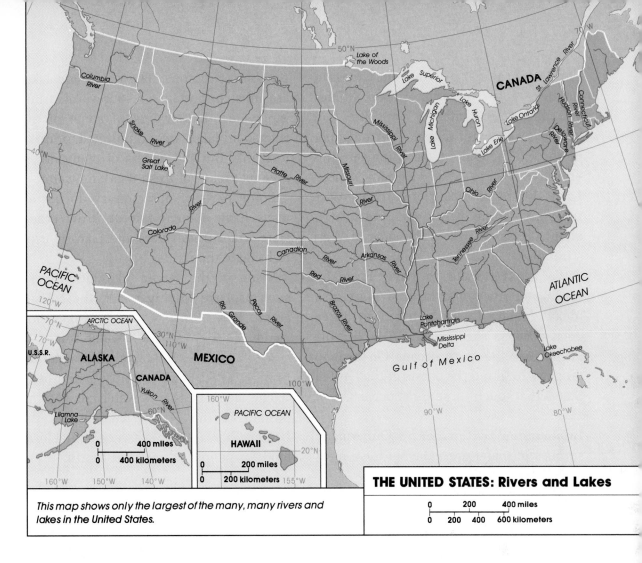

This map shows only the largest of the many, many rivers and lakes in the United States.

THE UNITED STATES: Rivers and Lakes

| 0 | 200 | 400 miles |
| 0 | 200 | 400 | 600 kilometers |

A wealth of water As you have learned, much of the earth's surface is water. From the beginning, great numbers of Americans, like people of all nations and ages, have chosen to live near oceans, lakes, and rivers. As you read this section and the next, you will find some of the reasons for this.

As you look at the map on page 263 and the map above, you will notice many rivers. Although there are hundreds and hundreds of beautiful rivers in the United States, only the largest are shown on these maps. Among those labeled are the nine rivers that are over 1,000 miles (1,600 km) in length.

The most important river in our country is the Mississippi. On the map above, trace the route of the Mississippi from its **source** in Minnesota to its **mouth** in Louisiana. A **delta** has formed here where the Mississippi empties into the Gulf of Mexico. A delta is a low, level piece of land at the mouth of a river. It is found where a river has formed more than one **channel.** Find the Mississippi Delta on the map above.

Our country also has a great many lakes. The largest of these are the Great Lakes. In fact, they are among the largest lakes in the world. These five huge lakes stretch from Minnesota to New York.

They are, in order of size from largest to smallest, Lakes Superior, Huron, Michigan, Erie, and Ontario. We share four of these lakes with Canada, our neighbor to the north. Only Lake Michigan lies entirely within the United States. Lake Michigan is more than twice the size of nine of our states. And it is about the same size as the state of West Virginia.

We are fortunate to have so many freshwater rivers and lakes. We are also lucky enough to be bounded by three great oceans. They are the Atlantic, the Pacific, and the Arctic oceans. On the map on page 263, find the coasts of the United States that touch these three oceans.

Importance of water Our many sources of water are valuable for a great number of reasons. The rivers and lakes are most important as sources of drinking water. The waters of some of our rivers and lakes are too **polluted,** or dirty, to drink. But the waters of many others give us plenty of fresh drinking water.

Some parts of our country do not always have enough rain to grow crops. Here water from rivers and lakes is used to **irrigate** the fields.

Some of the larger lakes and rivers, such as Lake Michigan and the Mississippi River, serve as transportation routes. Ships use these water routes to carry all kinds of goods and materials from one part of the country to another.

The larger bodies of water are also important to the fishing business in the United States. Fish are very valuable as food for people all over the world.

Barges like these on the Mississippi in Arkansas use our waterways to carry goods.

Some rivers, such as the Tennessee and the Niagara, provide electric power. The water from these rivers turns large generators. The generators change the power of moving water into electric power. Power from this source is known as **hydroelectric power.** The electricity can be used to light our homes. It can be used to run factory machines that make thousands of products.

Our lakes and rivers also give us beautiful places just to enjoy. Many people love to swim or boat. Others like to go fishing. People like to spend their vacations near many of our lakes and rivers.

Our oceans are also important for many reasons. The Atlantic, the Pacific, and the Arctic oceans are all sources of fish. Fine beaches along the Pacific and Atlantic attract thousands of visitors each year. The Atlantic and Pacific oceans also serve as major ocean highways to countries all over the world.

This hydroelectric plant is on the Colorado River.

People of all ages enjoy the water.

As you know, many Americans live near water. Look at the population map on page 259. You can see that many large cities have grown up near our ocean coasts and along our lakes and rivers. Now you know why that is so.

CHECKUP
1. Name three important landforms in the United States.
2. What is the difference between an island and a peninsula?
3. In which state is the source of the Mississippi River located? Where is the mouth of the Mississippi?
4. Name at least four important ways people in the United States use their lakes, rivers, and oceans.

The Earth and the Sun

VOCABULARY
weather	seasons
climate	axis
temperature	rotation
precipitation	revolution

Weather   Have you ever planned a picnic and had to call it off because it rained? Have you ever felt like flying a kite, only to discover that there was no wind? Have you ever wanted to go swimming but decided it was too cold? Has your school ever closed because of a snowstorm? If any of these things happened to you, your plans were changed because of the **weather.**

Weather is the condition of the air at a certain time. Rain, snow, wind, heat, and cold are all part of the weather. The weather may be hot or cold. It may be sunny or cloudy. It may be dry or wet. It may be raining or snowing. It may be windy or calm. Our big country has many different kinds of weather, just as it has many different kinds of land.

Climate   The kind of weather a place has over a long period of time is its **climate.** The two most important parts of any place's climate are **temperature** and **precipitation.** Temperature refers to the amount of heat in the air. Precipitation is rain, snow, mist, sleet, or hail.

Which of these three places gets the most precipitation? The least?

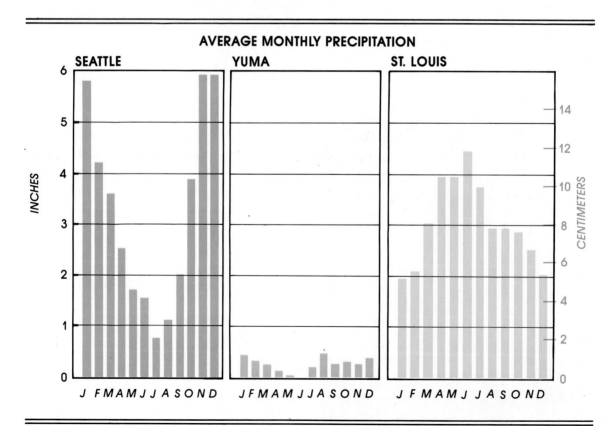

AVERAGE MONTHLY PRECIPITATION

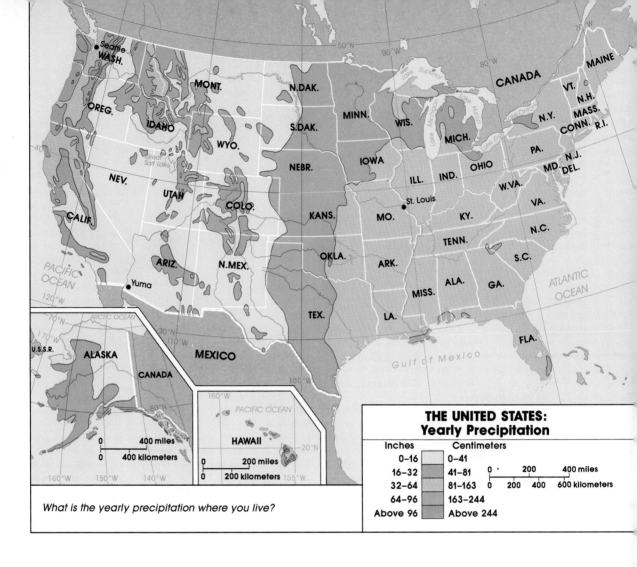

THE UNITED STATES:
Yearly Precipitation

Inches	Centimeters
0–16	0–41
16–32	41–81
32–64	81–163
64–96	163–244
Above 96	Above 244

What is the yearly precipitation where you live?

You probably know more about the climate where you live than you think you do. Of course, on some days it may rain when you don't expect it to. And a day that you expect to be hot and sunny may turn out to be chilly and windy. But most of the time you know the times of the year, or **seasons,** in which you can expect warm or cold weather. You know the months that have the most rain or snow.

Precipitation   Maps can help us learn a great deal about rain and snow in the United States. Look at the map of yearly precipitation above. Yearly precipitation is the total amount of precipitation that falls during a year. Find your state on the map. Now look in the key to discover how many inches or centimeters fall in your area. Which are the driest parts of our country? Which are the wettest?

You remember that graphs also help you learn important facts. You might want to know how much rain or snow falls from month to month in a certain place. You could look at a precipitation graph. On page 268 you will see precipitation graphs for Seattle, Washington; Yuma, Arizona; and St. Louis, Missouri. The graphs show the average amounts of rain or snow that fall in each of these cities each month of the year.

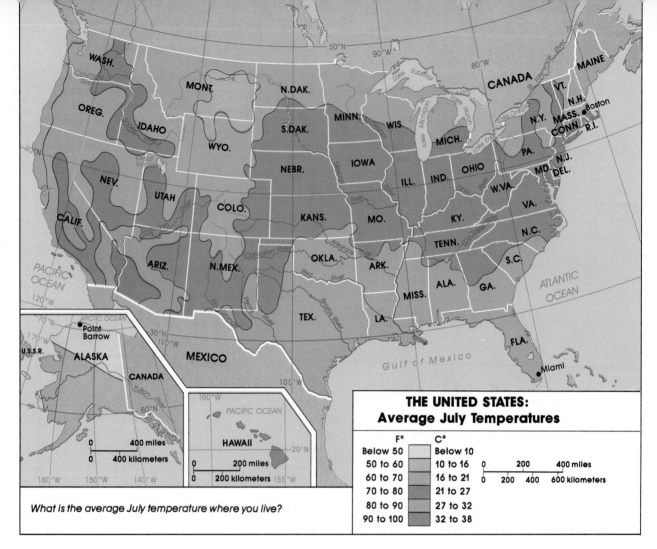

What is the average July temperature where you live?

Temperature   In most parts of our country, one season is generally hotter than the others, and one is colder than the others. Look at the map above. This map shows the average July temperatures in the United States. Find your state. What is the average July temperature in your part of the state? How did the key help you find out?

Southeastern California and southwestern Arizona have the hottest Julys in the United States. Alaska has the coldest.

Now look at the map on page 271. This map shows the average January temperatures. What is the average January temperature where you live? This map shows that Hawaii and the southern tip of Florida are the hottest places in the United States in January. Northern Alaska is the coldest. It has an average January temperature of less than −10° Fahrenheit (−23°C).

A graph is helpful if you want to know average temperatures for each month of the year for any one place. The graphs on page 271 show the average monthly temperatures for Point Barrow, Alaska; Boston, Massachusetts; and Miami, Florida. Where is it warmest in May? Where is it coldest? In which place does the temperature stay about the same all year long?

Which place has the greatest difference between winter and summer temperatures?

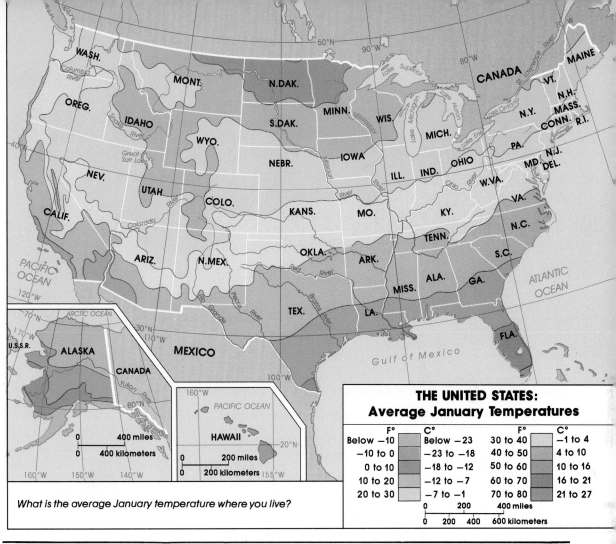

THE UNITED STATES:
Average January Temperatures

F°	C°		F°	C°
Below −10	Below −23		30 to 40	−1 to 4
−10 to 0	−23 to −18		40 to 50	4 to 10
0 to 10	−18 to −12		50 to 60	10 to 16
10 to 20	−12 to −7		60 to 70	16 to 21
20 to 30	−7 to −1		70 to 80	21 to 27

What is the average January temperature where you live?

AVERAGE MONTHLY TEMPERATURES

POINT BARROW   BOSTON   MIAMI

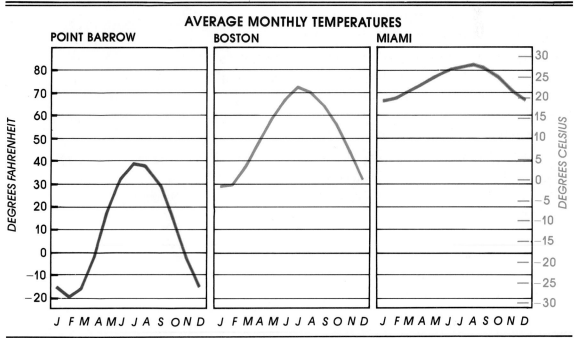

In this picture taken from Apollo 8, the earth seems to rise over the moon.

Spinning in space When you ride on a highway, you might be moving along at a speed of about 55 miles (90 km) an hour. If you fly in a jet plane, you might be traveling 560 miles (900 km) an hour. What is the fastest speed you have ever reached? Do you think you have ever moved at a speed of 795 miles (1,280 km) an hour? How would you like to speed along at 67,000 miles (107,800 km) an hour?

You may never have known it, but every day you move at a speed of 795 miles an hour. You also travel 67,000 miles an hour. This may sound strange to you. But it is true.

The first speed, 795 miles an hour, is the speed at which the earth turns, or rotates, on its **axis** every day. The earth's axis is an imaginary line that goes through the earth from the North Pole to the South Pole.

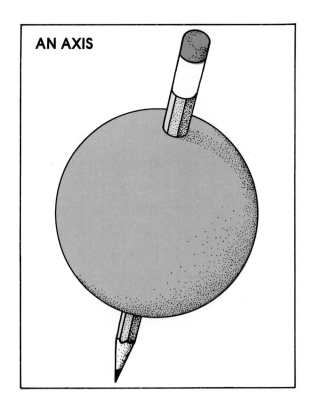

AN AXIS

In this drawing the pencil acts as the axis for the ball. Our earth spins on its axis in the same way. It makes one complete turn every 24 hours.

272

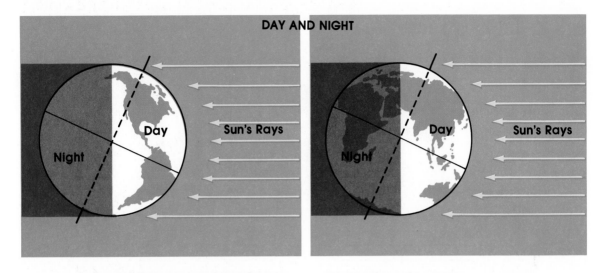

DAY AND NIGHT

The dotted line is the earth's axis. The solid line is the equator. When it is night on one side of the earth it is day on the other.

Suppose you were to push a pencil through the middle of a rubber ball. Then suppose you held the pencil steady while turning the ball around the pencil. Your ball would be doing the same thing that the earth does when it turns on its imaginary axis. The only difference would be that the ball had a pencil as an axis.

The earth's 24-hour **rotation** on its axis causes our day and night. Our heat and light come from the sun. Only about half the earth can receive the sun's rays at any given time. When our half of the earth receives the sun's rays, it is our daytime. When the other half of the earth is getting the heat and light of the sun's rays, it is our nighttime.

If the earth did not turn on its axis, the same side would always face the sun. The other half of the earth never would. If this happened, the side facing the sun would become too hot for people to live there. The side of the earth turned away from the sun would become too cold for people to live.

Journey around the sun   The earth takes 365 days to move once around the sun. So besides rotating on its axis once in every 24 hours, the earth also moves around the sun once in every year. This **revolution** is a journey of about 595 million miles (960 million km). The earth makes this journey at a speed of about 67,000 miles an hour. That means that in the past minute you have moved more than 1,000 miles (1,600 km)!

This yearly journey has a great deal to do with our climate. The revolution of the earth around the sun causes our seasons. Look carefully at the diagram on page 274. Notice that the axis of the earth is tilted. This tilt never changes. It stays the same throughout the earth's 365-day journey around the sun.

Now look at the position of the earth on June 22. June 22 is the beginning of summer in the Northern Hemisphere. You can see that the northern part of the earth is tilted toward the sun. That means the strongest, most direct rays of the sun

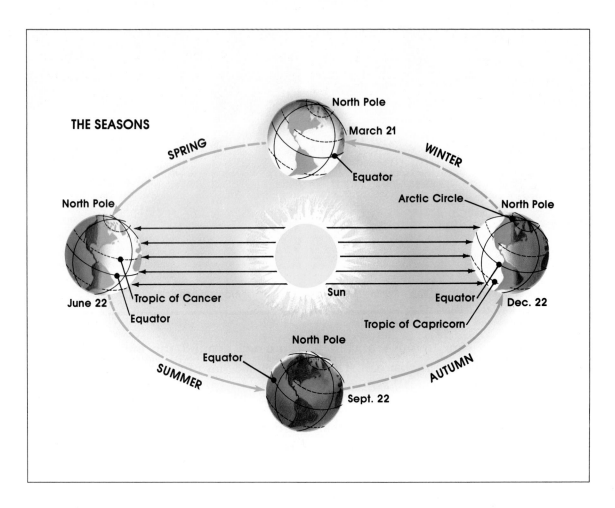

THE SEASONS

SPRING

WINTER

North Pole

March 21

Equator

Arctic Circle

North Pole

North Pole

Tropic of Cancer

Equator

Sun

Equator

Dec. 22

June 22

Tropic of Capricorn

Equator

North Pole

SUMMER

Sept. 22

AUTUMN

This diagram shows why there are seasons. The labels give the seasons for the Northern Hemisphere.

are shining on the Northern Hemisphere. When we receive the most direct rays of the sun, we have our summer.

The seasons in the Southern Hemisphere are just the opposite of those in the Northern Hemisphere. June 22 is the beginning of winter in the Southern Hemisphere. At that time the Southern Hemisphere is tilted as far away from the sun as it ever gets, so the sun's rays reach the Southern Hemisphere at a slant.

In December, January, and February, when it is winter in the Northern Hemisphere, it is summer in the Southern Hemisphere. At that time, the sun's rays reach the Northern Hemisphere at a slant while shining more directly on the Southern Hemisphere. December 22 is the first day of winter in the Northern Hemisphere. It is the first day of summer in the Southern Hemisphere. May is an autumn month in the Southern Hemisphere.

CHECKUP

1. What is weather? Climate?
2. What kinds of precipitation are there?
3. What causes day and night?
4. What causes the seasons?

Natural Resources

Riches of the earth   How long do you think you could live without fresh air or clean water? Without good soil, where would we grow our food crops? Air, water, and soil are **natural resources.** Natural resources are all the things found in and on the earth that are useful to people. They are not made by people. They are provided by nature. Without some of these resources we couldn't live.

You know that the United States is a rich and powerful country. One of the most important reasons for this is that we have so many natural resources. On pages 265–267, you read about how important water is to people in the United States. But there are many other valuable natural resources in our country.

Forests   Forests are a great natural resource. From trees come lumber and other products. Lumber is used for building houses, furniture, and many other things. The United States is the second largest lumber-producing country in the world.

A great deal of wood from our forests is made into pulp for paper products. The paper in this book is made from wood. We use more lumber and paper than any other country in the world.

Which nation produces the most lumber?

Which state produces the most lumber?

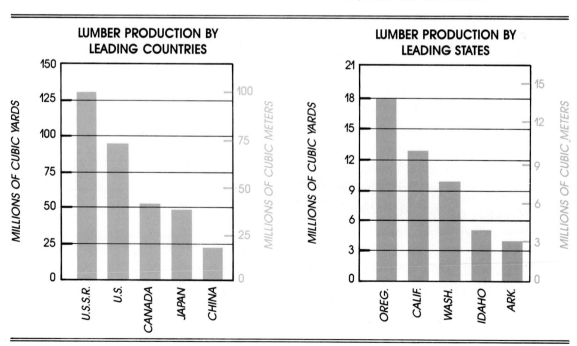

LUMBER PRODUCTION BY LEADING COUNTRIES

LUMBER PRODUCTION BY LEADING STATES

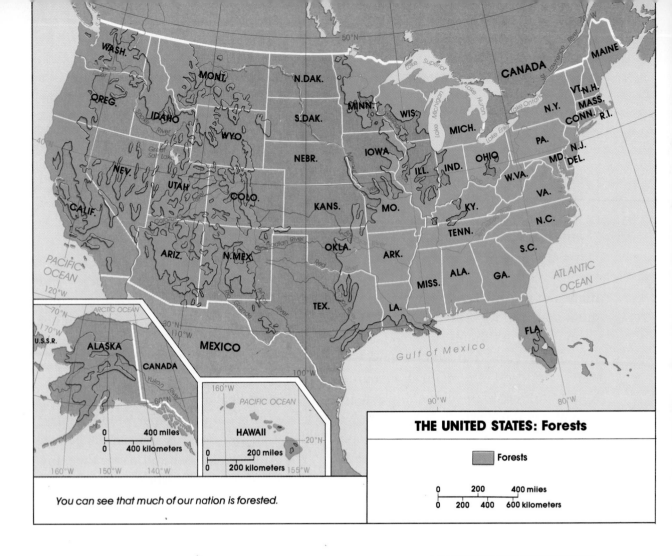

THE UNITED STATES: Forests

Forests

0   200   400 miles
0 200 400 600 kilometers

You can see that much of our nation is forested.

There are almost 740 million acres (300 million ha) of forests in the United States. Almost every part of our country has some forest land. Some large forests are found in all the regions of the United States. But the most important forests for lumbering are in the Pacific region. You will learn more about these great forests when you read about the resources of the Pacific region in Chapter 21.

Fuels Natural gas, **petroleum,** and coal are **fuels.** Fuels are very important to all of us. They are necessary to the life of the United States. Fuels give us the energy that runs our cars, buses, trucks, trains,

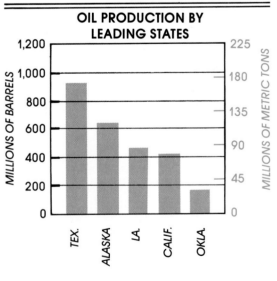

OIL PRODUCTION BY LEADING STATES

Which state produces about 600 million barrels of oil a year? About 900 million barrels?

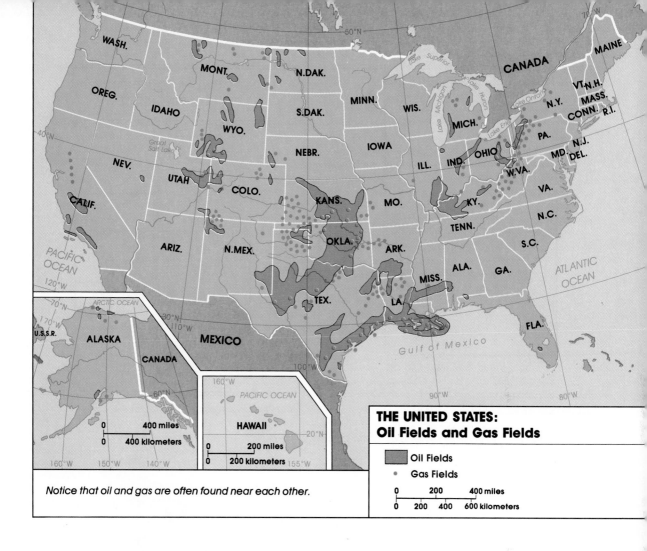

**THE UNITED STATES:
Oil Fields and Gas Fields**

Oil Fields

• Gas Fields

Notice that oil and gas are often found near each other.

ships, and airplanes. Fuels are used to heat or cool our homes and factories. They also provide electricity to run machines in our factories.

The United States is the second largest oil-producing country in the world. More than half of our states produce oil. Look at the graph on page 276. You can see that Texas, Alaska, Louisiana, California, and Oklahoma are the leading producers of oil in our country. Find these states on the map above.

Although oil was discovered in northern Alaska in 1968, it took a long time to solve the problems involved in getting the oil. It was not until the late 1970s that Alaska became one of our five leading producers of oil.

The United States is rich in oil. But we use huge amounts of it. When trees are cut down in our forests, new trees can be planted. But once oil is taken from the earth, it cannot be put back. So our supplies are running out. Today we get about a quarter of our oil from other countries. Much of that oil comes from four countries: Mexico, Saudi Arabia, Nigeria, and the United Kingdom. We also get oil from Indonesia, Canada, Venezuela, and several other countries.

Look at the map above. Find all the states that produce natural gas. This

UNITED STATES OIL PRODUCTION, 1955-1990

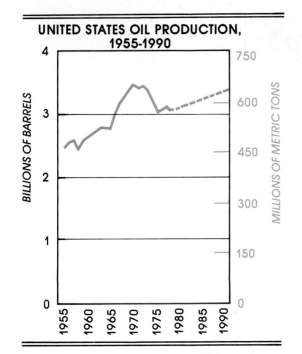

BILLIONS OF BARRELS

MILLIONS OF METRIC TONS

Oil production increased sharply in which years?

COAL PRODUCTION BY LEADING STATES

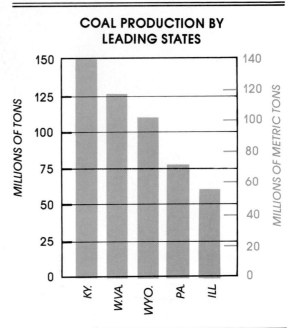

MILLIONS OF TONS

MILLIONS OF METRIC TONS

KY. W.VA. WYO. PA. ILL

Find these five states on the map at the right.

You can see how big this coal shovel is by comparing it with the bulldozer.

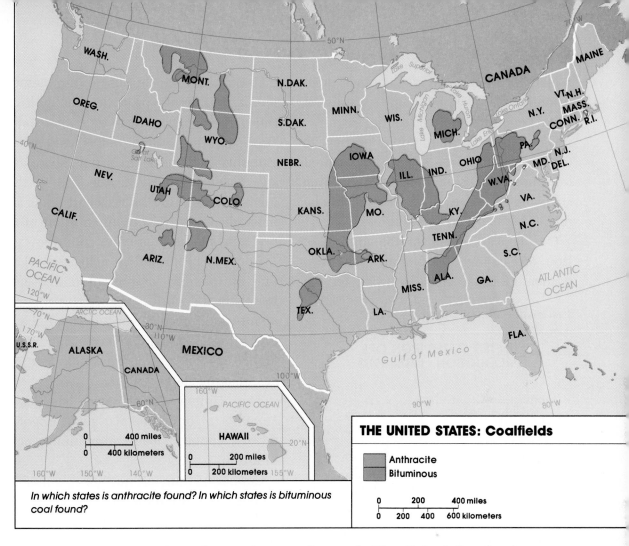

THE UNITED STATES: Coalfields

- Anthracite
- Bituminous

0   200   400 miles
0   200   400   600 kilometers

In which states is anthracite found? In which states is bituminous coal found?

country has huge supplies of natural gas. More are being found every year. However, Americans burn great amounts of gas every year. Millions of Americans use natural gas. We use it to heat our homes and cook our food. We are using up this natural resource faster than we can find new supplies. Once gone, natural gas, like oil, cannot be replaced.

Another natural resource that is an important source of energy is coal. This fuel is used to make half of all the electricity used in this country. The United States has the largest known **reserves** of coal in the world. Coal reserves are supplies of coal that have not been mined. But we know that they are in the earth and can

be used. The United States mines more coal than any other country. In 1970 about 145,000 people worked in our coal mines. By 1980 about 100,000 more people were working in these mines.

Look at the map above. You can see that coal is found in many of our states. There is more than one kind of coal. **Anthracite** (an′ thrǝ sīt), or hard coal, is found in several states. Of these states, Pennsylvania produces the most. Mining of **bituminous** (bǝ tü′ mǝ nǝs) coal, or soft coal, is also important in Pennsylvania. The map above shows you that soft coal is found in many states. The right-hand graph on page 278 shows the leading coal-mining states.

Metals   Metals are yet another great resource. The United States' supply of metals is one of the world's richest.

One of our most important metals is iron. It is found in a kind of rock called iron **ore.** By using heat from burning coal, the iron can be melted out of the rock. This is called **smelting.**

Our largest center for the mining of iron ore is the Mesabi Range in Minnesota. Find the Mesabi Range on the

Steel is made from iron ore.

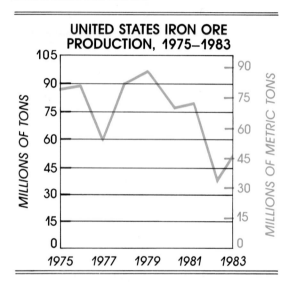

UNITED STATES IRON ORE PRODUCTION, 1975–1983

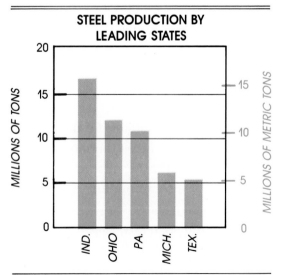

STEEL PRODUCTION BY LEADING STATES

map on page 281. Because of the Mesabi mines, Minnesota produces about three times as much iron ore as any other state. However, the United States uses great amounts of this resource, too. There are still huge amounts of iron ore in the Mesabi Range. But the very best ore is almost all used up. Now much of our iron ore comes to us from other countries.

Iron can be turned into steel. Steel is one of the most important and useful metals in the world. You will learn more about steelmaking when you read about the Middle Atlantic states. The lower graph on this page shows our leading steelmaking states.

The United States also has large amounts of other metals, such as gold, silver, copper, lead, aluminum, and uranium.

Copper is one of our most valuable metals. Its most important use is in the making of electric wire. Most of the wires that carry the electricity that we use in our homes, factories, and offices are made of copper. You might not even be able to turn on a light in your home if it were not for copper wire. The map on page 281 shows where copper is found in the United States. Again, in spite of our great reserves of copper, we use more than we can mine. So we must buy copper from other countries.

Uranium is a metal that is our newest source of energy. For many years no one knew that it was a valuable resource. Then it was found to be the main source of a new kind of energy. It is called **atomic energy,** or **nuclear energy.** This kind of energy can produce electricity, just as oil and coal can.

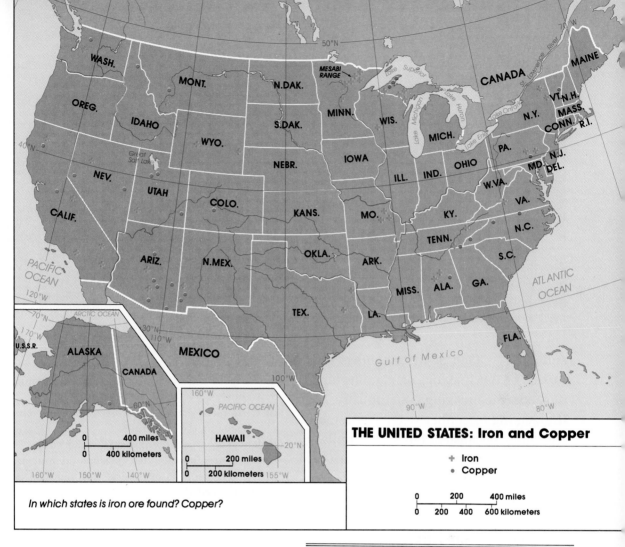

In which states is iron ore found? Copper?

THE UNITED STATES: Iron and Copper

+ Iron
• Copper

Soil and agriculture Without soil, we would have no crops. Without crops, we would not have enough food. The soil and climate in many parts of our country are very good for growing crops. The United States is the world's leading agricultural, or farming, country. We are one of the few countries in the world that grow more food than we can use. Much of our food is sent to other countries. Wheat in particular is shipped in huge amounts to other lands.

Look at the graph at the right. You can see that California is the leading farming state. Look at the graphs on pages 282–283. Name the five leading wheat states, corn states, and cotton states.

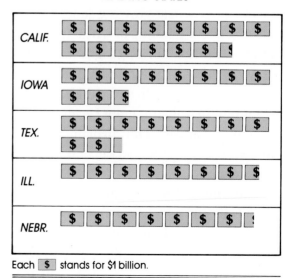

FARM PRODUCTION BY LEADING STATES

Each $ stands for $1 billion.

What is the value of farm production in Iowa?

This is the final assembly area of an airplane factory near Seattle, Washington.

Industry   One of the meanings of *industry* is the making, or manufacturing, of goods. Steelmaking is an industry. So is the making of copper wire. These industries grew because of our rich supplies of natural resources. Steelmaking uses coal and iron ore. To make copper wire, copper ore is needed.

The United States has a big textile, or cloth-making, industry. This developed because our rich soils grow fine cotton. The wheat-**milling** industry grew because of our rich wheat-growing lands. Wheat milling is the grinding of wheat into flour. Lumber milling, turning logs into lumber, grew because of our great forests. Oil refining, making oil and other products from raw petroleum, grew because of our rich oil reserves. The airplane and automobile industries also depend on many resources.

These industries and many others provide millions of jobs for Americans. The steel industry alone gives jobs to more than half a million people. You will learn more about these industries as you read about the different regions in our nation.

CHECKUP

1. Name at least four of our important natural resources.
2. What metal has recently been found to be a valuable source of energy?
3. Which is our most important farming state?
4. Name one industry that depends on iron ore, one that depends on forests, and one that depends on good soil.

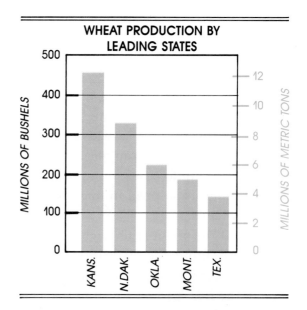

How much wheat does Kansas produce each year?

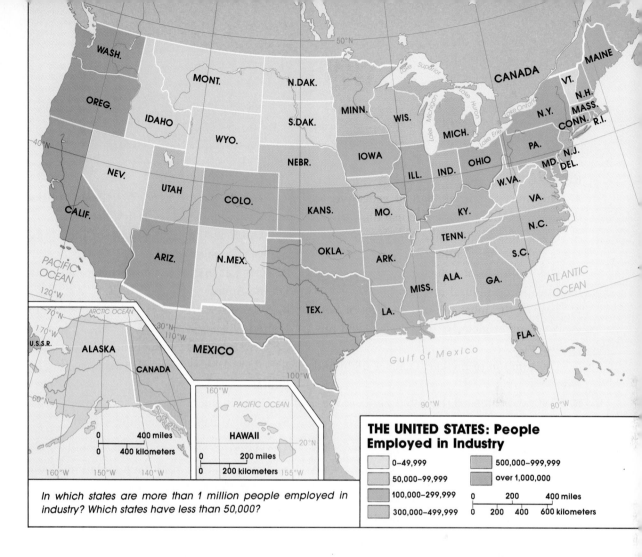

THE UNITED STATES: People Employed in Industry

- 0–49,999
- 50,000–99,999
- 100,000–299,999
- 300,000–499,999
- 500,000–999,999
- over 1,000,000

In which states are more than 1 million people employed in industry? Which states have less than 50,000?

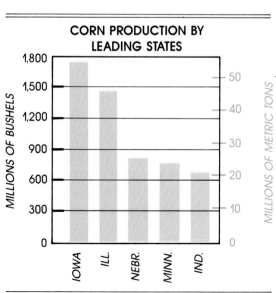

CORN PRODUCTION BY LEADING STATES

MILLIONS OF BUSHELS / MILLIONS OF METRIC TONS

IOWA, ILL., NEBR., MINN., IND.

How much corn does Illinois produce each year?

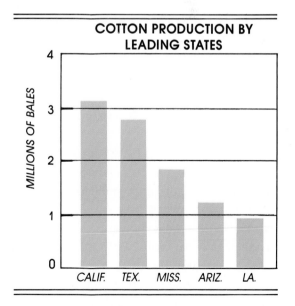

COTTON PRODUCTION BY LEADING STATES

MILLIONS OF BALES

CALIF., TEX., MISS., ARIZ., LA.

How much cotton does California produce each year?

14/CHAPTER REVIEW

KEY FACTS

1. The most important part of geography is the study of the ways people use the earth.

2. Three important tools of geography are maps, tables, and graphs.

3. The United States has a huge variety of landforms and natural resources.

4. Two of the most important parts of both weather and climate are temperature and precipitation.

5. The rotation of the earth causes night and day.

6. The revolution of the tilted earth around the sun causes the seasons.

VOCABULARY QUIZ

Beside the number of each sentence, write the word or words that best completes the sentence. Write on a sheet of paper.

1. Two parts, or _____, of the United States are the Mountain West and the Southeast.

2. The _____ _____ of most of Alaska is less than 5 people per square mile (2 per sq km).

3. At the mouth of the Mississippi River a ____ has formed.

4. Electricity created by the force of moving water is called _____ power.

5. Rain, sleet, snow, mist, and hail are all forms of _____.

6. The earth rotates on its ____ .

7. It takes a year for the earth to complete one _____ around the sun.

8. Another name for oil is _____ .

9. Hard coal is called _____ .

10. Soft coal is called _____ coal.

REVIEW QUESTIONS

1. What is the difference between a political map and a physical, or relief, map?

2. Which is the largest state in the United States? The smallest?

3. Name at least five landforms found in the United States.

4. Where are the highest mountains in the United States found?

5. Which state is made up entirely of islands?

6. What is the difference between weather and climate?

7. Why do we have night and day?

8. What causes the changing seasons?

ACTIVITIES

1. In an almanac, find the population of your state for the past ten censuses. Make a line graph to show how the population has changed. Show the number of people along the side and the years across the bottom of the graph. Give your graph a title. If you live in Alaska or Hawaii, use the United States population instead.

2. In an almanac, find the names of the world's ten largest lakes. Label the lakes on a world map. How many of the Great Lakes are labeled on your map?

3. Keep a record of the weather in your area for a few weeks. Record the temperature at the same time of day each morning and afternoon. Note whether it was raining, snowing, sunny, cloudy, or foggy. What was the highest morning temperature? The lowest? What was the highest afternoon temperature? The lowest? What were the average morning and afternoon temperatures? How often was there precipitation? Were most days sunny or cloudy?

READING A MAP: WORLD POPULATION DENSITY

SKILLS PRACTICE

On page 259 of this chapter you saw a map of population density in the United States. That map also shows the 25 largest cities in the United States. The map below shows population density in the whole world. It also shows the world's 25 largest cities. Use the map below, as well as the map on page 259, to answer the following questions. You may need to refer to the Atlas, pages 466–475, as well.

1. Are any of the 25 largest cities in the United States located in your state? How many?

2. Name the cities in the United States that have more than 1 million people.

3. Which state, Nevada or Massachusetts, has a higher population density?

4. Which of the 25 largest cities in the United States is located at 30° north latitude and 90° west longitude?

5. How many of the cities shown on the United States population map are within 100 miles (160 km) of a large body of water?

6. Two states each have three or more cities among the 25 largest cities in the United States. Name them.

7. Name the city in the United States that is one of the 25 largest cities in the world.

8. Which continent has the largest number of cities that are among the 25 largest cities in the world?

9. What is the southernmost city shown on the world population map?

10. What is the northernmost city shown on the world population map?

11. How many people per square mile are there in most of Australia? Per square kilometer?

12. What is the population density in most of central India?

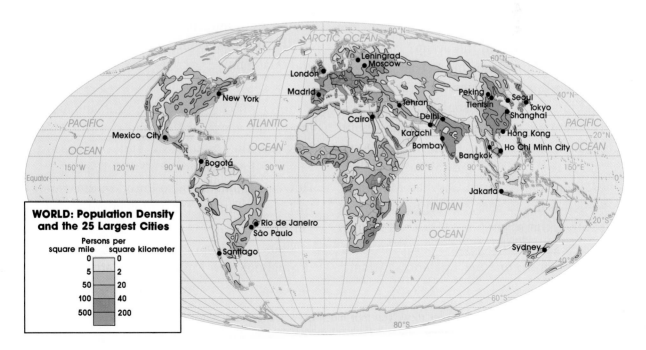

WORLD: Population Density and the 25 Largest Cities

Persons per

square mile	square kilometer
0	0
5	2
50	20
100	40
500	200

The Land and Climate

VOCABULARY

landscape	sound
promontory	temperature
elevation	extreme
upland	

The Atlantic coast   The United States is a huge nation of about 3,619,000 square miles (9,373,000 sq km). It is divided into 50 states. As we said earlier, it would be hard to study all 50 states at once, so we will divide them into 7 regions.

The first region, New England, has six states. They are Maine, New Hampshire, Vermont, Massachusetts, Rhode Island, and Connecticut.

The two main features of the New England **landscape** are coastline and mountains. Five of the six states are along the Atlantic coast. Which New England state does not border on the ocean?

Along Maine's northern coast are many bays and **promontories.** High, rocky land that juts out into the sea along a coastline is called a promontory. The highest point on the Atlantic coast is on Mount Desert Island in Acadia (ə kā′ dē ə) National Park, Maine. Here is found Cadillac Mountain, which is 1,530 feet (467 m) high. Farther south, there are stretches of sandy beaches as well as jagged coastline. A famous feature of New England's Atlantic coast is Cape Code in Massachusetts. Part of this peninsula is Cape Cod National Seashore.

The Appalachian Mountains   The second main feature is the mountain range known as the Appalachian Mountains. In the United States, this range extends from Maine south through all the rest of the New England states except Rhode Island. In New Hampshire, the Appalachians are called the White Mountains. The highest peak in the White Mountains is Mount Washington. With an **elevation** of 6,288 feet (1,917 m), Mount Washington is also the highest point in New England. In Vermont, the Appalachians are called the Green Mountains. In Massachusetts, the Appalachians are called the Berkshires. The Appalachians continue south through Connecticut and the Middle Atlantic and southern states as far as northern Georgia and Alabama.

Other features   Rolling hills and **uplands** make up most of the countryside between the mountains and the coast. Most of the lowlands are along the coast. However, some are also found in the central areas and in the Connecticut River valley.

There are many rivers and lakes throughout New England. The largest lake

The map shows you that much of New England is covered by the Appalachians. The photograph shows the rugged, rocky shores typical of the Maine coast.

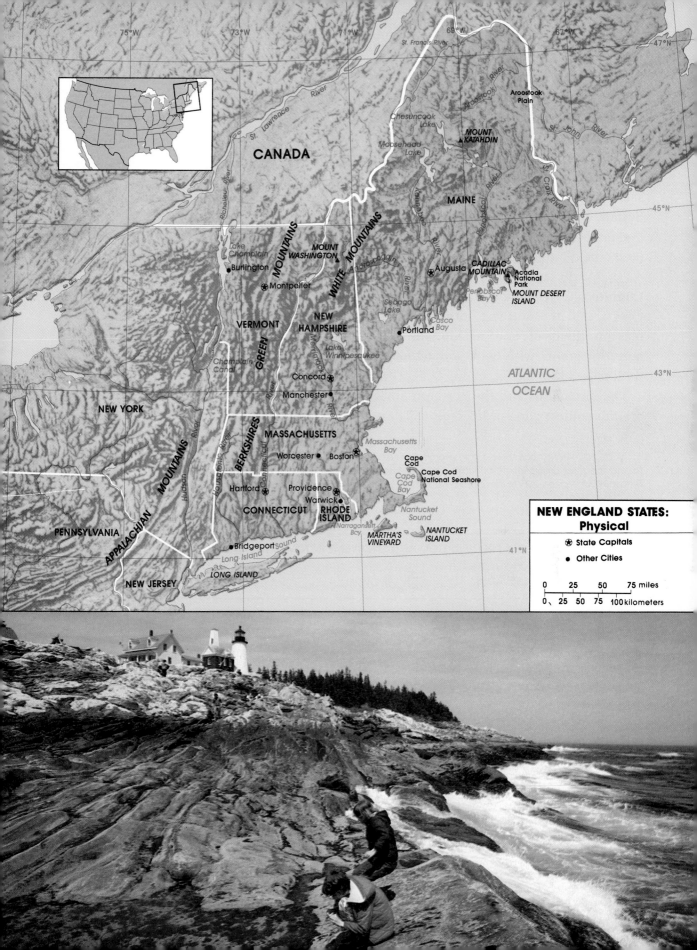

CANADA

St. Francis River

Aroostook
Plain

MOUNT
KATAHDIN

Chesuncook
Lake

Moosehead
Lake

MAINE

St. John River

St. Croix River

Lake
Champlain

Burlington

MOUNTAINS

MOUNT
WASHINGTON

WHITE MOUNTAINS

Augusta

CADILLAC
MOUNTAIN

Acadia
National
Park

MOUNT DESERT
ISLAND

Penobscot
Bay

Montpelier

VERMONT

NEW
HAMPSHIRE

Androscoggin River

Sebago
Lake

Casco
Bay

Portland

GREEN

Champlain
Canal

Lake
Winnipesaukee

ATLANTIC
OCEAN

Concord

Manchester

Merrimack River

NEW YORK

BERKSHIRES

MASSACHUSETTS

Worcester

Boston

Massachusetts
Bay

Cape
Cod

Cape Cod
National Seashore

APPALACHIAN MOUNTAINS

Hudson River

Housatonic River

Connecticut River

Hartford

Providence

Warwick

CONNECTICUT

RHODE
ISLAND

Cape
Cod
Bay

Nantucket
Sound

PENNSYLVANIA

Bridgeport

Narragansett
Bay

Long Island
Sound

MARTHA'S
VINEYARD

NANTUCKET
ISLAND

LONG ISLAND

NEW JERSEY

NEW ENGLAND STATES:
Physical

✪ State Capitals

● Other Cities

0   25   50   75 miles

0   25 50 75 100 kilometers

is Lake Champlain, which is between Vermont and New York State and extends into Canada. The longest river is the Connecticut River. It begins in New Hampshire and flows along the New Hampshire–Vermont border, through Massachusetts, and empties into Long Island **Sound.** Among the other large rivers are the Penobscot (pə näb′ skət), Kennebec (ken ə bek′), and Merrimack.

Climate   The mountains, the Atlantic Ocean, and the northern location all affect the climate of New England. The table and the graph will help you to better understand this region.

The mountains and the northern areas are the coldest parts of the region. These areas also have greater **temperature extremes.** Temperature extremes are the highest and lowest recorded temperatures. Along the coast, it is milder throughout the year.

Every month has some precipitation. Winters with 100 inches (254 cm) of snow are common in parts of Maine. Snowfall is heavy throughout the rest of New England as well. Cloudy and overcast skies are also common to this area.

Mount Washington is the windiest place in the United States. The average daily wind speed is 35 miles (56 km) per hour. Wind speeds greater than 230 miles (370 km) per hour have been recorded there.

You can see that some parts of New England have very severe winters. How-

For each city, the first bar shows total precipitation. The second bar shows snowfall alone. To find the total precipitation, scientists figure out how much rain the snow is equal to. Then they add that amount to the rainfall. From 6 to 30 inches (15–76 cm) of snow equals 1 inch (2.5 cm) of rain.

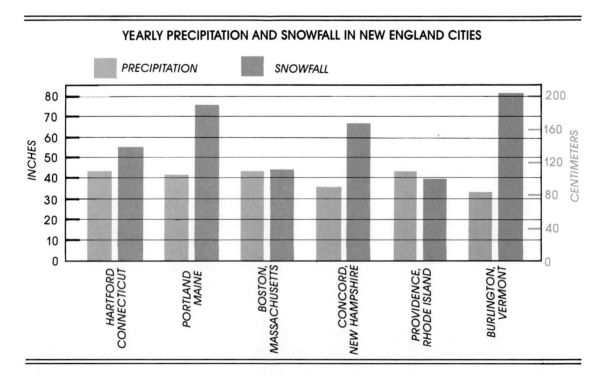

YEARLY PRECIPITATION AND SNOWFALL IN NEW ENGLAND CITIES

TEMPERATURE, NEW ENGLAND CITIES								
Weather station	Average January temperature		Average July temperature		Temperature extreme °F		Temperature extreme °C	
	°F	°C	°F	°C	High	Low	High	Low
Hartford, Conn.	25	−4	73	23	102	−26	39	−33
Portland, Maine	22	−6	68	20	103	−39	39	−39
Boston, Mass.	29	−2	73	23	102	−2	39	−24
Concord, N.H.	21	−6	70	21	102	−37	39	−38
Providence, R.I.	28	−2	72	22	104	−13	40	−25
Burlington, Vt.	17	−8	70	21	101	−30	38	−34

ever, winter is only one part of the New England climate. Fresh spring growth and autumn colors mark changing seasons. Coastal winds, though harsh in winter, are cooling and relaxing in the summer.

CHECKUP

1. What are the two main features of the New England landscape?
2. Name two factors that affect New England's climate.
3. What are the coldest parts of New England? The mildest?

Mining, Fishing, and Other Industries

VOCABULARY

mineral	spermaceti
quarry	synthetic
fleet	armory
quota	import
trawler	

Minerals The resources of New England, like the landscape and climate, are varied. Sand, gravel, and stone are found in all the states. These **mineral** resources are needed for many types of construction. From the **quarries** of northern New England come granite, slate, and marble, which are used in buildings throughout the United States.

Vermont is a leading source of talc in the United States. Talc is a soft mineral that when ground into a powder is used in making crayons, paint, paper, soap, and talcum powder. In slab form it is used in electrical insulation and as furnace insulation.

Vermont ranks second in the United States in the production of asbestos and slate. Asbestos is a fire-resistant mineral used for purposes similar to those of slab talc. Slate is a hard, blue-gray, layered rock well known to students of earlier days. Their lessons were written on a slate chalkboard in the front of the classroom. Many students had smaller slates for use at their seats. Slate roofs are still found on some old buildings. Slate roofs are fireproof and don't wear out. However, they are brittle and break quite easily, which is one reason that slate is no longer in common use for roofs.

A huge slab of stone is lifted from a quarry by a motor-driven pulley.

Quarrying   It is difficult to get granite, marble, and slate from the ground and prepare these stones for use. Some stone is taken from underground mines and some from deep quarries or open pits. Workers use torches on the slabs of stone. The heat of the torch makes the stone expand and crack. A skillful worker can crack a slab of stone in just the right way.

Stone cutters use special saws to cut the huge slabs of granite and marble into more manageable sizes and shapes. Some slabs are cut into smaller slabs for steps, blocks for buildings, or tiles for floors. Polishing machines are used to smooth the surface of the hard, heavy stone.

Some craftworkers do the carving and sculpturing of granite and marble. Others carve inscriptions on the polished surface of the stone.

Fishing   Fishing is an industry that has a long tradition in New England. As the colonists settled along the New England coast, they found the tall pine, fir, and oak trees to be good resources for shipbuilding. Soon fishing **fleets** were sailing out of harbors from Maine to Connecticut. They searched far into the North Atlantic Ocean for cod, flounder, halibut, and haddock. Mackerel and herring were most often found swimming in large schools in the waters off the coast. Here also were found lobsters and other shellfish.

Fishing remains important to this day. However, there have been many changes. For many years fishing fleets from other countries had such good catches that they were using up the stock of fish in the rich fishing grounds of the Atlantic. The New England fish catch dropped from about 700 million pounds (320 million kg) in 1965 to less than 500 million pounds (227 million kg) in 1975.

In 1977 the United States extended its fishing zone from 12 nautical miles (22 km) to 200 nautical miles (370 km). (Nautical miles are longer than the miles we use on land.) This meant that foreign fishing fleets needed permits to fish within 200 nautical miles of our coast. Our own fleets have had to limit their catches. Some types of fish, like cod, flounder, and haddock, were becoming so scarce that **quotas** were set up. Limiting catches would let the fish supply grow.

Changes have also been made in the fishing vessels themselves. Boats with sails are now used almost entirely for pleasure. Today's fishing **trawler** is likely to have a large diesel engine, a radio, sonar, and refrigerated areas for storing the catch. The radio allows a captain to talk to other captains in the fleet, as well as to people on shore. Sonar uses sound waves to find schools of fish.

Diesel power, good quarters for the crew, and refrigeration make it possible to travel farther after the schools of fish. (Of course, that in turn means the captain and the crew are away from their families longer.) With the extension of the zone,

A load of pollack and other kinds of fish has just been dumped into this fishing boat from Gloucester, Massachusetts.

better equipment, and quotas on the catches, the fish catch has grown. It is now about as big as it was in 1965.

Whaling   Once, New England ports sheltered many whaling ships, as well as fishing boats. Whales provided many valuable products. People burned whale oil in their lamps. From the whale oil, they got a waxlike solid called **spermaceti** (spėr mə set′ ē), which they used in making candles. They used whalebone in making fans and other articles.

In the early days, whales were caught in the coastal waters of New England. In time, however, whales became scarce there. As the years passed, whaling captains hunted the giant creatures in distant waters. New England whaling ships sailed around the southern tip of South America and then far north in the Pacific Ocean. Sometimes a whaling ship would be away from its home port for as long as 2 or 3 years.

Many sailors never returned from these long voyages. A whale could crush a whaleboat with one blow of its giant tail. Indeed, huge whales now and then sank the whaling ships themselves.

For more than 50 years after the Revolutionary War, whaling remained important. Then people learned how to get petroleum from the earth. When this happened, whale oil was no longer needed for lamps. The New England whalers turned to fishing or other jobs, and the old whaling ships slowly rotted in the harbors.

Textiles   For many years New England was the most important manufacturing center in America. Here were the necessary harbors, trading ships, skilled workers, and water power. Manufacturing is still important in New England but the products have changed somewhat.

One of the most important and earliest industries of New England was textile manufacturing. You read about Samuel Slater and the first textile mill in Chapter 8. You may remember that in the nineteenth century, northern mills made cloth from cotton grown on southern plantations.

During the first half of the twentieth century, most of New England's cotton mills either closed down or moved to the southeastern states. Here the mills were near the cotton supply. Also, wages were lower in the South. Some New England cotton mills closed because there was less demand for cotton. People wanted the new **synthetic** materials instead.

New England is still a leading producer of textiles. Today, however, the mills are more likely to produce woolens. Most of the raw wool comes from New Zealand and Australia. It is carried by ship to Boston Harbor. From there it goes to spinning and weaving mills in nearby cities. Here, fine woolen cloth is made.

Shipbuilding   Although tall-masted trading ships are a part of history, shipbuilding is still important in New England. Some of today's shipbuilders make sailboats and yachts for recreational use. Others work in the shipyards that build modern vessels. Nuclear-powered submarines for the United States Navy are built at Groton, Connecticut, near New London. There are other shipyards along the New England coast.

Small, delicate, precise instruments are needed for modern ships. Skilled workers in New England make these instruments, as well as electronic equipment, computers, gauges, and other equipment.

Silverware and firearms   In a sense, precision manufacturing has long been a part of the story of New England. Silverware and firearms, both of which take great skill in manufacturing, have been made in New England since the colonial days. Paul Revere is famous for his midnight ride. He is almost as well known for his skill as a silversmith. Even today, a certain style of bowl is called the Revere bowl. Of course, Revere was not the only New England silversmith. There were others who made fine silver. And people today still look to New England for beautiful examples of the craft.

Many of our soldiers in the Revolutionary War were armed with guns produced at Springfield, Massachusetts. The **armory** here has made firearms for United States soldiers for most of our history. Now there is a museum at the Springfield armory. There the history of firearms can be studied. Hartford, Connecticut, was the home of one of the country's best-known guns: the Colt six-shooter revolver. Many high quality sporting guns are still made in Connecticut and Massachusetts.

Leather   The leather goods industry is another New England industry that is no longer as large as it once was. Leather goods, such as saddles, harnesses, and footwear, were made from colonial days to the early 1900s. Then came the auto-

In this picture of the shipyard at Quincy, Massachusetts, you can see three tankers under construction. They will carry liquified natural gas.

mobile. You can guess what happened to the demand for saddles and harnesses then.

Shoe manufacturing has suffered for different reasons. A greater variety of materials are being used in the making of shoes. Leather is still important, but many shoes are made of synthetics. These shoes usually cost less than leather shoes, so there is less demand for leather shoes. A second reason is that much footwear is now **imported** from foreign countries. The value of imported footwear grew from $629 million in 1970 to over a billion dollars in 1975. By 1982 the value of imported footwear was more than $3.4 billion. The next time you buy a pair of shoes, look at either the shoes or the box they came in to see where they were made.

Shoes are still being made in New England, especially in Massachusetts. Maine has developed a reputation for moccasins and outdoor leather boots. Boots, moccasins, and other leather products have made leather a major industry in Maine today.

CHECKUP

1. Name two minerals found in New England and tell how each is used.
2. Why were quotas set up for United States and foreign fishing fleets?
3. How have synthetic materials changed both the textile and the shoe industries?

293

Agriculture and Forests

Hay, livestock, and vegetables New England's soil is not suited for all kinds of agriculture. In some places it is quite rocky and too thin for raising crops like wheat or oats. However, the cool, moist climate and thin soil is suited to raising hay. Some of the land can be used for the grazing of dairy cattle. Raising chickens is another important farming activity in each of the six states. Neither chickens nor cattle need level land, and there is a ready market for both nearby. New England does not grow enough feed for these farm animals. Farmers depend on farms in the North Central states for grain for their **livestock.** Small patches of level land are used to raise vegetables, which are sold at roadside stands or in nearby towns and cities.

Growing tobacco There is some level land along the coast and in the river valleys and in the central regions. Here the land is more **fertile** and better suited to raising crops. One crop that is raised in the fertile lands of Connecticut and Massachusetts is tobacco. From colonial times, farmers living in the Connecticut River valley have grown tobacco. Not as much tobacco is grown today as it was 30 or 40 years ago. However, tobacco still is a good **cash crop** because it gives more **income** per acre than most other crops.

Growing potatoes In northeastern Maine's Aroostook (ə rüs′ tək) River valley, the soil is rich and silty, or fine-grained. Summers are cool and moist. Even though the growing season is short, it is long enough to raise good potato crops. The Aroostook Valley has become famous for fine quality potatoes. The business of raising potatoes makes up nearly 60 percent of Maine's income from crops.

The Aroostook Valley is not very close to the major cities, but potatoes keep very well and are easy to transport. A cool dry place is suitable for storage. Maine potatoes are sold throughout the United States and Europe.

Blueberries and cranberries Two other important New England crops are grown in the eastern parts of Maine and Massachusetts. The two crops are blueberries and cranberries. You have probably enjoyed eating both fruits without knowing where they were grown. Maine is the leading producer of low-bush blueberries in the United States. The bushes, which are 6 to 18 inches (15 cm to 45 cm) high, grow wild in the fields and on the hillsides of Maine. The berries ripen in August. At that time, Indian families come from Maine's northern neighbor, New Brunswick, Canada, to help with the harvest. Most of the berries are shipped to other parts of the country. Some are shipped fresh. Others are frozen or canned.

Workers on Cape Cod guide cranberries to a pipe that carries them into a truck.

The second crop, cranberries, is popular throughout the United States during the Thanksgiving and Christmas holidays. The **bogs** near Cape Cod, Massachusetts, are the major source of the nation's cranberries. Bogs are wet swampy lands. They are drained when the plants need to be cared for. Then the water is allowed to flood the bogs again. When the bogs are flooded, the water helps to keep weeds from growing. Flooding also helps to keep the plants from freezing in early spring and late fall. The ripe berries are harvested in the fall.

A forested region   Overall, about 75 percent of New England is forested. Maine, New Hampshire, and Vermont have the highest percentages of forested land. Several kinds of trees are found in New En-

gland forests. Pine and spruce are quite common. Both are **evergreens** and keep their needles all year. You may be familiar with the types of pine and spruce that are used as Christmas trees. New England forests also have **deciduous** (di sij′ ú əs) trees, such as oak and chestnut, which lose their leaves in the fall.

To the Native Americans, and later to the Europeans who settled in New England, the forests played an important role. The forests sheltered the game that provided food and clothing. Both Indians and colonists used firewood in cooking and heating. Logs and lumber were used for homes and other buildings and for furniture. As you know, the lumber from coastal forests was used in shipbuilding. And as you will see, the sugar maple yielded yet another valuable product.

Maple syrup   Have you ever had maple candy from Vermont? Perhaps you have had real maple syrup on pancakes or waffles. The flavor of real maple syrup is different from that of pancake syrup, which contains only a little maple syrup.

The history of Vermont maple syrup and candy goes back to pioneer days. For many early settlers, maple syrup and candy were the only sweets. To make the syrup and candy, the settlers collected sap from certain kinds of maple trees. This was done in early spring. Often the snow was still on the ground and the air was cold and wintry. However, within the tree, the sap had begun to rise. The settler bored a hole into the tree and placed a tap in the hole. The sap flowed slowly through the tap and into a container. Each day while the sap was rising, a collector went from tree to tree emptying the containers. The sap was taken to the sugarhouse where it was boiled for a long time to remove most of the water. Nearly 40 buckets of sap were needed to produce one bucket of syrup. Today, some farmers use the same methods to get the sap. Others use a system of plastic tubing to carry the sap from the taps to the sugarhouse. That way there is no need to go from tree to tree collecting buckets.

Trees, a renewable resource   The Indians left the forests almost untouched. However, the colonists cleared huge areas of forests for their farms and towns. There was so much forest land that no one worried about how much wood was cut. Today, the demand for wood products is so high that we must keep track of the amount of wood we cut. Fortunately, forests are a **renewable resource.**

The boy in the picture (left) *is emptying a bucket of sap into a pail. The horse-drawn wagon in the background will carry the sap to the sugarhouse. This system of plastic tubing* (right) *carries the sap directly to the sugarhouse.*

In order to have a supply of wood in the future, people now treat trees as "crops." Only large, older trees that yield large amounts of good lumber are cut. New trees are planted to take their place. Sometimes the planting is done even before the old trees are harvested.

Many lumber and paper companies own large **tracts** of forested land. National and state governments also control large forested areas. Many farmers set aside parts of their land for growing trees.

This crane is loading logs onto the truck that will take them to the papermill.

Cutting timber   In the past, workers called **lumberjacks** cut down trees with axes and handsaws. Sometimes two people would work together with a two-man saw, but the lumberjack's job was still difficult and dangerous. For this reason, legends developed about the strength and daring of the lumberjack.

Today the colorful lumberjack, equipped only with a sharp axe and handsaw, lives only in legends. Hand tools are still used for some jobs, but most cutting is done with powerful chain saws. Power saws have made lumbering easier, although it is still hard work.

Hauling timber   After trees are felled and the branches trimmed off, the logs must be hauled out of the forest. Until about 60 years ago, this job was done by teams of horses or oxen. In the spring, when the snow melted, the ground was too muddy for the animals to get through. So the logs were cut in winter while the ground was still frozen. The oxen dragged the logs down the mountains and hills to rivers like the Kennebec and Penobscot. Then in the spring when the ice melted, the lumberjacks would guide huge log drives down the swiftly flowing rivers to the sawmills.

Today trucks have replaced both the oxen and the log drives. Most woodcutting is still done in the winter, because the logging roads become seas of mud in the spring. It is as hard for the trucks to get through as it once was for the oxen. Very few logs are moved by water.

Uses of timber   Today, as in colonial times, timber has many uses. Some trees are cut for **saw timber.** Lumber used in the building trades comes from saw timber. Some trees are used for making plywood and furniture. A few are very carefully chosen for use in boatbuilding. Smaller trees are cut for pulpwood, which is used in making paper.

Pulpwood and paper are major industries in New England. Maine is a pulpwood leader not only in New England, but in the nation as a whole. New England is noted for fine paper. Some paper is sold nationally, and some is sent to foreign markets.

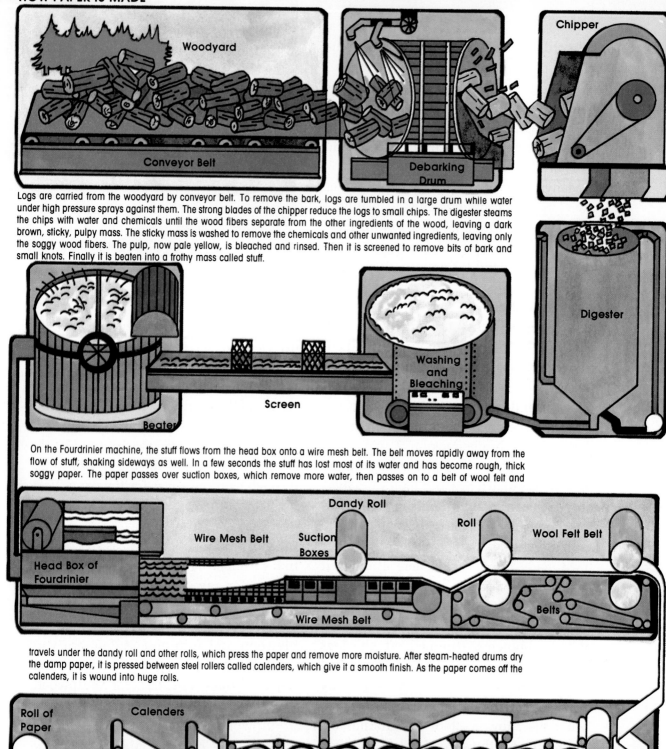

Woodyard

Conveyor Belt

Debarking Drum

Chipper

Logs are carried from the woodyard by conveyor belt. To remove the bark, logs are tumbled in a large drum while water under high pressure sprays against them. The strong blades of the chipper reduce the logs to small chips. The digester steams the chips with water and chemicals until the wood fibers separate from the other ingredients of the wood, leaving a dark brown, sticky, pulpy mass. The sticky mass is washed to remove the chemicals and other unwanted ingredients, leaving only the soggy wood fibers. The pulp, now pale yellow, is bleached and rinsed. Then it is screened to remove bits of bark and small knots. Finally it is beaten into a frothy mass called stuff.

Digester

Washing and Bleaching

Screen

Beater

On the Fourdrinier machine, the stuff flows from the head box onto a wire mesh belt. The belt moves rapidly away from the flow of stuff, shaking sideways as well. In a few seconds the stuff has lost most of its water and has become rough, thick soggy paper. The paper passes over suction boxes, which remove more water, then passes on to a belt of wool felt and

Dandy Roll

Roll

Wire Mesh Belt

Suction Boxes

Wool Felt Belt

Head Box of Fourdrinier

Wire Mesh Belt

Belts

travels under the dandy roll and other rolls, which press the paper and remove more moisture. After steam-heated drums dry the damp paper, it is pressed between steel rollers called calenders, which give it a smooth finish. As the paper comes off the calenders, it is wound into huge rolls.

Roll of Paper

Calenders

Drying Drums

Making paper   The first step in supplying pulpwood for the mill is planting and caring for trees. Spruce and pine are commonly grown for pulpwood. When the trees are ready for harvesting, workers may clear an area by cutting all the trees. If the trees vary in size, the workers cut down only the older trees, leaving the younger trees to grow. The fallen trees are trimmed of their branches, and cut into logs about 4 feet (1 m) long. Machines load them on large trucks that haul the logs to the mill.

At the mill, the bark is removed and the logs are cut into chips or ground up. The chips (or ground wood) are mixed with water and chemicals to form the pulp. As you can see in the drawing, the pulp passes through a number of machines. After the last stage shown in the drawing, the processes differ according to the kind of paper being made.

Pulp, paper, and the environment
Pulp mills need a lot of water. Many mills are on freshwater streams and rivers. In the past, the water and chemicals used in making paper were dumped into the streams. The water became polluted. Now at most mills the chemicals are removed and the water is cooled before it goes into the streams. The animals and plants that need the streams again have fresh, clean water.

Not all paper is made from newly cut pulpwood. When you have time, look at your notebook or at other paper supplies in your room or at home. On some paper goods or their wrappers, you will see a stamp saying that the paper is **recycled.** That means it is made of paper that has been used before. The used paper was collected, perhaps in a paper drive. Then the collected paper went through processes like the ones described earlier.

CHECKUP

1. In what ways do the soil and climate affect the types of crops grown in New England?
2. What are four important crops grown in this region?
3. Name three ways the early colonists and Indians used the forests.
4. How are forests used today?

Tourism, People, and Communities

—VOCABULARY—

tourism	gristmill
broadleaf	urban
foliage	metropolitan
landmark	area

Tourism   In a way, **tourism** is one of New England's important industries. All kinds of businesses are helped by the tourists who come to New England throughout the year. Tourists need restaurants, motels, and gas stations. They buy many different things, from magazines to suntan oil to skis. Many businesses have opened just to take care of the needs and wants of tourists.

Camping   Some visitors come to New England to camp in the national and state forests and parks. Most camping grounds have picnic tables, places for cooking, and safe, clear, water. Nature trails allow hikers to enjoy the beauty of the woods and

This peaceful Connecticut village is typical of many New England villages.

to see the many living things found there. These forests and parks are a welcome change for people who spend most of the year in the city.

Beautiful foliage   The maple, oak, beech, and other **broadleaf** trees give New England a resource other than lumber and paper. Each autumn the leaves of these trees change from green to bright red, yellow, orange, and other colors. The brilliant **foliage** attracts tourists who plan fall trips just to see the wooded hills and valleys in full color.

Winter sports   The New England winter also brings visitors. These people come for winter sports, especially skiing. In the mountains of Vermont alone, there are more than 50 ski areas. In most winters there is plenty of snow. However, if nature does not provide snow, snowmaking machines are put to work.

Coastal attractions   Another tourist attraction is the seacoast. The Maine coast is dotted with small islands, about 2,000 of them between New Brunswick and New Hampshire. The bays and promontories make a rugged, rocky coast that many people enjoy. Acadia National Park, much of which is on Mount Desert Island, just to the northeast of Penobscot Bay, has more than 3 million visitors a year. There they enjoy fishing, boating, and just watching the sea. Southeastern Maine's Old Orchard Beach, near Portland, is one of the few sandy beaches in northern New England. It attracts tourists from up and down the coast.

As we mentioned earlier, one of the nation's most famous landscape features is Cape Cod in Massachusetts. Cape Cod has the shape of a hook. The body of water within the hook is Cape Cod Bay. As you may know, the *Mayflower* anchored in Cape Cod Bay while some of the Pilgrims explored the coastline for a place to settle. Now Cape Cod is a national tourist attraction. It is crowded with visitors during the summer months. Some people return to Cape Cod year after year.

Historic sites   A different type of attraction found in New England is the restored village. Mystic, Connecticut, was a seaport in the 1800s. Today, Mystic Seaport, a museum, has restored a large area so that you can see how people lived in a coastal village more than a hundred years ago. You can see how people dressed,

These children have just skied through a covered bridge near Franconia, New Hampshire.

Crew members work in the rigging of a sailing ship at Mystic Seaport in Connecticut.

the tools they used, and the homes and stores they built. Up the coast, in Maine, near the mouth of the Kennebec River, the Bath Iron Works and Marine Museum help one to understand old methods of shipbuilding and America's seafaring history.

Both Plymouth Rock, where the Pilgrims came ashore from the *Mayflower*, and the reconstructed village, Plimoth Plantation, facing Cape Cod Bay, can be visited throughout the year. Docked nearby is a full-sized model of the *Mayflower*. As you explore the small ship, you get a feeling for the crowded conditions of the passengers and crew. At Sturbridge, in south central Massachusetts, is another reconstructed village. Here one can see how people lived in the early 1800s.

Throughout New England there are reminders of our nation's past. Tourists enjoy traveling through small rural villages that at first glance seem to have changed very little since they were first founded 200 or 300 years ago. It is still possible to find covered bridges that were built across small, clear streams more than 100 years ago. There are old farm and village homes that served as stops for runaway slaves using the Underground Railroad. You read about that route to freedom earlier.

Historic **landmarks** abound in New England towns. You could spend several days visiting those in Boston alone. In fact, one thing that ties the New England states together is their historic flavor. Of course, much of New England is very up-to-date. But as one travels through the region, one gets a feeling for history that is found in few other parts of the nation.

A region of villages More than 12 million people live in the six New England states. Only about one of every four lives in either a small village or a rural setting, even though much of the region is dotted with small villages.

Many villages got their start at a crossroads for travelers more than a century ago. Many are found on a stream or river that provided a water supply, waterpower for a **gristmill,** and sometimes a means of transportation. Some villages were once thriving communities that grew up around a textile mill, a leather factory, or a sawmill. When these small factories closed down, people began to move away. You can still find small communities based on one industry, such as a quarry or a papermill. Other communities vary in population depending on the season. A coastal village that swarms with people in the summer may be practically deserted in the winter.

A region of cities The largest **urban** area in New England begins just north of Boston, Massachusetts. It stretches southward through Connecticut. In fact, the eastern coast as far south as Washington, D.C., is one big urban area. In three of the six New England states—Connecticut,

Massachusetts, and Rhode Island—about four out of every five people live in an urban setting. In two of these states, the capital is also the largest city. Vermont, with the lowest portion of its people living in urban areas, also has the smallest capital. The table at the bottom of the page lists each New England state and names the capital and largest city and gives the population of each.

There are different ways of reporting the population of cities. The table below shows the population of the city itself. Sometimes you will see population figures for **metropolitan areas.** These figures are much larger. A city's metropolitan area includes the city and all the smaller towns and cities around the city. Look at the map on page 306. Find the cities of Cambridge, Newton, and Waltham. These are all part of Boston's metropolitan area. This area has a population of almost 3 million. The Hartford metropolitan area has over 700,000; that of Providence, more than 900,000.

Growth of cities The cities of New England have grown at different rates. We know this because every 10 years, beginning in 1790, the government has taken a census. The graph on page 303 shows the

NEW ENGLAND STATES: CAPITALS AND LARGEST CITIES				
State	Capital	Population	Largest city	Population
Connecticut	Hartford	136,000	Bridgeport	144,000
Maine	Augusta	22,000	Portland	61,000
Massachusetts	Boston	561,000	Boston	561,000
New Hampshire	Concord	30,000	Manchester	92,000
Rhode Island	Providence	156,000	Providence	156,000
Vermont	Montpelier	8,000	Burlington	38,000

population changes that have taken place in six cities since 1800.

There are many different reasons for the changes. The graph does not show which nearby communities were within the city limits in one year and not in another. Industries may have closed down or moved away. There are probably many more reasons for the changes in population. Find each of these six cities on the map on page 306. Does location help to explain how any city grew?

Like many cities today, three of these cities are losing population. Which three are they?

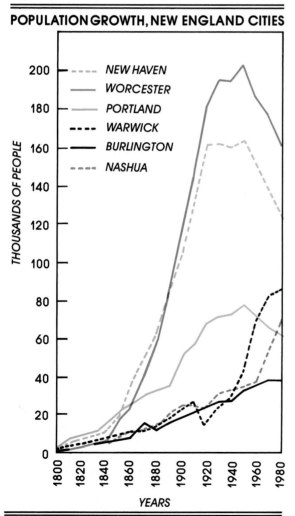

POPULATION GROWTH, NEW ENGLAND CITIES

Six cities   You have been introduced to a number of cities in this chapter. The table on page 302 listed the capital and largest city in each New England state. On the graph you saw how the population of six New England cities has changed over the years since 1800. You read about Mystic, an early port; the armory at Springfield; and the shipyard at Groton. Now let's look more closely at six New England cities.

Boston   By far the largest city in New England, Boston is the capital of Massachusetts. It is one of the 25 largest cities in the United States. There are about 561,000 people in Boston. About 2,760,000 people live in the metropolitan area. This area takes in about 90 smaller cities, towns, and other communities.

Boston is an important port city. It is also a center of trade, transportation, banking, and insurance. Within the city, the major industries are electronics and publishing. Among the hundreds of industries in the Boston area are food processing and the manufacture of machinery, medical instruments, and optical instruments. Fishing fleets supply the large seafood markets in the city.

Cultural and educational opportunities abound in Boston. Lovers of music find hundreds of concerts to attend. There are many art galleries and museums, as well as a museum of natural science, a planetarium, and an aquarium. Boston and the Boston area are the home of many colleges and universities. Among them are the well-known schools of Harvard, M.I.T., Tufts, Wellesley, and Brandeis (bran' dĭs).

The Old State House in Boston sits in the midst of the hustle and bustle of a busy city.

Boston was founded in 1630 by Puritan colonists. In the Revolutionary period, it was the site of the Boston Massacre, the Boston Tea Party, and other important events. Today, one can relive Boston's history as one follows the Freedom Trail. This is a 1½-mile (2.4 km) route that takes one past Beacon Hill, the Boston Common, the Old North Church, and other places of historic interest.

Burlington   With a population of about 38,000, Burlington is the largest city in Vermont. Burlington's location has helped to make it one of Vermont's resort centers. The city is built on a hillside overlooking Lake Champlain. The famous Green Mountains are just 20 miles (30 km) to the

east. In the summer, tourists are attracted by the cool climate and by boating on Lake Champlain. Iceboat racing, skiing, and other outdoor sports bring tourists in the winter.

Burlington is a port city. Ships from the St. Lawrence River can reach Lake Champlain by way of a canal and the Richelieu (rish′ ə lü) River in Canada. Ships traveling south from Lake Champlain use a canal and the Hudson River. Oil and gasoline are the major products carried by ships in the harbor. In addition to being a transportation and trade center, Burlington is Vermont's leading manufacturing center. Industries in the city make steel for building, electronics equipment, aircraft, appliances, and cereal.

Concord   Concord is located on the Merrimack River in southern New Hampshire. It is the state's capital and third largest city. With a population of 30,000, it is the smallest of the six cities being described. When Concord was founded in 1659, it was called Penny Cook, after the Indian name *Penacook*, which means "a crooked place." The Indians gave it this name because of the many bends in the river. Later the name was changed to Rumford, after a local settler. Then in 1765 it was given the name Concord. The city became the state capital in 1808. The government offices in Concord are housed in several beautiful buildings. The State House, or capitol building, is made of granite from nearby quarries and marble from Vermont.

Printing is Concord's leading industry. More than 50 nationally sold magazines are printed in Concord. Electronic equipment, leather goods, and wood products are also made in Concord. The city is a center of retail trade.

New Haven New Haven is on the north shore of Long Island Sound. The city's population is about 125,000. About 416,000 people live in the metropolitan area. This port city is the third largest city in Connecticut. Oil tankers outnumber other cargo ships in New Haven Harbor.

The New Haven area has about 1,000 industrial companies. These companies make such goods as guns, electrical appliances, machine tools, hardware, toys, and rubber goods.

Founded by the Puritans in 1638, New Haven is an educational and cultural center for southern Connecticut. It is well known for its fine museums and galleries. It is the home of Yale University, the third oldest school of higher learning in the United States.

Portland Portland is the largest city in Maine. Its city population is about 61,000. About 183,000 people live in the metropolitan area. Most of the city is on two hills overlooking Casco Bay. Portland's deepwater port is the Atlantic coast's second busiest oil shipping center. A pipeline carries oil from Portland to Montreal, Canada.

Much of the activity found in Portland has to do with the sea. Besides being an important oil port, the city is also busy with a growing fishing industry, seafood processing plants, and shipbuilding. Other industries include printing and the manufacture of metal products, clothing, and electronic parts.

Portland is the birthplace of Henry Wadsworth Longfellow, a well-known poet. There are many buildings of historic interest in the city. In what is now the city of South Portland stands the oldest lighthouse in the nation, the Portland Head Light. A branch of the University of Maine is located in Portland.

Providence Providence is Rhode Island's capital and largest city. Its city population is about 156,000. About 918,000 people live in the metropolitan area. The city was founded by Roger Williams in 1636. The port at Providence has been important since the early days of our nation. It has more than 10 miles (16 km) of waterfront, and is the third largest port in New England.

The manufacture of jewelry and of silverware are the city's leading industries. Other products include textiles, machinery, and rubber goods.

One of Providence's features is its fine collection of historic homes and buildings. People in the city have worked to restore and preserve many homes built before the Revolutionary War. Brown University, one of the oldest schools of higher learning in the United States, is found in Providence.

CHECKUP

1. Many different businesses depend upon tourists. Name as many of those businesses as you can.
2. What are some of the reasons tourists have for visiting New England?
3. Describe the difference between the population of a city and the population of a city's metropolitan area.
4. Choose two of the six cities described on the past few pages. How are they alike? Different?

305

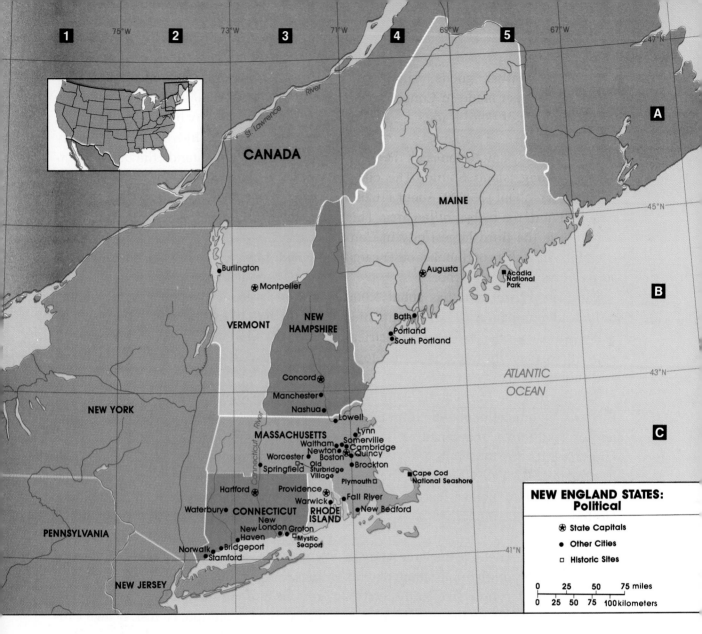

NEW ENGLAND STATES: Political

- ⊛ State Capitals
- ● Other Cities
- ▫ Historic Sites

| 0 | 25 | 50 | 75 miles |
| 0 | 25 50 | 75 | 100 kilometers |

This map has a grid system like the one on the map of Wyoming on page 21. This time the lines of latitude and longitude form the grid. Find Stamford on the list above. The letters C-2 mean it is in box C-2. Find Stamford in box C-2 on the map.

THE NEW ENGLAND STATES	Connecticut	Maine	Massachusetts	New Hampshire	Rhode Island	Vermont
Source of Name	From an Indian word *Quinnehtukput*, meaning "beside the long tidal river"	First used to distinguish the mainland from the offshore islands. It has been considered a compliment to Henrietta Maria, queen of Charles I of England. She was said to have owned the province of Mayne in France.	From two Algonquin words, meaning "great mountain place"	From the English county of Hampshire	From the Greek island of Rhodes	From the French *vert mont*, meaning "green mountain"
Nickname(s)	Nutmeg State; Constitution State	Pine Tree State	Bay State; Old Colony State	Granite State	Ocean State	Green Mountain State
Capital	Hartford	Augusta	Boston	Concord	Providence	Montpelier
Largest Cities	Bridgeport Hartford New Haven	Portland Lewiston Bangor	Boston Worcester Springfield	Manchester Nashua Concord	Providence Warwick Pawtucket	Burlington Rutland Bennington
Population Rank	27	38	12	41	42	48
Population Density Rank	4	36	3	20	2	30
Area Rank	48	39	45	44	50	43
State Flag						
State Bird	American robin	Chickadee	Chickadee	Purple finch	Rhode Island Red	Hermit thrush
State Flower	Mountain laurel	White pine cone & tassel	Mayflower	Purple lilac	Violet (unofficial)	Red clover
State Tree	White oak	White pine	American elm	White birch	Red maple	Sugar maple
State Motto	*Qui transtulit sustinet* (He who transplanted still sustains)	*Dirigo* (I direct)	*Ense petit placidam sub libertate quietem* (By the sword we seek peace, but peace only under liberty)	Live free or die	Hope	Vermont, freedom and unity
Interesting Facts	In 1954 the world's first atomic-powered submarine, the *Nautilus*, was launched from Groton. *The Courant*, published in Hartford, is the oldest United States newspaper still being published.	Maine leads the nation in lobster production, and leads the world in the production of the flat tins of sardines. Eastport is farther east than any other city in the United States.	The first shots of the Revolutionary War were fired in Lexington and Concord. Harvard is the oldest university in the United States.	New Hampshire's vote was the deciding vote that ratified the United States Constitution.	Although it is the smallest state in the nation in physical size, it is the nation's leader in the production of costume jewelry and lace.	Vermont leads the nation in the production of maple syrup. It is also the birthplace of the Morgan horse.

307

15/CHAPTER REVIEW

KEY FACTS

1. The Atlantic coast and the Appalachian Mountains are the two main landscape features of New England.

2. The climate of New England is affected by its northern location, the Appalachian Mountains, and the Atlantic Ocean.

3. New England's industries, such as fishing, lumbering, and the manufacture of textiles and other products, have undergone major changes since colonial times.

4. The landscape and climate of New England affect the type of farming in the region.

5. The location of communities is influenced by such things as transportation, landscape, and water and other resources.

VOCABULARY QUIZ

Beside the number of each sentence write the letter of the word that best completes the sentence. Write on a sheet of paper.

a. renewable   f. synthetic
b. elevation   g. trawlers
c. landscape   h. quarries
d. foliage   i. bogs
e. promontory   j. metropolitan

1. Plains, mountains, and other physical features make up the _____ of a region.

2. Today, _____ materials are often used instead of natural materials.

3. Fishes and forests are _____ resources.

4. A _____ area includes a central city and the nearby communities.

5. Slate, marble, and other kinds of stone are dug from _____.

6. The _____ of Cadillac Mountain is 1,530 feet (467 m).

7. Today, fishing _____ are equipped with sonar, radio, and refrigerated areas.

8. Each fall, the _____ of broadleaf trees turns to red, yellow, and other bright colors.

9. A _____ is high rocky land that juts out into the ocean.

10. Cranberries are grown in _____.

REVIEW QUESTIONS

1. Describe the New England climate.

2. Name three important rivers of New England.

3. Name three industries of New England.

4. Name four New England farm products.

5. In which two New England states is the capital also the largest city? Which state capital is the smallest? The largest?

6. Name two New England cities. What is each noted for?

ACTIVITIES

1. Plan a route that you would follow if you were to spend a year in New England. On an outline map, show your route and the places you would visit. Label seasonal attractions, such as swimming and skiing, as well as points of interest. Be sure to make a map key. To go with your map, make a pamphlet in which you briefly describe each place you plan to visit.

2. Write a report about an imaginary New England village. In the report, name your village, tell where it is, why it was founded at this particular spot, and describe the area. Give the size of the population in the first year, 10 years later, 50 years ago, and today. Tell how the village has changed and describe some of the results of those changes. Make a map of the village.

READING A MAP: A NATIONAL PARK

SKILLS PRACTICE

Use what you have learned about map reading to answer the following questions.

1. On the map on this page, find the name of the island on which most of Acadia is located. What is the island's name?

2. What color is used for Acadia National Park? What color is used for other land?

3. In addition to the main island, several other islands are labeled on the map. What are their names?

4. How many bodies of water are labeled on the map? What are they?

5. What route would you take to get from Southwest Harbor to Pretty Marsh?

6. How would you get from Bar Harbor to Seal Harbor?

As you may remember from Chapter 1, symbols as well as labels are used on many maps. The symbols are explained in the key.

7. Find the symbol for campgrounds in the key. How many campgrounds are shown on the map?

8. Find the symbol for lighthouses. How many are shown on the map?

9. Find the symbol for the national park headquarters. Find the headquarters on the map. What town is nearby?

In Chapter 1, you learned how to use a grid system when you worked with a map of Wyoming. A grid system is made up of lines that form boxes where they cross one another. The rows and columns are labeled with letters and numbers.

10. Which town is in box A-3? B-2? C-1?

11. Which body of water is entirely within box C-2?

As you learned, the part of map that helps you find distances is called the scale. Use the scale to answer questions 12 to 14.

12. About how far is it from Bar Harbor to Seal Harbor, measuring in a straight line?

13. About how far is it in a straight line from Salisbury Cove to the southernmost lighthouse?

14. About how long is the main island at its longest point? About how wide is it at its widest point?

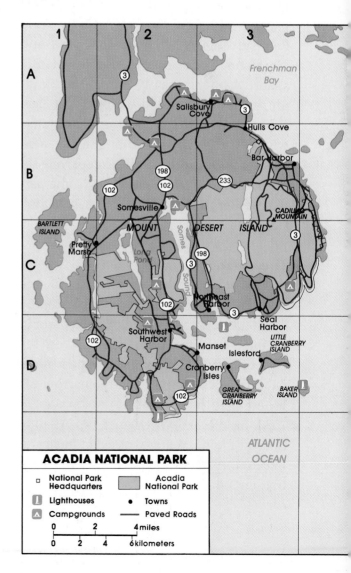

ACADIA NATIONAL PARK

□ National Park Headquarters
▨ Acadia National Park
▯ Lighthouses
● Towns
◭ Campgrounds
— Paved Roads

0   2   4 miles
0   2   4   6 kilometers

16 The Middle Atlantic States Today

The Land

VOCABULARY
bay	valley
harbor	foothill

Where is it? The Middle Atlantic region is just where its name tells us it is. Look at the map of the United States on pages 14–15. Find the states of New York, Pennsylvania, New Jersey, Delaware, and Maryland. These are the Middle Atlantic states. And they really are in the "middle." They are located between the New England states and the southeastern states, which you will learn about in the next chapter. Notice that all except one of the Middle Atlantic states have some part that borders on the Atlantic Ocean. Which state does not?

The Atlantic Coastal Plain One of the most important landforms of the Middle Atlantic region is the Atlantic Coastal Plain. You read about this plain in Chapter 14. Find this large area on the map on page 311. In which of the Middle Atlantic states is the plain the narrowest? Where is it the widest?

Along the eastern edge of the Atlantic Coastal Plain are many miles of **bays** and **harbors.** A bay is a part of a sea or ocean that cuts deep into the land. Harbors are protected waters where ships can anchor safely. On the map on page 311 find Chesapeake, Delaware, and New York bays. In which states do you find them? Did you name Maryland and Virginia for Chesapeake Bay? For Delaware Bay did you name New Jersey and Delaware? Did you also include Pennsylvania? For New York Bay did you name New York and New Jersey?

These three bays were also important in the history of our country. Ships carrying settlers and goods were able to enter the country by way of the deep, protected harbors formed by these great bays. The harbors are still important today. Ocean-going ships from many ports and even many nations travel in these bays on their way to and from the ports on the shores of the bays.

Also along the eastern edge of the Middle Atlantic region stretch mile after mile of fine sandy beaches. Every summer thousands of families visit these beaches to swim and sail and enjoy the sun and the cool ocean breezes.

The Appalachian Mountain system From the Atlantic coast, the broad plain of flat or gently rolling lowland stretches westward and begins to change. The land becomes rougher. Slowly the plain gives

On the map you can see the two most important landforms of the Middle Atlantic states: the Atlantic Coastal Plain and the Appalachian Mountains. The picture shows people enjoying a beach on the Atlantic Ocean.

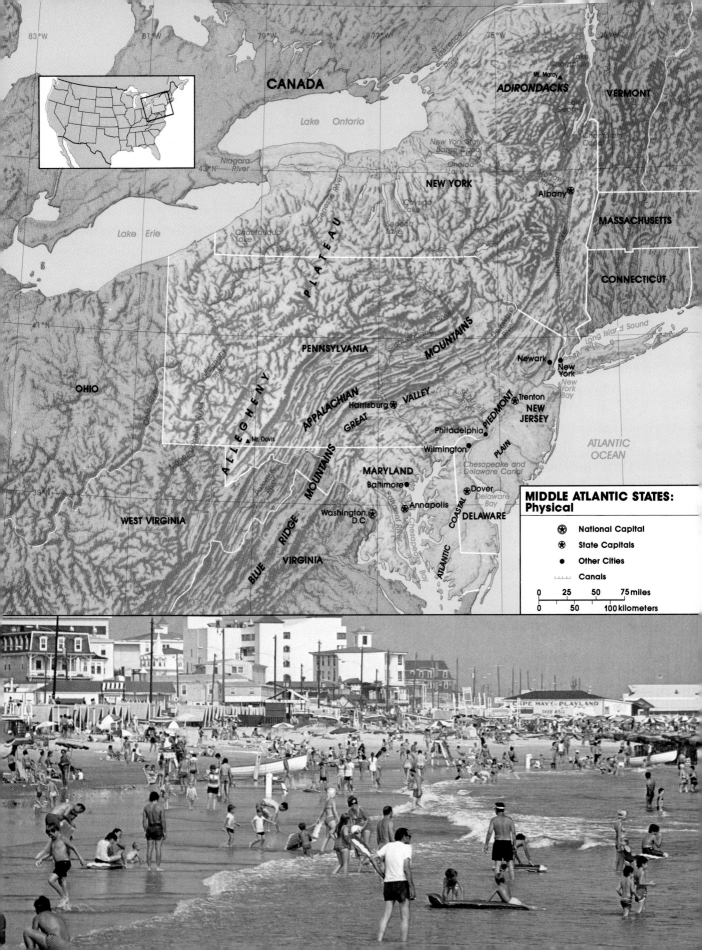

CANADA

Lake Ontario

Niagara River

VERMONT

Mt. Marcy ▲

ADIRONDACKS

Lake Champlain

New York State Barge Canal

Oneida Lake

NEW YORK

Geneseo River

Cayuga Lake

Genesee Lake

Chautauqua Lake

Albany ⊛

MASSACHUSETTS

CONNECTICUT

Lake Erie

P L A T E A U

Hudson River

Long Island Sound

OHIO

PENNSYLVANIA

Susquehanna River

Allegheny River

MOUNTAINS

Delaware River

Newark •

Newark ● New York

New York Bay

A L L E G H E N Y

APPALACHIAN

GREAT

VALLEY

Harrisburg ⊛

Trenton ⊛

PIEDMONT

NEW JERSEY

Mt. Davis •

Schuylkill River

Philadelphia ●

Wilmington ●

PLAIN

ATLANTIC OCEAN

Monongahela River

Youghiogheny River

MOUNTAINS

MARYLAND

Baltimore ●

Chesapeake and Delaware Canal

Dover ⊛

Delaware Bay

DELAWARE

BLUE

RIDGE

Washington, D.C. ⊛

Potomac River

Annapolis ●

Chesapeake Bay

COASTAL

WEST VIRGINIA

VIRGINIA

ATLANTIC

MIDDLE ATLANTIC STATES: Physical

⊛ National Capital

⊛ State Capitals

● Other Cities

⊔⊔⊔⊔ Canals

0	25	50	75 miles
0	50		100 kilometers

CAPE MAY'S PLAYLAND
SKEE BALL

way to a belt of low, tree-covered hills and rich green **valleys.** These are the **foothills** of the great Appalachian system.

The Appalachian Mountain system is a huge area of mountains, plateaus, and valleys. You remember from Chapter 15 that the Appalachian system in the United States starts in Maine and runs south through New England. This same system of mountain ranges continues southwest through the Middle Atlantic region. The Appalachian ranges include, among others, the high peaks of the Adirondacks in New York and the older, lower Blue Ridge Mountains that begin in the southern part of Pennsylvania.

Among the forested mountains of the Appalachians are many valleys. The most important of these is called the Great Valley. Find this valley on the map on page 311. The Great Valley is important because of its fine farmland. It also forms part of a route that leads through the mountains to the land west of the Appalachians.

Look at the map on page 311. What kind of landform do you find west of the Appalachians? In what states do you find the Allegheny Plateau?

Rivers and lakes   Among the important physical features of the Middle Atlantic region are its many beautiful lakes and rivers. The rivers that flow through the Middle Atlantic states played an important part in our country's history. They were the routes by which explorers and settlers could most easily reach new lands from the Atlantic coast.

One of the most important of these rivers is the great Hudson. The Hudson River flows south through the Appalachian Mountains. On the map on page 311 trace the Hudson River from its mouth in New York Bay to the place where it meets the Mohawk River. What city grew up near this point?

Three other important rivers flow south and east through the Appalachians. Find the Delaware, Susquehanna (səs kwə han' ə), and Potomac rivers on the map. Which two of these rivers form state boundaries? Which two rivers flow into Chesapeake Bay?

The Middle Atlantic region is well known for its fine lakes. The biggest by far are Lakes Ontario and Erie. These are two of the Great Lakes that form a boundary between the United States and Canada, our neighbor to the north. Find these two lakes on the map on page 311. Can you trace a water route by which people and goods can move from New York Bay to Lake Ontario and Lake Erie?

While Lakes Ontario and Erie are the two most important lakes in the Middle Atlantic states, there are hundreds of beautiful lakes scattered all through the Middle Atlantic states. These lakes draw thousands of visitors each year. People come not only in the summer to swim and sail, but also in the winter months to take part in winter sports such as ice-skating and iceboating.

CHECKUP

1. Name the states in the Middle Atlantic region.
2. Why were the rivers in this region important in our country's history?
3. The foothills to the west of the Atlantic Coastal Plain are the edge of what mountain system?
4. Which two Great Lakes are in this region?

Climate and Natural Resources

Temperature The word *middle* in *Middle Atlantic* region also tells us something about the climate. The weather in most of this region is hardly ever extremely hot or cold for very long at a time. However, the winters are longer and colder in the northern parts and in the high mountains. The temperature in these areas often drops below 0°F (−18°C). In the Adirondacks, temperatures have been recorded well below −40°F (−40°C).

These children in Buffalo are enjoying the snow, but shoveling a path to the house must have been hard.

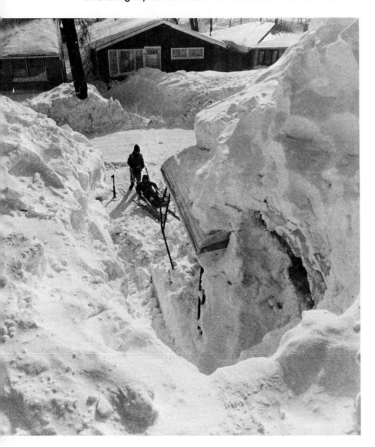

But the *average* winter temperatures of the Middle Atlantic region are not nearly so cold. Look at the map of average January temperatures on page 271 in Chapter 14. Find the average temperatures of the Middle Atlantic states. You can see that the word *middle* can be used to describe them.

In the summer also this area has "middle" temperatures. Sometimes July temperatures in the lower elevations and in the more southern parts may get as high as 100°F (38°C), or even higher. However, the average temperature is about 75°F (24°C) in the summer. Look at the map of average July temperatures on page 270 in Chapter 14. Find the average July temperatures for each of the Middle Atlantic states.

Precipitation The amounts of rain and snow that fall in the Middle Atlantic region also vary. The mountain areas tend to have much more precipitation than some of the other parts. In some mountain areas, precipitation is more than 50 inches (127 cm) every year. In Wilmington, Delaware, there is an average of about 40 inches (102 cm).

Buffalo is a city on Lake Erie in New York state. During a recent winter, Buffalo had 175.6 inches (446 cm) of **sleet,** or frozen rain, and snow. If all that snow and sleet had been on the ground at one time, it would have been more than 14 feet (4 m) high. Of course, that was an unusual winter. But the yearly average is over 80 inches (203 cm). On the other hand, southern New Jersey, Delaware, and Maryland have only about 20 inches (51 cm) of snow a year.

Soil and water   The Middle Atlantic states are rich in some of our most important resources. There is enough sunshine, rain, and good, fertile soil in these states to grow feed for herds of dairy cattle as well as fine crops of vegetables and fruit.

Beautiful woodlands cover many of the hills and slopes of the Middle Atlantic region. These woodlands supply very little lumber for building and making paper. But they do provide a home for the many birds and animals that live in these states. And the woodlands also give people a place to enjoy the quiet beauty of trees, flowers, and small streams.

You have already learned something about how important water is for transportation and recreation in the Middle Atlantic states. This region also has a good supply of clean drinking water, although some of its rivers and streams have become too polluted, or dirty, for people to use or for fish to live in.

You read earlier that since colonial times New England's fast-moving rivers have made power to run machines. Some of the states in the Middle Atlantic region also have waterpower that can be changed into electricity. In the Middle Atlantic region, where the coastal plain meets the foothills of the Appalachians, there are many rivers and waterfalls. These gave waterpower that ran some of the country's earliest factories.

Turn to the map on page 311 and find the Niagara River between Lakes Erie and Ontario. Between these two lakes the river makes a huge drop. At this point are great waterfalls. About 200,000 tons (181,400 t) of water rush over the falls every min-

Niagara Falls is split into two parts: American Falls (left) and Horseshoe Falls on the Canadian side of the river (center).

ute. Much of this tremendous power is turned into electricity by large power plants. This electricity is used in homes and factories on both the Canadian and the American sides of the falls.

Fuels   The first oil well in the United States was drilled in the Middle Atlantic region. In 1859, a man named Edwin Drake drilled this early well in western Pennsylvania. For a long time most of the oil produced in the United States came from this area.

Oil and natural gas still come from these fields. But Pennsylvania is no longer one of our leading oil states. The huge coalfields in the Appalachians of western Pennsylvania are a far more important source of fuel than Pennsylvania's oil fields. The map on page 279 of Chapter 14 shows you that these fields stretch from the Middle Atlantic region to Alabama.

CHECKUP

1. What parts of the Middle Atlantic region tend to have the coldest winters?
2. What word would you choose to describe the climate of the Middle Atlantic region?
3. Name at least three resources of the Middle Atlantic region.

Farming and Industry

Food for the cities   The millions of people in the Middle Atlantic states need huge amounts of food. They need the products that are raised on farms. And although cities cover much of the land in the Middle Atlantic region, there are still farms in every one of the Middle Atlantic states. In fact half of Delaware and a third of Pennsylvania are farmland. There are fewer farms than there once were. And very few people work on the farms. But still the farms of the Middle Atlantic region are able to supply a great deal of the needed food. Modern methods and machinery make that possible.

New York and Pennsylvania are well known for their dairy farms. Pennsylvania is one of the leading milk-producing states in the country. These two states also raise cattle for meat. In every Middle Atlantic state, **poultry** farms supply eggs and chickens for the city markets. As you know, fine crops of fruits and vegetables abound in the Middle Atlantic states. Southern Delaware farms are well known for sweet white corn. The soil and climate are also well suited for growing potatoes and strawberries. Maryland's farms grow rich crops of barley, wheat, and soybeans. Southwestern New Jersey is known for its fine **truck farms.** Truck farms are farms on which many different vegetables are grown in large amounts to be sold in markets.

Food from the sea   Some of the food produced in the Middle Atlantic states comes from the sea. Many harbors along the coasts of New Jersey, Delaware, and Maryland are fishing ports. Fishing boats leave from these ports every day for deeper waters. They return with fine catches of many kinds of fish. Much of the catch is frozen in nearby plants. Then the catch is sent to cities all over the United States.

The waters of Chesapeake and Delaware bays are noted for their valuable catches of shellfish, such as crabs, clams, lobsters, and oysters.

After picking up a load of milk, a truck driver stops to talk with a farmer in Pennsylvania. In the pasture is part of the farmer's herd of Holstein cows.

The Manufacturing Belt   The Middle Atlantic region is one of the greatest industrial areas in the Americas. Millions of dollars worth of goods are made and sold in the Middle Atlantic region. In fact, it has been called the **Manufacturing Belt** of the United States. About 22 out of every 100 workers in the Middle Atlantic region have jobs in factories and mills. They make machines, chemicals, clothes, ships, cameras, cloth, paper, and many, many more kinds of goods.

One of the important industries of this area is the manufacture of synthetics. This industry had its beginning in 1802 when gunpowder mills were first built along the Brandywine River in Delaware. With the discovery of nylon and other fabrics about 40 years ago, large **petrochemical** industries grew. It is quite likely that much of your clothing is made from synthetic fabrics, such as nylon or Dacron.

Iron   Industry has been important in the Middle Atlantic region since iron ore was first discovered in eastern Pennsylvania in the eighteenth century. The early settlers also found great amounts of limestone, another ingredient needed to make iron. The settlers burned wood from the great forests to make charcoal. Then they burned the charcoal to make the high heat needed to melt the iron from the ore. The limestone and iron ore were heated together in stone furnaces to make liquid iron. Later, the iron cooled and hardened. From the iron the settlers made their own pots and kettles, tools and nails, and many other necessary goods.

Later, Pennsylvania's rich coal supplies were discovered. Then the ironmakers used coal instead of charcoal to heat their furnaces.

Pittsburgh and steel   As you read in Chapter 14, iron can be turned into steel. Steel can be used to make even more things than iron can. Steel is one of the most important products in the world today. Just think of all the cars, tall buildings, strong bridges, and hundreds of other things that are made at least partly of steel. Today more than 600,000 people in the United States have jobs that have something to do with making steel.

After the Civil War there was a need for more and more steel. Pennsylvania could not mine enough iron to meet this need. Steel mills had to get iron ore from other parts of the country. Mines as far away as the Mesabi mines in Minnesota began shipping ore to the city of Pittsburgh in western Pennsylvania. The ore from these mines could travel most of the way by water.

On the map on page 324 find the port city of Pittsburgh. It is located at the point where the Allegheny (al ə gā′ nē) and Monongahela (mə nän gə hē′ lə) rivers meet to form the Ohio River.

Now turn to the map of the United States on pages 14–15. Find the city of Duluth (də lüth′), Minnesota, on Lake Superior. Iron ore from the Mesabi mines was loaded on barges at Duluth. From Duluth, the barges went across Lakes Superior, Huron, and Erie to the port city of Erie, Pennsylvania. Trace the route of the iron ore barges on the map of the United States. From the port of Erie the

HOW STEEL IS MADE

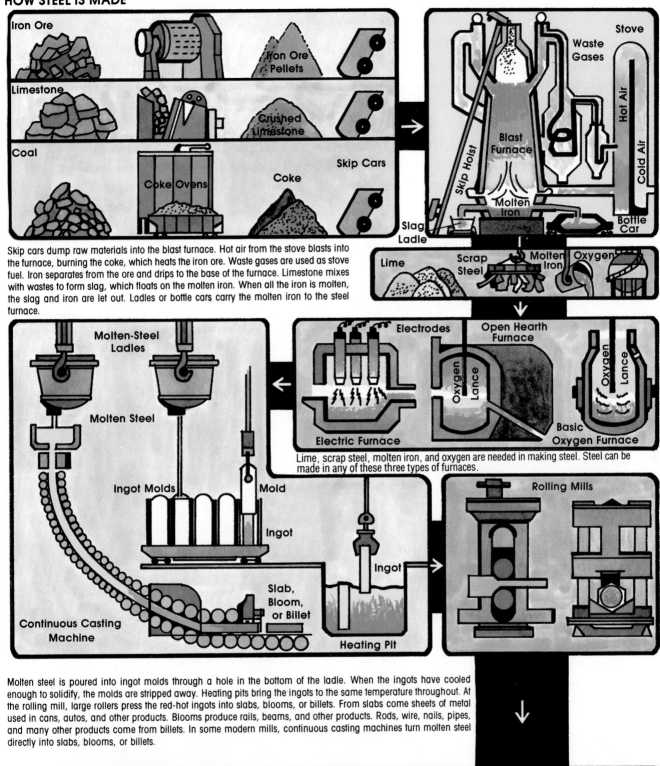

Iron Ore • **Iron Ore Pellets** • **Skip Cars**

Limestone • **Crushed Limestone**

Coal • **Coke Ovens** • **Coke**

Waste Gases • **Stove** • **Blast Furnace** • **Hot Air** • **Cold Air** • **Skip Hoist** • **Molten Iron** • **Bottle Car** • **Slag Ladle**

Skip cars dump raw materials into the blast furnace. Hot air from the stove blasts into the furnace, burning the coke, which heats the iron ore. Waste gases are used as stove fuel. Iron separates from the ore and drips to the base of the furnace. Limestone mixes with wastes to form slag, which floats on the molten iron. When all the iron is molten, the slag and iron are let out. Ladles or bottle cars carry the molten iron to the steel furnace.

Lime • **Scrap Steel** • **Molten Iron** • **Oxygen**

Electrodes • **Open Hearth Furnace** • **Oxygen Lance** • **Electric Furnace** • **Basic Oxygen Furnace**

Lime, scrap steel, molten iron, and oxygen are needed in making steel. Steel can be made in any of these three types of furnaces.

Molten-Steel Ladles • **Molten Steel** • **Ingot Molds** • **Mold** • **Ingot** • **Rolling Mills** • **Slab, Bloom, or Billet** • **Ingot** • **Continuous Casting Machine** • **Heating Pit**

Molten steel is poured into ingot molds through a hole in the bottom of the ladle. When the ingots have cooled enough to solidify, the molds are stripped away. Heating pits bring the ingots to the same temperature throughout. At the rolling mill, large rollers press the red-hot ingots into slabs, blooms, or billets. From slabs come sheets of metal used in cans, autos, and other products. Blooms produce rails, beams, and other products. Rods, wire, nails, pipes, and many other products come from billets. In some modern mills, continuous casting machines turn molten steel directly into slabs, blooms, or billets.

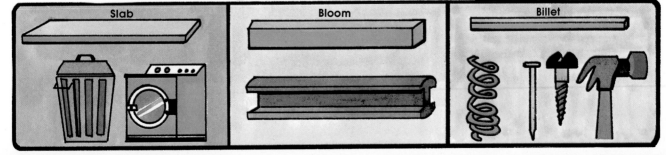

Slab • **Bloom** • **Billet**

iron continued its journey by way of railroad and the Allegheny River to Pittsburgh. Iron is carried along the same route today.

River barges could also bring coal and limestone to Pittsburgh for the giant furnaces and steel mills. And the rivers could carry the products of Pittsburgh's mills and factories to markets in other parts of the country. Pittsburgh became the most important center of steelmaking in the Americas.

Today much of the iron ore used in the Middle Atlantic states comes from other countries. It is shipped by boat and rail from places as close as Canada and as far away as Venezuela (ven əz wā′ lə) in South America. Other important steelmaking centers have grown up in Pennsylvania, as well as in Illinois, Indiana, Ohio, New York, and Maryland. However, steelmaking is still one of Pittsburgh's most important industries. And the steel mills in and around the city make a large part of the steel that Pennsylvania produces.

CHECKUP

1. Name four farm products of the Middle Atlantic region.
2. For what foods are the waters of Chesapeake and Delaware bays noted?
3. For what product was Pittsburgh most noted?

In this view of Pittsburgh, you see the Golden Triangle, the point at which the Allegheny River (left) and the Monongahela (right) meet to form the Ohio River.

Cities

┌─VOCABULARY─────────────────────────┐
│ commerce   megalopolis   │
└────────────────────────────────────┘

A region of great cities   Look at the population density map on page 259 in Chapter 14. You can see that some of the most densely populated areas in the United States are in the Middle Atlantic region. In fact, New Jersey is the most densely populated state in the country. There are an average of 965 people per square mile (373 people per sq km) living in New Jersey.

About 79 out of every 100 people in the Middle Atlantic region live in urban areas. The table below shows how many people live in each of the Middle Atlantic states. It also shows what percentage of those people live in urban areas.

Perhaps people know the Middle Atlantic region best for its cities. Cities are very important to the people of the Middle Atlantic states. Most of the factories and mills in this great industrial region are found in and around the cities. So are most of the banks and offices, stores and businesses of every kind.

Huge cargo containers are lined up on the dock ready to be loaded on this Australian ship at Port Elizabeth.

Importance of ports   Many of the great cities of the Middle Atlantic region are port cities. They are on harbors or bays, rivers or lakes, or even canals. The five largest cities in the Middle Atlantic states are New York, Philadelphia, Baltimore, Washington, D.C., and Pittsburgh. Find them on the map on page 324. You will see that all these cities, except Washington, are ports. On what bodies of water are the cities located?

One of the major reasons these cities grew big and important was ease of transportation. In the early days of our country, travel by water was easier and faster than travel over land. Explorers used the waterways to get into the wilderness. As settlers move westward, many of them used water routes. Waterways were important for shipping of goods and supplies to and from the different settlements. Water travel made trade with other countries possible.

The port cities of the Middle Atlantic region became centers of trade and

URBAN POPULATION OF THE MIDDLE ATLANTIC STATES

State	Total population	Percent urban
New York	17,735,000	85
New Jersey	7,515,000	89
Pennsylvania	11,901,000	69
Delaware	613,000	71
Maryland	4,349,000	80

commerce. *Commerce* means the buying and selling of goods. Many of these cities are still important commercial and shipping centers. Goods from other parts of the United States and from all over the world pass through these busy ports. The table below lists five of the largest ports in the Middle Atlantic region. It also shows how many tons of cargo, or goods, are loaded and unloaded at their busy docks each year. You can see that the port of New York is the busiest port in the Middle Atlantic region. It is also the second busiest port in the whole country.

MAIN SEAPORTS OF THE MIDDLE ATLANTIC REGION (Figures are rounded)	
Port	Short tons of cargo per year
New York, N.Y., and New Jersey	149,300,000
Baltimore	40,800,000
Philadelphia	31,900,000
Pittsburgh	28,300,000
Marcus Hook, Pa.	23,900,000
Paulsboro, N.J.	18,800,000

New York City New York is the most populated city in the United States. About 7 million people make their homes in this great city. And many more millions of people live in the New York metropolitan area. This area includes all the smaller cities and towns around New York City. Look at the map on page 324. Find the cities of Newark, Elizabeth, Paterson, and Jersey City in New Jersey and the city of Yonkers in New York State. These cities and more in Connecticut, New York, and New Jersey are all part of the New York metropolitan area. There would not be room on the map to show all the smaller towns and cities around New York City. Every day thousands of people from these communities travel into the city to their jobs.

New York is one of the most important business, banking, trading, and manufacturing centers in the world. Two of its largest industries are the manufacturing of clothing and publishing of books. You might be wearing something right now that was made in New York City. And some of your schoolbooks may have come from there also.

Welcome to America Since the Dutch settled in New Amsterdam in 1624, New York has welcomed millions of new Americans. Perhaps the Statue of Liberty in New York Harbor was the first thing your parents or grandparents or great-grandparents saw when they arrived in America.

For more than 350 years people from all over the world have poured into this country through New York Harbor. Most of them have come in search of more freedom and a better life. From New York, many of these immigrants have gone on to help build every corner of America. But many have stayed in New York to make it one of the world's most interesting and exciting cities.

Philadelphia Philadelphia is the biggest city in Pennsylvania and the fifth largest city in the United States. It is one of the busiest ports and manufacturing centers in the Middle Atlantic region. Look at the map on page 324. Find

The first balloon in the United States to carry people took off from Philadelphia in 1793. That historic event and others are celebrated during the city's Freedom Week festival.

visit the fine old buildings where great leaders such as Thomas Jefferson and Benjamin Franklin planned a new kind of government.

Philadelphia is well known for its lovely old buildings and tree-shaded streets. But it is also a modern city with tall buildings and busy streets crowded with cars and buses. And like other important Middle Atlantic cities, its airports, railroad stations, and highways make it a transportation center as well.

Baltimore   Baltimore, on Chesapeake Bay, is another of the great Middle Atlantic ports. Ships loaded with oil, wheat, coal, automobiles, iron, and steel move through its deep harbor.

Find Baltimore on the map on page 324. Move your finger past Baltimore northward on Chesapeake Bay. Do you see the waterway that connects Chesapeake Bay with the mouth of the Delaware River? This is the Chesapeake and Delaware Canal. It allows ships to travel from Baltimore to Philadelphia without having to go southward and around Virginia's Cape Charles to Delaware Bay. Ships taking this route pass the busy cities of Wilmington, Delaware, and Camden, New Jersey, as well as the ports of Marcus Hook, Pennsylvania, and Paulsboro, New Jersey.

Baltimore is the most southern city of the Middle Atlantic region's great Manufacturing Belt. Its factories make millions of dollars worth of goods. These include all kinds of products made of metal. One of the largest steel mills in the country is found in Baltimore. And from its earliest days, Baltimore has been famous as a shipbuilding city.

Philadelphia where the Delaware River meets the Schuylkill (skül' kil) River. Huge oceangoing ships can travel from the Atlantic Ocean into Delaware Bay. From there they can move through deep channels in the Delaware River until they reach the busy docks of Philadelphia's waterfront.

Old and new   Philadelphia was carefully planned and laid out by William Penn in 1682. Later, it was the scene of stirring events in our nation's history. Today, thousands of visitors come to Philadelphia to see Independence Hall where the Declaration of Independence was signed in 1776. They come to see the famous Liberty Bell that rang out the news that a new nation was born. They

Regions Depend on One Another

Washington, D.C., as the nation's capital, connects the Middle Atlantic region with every other state. There are other ways in which these states are related to other parts of the nation.

Port cities, such as New York, Philadelphia, and Baltimore, provide for the entry of goods from other nations. These goods are then shipped to other parts of the United States. At the port of Wilmington, Delaware, you can see hundreds of cars that have been imported from Europe. They will be loaded on auto transport trailers and moved west, south, and north. At the same port, you will see American-made cars waiting to be exported to other countries.

The Middle Atlantic states depend upon the North Central states for grain. Can you think of other goods that might be exchanged between these two regions?

Have you ever listed all the things you use during just one day? If you do that and then find out where they come from, the interconnections begin to show up quickly. Pennsylvanians drink Florida orange juice and visit Florida in the winter to enjoy the sunshine. New Yorkers depend upon Texas and Mississippi for cotton, but create designs for clothing that is manufactured in the Southeast. Can you think of an example of how New Jersey is connected with other parts of the nation?

Washington, D.C. On the map on page 324 find the capital city of each state in the Middle Atlantic region. What tells you they are the capital cities? Each of these cities is the center of the state's government. Here the state leaders work at managing the affairs of the state.

The United States also has a capital city. It is the city of Washington in the District of Columbia—Washington, D.C., for short. Find Washington, D.C., on the map on page 324. It looks as though it is in the state of Maryland. But Washington is not part of any state. It is built on land given to the national government by Maryland when George Washington was President.

Washington is on the Potomac River. But Washington is not an important port city. Neither is it a city of factories and mills. There are few big business companies in Washington. But Washington, D.C., is the most important city in America to all of us. The main business of Washington is the government of the United States. More people in and around Washington work at government jobs than at any other kind.

The President of the United States lives and works in Washington. In this city, senators and representatives from every state of the Union make the laws that rule our land. In Washington the Supreme Court, the highest court of the land, makes decisions that affect every one of us every day of our lives.

An exciting visit Every year millions of people come to visit their country's capital. They walk down the broad avenues that were planned by a French en-

Congress meets in the Capitol in Washington, D.C., our nation's capital.

gineer, Pierre Charles L'Enfant, before the city was built. They visit the White House, where the President lives, and the Capitol, where the Senate and House of Representatives meet. They visit the Supreme Court Building. Here they may even watch the nine judges of the Court at work. On the banks of the Potomac River, visitors admire the lovely buildings that were built to honor two of our country's great heroes—George Washington and Thomas Jefferson. From the top of the Washington Monument, people can look out over one of the most beautiful cities in the world.

Megalopolis   You have been learning about some of the cities of the Middle Atlantic region. And, of course, there are other important cities in the Middle Atlantic states, many more than we have room to tell about. Most of the cities are on the Atlantic Coastal Plain. Many of them have spread out far from their centers. Their metropolitan areas include many suburbs. Suburbs are the cities, towns, and villages that surround a large city.

The groups of cities and suburbs have spread so far into the countryside that they touch each other. Look at the map on pages 14–15. You can see that the area from Boston in New England to Washington, D.C., seems to be one huge city. This kind of city area is called a **megalopolis** (meg ə lop′ ə lis).

This is a very important area. It has millions of people, thousands of factories and businesses, many busy ports, and miles of highways and railroads. But many people feel that we must try to keep some green countryside and open spaces between the cities. Why do you think they feel that this is important?

CHECKUP

1. Which is our most densely populated state?
2. Name four large cities in the Middle Atlantic region.
3. What is a megalopolis?

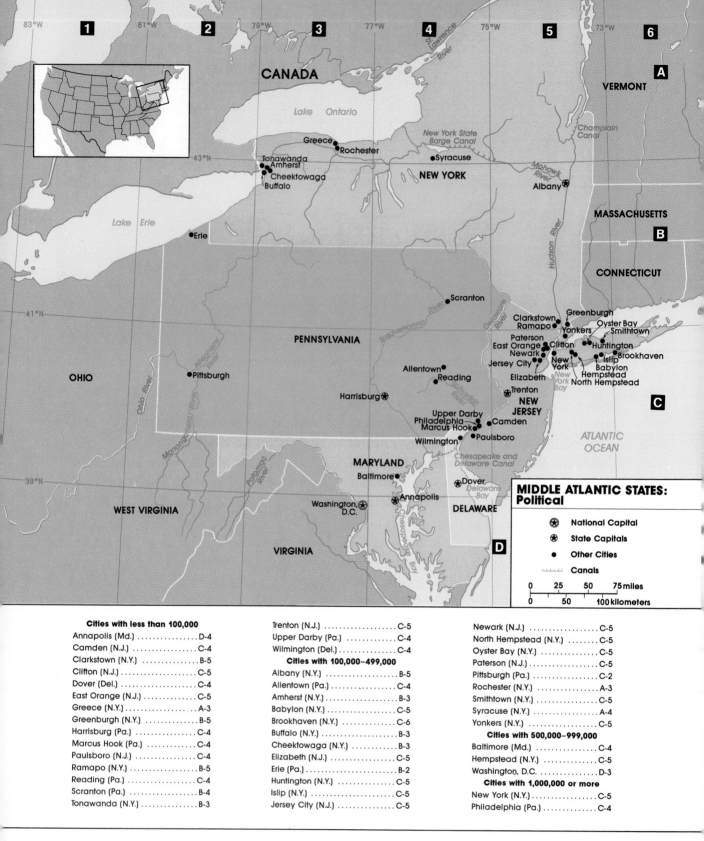

MIDDLE ATLANTIC STATES: Political

Symbol	Meaning
⊛	National Capital
✪	State Capitals
●	Other Cities
⌇⌇⌇	Canals

0   25   50   75 miles
0   50   100 kilometers

Cities with less than 100,000
Annapolis (Md.) D-4
Camden (N.J.) C-4
Clarkstown (N.Y.) B-5
Clifton (N.J.) C-5
Dover (Del.) C-4
East Orange (N.J.) C-5
Greece (N.Y.) A-3
Greenburgh (N.Y.) B-5
Harrisburg (Pa.) C-4
Marcus Hook (Pa.) C-4
Paulsboro (N.J.) C-4
Ramapo (N.Y.) B-5
Reading (Pa.) C-4
Scranton (Pa.) B-4
Tonawanda (N.Y.) B-3

Trenton (N.J.) C-5
Upper Darby (Pa.) C-4
Wilmington (Del.) C-4

Cities with 100,000–499,000
Albany (N.Y.) B-5
Allentown (Pa.) C-4
Amherst (N.Y.) B-3
Babylon (N.Y.) C-5
Brookhaven (N.Y.) C-6
Buffalo (N.Y.) B-3
Cheektowaga (N.Y.) B-3
Elizabeth (N.J.) C-5
Erie (Pa.) B-2
Huntington (N.Y.) C-5
Islip (N.Y.) C-5
Jersey City (N.J.) C-5

Newark (N.J.) C-5
North Hempstead (N.Y.) C-5
Oyster Bay (N.Y.) C-5
Paterson (N.J.) C-5
Pittsburgh (Pa.) C-2
Rochester (N.Y.) A-3
Smithtown (N.Y.) C-5
Syracuse (N.Y.) A-4
Yonkers (N.Y.) C-5

Cities with 500,000–999,000
Baltimore (Md.) C-4
Hempstead (N.Y.) C-5
Washington, D.C. D-3

Cities with 1,000,000 or more
New York (N.Y.) C-5
Philadelphia (Pa.) C-4

Look at the list of cities above. Then find on the map the two cities with 1 million or more people.

THE MIDDLE ATLANTIC STATES	Delaware	Maryland	New Jersey	New York	Pennsylvania
Source of Name	From Delaware River and Bay; named in turn for Sir Thomas West, Lord De La Warr	In honor of Henrietta Maria (queen of Charles I of England)	From the Channel Isle of Jersey	In honor of the English Duke of York, who later became King James II of England	In honor of Admiral Sir William Penn, father of William Penn. It means "Penn's Woodland."
Nickname(s)	Diamond State; First State	Free State; Old Line State	Garden State	Empire State	Keystone State
Capital	Dover	Annapolis	Trenton	Albany	Harrisburg
Largest Cities	Wilmington Newark Dover	Baltimore Rockville Hagerstown	Newark Jersey City Paterson	New York Hempstead Brookhaven	Philadelphia Pittsburgh Erie
Population Rank	47	19	9	2	4
Population Density Rank	7	5	1	6	8
Area Rank	49	42	46	30	33
State Flag					
State Bird	Blue hen chicken	Baltimore oriole	Eastern goldfinch	Bluebird	Ruffed grouse
State Flower	Peach blossom	Black-eyed Susan	Purple violet	Rose	Mountain laurel
State Tree	American holly	White oak	Red oak	Sugar maple	Hemlock
State Motto	Liberty and independence	*Fatti maschii, parole femine* (Manly deeds, womanly words)	Liberty and prosperity	*Excelsior* (Ever upward)	Virtue, liberty, and independence
Interesting Facts	Delaware was the first state to ratify the Constitution in 1787. It is the home of the largest chemical company in the world.	The land for Washington, D.C., our nation's capital, was given to the United States government by Maryland.	The first baseball game on record took place in Hoboken on June 19, 1846. West Orange is the home of Thomas Alva Edison.	West Point is the home of the United States Military Academy. New York City is the world's largest seaport and headquarters for the United Nations.	The Declaration of Independence was signed at Independence Hall in Philadelphia. The world's largest chocolate and cocoa factory is in Hershey. The first oil well in the United States was drilled in Titusville.

325

16/ CHAPTER REVIEW

KEY FACTS

1. Important features of the Middle Atlantic region include the bays and waterways, the Appalachians, and the Atlantic Coastal Plain.
2. The climate and soil of the Middle Atlantic region are suited to truck, dairy, and poultry farming.
3. Waterpower and coal are important energy resources of the Middle Atlantic region.
4. Important industries of the Middle Atlantic region include the manufacture of petrochemicals, iron, and steel.
5. Most of the Middle Atlantic region is heavily urban.

VOCABULARY QUIZ

Write the letter of the term next to the number of its description. Write on a sheet of paper.

a. foothills	**f.** truck farm
b. megalopolis	**g.** suburbs
c. sleet	**h.** petrochemical
d. commerce	**i.** temperature
e. harbor	**j.** Manufacturing Belt

1. The cities, towns, and villages that surround a large city
2. A protected place along a coast where ships load and unload goods
3. A landform often found between plains and mountains
4. The hotness or coldness of the air
5. Frozen rain
6. A vegetable farm
7. A term used to describe the huge industrial area of the Middle Atlantic region
8. A term used to describe industries that produce such materials as nylon or Dacron
9. A huge urban area made up of many cities and their suburbs
10. The buying and selling of goods

REVIEW QUESTIONS

1. Name the Middle Atlantic states.
2. Describe the physical features and climate of the Middle Atlantic region.
3. Name three important resources of the Middle Atlantic region.
4. Explain why the harbors and waterways of the Middle Atlantic region were important in the past and are still important today.
5. In which city is each of the following found: Liberty Bell, White House, Statue of Liberty?
6. Choose two of the cities described in the chapter and tell why each is important.

ACTIVITIES

1. Steel and petrochemicals are major products of the Middle Atlantic region. Look in an encyclopedia to find the kinds of products made from petrochemicals. Then label one sheet of paper *Steel Products* and another *Petrochemicals*. List as many items as you can find at home and in school that are made from these two products.
2. Choose two cities described in this chapter. (Do not choose a city in which you live.) For 2 weeks, look in your local newspaper for articles about the two cities.

First separate the articles by city. Then group the articles for each city. Put all the sports stories together, all the crime stories together, and so on. Then compare the two sets of articles. How do they show you that the two cities are alike? Different?

16/SKILLS DEVELOPMENT

READING A TABLE

OUR LARGEST CITIES

In this chapter you read about several of our nation's largest cities. You saw a map showing our largest cities in Chapter 14. On this page is a table that gives you some further information about our largest cities.

SKILLS PRACTICE

Use the table at the right as you answer the following questions. Write your answers on a separate sheet of paper.

1. How many of the cities are in New England?

2. How many of the cities are in the Middle Atlantic region?

3. How many cities have a population of over 1 million?

4. How many of the cities are in each of the following regions? (Hint: The states in each region are shown on the map on page 255.)

   a. Southeast   **d.** Mountain West

   b. South Central   **e.** Pacific

   c. North Central

5. Which states each have four cities on the table?

6. Which states each have two cities on the table?

7. What is the population of our fourteenth largest city? What city is it?

8. What is the population of our eighth largest city? What city is it?

9. Which two pairs of cities have almost the same population?

10. How many cities have a population of less than 500,000?

OUR NATION'S THIRTY LARGEST CITIES

City	Population	Rank
New York, N.Y.	7,086,000	1
Los Angeles, Calif.	3,022,000	2
Chicago, Ill.	2,997,000	3
Houston, Tex.	1,726,000	4
Philadelphia, Pa.	1,665,000	5
Detroit, Mich.	1,139,000	6
Dallas, Tex.	944,000	7
San Diego, Calif.	916,000	8
Phoenix, Ariz.	824,000	9
San Antonio, Tex.	819,000	10
Baltimore, Md.	774,000	11
Indianapolis, Ind.	708,000	12
San Francisco, Calif.	692,000	13
San Jose, Calif.	659,000	14
Memphis, Tenn.	646,000	15
Washington, D.C.	633,000	16
Milwaukee, Wis.	632,000	17
Columbus, Ohio	571,000	18
New Orleans, La.	565,000	19
Boston, Mass.	561,000	20
Cleveland, Ohio	559,000	21
Jacksonville, Fla.	556,000	22
Denver, Colo.	506,000	23
Seattle, Wash.	490,000	24
Nashville, Tenn.	455,000	25
Kansas City, Mo.	445,000	26
El Paso, Tex.	445,000	27
St. Louis, Mo.	437,000	28
Atlanta, Ga.	428,000	29
Oklahoma City, Okla.	428,000	30

Figures are rounded to the nearer thousand.

327

CHAPTER 17

The Southeast States Today

The Land

The region The Southeast has ten states: Virginia, West Virginia, Kentucky, Tennessee, North Carolina, South Carolina, Georgia, Florida, Alabama, and Mississippi.

Much of the Southeast is covered by coastal plains. Of course, there are other kinds of landforms, too. They include mountains and inland plains. The climate of much of the Southeast is hot and wet. However, in the mountains it is more **temperate.** A temperate climate is one that is neither extremely hot or cold nor extremely wet or dry.

The coastal plains The Atlantic Coastal Plain, which you learned about earlier, continues on from the Middle Atlantic states through Virginia, North and South Carolina, Georgia, and Florida. The Gulf Coastal Plain is the plain along the Gulf of Mexico. It stretches west from Florida into Alabama and Mississippi. Both the Atlantic Coastal Plain and the Gulf Coastal Plain reach inland as much as 200 miles (320 km) in many areas.

The swamps Here and there along both coastal plains are large swamps and **tidewater** areas. Tidewater is a name that is given to low-lying coastal land that is often flooded with seawater. When the land is covered with water, it is hard to tell where the sea ends and land begins. One way in which swamps differ from tidewater is that swamps are *always* under water.

The Everglades From Lake Okeechobee south, much of Florida is swampland known as The Everglades. There are towns and cities along the seacoasts, but much of the inland area is given over to wildlife refuges and parks. A wildlife refuge is a place set aside for wild animals. Hunting is not allowed. People may not build on the land or make roads through it. The best known park is Everglades National Park in Florida.

Many kinds of plants grow in The Everglades. Sawgrass covers acre after acre, but shrubs and trees, such as cypress, palm, and mangrove, have taken over large areas, too. Because there is a warm, wet climate, plants grow rapidly.

The Everglades is home to an amazing number of animals. There are hundreds of birds—egrets, herons, pelicans, cranes, and others. Alligators, crocodiles, turtles, snakes, snails, and raccoons all make

On the map find the Atlantic Coastal Plain and the Gulf Coastal Plain. The picture shows part of a chain of islands that stretches from Florida 150 miles (240 km) into the Gulf of Mexico.

THE SOUTHEAST STATES: Physical

⊛ State Capitals ▢ National Parks

● Other Cities ⟿ Swamp

| 0 | 50 | 100 | 150 miles |
| 0 | 100 | | 200 kilometers |

ILLINOIS

INDIANA

OHIO

PENNSYLVANIA

NEW JERSEY

MARYLAND

DELAWARE

WEST VIRGINIA

Huntington

Charleston

Louisville

Frankfort

MISSOURI

KENTUCKY

Mammoth Cave National Park

Lake Cumberland

Shenandoah National Park

Richmond

VIRGINIA

Colonial National Historical Park

Chesapeake Bay

Roanoke River

Kerr Lake

Great Dismal Swamp

Great Dismal Swamp National Wildlife Refuge

Virginia Beach

Roanoke Island

Kentucky Lake

Nashville

TENNESSEE

Great Smoky Mountains National Park

Mitchell

Charlotte

Raleigh

NORTH CAROLINA

ATLANTIC COASTAL PLAIN

Outer Banks

Cape Hatteras National Seashore

Pamlico Sound

Cape Lookout National Seashore

ARKANSAS

Memphis

Wheeler Lake

Guntersville Lake

Hartwell Reservoir

Sidney Lanier

Columbia

SOUTH CAROLINA

L.M. Smith Reservoir

Clark Hill Reservoir

Lake Marion

Birmingham

Atlanta

MISSISSIPPI

ALABAMA

GEORGIA

Charleston

Jackson

Montgomery

Columbus

LOUISIANA

Big Black River

Pearl River

Chattahoochee River

GULF COASTAL PLAIN

Okeefenokee Swamp

Tallahassee

Jacksonville

ATLANTIC OCEAN

Biloxi

Gulf of Mexico

FLORIDA

Cape Canaveral

Lake Okeechobee

The Everglades

Everglades National Park

Biscayne National Park

Florida Keys

APPALACHIAN MOUNTAINS

CUMBERLAND PLATEAU

ALLEGHENY PLATEAU

CUMBERLAND MOUNTAINS

BLUE RIDGE MOUNTAINS

PIEDMONT

88°W 84°W 80°W 76°W 72°W

38°N 34°N 30°N 26°N

A snowy egret looks for food while an alligator basks in the sun. These are just two of the many, many animals that make their home in The Everglades of Florida.

their home in The Everglades. The rare sea cow, or manatee, lives in The Everglades, as do thousands of insects.

The Florida Keys   A string of islands stretches southwest from the tip of Florida. These islands are the Florida **Keys.** They are little bits of land, barely above sea level, made of **coral** and limestone. The keys reach 150 miles (240 km) into the Gulf of Mexico. They are connected to one another by at least 40 bridges. A highway runs most of the length of the keys.

The Outer Banks   Another interesting group of islands is found along North Carolina's coast. The Outer Banks, as these islands are called, are a line of **barrier islands.** These sandy strips of land are called barrier islands because they form a barrier that protects the mainland.

The Outer Banks were once a part of a major disaster area for sailing vessels. The water is shallow here, and there are **shoals** and **reefs.** Shoals are underwater sand bars. The water above them is very shallow. Reefs are chains of rocks at or near the surface of the water. There have been hundreds of shipwrecks along the Outer Banks. Lighthouses now warn ships of the offshore danger.

Two large sections of the Outer Banks are taken up by Cape Hatteras National Seashore and Cape Lookout National Seashore. Another area is a wildlife refuge. One of the few villages is Kitty Hawk, where the Wright brothers made the first successful airplane flight.

The Piedmont   The Atlantic Coastal Plain rises gently to the Piedmont. The Piedmont is the upland area that lies between the Coastal Plain and the Appalachian Mountains. At the eastern edge of the Piedmont is the Fall Line, which begins in the north. It stretches south as far as Georgia. The Fall Line marks the point at which one finds waterfalls on the rivers flowing toward the coast. The waterfalls were a source of power in colonial days. Here too, the rivers change from swift-flowing streams into slow, gentle rivers that the ships of the time could use.

Ridges and plateaus   To the west of the Piedmont are the Appalachians. These mountains cover a large part of the Southeast. The Blue Ridge Mountains form the easternmost range of the Appalachians. This range begins in Pennsylvania and continues south to Georgia. The highest point of the Appalachians is in the Blue Ridge Mountains. It is Mount Mitchell in North Carolina.

West of the Blue Ridge Mountains in the north is the Allegheny Plateau. The Cumberland Mountains are south of this rugged plateau. The Cumberland Mountains are really a part of the Cumberland Plateau. The Cumberland Plateau stretches from West Virginia south through Kentucky, Virginia, and Tennessee to northern Alabama.

Hills and lowlands   As you travel westward, the mountains and plateaus give way to rolling hills. In Kentucky, this area is known as Bluegrass country. The

Kentucky's Bluegrass country is noted for its horse farms, on which fine horses like this mare and foal are raised.

name comes from the blue flowers in the grass that carpets the hills. Finally, in western Kentucky and Tennessee, you find yourself in lowlands. These lowlands are the Ohio and Mississippi river valleys.

Rivers   Throughout the southeastern states there are many rivers and streams. The Mississippi River forms the western border of Tennessee and most of that of Mississippi. You will learn more about this great river later. The Ohio River, another of our great rivers, borders West Virginia and Kentucky. The Cumberland River begins in Kentucky and loops down into Tennessee before flowing back through Kentucky to join the Ohio.

A fourth river, the Tennessee, is very important to the Southeast. At one time, the Tennessee and other nearby rivers flooded the land each spring. Then in 1933, Congress set up the Tennessee Valley Authority, or TVA, as it is called. The TVA built dams to help control the flooding. The TVA also provides water for irrigation, generates electricity, manufactures fertilizer, and has introduced soil conservation methods to many people in the area. In addition, the Tennessee River has been made navigable from Knoxville, Tennessee, to Paducah, Kentucky, where it joins the Ohio River.

CHECKUP

1. Describe one way in which a swamp differs from a tidewater.
2. What line marks the point at which waterfalls generally occur as rivers flow toward the coast?
3. Name at least four different landforms found in the Southeast.
4. What are shoals and reefs?

Climate

Temperature   In some places in the Southeast, the temperature rarely goes below 60°F (16°C), even in January. At others, the average January temperature is about 32°F (0°C). In general, the warmest places are in the southern coastal plains and in the lowlands west of the mountains. In these low-lying areas, there are long periods of warm weather. The **frost-free** season is the period when the temperature is always above freezing. This season lasts 6 months or more in most places near the coast. This makes for a long growing season throughout much of the Southeast.

The coolest parts of the Southeast are in the hills and mountains. In fact, elevation is one of the main reasons for temperature differences in the Southeast. But elevation is not the only reason for these differences. Otherwise Norfolk, Virginia, and Miami, Florida, would have the same climate. They are both on the Atlantic Coastal Plain, and both are less than 30 feet (9 m) in elevation. Yet Norfolk's average yearly temperature is 59°F (15°C), while Miami's is 76°F (24°C). The difference is that Miami is closer to the Equator (0° latitude) than Norfolk is. Miami is at about 26° north latitude; Norfolk is at about 37° north latitude.

The table at the top of this page shows you how latitude affects temperature. Each city on the table is at about the same elevation, but the latitude is different.

TEMPERATURE AND LATITUDE

City	Latitude	Average yearly temperature
Norfolk, Va.	37°N	59°F (15°C)
Wilmington, N.C.	34°N	64°F (18°C)
Savannah, Ga.	32°N	66°F (19°C)
Tampa, Fla.	28°N	72°F (22°C)
Miami, Fla.	26°N	76°F (24°C)

Which city is farthest from the Equator? Which is closest to the Equator? What happens to the temperature as you move closer to the Equator?

The table at the bottom of this page shows how elevation affects temperature. The places on the table are paired by latitude, but have different elevations. Which place in each pair has the warmer temperature: the place with the high elevation, or the one with the low elevation?

Precipitation   Most of the precipitation in the Southeast is rain. Snow is rare

TEMPERATURE AND ELEVATION

City	Elevation	Average yearly temperature
Charleston, S.C.	40 ft (12 m)	65°F (18°C)
Atlanta, Ga.	1,010 ft (308 m)	61°F (16°C)
Raleigh, N.C.	434 ft (132 m)	59°F (15°C)
Asheville, N.C.	2,140 ft (652 m)	56°F (13°C)
Norfolk, Va.	24 ft (7 m)	59°F (15°C)
Roanoke, Va.	1,149 ft (350 m)	56°F (13°C)
Richmond, Va.	164 ft (50 m)	58°F (14°C)
Beckley, W. Va.	2,504 ft (763 m)	51°F (11°C)

except in the mountain and northernmost areas. Even in the northern areas, the amount of snow that falls in a whole year is about the same as the amount that falls in one good New England storm.

Rainfall varies in the Southeast from about 40 inches (100 cm) a year to almost 70 inches (180 cm). The rainiest places are along the coasts. In these places, the most rain falls during the summer, when the temperature is at its highest. This combination causes hot, **humid** summers.

Hurricanes The coastal states may not get much snow, but they do have storms. **Hurricanes** often pass through the area. These storms have rapidly spinning walls of moist air around an inner area, or "eye," that is calm and cloudless. The "eye" alone may be several miles across, while the storm as a whole may be 100 to 300 miles (160–480 km) wide.

The hurricanes that affect the United States form over the Atlantic Ocean east of the Caribbean. They move west and northwest into the Caribbean and the Gulf of Mexico, striking the lands in their path. Many hurricanes leave their westward path and head north and northeast. Fortunately, some storms then blow out to sea. Others strike the Gulf or Atlantic coast, battering everything in their path with winds that reach 75 to 125 miles (120–200 km) an hour.

CHECKUP

1. In what parts of the Southeast would you be likely to find the coolest temperatures?
2. In this region, when does most rain occur? What part of the region gets the most rain?

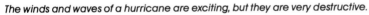

The winds and waves of a hurricane are exciting, but they are very destructive.

Agriculture, Industry, and Resources

Agriculture   One of the major crops in the Southeast is **citrus fruit.** Florida leads the United States in citrus production. As you drive through the Florida peninsula, you can see orange, lemon, lime, and grapefruit groves along the highways. In the cities and suburbs, many homeowners have citrus trees.

Croplands in the Southeast are also used to raise cash crops of tomatoes, lettuce, and many other vegetables. Two or three crops can be grown in a year in many places.

In Virginia, along the sandy coastal plain, there are large fields of potatoes, tomatoes, and strawberries. Peaches are grown from Georgia through Delaware. South Carolina leads the Southeast in peach production. Peanuts are grown from Virginia through Georgia and Alabama. Georgia is the United States' leading producer of peanuts. Other food crops include apples, corn, pecans, and sweet potatoes.

Not all crops are used for food. Two important nonfood crops from the Southeast are tobacco and cotton. Tobacco is grown in much of the Southeast. The leading states in tobacco production are North Carolina, Kentucky, and Tennessee.

In the 1800s, cotton was one of the most important crops in the South. It

The climate in many parts of the Southeast is good for cotton. This machine harvests the cotton bolls.

is still an important crop, although not as much cotton is planted now. Today farmers in Mississippi, Alabama, and Tennessee are the Southeast's leading producers of cotton.

Cotton needs a growing season of at least 6 months. It also needs plenty of rain in the spring and summer, and fairly dry weather during the fall harvest season. For these reasons, most of the cotton is grown in the inland areas, which are drier than the coastal areas.

The Southeast is important for its livestock, too. Cattle are raised in all ten states. Georgia, Alabama, North Carolina, and Mississippi rank second through fifth in the production of meat chickens in the United States. Hogs are important in several states.

Tourism   One of the largest industries of the Southeast is tourism. Florida's income from tourism is about eight times as large as that of any other state in the Southeast. The warm, sunny weather attracts many travelers. Walt Disney World, the Gulf Coast and Atlantic beaches, the Florida Keys, The Everglades, the Kennedy Space Center at Cape Canaveral, and other interesting places bring many visitors.

There are historic sites throughout the Southeast. One of the best known is Williamsburg, Virginia. Williamsburg has been restored to show visitors what homes looked like, how people dressed, and the work people did when our country was very young.

Near Williamsburg is the site of Jamestown. Here one can see ruins of the old settlement. Both Williamsburg and the Jamestown site are part of the Colonial National Historical Park. Near the Jamestown site is a state park in which you can see some reconstructed homes. These homes give you an idea of the way people of Jamestown lived. Also in this park are full-sized models of the ships that brought the colonists to Jamestown.

A visitor to Charleston, South Carolina, finds the nation's oldest museum and the Fort Sumter National Monument, where the first shots of the Civil War were fired.

Another interesting place to visit is St. Augustine, Florida. This town is the oldest existing European settlement in what is now the United States.

People who like camping, hiking, and other outdoor activities find much to enjoy in the Southeast. Wildlife abounds in the parks and elsewhere. Thousands of kinds of plants grow in the warm climate. Many lakes and streams offer freshwater fishing, and people can go deep-sea fishing in the waters off the coast. Throughout the area, tourists can observe the nesting areas of **migratory birds.** Migratory birds are birds that fly south for the winter.

The first shots of the Civil War were fired at Fort Sumter in the harbor of Charleston, South Carolina. Confederate forces fired on the Union troops holding the fort.

These boys and girls are backpacking in the Great Smoky Mountains. Judging by their faces, it's time to rest.

One park that offers many of these attractions is the Great Smoky Mountains National Park. This park is along the border between Tennessee and North Carolina. It draws more than 11 million visitors a year. Another well-known park is Mammoth Cave National Park in south-central Kentucky. People from all over the United States come to the park to explore the cave.

Fishing   Another important industry of the Southeast is fishing. From Chesapeake Bay come crabs, oysters, and menhaden (men hā' dən). Menhaden is a kind of fish that is either used as bait or made into fertilizer and oil.

From the Atlantic Ocean and the Gulf of Mexico come oysters, scallops, crabs, lobsters, shrimp, menhaden, and red snappers. The red snapper is a food fish. Fish catches in Virginia, North Carolina, and Mississippi are among the ten largest in the United States.

Tree farming   At one time almost all of the Southeast was forested. Now much of the land has been cleared so people can use it for other purposes. However, there is still a large demand for lumber. Hardwoods, such as maple and oak, are needed for furniture and for use in building. Papermills need softwoods, such as pine and poplar. Softwoods are also used for some kinds of furniture and for building. **Tree farming** has become important in meeting the demand for these different kinds of lumber. A tree farm may be a few acres of a farmer's land. Or it may be a huge tract owned by a lumber company. Scientists work on these large tree farms, developing new, fast-growing kinds of trees. There are more tree farms in Mississippi than in any other state.

The coniferous trees of the woodlands and tree farms of the coastal plains provide the raw materials for the paper industry. As in New England, many mills have polluted the air and water. Now state and national laws are helping to control pollution.

Textiles   Many industries of the Southeast are directly related to agriculture. One such industry is the textile industry. Mills from Virginia through Georgia make not only cotton but also rayon, nylon, and other synthetics. Good workers, well-run plants, and good transportation have helped to make southern mills our leading producers of textiles. South Carolina leads the nation in textile production.

Food processing   Citrus products from Florida reach all parts of the United States. Much of the fruit chosen to be

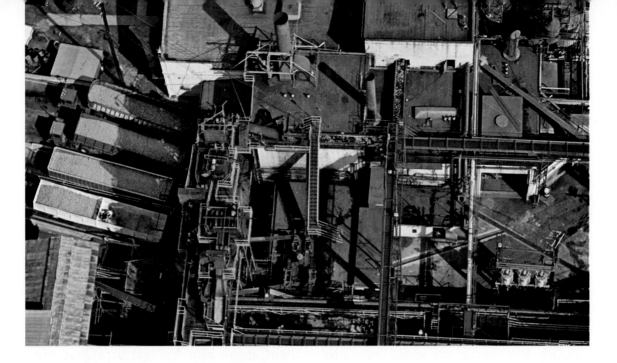

Several truckloads of fruit start their journey through this citrus-processing plant. Notice the fruit on the conveyor belt in the center of the picture.

sent fresh is handpicked before it is fully ripe. The fruit is then cleaned, dyed, labeled, and sorted by size. Finally it is packed into crates and shipped to markets all across the country.

Fruit that is to be made into frozen or canned juice is loaded into large trucks after it is picked. These big tractor-trailer trucks hold tons of oranges or other fruits. At the food-processing plant, the load is weighed. Then it is emptied by raising the whole trailer up so the fruit rolls out. Almost the whole process, from emptying the truck to filling the cans with juice, is handled by machines. Workers operate the machines and make sure they are running properly.

Canning and freezing vegetables is another important food-processing industry. Most ripe vegetables, like fruits, spoil within a short time after picking. When these foods are canned, dried, or frozen, they can be enjoyed throughout the year.

Minerals   Several important resources are found underground in the Southeast. There are large deposits of oil and gas. Mines in Alabama and Georgia are among our leading sources of bauxite. Bauxite is used in making aluminum. Mines in Florida, North Carolina, and Tennessee are leaders in phosphate production. This mineral is used in fertilizers.

You might not think of stone, gravel, sand, and clay as important natural resources. After all, you can pick up a stone or a handful of gravel or sand in many places. However, these materials are important. Our highways and many construction projects could not be completed without them. The Southeast is an important source of these resources.

Coal   Large amounts of coal are mined in the Southeast. More than half our coal comes from a huge coalfield that stretches from Pennsylvania into Alabama, a distance of more than 700 miles (1,100 km). Kentucky ranks first in the United States in coal production; West Virginia, second.

At one time coal was the main fuel in use in the United States. Then more and more people began using oil and gas. As a result, many coal mines were closed. Now we have begun to run out of oil and gas. Both fuels have become very expensive. Coal is once again important.

Some coal is near the surface of the earth. It can be mined by a method called **strip mining.** Large earthmovers are used to clear away the **overburden,** or layers of earth that cover the coal. Once the overburden has been removed, machines like the one in the picture on page 278 dig the coal and load it into trucks to be hauled away.

Strip mining is safer and less costly than underground mining. However, strip mining destroys the land. Mining com-panies must now restore the land after the coal has been mined. Restoring the land is costly. However, not restoring it is even more costly in the long run. If the land is left without its topsoil and plant cover, the remaining earth **erodes.** Few plants will grow in the poor soil. Large areas of land become both unsightly and of little value.

Underground mines are used when the **seam** of coal is deep in the ground. Although today's miners use machines, underground mining is a difficult job. Each day the miners ride an elevator that takes them deep into the earth. When they leave the elevator, they find themselves in a system of tunnels and "rooms" that have been hollowed out of the earth. These rooms may be only about as high as the seam is thick. Often, this means that the ceiling is not high enough to allow miners to stand upright. The miners sit in long, low machines that dig out the coal.

Underground mining has always been a dangerous job. Sometimes there are cave-ins, and miners are crushed. Sometimes the digging releases poisonous or explosive gases. Coal dust presents further problems. When there is a lot of coal dust in the air, the dust may explode. Miners who breathe coal dust for many years often get a disease called black lung. Laws today help to protect the miners. There are fewer deaths and injuries than there once were, but mining can still be dangerous.

From this picture, you can see why land that has been strip mined needs to be reclaimed.

CHECKUP

1. Which state is the leading grower of citrus?
2. Name at least four tourist attractions found in the Southeast. Tell where each is found.
3. Which state is the leading coal producer?

Population and Cities

Population   Florida has the largest population of the southeastern states and the sixth largest population of the 50 states. It is one of the five fastest growing states in the United States. Most people in Florida live in cities.

West Virginia has the smallest population of the southeastern states. Less than half the people live in cities.

The table shows the population of each southeastern state, the number of cities with populations of 100,000 or more, and the percent of the population living in urban areas.

Cities   Only two southeastern cities have populations of more than 500,000. They are Memphis, Tennessee, and Jacksonville, Florida, two of the 25 largest cities in the United States.

At one time, the Southeast had few large cities. Today, however, much manufacturing has moved to the Southeast. New industries have developed. *Manufacturing cities* have grown with these industries. Cities have developed as *trade centers*, where the goods produced by industry are sold. Because the goods must be shipped to other places, *port cities* have increased in size. The increase in tourism has brought growth to another kind of city, the *resort city*. Of course, none of the cities is just a trade center, just a resort, or just a port. Miami, for example, started

SOUTHEASTERN STATES: POPULATION AND CITIES			
States	Population	Percent urban	Cities of 100,000 or more people
Florida	10,976,000	84	9
North Carolina	6,165,000	48	5
Georgia	5,837,000	62	4
Virginia	5,636,000	66	9
Tennessee	4,717,000	60	4
Alabama	3,990,000	60	4
Kentucky	3,723,000	51	2
South Carolina	3,300,000	54	1
Mississippi	2,598,000	47	1
West Virginia	1,952,000	36	0

as a resort. Now the city is important in manufacturing and transportation, too. In the next few pages, we'll look at Miami and some other cities.

Atlanta   With a population of about 428,000 Atlanta is the largest city in Georgia. Atlanta has served as Georgia's capital since the time of the Civil War. The National Center for Disease Control is in Atlanta. At this center, people look for ways to control outbreaks of diseases that spread from one person to another.

Atlanta is a leading industrial center. Airplanes, automobiles, chemicals, textiles, furniture, and many other products are made in and around Atlanta.

Atlanta is the Southeast's center for foreign trade. Governments from about 11 countries have set up **consulates** in Atlanta. The people in the consulates help make trade agreements between business people from their countries and business people in and around Atlanta.

Birmingham   Birmingham, Alabama, has been the Southeast's leading iron- and steel-producing center for over 100 years. The city is near the coal, limestone, and iron ore needed to make iron and steel. Railways provide transportation for these raw materials and for the finished products. Since the 1940s the city has tried to attract new industries so that it would not be dependent on just one industry. Now food-processing and chemical plants are among Birmingham's many industries.

Charleston, South Carolina   Charleston is a small city with a population of about 70,000, although the metropolitan area has about 430,000 people. Charleston is one of the oldest cities in the United States. At the time of the Revolutionary War, Charleston was the most important city and port south of Philadelphia. It served as the business and cultural center of the area. Charleston still serves as a port for both trade and military purposes.

Charleston, West Virginia   The resources near Charleston, West Virginia, have helped the city grow into the major trade and industrial center of the state. Coal, chemicals, limestone, lumber, salt, clay, and gas are leading products of the city's industries.

Charlotte   Charlotte is the largest city in North Carolina. With more than 670 manufacturing companies, it is a major industrial center. The chief products are chemicals, cloth, foods, and machinery. Charlotte is also a very important trucking center. Charlotte became a city before the Revolutionary War.

Jackson   Jackson is the capital and by far the largest city in Mississippi. Jackson has about 204,000 people, while the other cities in the state have less than 60,000 people each. Jackson's central location has helped it grow as a center of transportation. This in turn helped it grow as a trading and manufacturing center. A nearby supply of gas also helped the city bring in industry.

Louisville   Louisville (lü′ i vil) is the largest city in Kentucky. This important transportation center is on the banks of the Ohio River. Plastics, automobiles, meat-packing, and tobacco are a few of the city's important industries. The world's largest publisher of Braille books and magazines is in Louisville. Braille books are books for blind people. The well-known Kentucky Derby horse race is held in Louisville.

This part of Charleston, South Carolina, has been restored to show the way it looked many years ago.

Memphis   This Tennessee city serves as a trade center for much of the South Central region of the United States, as well as for western Tennessee. Cotton and livestock and many other agricultural products are marketed in Memphis.

Memphis is a transportation center for the area, too. Located on the Mississippi River, it is one of the major North American ports.

Miami   Miami, Florida, is one of the newer cities of the United States. It was founded in 1870 and officially became a city in 1896. This city is home to many thousands of Cuban refugees. People whose lives and property have been in danger have been fleeing from Cuba since the revolution there in 1959. Most of them have come first to Florida. Many of them have stayed there.

Tourism is Miami's leading industry, although the city is a transportation center because of its major air, sea, and rail connections. The city also is the nation's third largest center of the **garment,** or clothing, industry.

Norfolk   Norfolk, Virginia, is the largest of a group of cities around the Port of Hampton Roads. The other cities that share the port are Portsmouth, Newport News, and Hampton. More goods are **exported** from the Port of Hampton Roads than from any other Atlantic port. The Port of Hampton Roads is the biggest coal port in the world. The largest naval base in the United States is located in Norfolk. The harbor and the city's airlines, railroads, and highways have helped make Norfolk the largest city in Virginia.

Several ships are berthed at this Norfolk navy base. Among them are aircraft carriers and cargo ships.

Rural areas   Of course, not all of the Southeast is made up of cities. Many areas have few people living in them. Farming areas usually have a low population density. Certain physical features account for other areas of low population density.

Look at the population density map on page 259. What physical feature accounts for the low population density in most of southern Florida? If you can't remember, look at the map on page 329. What physical feature accounts for the area of low population density that runs northeast to southwest through the middle of the southeastern region? Let's see why this area has such a low population density.

Appalachia   People settled in the many small valleys of the Appalachians as early as the seventeenth century. Here they built farms just big enough to meet their own needs. Travel was difficult in this hilly land. There wasn't enough good farmland for the large farms that

The old crafts have undergone a revival in Appalachia. (Left) An old woman teaches the art of making brooms. (Right) Fairgoers watch a potter demonstrate her craft.

need a market in which to sell crops. For these reasons, few towns grew up in Appalachia, as this region is called. Because there were so few ways of making a living, many young people left Appalachia as soon as they were old enough to look for work. During the 1800s, some coal-mining towns were built. However, many of these almost disappeared when the demand for coal fell off. For those who remained in Appalachia, life was hard. **Poverty** was widespread.

Even today, Appalachia remains a region of small farms and villages. However, some of the mining towns are again beginning to grow because of the renewed need for coal. Modern fertilizers and farming methods have helped farmers in the area to grow larger crops. This means

they have more money to spend in nearby towns and villages. The TVA brought electricity to some parts of Appalachia. This in turn allowed businesses to develop. Ski resorts and campgrounds in the area bring tourists who want the same kinds of services they find at home. New roads have made travel easier. Appalachia is becoming less isolated. For these reasons, there is less poverty in the area. More young people are staying in the region. Life in Appalachia is becoming more and more like life in the rest of the nation.

CHECKUP

1. What are the two largest cities of the Southeast?
2. Name three cities that serve as ports. Locate each city on a map.
3. What are three things that are happening to bring change to Appalachia?

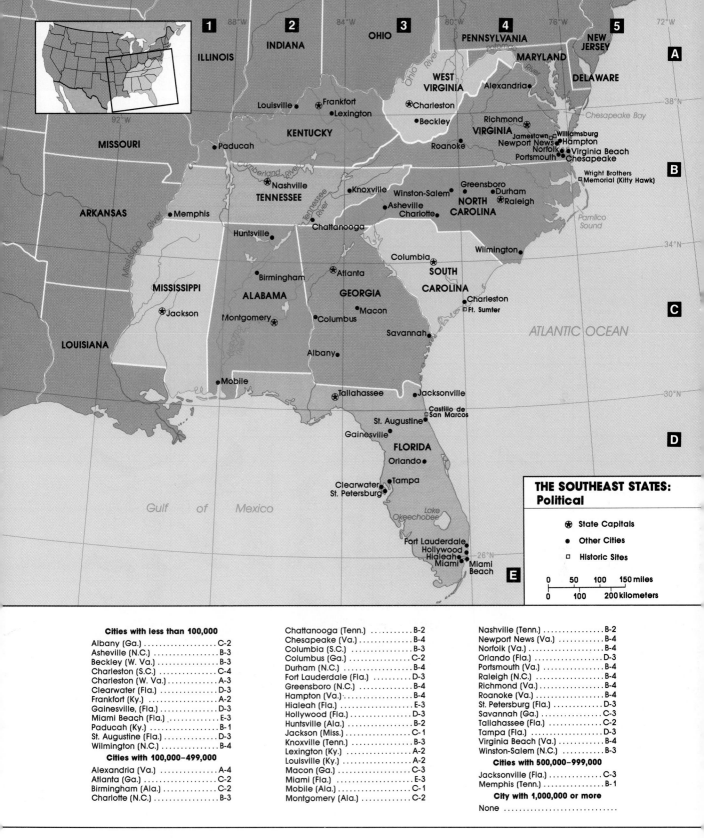

The map shows the following labels:

Top border grid numbers: 1, 2, 3, 4, 5

Longitude: 88°W, 84°W, 80°W, 76°W, 72°W, 92°W

Latitude: 38°N, 34°N, 30°N, 26°N

Side grid letters: A, B, C, D, E

States and regions:
ILLINOIS, INDIANA, OHIO, PENNSYLVANIA, NEW JERSEY, MARYLAND, DELAWARE, WEST VIRGINIA, VIRGINIA, KENTUCKY, MISSOURI, TENNESSEE, ARKANSAS, NORTH CAROLINA, MISSISSIPPI, ALABAMA, GEORGIA, SOUTH CAROLINA, LOUISIANA, FLORIDA

Water bodies:
Ohio River, Chesapeake Bay, Cumberland River, Tennessee River, Mississippi River, Pamlico Sound, ATLANTIC OCEAN, Gulf of Mexico, Lake Okeechobee, Potomac

Cities and sites:
Louisville, Frankfort, Lexington, Charleston, Alexandria, Beckley, Richmond, Jamestown, Williamsburg, Newport News, Hampton, Norfolk, Virginia Beach, Portsmouth, Chesapeake, Roanoke, Paducah, Nashville, Knoxville, Winston-Salem, Greensboro, Durham, Wright Brothers Memorial (Kitty Hawk), Memphis, Asheville, Charlotte, Raleigh, Huntsville, Chattanooga, Wilmington, Columbia, Jackson, Birmingham, Atlanta, SOUTH CAROLINA, Charleston, Ft. Sumter, Montgomery, Macon, Columbus, Savannah, Albany, Mobile, Tallahassee, Jacksonville, Castillo de San Marcos, St. Augustine, Gainesville, Orlando, Clearwater, Tampa, St. Petersburg, Fort Lauderdale, Hollywood, Hialeah, Miami, Miami Beach

Legend:

THE SOUTHEAST STATES:
Political

⊛ State Capitals
● Other Cities
□ Historic Sites

0 50 100 150 miles
0 100 200 kilometers

Cities with less than 100,000

City	Grid
Albany (Ga.)	C-2
Asheville (N.C.)	B-3
Beckley (W. Va.)	B-3
Charleston (S.C.)	C-4
Charleston (W. Va.)	A-3
Clearwater (Fla.)	D-3
Frankfort (Ky.)	A-2
Gainesville, (Fla.)	D-3
Miami Beach (Fla.)	E-3
Paducah (Ky.)	B-1
St. Augustine (Fla.)	D-3
Wilmington (N.C.)	B-4

Cities with 100,000–499,000

City	Grid
Alexandria (Va.)	A-4
Atlanta (Ga.)	C-2
Birmingham (Ala.)	C-2
Charlotte (N.C.)	B-3
Chattanooga (Tenn.)	B-2
Chesapeake (Va.)	B-4
Columbia (S.C.)	B-3
Columbus (Ga.)	C-2
Durham (N.C.)	B-4
Fort Lauderdale (Fla.)	D-3
Greensboro (N.C.)	B-4
Hampton (Va.)	B-4
Hialeah (Fla.)	E-3
Hollywood (Fla.)	D-3
Huntsville (Ala.)	B-2
Jackson (Miss.)	C-1
Knoxville (Tenn.)	B-3
Lexington (Ky.)	A-2
Louisville (Ky.)	A-2
Macon (Ga.)	C-3
Miami (Fla.)	E-3
Mobile (Ala.)	C-1
Montgomery (Ala.)	C-2
Nashville (Tenn.)	B-2
Newport News (Va.)	B-4
Norfolk (Va.)	B-4
Orlando (Fla.)	D-3
Portsmouth (Va.)	B-4
Raleigh (N.C.)	B-4
Richmond (Va.)	B-4
Roanoke (Va.)	B-4
St. Petersburg (Fla.)	D-3
Savannah (Ga.)	C-3
Tallahassee (Fla.)	C-2
Tampa (Fla.)	D-3
Virginia Beach (Va.)	B-4
Winston-Salem (N.C.)	B-3

Cities with 500,000–999,000

City	Grid
Jacksonville (Fla.)	C-3
Memphis (Tenn.)	B-1

City with 1,000,000 or more

None . . . .

Which two cities have populations greater than 500,000? Find them on the map. What places shown on the map would you like to visit?

THE SOUTHEAST STATES	Alabama	Florida	Georgia	Kentucky	Mississippi
Source of Name	From the Alibamu Indian tribe meaning "I clear the thicket."	From the Spanish, (*pascua florida*) meaning "feast of flowers"	In honor of George II of England	From an Iroquoian word *Ken-tah-ten* meaning "land of tomorrow"	From an Indian word meaning "Father of Waters"
Nickname(s)	Yellowhammer State	Sunshine State	Peach State; Empire State of the South; Goober State	Bluegrass State	Magnolia State
Capital	Montgomery	Tallahassee	Atlanta	Frankfort	Jackson
Largest Cities	Birmingham Mobile Montgomery	Jacksonville Miami Tampa	Atlanta Columbus Savannah	Louisville Lexington Owensboro	Jackson Biloxi Meridian
Population Rank	22	6	11	23	31
Population Density Rank	26	11	21	23	31
Area Rank	29	22	21	37	32
State Flag					
State Bird	Yellowhammer	Mockingbird	Brown thrasher	Kentucky cardinal	Mockingbird
State Flower	Camellia	Orange blossom	Cherokee rose	Goldenrod	Magnolia
State Tree	Southern pine (longleaf)	Sabal palm	Live oak	Coffeetree	Magnolia
State Motto	*Audemus jura nostra defendere* (We dare defend our rights.)	In God we trust	Wisdom, justice, and moderation	United we stand, divided we fall	*Virtute et armis* (By valor and arms)
Interesting Facts	Montgomery was the first capital of the Confederacy. George Washington Carver did his famous research on the peanut at Tuskegee Institute.	Nearly three fourths of the nation's oranges and grapefruit are produced here. The manned space flights are launched from the John F. Kennedy Space Center.	It is the largest state east of the Mississippi. It is called the "Goober State" because the state leads the nation in the production of goobers, or peanuts.	It is the nation's largest producer of coal. The federal government's huge gold supply is kept at Fort Knox.	The Petrified Forest near Flora has giant stone trees as old as 30 million years. There are more tree farms in Mississippi than in any other state.

344

THE SOUTHEAST STATES	North Carolina	South Carolina	Tennessee	Virginia	West Virginia
Source of Name	In honor of Charles I of England	In honor of Charles I of England	From the name of a Cherokee Indian village—Tanasie	In honor of Queen Elizabeth I of England	In honor of Queen Elizabeth I of England
Nickname(s)	Tar Heel State	Palmetto State	Volunteer State	The Old Dominion; Mother of Presidents	Mountain State
Capital	Raleigh	Columbia	Nashville	Richmond	Charleston
Largest Cities	Charlotte Greensboro Raleigh	Columbia Charleston North Charleston	Memphis Nashville-Davidson Knoxville	Virginia Beach Norfolk Richmond	Huntington Charleston Wheeling
Population Rank	10	24	17	13	34
Population Density Rank	17	19	18	16	25
Area Rank	28	40	34	36	41
State Flag					
State Bird	Cardinal	Carolina wren	Mockingbird	Cardinal	Cardinal
State Flower	American dogwood	Carolina yellow jessamine	Iris	American dogwood	Rhododendron
State Tree	Pine	Palmetto	Tulip poplar	Flowering dogwood	Sugar maple
State Motto	*Esse quam videri* (To be rather than to seem)	*Animis opibusque parati* (Prepared in mind and resources) *Dum spiro spero* (While I breathe, I hope)	Tennessee—America at its best	*Sic semper tyrannis* (Thus always to tyrants)	*Montani semper liberi* (Mountaineers are always free)
Interesting Facts	On December 17, 1903, the Wright brothers made their first flight from Kitty Hawk. The dangerous Cape Hatteras, off the coast, is known as the "Graveyard of the Atlantic."	It was the first state to withdraw from the Union before the Civil War. On April 12, 1861, Confederate troops fired the opening shots of the Civil War on Fort Sumter in Charleston Harbor.	It is called the Volunteer State because it is known for its tradition of excellent military service. Davy Crockett and President Andrew Jackson were natives of Tennessee.	Eight presidents of the United States were born in Virginia. They include Washington, Jefferson, Madison, Monroe, W. Harrison, Tyler, Taylor, and Wilson. The first permanent English settlement was in Jamestown, 1607.	Free delivery of mail in rural areas was started here in 1896. The first natural gas well to be discovered in the nation was found in Charleston.

345

17/CHAPTER REVIEW

KEY FACTS

1. Important landforms of the Southeast include swamps, the Piedmont, hills and plateaus, the Appalachian Mountains, and the Atlantic and Gulf coastal plains.

2. The Tennessee River system is used for shipping, recreation, irrigation, and power.

3. Climate is related to latitude and to elevation.

4. Much of the Southeast has a climate suited to growing a variety of important crops.

5. Major industries of the Southeast include tourism, textiles, food processing, fishing, lumbering, mining, and manufacturing.

6. The largest cities of the Southeast are Memphis and Jacksonville.

VOCABULARY QUIZ

Write the letter of the term next to the number of its description. Write on a sheet of paper.

a. barrier islands **f.** tidewater
b. overburden **g.** hurricane
c. temperate **h.** consulate
d. humid **i.** citrus
e. shoals **j.** refugees

1. Neither extremely hot nor extremely cold
2. Underwater sand bars
3. Islands along a coast that help protect the mainland
4. A storm with winds that reach speeds of 75 to 125 miles (120–200 km) an hour
5. A kind of fruit that includes lemons, oranges, and limes
6. Low-lying coastal land that is often flooded with water
7. People who flee from their homeland because their lives and property are in danger

8. The earth covering a deposit of coal
9. An office set up by the government of a foreign country to help business people work together
10. Having much moisture.

REVIEW QUESTIONS

1. Where are the Atlantic and Gulf coastal plains located?
2. Describe The Everglades of Florida.
3. What is the Piedmont? Where is it located?
4. What do the letters TVA stand for? What does the TVA do?
5. How are temperature and latitude related? Temperature and elevation?
6. Name two important crops of the Southeast.
7. What is strip mining?
8. Give an example of each of the following kinds of cities: port city, manufacturing city, trade center, resort city.
9. What was life like in Appalachia at one time? How is it changing?

ACTIVITIES

1. Choose several of the places named in the section on tourism that you would like to visit. Look in magazines or write for information about those places. Plan how you would travel to the places. Tell what kind of transportation you would use (plane, bus, car, train), and show your route on a map.

2. On the left side of a sheet of paper make a list of agricultural products from the Southeast. Draw another line to make a column. For each product, name one state that produces the product. In a third column list some of the uses of the product. For example, for the product peanuts you might list candy, peanut butter, and cooking oil.

17/ SKILLS DEVELOPMENT

RESEARCH SKILLS

CAREER AWARENESS

In the next few years, there will be large numbers of job openings for the kinds of workers named on the graph below. Do you know what kinds of work all these people do? What does a stenographer do? A retail trade sales worker? A chef? If you don't know, look in a dictionary or an encyclopedia.

SKILLS PRACTICE

Look at the graph. Answer these questions.

1. Which workers should find a job most easily?

2. Who would have more openings to choose from, a bookkeeper or a typist?

3. About how many openings will there be each year for custodians? For teachers?

If you are interested in finding out about other jobs, look in the index of an almanac under "Jobs," "Occupations," or "Employment." Several almanacs have tables giving the percent of change in the number of openings for many different jobs over a 10-year period. (A minus sign before the percent means that fewer people will be doing that job at the end of the 10 years than at the beginning.) Look for the kind of job you would like. Is the percent higher, or lower, than it is for most of the other jobs? Why is it important to know about job openings?

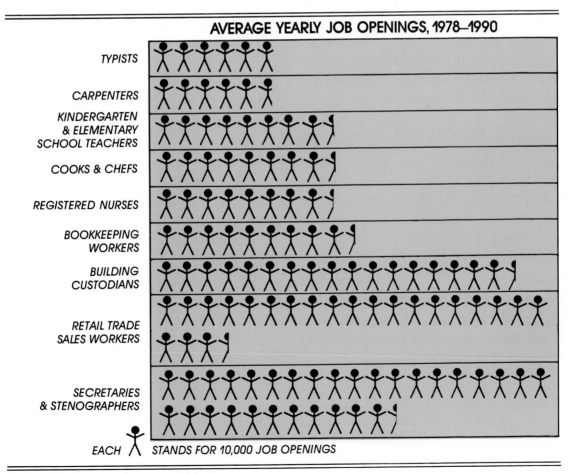

AVERAGE YEARLY JOB OPENINGS, 1978–1990

EACH ⋀ STANDS FOR 10,000 JOB OPENINGS

18 The South Central States Today

The Land and Climate

VOCABULARY

marshland	tornado
gulf	panhandle
silt	water vapor
levee	

Four similar states The South Central region has the fewest states. There are only four states. They are Arkansas, Louisiana, Oklahoma, and Texas. The land features of the South Central states range from low **marshlands** along the coast, to high plains, to mountains. Look at the map at the right. Notice that the Gulf Coastal Plain covers much of the region.

The four South Central states supply us with some very important resources and farm products. Deposits of oil and gas can be found in each of the four states. All four states have large forests that provide wood and paper products. All four states also have rich, fertile soil for growing farm crops. Cotton, grains, and fruit are only some of the products grown in each of the South Central states.

Land features The Gulf Coastal Plain is an important land feature of the South Central states. Gently rolling grasslands and valleys make up a large part of the South Central region.

The Mississippi River delta is in the Gulf Coastal Plain. The delta is in the low coastal marshland of Louisiana. The word *delta* comes from the Greek letter that looks like this Δ. River deltas often have a shape like the Greek letter.

The flow of a river causes deltas to form. Rivers usually flow into larger bodies of water, such as oceans or **gulfs.** A gulf is part of an ocean or sea that pushes into the land. **Silt,** or fine soil and ground stone, is carried by the flowing water. As the water slows down at the mouth of a river, the silt drops to the bottom. Over time the silt builds up at the river's mouth to form a delta.

There are several places in the South Central region where the land rises to become plateaus and mountains. Find the Ozark Plateau and the Ouachita (wäsh′ ə tô) and Guadalupe (gwäd′ əl üp) mountains on the map.

The Great Plains is a vast plain that stretches from southwestern Texas to the Canadian border. One part of the Great Plains in Texas is called *Llano Estacado* (lan′ ō es tə käd′ ō). These are Spanish words that mean "staked (stākt) plain." Early Spanish explorers found the area so flat that the only way they could find their way was to place stakes in the ground to show where they had been.

Can you find on the map all the rivers that form borders? Below the map is a photograph taken from a satellite showing part of the Mississippi Delta area. The river is the bright blue line. The cloudy blue area is mud and silt in the water.

THE SOUTH CENTRAL STATES:
Physical

⊛ State Capitals
● Other Cities
⊔⊔ Canal

0   50   100   150 miles
0   100   200 kilometers

This house remained standing in spite of the flood. Many others were swept away.

Rivers In Chapter 14 you learned that the source of the Mississippi River is in Minnesota. The Mississippi River is one of the nation's longest rivers. It is 2,348 miles (3,778 km) long. This major waterway serves as the eastern boundary of Arkansas and most of that of Louisiana. It forms a large part of the western boundary of Mississippi and all the western boundary of Tennessee. Look at the map of the United States in the Atlas, pages 468–469. What other states have the Mississippi River as a boundary?

The Mississippi has been a major transportation route throughout the history of the United States. Today it is still the busiest inland waterway in our country. Barges can travel on the Mississippi as far north as Minneapolis, Minnesota.

As you know, the river has left silt along the delta and coastal plain for hundreds of years. This has helped to make the land fertile and valuable for farming. However,

the river has also caused problems. There have been years when the river overflowed its banks and flooded the land. The flooding happened in the spring after the northern snows melted or after weeks of very heavy rain. The water flooded areas where the **levees** (lev′ ēz) along the river were not strong enough or high enough to hold back the increased flow of the river. A levee is a wide wall built with earth.

One of the worst floods took place in 1927. It forced more than 300,000 people living in the Mississippi River plain to flee their homes. In 1973 high water flooded more than 13 million acres (5 million ha) of land in nine states from Illinois to Louisiana. The flooding destroyed millions of dollars worth of crops. It delayed the planting of other crops. It cost about $193 million to repair the damage. Only the very large levee system prevented more damage.

The Rio Grande, like the Mississippi River, serves as a boundary. It lies between Mexico and Texas. From its source high in the Rocky Mountains in Colorado, the river travels 1,885 miles (3,033 km) to reach the Gulf of Mexico. *Rio Grande* is a Spanish name. In English it means "great river."

Other large rivers of the South Central region include the Arkansas River and the Red River. Barges can navigate the Arkansas River as far north as Tulsa, Oklahoma. Even though Tulsa is inland, it is a major port city.

The Red River flows through parts of each of the South Central states before it reaches the Mississippi River north of New Orleans. It is named the Red River because it carries red-colored silt. The land along the Arkansas and Red rivers has rich soil that is excellent for farming.

Climate   Warm waters from the area around the Equator flow into the Gulf of Mexico. These warm waters help control the climate of Louisiana and coastal Texas. Warm breezes blowing off the gulf help keep the summers warm and humid and the winters temperate. This means most

SOUTH CENTRAL STATES: YEARLY PRECIPITATION

Weather station	Inches	Centimeters
Little Rock	49	124
Baton Rouge	54	137
Oklahoma City	31	79
Lubbock	18	46
Houston	48	122

winters are mild. Although the temperature does go below freezing, snow is rare. The mild winters give farmers a long growing season.

Western Texas has a cool, dry climate. Central Texas and most of Oklahoma have a warm, dry climate. The climate of Arkansas is warm and rainy. As you can see, there are different types of climates in this region. Look at the charts to find the temperature and precipitation of certain cities in the South Central region.

Tornadoes   During the months from March to June, the South Central states can have one of the most feared of all storms—the **tornado.** The South Central region is part of what is called "Tornado

SOUTH CENTRAL STATES: TEMPERATURE

Weather station	Average January temperature °F	°C	Average July temperature °F	°C	Temperature extremes High °F	Low °F	Temperature extremes High °C	Low °C
Little Rock	40	4	81	27	108	−5	42	−21
Baton Rouge	51	11	82	28	103	10	39	−12
Oklahoma City	39	4	82	28	108	−4	42	−20
Lubbock	39	4	80	27	107	−16	42	−27
Houston	52	11	83	28	102	17	39	−8

The swirling winds of a tornado can cause nearly complete destruction. Yet right next to the storm track, there may be no damage at all.

Alley." This alley stretches from the Texas **panhandle** north to Nebraska and as far east as Ohio. A panhandle is a narrow strip of land.

Tornadoes often form in the late afternoon or early evening of a very hot, humid day. At such times, thick, dark clouds sometimes form into a cone-shaped cloud that becomes a high-powered, twisting windstorm. That storm is a tornado. Tornadoes make a roaring noise that sounds like a speeding train. **Water vapor** and dust picked up by the winds give the funnel its gray color.

In the center of the tornado, winds can swirl at speeds of 300 miles per hour (480 km per hr). The worst tornado on record was a mile (1.6 km) wide and traveled 220 miles (354 km) across three states at 60 miles (97 km) per hour.

CHECKUP

1. How was the Mississippi River delta formed?
2. What are the four kinds of climate found in the South Central region?
3. What is a tornado?

Agriculture

-VOCABULARY-

sorghum grain	feedlot
subtropical	overgraze
erosion	rodeo

A variety of crops   The kinds of crops that are grown in the South Central region are closely connected to the rainfall, temperature, and land features you have just learned about. Many types of crops are produced in these four states. Soybeans, rice, sugarcane, cotton, sweet potatoes, and citrus fruits grow well in the warm, moist climate of Arkansas, Louisiana, and the coastal plains of Texas. Winter wheat and **sorghum** (sôr' gəm) **grain** do well in the drier and more temperate areas of the region.

Along the Rio Grande in southern Texas and near the Gulf Coast, farmers grow citrus fruits and fresh vegetables. The long growing season, good rainfall, and irrigation from the river help to make citrus fruits and fresh vegetables important crops.

Cotton   Texas is the second largest cotton-producing state in the United States. Look at the table. How do the other three South Central states rank in the production of cotton? The combination of warm, wet climate and good soil helps to make cotton a very successful crop in this region.

Sugarcane   The **subtropical** climate of the lower delta area of Louisiana is very important for raising sugarcane. When sugarcane is harvested, the roots remain in the ground. As long as the roots do not

SOUTH CENTRAL STATES: RANK IN AGRICULTURAL PRODUCTION

Product	Ark.	La.	Okla.	Tex.
Sugarcane		3		4
Cotton	6	5	9	2
Soybeans	7	10		
Sweet potatoes		2		5
Rice	1	3		4
Citrus fruits				3
Winter wheat	10		2	3
Sorghum grain	7		5	1
Beef cattle			3	1

Only ranks of 1 through 10 are given.

freeze, the plant will keep producing for several years. The lower delta area often has several years in a row without frost. This means that sugarcane does not have to be replanted very often.

Sugarcane farmers, like most other farmers, need machines to help them. Machines prepare the fields and plant the cane. Machines are also used for weeding, harvesting, and loading the cane onto trucks to ship to sugar-processing plants. Here the machines of the factory take over. The cane is cut, washed, and crushed. The workers run, repair, and clean the machines. Manufacturing the cane syrup and sugar is also done with machines. The syrup and sugar are then shipped to markets and food-processing factories all over the United States.

Rice   Rice is another important crop grown in the South Central region. Arkansas, Louisiana, and Texas are three of the leading rice-growing states. To grow well, rice needs warm temperatures, from 70°F to 100°F (21°C–38°C). Rice also needs lots of water. Even though most of the places where rice is grown get 40 or more inches (100 cm) of rain every year, more water is needed. Rice fields are irrigated to be sure there is plenty of water.

Rice is a very important food for many people all over the world. Sometimes rice is used in cereals.

Winter wheat   From central Texas through Oklahoma, winter wheat is an important crop. Winter wheat is planted in the fall. Its roots grow strong before winter's cold weather arrives. In the spring the wheat begins to grow rapidly. It is ready for harvest in early summer.

By planting winter wheat the farmers help to prevent soil **erosion.** In this area of little rainfall, plant roots are needed to help keep the soil from blowing away. The wheat plants help hold the soil during the long, dry winter season.

Raising cattle   Cattle ranching is one of the best known and most important agricultural activities in Oklahoma and Texas. In large parts of Oklahoma and Texas the soil is too dry and poor for growing crops. But this dry grassland is used for grazing. It is where the cattle and sheep ranches are found.

Because this area is so dry, many ranchers drill wells to get the water their cattle need. The wells cost a lot of money but without them the huge herds of cattle could not be raised.

Most cattle do not go directly from the grazing lands to the marketplace. The grasslands do not provide enough food to fatten cattle. Instead the cattle are sent to **feedlots.** Here the animals are fed special diets that add pounds every day. When the cattle have gained enough weight they are sold for meat. The feedlot is then made ready for another herd.

Cattle ranching has been an important part of the history and growth of the United States. In Chapter 10 you read about the ranchers who were part of the fast growth of the Great Plains in the 1860s. In the early years of ranching, cattle were grazed on open land. But in the late 1800s, ranchers started fencing in their land. Ranches today are very large but they are not as large as in the frontier days.

The work of the cowhand hasn't changed much from the days of the Old West. Cowhands may ride in a jeep or even a helicopter instead of on a horse. However, they still watch over large herds of cattle all across the plains. Cattle must be moved from one grazing area to another to protect the grass from being **overgrazed.** Once a year, usually in the fall, there is a roundup. At the roundup, the young calves are branded with the letters of the ranch. The cattle are sorted. Some are sent to market and others are sent to feedlots.

The rodeo   Part of the colorful history of the West is the **rodeo.** The word *rodeo* is a Spanish word. In English it means "surround," or "round up." The rodeo started in the 1800s during the roundup. Along the trail to market, cowhands from different ranches would compete in riding and steer roping. Today, throughout Texas, Oklahoma, and other states in the West, the rodeo may be a monthly or yearly event.

Rodeos are held on large ranches, in small

This cowhand is still on top of the bull, but how long will he last? If he falls, the clown will make sure the bull doesn't hurt him.

towns, and in large cities. In most small towns the prize is also small. Sometimes there are no prizes. Cowhands compete just for the fun of it. Only a few people earn their living by competing in the large rodeos. Whether large or small, rodeos are exciting. The cowhands eagerly try to see who can manage a bucking horse, ride a kicking bull, rope a speeding calf, or wrestle a steer to the ground. Just about everyone likes a rodeo. The stands are filled with young and old cheering for their favorite cowhand.

CHECKUP

1. Why do cotton, sugarcane, and rice grow well in this region?
2. How does winter wheat help the farmers?
3. Why are large areas of Oklahoma and Texas used for raising cattle?

Resources and Industry

Mineral resources   Each South Central state has valuable mineral resources. One resource is found in the Crater of Diamonds State Park near Murfreesboro, Arkansas. This park has the only diamond mine in the United States. If you find a diamond when you visit the park you can keep it!

Arkansas also has our most important bauxite mines. The bauxite mines are southwest of Little Rock. As you know, bauxite is used to make aluminum. However, the supply does not meet our need for aluminum. More bauxite must be imported from Jamaica and Guinea.

Texas and Louisiana are the leading producers of sulfur in the United States. Sulfur is a pale yellow mineral. It has many uses that are important to us. Sulfur is used to make rubber. It keeps the rubber from becoming sticky in the summer and too hard and brittle in cold weather. Sulfur is also used to make matches, gunpowder, and insect sprays.

Louisiana and Texas are also our leading producers of salt. Salt has over 14,000 uses! Some uses are making glass, preserving meat, and processing leather.

Energy resources   The South Central states have very large deposits of oil and gas. As you know, oil and gas are major sources of energy that people all over the world need. Texas, Louisiana, and Oklahoma rank among the leading states in the United States in supplying these very important energy resources.

One of the world's largest sources of oil—close to 10 billion barrels (1.3 trillion t)—lies under the plains of Texas. That equals almost one third of the country's known supply of oil. There is more oil off the coast of Texas, in the earth under the Gulf of Mexico. One of the world's largest underground areas of natural gas is also found in Texas—in the northwestern panhandle. Most of Louisiana's 1,000 gas and oil fields are found in the southern marshlands. Oil has also been found off the Louisiana coast in the Gulf of Mexico. There are deposits of oil and gas throughout most of Oklahoma. The state has about 70,000 oil wells. Arkansas also has supplies of oil in the southwestern part of the state and of gas in the Arkansas River valley.

Exploring for oil   Before oil can be used it must be brought up from inside the earth. **Geologists,** who study the earth's surface and the layers of rock below the surface, look for good places to drill oil and gas wells. These scientists know what to look for from studying other oil- and gas-producing regions. But even with the geologists' knowledge, very often only one in ten wells will have oil or gas. Wells that don't yield oil or gas are known as dry wells or dry holes.

Geologists explore for new oil and gas reserves both on land and under the sea. In order to bring the oil and gas above the surface, many difficult problems have to be solved.

Drilling an ocean well How do you drill a well when the ocean floor is 100 feet (30 m) or more below the surface of the water? And that is just the beginning! A well may have to be drilled another 20,000 feet (6,100 m) before oil or gas is found. Drilling platforms have been designed that float on the ocean surface. The **derrick,** or tall steel frame, is anchored to the ocean floor. The platforms and derricks are built to hold up in the strong winds and high waves of a storm.

Workers are taken to and from the drilling platform by boat or helicopter. They live on the platform. They can sleep, eat, bathe, and watch TV or movies, as well as work on the platform. The workers stay on the platform for two or three weeks at a time.

A well that is 20,000 feet (6,100 m) deep may take more than a year to drill. The drilling goes on every day, 24 hours a day.

The drill goes through the soil and into the rock layers of the earth. The drill must be hard and sharp to break through the rock layers. The cutting edges on the drill are made of diamonds. Diamonds are hard enough to cut away the rock.

Steel pipe casings are hollow tubes that are 16 to 34 feet (5–10 m) long. They are placed one on top of the other inside the part of the well that is drilled. The casings are sealed together. They are also sealed on the outside with concrete. The casings keep the well from caving in. They also keep dirt, salt water, and other materials from getting into fresh water lying inside the rock layers.

If a well produces oil, the workers put in a pump that pumps oil until the well runs dry. The oil is sent to a pipeline. The pipeline sends the oil to a storage tank. Then it is moved to a **refinery.** In the refinery the oil is made into many prod-

This drilling platform is in the Gulf of Mexico. The boat brings pipes and other supplies to the platform. The helicopter is used mostly to bring people.

ucts. The final products are sent by railroad, truck, ship, or pipeline all over the United States.

Uses of oil   Oil is used in many ways. When we think of oil, we usually think about running our cars or heating our homes. But oil and gas have many other uses. Look at the pie graph. You can see that most petroleum is made into gasoline and fuel oil. Gasoline is used for cars. Fuel oil is used to heat homes and other buildings. It is also burned to make power for factories. Fuel oil also includes **diesel fuel,** which is used in trucks, buses, and some cars. Jet fuels are a mixture of oil products that are specially made for jet airplanes. Oil is made into other fuels, as well. They are used in camp stoves and in many other ways. Some of these fuels are also **solvents.** That is, they are used for such purposes as thinning paints or dissolving grease. Asphalt and road oil are used to make smooth, long-lasting road surfaces. Some oil is made into **lubricants.** These are oils and greases that are used to make a slippery coating between metal parts. The lubricants keep the metal parts from wearing out too fast.

As you read in Chapter 16, petroleum is also used to make petrochemicals. The products made from petrochemicals include medicine, fertilizer for growing food, plastics, and paint. Even some of the clothes you wear and the soap your clothes are washed in are made from petrochemicals.

Our country's demand for oil is very high. The United States has about 5 percent of the world's people. At the same time, we use 28 percent of the world's en-

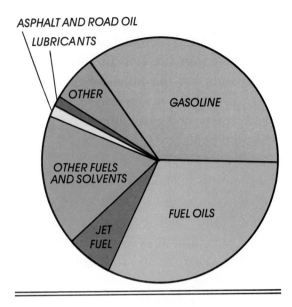

PETROLEUM PRODUCTS

About 2/3 of our oil is used for what two products?

ergy. Most of the energy we use comes from oil and gas. We have to import a lot of oil and gas to meet our needs. But every year there is less oil and gas in the earth. Therefore we must use our energy resources wisely. As you read in Chapter 17, coal has become an important energy resource again. Scientists are also trying to find other sources of energy. They are experimenting with heat from the sun and the ocean.

Oil spills   Oil spills are a danger that comes with shipping oil or drilling for it in the ocean. A spill may result from a problem with an offshore well or from an oil tanker that is broken up by a storm.

Oil spills can hurt people, beaches, plants, and wildlife. At sea or in a river the spilled oil is carried by the water's current. It may be carried up on a beach used by swimmers or sunbathers. It may also be carried into **tidal pools** and coastal marshlands. Tidal pools are pools of water left behind when the ocean moves away from the shore at low tide. Small forms of ocean life live in these pools. Marshlands are the home of many animals, especially water birds such as ducks, egrets, and gulls. Oil spills in areas near tidal pools and marshlands are likely to destroy or seriously hurt both animal and plant life. The feathers of water birds become covered with the thick oily substance. Globs of oil also sink to the bottom of the tidal pools and marshlands, polluting the water and killing the plants and animals.

Engineers, scientists, and government people are working together. They are trying to solve the problems of oil spills. They are learning how to control the spread of oil from spills.

Forests and lumber   Not all the South Central states' resources are underground. Forests cover almost half of Arkansas and Louisiana. In Arkansas this amounts to about 18 million acres (7 million ha) of land, and in Louisiana, about 15 million acres (6 million ha). Arkansas is among the top ten lumber-producing states in the United States. The lumber from both states is used for building materials and paper products. The paper in this book may have come from a tree grown in Arkansas or Louisiana.

Fishing   Fish are another resource that is important to this region. Fishing fleets work the waters of the Gulf of Mexico for shrimp, oysters, crabs, flounder, menhaden, and red snapper.

At present Louisiana is the leading state in the fishing industry. Texas also brings in large catches. But the people in the fishing industry of these two states are worried. They do not yet know whether offshore drilling will harm the fish. Both the fishing industry and the oil industry provide jobs for many people. It is hoped that these two important industries can work side by side in the Gulf of Mexico without causing problems for either.

Space exploration and electronics
Other industries of the South Central region include space exploration and travel, **electronics,** and tourism. The Lyndon B. Johnson Space Center in Houston, Texas, has played a very important role in the exploration of the moon, the planets, and outer space.

Electronics has become an important industry for Arkansas, Texas, and Oklahoma in the past few years. This industry needs highly skilled workers. People who

These children are visiting the Lyndon B. Johnson Space Center. Astronauts are trained at the center. The center keeps a constant watch over all its space flights.

Scenery like this view of the Rio Grande at Santa Elena Canyon attracts visitors to Big Bend National Park in Texas. Big Bend covers over 700,000 acres (280,000 ha) along the Rio Grande.

understand electronics have been able to improve televisions, radios, and other products. If you use a calculator or play video games, you are using electronic products that may have been made in one of these states. Our everyday lives are touched by the spacecraft and electronics industries of the South Central states.

Tourism All the South Central states attract visitors. People visit each of the four states for different reasons. Some people want to learn about the Native Americans. Over 10 percent of the Indians of the United States live in Oklahoma. The Cherokees, the largest of the tribes in Oklahoma, have built a village to show what an ancient Indian village was like. Members of the tribe take visitors around the village.

The Cowboy Hall of Fame is in Oklahoma City. This museum attracts people of all ages. It teaches them about the way of life of the cowhand.

The Gulf Coast, from the Mississippi River delta to the southern end of Padre (päd′ rē) Island in Texas, attracts many winter visitors. People want to escape from the cold North. They come to the Gulf Coast for boating, sight-seeing, sun-bathing, and sport fishing.

Another place people like to visit is the Alamo in San Antonio, Texas. The Alamo is an old Spanish mission that was made into a fort. In Chapter 8, you read about the famous battle that took place at the Alamo.

National parklands and forests also attract visitors. Padre Island National Seashore has about 80 miles (130 km) of sandy beaches.

CHECKUP

1. Why are bauxite, sulfur, and salt important mineral resources?
2. Which South Central state has one of the world's largest sources of petroleum?
3. Name at least five ways people use petroleum products.

359

Population and Cities

Population and capital cities   Six of the nation's 30 largest cities are found in the South Central region. These cities are Houston, Dallas, San Antonio, New Orleans, El Paso, and Oklahoma City.

Little Rock, the capital of Arkansas, is on the Arkansas River. About 158,000 people live in Little Rock. It is the largest city in the state. Little Rock is Arkansas' center of transportation and trading.

Austin is the capital of Texas, but it is smaller than several other Texas cities. The city was named after Stephen F. Austin, an important leader in the American settlement of Texas.

Baton Rouge (bat ən rüzh'), Louisiana's capital, is the second largest city in the state. The name *Baton Rouge* is French. In English it means "red stick." The city was named for a red pole that Indians raised in the 1700s to show the boundary between two of their nations.

Oklahoma City, the capital of Oklahoma, covers 604 square miles (1,564 sq km). It is the third largest city in land area in our nation. About one fourth of the people in the state live in or near Oklahoma City.

New Orleans   New Orleans is Louisiana's largest city. It lies on the Mississippi River. To the north of the city is the large, shallow Lake Pontchartrain.

The city's population of 565,000 is a mixture of people from many different cultures. The first people to live in the New Orleans area were American Indians. They were followed by French, Spanish, and African peoples. The mixing of these three groups has given New Orleans a culture that is rather different from most other American cities. New Orleans is like a European city in many ways.

New Orleans is also well-known for the Mardi Gras (mär' dē grä') festival. This exciting carnival lasts for several weeks. The main celebration takes place two weeks before Lent in the Christian calendar. Parades fill the streets and a holiday spirit takes over the city.

New Orleans is not just a tourist center. It is also an important center for shipping. The port of New Orleans is the busiest port in our country.

Houston   Houston, like New Orleans, is a port city. It is the third busiest port city in the United States. To reach the port of Houston, ships have to travel

This Mardi Gras float takes its theme from Around the World in Eighty Days, *a book by Jules Verne.*

through a deepwater channel. The channel connects Houston to the Gulf of Mexico 50 miles (80 km) away. With about 1,726,000 people, Houston is the largest city of the South Central region. Houston was founded in 1836. After the channel was built in 1914 the city of Houston grew very fast. It grew fast not only because of the port but also because of the rich oil deposits nearby.

Houston is a leader in oil refining, in petrochemical manufacturing, and in making parts for oil wells and pipelines. Oil refining is the city's most important industry.

San Antonio   San Antonio is a food-processing, industrial, and transportation center serving the farming and cattle-ranching country of western Texas. It is also a city with a rich culture. People in the city speak Spanish or English or both. Many shops display signs in both languages. About 820,000 people live in San Antonio.

Throughout the city there are many historic landmarks. These landmarks tell the story of the city's beginnings. They show the Spanish and Mexican influence.

Dallas/Fort Worth   Dallas and Fort Worth lie in north-central Texas. Only 30 miles (48 km) separate the two cities. Together they form the largest metropolitan area of the South Central states. Dallas is the second largest city of Texas. About 944,000 people live in Dallas, and about 401,000 people live in Fort Worth. Both cities are important in the aircraft industry. Fort Worth is one of our country's largest producers of airplanes.

Many companies in the Dallas-Fort Worth area provide goods and services related to Texas' huge oil industry. The area is also known as a very important transportation center. The Dallas-Fort Worth airport is one of the busiest airports in the United States. It lies between the two cities and in many ways is a city by itself. Seven interstate highways and a good railroad system also serve the area.

Hot Springs   Hot Springs is in the Ouachita Mountains of Arkansas. The city was named for its 47 hot **mineral springs.** Most of Hot Springs National Park is in the city. It is the only city in the United States that has most of a national park inside its borders.

About 36,000 people live in Hot Springs, but more than a million people visit the city every year. These people come to relax and bathe in the hot mineral water. The average temperature of the water is 145°F (63°C). The water is cooled down by about 40°F (22°C) before it enters the bathhouses.

The Native Americans were the first to enjoy the hot springs. In 1807 a permanent white settlement was founded here by a trapper. By 1832 the area had become the first national health and recreation center in the United States. Today most of the people who live in Hot Springs work at the hotels, bathhouses, racetracks, and restaurants built for the tourists.

CHECKUP

1. What is the capital city of Arkansas? Louisiana? Oklahoma? Texas?
2. Why is the Dallas-Fort Worth area important?

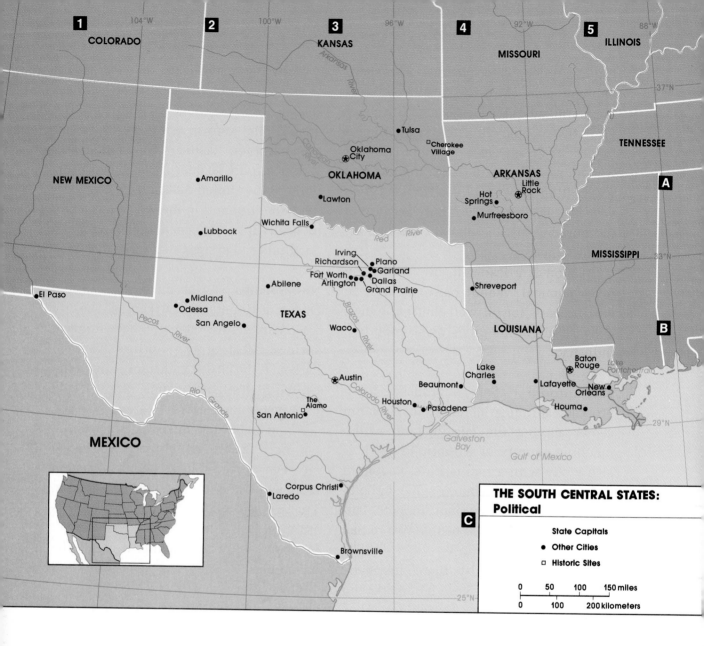

THE SOUTH CENTRAL STATES:
Political

State Capitals
- ● **Other Cities**
- □ **Historic Sites**

| 0 | 50 | 100 | 150 miles |
| 0 | 100 | 200 kilometers |

Cities with less than 100,000

Brownsville (Tex.) C-3
Grand Prairie (Tex.) B-3
Hot Springs (Ark.) A-4
Lafayette (La.) B-4
Lake Charles (La.) B-4
Lawton (Okla.) A-3
Midland (Tex.) B-2
Murfreesboro (Ark.) A-4
Plano (Tex.) A-3
Richardson (Tex.) B-3
San Angelo (Tex.) B-2

Cities with 100,000-499,000

Abilene (Tex.) B-3

Amarillo (Tex.) A-2
Arlington (Tex.) B-3
Austin (Tex.) B-3
Baton Rouge (La.) B-5
Beaumont (Tex.) B-4
Corpus Christi (Tex.) C-3
El Paso (Tex.) B-1
Fort Worth (Tex.) B-3
Garland (Tex.) B-3
Houma (La.) B-5
Irving (Tex.) B-3
Laredo (Tex.) C-3
Little Rock (Ark.) A-4
Lubbock (Tex.) A-2
Odessa (Tex.) B-2

Oklahoma City (Okla.) A-3
Pasadena (Tex.) B-4
Shreveport (La.) B-4
Tulsa (Okla.) A-4
Waco (Tex.) B-3
Wichita Falls (Tex.) A-3

Cities with 500,000-999,000

Dallas (Tex.) B-3
New Orleans (La.) B-5
San Antonio (Tex.) B-3

City with 1,000,000 or more

Houston (Tex.) B-4

Which city has a million or more people? Find it on the map. Which city is at 30°N by 90°W?
Which city is at 30°N by 98°W?

THE SOUTH CENTRAL STATES	Arkansas	Louisiana	Oklahoma	Texas
Source of Name	From a Quapaw Indian word meaning "downstream people"	In honor of Louis XIV of France	From two Choctaw Indian words meaning "red people"	From the Indian word *Tejas*, meaning "friends"
Nickname(s)	Land of Opportunity	Pelican State; Sportsman's Paradise; Creole State; Sugar State	Sooner State	Lone Star State
Capital	Little Rock	Baton Rouge	Oklahoma City	Austin
Largest Cities (1980 Census)	Little Rock Fort Smith North Little Rock	New Orleans Metropolitan Baton Rouge Shreveport	Oklahoma City Tulsa Lawton	Houston Dallas San Antonio
Population Rank	33	18	25	3
Population Density Rank	35	22	34	29
Area Rank	27	31	18	2
State Flag				
State Bird	Mockingbird	Brown pelican	Scissortailed flycatcher	Mockingbird
State Flower	Apple blossom	Magnolia	Mistletoe	Bluebonnet
State Tree	Pine	Bald cypress	Redbud	Pecan
State Motto	*Regnat populus* (The people rule)	Union, justice, and confidence	*Labor omnia vincit* (Labor conquers all things)	Friendship
Interesting Facts	Mammoth Spring, in the northern part of the state, is one of the largest springs in the world.	About 5,000 miles (8,000 km) of rivers and waterways can be navigated. Almost half of North America's wild ducks and geese spend the winter in Louisiana's coastal marshes.	Will Rogers, a famous cowboy humorist, was born in Oklahoma (then Indian Territory) in 1879. Tulsa has been called the "oil capital of the world."	Texas is the only state in the United States that can be divided into two, three or four states by permission of Congress.

363

KEY FACTS

1. Important physical features of the South Central region include the Gulf Coastal Plain, the Mississippi delta, the Ozark Plateau, the Great Plains, and the Mississippi River.

2. The South Central region is important for its agriculture, which includes crops and livestock.

3. Resources of the South Central region include fish, lumber, and large deposits of oil and gas, as well as other minerals.

4. The oil in the Gulf of Mexico is very important, but drilling for it and transporting it present the danger of oil spills.

5. The largest cities of the South Central region are Houston, Dallas, and San Antonio.

VOCABULARY QUIZ

Next to the number of the sentence, write the term that best completes the sentence. Write on a sheet of paper.

silt
tornado
levees
feedlots
overgrazed

erosion
geologists
refinery
lubricants
deltas

1. _____ along the Mississippi River help control flooding.

2. River _____ often have the shape of the Greek letter Δ.

3. Plant roots help prevent _____ of the soil.

4. A delta can be built up by deposits of __ carried by a river.

5. _____ study the earth's surface and the layers of rock below the surface.

6. _____ keep a machine's metal parts from wearing out too fast.

7. The swirling winds of a _____ can cause nearly complete destruction.

8. If cattle are left too long in one grazing area, the land will become _____ .

9. Cattle are sent to _____ to be fattened for market.

10. At a _____ , oil is made into many products.

REVIEW QUESTIONS

1. How did the Llano Estacado get its name?

2. Name three important rivers of the South Central region.

3. What effect do the warm breezes from the Gulf of Mexico have on the climate of Louisiana and coastal Texas?

4. Name at least four important agricultural products of the South Central states.

5. List one use for each of these minerals: bauxite, sulfur, and salt.

6. Why are the cutting edges on an oil drill made of diamonds?

7. Give an example of a petrochemical.

8. How does an oil spill harm plant and animal life?

9. Name the four South Central states and the capital of each.

ACTIVITIES

1. Do some research on cattle raising and meat-packing. Then make a chart on a large sheet of paper. Starting with cattle grazing on the range, show the main steps in getting beef to your table.

2. In an encyclopedia or other reference book, find out about the ways salt is obtained. Make drawings of the different processes. Make labels and captions for your drawings.

READING A MAP: UNITED STATES TIME ZONES

TIME ZONES

Earlier you learned that as the earth turns, one part of the earth gets lighter, while another gets darker. Because this is true, people have divided the earth into time zones.

Six of the 24 time zones are in the United States. Each zone is different by one hour from the zone next to it. New York City is in the Eastern Time Zone. Minneapolis is in the Central Time Zone. When it is 7 o'clock in New York, it is 6 o'clock in Minneapolis. In Denver, which is in the Mountain Time Zone, it is 5 o'clock. In the Pacific Time Zone, it is 4 o'clock. In the Alaska Time Zone, it is 3 o'clock; and in the Hawaii-Aleutian Time Zone, it is 2 o'clock.

At one time there were no standard time zones. Each town or city set its own times, based on the sun. You could ride 10 miles (16 km) down the road to the next town and arrive 20 minutes before you set out!

SKILLS PRACTICE

1. You live in Hawaii. Your grandmother lives in Georgia. You want to call her before she leaves for work, which she does at 8 A.M. her time. At what time, your time, should you place the call?

2. You live in New York. It is now 1 P.M. Eastern Standard Time. What time is it in Seattle? In Anchorage? In Phoenix?

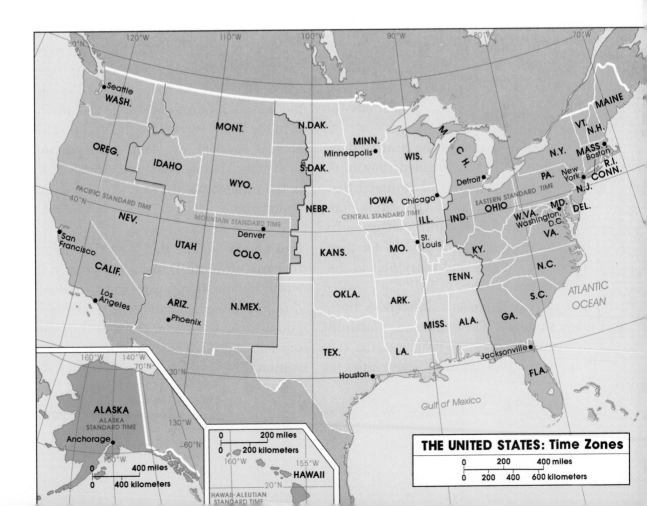

THE UNITED STATES: Time Zones

CHAPTER

19 The North Central States Today

The Land

The region   The North Central region is huge. It measures about 1,000 miles (1,600 km) from east to west and about 800 miles (1,300 km) from north to south. The 12 North Central states are Illinois, Indiana, Iowa, Kansas, Michigan, Minnesota, Missouri, Nebraska, North Dakota, Ohio, South Dakota, and Wisconsin.

What makes this group of states a region? The easiest answer to that question lies in the main physical feature: plains. Almost the whole region is covered by one kind of plain or another. Another answer lies in farming.

When people think of the Heartland, as this region is sometimes called, they think of the miles and miles of cropland that cover much of the area. They think, too, of the herds of beef cattle that graze in the western part of the region. Or they remember the Hay and Dairy Belt in the northeastern section.

Of course, there are differences from place to place. On one hand, you find thousands of acres of cropland. On the other, you find 8 of the 30 largest cities in the United States. You can drive for hundreds of miles and see nothing moving, other than a herd of cattle. You can also drive on streets clogged with the traffic of some of the most urbanized areas of the United States.

Landforms   In the eastern part of the region are the Central Lowlands. Along the western part of the North Central states is the Great Plains. The elevation of the region rises from east to west, until the plains meet the Rocky Mountains. However, the rise is so gradual that you do not notice it from the ground.

Most of the hills and mountains of the North Central states are fairly low. Even on the Ozark Plateau, the highest point is only 2,500 feet (762 m) high. One of the few places in which you find high mountains is in the Black Hills of South Dakota. This area is marked by steep **canyons** and high hills. Harney Peak in the Black Hills is the highest point of the North Central region.

Bad Lands   The **Bad Lands** are found in parts of South Dakota, Nebraska, and North Dakota. If you were to be suddenly dropped in the Bad Lands you might think you were on the moon. The Bad Lands are dry and rugged. There is little or no vegetation in the deep **gullies** and high, steep

On the map, find the only Great Lake that is entirely within the United States. The picture shows you the main physical feature of the North Central region: plains.

CANADA

Lake of the Woods

Lake Superior

MESABI RANGE

MOUNT CURWOOD

UPPER PENINSULA

MICHIGAN

Lake Huron

MONTANA

NORTH DAKOTA

Bismarck ✪

Fargo •

MINNESOTA

Lake Itasca

WHITE BUTTE

Lake Michigan

Lake Ontario

Niagara River

Minneapolis • ✪ St. Paul

WISCONSIN

Lake Winnebago

NEW YORK

SOUTH DAKOTA

Pierre ✪

BLACK

HARNEY PEAK

HILLS

Sioux Falls •

Red Lake

Madison ✪ • Milwaukee

Lansing ✪ • Detroit

Lake Erie

Cleveland •

WYOMING

BADLANDS

Missouri River

Minnesota River

Red River

IOWA

Cedar Rapids •

Chicago •

Fort Wayne •

PENNSYLVANIA

NEBRASKA

Des Moines •

CENTRAL LOWLANDS

INDIANA

OHIO

Columbus ✪

WEST VIRGINIA

North Platte River

Platte River

Omaha •

Lincoln ✪

Des Moines River

ILLINOIS

Springfield ✪

Indianapolis ✪

Wabash River

Illinois River

VIRGINIA

COLORADO

Kansas River

Topeka ✪

Kansas City •

MISSOURI

KANSAS

Jefferson City ✪

Wichita •

Arkansas River

OZARK PLATEAU

Mississippi River

Ohio River

KENTUCKY

NEW MEXICO

OKLAHOMA

ARKANSAS

TENNESSEE

TEXAS

MISSISSIPPI

ALABAMA

THE NORTH CENTRAL STATES: Physical

✪ State Capitals

• Other Cities

| 0 | 50 | 100 | 150 | 200 miles |

| 0 | 100 | 200 | 300 kilometers |

bluffs of the Bad Lands. North Dakota's highest peak, White **Butte** (byüt), is in the state's Bad Lands area.

Lakes   Thousands of years ago **glaciers** moved over much of the Northern Hemisphere. As they moved south, these large sheets of ice and packed snow helped to change the landscape. They carved out hollows and moved large masses of earth and huge boulders. After the ice ages passed, rivers and lakes were filled with water from the melted ice. These rivers and lakes have become an important part of the North Central states.

Four of the Great Lakes are part of the North Central region. The Great Lakes are so large that they are called **inland seas**. Their total area is greater than that of Indiana and Illinois.

Name	Area (sq mi)	Area (sq km)
Superior	31,700	82,100
Huron	23,010	59,600
Michigan	22,300	57,760
Erie	9,910	25,770
Ontario	7,340	19,010

THE GREAT LAKES: AREA

As you know, the lakes also serve as a part of an important water route—the St. Lawrence Seaway. Many cities, such as Detroit, Cleveland, Chicago, Milwaukee, and Duluth, have grown up along the shores of the lakes. Oceangoing ships travel between these cities and other ports in the United States and in other countries. The ships carry cargoes such as iron, grain, coal, and manufactured products.

The dry wastes of the Bad Lands are the result of years of wind erosion.

Rivers   Three of our major rivers are found in the North Central States. These are the Ohio, Missouri, and Mississippi rivers. The Ohio River flows along the southern borders of Ohio and Indiana and the southeastern edge of Illinois. There it reaches the Mississippi. The Missouri River enters the North Central region in North Dakota. It flows through 6 of the 12 states. Near the port city of St. Louis, the Missouri River joins the Mississippi River.

The Missouri has touched the lives of many people. Its spring floods have taken lives and destroyed farms, homes, and businesses. Nearly 90 dams have been built to help control the Missouri and the many rivers and streams that flow into it.

The mighty Mississippi River starts as a tiny stream in northern Minnesota in the Lake Itasca (ī tas′ kə) area. As it flows south it forms parts of the borders of the North Central states of Wisconsin, Iowa, Illinois, and Missouri.

CHECKUP

1. Where is the highest point of the North Central states found? How high is it?
2. Describe the Bad Lands.
3. Name the region's three major rivers.

Climate

VOCABULARY
water cycle   hail
evaporate

Temperature   In northern Minnesota and North Dakota, winter temperatures have reached −40°F (−40°C) or lower. In these same states, temperatures higher than 100°F (38°C) have been recorded in the summer months of July and August. Of course, these are extremes. But in much of the region the usual range is quite large, too.

The table helps to show the temperature pattern. Notice that the places with average January temperatures higher than 25°F (−4°C) are in the south. Those places with average January temperatures lower than 25°F are in the north. You can also see that as one travels west, summer temperatures are usually hotter and winter temperatures colder.

Another thing that affects temperatures in the North Central region is the presence of the Great Lakes. The Great Lakes help keep the temperatures from getting as hot or as cold as they do farther west.

NORTH CENTRAL STATES: AVERAGE TEMPERATURES						
Weather station	Average January temperature		Average July temperature		Average yearly temperature	
	°F	°C	°F	°C	°F	°C
Williston, N. Dak.	8	−13	70	21	41	5
International Falls, Minn.	2	−17	66	19	37	3
Sault Ste. Marie, Mich.	14	−10	64	18	40	4
Concordia, Kans.	26	−3	78	26	53	12
Columbia, Mo.	29	−2	77	25	54	12
Cincinnati, Ohio	32	0	76	24	55	13

The large bodies of water warm and cool more slowly than does the nearby land. Breezes coming across the lake warm the air in winter and cool it in summer. In Wisconsin, along the shore of Lake Michigan, the summer temperatures are lower and the winter temperatures higher than they are farther inland.

Precipitation   Like temperature, precipitation varies with the seasons and from place to place. Generally the northern and western parts of the North Central region receive the least precipitation. The most precipitation falls in the southeastern part along the Ohio River valley.

The area around the Great Lakes lies between the two extremes. The rivers and the Great Lakes and the many other lakes affect the precipitation. The **water cycle** diagram helps to explain how water from the rivers, lakes, and plants **evaporates** to form rain-bearing clouds.

The average yearly precipitation in the North Central states ranges from 15 to 47 inches (50–119 cm). It comes in the form of rain, snow, sleet, and **hail.** In the winter months snow may blanket the northern parts of North Dakota through Michigan as early as November and stay on the ground until April. In some areas, the yearly average snowfall is more than 100 inches (250 cm).

CHECKUP

1. How do the Great Lakes affect the temperatures of the region?
2. What is the water cycle?

Water evaporates and forms clouds. Clouds contain many tiny droplets of water. These tiny drops combine to form larger drops, which fall as precipitation.

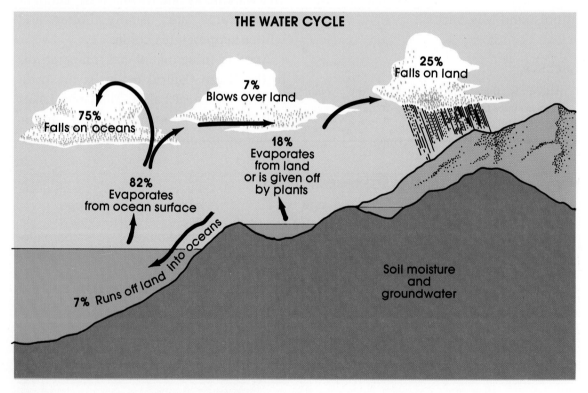

THE WATER CYCLE

25%
Falls on land

7%
Blows over land

75%
Falls on oceans

18%
Evaporates
from land
or is given off
by plants

82%
Evaporates
from ocean surface

7% Runs off land into oceans

Soil moisture
and
groundwater

Farmlands and Forests

PARTS OF A KERNEL OF WHEAT

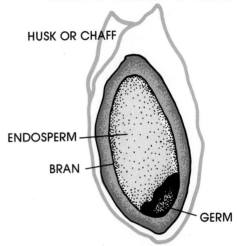

White flour is made from the endosperm of the wheat kernel. The whole kernel except the husk is used in making whole wheat flour.

Crops   Each of the 12 North Central states is part of our most important farming region. Much of the soil of the plains is fertile and deep. The frost-free season is long enough for many different kinds of crops. There is also enough rainfall for these crops.

The chief crops are corn and wheat. Soybeans, barley, oats, sorghum, rye, and hay are also very important. The table shows you how the North Central states rank in the United States in the production of these crops. Only ranks of one to ten are shown. Notice that the North Central region has all of the top ten corn-producing states, and at least half of the top ten soybean-producing states, oat-producing states, and hay-producing states.

Wheat   Winter wheat is grown in the warmer southern areas from Ohio westward to Nebraska and Kansas. As you may remember, it is also grown in Oklahoma and Texas. If you look at the map on the next page, you will see that these areas form a belt across the middle of the United States. This is the Wheat Belt.

THE NORTH CENTRAL STATES: RANK IN CROP PRODUCTION

State	Wheat	Corn	Soybeans	Barley	Oats	Sorghum	Rye	Hay
Illinois	—	2	1	—	—	—	—	—
Indiana	—	3	4	—	—	—	—	—
Iowa	—	1	2	—	4	—	—	2
Kansas	1	—	—	—	—	2	—	9
Michigan	—	8	—	—	6	—	7	—
Minnesota	7	5	5	4	2	—	3	3
Missouri	—	9	3	—	—	4	—	8
Nebraska	8	4	9	—	7	3	5	5
North Dakota	2	—	—	1	3	—	2	—
Ohio	—	6	6	—	8	—	—	—
South Dakota	9	10	—	7	1	6	1	2
Wisconsin	—	7	—	—	5	—	—	1

Spring wheat is grown in the cooler and drier parts of the region. This includes western Minnesota and North and South Dakota.

Wheat is one of the few grains that is not used chiefly for animal feed. Wheat is used in breads and other baked goods, in cereals, and in other foods. **Wheat germ** and wheat germ oil are used mostly to enrich other foods. The **bran** is one part of the grain that is used mostly in animal feeds. A kind of alcohol made from wheat is used in several products. A wheat paste is used in insect sprays and in coffee substitutes. The wheat stalks are used to make fertilizer and boxes.

Corn   Part of the Corn Belt is in just about the same area as the Wheat Belt. Unless you live in the area, you are probably wondering how that is possible. The answer to this small riddle lies in the huge amount of farmland in the Corn Belt and Wheat Belt areas. There is plenty of room for the huge crops of both corn and wheat, not to mention all the other crops.

If you drive through the Corn Belt, you may notice that the corn plants are all almost exactly the same. They are all about the same height and all have several large ears of corn at about the same place on the plant. This is because scientists have worked to improve the quality of the corn and to get a bigger **yield** from each plant.

Plants that are alike make the work of the farmer easier and more productive. Harvesting machines have been designed so they can be carefully set to the height of the ears. The more alike the plants are,

THE WHEAT BELT
- Spring Wheat
- Winter Wheat

The more dots in an area, the more wheat is grown there. Where is most wheat grown?

THE CORN BELT

The more dots in an area, the more corn is grown there. Where is most corn grown?

the more corn is harvested. This is also true of the harvesting machinery for other crops, such as wheat, oats, and soybeans.

Uses of corn   There are several kinds of corn. The two most important kinds are sweet corn and field corn. Sweet corn is the kind served as a vegetable with meals. Field corn is used mainly as animal feed, but it has many other important uses, too. You have probably eaten cornbread, which is made with corn flour or cornmeal. Many foods are sweetened with corn syrup. Corn oil is used in cooking and baking. It can be used in salad dressings and margarine. A kind of sugar called dextrose comes from corn. It is used as a sweetener and in the making of candy.

Many nonfood products are also made from corn. One that is becoming more and more important is alcohol. In some places it is now mixed with gasoline to make **gasohol.** Gasohol can be used instead of gasoline in automobiles and tractors. Other nonfood products made from corn are shellac, varnish, and plastics.

Cornstalks are also used. In some cases the stalks and even some ears of corn are left in the field. The stalks help keep the soil from blowing away. They also help to provide shelter or food for wild animals. Corncobs and cornstalks are used in making fiberboard and paper. Fiberboard is used in building.

Other crops   Most of the other large crops in the North Central states are used chiefly as animal feeds. Almost all sorghum and hay are used as feeds. Barley, rye, and oats are used largely for this purpose. Barley is also used in making malt. Barley grains, or "pearls," are used in soups, and barley flour is used in cereals and bread. Rye is used for bread and malt, also. The straw is used as a packing material and in making hats and other goods. Oats are used for cereals and baked goods. Soybeans are used in so many ways that we made a chart listing the main products made at least in part from soybeans.

Cattle and hogs   Cattle and hogs are also raised in the Corn Belt. Often cattle are raised in the dry grasslands of the Great Plains. Then they are sent to feedlots in the Corn Belt to be fattened before being shipped to market. Most hogs are not put out to graze, as cattle are. Rather, they spend their whole lives in pens.

A farmer knows how much of each kind of food and **vitamins** the animals need. He or she also knows how many weeks it will take for the animals to reach **market weight.** Market weight is the weight that an animal must reach before it is sent to market. If an animal is too light, the farmer doesn't make enough money. If the farmer lets the animals get too heavy, he or she will lose money on

If you have never heard of some of these products, look them up to find out what they are.

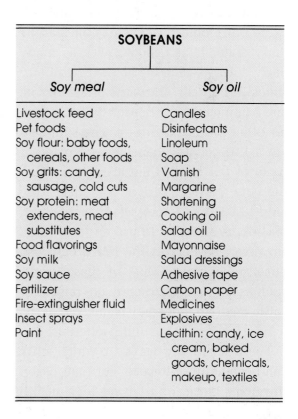

SOYBEANS	
Soy meal	*Soy oil*
Livestock feed	Candles
Pet foods	Disinfectants
Soy flour: baby foods, cereals, other foods	Linoleum
Soy grits: candy, sausage, cold cuts	Soap
	Varnish
Soy protein: meat extenders, meat substitutes	Margarine
	Shortening
	Cooking oil
Food flavorings	Salad oil
Soy milk	Mayonnaise
Soy sauce	Salad dressings
Fertilizer	Adhesive tape
Fire-extinguisher fluid	Carbon paper
Insect sprays	Medicines
Paint	Explosives
	Lecithin: candy, ice cream, baked goods, chemicals, makeup, textiles

Hogs spend all their lives in pens. When they are heavy enough, they are sent to slaughterhouses.

feed. This is why the quantity and quality of the food given to hogs in pens and cattle in feedlots is very carefully controlled. The proper amounts of each kind of food are mixed and given out automatically. That way a farmer can be sure the animals are being fed not only well, but as cheaply as possible.

Dairy farming   North of the Corn Belt is the Dairy Belt. Wisconsin is the leading dairy state. It has about twice as many dairy cows as each of the next two dairy states. Wisconsin and parts of Minnesota and Michigan are better for dairying than for other kinds of farming. The summers are a little cooler than they are in other parts of the North Central region. Often the countryside is hilly. This makes the land less suited to crops since most farm machinery is easier to use on level land. However, farmers in the Dairy Belt also raise some crops. Most of these crops, such as hay, oats, and corn, are raised for cattle feed. So much hay is raised that the name Hay and Dairy Belt is often used.

There are many ways in which milk can become unfit for use. For that reason the dairy farmer must meet high health standards in order to sell milk. Barns, milking machines, and milk storage areas have to meet cleanliness standards. If they are not met, the farmer will not be able to sell the milk. Cattle are inspected to be sure they are not diseased. The milk itself is tested often.

The farmer must also keep careful records of the cost of feeding and caring for each animal. The amount of milk from each cow is also recorded. The value of the milk from each cow must be greater than the cost of the cow's feeding and care. Careful record-keeping helps everyone. Milk buyers know the product will be safe. Milk prices are kept as low as possible because the farmer knows which cows are the best producers. Those cows will be kept, while the ones that don't give much milk will be replaced.

Forests and wood products   Much of the North Central region is forested. The more heavily forested areas are in the north and the south. In the west, there isn't enough rainfall for trees. Much of the central area has been cleared of trees.

Some forests are used for recreation. Others supply wood for lumber, furniture, and paper. Trees also help control erosion and flooding. When large forests are cut down, melting snow and heavy rains wash soil away and flood streams. Tree roots help hold the soil and absorb water.

CHECKUP

1. What are the two main crops of the North Central states?
2. Without looking back at the list of soybean products, how many can you name?
3. Why must a dairy farmer keep careful records?

Industry and Resources

VOCABULARY

pasteurize

grain elevator

wholesale market

by-product

radioactive

open-pit mine

The dairy industry   One of the many industries related to farming in the North Central states is the dairy industry. Milk from dairy farms is picked up by large milk trucks. Machines empty the farm's storage tanks and load the milk trucks.

The trucks deliver the milk to a processing plant. Here some of the milk is **pasteurized** and packaged in glass, plastic, or paper containers. Pasteurization is a process that makes milk safe to drink. Fresh milk is sent to markets, restaurants, and homes. Some milk is dried and packaged, and some is condensed and canned. Milk is also used to make cheese and butter.

Storing, transporting, and milling grain
A large business in the grain belt is grain storage and transportation. The highest building in many small farming communities is the **grain elevator.** After the harvest some farmers store grain on their farms. However, most farmers bring their truckloads of wheat and other crops to the local elevator. Here the crops are stored until they can be sold and shipped to processing plants.

Railroads are often used to move the grain from the elevators to the grain-processing plants. In the North Central states it is common to see a big diesel locomotive pulling a long line of railroad cars loaded with grain.

Duluth and Chicago are two important Great Lakes ports for shipping grain. Large barges loaded with grain can also be seen heading down the Mississippi and Missouri rivers on their way to New Orleans for shipment to other countries.

Grains are carried to different places depending on what they will be used for. Much of the wheat is taken to cities, such as Minneapolis, which has a large flour-milling industry. There the wheat is ground into flour and packaged. Some of the flour goes directly to large bakeries. Some is sent to a **wholesale market.** A wholesale market buys products in large quantities and sells them in smaller quantities to businesses. From the wholesale market, the flour goes to grocery stores and small bakeries.

Meat-packing   The people of the United States eat a huge amount of beef and a large amount of pork. Much of the meat comes from the North Central states.

Omaha, St. Louis, and Kansas City, Kansas, are among the North Central region's major meat-packing centers. Animals are brought from the feedlots to these centers. Here, in meat-packing plants, they are slaughtered and made ready for shipping in refrigerated trucks and railroad cars.

There is very little waste in the meat-packing process. Most of the meat and several of the organs, such as the heart and liver, are used as food for people. Animal hides are sold to companies that make leather goods. Pet foods are made from scrap meats and bone meal, or powdered bone. The soap you used this morning and even medicines are **by-products** of the meat-packing process. The fertilizers used to feed your house plants and the glue used to mend the broken pot are some other by-products.

Farm machinery   Another industry related to agriculture in the North Central states is the manufacture of farm machinery. More than half the country's farm machinery is made here. This industry has grown here for several reasons. First of all there is a good market. That is, there are people to buy the machinery. Farmers need plows and other farm machinery. Second, there are raw materials. The region has iron from which comes the steel to make the machinery. There is coal for power to run the factories and for making steel. Third, there is a good transportation network. Lakes, rivers, railroads, and highways are used to move both the raw materials and the finished products.

Minerals   The North Central region is an important source of underground resources. Minnesota is our leading source of iron ore. Coal deposits are found in most of the 12 states. The major coal-producing states within the region are Illinois, Indiana, and Ohio. Oil and gas are found in several states.

Deep tunnels dug into the Black Hills near Lead (lēd), South Dakota, produce about one fifth of the gold in the United States. Mining gold is difficult work. Explosives must be used in the deep tunnels to blast the ore. The ore must be loaded and brought to mills. There the ore is further treated with chemicals. About 5 tons of rock must be mined to get 1 ounce of gold (4 t of rock to get 25 g of gold).

The United States is the world's largest producer of lead. Missouri produces more of this very heavy but soft metal than any other state. Lead is useful to us in many ways. A lead layer is used in hospitals and clinics to protect the doctors and technicians who run X-ray machines. Lead is also used in nuclear plants to prevent leaks of **radioactive** materials. Lead is used to make ammunition for guns, type for large printing machines, and some kinds of paint.

As you know, cement, stone, gravel, and sand are important for building construction and for highways. Each North Central state is a source of one or more of these products.

Iron ore   Iron is found in Missouri, Michigan, Wisconsin, and Minnesota. As we said in Chapter 14, Minnesota's Mesabi Range is the leading source of iron ore in the United States. Although the richest ores have been used up, there are still large amounts of taconite. Taconite is a low-grade iron ore. This means it is more difficult and costly to separate the iron from the rest of the ore. Most mining in this area is done in **open-pit mines.** The world's largest open-pit mine is near Hibbing, Minnesota, in the Mesabi Range.

The iron is processed in plants near the mines. When the iron leaves the plant it is in the form of pellets that are about two-thirds iron. The pellets are then sent by rail to one of the ports on Lake Superior, such as Duluth or Superior. At these ports the iron pellets are emptied into storage bins. Conveyer belts move the pellets from the bins to ore carriers. The carriers move the iron to steel-manufacturing centers along the southern shores of Lake Michigan and Lake Erie. These centers produce about half the steel made in the United States. They include Gary, Cleveland, Toledo, Chicago, and Milwaukee, as well as several other cities in the area.

To reach these cities, the ore carriers travel on Lake Superior to Sault Ste. Marie (sü′ sānt′ mə rē′). From there the carriers use a canal to reach Lake Huron. To get from Lake Huron to Lake Erie, the carriers follow the St. Clair and Detroit rivers. These rivers and lakes and the canal, as well as other waterways, make up the St. Lawrence Seaway. Using the St. Lawrence Seaway, a ship can travel all the way from the Great Lakes to the Atlantic Ocean.

Automobiles   Factories in many cities of the North Central states make products from iron and steel. One of the most important of these cities is Detroit. Detroit is the auto and truck manufacturing center of the world.

Most cars and trucks are made in huge plants. These plants have thousands of workers, many of them highly skilled. Even so, much of the work is done by machines. Assembly lines play a big part in the making of cars. An assembly line is a moving belt on which part of the car is placed. Workers standing along the line add various pieces as the part passes them. Some plants may have several assembly lines. On one line, workers may build the frame of a car. On another line workers construct the body. Engines may be assembled on another. On the last assembly line the workers finish the auto with the parts from the other lines.

This is the world's largest open-pit iron mine, near Hibbing, Minnesota. The red color comes from the rust that forms in the iron ore.

Automobile makers need many other industries. Glass must be made for car windows. Car upholstery may be made from leather, cotton, wool, or synthetics. Other necessary products include paint, wiring, gasoline and oil, and tires. Of course, cars also need roads to drive on. So cement, asphalt, stone, and gravel are needed. You could name more materials. This list, though, shows how several industries can be involved in making one thing. The companies that make these products are found throughout the North Central states. Glass is made in Toledo, Ohio. Tires are made in Akron, Ohio. Other products are made in other cities.

CHECKUP

1. What is a grain elevator?
2. Name three nonfood products of the meat-packing industry.
3. Which state is the leading producer of iron? Lead? Which is a leading producer of gold?
4. What kind of work might a person on an automobile assembly line do?

These men are working on an assembly line in an automobile factory. They will perform the same job on each car as it passes along the line.

Population and Cities

Population   Nearly 60 million people live in the North Central states. The 12 states vary in population from less than 700,000 to more than 11 million. The state with the largest population is Illinois. It has over 10 million more people than the state with fewest people, North Dakota.

Throughout most of the states you will find large metropolitan centers, such as Chicago, Detroit, and St. Louis. There are about 40 cities with more than 100,000 people. Of these cities, six have more than 500,000 people. Two, Chicago and Detroit, have more than 1 million people.

Chicago   Chicago is the third largest city in the United States. About 3 million people live in the city. In the metropolitan area there are about 7 million people. Chicago is on Lake Michigan. It was this location that helped the city grow into a major center of business, industry, and transportation.

The port on Lake Michigan is one of the busiest in the United States. Ships carry grains, ores, and goods over Lake Michigan and along the St. Lawrence Seaway to the Atlantic Ocean. The Chicago Sanitary and Ship Canal connects Chicago with the Mississippi River.

The Chicago area is the home of more than 14,000 manufacturers. The largest of these make iron and steel, electrical equipment, and machinery. Other industries include publishing, foods, plastics, and construction.

Like other big cities, Chicago has many attractions. There is the Museum of Science and Industry, as well as several other museums. People can enjoy a symphony or an opera, a day at the zoo or the aquarium, an evening of ballet, or a picnic in one of the many parks. Several large libraries and many colleges and universities serve students in the area.

Downtown Chicago has hundreds of stores and office buildings. More than 300,000 people work in these stores and offices. Three of the ten largest skyscrapers in the world are in Chicago. In fact, the tallest building in the world, the Sears Tower, is in the city.

Cleveland   About 559,000 people live in Cleveland. The metropolitan area has about 2 million people. The city is the largest port on Lake Erie and the second largest city in Ohio. It is one of the 25 largest cities in the United States.

Coal from Pennsylvania and Ohio and iron from Minnesota are the two major cargoes handled in the Cleveland harbor. These two resources have helped make the city an important iron- and steel-manufacturing center. Other manufacturing includes petroleum products, automobiles, chemicals, tools, and electrical equipment. Cleveland has several museums, a large library, several colleges and universities, and many parks. The Cleveland Orchestra is well known throughout the United States.

Detroit   Detroit is the largest city in Michigan and the sixth largest city in the nation. More than 1 million people live in the city. More than 4 million people live in

Chicago's skyscrapers rise along Lake Michigan. At left is the Sears Tower.

the metropolitan area. Detroit is on the Detroit River between Lake Huron and Lake Erie.

Important industries include the making of auto parts, machine tools, iron products, hardware, chemicals, drugs, paint, and wire products, as well as automobiles and trucks. Detroit also has one of the largest salt mines in the United States. The mine is under the city!

St. Louis   With a population of about 437,000, St. Louis is the largest city in Missouri. It is one of the 30 largest cities in the United States and the nation's largest inland port.

St. Louis is second only to Detroit in the automobile industry. In fact, the area is important in the making of several kinds of transportation equipment. Airplanes,

The famous Gateway Arch in St. Louis is a **monument** to remind us that St. Louis was the starting point, or gateway, for many pioneers heading west.

barges, railroad cars, and tugboats are all made here. Chemicals, foods, and metals are also important.

Like other large cities, St. Louis offers something for just about every interest. For sports fans there are several sports teams. For music lovers there is a symphony orchestra and an opera company. Several colleges and universities and a number of museums help people learn about their world.

Other cities   There are many other large and important cities in the North Central states. Omaha is one of the nation's leading meat-packing centers. Minneapolis, Minnesota, is noted for electronics and precision instruments. Columbus is a center for the making of aircraft, appliances, and mining equipment. It is Ohio's capital and largest city. Kansas City, Missouri, is an important center for agricultural industries. It is also the country's leading maker of vending machines.

Indianapolis is the capital and largest city in Indiana. A major industrial, trans-portation, and shipping center, Indianapolis is the twelfth largest city in the United States. One of the most famous auto races in the United States—the Indianapolis 500—is held here each year.

Milwaukee is the largest city in Wisconsin. It is one of the 20 largest cities in the United States. Its location on Lake Michigan has helped it grow into a major industrial and shipping center.

Cincinnati is one of the largest cities in Ohio. It is an industrial and trade center on the Ohio River.

Two other cities in the North Central region are Des Moines (di moin') and Wichita. Although they are smaller than the cities we've discussed so far, both are large cities. Wichita, with about 289,000 people, is the largest city in Kansas. It makes more than half of the world's small airplanes. Des Moines is the capital and chief center of trade in Iowa. Its population of about 192,000 makes it the state's largest city.

Although neither North Dakota nor South Dakota has very large cities, each state has several smaller cities. Sioux (sü) Falls, South Dakota, with a population of 83,000, is the largest city of the two states. It is South Dakota's leading livestock and trade center. Bismarck is the capital of North Dakota. The second largest city in the state, it is a shipping center for agricultural products.

CHECKUP

1. In which three states is the capital city also the largest city?
2. What are the major industries in Chicago? Detroit? St. Louis?
3. What are the major cargoes handled at the port of Cleveland? Where do they come from?

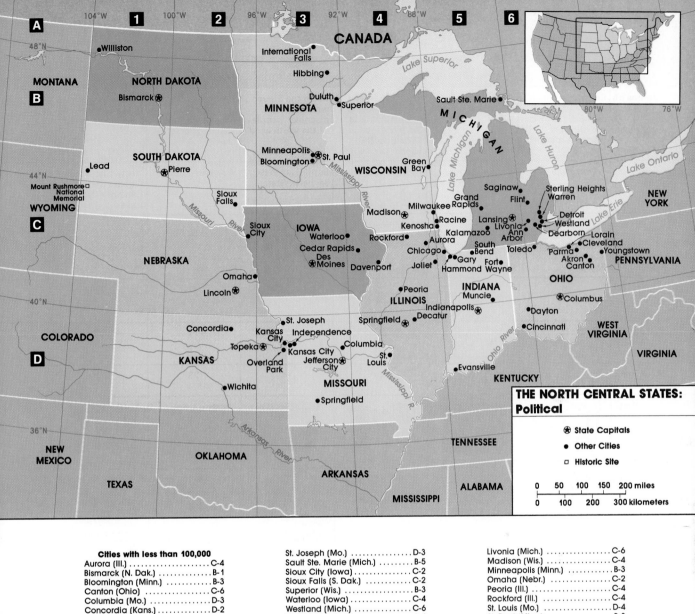

THE NORTH CENTRAL STATES: Political

- ⊛ State Capitals
- ● Other Cities
- □ Historic Site

| 0 | 50 | 100 | 150 | 200 miles |
| 0 | 100 | 200 | 300 kilometers |

Cities with less than 100,000

Aurora (Ill.) C-4
Bismarck (N. Dak.) B-1
Bloomington (Minn.) B-3
Canton (Ohio) C-6
Columbia (Mo.) D-3
Concordia (Kans.) D-2
Dearborn (Mich.) C-6
Decatur (Ill.) D-4
Duluth (Minn.) B-3
Green Bay (Wis.) B-4
Hammond (Ind.) C-5
Hibbing (Minn.) B-3
International Falls (Minn.) A-3
Jefferson City (Mo.) D-3
Joliet (Ill.) C-4
Kalamazoo (Mich.) C-5
Kenosha (Wis.) C-5
Lead (S. Dak.) B-1
Lorain (Ohio) C-6
Muncie (Ind.) C-5
Overland Park (Kans.) D-3
Parma (Ohio) C-6
Pierre (S. Dak.) B-1
Racine (Wis.) C-5
Saginaw (Mich.) C-6

St. Joseph (Mo.) D-3
Sault Ste. Marie (Mich.) B-5
Sioux City (Iowa) C-2
Sioux Falls (S. Dak.) C-2
Superior (Wis.) B-3
Waterloo (Iowa) C-4
Westland (Mich.) C-6
Williston (N. Dak.) A-1

Cities with 100,000–499,000

Akron (Ohio) C-6
Ann Arbor (Mich.) C-6
Cedar Rapids (Iowa) C-4
Cincinnati (Ohio) D-5
Davenport (Iowa) C-4
Dayton (Ohio) D-5
Des Moines (Iowa) C-3
Evansville (Ind.) D-5
Flint (Mich.) C-6
Fort Wayne (Ind.) C-5
Gary (Ind.) C-5
Grand Rapids (Mich.) C-5
Independence (Mo.) D-3
Kansas City (Kans.) D-3
Kansas City (Mo.) D-3
Lansing (Mich.) C-5
Lincoln (Nebr.) C-2

Livonia (Mich.) C-6
Madison (Wis.) C-4
Minneapolis (Minn.) B-3
Omaha (Nebr.) C-2
Peoria (Ill.) C-4
Rockford (Ill.) C-4
St. Louis (Mo.) D-4
St. Paul (Minn.) B-3
South Bend (Ind.) C-5
Springfield (Ill.) D-4
Springfield (Mo.) D-3
Sterling Heights (Mich.) C-6
Toledo (Ohio) C-6
Topeka (Kans.) D-3
Warren (Mich.) C-6
Wichita (Kans.) D-2
Youngstown (Ohio) C-6

Cities with 500,000–999,000

Cleveland (Ohio) C-6
Columbus (Ohio) D-6
Indianapolis (Ind.) D-5
Milwaukee (Wis.) C-5

Cities with 1,000,000 or more

Chicago (Ill.) C-5
Detroit (Mich.) C-6

How many state capitals have a population of less than 100,000 people? Between 100,000 and 499,000? Between 500,000 and 999,000?

THE NORTH CENTRAL STATES	Illinois	Indiana	Iowa	Kansas	Michigan	Minnesota
Source of Name	From the French version of an Indian tribe named the Illiniwek. It means "superior men."	Meaning "land of Indians"	From the Indian word *I-o-w-a* meaning "this is the place," or "The Beautiful Land"	From the Siouan word *Kansa*, meaning "people of the south wind"	From a Chippewa Indian word, *Michigama*, meaning "great lake"	From a Dakota Indian word meaning "sky-tinted water"
Nickname(s)	Prairie State	Hoosier State	Hawkeye State	Sunflower State; Jayhawk State	Wolverine State	North Star State; Gopher State; Land of 10,000 Lakes
Capital	Springfield	Indianapolis	Des Moines	Topeka	Lansing	St. Paul
Largest Cities	Chicago Rockford Peoria	Indianapolis Fort Wayne Gary	Des Moines Cedar Rapids Davenport	Wichita Kansas City Topeka	Detroit Grand Rapids Warren	Minneapolis St. Paul Duluth
Population Rank	5	14	29	32	8	21
Population Density Rank	10	15	32	38	14	33
Area Rank	24	38	25	14	23	12
State Flag						
State Bird	Cardinal	Cardinal	Eastern goldfinch	Western meadowlark	Robin	Common loon
State Flower	Violet	Peony	Wild rose	Sunflower	Apple blossom	Showy lady slipper
State Tree	White oak	Tulip	Oak	Cottonwood	White pine	Norway Pine
State Motto	State sovereignty, national union	The crossroads of America	Our liberties we prize and our rights we will maintain	*Ad astra per aspera* (To the stars through difficulties)	*Si quaeris peninsulam amoenam circumspice* (If you seek a pleasant peninsula, look around you)	L'Etoile du Nord (The North Star)
Interesting Facts	The first controlled chain reaction that created nuclear energy was produced by scientists at the University of Chicago. Scientists from around the world come to study the atom at the Fermi National Accelerator Laboratory, near Chicago.	The first international automobile race in the United States was held in Indianapolis in 1911. The Indianapolis 500 race is held every year on Memorial Day.	Grant Wood, a noted American painter, was an Iowan. Ninety-nine percent of Iowans can read and write. Sioux City has the largest popcorn processing plant in the United States.	Kansas lies midway between the Atlantic and Pacific Oceans. It is called the Sunflower State because the tall yellow prairie flower grows in most parts of the state.	Michigan has more than 11,000 inland lakes and about 150 waterfalls. Detroit is the "Automobile Capital of the World."	Minnesota produces most of the nation's supply of iron ore. The Northwest Angle in the Lake of the Woods is the most northern part of the United States excluding Alaska.

382

	Missouri	Nebraska	North Dakota	Ohio	South Dakota	Wisconsin
Source of Name	Named after a tribe called Missouri Indians. *Missouri* means "town of the large canoes."	From an Oto Indian word *Nebrathka*, meaning "flat water"	From the Dakotah tribe, meaning "allies"	From an Iroquoian word meaning "great river"	From the Dakotah tribe, meaning "allies"	French version (Ouisconsin) of Indian name for a river (Miskonsing), meaning "gathering of the waters"
Nickname(s)	Show Me State	Cornhusker State; Beef State; Tree Planters State	Sioux State; Flickertail State	Buckeye State	Sunshine State; Coyote State	Badger State
Capital	Jefferson City	Lincoln	Bismarck	Columbus	Pierre	Madison
Largest Cities	Kansas City St. Louis Springfield	Omaha Lincoln Grand Island	Fargo Bismarck Grand Forks	Columbus Cleveland Cincinnati	Sioux Falls Rapid City Aberdeen	Milwaukee Madison Green Bay
Population Rank	15	36	46	7	45	16
Population Density Rank	27	41	45	9	46	24
Area Rank	19	15	17	35	16	26
State Flag						
State Bird	Bluebird	Western meadowlark	Western meadowlark	Cardinal	Ring-necked pheasant	Robin
State Flower	Hawthorn	Goldenrod	Wild prairie rose	Scarlet carnation	American pasqueflower	Wood violet
State Tree	Flowering dogwood	Cottonwood	American elm	Buckeye	Black Hills spruce	Sugar maple
State Motto	*Salus populi suprema lex esto* (The welfare of the people shall be the supreme law)	Equality before the law	Liberty and union, now and forever: one and inseparable	With God, all things are possible	Under God the people rule	Forward
Interesting Facts	Missouri was one of the leading gateways to the West in pioneer days. St. Joseph was the eastern starting point of the Pony Express, and the Santa Fe and Oregon trails began in Independence.	The largest mammoth fossil ever found was discovered near North Platte. Nebraska's two national forests are the only national forests that have been planted by foresters.	The nation's largest coal reserves are here. Near Grenora there is a large glacial boulder covered with Indian picture writing. It is called Writing Rock.	Ohio is the birthplace of seven United States presidents: Grant, Hayes, Garfield, B. Harrison, McKinley, Taft, and Harding.	Carvings of the heads of George Washington, Thomas Jefferson, Theodore Roosevelt, and Abraham Lincoln were made on Mount Rushmore. It is one of the world's largest sculptures.	Wisconsin is the nation's leading producer of milk and cheese. More minks are raised in Wisconsin than in any other state.

383

KEY FACTS

1. Plains cover most of the North Central region.

2. The Great Lakes and the Mississippi and Missouri rivers, as well as the many other bodies of water, are important to the climate and industry of the North Central region.

3. The climate of the states in the North Central region varies with the location of the state.

4. Agricultural products from the North Central states help feed the entire nation.

5. Much of the North Central region's industry is closely related to its agriculture.

6. Mineral resources of the North Central region include lead, coal, gold, petroleum, and iron.

7. Detroit and St. Louis are two of the nation's leading cities in auto production.

8. The North Central region contains many of our largest cities, including Chicago, Detroit, and Indianapolis.

VOCABULARY QUIZ

Write the letter of the term next to the number of its description. Write on a sheet of paper.

a. grain elevator
b. wholesale market
c. bran
d. gasohol
e. radioactive
f. market weight
g. open-pit mine
h. vitamin
i. assembly line
j. Bad Lands

1. A fuel made from corn

2. A dry, rugged area with gullies and steep bluffs and little or no vegetation

3. A building in which wheat and other crops are stored

4. The weight that an animal must reach before it is sent to market

5. A market that buys products in large quantities and sells them in smaller quantities to other businesses

6. A moving belt that carries a certain part of a product past workers who add pieces to the part

7. A large hole dug in order to reach the iron ore near the earth's surface

8. A part of the wheat kernel

9. Giving off harmful rays

10. A substance necessary for good health

REVIEW QUESTIONS

1. How did glaciers change the landscape of the North Central region?

2. Explain the water cycle either in words or by drawing a labeled diagram.

3. Name at least four important crops of the North Central region.

4. Where are most cattle raised?

5. Which state is our nation's leading dairy state?

6. Why is the making of farm machinery a leading industry of the North Central region?

7. Explain how one industry can lead to the growth of other industries.

8. Which two cities in the North Central region have more than 1 million people?

ACTIVITIES

1. Make a list of the products used in the manufacture of an automobile. Next, group the products according to the natural resources used in them. Third, make a map to show the location of those resources.

2. Paul Bunyan was a legendary logger. Read about Paul and Babe, his blue ox. Then write a report or draw a picture describing one of his adventures.

DESCRIPTIVE WRITING

SETTING A SCENE

In this passage from the *Adventures of Huckleberry Finn*, by Samuel Clemens, Huck and his friend Jim have run away. They are riding down the Mississippi on a raft. As you read, notice how the author gives a clear picture of the scene—the quiet peacefulness, the carefree mood. Clemens does not say that it is summer, that it is quiet and peaceful, and so forth, but his description lets you know these things.

Words in brackets [ ] have been put in by the editor to help you understand certain words.

NIGHT ON THE RIVER

Soon as it was night, out we shoved; when we got her [the raft] out to about the middle, we let her alone, and let her float wherever the current wanted her to; then we . . . dangled our legs in the water and talked about all kinds of things. . . .

Sometimes we'd have that whole river all to ourselves for the longest time. Yonder was the banks and the islands, across the water; and maybe a spark—which was a candle in a cabin window; and sometimes on the water you could see a spark or two—on a raft or a scow [flat-bottomed boat], you know; and maybe you could hear a fiddle or a song coming over from one of them crafts. It's lovely to live on a raft. We had the sky, up there, all speckled with stars, and we used to lay on our backs and look up at them, and discuss about whether they was made, or only just happened. Jim he allowed [thought] they was made, but I allowed they happened; I judged it would have took too long to *make* so many. Jim said the moon could 'a' *laid* them; well, that looked

kind of reasonable, so I didn't say nothing against it, because I've seen a frog lay most as many, so of course it could be done. We used to watch the stars that fell, too, and see them streak down. Jim allowed they'd got spoiled and was hove [thrown] out of the nest.

Once or twice of a night we would see a steamboat slipping along in the dark, and now and then she would belch a whole world of sparks up out of her chimbleys [chimneys], and they would rain down in the river and look awful pretty; then she would turn a corner and her lights would wink out and her powwow shut off and leave the river still again; and by and by her waves would get to us, a long time after she was gone, and joggle the raft a bit, and after that you wouldn't hear nothing for you couldn't tell how long, except maybe frogs or something.

SKILLS PRACTICE

Now answer these questions about the passage. Write on a separate sheet of paper.

1. What did you read in the first and third paragraphs that let you know it was summer?

2. What descriptive word does the author use in place of the word *light*?

3. With what word does the author let you know that the sparks from the steamboat came out in bursts?

4. What words does the author use to tell you that the steamboat let out lots of sparks? What does he use instead of *fall down* to describe how they fell?

5. The discussion about the origin of the stars helps set the mood, too. Do you know why? What kinds of things would they talk about if they were worried or rushed or busy?

The Land and Climate

┌─VOCABULARY─────────────────┐
timberline	arroyo
intermontane	desert
Continental Divide	semidesert
	rain shadow
└────────────────────────────┘

The region   What do you think of when you see the words *the West*? Do you think of mountains and deserts, buffalo and cacti, ghost towns and gold mines? Perhaps you think of skiing or hiking. If any of these things come to mind, you already have some idea of what the Mountain West region is like. Let's see what else we can learn about the region.

There are eight states in the Mountain West. In the north, next to Canada, are Idaho and Montana. In the south, next to Mexico, are Arizona and New Mexico. In between these four states are Wyoming, Nevada, Utah, and Colorado.

One look at the map on the next page will show you the landform that makes this region a region and gives it its name. You can see that the outstanding physical feature is the Rocky Mountains. Even the parts of the region not covered by the Rocky Mountains are high. In fact, just about the only lowlands are those along rivers. Look at the map on page 263 to find elevations in this region.

The Great Plains   Along the eastern edge of the Mountain West is the high plain known as the Great Plains. You read about this important cattle and wheat area earlier. In the Mountain West, the Great Plains covers parts of Montana, Wyoming, Colorado, and New Mexico. The Great Plains slowly rises from east to west until it meets the Rocky Mountains.

The Rockies   In the United States, the Rockies stretch from New Mexico to Canada. They continue north through Canada into the northern part of our largest state, Alaska.

These rugged mountains are much higher than the Appalachians to the east. The highest peak in the Rockies is Mount Elbert in Colorado. In fact all of the highest peaks of the Rockies—those over 14,000 feet (4,270 m)—are in Colorado.

The Rockies are beautiful mountains. At the base are meadows and broadleaf trees. As you climb higher, you find fewer broadleaf trees and more evergreens. As you climb still higher, you find fewer trees of any kind. Those that do cling to the rocky soil are short and often are bent and twisted by the wind.

If you climb high enough, you come to the **timberline**. Beyond this line no trees grow. If you stop here and look up, you

Mount Elbert is the highest peak in the Rocky Mountains. It is 14,433 feet (4,399 m) high. Find it on the map at the right. What state is it in?

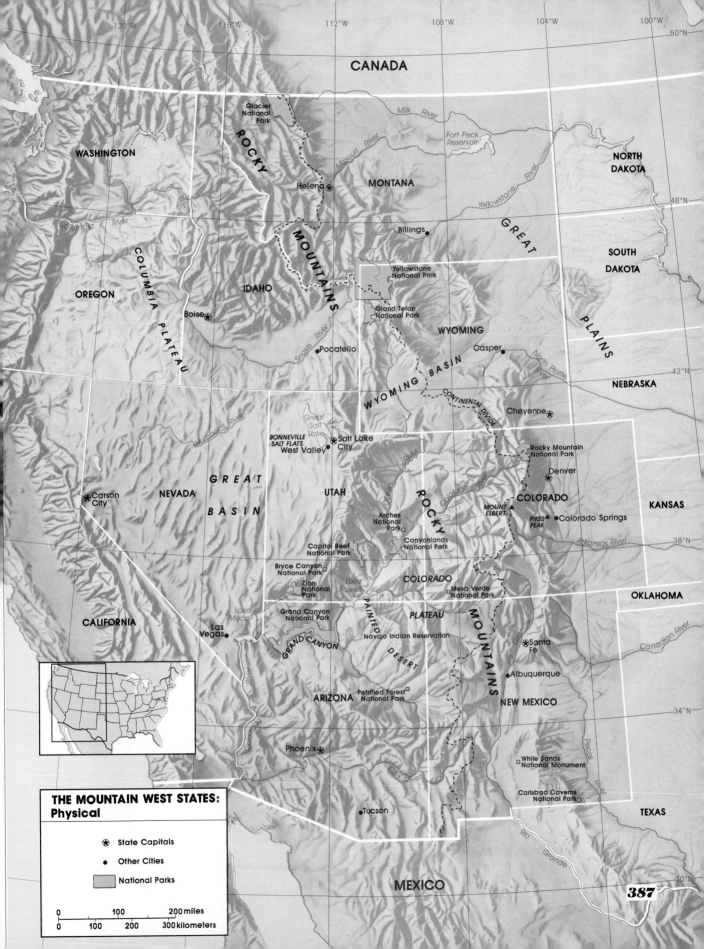

THE MOUNTAIN WEST STATES: Physical

CANADA

WASHINGTON

OREGON

Columbia River

COLUMBIA PLATEAU

Snake River

Humboldt River

Boise ⊛

Pocatello ●

IDAHO

ROCKY

MOUNTAINS

Glacier National Park

Helena ● ⊛

MONTANA

Milk River

Missouri River

Fort Peck Reservoir

Billings ●

Yellowstone River

Yellowstone National Park

Grand Teton National Park

WYOMING

Casper ●

North Platte River

NORTH DAKOTA

SOUTH DAKOTA

GREAT PLAINS

NEBRASKA

CONTINENTAL DIVIDE

WYOMING BASIN

Great Salt Lake

BONNEVILLE SALT FLATS

West Valley ●

Salt Lake City ⊛

Cheyenne ⊛

Rocky Mountain National Park

Denver ⊛

Carson City ●

NEVADA

GREAT

BASIN

UTAH

Green River

Colorado River

ROCKY

COLORADO

MOUNT ELBERT ▲

PIKES PEAK ▲ ● Colorado Springs

Arkansas River

KANSAS

Arches National Park

Capitol Reef National Park

Canyonlands National Park

Bryce Canyon National Park

Zion National Park

Lake Powell

COLORADO

Mesa Verde National Park

PLATEAU

MOUNTAINS

OKLAHOMA

Lake Mead

Grand Canyon National Park

Las Vegas ●

GRAND CANYON

PAINTED DESERT

Navajo Indian Reservation

Santa Fe ⊛

Rio Grande

Canadian River

CALIFORNIA

Colorado River

ARIZONA

Petrified Forest National Park

Albuquerque ●

NEW MEXICO

Pecos River

Phoenix ⊛

Gila River

White Sands National Monument

Tucson ●

Carlsbad Caverns National Park

Rio Grande

TEXAS

MEXICO

Legend

⊛ State Capitals

● Other Cities

▨ National Parks

0   100   200 miles
0   100   200   300 kilometers

50°N
46°N
42°N
38°N
34°N
30°N

120°W 116°W 112°W 108°W 104°W 100°W

will see that even the grass and flowers do not grow on the highest peaks. Sunlight gleams on the snow that covers these rocky peaks all year long.

Intermontane region   You have probably noticed that there are mountain ranges along the Pacific Coast of the United States. The land between these mountains and the Rocky Mountains is known as the **intermontane** region. *Inter* means "between." You can guess what *montane* means. So the intermontane region is the land between the mountains.

The intermontane region has three major parts: the Columbia Plateau, the Colorado Plateau, and the Great Basin.

The landforms of the intermontane region range from rugged cliffs to steep-sided canyons to sandy desert. The Grand Canyon is in this region. It has been formed over millions of years by the Colorado River. The moving water has slowly worn away the soil and carried it downstream. Today thousands of people visit Grand Canyon National Park in Arizona to see the beautiful result of this slow process.

The Continental Divide   You may have noticed a line on the map on page 387 marked **Continental Divide.** This line runs along the high ridges of the Rocky Mountains. The Continental Divide is important in terms of the rivers of North America. The rivers to the east of the Continental Divide flow generally toward the east. Rivers to the west of the Divide flow generally west.

Rivers and lakes   If we had to choose the most important river of the Mountain West, it would probably be the Colorado. This river and its tributaries supply water and hydroelectric power to people in seven states. Water from the Colorado system irrigates crops from Wyoming to southern California and New Mexico. Elec-

For millions of years the Colorado River has been forming the Grand Canyon.

tricity generated in power plants on the Colorado and its tributaries lights thousands of homes. People swim, fish, and go boating on lakes created by dams on the river.

In the northwest are the Snake River and the Salmon River, which flow into the Columbia River. The Columbia flows into the Pacific Ocean. These rivers are also used to supply water and power.

The streams and rivers that flow out of the Rockies into the Great Basin never reach the ocean. Instead they flow into lakes, such as the Great Salt Lake, or simply dry up in the dry, desertlike land. Many of the streams of the Great Basin and the Colorado Plateau have flowing water only following a heavy rainstorm or in spring when the snow melts in the mountains. Later they will slowly dry up until the next heavy rain or spring snow melt. The term **arroyo** is given to a dry streambed. An arroyo may be without flowing water for years.

Many rivers important to the North Central states and the South Central states start in the Rockies. Among these rivers are the Missouri and the Rio Grande. You can find others on a map.

Deserts   The intermontane lands south of the northern borders of Utah and Nevada are largely **desert** and **semidesert.** A desert is a dry land in which there is very little plant growth. You could describe a semidesert by saying that it is halfway between a desert and a grassland. A semidesert is not as dry and bare as a desert, yet it doesn't have as much rain or as much plant cover as a grassland.

Probably the best-known desert of the intermontane region is the Painted Desert in northern Arizona. This desert gets its name from its colorful soil and rock formations.

In New Mexico there are giant dunes of white "sand." The sand is not really sand but a mineral called gypsum. The gypsum comes from the bed of a lake that dries up each year, leaving behind large deposits of gypsum. The wind blows the gypsum into dunes. The White Sands National Monument is in this area.

In the area around Great Salt Lake in Utah one finds the Bonneville Salt Flats. The land here is covered with salt left behind by water that runs down off the mountains and dries up. Because the flats are so level, they are used for high-speed auto racing.

The desert and semidesert areas are by no means forgotten wastelands. In some places, thriving cities have grown up. Such cities include Las Vegas, Nevada; Salt Lake City, Utah; and Phoenix, Arizona. Irrigation has made fertile cropland out of other areas. Valuable minerals are mined here. In some places cattle and sheep can be grazed. Much of the area is a part of the national park system.

Climate   The story of climate in the Mountain West is a tale told by mountains. Generally, the higher one goes, the cooler the air is. The temperature change is about 3½°F for every 1,000 feet of elevation (2°C per 300 m). Pikes Peak is about 9,000 feet (2,700 m) higher than Denver. If the temperature in Denver is 72°F (22°C), the temperature on nearby Pikes Peak will be about 40°F (4°C).

389

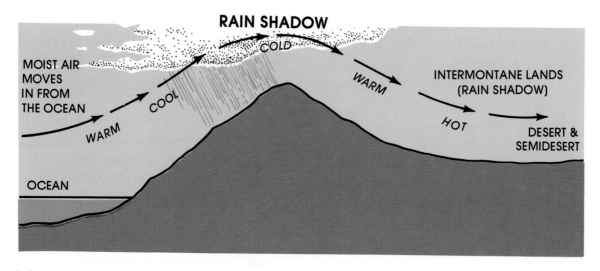

RAIN SHADOW

MOIST AIR MOVES IN FROM THE OCEAN

WARM

COOL

COLD

WARM

HOT

INTERMONTANE LANDS (RAIN SHADOW)

DESERT & SEMIDESERT

OCEAN

By the time the winds pass over the mountains, they have lost most of their moisture.

The mountains also affect precipitation. The winds that blow in off the Pacific Ocean are warm and wet. When they meet the mountains along the coast they are forced to rise. As they rise they are cooled. Cool air cannot hold as much moisture as warm air can.

The moisture in the air falls as rain or snow on the western slopes of the mountains along the coast. Meanwhile the winds continue on up and over the mountains. Now, however, the winds carry very little moisture. The air becomes warmer as it goes downhill and over the intermontane lands. This warm air can hold most of the moisture it does carry. It even absorbs moisture from the ground. As a result, very little rain falls on the intermontane lands. These lands are said to be in a **rain shadow.** The whole rain shadow process repeats itself as the winds rise up and over the slopes of the Rockies. However, the Great Plains are not quite as dry as the intermontane lands. They receive some rain from winds coming in from the north and south.

The range in daily temperature in the Mountain West is quite large, both in summer and in winter. In Phoenix during a winter's day, you might be warm enough without a jacket. When night fell, however, you would be reaching for a warm coat.

The range in record temperature extremes is huge. Phoenix has a record high of 118°F (48°C) and a low of 17°F (−8°C). Alamosa, Colorado, has a record high of 93°F (34°C) and a low of −50°F (−46°C).

The greatest average yearly precipitation is only about 19 inches (48 cm). This is true even though large amounts of snow fall in some places. The snow is dry and powdery. It doesn't equal as much rainfall as do the wet and heavy snows of some other parts of the United States.

CHECKUP

1. What is the timberline? The Continental Divide?
2. What does *intermontane* mean? Where is the intermontane region?
3. Why is the Colorado River important?
4. What is a rain shadow?

390

Agriculture, Resources, and Industry

VOCABULARY
shearing   fossil
oil shale

Farming   Water is one of the most important resources in the Mountain West. It often determines how people use their land. Only a few parts of the Mountain West have enough water for crops. Wheat is grown in the Great Plains and along the Snake River. The Snake River area of Idaho is well known for another crop, potatoes. Idaho leads the United States in the production of potatoes.

Irrigation allows crops to be raised in other places. Irrigated land in Arizona and New Mexico produces large amounts of cotton. Fruits and vegetables grow well in the irrigated lands of Utah and Arizona.

Ranching   Cattle raising makes up a large part of the agriculture of the Mountain West. Cattle ranches here are very large. It takes about 20 to 25 acres (8–10 ha) of good grassland to feed one cow. In the drier areas where there is less grass, it takes even more land. Many ranchers in the Mountain West use national forest lands as well as their own lands for grazing cattle. Even so, ranches of 20,000 acres (8,100 ha) are common. Some are more than 60,000 acres (24,300 ha). The average is about 4,000 acres (1,600 ha).

Because cows won't graze far from water, most ranchers in this dry land have to dig wells. The water is pumped into large troughs from which the cattle drink.

The Mountain West is well known for its sheep ranches, too. Five of the ten leading sheep-raising states are in the Mountain West. Sheep are hardy enough to live on lands that cannot be used for other kinds of farming.

During the fall, winter, and spring, the sheep are kept on pastures near the ranch. During the hot summer when the grass dries up, the sheep are taken into the hills where the grazing is better. The herds are watched over by sheep herders, or shepherds, and their dogs. These dogs are trained to keep the sheep from straying.

Most lambs are born in the spring. They go with their mothers to the hill pastures for the summer. By the time the lambs return in the fall they are old enough to be sold for meat.

Some sheep are raised for wool. **Shearing,** or cutting off the wool, takes place in the spring, after the very cold weather is gone. By the time the cold weather returns, the sheep have grown another coat of wool.

Minerals   The Mountain West is rich in minerals. Large deposits of copper, lead, potassium, iron, and molybdenum (mə lib' də nəm) are found here. Molybdenum is a silvery metal used to make blends of other metals stronger. Although the gold rush days are long gone, gold and silver are still mined in the Mountain West. Fuel resources include natural gas, oil, oil shale, coal, and uranium.

Oil shale   Shale is a kind of rock made of hardened clay, mud, or silt. **Oil shale** is shale that contains oil. There are rich

391

deposits of oil shale in Colorado, Utah, and Wyoming. Unfortunately, many problems must be solved before we can afford to remove the oil from the shale.

Coal   Most coal mines in the Mountain West region are strip mines. Sometimes an entire mountaintop is removed to expose the coal beneath. When this is done, the land can never be completely restored. Some of the coal is found under land used for grazing or crops. A choice has to be made as to how the land will be used. On one hand is our growing need for coal as a fuel. On the other is the need for the products of agriculture. The choice is not easy.

Uranium   Uranium is used to produce nuclear energy. New Mexico, Wyoming, Colorado, and Utah are leading sources of pitchblende, the ore from which we get uranium. This ore, like other nonrenewable resources, is limited. Processing the ore to get uranium that is pure enough to be used for nuclear energy is difficult and costly.

Less than 5 percent of the electrical energy used in the United States comes from nuclear power plants. About half of the states have nuclear power plants. Because of problems with such plants in the early 1980s, plans for new plants were stopped. If they can be made safe, perhaps more plants will be built.

Very strict laws govern the building and operation of nuclear power plants. These laws are needed because one of the byproducts of producing nuclear energy is radioactivity. When something is radioactive, it sends out rays that are very harmful. These rays can cause disease and death. Many people feel that the laws controlling nuclear power are not strong enough. In fact, they think that nuclear energy is too dangerous to use.

Tourism and national parks   In 1872 our Congress set up the first national park. This was Yellowstone National Park. Today there are about 50 national parks and about 300 monuments, memorials, and other areas under the care of the National Park Service. Nearly a quarter of them are in the Mountain West. Besides the areas under the care of the Park Service, there are many thousands of acres of land given over to national forests and wildlife refuges. In

Many tourists visit the Mountain West's national parks, such as Carlsbad Caverns in New Mexico.

Ski resorts are a major industry in the Mountain West. This woman and her instructor are at Snowmass in Colorado. She is using special poles designed for amputees.

fact, the federal government owns almost half of the land in the Mountain West states.

There are also many state parks in the Mountain West. With all this land set aside for the public, it makes sense that tourism is an important business in the Mountain West. Visitors come to camp, hike, boat, fish, ski, and enjoy the scenery.

In some places you can study the geologic history from **fossils,** rocks, and canyon walls. The remains of Indian villages nearly a thousand years old may be seen. Pueblos and cliff houses of long ago interest many people. Landmarks left by the Spaniards can be found in many places in the Southwest.

Places that show the history of our country's westward expansion during the 1800s can also be found. Old ranches, trading posts, and forts help to show how people lived here a hundred years ago.

Near Ogden, Utah, a marker shows the spot where the first transcontinental railroad was finished in 1869.

Other industries   The Mountain West is not as heavily industrialized as other parts of the United States. However, there is some manufacturing. Factories produce aircraft, electronics equipment, machinery, transportation equipment, wood products, foods, and chemicals. Sports clothing and equipment are two new products of the area. Printing and publishing have become well established in some of the cities.

CHECKUP
1. Why must cattle ranches in the Mountain West be so large?
2. Why is some land in the Mountain West used for raising sheep?
3. Name five important mineral resources of the Mountain West.

393

Population and Cities

┌─VOCABULARY─────────
│ oasis
└─────────────────────

Population   The Mountain West is growing very rapidly. Of the ten states whose populations are growing most rapidly, seven are in this region. It is not the region with the largest population. In fact three of the states are among the ten states with the smallest number of people. Throughout the eight states there are large areas of land where very few people live.

MOUNTAIN WEST, INCREASE IN POPULATION, 1970 to 1984 (Figures rounded to nearer percent)	
State	*Percent of increase*
Nevada	86
Arizona	72
Utah	56
Wyoming	54
Colorado	44
Idaho	40
New Mexico	40
Montana	19

The Navajo   The Navajo is one of several tribes of Indians living in the Mountain West. The ancestors of the Navajo people moved from Alaska and Canada to the southwestern part of the United States about 500 years before Columbus landed in the West Indies. Of course this took place before any of those places had their present names. Today most of the Navajo people live on a reservation. The Navajo reservation is the largest one in the United States. Most of it is in the northeastern

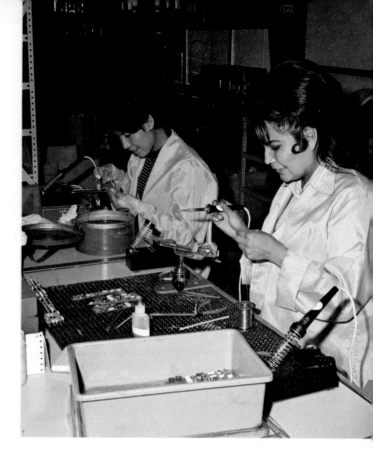

These women are working in the electronics factory on the Navajo reservation in Arizona.

corner of Arizona. Parts of the reservation are in New Mexico and Utah as well.

The Navajo have undergone the same kinds of problems that have faced other Native American peoples. Some of these troubles are discussed in Chapter 10. However, life on the reservation is slowly improving. Many Navajo raise sheep or grow crops. Because the soil is so dry and poor, most of these people work very hard for very little return.

However, the Navajo people now own a lumber mill and an electronics company. These businesses give a good income to many Navajo workers. Skilled Navajo craftworkers make turquoise and silver jewelry and weave blankets. These beautiful articles are sold throughout the United States.

Another major change on the reservation is the opening of coal mines. While the mines are a source of income for the Navajo, they are also a source of conflict. The money from the mines helps the Navajo to buy food and clothing and to give their children a better education. But Navajo tradition and culture always preserved the natural landscape. Coal mining changes it.

Cities   The two largest cities in the Mountain West are Phoenix and Denver. These two cities are among the 25 largest in the United States. Four of the nation's ten fastest growing cities are in the Mountain West. They are Mesa, Aurora, Tempe, and Colorado Springs.

Phoenix   The capital of Arizona, Phoenix is also the state's largest city. It got its start in 1870, when a few pioneers settled on the ruins of an ancient Indian village. Since then Phoenix has been growing rapidly, both in population and in area. In 1940 its population was about 65,000. By the late 1970s, the population of the city alone was more than ten times that large. The metropolitan area had about 1½ million people. In the 1870s, Phoenix was a few homes. Phoenix today sprawls over more than 250 square miles (650 sq km).

Phoenix has grown for many reasons. Irrigation of the desert has made it possible to grow vegetables and citrus fruit. The dry, clear air brings people for health reasons. With people come industries. Thousands of people have found jobs with the new electronics, aircraft, chemical, and other industries.

Denver   Because Denver is 5,280 feet (1,609 m) above sea level, it is often given the nickname of "The Mile-High City." (One mile [1.6 km] equals 5,280 feet.) Denver lies on the western edge of the Great Plains. From many places in the city you can see the Rocky Mountains rising in the distance.

Denver is Colorado's capital and largest city. It got its start as a mining town. When the mining boom was over, Denver did not become a ghost town. The city was in the middle of a large agricultural area. Denver became a center of trade for cattle, wheat, and other such products of the area.

Today the city is an important manufacturing and distributing center as well. Aerospace, food processing, luggage, and rubber goods are among Denver's many industries. The federal government has so many offices in the city that Denver is often called the "Washington of the West." A mint, an air force base, an arsenal, an army medical center, and a nuclear energy plant are among the many federal installations in the Denver area.

Salt Lake City   Salt Lake City is Utah's capital and largest city. About two thirds of the state's people live in or near Salt Lake City. The city was founded on the Great Salt Lake in 1847 by a religious group called the Mormons. This group had been persecuted first in New York State and then in Illinois. The Mormons moved to the Utah desert because they hoped to be far enough away from other people to be safe from persecution.

It took much hard work to build the farms and homes of the Mormon settle-

At this plant near Salt Lake City, coal is crushed and mixed with water to form a soupy mass called slurry. The slurry can then be piped to its destination.

ment. Irrigation was needed before even the smallest of gardens would produce.

Today this **oasis** in the desert is still largely Mormon. In fact about 70 percent of Utah's population is Mormon. In the heart of the city is the huge Mormon Temple, which took 40 years to build. Nearby is the Tabernacle, a large domed building. The Tabernacle is used for meetings and for concerts given by the famous Mormon Tabernacle Choir.

Salt Lake City is not just a religious center. It is a center for tourists who come to see the Great Salt Lake and the Temple and Tabernacle, and for skiers who visit the many ski resorts in the nearby mountains. Salt Lake City has many thriving businesses, including oil refining, electronics and clothing manufacturing, copper smelting, and printing. It is a trade center for agricultural and mining products.

CHECKUP

1. Which Mountain West state is growing most rapidly?
2. Why is coal mining a source of conflict among the Navajo?
3. What are the two largest cities in the Mountain West?
4. What group founded Salt Lake City?

Cities with less than 100,000		
Alamoso (Colo.) D-4	West Valley C-2	Pueblo (Colo.) C-4
Arvada (Colo.) C-4	**Cities with 100,000–499,000**	Reno (Nev.) C-1
Boulder (Colo.) C-4	Albuquerque (N. Mex.) D-4	Salt Lake City (Utah) C-3
Carson City (Nev.) C-1	Aurora (Colo.) C-4	Tempe (Ariz.) E-3
Cheyenne (Wyo.) C-4	Boise (Idaho) B-1	Tucson (Ariz.) E-3
Helena (Mont.) A-2	Colorado Springs (Colo.) C-4	**Cities with 500,000–999,000**
Provo C-3	Glendale (Ariz.) E-2	Denver (Colo.) C-4
Santa Fe (N. Mex.) D-4	Lakewood (Colo.) C-4	Phoenix (Ariz.) E-2
Scottsdale (Ariz.) E-3	Las Vegas (Nev.) D-2	**City with 1,000,000 or more**
	Mesa (Ariz.) E-3	None ....

Despite its great size, the Mountain West is a region with few large cities. Which two states have no cities with a population of 100,000 or more?

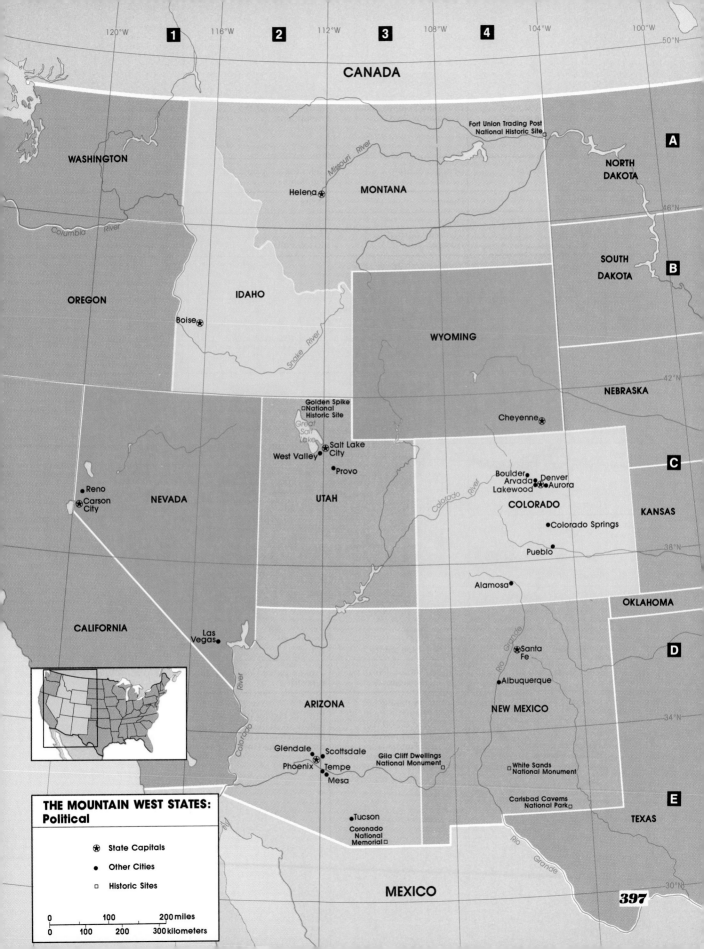

THE MOUNTAIN WEST STATES: Political

1 **2** **3** **4**

A **B** **C** **D** **E**

CANADA

WASHINGTON

MONTANA

Helena ✪

Boise ✪

IDAHO

OREGON

Columbia River

Missouri River

Snake River

Fort Union Trading Post
National Historic Site □

NORTH DAKOTA

SOUTH DAKOTA

WYOMING

NEBRASKA

Golden Spike □ National Historic Site

Great Salt Lake

Salt Lake City ✪

West Valley •

Provo •

UTAH

Cheyenne ✪

Boulder •
Arvada ✪ Denver
Lakewood • Aurora

COLORADO

Colorado River

Colorado Springs •

Pueblo •

Alamosa •

KANSAS

Reno •

Carson City ✪

NEVADA

CALIFORNIA

Las Vegas •

Colorado River

OKLAHOMA

Santa Fe ✪

Albuquerque •

ARIZONA

NEW MEXICO

Rio Grande

Glendale •
Phoenix ✪ Scottsdale •
Tempe •
Mesa •

Gila Cliff Dwellings
National Monument □

White Sands
National Monument □

Carlsbad Caverns
National Park □

TEXAS

Tucson •

Coronado
National
Memorial □

Rio Grande

MEXICO

THE MOUNTAIN WEST STATES: Political

✪ State Capitals

• Other Cities

□ Historic Sites

0   100   200 miles

0   100   200   300 kilometers

50°N
120°W 116°W 112°W 108°W 104°W 100°W
46°N
42°N
38°N
34°N
30°N

397

THE MOUNTAIN WEST STATES	Arizona	Colorado	Idaho	Montana
Source of Name	From Indian *Arizonac*, meaning "little spring"	From the Spanish, meaning "ruddy" or "red"	Means "gem of the mountains"	A Latinized Spanish word meaning "mountainous region"
Nickname(s)	Grand Canyon State	Centennial State	Gem State; Spud State; Panhandle State	Treasure State
Capital	Phoenix	Denver	Boise	Helena
Largest Cities	Phoenix Tucson Mesa	Denver Colorado Springs Aurora	Boise Pocatello Idaho Falls	Billings Great Falls Butte-Silver Bow
Population Rank	28	26	40	44
Population Density Rank	40	37	43	48
Area Rank	6	8	13	4
State Flag				
State Bird	Cactus wren	Lark bunting	Mountain bluebird	Western meadowlark
State Flower	Flower of saguaro cactus	Rocky Mountain columbine	Syringa	Bitterroot
State Tree	Paloverde	Colorado blue spruce	White pine	Ponderosa pine
State Motto	*Ditat Deus* (God enriches)	*Nil sine Numine* (Nothing without Providence)	*Esto perpetua* (May you last forever)	*Oro y plata* (Gold and silver)
Interesting Facts	Millions of tourists visit the Grand Canyon, the Painted Desert, and the Petrified Forest each year. London Bridge, at Lake Havasu City, is a stone bridge that was brought here from London, England.	Colorado is the highest state in the nation with an elevation of 6,800 feet (818 m). Eisenhower Memorial Tunnel is the world's highest tunnel for vehicles. It is 11,000 feet (3,400 m) above sea level.	In 1955, Arco was the first town to receive its power supply from nuclear energy. Hells Canyon is the deepest canyon in the United States.	More than 50 glaciers can be found on the rugged mountain slopes of Glacier National Park.

398

THE MOUNTAIN WEST STATES	Nevada	New Mexico	Utah	Wyoming
Source of Name	Spanish "snowcapped"	From the country of Mexico	From the Ute tribe, meaning "people of the mountains"	From a Delaware Indian word meaning "upon the great plain"
Nickname(s)	Sagebrush State; Silver State; Battle-born State	Land of Enchantment; Sunshine State	Beehive State	Equality State
Capital	Carson City	Santa Fe	Salt Lake City	Cheyenne
Largest Cities	Las Vegas Reno North Las Vegas	Albuquerque Santa Fe Las Cruces	Salt Lake City West Valley Provo	Casper Cheyenne Laramie
Population Rank	43	37	35	49
Population Density Rank	47	44	42	49
Area Rank	7	5	11	9
State Flag				
State Bird	 Mountain bluebird	 Roadrunner	 Sea gull	 Meadowlark
State Flower	 Sagebrush	 Yucca	 Sego lily	 Indian paintbrush
State Tree	 Single-leaf piñon	 Piñon	 Blue spruce	 Cottonwood
State Motto	All for our country	*Crescit eundo* (It grows as it goes)	Industry	Equal rights
Interesting Facts	This state has less rainfall than any other state in the United States. One of the world's largest dams, the Hoover Dam, is located near Las Vegas.	The world's first atomic bomb was exploded in the desert near Alamogordo on July 16, 1945. El Camino Real, Spanish for the Royal Road, is the oldest road in the United States.	Great Salt Lake is the largest natural lake west of the Mississippi River and is almost five times as salty as the ocean.	In 1872, Yellowstone became the first national park in the United States. In 1906, Devil's Tower became the first national monument.

KEY FACTS

1. Mountains, high plateaus, steep canyons, and deserts are the major land features of the Mountain West.

2. The Colorado River is used for irrigation, water supply, waterpower, and recreation.

3. The intermontane lands are dry because they are in a rain shadow.

4. Cattle and sheep raising make up a large part of the agriculture of the Mountain West.

5. The Mountain West has many important mineral resources.

6. The population of the Mountain West is growing rapidly.

VOCABULARY QUIZ

Next to the number of the sentence write the term that best completes the sentence. Write on a sheet of paper.

reservation   Continental Divide
desert   oil shale
arroyo   timberline
oasis   shearing
intermontane   fossil

1. The land between the Rockies and the mountains near the Pacific coast is known as the _____ region.

2. Rivers to the west of the _____ flow generally west.

3. You can tell you are crossing an _____ when you see the stones polished by the water that sometimes flows there.

4. Most Navajo live on the _____ in northeastern Arizona.

5. When you find a rock that shows the imprint of a plant leaf or that of an animal's skeleton, you have found a _____ .

6. The green trees and lawns of Salt Lake City create an _____ in the desert.

7. No trees grow above the _____ on a mountain slope.

8. A _____ is a land with very little rainfall and very few plants.

9. Clipping wool from sheep is called _____ .

10. It is difficult to get oil from the kind of rock known as _____ .

REVIEW QUESTIONS

1. Describe how the vegetation changes as you climb the high mountains of the Rockies.

2. What are the three major parts of the intermontane region?

3. Why is the Colorado River system important to the people of the Mountain West?

4. What is a rain shadow?

5. Which state produces the most potatoes?

6. Name at least four mineral resources of the Mountain West.

7. Why do some people object to the use of nuclear energy?

8. Which park was the first national park?

9. Why is coal mining a source of conflict for the Navajo?

10. What are the two largest cities of the Mountain West?

ACTIVITIES

1. Make a booklet of national parks found in the Mountain West. In the booklet tell where the park is located, its size, and when it was founded. Then give a description of its most important features.

2. Read about life on a Navajo reservation. List the things a Navajo boy or girl might do during one day. Which activities are like your own? Which are different?

LEARNING WORD ORIGINS

SOURCES OF WORDS

Words, like people and nations, have histories. There are people who study the history of words, just as there are people who study the history of nations. There is a lot to study, because languages have been growing and changing since the first word was spoken.

There are many reasons why this is true. Every time people make or discover something new, they need a new word. Also, people do not remain in one place. When they move, they take their language with them. Some of their words are adopted into the language of the people in the new land. Or if the immigrants are also the conquerors, they adopt some of the words of the original inhabitants. English, especially American English, is full of such words. *Arroyo, mesa, pueblo,* and *lariat* are a few of the words of Spanish origin that have become part of our vocabulary. From Native Americans, we borrowed *moccasin, canoe, succotash, kayak,* and a number of other words. The French, Dutch, and other settlers gave us still more words.

AMERICAN PLACE-NAMES

American place-names have many different origins. Here again we find words from several different languages. We also find places named after places in the homeland of the first settlers of an area. In addition there are places named after local people or after saints, Presidents, royalty, or other famous people. Many place-names describe a physical feature, a plant, an animal, or an event. Place-names can come from the Bible or other works of literature. Some place-names are made-up words. A large number of names are borrowed from Indian words.

The list below gives the origin of some place-names in the Mountain West.

Name	Source
Humboldt River	After Alexander von Humboldt a German traveler and explorer
Bitterroot Mountains	After the bitterroot plant
Big Horn Mountains	After the mountain sheep
Gila River	After an Indian tribe
Boise	From the French word *bois* "wooded"
Ogden	After a local man
Pueblo	Spanish word meaning "town." (It was the only settlement in the area, so it was just called "the town.")
Cheyenne	From an Indian tribal name
Nevada	Spanish word meaning "snowy"
Moscow	After the Russian city of that name

SKILLS PRACTICE

Now look at the following place-names. Try to guess the origin of each. Check your guesses in an encyclopedia, a dictionary, or a book of place-name origins, such as *American Place-Names,* by George R. Steward (New York: Oxford University Press, 1970).

1. Phoenix
2. Boulder
3. Carson City
4. Havre
5. Trinidad
6. Yellowstone
7. Rio Grande
8. Utah
9. Aurora
10. Alamosa
11. Cody
12. Helena
13. Santa Fe
14. Lewis Range

The Land and Climate

VOCABULARY

earthquake	permafrost
volcano	tundra
ocean current	

The region The Pacific region stretches from the northernmost point in the United States—Point Barrow, Alaska, at about 71°N—to the southernmost point in the United States—Ka Lae (kä lä′ ā), a cape in Hawaii at about 19°N. The Pacific region has five states: Alaska, California, Hawaii, Oregon, and Washington. Unlike the states in the other regions, these five states are not all together in one part of our nation. California, Oregon, and Washington are next to one another along the Pacific coast. Alaska and Hawaii, however, are both far away. Neither state borders any other state.

The Pacific region is one of great contrasts. At 20,320 feet (6,194 m), Mount McKinley in Alaska is the highest point in all of North America. The lowest point in North America is Death Valley in California at 282 feet (86 m) below sea level. On the coasts you find beaches of bright white sand and beaches with deep black sand. You also find places with steep, rocky cliffs at the water's edge. There are barren deserts and lush jungles. The vari-ety of climates ranges from the cold, dry Arctic of Alaska to the hot, wet tropics of Hawaii.

Landforms Mountains and valleys are important landforms of the Pacific region. Look at the map on the next page. Notice the mountain system called the Coast Ranges, which stretches from southern California to northern Washington. Inland from these mountains are the Cascades and the Sierra Nevada. Find these mountains on the map, too.

Between the Coast Ranges and these inland mountains are some of the most fertile valleys in our nation. The largest of these is the Central Valley of California. In Alaska the two major mountain ranges are the Brooks Range in the north and the Alaska Range in the south. Between the two is the Yukon River valley. Hawaii is also mountainous. In fact, the islands are the tops of submerged mountains.

Waterways The Pacific Ocean washes the shores of all five states. There are many important harbors along the coast, including Washington's Puget (pyü′ jət) Sound and California's San Francisco Bay. In the Gulf of Alaska there are several ports, and of course Hawaii has a number of ports, too.

Name the islands that make up the state of Hawaii. Notice the Alaska panhandle—the narrow strip of the state that extends south along Canada's western border.

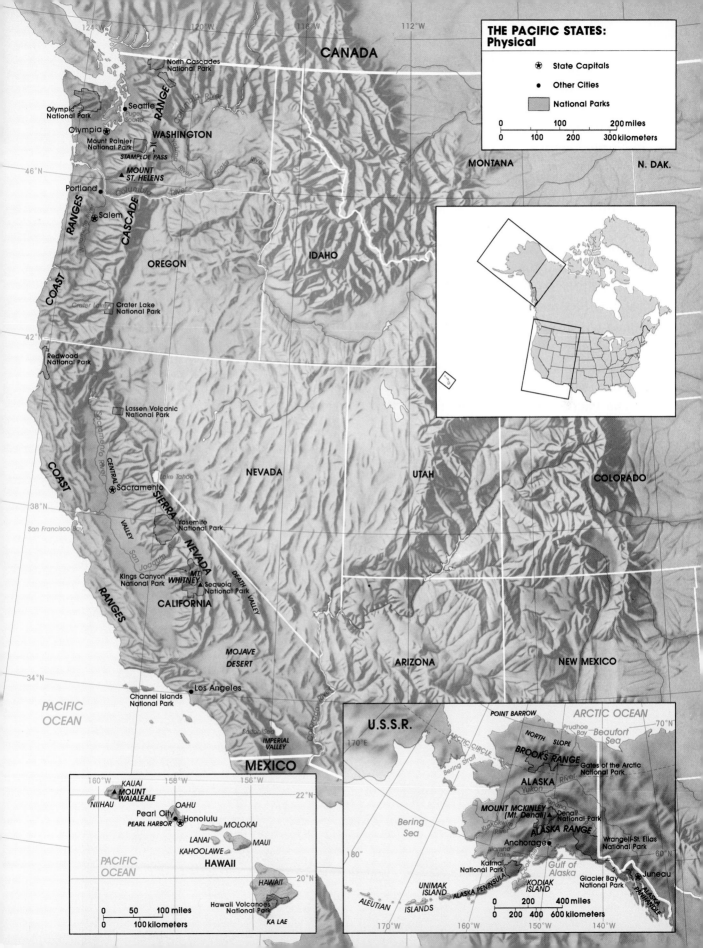

The longest river in the Pacific states is the Yukon River, which begins in Canada and flows through Alaska to the Bering Sea. The Yukon is the third largest river in North America.

Another important waterway is the Columbia River. This river is important for shipping, irrigation, waterpower, and fishing. It ranks as one of the world's most important salmon (sam' ən) streams.

In California, the San Joaquin (san wä kēn') and Sacramento rivers are a part of a statewide water plan. Rivers, canals, and aqueducts bring water from northern rivers and lakes to the dry parts of the state. California also uses water from the Colorado River.

The Pacific region contains two of the world's deepest lakes: Crater Lake in Oregon and Lake Tahoe on the border between California and Nevada. In the Western Hemisphere, only Canada's Great Slave Lake is deeper than these two lakes.

Another interesting lake is the Salton Sea in southern California. It is actually a lake, but is called a sea because it has salt water. The Salton Sea formed in an area that is about 280 feet (85 m) below sea level. Most of the water that created the lake came from the Colorado River when it flooded and left its course in the early 1900s. Since the Salton Sea now has no rivers flowing out of it, the water is saltier than ocean water.

Climate   Three main factors affect the climates of the Pacific states: mountains, ocean currents, and latitude. Hawaii is the warmest of the five states. It lies in the tropics, near the Equator. Hawaii also has one of the wettest spots on the earth. The north slope of Mount Waialeale (wī äl ā äl' ā) on the island of Kauai (kou' ī) gets about 450 inches (1,125 cm) of rain a year. Warm, moist winds come in from the ocean, dropping most of their moisture on the

Crater Lake formed in the cone of a volcanic mountain. Wizard Island, shown in the picture, is also a volcanic formation. The lake's greatest depth is 1,932 feet (589 m).

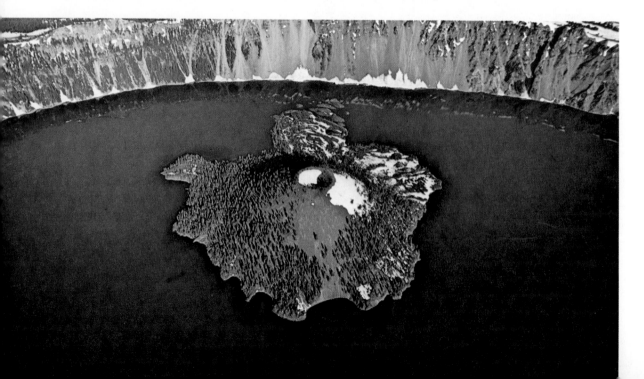

Earthquakes and Volcanoes

People in the Pacific region experience two of nature's most violent forces: **earthquakes** and **volcanoes.**

An earthquake is a movement of the ground. A small earthquake can be just a gentle shaking or a sharp jolt. Although the motion usually lasts no more than a few minutes, a large earthquake can cause great damage. Large cracks form in the earth's surface. Roads buckle, bridges collapse, and buildings tumble to the ground. The side effects can include fires, floods, landslides, and tidal waves. In the Pacific states, earthquakes occur most often in California and Alaska.

A volcano is an opening in the ground through which melted rock and other materials pour. These materials are deep inside the earth. From time to time they push up through a weak spot in the earth's surface, and a volcano is born. A volcanic eruption may send clouds of ash, gases, and water vapor shooting into the air. Lava, or melted rock, may flow from a volcano for days.

Many of the mountains in the Pacific states were formed by volcanoes. Several Hawaiian Islands are the tops of volcanic mountains. A recent eruption in the United States was that of Mount St. Helens in 1980. The eruption blew off the peak, sending tons of mud sliding down the mountainside. The mudslide swept away houses and bridges. A blast of hot gases shot out of the side of the mountain, burning everything in a path 15 miles (24 km) wide and 8 miles (13 km) long. A rain of ash fell over much of the land, damaging forests and crops, choking streams, lakes, and roads, and sending thousands of people to shelter.

northern and eastern slopes of Waialeale and the other mountains of the Hawaiian Islands. The southern and western sides are in a rain shadow and get much less rain.

The rain-shadow effect is at work in other parts of the Pacific states, too. The Central Valley and the lands to the east of the Cascades and the Sierra Nevada are all quite dry.

In fact, most of California has a dry climate. Winds bearing rain blow off the ocean only in winter. Rainfall in summer is very rare. The yearly average precipitation is less than 20 inches (50 cm) in most places. Summers are hot, and winters are warm in most of central and southern California.

The lands along the coast from northern California to the Alaskan peninsula and the Aleutian Islands are affected by a warm **ocean current.** (An ocean current is a movement of the surface water in a regular path.) These lands have plenty of rainfall and milder temperatures than do the inland areas at the same latitudes.

Snowfall is heavy in southern Alaska and in the high mountains of Washington, Oregon, and northern California. One weather station in Washington, Stampede Pass, has an average yearly snowfall of 442 inches (1,123 cm).

These ballplayers are saluting the flag before the start of Fairbanks, Alaska's annual midnight sun baseball game.

Northern Alaska is very cold and quite dry. The weather station at Barrow has an average yearly temperature of 9°F (−23°C). It has an average yearly precipitation of only 5 inches (13 cm). It is so cold here that only the top few inches of the ground ever thaw. Below that is **permafrost,** or ground that stays frozen all year long. Barrow is in the **tundra.** The tundra is a treeless plain. It is so dry and cold that very few kinds of plants can live there.

Central Alaska receives more rainfall than the tundra area. Along the Yukon River valley, winters are cold and harsh. Summers are short and cool. The growing season may last only 100 days. However, it is possible to grow some vegetables and grains.

Midnight sun   In the Arctic region of Alaska and in other Arctic lands, day and night are different from our day and night. At the North Pole, the sun does not set at all from the end of March to the end of September. From September to March the sun doesn't rise. Night lasts for 6 months and day lasts for 6 months. As you move away from the Pole, you find that the sun does rise and set during each 24-hour period.

Even so, from March to September, daylight lasts for a long time in the Arctic. The sun is still out at midnight in some places. In winter, the opposite is true. Then the sun is only out for a short time during each 24-hour period. At the Arctic Circle there is one 24-hour period of darkness in the winter and one 24-hour period of sunlight in the summer.

CHECKUP

1. What is the highest point in North America? The lowest?
2. What are the two main physical features of the Pacific region?
3. What three main factors affect the Pacific climates? How do they do so?

406

Agriculture, Resources, and Industry

—VOCABULARY—
fish hatchery

Agriculture California's farmlands are among the richest in the world. The warm, sunny climate and rich soil are ideal for many crops. Water, the missing ingredient, is supplied by irrigation. It is not surprising, then, that California leads the nation in farm production and in the amount of land used for farming. (The graph on page 281 in Chapter 14 shows you which five states lead the nation in farm production.) California's two most important farming areas are the Central Valley and the Imperial Valley. The Imperial Valley is in southern California near the Salton Sea.

This orange grove near Bakersfield, California, gives you an idea of the vastness of California's agriculture. Bakersfield is at latitude 35°N and longitude 119°W. It is near the southern end of the Central Valley.

Many crops are grown in these fertile valleys. There are citrus fruit, grapes, apricots, dates, and figs. There are vegetables, such as lettuce, tomatoes, and artichokes. Among the other important crops are rice and cotton. Cattle and other livestock are also raised.

The chief farmlands of Washington and Oregon are found in the Willamette (wə lam′ ət), Yakima (yak′ ə mô), and Columbia river valleys and in the lowlands south of Puget Sound. Many different types of crops are grown in these areas. Washington apples are sold throughout the nation. There are many vegetable farms and dairy farms. This area has become famous for farms that grow roses and other flowers. Large wheat crops are grown on the dry plateau of eastern Washington.

Most of Alaska's farmlands are near Anchorage and Fairbanks. Potatoes, vegetables, and hay are among the most important crops. Blueberries and strawberries are harvested during the short growing season. Cattle and poultry are also raised. Most of the products are used locally.

Sugarcane and pineapple are Hawaii's two most important crops. Both crops are grown on large plantations. Hawaii is one of the world's leaders in pineapple production. Both fresh and canned pineapple are exported.

A third important export crop is coffee. Coffee is grown on the cooler mountain slopes rather than on the level land used for fields of sugarcane and pineapple.

On the islands of Maui (mou′ ē) and Hawaii, cattle ranching is big business. Most of the beef raised on the islands is sold in Hawaiian markets.

Forests   Four of the five Pacific states have important lumbering industries. About half of Washington and Oregon, about one third of Alaska, and about two fifths of California are forested. Oregon is our leading lumber state. It produces about one fifth of the nation's lumber and nearly three fourths of the plywood. The graph on page 275 in Chapter 14 shows you that Oregon produces about twice as much lumber as Washington, the state with the third highest lumber production. Which state is second?

Between the Cascades and the Coast Ranges in Washington and Oregon are huge forests of pine and other evergreens. The mild temperatures and plentiful rainfall are ideal for growing trees. Lumbering has been going on in this area for over 100 years. Sawmills, pulp and paper mills, and furniture factories make wood processing a leading industry of the area. Most of the lumber and wood products are shipped from Portland and ports along Puget Sound.

Timber is one of Alaska's leading products. Most of it comes from the southern coastal area and from the Yukon River valley. The growth of Alaska's industry and population has increased the local demand for wood products. Much lumber is also shipped to other markets.

California is famous for its huge redwood trees. One kind of redwood, the coast redwood, grows near the ocean, where it receives moisture from winds coming in off the Pacific. The other kind, the giant redwood, grows on the western slopes of the Sierra Nevada. Both kinds of redwoods can grow to enormous size, although the coast redwood is the taller of

These two girls must feel like ants next to these huge redwoods. Redwoods grow to such great heights that their tops are often broken off by lightning.

the two. One coast redwood was reported to be 385 feet (117 m) high, and one giant redwood measured 325 feet (99 m). Redwoods can be as much as 30 feet (9 m) in diameter. Redwoods live for hundreds of years. Some of the largest redwoods are thought to be about 3,500 years old.

People do not agree on what should be done with the redwoods. Some people think they should be cut for lumber. The lumber is valuable for building, furniture, and other things. A single coast redwood can provide more than enough lumber for several houses. Other people feel that the remaining redwoods should be preserved for future generations to enjoy.

Fishing   The Pacific states have an important fishing industry. Salmon play a large role in that industry. Salmon hatch in freshwater streams. They live in the

streams until they are at least 2 years old. Then they swim downstream and head far out to sea. After 2 or more years there, they return to the streams where they were hatched to lay their eggs. Soon after the eggs are laid, the salmon die.

Not all the salmon make it upstream to lay their eggs. Gulls and bears feed on the returning salmon. And when the salmon are running, fish canneries are busy 24 hours a day processing the catch.

Some streams and rivers are no longer available to salmon. Some streams are too polluted. On others, dams have been built. Unless fish ladders are also built, the dams keep the fish from making their journey. A fish ladder is a series of pools, set up like steps, that fish can use to get past a dam. From Alaska to northern Cal-

Low walls called weirs separate the pools of a fish ladder. The raised section of the weir makes a backwater where fish can rest. Fish either jump the weirs or swim through holes near the weir's bottom.

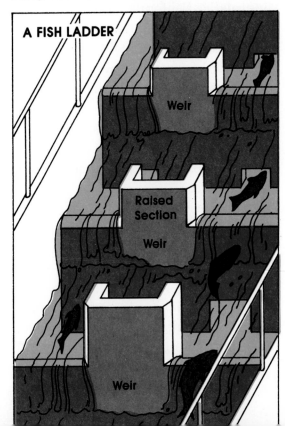

A FISH LADDER

Weir

Raised
Section

Weir

Weir

ifornia, **fish hatcheries** have been developed to offset the loss. Millions of eggs are hatched. When the young salmon have grown large enough, they are released in the streams and head out to sea.

Shellfish, especially crabs, are also important along the coast from northern California to Alaska. California port cities have fishing fleets that bring in catches of tuna and halibut.

Other products of the sea include otters, seals, and whales. All three were hunted for years until very few were left. Now some countries are trying to work together to control the numbers taken. Seals and otters have become tourist attractions at several places along the rocky Pacific coast. Tourists also come to watch the whales that migrate seasonally along the coast from the Arctic Ocean and the North Pacific Ocean to southern waters and back again.

Minerals   California leads the five Pacific states in the production of many minerals. It ranks first in the nation in the production of several of those minerals. It is the third largest producer of iron ore. The state has been one of our leading producers of oil for many years. However, the known reserves are being used up. California's oil production is not as large as it once was.

The discovery of gold near Sacramento in 1848 brought thousands of people to California. Gold is still mined but is no longer a leading mineral resource of California.

Like California, Alaska had a gold rush. Some gold is still mined along the Yukon River, but more interest is now given to the large oil and gas deposits near Prudhoe Bay on Alaska's North Slope. The North Slope is a broad, frozen tundra between the Brooks Range and the Beaufort Sea. In area it is about the size of the state of Washington. Geologists believe the North Slope has one of the largest oil reserves in North America.

The oil cannot be shipped out by tanker, because Prudhoe Bay is blocked with ice for much of the year. To get the oil from Prudhoe Bay to the places where it is needed, a large pipeline was built. The pipeline goes to Valdez, a port in southern Alaska. The 48-inch (122-cm) pipeline crosses three mountain ranges and 350 rivers and streams on its 800-mile (1,300-km) course. From Valdez the oil is taken by tanker to refineries in Washington and California. Much oil is exported to Japan and other nations.

Not everyone wanted the Alaskan pipeline to be built. Many people were worried about the danger of oil spills if the pipe were to break. Others worried that the warm oil carried by the pipe would melt the top layers of the permafrost and upset the natural balance. Our nation's demand for oil was so great that the pipeline was built in spite of these dangers. However, great care was taken in planning the pipeline so that the natural world would be hurt as little as possible. So far it seems to have done little damage.

Other industries   Tourism is a leading industry in each of the five Pacific states. People hike and camp in the breathtakingly beautiful mountains. They hunt and fish in the forests and streams. In California and Hawaii, they enjoy the surf and

As you can see, the Alaskan pipeline crosses some pretty rugged country. This picture was taken 80 miles (130 km) north of Valdez. Notice the mountains in the background.

sunny beaches. People come to visit the twenty national parks in the Pacific states. These parks include Yosemite in California, Olympic in Washington, Crater Lake in Oregon, Denali in Alaska, and Hawaii Volcanoes in Hawaii.

The nation's largest aerospace manufacturing center is in southern California. Another large center is in Washington. Both passenger planes and military planes are built in these two centers.

Food processing is important in the cities near the farming centers. Most of the other industries of California, Washington, and Oregon make products that are the result of modern scientific developments. Among them are televisions, radios, and other electronic products. Southern California's dry, sunny climate made it an ideal place for the growth of the entertainment industry. Many movies and television programs are produced here.

CHECKUP

1. Which is our leading farming state? Lumbering state?
2. What is unusual about redwoods? Salmon?
3. What is Alaska's most important mineral resource?

Population and Cities

Population   The Pacific region has the state with the largest number of people (California) and the state with the smallest number (Alaska). Alaska not only has the fewest people, but also the fewest people per square mile of the 50 states. It is the largest state in area and smallest in number of people.

The region's largest population centers are on or near the coast. They include five of the 25 largest cities in the United States: Los Angeles, San Diego, San Francisco, and San Jose (san ə zā') in California, and Seattle on Puget Sound in Washington.

During the 1970s, Alaska's population grew rapidly. Many people moved into the state from other parts of the United States. Among those who moved in were people who worked on building the Alaskan pipeline and a smaller number who came to set up **homesteads** in the Alaskan wilderness.

The older residents include whites, Inuit (in yü' it), or Eskimos, Indians, and Aleuts (ə lüts'). Aleuts are the native people of the Aleutian Islands. The Eskimos, Indians, and Aleuts combined make up about 15 percent of Alaska's population.

Of Hawaii's more than 1 million residents, only about 8 percent have all Hawaiian ancestors. The population is made up of the descendants of immigrants from many parts of the world. People from Japan, the Philippines, China, Polynesia, Portugal, and the United States were among the early settlers. Their descendants have stayed on the islands.

Mexican Americans   There are about 9 million Mexican Americans living in the United States. More Mexican Americans live in California than in any other state. The roots of Mexican Americans can be traced back to the great Indian civilizations of Mexico and to the Spanish settlers of that nation. By the mid-1800s, over 75,000 Spanish-speaking persons lived in

---

Cities with less than 100,000
Barrow (Alaska) H-8
Eugene (Oreg.) B-1
Fairbanks (Alaska) I-9
Hayward (Calif.) D-1
Hilo (Hawaii) G-7
Inglewood (Calif.) E-2
Juneau (Alaska) J-10
Kailua (Hawaii) F-6
Ketchikan J-10
Olympia (Wash.) A-1
Ontario (Calif.) D-2
Orange (Calif.) E-2
Pearl City (Hawaii) F-6
Pomona (Calif.) D-2
Salem (Oreg.) B-1
Sitka (Alaska) J-10
Thousand Oaks (Calif.) D-2
Valdez (Alaska) I-9

Cities with 100,000–499,000
Anaheim (Calif.) E-2
Anchorage (Alaska) I-9
Bakersfield (Calif.) D-2
Berkeley (Calif.) D-1
Concord (Calif.) D-1
Eugene (Oreg.) B-1
Fremont (Calif.) D-1
Fresno (Calif.) D-2
Fullerton (Calif.) E-2
Glendale (Calif.) D-2
Garden Grove (Calif.) E-2
Honolulu (Hawaii) F-6
Huntington Beach (Calif.) E-2
Long Beach (Calif.) E-2
Modesto (Calif.) D-1
Oakland (Calif.) D-1
Oxnard (Calif.) D-2
Pasadena (Calif.) D-2

Pomona (Calif.) D-2
Portland (Oreg.) B-1
Riverside (Calif.) E-2
Sacramento (Calif.) C-1
San Bernardino (Calif.) D-2
Santa Ana (Calif.) E-2
Seattle (Wash.) A-1
Spokane (Wash.) A-2
Stockton (Calif.) D-1
Sunnyvale (Calif.) D-1
Tacoma (Wash.) A-1
Torrance (Calif.) E-2

Cities with 500,000–999,000
San Diego (Calif.) E-2
San Francisco (Calif.) D-1
San Jose (Calif.) D-1

City with 1,000,000 or more
Los Angeles (Calif.) D-2

Compare this list of cities with the lists on pages, 306, 324, 343, 362, 381, and 396. Which region has the most cities with a population of 500,000 to 999,000?

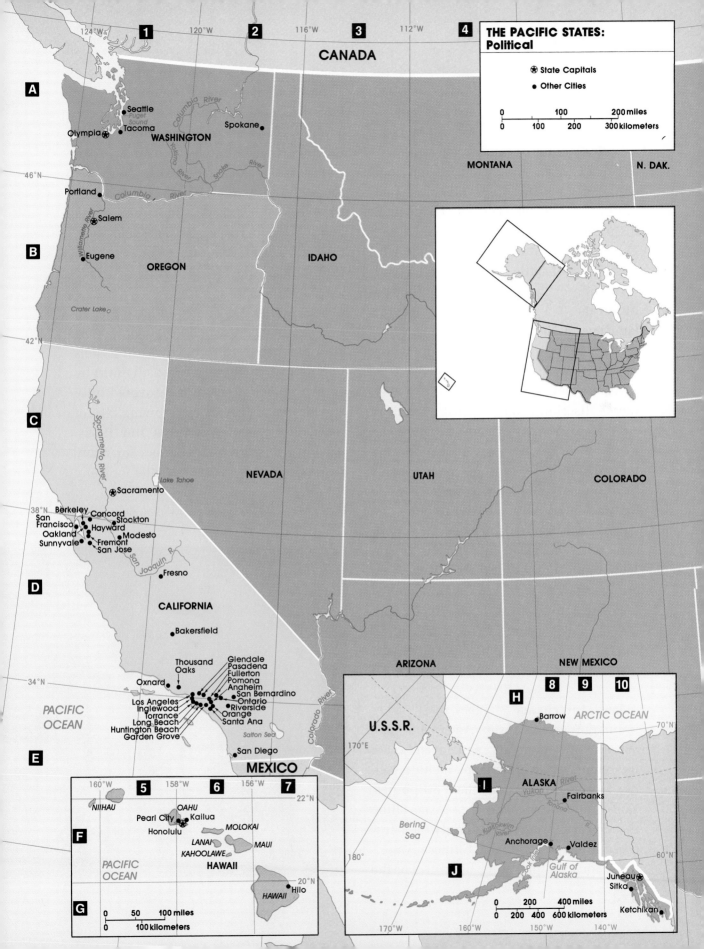

THE PACIFIC STATES: Political

⊛ State Capitals
● Other Cities

0   100   200 miles
0   100   200   300 kilometers

CANADA

MONTANA   **N. DAK.**

WASHINGTON
Seattle
Tacoma
Olympia ⊛
Spokane

OREGON
Portland
Salem ⊛
Eugene

IDAHO

Columbia River
Yakima River
Snake River
Willamette River
Crater Lake

46°N
42°N

NEVADA   **UTAH**   **COLORADO**

Sacramento River
Lake Tahoe
Sacramento

Berkeley   Concord
San   Stockton
Francisco Hayward   Modesto
Oakland
Sunnyvale Fremont
           San Jose

San Joaquin R.

Fresno

CALIFORNIA

Bakersfield

38°N

Thousand   Glendale
Oaks   Pasadena
            Fullerton
Oxnard   Pomona
            Anaheim
Los Angeles San Bernardino
Inglewood   Ontario
Torrance   Riverside
Long Beach   Orange
Huntington Beach Santa Ana
Garden Grove

San Diego

ARIZONA   **NEW MEXICO**

Colorado River
Salton Sea

34°N

PACIFIC OCEAN

MEXICO

HAWAII
NIIHAU
OAHU
Pearl City   Kailua
Honolulu
LANAI   MOLOKAI
KAHOOLAWE   MAUI

PACIFIC OCEAN

HAWAII
Hilo

160°W   158°W   156°W
22°N
20°N

0   50   100 miles
0   100 kilometers

U.S.S.R.

ARCTIC OCEAN
Barrow

ALASKA
Fairbanks
Anchorage   Valdez
Juneau ⊛
Sitka
Ketchikan

Yukon River
Kuskokwim River
Tanana R.

Bering
Sea

Gulf of
Alaska

70°N
60°N

170°E   180°   170°W   160°W   150°W   140°W

0   200   400 miles
0   200   400   600 kilometers

the West before it became part of the United States. The gold rush in 1849, however, brought so many English-speaking settlers to the West that Mexican Americans were outnumbered.

The Mexican Americans shared their knowledge of farming, ranching, and mining with the newcomers. They taught them methods of mining gold and silver. They also taught them how to tame wild horses, brand cattle, and irrigate the land.

In spite of this, there was conflict between the two groups. Each had its own language, religion, and customs. Many English-speaking settlers thought of the Mexican Americans as "foreign."

As the new settlers came into power, they discriminated against Mexican Americans. Many Mexican Americans had to settle for poorer jobs, education, and housing. In spite of this, many people have moved from Mexico to the United States. They continue to do so today.

In recent years, many Mexican Americans have organized into groups to gain more opportunities for themselves. These groups draw attention to the problems of Mexican Americans throughout the country. They also encourage Mexican Americans to take pride in themselves and in their history, both Mexican and American.

Asian Americans   Like most other immigrant groups, Asian Americans have suffered from unfair and even cruel treatment. Asian Americans include people from China, Japan, the Philippines, Korea, and other nations of Asia. Often these people were allowed only the hardest and lowest-paid jobs. Chinese Americans, for example, were hired to lay the track for the transcontinental railroad. Thousands of Japanese Americans were forced to give up their jobs and homes and to live in camps during World War II. Despite these and other hardships, Asian Americans have made good lives for themselves in the United States. They have been able to keep a sense of pride in their Asian heritage. At the same time, they have made important contributions to American life.

Alaskan cities   There are few cities in our largest state. Anchorage, the largest city, has about 40 percent of the state's population. Anchorage was badly hurt by an earthquake in 1964. It recovered fully and has been the fastest growing city of the nation during the 1970s and 1980s. Anchorage is the headquarters for many large businesses. It is also a center for many

United States Senator Daniel Inouye (Hawaii) is a well-known Asian American.

These men are using an outrigger canoe near Honolulu. The first Hawaiians came from Polynesia in outriggers.

lulu's leading industry is tourism. Each year about three million people visit the city's famous Waikiki Beach.

Tourists and residents alike are interested in the history of Hawaii's rulers. Iolani Palace near Honolulu is the nation's only royal palace. Here you can see robes and other treasures of the monarchs who ruled the islands during the 1800s.

Portland   Oregon's largest city, Portland, is near the junction of the Columbia and Willamette rivers. Even though it is 100 miles (160 km) inland, it is a major deepwater port. At the port, ships are loaded with lumber, grain, wool, and bauxite. Waterpower has also helped the city grow as a manufacturing and trading center.

Seattle   In the 1890s Seattle was the nation's chief link to the Alaskan gold fields. During the building of the big Alaskan pipeline the city was again the chief link. Aircraft manufacturing and shipbuilding are the major industries today. Other industries include lumbering; fishing; and the manufacture of chemicals, food products, and metals.

Seattle is built on several hills. Within the city borders are four lakes and many small parks that help to make the city a pleasant place to live in.

Los Angeles   Los Angeles is by far the largest city of the Pacific region. It is the nation's second largest city. The rich farmland in the area and nearby oil deposits have helped Los Angeles become the region's most important trade and manufacturing center.

government offices although it is not the state capital. The mountains around Cook Inlet on the Gulf of Alaska form a beautiful backdrop for the city of Anchorage.

Many of Alaska's cities are near waterways or along the coast. Juneau, the capital, is on the Alaskan panhandle. Ketchikan and Sitka in the southeast are lumbering and fishing centers. Valdez is a port city. On the Arctic coast is Barrow, our nation's northernmost community. Fairbanks, in the interior, was a supply center during Alaska's gold rush. It is still a commercial and mining supply center.

Hawaiian cities   Hawaii's few cities include Hilo (hē′ lō), Kailua (kī lü′ ə), Pearl City, and Honolulu. Honolulu is the capital and largest city. It is also the state's industrial and commercial center. Hono-

Los Angeles has two major problems. One is water. Like the rest of southern and central California, the Los Angeles area is very dry. With such a big population, the demand for water is very large. About three quarters of the city's water must be carried by aqueduct from several different sources. These sources are streams in the Sierra Nevada, the Owens River in eastern California, the Colorado River, and the Feather River in northern California. As more people move into the Los Angeles area, the problem of providing water is becoming very serious.

The second problem is a result of the great number of industries in and around Los Angeles and of the huge number of automobiles that fill the highways of the area. Industrial fumes and auto exhaust sometimes combine to form a low-hanging cloud of polluted air called **smog.** Because the mountains around the city form a sort of pocket, the smog often remains over the city for days and even weeks at a time. Los Angeles is working on this problem, but has not completely solved it.

San Diego   San Diego is one of the nation's ten largest cities. San Diego's natural harbor is the home of a large fishing fleet and a United States Navy base. A center for oceanic studies has also been set up in San Diego. Aircraft, food processing, and electronic industries all help the city's growth.

San Francisco   San Francisco is built along the waterfront on San Francisco Bay and on steep hillsides. Many people think it is one of our most beautiful cities.

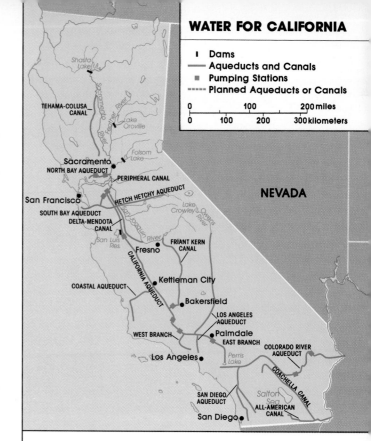

You can see that getting water to the cities and farms of central and southern California is a major project.

The city was nearly destroyed by an earthquake and fire in 1906. Food processing, oil refineries, chemical plants, and electronics are among the industries of the Bay area. The port of San Francisco is the largest on the Pacific coast.

San Francisco also has one of the country's largest Chinese American populations. You can see signs written in Chinese, hear people speaking the language, and shop in markets or eat in restaurants specializing in Chinese foods.

CHECKUP

1. People of many different races and nations have settled in the Pacific states. How would this make the Pacific states an interesting place to live?
2. Which two Pacific cities would you most like to visit? Why?

THE PACIFIC STATES	Alaska	California	Hawaii	Oregon	Washington
Source of Name	Change of Aleut word meaning "great land" or "that which the sea breaks against"	From a book *Las Sergas de Esplandián* by Garcia Ordóñez de Montalvo (c 1500)	Uncertain; maybe named by traditional discoverer: Hawaii Loa; or named after Hawaii (Hawaiki) traditional Polynesian home	Named for a river the French called the Ouragon, which means "hurricane"	In honor of George Washington
Nickname(s)	The Last Frontier; Land of the Midnight Sun	Golden State	Aloha State	Beaver State	Evergreen State; Chinook State
Capital	Juneau	Sacramento	Honolulu	Salem	Olympia
Largest Cities	Anchorage Fairbanks Juneau	Los Angeles San Diego San Francisco	Honolulu Pearl City Kailua	Portland Eugene Salem	Seattle Spokane Tacoma
Population Rank	50	1	39	30	19
Population Density Rank	50	13	12	39	28
Area Rank	1	3	47	10	20
State Flag					
State Bird	Willow ptarmigan	California valley quail	Nene (Hawaiian goose)	Western meadowlark	Willow goldfinch
State Flower	Forget-me-not	Golden poppy	Hibiscus	Oregon grape	Rhododendron
State Tree	Sitka spruce	California redwood	Kukui	Douglas fir	Western hemlock
State Motto	North to the future	*Eureka* (I have found it)	*Ua mau ke ea o ka aina i ka pono* (The life of the land is perpetuated in righteousness)	The Union	*Al-Ki* (Indian word meaning "by and by")
Interesting Facts	The United States purchased the territory of Alaska from Russia in 1867 for about 2¢ an acre. Mt. McKinley (20,320 ft; 6,190 m) is the highest peak in the United States.	The highest temperature in the United States and the lowest point below sea level are both found in Death Valley. The coast redwoods are the tallest living things in the world.	One fifth of all the pineapples grown in the world are produced in Hawaii. Hilo is the wettest city in the United States with 133.57 in. (3,393 mm) annual rainfall.	Oregon is a leader in the production of nuts, lumber, and orchard fruits. Crater Lake is the deepest (1,932 ft; 589 m) natural lake in the United States.	Grand Coulee Dam, across the Columbia River, is the largest concrete dam and the greatest single source of water power in the United States. The eruption of Mount St. Helens on March 27, 1980, was the first volcanic eruption in the continental United States since 1914.

417

KEY FACTS

1. The Pacific region has the northernmost and southernmost points in the United States, as well as the highest and lowest points.

2. Mountains and valleys are important landforms of the Pacific region.

3. Mountains, ocean currents, and latitude affect the climates of the Pacific states.

4. Agriculture is important in several parts of the Pacific region, but California is our leading state in farm production.

5. The Pacific region's resources include lumber, fish, and oil and other minerals.

6. Five of our 25 largest cities are in the Pacific region.

VOCABULARY QUIZ

Write the letter of the term next to the number of its description. Write on a sheet of paper.

a. tundra   **f.** smog
b. volcano   **g.** Aleutian
c. heritage   **h.** current
d. permafrost   **i.** earthquake
e. fish ladder   **j.** fish hatchery

1. Movement of water in a regular path

2. An eruption of gases, ash, and molten rock through a weak spot in the earth's surface

3. A place where fish are raised

4. Ideas, values, and customs passed on by one's ancestors

5. A treeless plain that is so dry and cold that only a few kinds of plants can live there

6. One of the islands that form an arc extending out from the Alaskan peninsula

7. A series of pools that make it possible for fish to travel past a dam in a river

8. A low-lying, cloudlike layer in the air formed by a mixture of pollutants

9. A movement of the ground that makes cracks in the earth's surface

10. A layer of earth that remains frozen

REVIEW QUESTIONS

1. What are the highest and lowest points in North America?

2. Why is the Salton Sea salty?

3. What effects do mountains, ocean currents, and latitude have on the climates of the Pacific region?

4. What are California's two most important farming areas?

5. Which state is our leading lumber state?

6. What is unusual about redwood trees? What is the disagreement concerning redwoods?

7. What mineral resource do we get from the North Slope? How does the resource get to the places where it is needed?

8. Why is life so often difficult for immigrant groups, such as Mexican Americans and Asian Americans?

9. Name five of the large cities of the Pacific states.

ACTIVITIES

1. You want to travel along the coast from San Diego to Anchorage. What distance will you travel? What are the major cities that you will see along the route? Describe the weather that you might find.

2. For one week collect newspaper articles dealing with the Pacific states. How many different topics are included in your articles? (Climate, jobs, resources, industries, etc.) Which state is mentioned most often? How many articles deal with problems? Is one problem mentioned more often than others?

READING CLIMOGRAPHS

TEMPERATURE

On this page there are two special kinds of graphs. They are called climographs because they show temperature and precipitation, two important parts of climate. Each climograph has temperature scales on the left side. They are printed in red. The scale on the outside is for Fahrenheit temperatures. The scale on the inside is for Celsius temperatures. The months of the year are given along the bottom of the graph. The average temperature for each month is shown by a red line.

SKILLS PRACTICE

Now use the temperature information on the climographs to answer these questions.

1. Which place is warmer?

2. Is the average January temperature above or below freezing (32°F or 0°C) in Juneau?

3. Which three months have the same temperature in Los Angeles?

PRECIPITATION

On the right side of the graph are the scales for precipitation. They are printed in blue. Centimeters are given on the inside; inches, on the outside. The blue bars show the average monthly precipitation.

SKILLS PRACTICE

Look at the blue bars and answer these questions.

1. Which place is wetter?

2. Which place has no precipitation from May through October?

3. What is the greatest amount of precipitation for any one month in Juneau? In Los Angeles?

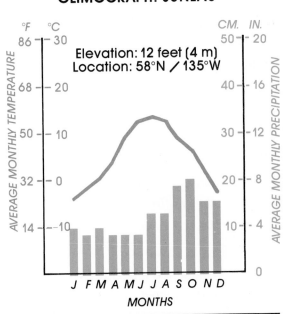

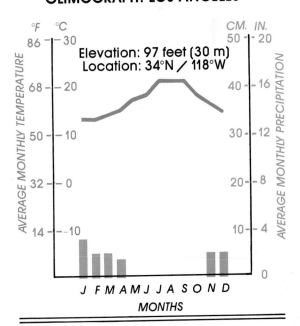

6/UNIT REVIEW

1. The United States may be divided into seven regions. — *Name the seven regions. Be ready to point out on a map the states in each region.*

2. The major landforms in the United States include mountains and plains. — *What are two major mountain ranges? What is the high, dry inland plain that stretches from Texas to North Dakota? Name the two plains along the southern and eastern coasts of the United States.*

3. The oceans and other bodies of water are extremely important to the United States. — *What three oceans form parts of the United States border? Name the five Great Lakes. Name at least three of our major rivers. In what ways are waterways important to us?*

4. Climate in the United States depends on many things, including distance from the ocean or other major body of water; latitude; elevation; and location in relation to mountains. — *What effect does elevation have on temperature? Why is the Great Basin so dry? Which would be warmer and wetter, a place near the Atlantic coast, or a place in the interior at the same latitude?*

5. Agriculture is important in many parts of the United States, including much of the North Central region, California, Texas, and the Southeast. — *What are some of the important agricultural products of each of these areas?*

6. Each region of the United States has important resources. — *Where are our major forests? Major deposits of petroleum, natural gas, and coal? Name some of the important metal resources of the United States.*

7. Manufacturing is important throughout our nation, although some parts of the country have more industry than others. — *Where is the Manufacturing Belt? What are some of our major industries? How do industries depend on one another and upon natural resources?*

8. Population density in the United States varies from near 0 to more than 500 people per square mile (200 per sq km). — *Where do you find the areas of greatest population density? Of least density?*

9. The population of the United States is made up of people of varying ancestry. — *Why, do you think, have some groups been accepted and others not? Read about one group that has suffered discrimination. Make a report on what is being done to improve the situation.*

Canada and Latin America

22 Canada

History and Government

┌─ VOCABULARY ─────────────────────────┐
banks	Commonwealth
province	official language
descent	Separatist
└──────────────────────────────────────┘

Indians and Inuit   In Chapter 3 you learned that the first people who came to live in North America came from Asia. They probably came by way of Alaska. Those people were the ancestors of the Indians and Inuit of Canada. The Inuit settled in the Arctic area of Canada. They lived by hunting and fishing. The Indians who came to Canada went farther south than the Inuit. They lived in central and southern Canada.

Of the 24 million people in Canada today, fewer than 20,000 are Inuit. Some Inuit still live in northern Canada. Some of them still hunt and fish for a living. Others work in industry, especially mining and transportation. There are about 300,000 Indians in Canada today. Many of them live on reserves, or reservations.

The first Europeans   The first Europeans who came to Canada were explorers. They explored the eastern coast of what is now Canada and the United States. They caught fish on the Grand Banks. **Banks** are a part of the seafloor. They rise above the floor around them. Banks do not rise high enough to be a danger to ships, however. The Grand Banks are just off the island of Newfoundland (nü′ fənd lənd). The explorers came ashore to dry their fish and repair their boats. But few of these people made their homes here.

One French explorer, Jacques Cartier, sailed his ship up the St. Lawrence River as far as the present city of Montreal (män trē ôl′). On his return to France, he described the rich soil in the valley of the St. Lawrence River. This land was very different from the rugged coast of eastern Canada. Here people could settle and till the soil.

French and British settlers   French settlers began coming to Canada in the early 1600s. These early settlers built farms and villages in the St. Lawrence Valley. Most of them lived in what is now the **province** of Quebec (kwi bek′). A province is somewhat like a state in the United States. This French colony was called New France.

People also came to Canada from Great Britain. They settled in what is now New Brunswick, Prince Edward Island, and Nova Scotia (nō′ və skō′ shə). They also settled on Newfoundland.

On the map find landforms that are shared by Canada and the United States. The women in the picture show their Scots heritage in dress and in dance (a sword dance).

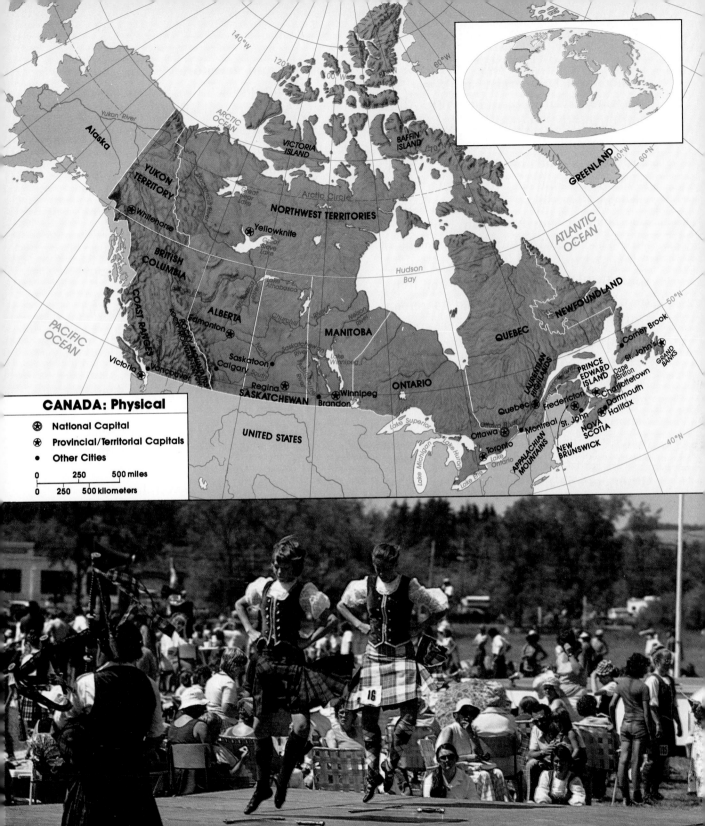

CANADA: Physical

- ⊛ National Capital
- ✳ Provincial/Territorial Capitals
- • Other Cities

| 0 | 250 | 500 miles |
| 0 | 250 | 500 kilometers |

Alaska

ARCTIC OCEAN

Yukon River

YUKON TERRITORY

✳ Whitehorse

BRITISH COLUMBIA

COAST RANGES

PACIFIC OCEAN

Victoria ✳ • Vancouver

ALBERTA

Edmonton ✳

Calgary •
Regina ✳
SASKATCHEWAN

Saskatoon •

VICTORIA ISLAND

Great Bear Lake

Arctic Circle

NORTHWEST TERRITORIES

Yellowknife ✳

Great Slave Lake

Lake Athabasca

Churchill River

Nelson River

Saskatchewan River

Lake Winnipeg

MANITOBA

Winnipeg ✳
Brandon •

UNITED STATES

Lake Superior

Lake Michigan

Lake Huron

ONTARIO

Toronto ✳
Lake Ontario
Lake Erie

BAFFIN ISLAND

Hudson Bay

GREENLAND

ATLANTIC OCEAN

NEWFOUNDLAND

QUEBEC

LAURENTIAN HIGHLANDS

Corner Brook •
St. John's ✳

GRAND BANKS

PRINCE EDWARD ISLAND
Cape Breton
Charlottetown ✳

Quebec ✳
Fredericton ✳
Montreal • Dartmouth •
St. John • Halifax ✳
Ottawa ⊛
NEW BRUNSWICK
NOVA SCOTIA

APPALACHIAN MOUNTAINS

New France remained a colony of France until 1760. France and Great Britain were at war in the mid-1700s. At the end of the war, France had to turn over New France to Britain. Great Britain then had Canada and the American colonies that later became the United States. When the American colonies gained their independence in the American Revolution, however, Great Britain kept control of Canada. After the American Revolution, some British settlers who had been living in the United States wanted to remain British citizens. Many of these people moved to Canada.

Today, about 45 percent of Canada's people are of British **descent**. Another 26 percent are of French descent. Most of Canada's more than 6 million French Canadians still live in the province of Quebec.

Other peoples Through the 1800s, English, Irish, and Scots people continued to settle in Canada. Beginning in the late 1800s, people began moving to Canada from other European countries. There was a great wave of immigration from that time until World War I began in 1914. The people who came in that period settled mostly in the new industrial cities and on the farmlands of the prairies.

The next great period of immigration came in the 15 years after World War II. Between 1946 and 1961 about 2 million people came to Canada from Europe. These people were German, Dutch, Italian, Polish, and Scandinavian. Their descendants and about 35,000 black people and over 150,000 Japanese, Chinese, and other Asians make up most of the rest of Canada's population today.

Provinces and territories In 1867, Great Britain passed the British North America Act. It created a new government for Canada, which became known as the Dominion (də min' yən) of Canada. Under this act, Canada was divided into provinces. In 1867 there were four provinces—New Brunswick, Nova Scotia, Ontario, and Quebec. By 1905 five more provinces had been added—Manitoba, British Columbia, Prince Edward Island, Alberta, and Saskatchewan (sə skach' ə wən). In 1949 Newfoundland became Canada's tenth province. This province is made up of the island of Newfoundland plus part of northeastern Canada.

In addition to the ten provinces, Canada also has two territories. The Yukon Territory was formed in 1898, the Northwest Territories in 1912. Find each province and territory on the map on page 434.

Canada never fought a war for independence. Instead, Great Britain slowly allowed Canadians more and more power in running their country. In 1931 Canada became, for practical purposes, an independent country. The last ties with Great Britain were broken in 1982.

A Commonwealth nation If you have ever visited Canada, you probably noticed many photographs of Queen Elizabeth II of Great Britain. That is because in a way Queen Elizabeth II is also queen of Canada. Canada is a member of the **Commonwealth**. The Commonwealth is made up of independent countries that were once ruled by Great Britain. The countries in the Commonwealth include, among others, Australia, New Zealand, and India. The countries of the Commonwealth share their ideas on many things, such as education, food production, and health. Government leaders from the Commonwealth countries meet to discuss such matters as trade between countries. The Commonwealth countries work together as much as possible. They share a bond as members of the Commonwealth. The queen is a symbol of that bond.

Canada's government   Canada, like the United States, has a federal form of government. The federation is made up of the ten provinces and the two territories. Each province has its own government.

A member of the Royal Canadian Mounted Police stands guard before the Parliament building in Ottawa.

The territories are run mainly by the federal government, although they do have some self-government.

The head of the government of Canada is the prime minister. Canada also has a governor general who is appointed by Queen Elizabeth II on the recommendation of the prime minister. The lawmaking body of Canada is called Parliament. It has two houses—the Senate and the House of Commons. The people of Canada vote for the members of the House of Commons. The members of the Senate are appointed by the governor general. The House is the more powerful of the two bodies.

The capital of Canada is Ottawa, in Ontario. Like Washington, D.C., Ottawa is chiefly a government city. Its major purpose is to carry on the business of government.

Two languages   There are two **official languages** in Canada—English and French. English is the language of most Canadians. In the province of Quebec, where most French Canadians live, French is the chief language. Some French Canadians, called **Separatists,** want the province of Quebec to separate from Canada and become an independent country. In 1980 the people of Quebec voted against doing that.

CHECKUP

1. How did Canada come to be subject to Great Britain?
2. What is the Commonwealth?
3. What is the head of the government of Canada called?
4. What are the two official languages of Canada?

The Land and Climate

A vast country   Canada is the second largest country in the world. Only the Soviet Union is larger in area. The country of Canada covers most of the northern half of North America. Canada, like the United States, spreads "from sea to shining sea." The Atlantic Ocean is on the east; the Pacific Ocean is on the west. Now look at the map on page 427. Trace the boundary between Canada and the United States.

There are many ways in which Canada and the United States are alike. They are almost the same size, although Canada is a little larger. You can see the same kinds of gas stations. You can buy United States newspapers and even pay for them with United States money. And most people speak English. But there is at least one important difference. Canada is much less densely populated. There are large areas of the country in which no people live. Let us see why this is so.

Climate and vegetation   Large parts of Canada are too cold for most people. In many places the growing season is too short for crops. Often the land is too mountainous or rocky for farming.

Generally speaking, the farther north one travels in the United States, the colder the climate becomes. Canada is even farther north than the United States, excluding Alaska. In most of Canada, the winters are long and cold. January temperatures average below 0°F (-18°C) in more than two thirds of Canada. In the islands in the Arctic Ocean, January temperatures average below -40°F (-40°C).

Northern Canada has short, cool summers. These summers are not warm enough or long enough for crops to be grown. In the far northern areas the summer may last only a few weeks. In southern Canada the summers are warmer and longer. Crops can be raised in southern Canada. Most of Canada's farmland is in the south.

Much of Canada is covered by forests. These forests are one of Canada's most important resources. To the north of the forest areas is the tundra. Trees do not grow in the tundra because of the shortage of rain and the long, cold winters. Some plants, however, do grow here.

The Appalachian region   In Chapter 14 you learned that it is helpful to divide a large country into regions in order to study it. A physical region is one in which the land features are like one another. Canada has five such regions. They are (1) the Appalachian region, (2) the St. Lawrence Valley and Lakes Peninsula, (3) the Canadian Shield, (4) the plains region, and (5) the western mountain region. Find these five regions on the map.

The Appalachian Mountains are found in both the United States and Canada. In the United States these mountains stretch from Alabama to Maine. In Canada the Appalachian region is made up of the three **Maritime** Provinces—New Brunswick, Nova Scotia, and Prince Edward Island—plus the island of Newfoundland. *Maritime* means "having to do with the

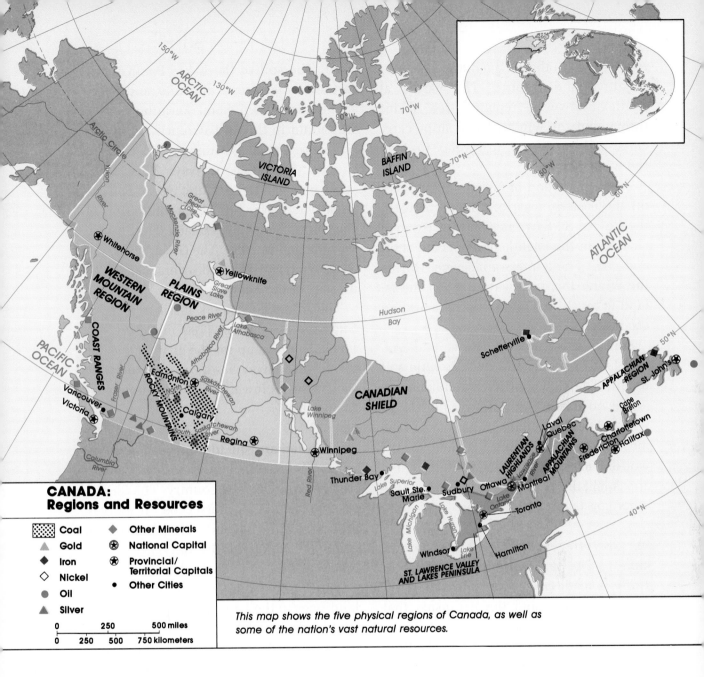

CANADA:
Regions and Resources

▨	Coal	◆	Other Minerals
▲	Gold	✪	National Capital
◆	Iron	✪	Provincial/Territorial Capitals
◇	Nickel	•	Other Cities
●	Oil		
▲	Silver		

0   250   500 miles

0   250   500   750 kilometers

This map shows the five physical regions of Canada, as well as some of the nation's vast natural resources.

sea." The Appalachian region also includes a small part of Quebec southeast of the St. Lawrence River. As you can see on the map above, this region borders on the Atlantic Ocean.

Most of the Appalachian region is made up of low hills. The hills have a mixture of hardwood trees and **conifers.** The summers here are cool. The winters are long, and there is a great deal of snow.

Most people in the Maritime Provinces live close to the coast, where the soil is better than in the hills. Farming is the chief occupation. Farmers raise dairy cattle and beef cattle. They grow potatoes, fruits, cereals, and feed crops.

There are no large cities in the Maritime Provinces. The chief city is Halifax, Nova Scotia. In winter the St. Lawrence River is frozen. Ships cannot reach such other Canadian cities as Montreal and Quebec. The harbor at Halifax, however, remains free of ice throughout the winter. Large ships carry cargo and passengers to Halifax through the winter months.

The large island of Newfoundland lies off the eastern coast of Canada between the Gulf of St. Lawrence and the Atlantic Ocean. On the island, summers are short and cool. The winters are severe. During the winter the only way to reach the island is by air. Ice blocks the seas around the island.

Forests cover much of Newfoundland. The land is rocky, and there is little soil to till. The riches of Newfoundland are found off its eastern coast on the Grand Banks. The Grand Banks area is one of the most important fishing grounds in the world. Each year thousands of tons of fish are caught on the Grand Banks and off the other coasts of the Maritimes.

St. Lawrence Valley and Lakes Peninsula   The next region you are going to study is made up of the valley of the St. Lawrence River and the peninsula that borders on three of the Great Lakes—Lake Ontario, Lake Huron, and Lake Erie. This is the smallest land region in Canada. Yet it is one of the most important regions in the country. In fact, about one half of Canada's people live here. Canada's two largest cities—Montreal and Toronto—are in this region. Ottawa, the capital of Canada, is also in this region.

This area is made up of lowlands. The relief is gentle. It goes from flatland to rolling hills. Farming is important here even though the winters are long and hard. The soil of the Lakes Peninsula is fertile. Large crops of fruits and vegetables are grown here. Farming is also important in the St. Lawrence Valley.

This region is also important because of the St. Lawrence Seaway. This water route between the Atlantic Ocean and the Great Lakes was built by a joint effort of the United States and Canada. The Seaway was opened in 1959. The Great Lakes, the St. Lawrence River, and several canals are all part of the Seaway.

The Atlantic Ocean is at sea level. Lake Superior is 600 feet (180 m) above sea level. To make up for the changing water level, the Seaway has a series of **locks.** A lock raises or lowers ships from one level to another.

The Canadian Shield   The largest region of Canada is the Canadian Shield. It covers about half the country. The Shield is shaped like a horseshoe. It curves around Hudson Bay and includes the Arctic islands north of Hudson Bay.

Low hills cover much of the Canadian Shield. Toward the east and southeast the land rises to the Laurentian (lô ren′ chən) Highlands, which border the St. Lawrence River. The land becomes even more mountainous along the rugged coast in the east.

The Shield is made up of very old and very hard rocks. Many thousands of years ago, during the Ice Age, great sheets of ice covered this region. They scraped away the soil. Then they dug out hollows in the land. The ice has long since gone. The hollows are now filled with water. Lakes and swamps have formed in these hollows. New soil forms very slowly. So there

HOW A CANAL LOCK WORKS

A lock has a watertight gate at each end. Water is let into or out of the lock to raise or lower a ship. In many canals, locks are built in pairs so that ships can go in both directions at the same time.

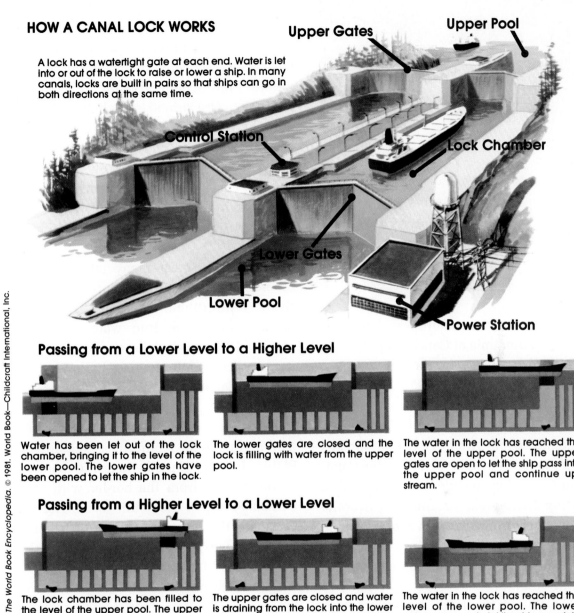

Upper Gates

Upper Pool

Control Station

Lock Chamber

Lower Gates

Lower Pool

Power Station

Passing from a Lower Level to a Higher Level

Water has been let out of the lock chamber, bringing it to the level of the lower pool. The lower gates have been opened to let the ship in the lock.

The lower gates are closed and the lock is filling with water from the upper pool.

The water in the lock has reached the level of the upper pool. The upper gates are open to let the ship pass into the upper pool and continue upstream.

Passing from a Higher Level to a Lower Level

The lock chamber has been filled to the level of the upper pool. The upper gates are open and the ship is passing into the lock.

The upper gates are closed and water is draining from the lock into the lower pool.

The water in the lock has reached the level of the lower pool. The lower gates are open to let the ship pass into the lower pool and continue downstream.

is little soil over much of the Shield. As a result, crops cannot be grown. Few people live in the Canadian Shield because of its poor soil and cold climate.

Great forests spread across the southern half of the Canadian Shield. Lumbering has developed in places that can be reached by land or by water. Logs are floated down the many rivers in the Shield. The logging industry and industries related to it are very important to Canada. Canada exports a great deal of lumber. It also makes wood pulp and paper. Paper companies in the United

Copper is smelted at this plant near Sudbury. Copper is just one of the Shield's many mineral resources.

States and in many European countries buy large amounts of Canadian pulp. The forests also shelter fur-bearing animals. Some animals are trapped for their furs.

To the north of the forests is the tundra. This part of the Canadian Shield stretches to the Arctic Ocean. It spreads over the thousands of islands in the Canadian Arctic. Few people live in the tundra. During the summer, the Inuit live near the coast where they can catch fish. But in the winter the sea is frozen. Many of the Inuit then find shelter within the forests to the south.

The Shield has large deposits of copper, lead, and zinc. The world's largest deposit of nickel is near Sudbury, Ontario. Nickel is used to make certain kinds of steel. About one third of the world's nickel comes from Sudbury. **Pitchblende** is found in the northern part of the Shield. Uranium comes from pitchblende. Large amounts of gold are also mined in the Shield.

Iron is one of the most important resources found in the Shield. This ore has long been mined along the southwestern edge of the Shield. Large amounts of iron have been discovered in the interior of the Shield. Find Schefferville on the map on page 427. Ore mined at Schefferville is brought by railroad to ports on the St. Lawrence River. From these ports ships carry the ore to ironworks on the Great Lakes. There are major ironworks at Hamilton in Canada and at Buffalo, Cleveland, Detroit, and Chicago in the United States.

There are a great many lakes in the Shield. The lakes are the source of many rivers. Within the Shield and at its edge, these rivers break into waterfalls and rapids. These waterfalls and rapids are used to produce hydroelectric power for many of Canada's industries.

The plains   The Canadian plains are part of the same landform as the Great Plains in the United States. Canada's plains stretch from the border with the United States in the south to the Arctic Ocean in the north. In the south, where the Canadian plains meet those of North Dakota and Montana, the plains are several hundred miles wide. They narrow in the north.

The plains are not level. They rise slowly toward the Rocky Mountains on the west. The plains are also broken by hilly ridges that form a series of giant steps.

The northern plains are very much like the Canadian Shield. There are forests and then, farther north, tundra. Some of the forests have been cleared for farming. The climate in the northern plains is wetter than that of the southern plains.

430

The plains of southern Canada are the nation's bread-basket. Here combines are harvesting wheat.

The southern part of the plains is covered with prairies. Toward the east, these grasslands have been plowed, and wheat, corn, and feedstuffs are grown. Canada is one of the world's leading producers of wheat. Most of that wheat is grown on the prairies. In the western part of the prairies the climate is drier. Fewer crops can be grown, but ranching is important.

The plains region is a very important part of Canada. Much of the country's farmland is in the plains. In addition, there are large deposits of oil, coal, and gas. Many people have moved to the plains. Manufacturing has developed in the cities. A number of Canada's largest cities are in the plains. They include Winnipeg, Calgary, and Edmonton. These cities are shown on the map on page 434.

Western mountain region The Appalachian Mountains and the plains are found in both Canada and the United States. Two western mountain ranges also stretch north and south through Canada and the United States. These two ranges are the Rocky Mountains and the Coast Ranges. Together they form Canada's fifth region, the western mountain region.

The Coast Ranges rise steeply from the Pacific Ocean. There is little flat land between the ocean and the mountains. Warm ocean currents make the climate along the coast milder than that of any other part of Canada. Moist winds from the ocean blow onto the mountains. This results in a very heavy rainfall. Many areas of Canada's west coast have more than 100 inches (250 cm) of rain in a year. Hundreds of rivers also rush down to the sea from the mountains.

The Canadian Rockies are among the highest mountains in the world. They rise steeply from the plains. Transportation across the mountains is difficult. However, there are a number of passes. Some roads and railroads have been built through these passes.

The Canadian Rockies are noted for their beauty. Shown here is Lake Moraine in Banff National Park in Alberta.

Lumbering is important in several parts of Canada. This sawmill is on the Fraser River near Vancouver.

The western mountains are rich in resources. There are deposits of coal, copper, gold, silver, iron, zinc, and **tungsten.** Mining is a major industry in this region.

The rivers of the western mountains are used to produce hydroelectric power. Much of this power is used to refine the ores mined in the mountains. Three of the major rivers of this region are the Fraser, the Columbia, and the Yukon. The Fraser flows from the Canadian Rockies to the Pacific Ocean. The Columbia flows from the mountains southward into the United States. The Yukon River flows into Alaska from northwestern Canada.

The western mountains are important for their resources. Because of their rivers, lakes, and beauty, the mountains also attract thousands of visitors every year.

CHECKUP

1. Name the five regions of Canada and tell why each is important.
2. Why is the St. Lawrence Seaway important?
3. Name two major mountain ranges of western Canada.

Cities

Cities   Look at the map on page 434. You can see that most of Canada's cities are in Ontario, Quebec, and the southern parts of Manitoba, Saskatchewan, Alberta, and British Columbia.

Most cities in Canada began as trading centers for the areas around them. They are still important trading centers. Today they are also important centers for manufacturing. Manufacturing is Canada's most important **economic activity.** (Mining and agriculture are the second and third most important activities.) An economic activity is one that has to do with the production or selling of goods or services.

The table shows Canada's ten largest cities and their populations. Find each of these cities on the map on page 434.

CANADA'S TEN LARGEST CITIES (Figures are rounded)	
City and Province	*Population*
Montreal, Quebec	980,000
Toronto, Ontario	599,000
Calgary, Alberta	593,000
Winnipeg, Manitoba	564,000
North York, Ontario	559,000
Edmonton, Alberta	532,000
Vancouver, British Columbia	414,000
Mississauga, Ontario	315,000
Hamilton, Ontario	306,000
Ottawa (Ontario)	295,000

CHECKUP

1. What are Canada's three most important economic activities?
2. Name five of Canada's ten largest cities.

(Top) The names of these sidewalk cafes in Montreal reveal the French heritage of many Canadians. (Left) Toronto, the capital of Ontario, has a very modern city hall. (Right) Vancouver's protected harbor and its location on the Fraser River have helped the city become one of Canada's largest cities.

433

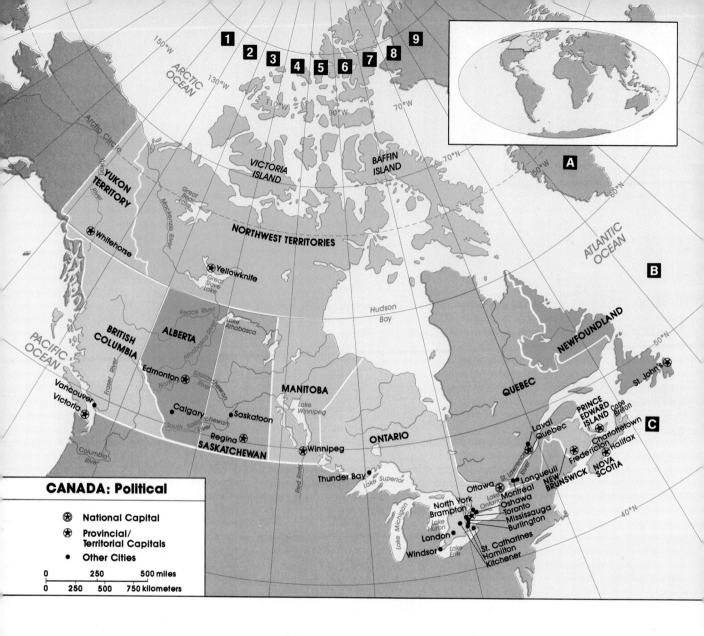

CANADA: Political

⊛ National Capital

⊛ Provincial/
   Territorial Capitals

• Other Cities

0   250   500 miles
0   250   500   750 kilometers

Cities with less than 100,000

Charlottetown, P.E.I.	C-8
Fredericton, N.B.	C-8
St. John's, Newf.	C-9
Victoria, B.C.	C-2
Whitehorse, Y.T.	A-1
Yellowknife, N.W.T.	A-3

Cities with 100,000–499,000

Brampton, Ont.	C-7
Burlington, Ont.	C-7

Halifax, N.S.	C-8
Hamilton, Ont.	C-7
Kitchener, Ont.	C-6
Laval, Que.	C-7
London, Ont.	C-6
Longueuil, Que.	C-7
Mississauga, Ont.	C-7
Oshawa, Ont.	C-7
Ottawa	C-7
Quebec, Que.	C-7
Regina, Sask.	B-4
St. Catharines, Ont.	C-7

Saskatoon, Sask.	B-4
Thunder Bay, Ont.	C-6
Vancouver, B.C.	C-2
Windsor, Ont.	C-6

Cities with 500,000–999,000

Calgary, Alta.	B-3
Edmonton, Alta.	B-3
Montreal, Que.	C-7
North York, Ont.	C-7
Toronto, Ont.	C-7
Winnipeg, Man.	B-5

Most of Canada's cities and most of the people are in the southern part of the nation.
Which cities have 500,000 or more people? Which capitals have less than 100,000 people?

CANADA

COUNTRY		TOTAL AREA	POPULATION AND POPULATION DENSITY	CAPITAL CITY AND POPULATION	LANGUAGE(S)	OTHER FACTS
	Canada	3,840,019 sq mi (9,922,330 sq km)	24,900,000 6 per sq mi (2 per sq km)	Ottawa 304,500	English*, French*	The United States and Canada together guard North America through the North American Air Defense Command.

PROVINCES		TOTAL AREA	POPULATION AND POPULATION DENSITY	CAPITAL CITY AND POPULATION	LANGUAGE(S)	OTHER FACTS
	Alberta	246,358 sq mi (638,233 sq km)	2,341,000 9 per sq mi (4 per sq km)	Edmonton 532,246	English	Columbia Ice Field, consisting of huge glaciers formed during the Ice Age, is found in Alberta.
	British Columbia	344,573 sq mi (892,677 sq km)	2,801,000 8 per sq mi (3 per sq km)	Victoria 64,379	English	Gold found near the Fraser River caused rapid settlement of interior sections of British Columbia from 1850 to 1860.
	Manitoba	211,414 sq mi (547,704 sq km)	1,043,000 5 per sq mi (2 per sq km)	Winnipeg 564,473	English, French, German, Ukrainian	The International Peace Garden found in Manitoba honors friendship between the United States and Canada.
	New Brunswick	27,626 sq mi (71,569 sq km)	706,000 25 per sq mi (10 per sq km)	Fredericton 43,723	English, French	Reversing Falls is a waterfall on a New Brunswick river that empties into the Bay of Fundy. At high tide, water from the bay rushes *up* the falls.
	Newfoundland	143,451 sq mi (371,635 sq km)	576,000 4 per sq mi (2 per sq km)	St. John's 83,770	English, French	In 1901 Marconi received the first transatlantic wireless signal at Cabot Tower on Signal Hill, St. John's.
	Nova Scotia	20,397 sq mi (52,841 sq km)	857,000 42 per sq mi (16 per sq km)	Halifax 114,594	English, French	*Nova Scotia* (Latin for *New Scotland*) is almost completely surrounded by water.
	Ontario	353,860 sq mi (916,734 sq km)	8,754,000 25 per sq mi (9 per sq km)	Toronto 599,217	English, French, German, Italian	Ontario was a refuge for southern slaves in the 1850s. It has about one fourth of the world's nickel ore.
	Prince Edward Island	2,184 sq mi (5,660 sq km)	124,000 57 per sq mi (22 per sq km)	Charlottetown 15,282	English, French	The smallest province, Prince Edward Island is known for its long white and red sandy beaches and its fertile red soil.
	Quebec	524,055 sq mi (1,357,655 sq km)	6,478,000 12 per sq mi (5 per sq km)	Quebec City 166,474	French, English	Chubb Crater, one of the world's largest meteor craters, is located in northwestern Quebec.
	Saskatchewan	220,064 sq mi (570,113 sq km)	991,000 5 per sq mi (2 per sq km)	Regina 162,613	English, French, German	This province, called Canada's Breadbasket, is the greatest wheat-growing region in North America.

TERRITORIES		TOTAL AREA	POPULATION AND POPULATION DENSITY	CAPITAL CITY AND POPULATION	LANGUAGE(S)	OTHER FACTS
	Northwest Territories	1,253,106 sq mi (3,246,389 sq km)	47,000 0.04 per sq mi (0.01 per sq km)	Yellowknife 9,483	English	This region covers almost a third of Canada. The source of the Mackenzie River, Canada's longest river, is here.
	Yukon Territory	205,292 sq mi (531,844 sq km)	23,000 0.1 per sq mi (0.04 per sq km)	Whitehorse 14,814	English	Mount Logan, in the St. Elias Mountains, rises 19,520 feet (5,950 m) and is the highest point in Canada.

*Official language(s)

435

KEY FACTS

1. The earliest Canadians were Indians and the Inuit.

2. Canada has two official languages—English and French.

3. Canada is larger than the United States, but has about one tenth as many people.

4. Canada has many natural resources.

5. The main economic activities of Canada are manufacturing, mining, and agriculture.

VOCABULARY QUIZ

Write the letter of the term next to the number of its description. Write on a separate sheet of paper.

a. St. Lawrence Seaway   **f.** province

b. tundra   **g.** federal

c. hydroelectric power   **h.** Ice Age

d. Grand Banks   **i.** pitchblende

e. prime minister   **j.** plains

1. A treeless region in northern Canada

2. A source of uranium

3. Waterpower

4. Links the Atlantic Ocean and the Great Lakes

5. A rich fishing ground

6. An important farming area

7. Canada's form of government

8. A political division similar to a state

9. A time when sheets of ice spread outward from the Arctic

10. The head of Canada's government

REVIEW QUESTIONS

1. From which two groups of European settlers are most Canadians descended?

2. Where do most French Canadians live?

3. How is Canada's government organized?

4. What is the Commonwealth?

5. Name the five physical regions of Canada.

6. In what part of Canada do most of Canada's people live?

7. Why is the Canadian Shield an important region even though few people live there?

ACTIVITIES

1. In an encyclopedia or other reference book, find out about these four explorers: John Cabot, Henry Hudson, Jacques Cartier, and Samuel de Champlain. Write a report telling the following: (**a**) What country did each explorer work for? (**b**) What area of Canada did he explore? (**c**) When did he explore this area?

2. Prepare a report on the Separatist movement in Canada. Your report should tell why some French Canadians think the province of Quebec should become an independent country. You can find this information in an encyclopedia.

3. Prepare an oral report on people who explored the Arctic. This information can be found in an encyclopedia.

4. Make a chart that lists Canada's prime ministers and governors general from 1867 to the present. Tell the years in which each person served. The information for this chart can be found in an encyclopedia.

5. Imagine that you have moved from the island of Newfoundland to the prairies of southern Saskatchewan. Write a letter to a friend describing the differences you find.

6. Plan a summer vacation for someone who will visit Canada for 2 weeks. Plan the trip so the visitor will learn about the great variety in Canada's land and vegetation.

READING A MAP: CONTOURS

SKILLS PRACTICE

To measure your height, you would measure the distance from the bottom of your feet to the top of your head. The bottom of your feet would be your *base*. The earth's hills and mountains are also measured from base to top. The base for all hills and mountains is sea level. Find sea level (0 feet) on the drawing of the mountains (**A**). The lines on the drawing are contour lines.

Contour lines are a good way to show elevation. All points along one contour line are the same distance above sea level. Find the 500-foot contour line on the drawing (**A**). Now find it on the contour map of the mountains (**B**). What is the highest contour line shown on the drawing? What is the highest contour line shown on the map?

Sometimes color is added between contour lines (**C**). What does the yellow stand for? What is the elevation of the orange part? Can you find the same part on the drawing (**A**)?

Elevation can be shown in this same way on maps of any part of the world. Map D shows part of Canada. What is the elevation of the land near the mouth of the Fraser River? What is the elevation of the highest places in this part of British Columbia? Where are the lowest places found?

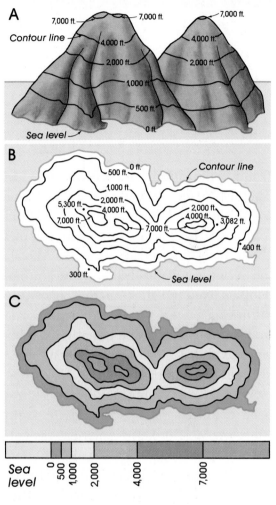

Feet above sea level

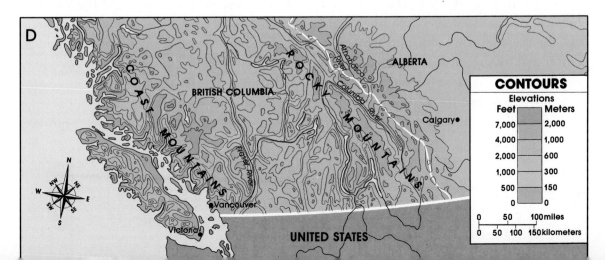

CHAPTER

23 Latin America

Latin America Yesterday and Today

┌─VOCABULARY─────────────────┐
| developed   mestizo |
| country |
| developing |
| country |
└────────────────────────────┘

From exploration to colonization   In Chapter 3 you learned what the terms *Latin America*, *Middle America*, and *Central America* mean. You also learned about such Indian peoples as the Mayas, the Aztecs, and the Incas. These Indian peoples lived in Latin America before any Europeans came to the Americas. The first Europeans to come to Latin America were explorers. You learned about some of them in Chapter 4.

After the explorers came, several European countries set up colonies in Latin America. Most of Latin America was colonized by two countries—Spain and Portugal. Portugal set up the colony of Brazil in South America. Spain made settlements in most of the rest of South America and in Middle America. Great Britain, France, and the Netherlands also set up colonies in Latin America. They colonized many of the islands in the Caribbean Sea. They also had colonies in the northern part of South America—British Guiana, French Guiana, and Dutch Guiana. (If you need help pronouncing Latin American place-names, see page 458.) British Guiana later became the country of Guyana. Dutch Guiana became Surinam. French Guiana is still a colony of France.

Colonies of Spain and Portugal   Beginning in about 1500, people from Spain and Portugal began settling in Latin America. Some of them planned to stay only a short time. They hoped to become rich quickly. So they looked for such riches as gold and silver. Others set up plantations. On these large farms, crops such as sugarcane, cotton, or fruit were grown.

The Europeans made slaves of many Indians. These Indians did much of the hard work in the mines and on the plantations. Also, black people were brought from Africa as slaves.

Independence   Most of Latin America remained under Spanish or Portuguese rule for about 300 years. Between 1791 and 1824, however, most of the Spanish colonies in Latin America fought wars to gain their independence. Brazil gained its independence from Portugal in 1822 without having to fight a war.

Though Spain lost most of its colonies in Latin America, it kept two important

What are Mexico's two mountain ranges? Find the meaning of oriental and occidental in a dictionary. What mountain range runs almost the entire length of South America?

LATIN AMERICA: Physical

⊛ National Capitals

● Other Cities

0   500   1,000 miles

0   500   1,000   1,500 kilometers

LATIN AMERICA: Political

- ✪ National Capitals
- • Other Cities

0   500   1,000 miles

0   500   1,000   1,500 kilometers

Which nation has five cities with 1 million or more people? How many cities of 1 million or more people are capital cities?

islands in the Caribbean Sea—Puerto Rico and Cuba—until 1898. Then after the Spanish-American War, Cuba became independent and Puerto Rico was given to the United States.

Before the Spanish colonies became independent, there were boundaries between the colonies. These boundaries ran across mountains and through forests. It was not certain just where the boundaries were. After the colonies became independent, each new country wanted to have as much land as it could. Since the boundaries were not certain, this caused problems. Often different countries claimed the same land. These claims led to wars. Some of these boundary problems remain today.

Latin America today   One way to divide the world is into "**developed countries**" and "**developing countries.**" Developed countries are highly industrialized.

Developing countries are becoming industrialized. Developed countries are richer, developing countries are poorer. Most of Latin America is a developing area.

There are parts of Latin America, however, that are highly developed. There are large cities that are much like cities in the United States, Canada, and Europe. There are industries. There is great wealth. In developed countries, many people share in the wealth of the country. That is not true in much of Latin America. Although there are people with wealth, there are a great many more people who are very poor. They have poor food, clothing, and shelter. Many of them have not had much education.

In much of Latin America, workers produce a great deal less than workers in developed countries. There are fewer goods from the factories. There are smaller harvests from the land. In many areas, there is subsistence farming. That means a farm family grows enough food to meet its own needs, but there is little, if any, left to sell. Workers in Latin America work as hard as workers in developed countries. But in much of Latin America, workers have fewer machines and tools than workers in developed countries. The tools they have are simpler than the tools of workers in developed countries.

People of Latin America   There are more than 375 million people living in Latin America. About three fifths of those people live in urban areas. The other two fifths live in rural areas.

Most Latin Americans are of European descent. However, more than 20 million people of Latin America are Indians. They make up a large part of the population of Bolivia, Ecuador, and Peru. Some of the people of Latin America are **mestizos** (mes tē′ zōz). That means they have a mixed heritage—white and Indian. Mestizos make up a large part of the population in Chile, Colombia, El Salvador, Honduras, Mexico, Nicaragua, Paraguay, and Venezuela. Many of the people in Barbados, Haiti, and Jamaica are black. Cuba, the Dominican Republic, Panama, and Trinidad and Tobago have many people with mixed black and white ancestry.

CHECKUP

1. Name three Indian peoples who lived in Latin America before any Europeans came to the Americas.
2. Which two European countries colonized most of Latin America?
3. Define *subsistence farming* and *mestizo*.

Mexico

VOCABULARY
henequen

The land   Mexico is the Latin American country that is nearest to the United States. Look at the map on page 440. You can see that Mexico is south of the United States. The boundary between the two countries is 1,934 miles (3,112 km) long. It begins in the west at the Pacific Ocean. It then runs across the mountains and desert until it reaches the Rio Grande. This river forms the rest of the boundary.

Mexico is the largest country of Middle America. From the border of the United States, it stretches 1,600 miles (2,600 km) to the border of Guatemala. Look again at the map on page 440. You can see that Mexico narrows toward the south. Then it juts to the north at the Yucatán Peninsula.

Most of Mexico is a high plateau. This plateau is bordered on the east and west by mountain ranges. To the east is the Sierra Madre Oriental. To the west is the Sierra Madre Occidental. These two ranges come together in the rugged mountains that lie to the south of Mexico City. Southeast of these mountains the land drops suddenly to the lowlands of the Yucatán.

Climate   There are few countries in the world with as much variety in climate as Mexico has. The mountains are cool most of the year. The plateau is very hot in summer, and warm in winter. It is also very dry. The lowlands in the south, including the Yucatán Peninsula, are hot

442

and wet. Part of the lowlands is covered with dense forest. The rainfall varies from one part of the country to another.

Agriculture   Only about one eighth of the land in Mexico is used for farming. The rest of the land is too mountainous or too dry. Much of the land that is farmed is of poor quality. Also, large parts of Mexico have very little rainfall. The best cropland is in the southern part of the plateau in central Mexico. Cattle are grazed in the northern part of the plateau because it is too dry for crops.

Corn is the most widely grown crop. More farmland is used for corn than for any other crop. Corn is the basic food of the Mexican people. Beans, wheat, cotton, sugarcane, and coffee are also major crops. Rice and **henequen** (hen' ə kin), which is used to make rope, are also grown. Fruits and vegetables are important crops, too. In fact, many of the fruits and vegetables eaten in the United States come from Mexico.

The growing of crops to be sold is called commercial agriculture. This kind of farming has increased in Mexico in recent years. But much of Mexico's agriculture is still subsistence farming. Most farms are small family farms.

Manufacturing and cities   Most of Mexico's factories are in or near Mexico City. Motor vehicles are made in Mexico City. There are also smelters to process silver, lead, and zinc ores. Mexico City also has chemical and engineering industries, as well as steel plants. Mexico City is also Mexico's capital and largest city. It has about 9 million people.

There are other important cities in Mexico. Guadalajara, Mexico's second largest city, has many industries. Puebla is an important center for making textiles. Motor vehicles are made in Monterrey and Mazatlán. Monterrey and Monclova have blast furnaces and steelworks.

Mineral resources   The map on page 444 shows natural resources in Middle America and the Caribbean. Mexico is rich in mineral resources. It is one of the world's leading producers of silver. It is a major source of lead, zinc, and sulphur. It

More people live in Mexico City than in any other city in the Western Hemisphere.

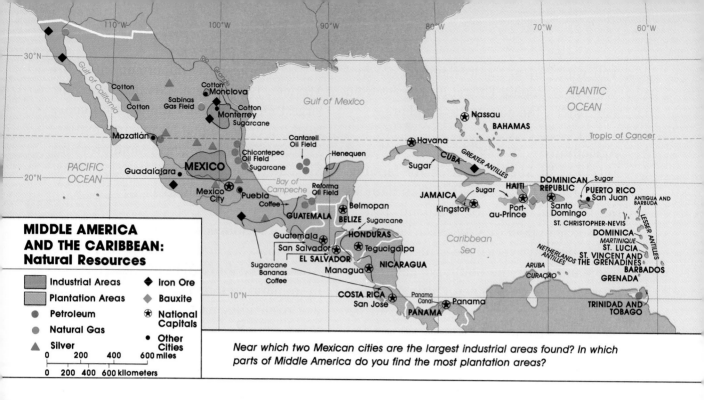

MIDDLE AMERICA AND THE CARIBBEAN: Natural Resources

▨ Industrial Areas	◆ Iron Ore
▨ Plantation Areas	◆ Bauxite
● Petroleum	✪ National Capitals
● Natural Gas	
▲ Silver	• Other Cities

0   200   400   600 miles
0   200   400   600 kilometers

Near which two Mexican cities are the largest industrial areas found? In which parts of Middle America do you find the most plantation areas?

---

produces copper and gold as well. Most of these ores are taken from mines in the Sierra Madre and the plateau of northern Mexico.

Mexico's major resource, though, may be oil. For a long time, wells in the lowlands near the Gulf of Mexico have produced oil. In recent years, large amounts of oil have been discovered in the southern part of the country. Since that time Mexico has been producing larger and larger amounts of oil. Mexico has become one of the world's leading producers of oil. Find the petroleum deposits on the map above. Name some of Mexico's other resources shown on the map.

CHECKUP

1. How does Mexico compare in size with the other countries of Middle America?
2. About how much of Mexico's land is used for farming?
3. What is Mexico's capital?
4. Name five of Mexico's important mineral resources.

444

Central America and the Caribbean

┌─VOCABULARY───────────────┐
│ **tropical rain forest** │
│ **cacao** │
└──────────────────────────┘

Central America   The area between Mexico and South America is Central America. Mountains cover most of Central America. Between the mountains and the sea are narrow coastal plains. Central America is a hot region with a heavy rainfall.

Much of Central America is covered with **tropical rain forests.** These are forests that grow in hot, wet lands. Trees and vines grow thickly in such forests. The rain forests of Central America were once a major source of mahogany and other kinds of hardwood lumber. Now large parts of the forest have been cleared to make room for plantations. Such crops as bananas, coconuts, coffee, and **cacao** (kə kā′ ō) are grown on these plantations. Many of these crops are exported to the United States.

There are seven countries in Central America. They are Guatemala, Belize, El Salvador, Honduras, Nicaragua, Costa Rica, and Panama. Find these countries on the map on page 444.

Central America is also the site of the Panama Canal, which joins the Atlantic and Pacific oceans and divides the Republic of Panama into two parts. In 1903, the United States gained the rights to the narrow strip of land through which the canal was to be built. This strip was called the Canal Zone. The canal, which took ten years to build, was completed in 1914. In 1978, the United States Senate voted to return the Canal Zone to the Republic of

Electric "mules" help an Israeli ship move through the Panama Canal. It takes 15 hours for a ship to travel the entire length of the canal.

Panama but keep the rights to the actual canal. On December 31, 1999, we will turn over the rights to the canal as well.

The Caribbean   Have you ever wondered what the floor of an ocean looks like? The floors of the Atlantic and Pacific oceans are vast, wavy plains. From the floor, mountain ranges rise to great heights. Most of these ranges, of course, are covered by water. Some, however, are high enough to reach the surface of the oceans. Their peaks form islands. There are hundreds of such islands in the Caribbean Sea.

The islands of the Caribbean form an arc. It begins near the Yucatán Peninsula in Mexico and reaches almost to South America. The three main groups of islands in this region are the Greater Antilles, the Lesser Antilles, and the Bahamas. The Greater Antilles are made up of the islands of Cuba, Jamaica, Puerto Rico, and Hispaniola. Hispaniola is divided into two countries—Haiti and the Dominican Republic. The Lesser Antilles and the Bahamas are both made up of a number of smaller islands.

Most of the Caribbean islands are mountainous. The climate is warm in winter and hot and wet in summer. Sugarcane is the most important crop in these islands. Coconuts, bananas, and other tropical fruit are also grown. Tourism is important to many of the larger islands.

Cuba   Cuba is the largest island in the Caribbean. Its population is about 10 million. Cuba is a long, narrow island. Much of it is low and flat with fertile soil. The most important crop of Cuba is sugarcane. Much of the sugar from this crop is exported. Tobacco, pineapples, citrus fruit, and coffee are also grown for export. A range of hills in the southeast contains deposits of iron, manganese, and copper.

Cuba was once a colony of Spain. Its capital, Havana, was founded by the Spaniards soon after they came to the Americas. Havana is Cuba's largest city. It has a population of about 2 million. Havana has industries that process the farm products of the island. The city also handles most of Cuba's export trade.

Jamaica

Jamaica The island of Jamaica was once a British colony. It is now an independent country. Jamaica has about 2 million people.

Jamaica is a mountainous island. Sugarcane and bananas are the chief crops. Tobacco, coffee, cacao, spices, and citrus fruit are also grown. Jamaica is also an important source of bauxite. Much of this bauxite is shipped to the United States to be refined into aluminum.

The chief city of Jamaica is Kingston, on the south coast of the island. Most of Jamaica's trade passes through this city.

Haiti and the Dominican Republic

Since Haiti and the Dominican Republic share the island of Hispaniola, their geographic features are very much alike. In other ways the two countries are very different. Haiti's culture is French, although the people are of African descent. The culture of the Dominican Republic is Spanish. The country has a mixed Spanish and African population. Haiti is more densely populated than the Dominican Republic. Both countries produce sugar and coffee for export.

Port-au-Prince is the capital and chief city of Haiti. Santo Domingo is the capital and chief city of the Dominican Republic.

Puerto Rico Christopher Columbus landed in Puerto Rico in 1493. He claimed the island for Spain. Spain controlled Puerto Rico until 1898. In that year Spain turned the island over to the United States.

The people of Puerto Rico are United States citizens, but Puerto Rico is self-governing. The United States gives aid and protection to the island. The Puerto Rican government, however, has control in all local matters. Some Puerto Ricans would like the island to become one of the states of the United States. Other Puerto Ricans want the island to be an independent country.

More than half of Puerto Rico is farmland. Most of the farms are small. Sugarcane is the chief crop. Coffee, tobacco, bananas, and other fruit are also grown. Puerto Rico has more than 2,600 factories. They turn out chemicals, food, and metal products, as well as clothing. Tourism is also an important industry in Puerto Rico.

San Juan is Puerto Rico's capital and largest city.

CHECKUP

1. When will the Panama Canal be returned to the Republic of Panama?
2. Name the countries of Central America.
3. What is the largest island in the Caribbean?

At left center is Huascarán (wäs kə rän'), the highest peak in the Peruvian Andes.

South America

The land   South of Middle America and the Caribbean lies the huge continent of South America. Much of South America's coastline is straight and even. There are few bays and openings into the interior of the continent. For that reason it was difficult for early explorers to go very far inland from the coast. Even today little is known about some parts of the interior.

The chief physical features of South America are easy to understand. A range of giant mountains, the Andes, runs along the west coast. There is a narrow plain between the Pacific Ocean and the Andes.

To the east of the mountains there are the wide plains and plateaus that make up most of South America.

Let us look more closely at these physical features. The Andes run along the west coast of South America for almost 5,000 miles (8,000 km). The Andes are among the highest mountains in the world. There are several peaks in this range that are higher than any in the United States. Very few roads and railroads cross the Andes.

To the east of the Andes there are two high plateaus. The largest and highest of the two is the one known as the Brazilian Highlands. The Brazilian Highlands are on the east side of the continent. The other plateau is known as the Guiana Highlands. The Guiana Highlands are in the northern part of the continent.

447

The plains of South America have been built by the great rivers of the continent. The plain of the Orinoco River lies between the Guiana Highlands and the northern Andes. It is called the **Llanos.** *Llanos* is Spanish for "plains."

Between the Guiana Highlands and the Brazilian Highlands is the plain of the Amazon River. This vast plain is very flat and stretches for thousands of miles. It is known as the Amazon Basin.

Between the Brazilian Highlands and the southern Andes lie the plains of the Paraná and Paraguay rivers. This area is called the **Chaco.** Farther south, in Uruguay and Argentina, the plains are called the **Pampas.** The plains become narrower toward the southern end of the continent. That area is called **Patagonia.**

Climate and vegetation   The Amazon River flows very close to the Equator. The Amazon Basin is always hot and humid. The heavy rainfall helps trees to grow. Most of the basin is covered with thick rain forest. It is very difficult to travel in this area. There are no railroads and very few roads. Most travel is by boat. Few people live in the forests of the Amazon Basin.

If you were to travel either north or south, away from the Amazon, you would find that the climate and vegetation change. It is still hot for most of the year. But the rainfall is less. It comes mostly in the summers. The winters are fairly dry.

When the climate changes so does the vegetation. Rain forests grow only where it is wet throughout the year, as in the Amazon Basin. Where the rainfall comes in one or two seasons, the vegetation is more open. It is made up of grassland with scattered trees. This kind of vegetation is called **savanna.** The Guiana Highlands and the Brazilian Highlands are covered mostly with savanna.

The Chaco has both savanna and forests. There are large swampy areas, too. The summers are hot and wet, and the winters warm and dry.

The Pampas are much drier than the Amazon lowlands. Summers are hot, but winters are cool. This leads to another change in vegetation. There are almost no trees. The land is a grassland like the Great Plains in the United States.

Patagonia, south of the Pampas, has a cool dry climate. Summers are cool, and winters cold. Some parts of Patagonia are as dry as a desert.

West of the Andes, along the narrow coastal plain, there are a number of climates. Near the Equator it is hot and humid throughout the year. Rain forests grow on this part of the plain. North and south of the Equator, there are savannas. The southern savanna is small. It soon gives way to desert. The plains along the coast of southern Peru and northern Chile are desert. Rainfall is less than 10 inches (25 cm) a year. On much of the land there is little or no plant life. South of the desert, in central Chile, is a small area with hot, dry summers and warm, rainy winters.

As you travel from central Chile to southern Chile, the climate becomes cooler and wetter. Southern Chile is cool in summer and cold in winter.

CHECKUP

1. Where is the Chaco? Patagonia?
2. What is a savanna?

The Countries of South America

┌─VOCABULARY──────────────────┐
| nitrate   altiplano |
| landlocked |
└──────────────────────────────┘

Twelve countries   South America has 12 countries. There are also two other political units that are not independent countries. French Guiana is controlled by France. The Falkland Islands, off the coast of southern Argentina, are a colony of the United Kingdom. These islands are also claimed by Argentina. The two countries fought over the islands in 1982, but the islands remained British. You can find the Falklands on the map on page 440.

Brazil   Brazil is the largest country of Latin America. It is only a little smaller in area than the United States. But it has about half as many people. The people of Brazil speak Portuguese.

Brazil has two giant regions: the Amazon Basin in the north and the Brazilian Highlands in the south. At one time the Amazon Basin was the world's main source of rubber. As a result, a number of towns grew up along the rivers in this area. The city of Manaus grew as a result of the rubber industry. Now Brazil produces less than one percent of the world's rubber. When the rubber industry died out, so did many of the towns and cities.

Brazil has very large reserves of iron ore. Most of the iron that is mined here is exported to other countries. Brazil also has rich deposits of manganese and other important minerals.

Brazil is becoming an important manufacturing country. The meat-packing industry is very large. The textile industry is growing. Clothing, paper, hardware, chemicals, paints, and rubber are also manufactured.

The growth of manufacturing has led to the rapid growth of cities in Brazil. There are about 50 cities with populations of over 100,000. Rio de Janeiro is a great port and a leading industrial center of Brazil. It has

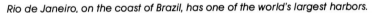

Rio de Janeiro, on the coast of Brazil, has one of the world's largest harbors.

over 5 million people. São Paulo, Brazil's largest city, has about 8 million people. São Paulo is an industrial and commercial center. There are many ports and industrial cities along the Atlantic coast. They include Pôrto Alegre, Salvador, Recife, and Fortaleza. Belém and Manaus are important river ports.

Until 1960 Rio de Janeiro was the capital of Brazil. Then the capital was changed to Brasília. You can see on the map on page 440 that most of Brazil's cities are along the coast. That is where most of Brazil's people live. Brasília was built farther inland. The government did this to encourage people to move to the vast interior of the country.

Brazil is the world's largest coffee producer. People began growing coffee about 100 years ago in the hills behind Rio de Janeiro. Today Brazil produces about one third of the world's coffee. The port of Santos handles most of the coffee export. Sugarcane, cotton, tobacco, cacao, and bananas are also important crops. The raising of cattle, horses, sheep, goats, and hogs is becoming more important.

Brazil is trying to develop agriculture in the interior of the country. Most of the interior is in the Amazon Basin. Until now most of Brazil's farms and ranches have been within 500 miles (800 km) of the Atlantic coast. What do you know about the land and climate of the Amazon Basin that tells you why this is so?

Guyana, Surinam, and French Guiana

Guyana, Surinam, and French Guiana are on the northern coast, between Venezuela and Brazil. They all have damp, forested lowlands. Sugarcane is the major crop in all three lands. Rice, cacao, and coconuts are also grown. Guyana and Surinam are both sources of bauxite.

Georgetown is the chief city and port of Guyana. Paramaribo is Surinam's capital and largest city. The capital and chief port of French Guiana is Cayenne.

Venezuela   Venezuela has three regions. In the northern part of the country there is the Andes region. South of the Andes is the Llanos in the valley of the Orinoco River. The third region is made up of part of the Guiana Highlands.

Mining is Venezuela's most important industry. Venezuela is one of the world's leading producers of oil. Over 60 percent of the oil produced in South America comes from Venezuela. Lake Maracaibo, in northern Venezuela, is the center of the oil industry. Find Lake Maracaibo on the map on page 454. Venezuela also has some of the world's largest iron deposits. Iron is mined in the Guiana Highlands.

Two of Venezuela's major crops, coffee and sugarcane, are grown in the valleys of the Andes. Cattle are raised in the lowlands of the Orinoco River.

Caracas is Venezuela's capital and chief city. This large modern city is in the mountains of northern Venezuela.

Paraguay   Paraguay is a small inland country on the northern part of the Chaco. It is made up of savanna-covered plains and low plateaus that rise gently westward toward the Andes. Paraguay is mainly an agricultural country. Livestock is raised on the savanna for meat, wool, and hides. Crops include corn, sugarcane, and tobacco.

Most of the people live in the eastern part of the country, between the Paraguay and the Paraná rivers. Paraguay's only large city is its capital, Asunción.

Uruguay   Uruguay lies farther south than Paraguay, and is bordered on the east by the Atlantic Ocean. Uruguay has very good grazing land. Cattle and sheep are raised on the cool, dry grasslands. Uruguay's chief exports are animal products—meats, hides, and wool.

Uruguay has one large city, Montevideo. It is the country's capital and chief port. Montevideo is on the Río de la Plata.

Argentina   Argentina lies between the Andes and the Atlantic Ocean. Most of Argentina is a vast, grass-covered plain. In northern Argentina is the Chaco. Because of the swamps and forests, much of the Chaco is difficult to cultivate. But agriculture is developing slowly in the Chaco.

South of the Chaco are the Pampas. Most of Argentina's crops are grown in the rich soil of the Pampas. Wheat, corn, flax, sunflower seeds, and feed crops are the chief agricultural products. Cattle raising is also important on the Pampas.

South of the Pampas is Patagonia. This cold, dry area has very few people and very little agriculture. Some sheep are raised for their wool. There are deposits of coal, iron, and oil in Patagonia.

Agriculture is the chief occupation of the people of Argentina. However, people do other kinds of work, too. Argentina's three main industries are meat-packing, food processing, and textiles. The major manufacturing cities are the capital, Buenos Aires, and Córdoba and Rosario.

Chile   Chile is a strangely shaped country. It lies between the Pacific Ocean and the Andes. Chile is nearly 2,400 miles (3,900 km) long. Yet it is only about 200 miles (320 km) at its widest point.

In northern Chile is the Atacama Desert. This is one of the driest areas on the earth. Yet it is very important because of its mineral resources. Chile is one of the world's leading copper producers. Much of its copper comes from this area. Also, **nitrate** salts have formed over the surface of the Atacama Desert. Nitrates are used to make fertilizers. Chile exports large amounts of nitrates.

In central Chile, wheat is the chief food crop. Corn, fruits, vegetables, and feed crops are also grown. Cattle raising is also important.

Most of Chile's people live in this region. Chile's two largest cities are in

This mine in Chile is the world's largest copper mine.

central Chile. Santiago, the capital, has over 3 million people. It is the largest city on the west coast of South America. Valparaíso is Chile's largest seaport.

In southern Chile, the land is rugged and mountainous. There are no cities in this cold, wet land. Some sheep are raised and there is also some lumbering.

The Andean countries   There are four more countries in South America—Bolivia, Peru, Ecuador, and Colombia. All four lie partly in the Andes and partly in the great forested plain that is drained by the Amazon River. There is little good farmland in any of these countries. Transportation is poorly developed. It is very difficult to reach the plains in the Amazon Basin from the coast of the Pacific Ocean. These four countries all have small populations. Many of the people in these four countries are Indians or mestizos.

Bolivia   Bolivia has no coastline. Like Paraguay, it is a **landlocked** country. Most of Bolivia lies on a very high plateau called the **altiplano**. The altiplano is surrounded by mountains. To the east there are forested lowlands.

Most of Bolivia's people live on the altiplano. The major cities are there. The capital of Bolivia is Sucre, but most of the government offices are in La Paz. La Paz is Bolivia's largest city.

The people of Bolivia use their crops themselves. Crops are not exported. Mining is Bolivia's major industry. Bolivia is one of the world's leading producers of tin. Silver, lead, and zinc are also mined. Bolivia does export some of these metals.

Peru   Peru borders on the Pacific Ocean. The country has three regions, the narrow coastal plain on the west, then the high mountains, and the Amazon plains on the east.

Peru was the home of the Inca Indians. Most of the descendants of the Incas, like many other South American Indians, live in the mountains. The descendants of the Spanish settlers live mostly on the lower western slopes of the mountains and along the coast. Most of Peru's cities are on the coastal plain. Lima, the capital, has about 3 million people.

Coffee, sugarcane, and tropical fruit are grown along the coastal plain. In the mountains some grain crops and potatoes are grown. In recent years the waters off the coast of Peru have become one of the great fishing areas of the world.

There are rich mineral resources in the Andes. Copper, silver, gold, lead, zinc, and iron are mined in the mountains.

Ecuador   The Equator crosses the country of Ecuador. That is how the country gets its name, for the Spanish word for *equator* is *ecuador*. Quito, the capital, is almost on the Equator. However, because Quito is 9,350 feet (2,850 m) above sea level, it has one of the most pleasant climates in the world.

Many of Ecuador's people grow corn, wheat, and potatoes for their own needs. The chief cash crops are bananas, cacao, and coffee.

The mountains of Ecuador are said to contain great mineral wealth. A little gold and silver have been mined, but mining is not a major industry in the country. Ecuador does produce some oil, however.

The workers above are packing coffee beans. Coffee is one of Ecuador's major crops.

Colombia Colombia is bordered by the Pacific Ocean and the Caribbean Sea. It stretches across the Andes to the plains of the Orinoco and Amazon rivers. Colombia is made up of three regions. There are hot, wet coastal lowlands in the northwest and west. The second region is in the northern Andes. Most of Colombia's people live in the valleys of the Andes. Bogotá, Colombia's capital and largest city, is in this region. The third region of Colombia is the Llanos. This plain makes up about three fifths of the country but has only a small part of the people.

Commercial farming is important only in the second region—the Andes. Coffee, cotton, cacao, sugarcane, and bananas are Colombia's important cash crops. Some oil and small amounts of iron and coal are produced. There is a small but growing steel industry.

The future South America is rich in resources. It has great amounts of many different minerals. It has rich farmland and huge forests. Making use of these resources will take time. There has been quite a lot of development of resources in South America in the past 25 years. The governments and people of South America are working to continue that development.

CHECKUP

1. List the 12 countries of South America. Which is the largest?
2. Which country produces the most oil?
3. Name the capitals of Argentina, Brazil, and Venezuela.

453

SOUTH AMERICA: Natural Resources

Agricultural Area

Manufacturing Area

Cattle
Copper
Iron
Petroleum
Bauxite
Manganese
Tin
Nitrates
National Capitals
Other Cities

Diamonds
Fish
Gold
Forest Products
Sheep

Caribbean Sea

ARUBA (NETH.) CURAÇAO (NETH.)

Barranquilla

Bananas

Maracaibo

Lake Maracaibo

Caracas

Coffee
Sugarcane
Cacao

VENEZUELA

Orinoco River

Cauca River

Kaieteur Falls

GUYANA

Georgetown

Paramaribo — Sugarcane

Cayenne

Medellín
Coffee
Bogotá

Cali

COLOMBIA

Coffee

Magdalena River

SURINAM

FRENCH GUIANA

GUIANA HIGHLANDS

Quito

Cacao
Bananas

ECUADOR

Guayaquil

Manaus

Amazon River

Belém

Cotton   Fruit

Fortaleza

Sugarcane

PERU

Cotton

Lima

ANDES

Lake Titicaca

BOLIVIA

La Paz

Lake Poopó

Sucre

PACIFIC OCEAN

Chaco

Paraguay River

PARAGUAY

Asunción

BRAZIL

Brasília

BRAZILIAN HIGHLANDS

São Francisco River

Recife

Cacao
Sugarcane

Salvador

Sugarcane

Coffee

Belo Horizonte

Bananas

Sugarcane

Coffee

Nova Iguaçu

São Paulo

Santos

Rio de Janeiro

Curitiba

ATLANTIC OCEAN

Equator

Atacama Desert

Córdoba

Rosario

Buenos Aires

Valparaíso
Santiago

Grapes

CHILE

ARGENTINA

ANDES

Salado River

Uruguay River

Paraná River

Grain

Pôrto Alegre

URUGUAY

Montevideo

Río de la Plata

Grain

Pampas

Colorado River

Patagonia

Tropic of Capricorn

Strait of Magellan

FALKLAND IS. (U.K.)

TIERRA DEL FUEGO

0   250   500   750 miles

0   250   500   750 kilometers

80°W   70°W   60°W   50°W   40°W

10°N

0°

10°S

20°S

30°S

40°S

50°S

COUNTRY	TOTAL AREA	POPULATION AND POPULATION DENSITY	CAPITAL CITY AND POPULATION	LANGUAGE(S)	OTHER FACTS
Mexico	761,601 sq mi (1,972,547 sq km)	75,700,000 99 per sq mi (38 per sq km)	Mexico City 8,988,000	Spanish*, Maya, Mixtec, Nahuatl, Otomi, Tarascan, Zapotec	Mexico is a world leader in silver production. Mexico City is on the site of the ancient Aztec capital.
Antigua and Barbuda	171 sq mi (442 sq km)	100,000 585 per sq mi (226 per sq km)	St. John's 22,000	English	Formerly part of the British West Indies, Antigua and Barbuda became an independent nation on November 1, 1981.
Bahamas	5,380 sq mi (13,934 sq km)	200,000 37 per sq mi (14 per sq km)	Nassau 102,000	English*	Christopher Columbus first sighted land at San Salvador in the Bahamas on October 12, 1492.
Barbados	166 sq mi (431 sq km)	300,000 1,807 per sq mi (696 per sq km)	Bridgetown 9,000	English*	Barbados is an island country that lies about 250 miles (402 km) north of Venezuela.
Belize	8,867 sq mi (22,965 sq km)	200,000 23 per sq mi (9 per sq km)	Belmopan 3,000	English*, Spanish, Creole	The last Central American country to become independent, Belize was, until 1981, a colony of the United Kingdom.
Costa Rica	19,653 sq mi (50,901 sq km)	2,400,000 122 per sq mi (47 per sq km)	San José 259,000	Spanish*	The Spanish words costa rica mean "rich coast." Columbus explored Costa Rica in 1502 looking for gold.
Cuba	44,218 sq mi (114,524 sq km)	9,800,000 222 per sq mi (86 per sq km)	Havana 1,925,000	Spanish*	Cuba is an island nation located 90 miles (140 km) south of Key West, Florida.
Dominica	290 sq mi (751 sq km)	100,000 345 per sq mi (133 per sq km)	Roseau 18,000	English*, French patois	Dominica, an island republic, gained full independence on November 3, 1978.
Dominican Republic	18,704 sq mi (48,443 sq km)	6,200,000 331 per sq mi (128 per sq km)	Santo Domingo 1,318,000	Spanish*	Santo Domingo was the first city to be founded by Europeans in the Western Hemisphere.
El Salvador	8,124 sq mi (21,041 sq km)	4,700,000 579 per sq mi (223 per sq km)	San Salvador 407,000	Spanish*, Nahua	El Salvador is the smallest mainland country in the Western Hemisphere.
Grenada	133 sq mi (344 sq km)	100,000 752 per sq mi (291 per sq km)	St. George's 27,000	English*, French dialect	An island nation in the Caribbean Sea, Grenada is one of the world's leading producers of nutmeg.
Guatemala	42,042 sq mi (108,889 sq km)	7,900,000 188 per sq mi (73 per sq km)	Guatemala City 836,000	Spanish*, Maya Indian dialects	Guatemala's Volcán Tajumulco, rising 13,845 feet (4,220 m), is the highest mountain in Central America.
Haiti	10,714 sq mi (27,750 sq km)	5,700,000 532 per sq mi (205 per sq km)	Port-au-Prince 306,000	French*, Haitian, Creole	Haiti is the oldest black republic in the world. The Indian word haiti means "high ground."
Honduras	43,277 sq mi (112,088 sq km)	4,100,000 95 per sq mi (37 per sq km)	Tegucigalpa 274,000	Spanish*	Honduras is among the world's top ten leading producers of bananas.
Jamaica	4,244 sq mi (10,991 sq km)	2,300,000 542 per sq mi (209 per sq km)	Kingston 112,000	English*	The name Jamaica comes from the Arawak Indian word xaymaca, which means "island of springs."
Nicaragua	57,143 sq mi (148,000 sq km)	2,800,000 49 per sq mi (19 per sq km)	Managua 623,000	Spanish*	Nicaragua is the largest Central American country. Cotton is this nation's most important product.
Panama	29,306 sq mi (75,903 sq km)	2,100,000 72 per sq mi (28 per sq km)	Panama City 460,000	Spanish*, English, Indian dialects	Panama is sometimes called "the Crossroads of the World" because of the Panama Canal.
Puerto Rico	3,435 sq mi (8,897 sq km)	3,400,000 990 per sq mi (382 per sq km)	San Juan 433,000	Spanish*, English*	Puerto Rico is an outlying area of the United States with its own commonwealth government.
St. Christopher-Nevis	104 sq mi (261 sq km)	60,000 577 per sq mi (230 per sq km)	Basseterre 16,000	English	This nation became independent on September 19, 1983. St. Christopher is nicknamed St. Kitts.
St. Lucia	238 sq mi (616 sq km)	100,000 420 per sq mi (162 per sq km)	Castries 15,500	English*, French patois	St. Lucia is an island with thick tropical forests. Bananas are the chief crop.
St. Vincent and the Grenadines	150 sq mi (388 sq km)	100,000 667 per sq mi (257 per sq km)	Kingstown 22,000	English*, French patois	Soufrière is an active volcano and the highest point (4,048 feet; 1,234 m) on St. Vincent.
Trinidad and Tobago	1,980 sq mi (5,128 sq km)	1,200,000 606 per sq mi (234 per sq km)	Port of Spain 63,000	English*, French, Spanish, Hindi	Calypso music and the limbo dance originated on this two-island nation.

*Official language(s)

455

COUNTRY	TOTAL AREA	POPULATION AND POPULATION DENSITY	CAPITAL CITY AND POPULATION	LANGUAGE(S)	OTHER FACTS
Argentina	1,072,067 sq mi (2,776,654 sq km)	29,100,000 27 per sq mi (10 per sq km)	Buenos Aires 2,908,000	Spanish*	Nine out of ten people in Argentina can read and write. This nation has the world's largest beef exports.
Bolivia	424,162 sq mi (1,098,581 sq km)	5,900,000 14 per sq mi (5 per sq km)	La Paz 655,000 and Sucre 64,000	Spanish*, Quéchua, Aymara	Bolivian forests have more than 2,000 kinds of trees. Mount Chacaltaya has the world's highest ski run.
Brazil	3,286,470 sq mi (8,511,957 sq km)	131,300,000 40 per sq mi (15 per sq km)	Brasília 272,000	Portuguese*	Brazil leads the world in coffee production and is the largest and most populous Latin American country.
Chile	286,396 sq mi (741,766 sq km)	11,500,000 40 per sq mi (16 per sq km)	Santiago 3,449,000	Spanish*	The Chuquicamata copper mine in Chile produces more copper than any other mine in the world.
Colombia	455,355 sq mi (1,179,369 sq km)	27,700,000 56 per sq mi (22 per sq km)	Bogotá 4,294,000	Spanish*	Colombia's Pacific coast is the rainiest spot in the Americas with an annual rainfall of 350 inches (889 cm).
Ecuador	105,685 sq mi (273,724 sq km)	8,800,000 83 per sq mi (32 per sq km)	Quito 743,000	Spanish*, Quéchua, Jibaro	The world's highest active volcano, Cotopaxi, 19,347 feet (5,897 m), is in northern Ecuador.
French Guiana	35,135 sq mi (91,000 sq km)	67,000 2 per sq mi (1 per sq km)	Cayenne 34,000	French*	The French started using Devil's Island as a prison colony during the French Revolution, 1789-1799.
Guyana	83,000 sq mi (214,969 sq km)	800,000 10 per sq mi (4 per sq km)	Georgetown 188,000	English, Hindi, Urdu	Guyana is one of the world's leading producers of bauxite. King George VI waterfall drops 1,600 feet (488 m).
Paraguay	157,047 sq mi (406,752 sq km)	3,500,000 22 per sq mi (9 per sq km)	Asunción 514,000	Spanish*, Guarani	Paraguay's flag is the only national flag with one design on the front and another on the back.
Peru	496,222 sq mi (1,285,216 sq km)	19,200,000 39 per sq mi (15 per sq km)	Lima 2,862,000	Spanish*, Quéchua*, Aymara	The world's second largest river, the Amazon, begins in the Andes Mountains of northern Peru.
Surinam	63,251 sq mi (163,820 sq km)	400,000 6 per sq mi (2 per sq km)	Paramaribo 151,500	Dutch*, Taki-taki	About 80 percent of Surinam is covered by mountainous rain forests. The nation is a leading producer of bauxite.
Uruguay	68,548 sq mi (177,539 sq km)	3,000,000 44 per sq mi (17 per sq km)	Montevideo 1,238,500	Spanish*	Uruguay is the smallest country in South America. Pasturelands cover 80 percent of the land area.
Venezuela	352,143 sq mi (912,050 sq km)	18,000,000 51 per sq mi (20 per sq km)	Caracas 1,754,500	Spanish*	Angel Falls in the Guiana Highlands is the world's highest waterfall, plunging 3,212 feet (979 m).

*Official language(s)

KEY FACTS

1. There were various Indian groups living in Latin America before any Europeans came to the Americas.

2. Most of Latin America was colonized by Spain and Portugal.

3. Although parts of it are highly developed, Latin America is considered a developing area.

4. Many countries in Latin America are rich in mineral resources.

VOCABULARY QUIZ

Beside the number of the sentence, write the word that best completes the sentence. Write on a sheet of paper.

subsistence   bauxite
developed   cacao
plantation   developing
mestizo   Pampas
commercial   savanna

1. A large farm on which such crops as sugarcane and cotton are grown is a _____ .

2. A _____ is a person of mixed white and Indian ancestry.

3. Aluminum is obtained from the mineral _____ .

4. The raising of crops to be sold is called _____ agriculture.

5. A _____ country is one that is highly industrialized.

6. The raising of only enough crops and livestock to meet the needs of a farm family is called _____ farming.

7. A country that is becoming industrialized is called a _____ country.

8. The chocolate in a candy bar comes from a crop called _____ .

9. _____ is a kind of vegetation with grassland and scattered trees.

10. A plains area in South America that is similar to the Great Plains is the _____ .

REVIEW QUESTIONS

1. Which two European countries colonized most of Latin America?

2. Explain three ways in which developed and developing countries are different.

3. What is the difference between subsistence farming and commercial agriculture?

4. What is the largest country in Middle America and what is its capital?

5. List the 12 countries of South America.

6. Name the 7 countries of Central America.

ACTIVITIES

1. Make a report on one of the following topics: "Animals of the Galapagos Islands," "The Pan American Highway," "Llamas of the Andes," or "The Deadly Piranha."

2. Look in an encyclopedia to find information on Simón Bolívar, José de San Martin, Francisco Miranda, Bernardo O'Higgins, Miguel Hidalgo y Costilla or Toussaint L'Ouverture. Write a report on how any two of these men helped Latin American colonies become independent.

3. Prepare an oral report on the Amazon River. In an encyclopedia or other reference book find out these facts about the river:

a. How long is it?

b. How wide is it at its widest point?

c. How many tributaries does it have?

d. What are some of the major ports on the river?

USING PRONUNCIATION SYMBOLS

SKILLS PRACTICE

In this book, words that may be hard to pronounce are respelled in parentheses, using a system of pronunciation symbols. Such a system is needed because so many letters have more than one sound. The letter *a* for example, can be pronounced with the sound you hear in *map*, *page*, *mare*, or *harm*. A pronunciation symbol stands for only one sound. The vowel sounds in the four words above have these four symbols: a, ā, ã, and ä.

An accent, or stress mark, is used after one of the syllables in each respelling used in this book. The accent tells you that that syllable gets the most stress. Which syllable is stressed in the word *Cayenne* in the list below?

One important symbol is called a schwa(ə). This is the sound heard in many unstressed syllables. The schwa sound can be spelled with any of the vowels. Which vowel is used to spell the schwa in *La Paz*?

The Key to Pronunciation for this book is on page 476. Use it to help you pronounce the names below. Which country name rhymes with *hilly*? With *Katie*? Write your name and a friend's name using pronunciation symbols. Don't forget the accents.

Altiplano	äl ti plä′ nō	
Amazon	am′ ə zän	
Antigua	an tēg′ ə	
Antilles	an til′ ēz	
Argentina	är jən tē′ nə	
Asunción	ə sün sē ōn′	
Atacama	ät ə käm′ ə	
Bahamas	bə häm′ əz	
Barbados	bär bād′ əs	
Belém	bə lem′	
Belize	bə lēz′	
Bogotá	bō gə tô′	
Bolivia	bə liv′ ē ə	
Brasília	brə zil′ yə	
Brazil	brə zil′	
Buenos Aires		
	bwā nə sar′ ēz	
Caracas	kə rak′ əs	
Cayenne	kī en′	
Chaco	chäk′ ō	
Chile	chil′ ē	
Colombia	kə ləm′ bē ə	
Córdoba	kôrd′ ə bə	
Costa Rica	käs tə rē′ kə	
Cuba	kyü′ bə	
Dominica	däm ə nē′ kə	
Dominican (Republic)		
	də min′ i kən	
Ecuador	ek′ wə dôr	
El Salvador	el sal′ və dôr	
Falkland	fô′ klənd	

Fortaleza	fôrt əl ā′ zə
(French) Guiana	gē an′ ə
Grenada	grə nād′ ə
Guadalajara	gwäd ə lə här′ ə
Guatemala	gwät ə mäl′ ə
Guiana	gē an′ ə
Guyana	gī an′ ə
Haiti	hāt′ ē
Havana	hə van′ ə
Hispaniola	his pən yō′ lə
Honduras	hän dur′ əs
Jamaica	jə mā′ kə
La Paz	lə paz′
Lima	lē′ mə
Llanos	lan′ ōz
Manaus	mə nous′
Maracaibo	mar ə kī′ bō
Mazatlán	mäs ə tlän′
Mexico	mek′ si kō
Monclova	mông klō′ və
Monterrey	mänt ə rā′
Montevideo	mänt ə və dā′ ō
Nicaragua	nik ə räg′ wə
Orinoco	ōr ə nō′ kō
Pampas	pam′ pəz
Panama	pan′ ə mä
Paraguay	par′ ə gwī
Paramaribo	par ə mar′ ə bō
Paraná	par ə nä′
Patagonia	pat ə gō′ nyə
Peru	pə rü′

Port-au-Prince	pôrt ō prins′
Pôrto Alegre	pôrt ü ə leg′ rə
Puebla	pü eb′ lə
Puerto Rico	pwert ə rē′ kō
Quito	kē′ tō
Recife	rə sē′ fə
Rio de Janeiro	
	rē′ ō dā zhə ner′ ō
Río de la Plata	
	rē′ ō də lə plät ə
Rosario	rō zär′ ē ō
St. Lucia	sānt lü′ shə
Salvador	sal′ və dôr
San Juan	san wän′
Santiago	sant ē äg′ ō
Santo Domingo	
	sant əd ə min′ gō
Santos	sant′ əs
São Paulo	sou pou′ lü
Sierra Madre Occidental	
	sē er′ ə mäd′ rē äk sə den täl′
Sierra Madre Oriental	
	sē er′ ə mäd′ rē ōr ē en täl′
Sucre	sü′ krā
Surinam	sur′ ə nam
Tobago	tə bā′ gō
Trinidad	trin′ ə dad
Uruguay	ur′ ə gwī
Valparaíso	väl pä rä ē′ sō
Venezuela	ven əz wā′ lə
Yucatán	yü kə tan′

7/UNIT REVIEW

1. Two of the world's largest forest areas are in Canada and in South America. — *What are the chief differences between them?*

2. The United States imports a great deal of lumber. — *Which of these two forest regions, do you think, is the more valuable to us, that of Canada or that of South America?*

3. Imagine that you are traveling from Ecuador on the Equator (a) southward to Cape Horn, and (b) northward to Alaska. — *List the kinds of climate that you would experience in each journey. What similarities would you find?*

4. The Panama Canal links the Atlantic Ocean with the Pacific. — *Which countries of the Western Hemisphere, do you think, benefit most from the canal? Why?*

5. Both Canada and Latin America are very rich in minerals. — *List some that are obtained from both.*

6. Canada is more developed than most of Latin America. — *List facts that show that this is so.*

7. Climate exerts a great influence on human activity. The Canadian northlands and the Amazon forest are both difficult environments. — *Explain how each limits human activity and development.*

8. North America, Central America, and South America are linked by a chain of mountains. — *Describe the changes of name and of form that these mountains undergo between Alaska and southern Chile.*

9. Two countries make up Anglo, or English-speaking, America, while there are over 30 in Latin America. — *If Latin America had been made up of only two or three countries, would its development have been different? How?*

10. Both Canada and Latin America contain very large areas in which very few people live. — *Name some of them, and explain why their population is so small.*

11. The Canadian Shield and the Brazilian plateau are both plateau regions made up of old, hard rock, yet they differ greatly in the ways in which they have been developed. — *What are the chief differences between them?*

EPILOGUE: Looking Forward

Responsibilities and roles "And so, my fellow Americans, ask not what your country can do for you—ask what you can do for your country." It was with these words that President John F. Kennedy challenged Americans in his first moments as President. The challenge remains for each of us today.

You have learned a lot this year about the rights and freedoms Americans enjoy. But rights always involve responsibilities. This is true for young people as well as adults. It is true for you today.

You will have many different life roles—parts you will play in relation to others, to your work, and so on. These roles have already begun for you. They will expand as you get older. They can help you carry out your responsibilities to our nation.

Role 1: Family membership Each of you belongs to some type of family. You will remain a family member all your life. Right now you are a son or daughter, and perhaps a sister or brother. One day you might be in charge of your own family.

Have you ever stopped to think about your responsibilities as a family member? What jobs do you have that help your family throughout the week? What feelings do you share? What things do you learn? Your family is a very important training ground for life. You are learning to get along and work closely with others. You are learning you cannot always do things the way you want. You are learning to share joys and sorrows.

Do you remember reading in Chapter 2 about United States history being a family history? Your family helps you learn how to live in a much larger family—the United States of America!

Role 2: Your job Every job done cheerfully and to the best of your ability helps the United States become a better place. All jobs are important and worthwhile. The person who keeps the country clean, who makes the goods we buy, who works in an office, is as important as the person who runs the country.

Even if you do not have a paper route, mow lawns, babysit, or shovel snow, all of you have a job right now. It is studying and working hard in school. It is following the rules of the school. It is listening carefully to your teacher. It is cooperating with other students. It is coming to school every day unless you are sick.

True, you will not be paid in money for your school job. But you can be proud of a job well done. You can learn a great deal about rights and responsibilities. And you can become prepared for a paying job later on that will be suited to your abilities and that you will enjoy.

Role 3: Your spare time Americans have more and more leisure time. What is done with that time is important for our future as a nation. This is as true for you as it is for adults.

It is fun to watch TV. Many shows are interesting and educational. But many of us watch too much TV. Many times we do

not think about what we watch. And, sadly, many of us cannot think of anything else to do besides watch TV.

You can do things to help build your body. Walking, biking, rollerskating, and playing ball are good activities. Can you think of others?

You can do things to build your mind. Stamp collecting, reading, and writing poetry are great hobbies. Can you think of other hobbies that are fun and make you think?

Are there people in your neighborhood who could use some help and friendship? Is there a walk-a-thon or some other event you could enter to raise money for others? Do you take time to look around you or to just sit and think? What are some other things that you rarely do that you could use your free time for?

All the great people you have read about in this book used their time in many different ways to make our country a better place. This country will be a better place if you too use your time wisely.

Role 4: As citizen All the things we have said make up your role as a citizen of this nation and the world. In the future you will vote and be more involved in community, national, and world events. But you are a citizen *now*.

You have learned how your country was born and what shaped it. You have to take those same ideas of freedom and equality to heart. You have to be willing to stand up for them.

You have to be willing to do things *now* to make the United States and the world better. You can encourage adults to vote. You can try to understand important events and people so you will be able to vote one day. You can complain if you are treated unfairly when buying things. You can help your family recycle papers, bottles, and cans. You can save energy. You

the future. But we do know one thing from our study of history—the future will be very different from the past or present. History is a record of change.

Think about this example. My grandfather came to the United States as a baby in the early 1890s. He came to a country that was hardly involved in world affairs. There were no cars or airplanes, no television, no computers. Most homes did not have electricity. The list of differences between then and now could go on and on. Does it make sense to expect that the United States will be the same 90 years from now as it is today? Of course not! In fact, it will probably change at a faster rate than it did for my grandfather.

We must understand that almost anything can happen in the future. Imagine telling my grandfather back in the 1890s that the United States would fight in two world wars; that people could sit at home and see pictures of events happening on the other side of the world. Imagine telling him that he would be able to fly across the country in hours; that the United States would send people to the moon. He would not have believed it. Yet he has seen it all happen. And we are being told some things just as unbelievable. Colonies in space! Average age of over 100 years! Robots to do housework! We must understand that the future is full of exciting possibilities.

But do we want just anything to happen? Are there some things that should not happen even though they are possible? What would we like to have happen in the future? Can we choose our future by working for certain goals? Let's look at two possible choices for the future.

can decide *now* to stay away from crime, drugs, and other harmful things. You can try to influence friends who want to do things you know are not right. You can get involved in scout groups, church groups, or community groups that can help you find ways to make things better.

The right of citizenship is given to you. Whether you are a *good* citizen or a *bad* citizen is up to you.

President Kennedy also spoke these words: "Now the trumpet summons us again— . . . [a call to] struggle against the common enemies of man: tyranny, poverty, disease, and war itself." In thousands of ways you can answer that trumpet call for your nation and your world!

The future: changes and choices   No one knows exactly what will happen in

One choice   Imagine a world 90 years from now. Four people share one tiny room. The smell from the outside is hard to bear. People allow garbage to just lie there in the streets.

When did people stop caring? Perhaps it was when the nuclear war destroyed cities, crops, and much of the world population. Perhaps it was when the factories stopped because there wasn't enough energy to run them. Perhaps it was when there was no more drinkable water in the pollution-choked lakes and streams.

You think of the masses of people starving around the world. There are four times as many people as there were 100 years ago. You think of the way things were when you were a child. There was still time then to make this a better world. . . .

Another choice   Imagine a different world 90 years from now. You may be about 100 years old. You have just finished playing a round of space tennis. You have a great deal of leisure time. You have retired from an active business life, but you still receive computer calls to give advice and help. Your many friends live all over the world—in domed cities or underwater cities. They may even live out of this world—in the lunar space colony where you once lived.

You live in a safe world. There has not been the least hint of war in 50 years. Nations finally realized that their abilities and resources were better used to provide food and shelter for their people than to make war. Nations cooperate with one another. The awful threat of nuclear war has turned the thoughts of most people to peace.

Solar energy storage cells store the sun's power and provide all the energy anyone needs. It is cheap and easy to drive your plane-mobile and to power all the appliances in your home.

Pollution is something your great-grandchildren study in history books. You cannot remember the last time you saw trash and waste on the ground. The air is clean; the streams are pure.

You think of how happy you are to have helped to make this a better world. . . .

The choice is yours   Neither of these stories will ever come entirely true. Maybe the truth lies somewhere in the middle. But will we do our part to make a better country? A better world? Remember, not to decide is to decide. To take no action will result in a poorer world. We must choose what kind of world we want, and work for it.

A fable   There was once a wise old woman who lived back in the hills. All the children used to come and ask her questions. She always gave the right answers.

There was a naughty little troublemaker among the children. One day he caught a tiny bird and held it in his cupped hands. Then he gathered his friends around. He said, "Let's trick the old woman. I'll ask her what I'm holding in my hands. Of course, she'll answer that I have a bird. Then I'll ask her if the bird is living or dead. If she says the bird is dead, I'll open my hands and let the bird fly away. If she says the bird is alive, I'll quickly crush it and show her the dead bird. Either way, she'll be wrong."

The children agreed that this was a clever plan. Up the hill they went to the old woman's hut.

"Old woman, we have a question for you," they all shouted.

"What's in my hands?" asked the little boy.

"Why, it must be a bird," replied the old woman.

"But is it living or dead?" demanded the excited boy.

The old woman thought for a second and then replied, "It is as you will, my child."

So it is with the United States. Our country's future is in *your* hands. "It is as you will, my child."

PRESIDENTS AND VICE-PRESIDENTS OF THE UNITED STATES

President	Birth-death	State*	Term	Party	Vice-President
George Washington	1732–1799	Va.	1789–1797	None	John Adams
John Adams	1735–1826	Mass.	1797–1801	Federalist	Thomas Jefferson
Thomas Jefferson	1743–1826	Va.	1801–1805	Democratic-	Aaron Burr
			1805–1809	Republican	George Clinton
James Madison	1751–1836	Va.	1809–1813	Democratic-	George Clinton
			1813–1817	Republican	Elbridge Gerry
James Monroe	1758–1831	Va.	1817–1825	Democratic-	Daniel D. Tompkins
				Republican	
John Quincy Adams	1767–1848	Mass.	1825–1829	National	John C. Calhoun
				Republican	
Andrew Jackson	1767–1845	Tenn.	1829–1833	Democratic	John C. Calhoun
			1833–1837		Martin Van Buren
Martin Van Buren	1782–1862	N.Y.	1837–1841	Democratic	Richard M. Johnson
William H. Harrison	1773–1841	Ohio	1841	Whig	John Tyler
John Tyler	1790–1862	Va.	1841–1845	Whig	....
James K. Polk	1795–1849	Tenn.	1845–1849	Democratic	George M. Dallas
Zachary Taylor	1784–1850	La.	1849–1850	Whig	Millard Fillmore
Millard Fillmore	1800–1874	N.Y.	1850–1853	Whig	....
Franklin Pierce	1804–1869	N.H.	1853–1857	Democratic	William R. King
James Buchanan	1791–1868	Pa.	1857–1861	Democratic	John C. Breckinridge
Abraham Lincoln	1809–1865	Ill.	1861–1865	Republican	Hannibal Hamlin
			1865		Andrew Johnson
Andrew Johnson	1808–1875	Tenn.	1865–1869	Democratic	....
Ulysses S. Grant	1822–1885	Ill.	1869–1873	Republican	Schuyler Colfax
			1873–1877		Henry Wilson
Rutherford B. Hayes	1822–1893	Ohio	1877–1881	Republican	William A. Wheeler
James A. Garfield	1831–1881	Ohio	1881	Republican	Chester A. Arthur
Chester A. Arthur	1830–1886	N.Y.	1881–1885	Republican	....
Grover Cleveland	1837–1908	N.Y.	1885–1889	Democratic	Thomas A. Hendricks
Benjamin Harrison	1833–1901	Ind.	1889–1893	Republican	Levi P. Morton
Grover Cleveland	1837–1908	N.Y.	1893–1897	Democratic	Adlai E. Stevenson
William McKinley	1843–1901	Ohio	1897–1901	Republican	Garret A. Hobart
			1901		Theodore Roosevelt
Theodore Roosevelt	1858–1919	N.Y.	1901–1905	Republican	....
			1905–1909		Charles W. Fairbanks
William H. Taft	1857–1930	Ohio	1909–1913	Republican	James S. Sherman
Woodrow Wilson	1856–1924	N.J.	1913–1917	Democratic	Thomas R. Marshall
			1917–1921		Thomas R. Marshall
Warren G. Harding	1865–1923	Ohio	1921–1923	Republican	Calvin Coolidge
Calvin Coolidge	1872–1933	Mass.	1923–1925	Republican	....
			1925–1929		Charles G. Dawes
Herbert C. Hoover	1874–1964	Calif.	1929–1933	Republican	Charles Curtis
Franklin D. Roosevelt	1882–1945	N.Y.	1933–1937	Democratic	John N. Garner
			1937–1941		John N. Garner
			1941–1945		Henry A. Wallace
			1945		Harry S. Truman
Harry S. Truman	1884–1972	Mo.	1945–1949	Democratic	....
			1949–1953		Alben W. Barkley
Dwight D. Eisenhower	1890–1969	N.Y.	1953–1957	Republican	Richard M. Nixon
			1957–1961		Richard M. Nixon
John F. Kennedy	1917–1963	Mass.	1961–1963	Democratic	Lyndon B. Johnson
Lyndon B. Johnson	1908–1973	Texas	1963–1965	Democratic	....
			1965–1969		Hubert H. Humphrey
Richard M. Nixon	1913–	N.Y.	1969–1973	Republican	Spiro T. Agnew
			1973–1974		Agnew/Ford
Gerald R. Ford	1913–	Mich.	1974–1977	Republican	Nelson R. Rockefeller
James Earl Carter	1924–	Ga.	1977–1981	Democratic	Walter Mondale
Ronald Reagan	1911–	Calif.	1981–1985	Republican	George Bush
			1985–		George Bush

*State of residence at election

Atlas

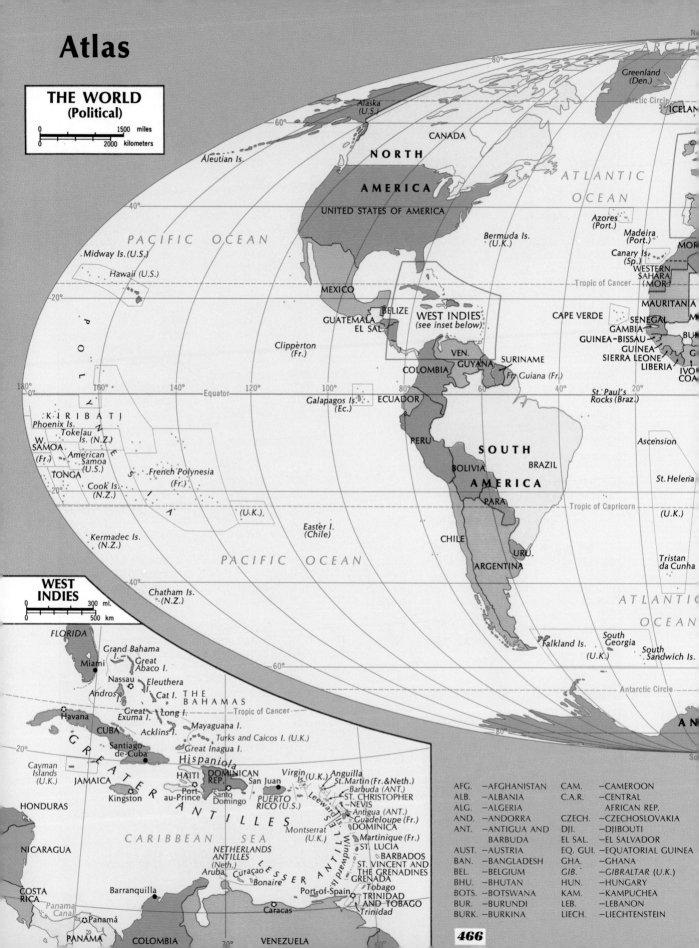

THE WORLD
(Political)

0 · · · 1500 miles
0 · · · 2000 kilometers

NORTH AMERICA

Greenland (Den.)

Arctic Circle

ICELAN

Alaska (U.S.)

CANADA

Aleutian Is.

ATLANTIC OCEAN

UNITED STATES OF AMERICA

PACIFIC OCEAN

Azores (Port.)

Madeira (Port.)

MOR

Bermuda Is. (U.K.)

Canary Is. (Sp.)

WESTERN SAHARA (MOR

Midway Is. (U.S.)

Hawaii (U.S.)

MEXICO

Tropic of Cancer

WEST INDIES (see inset below)

CAPE VERDE

MAURITANIA

BELIZE

GUATEMALA
EL SAL.

Clipperton (Fr.)

SENEGAL
GAMBIA
GUINEA-BISSAU
GUINEA
SIERRA LEONE
LIBERIA

BU

G

IVO
COA

VEN.
COLOMBIA GUYANA SURINAME
Fr. Guiana (Fr.)

Galapagos Is. (Ec.)

ECUADOR

Equator

St. Paul's Rocks (Braz.)

P O L Y

KIRIBATI

Phoenix Is.

Tokelau
Is. (N.Z.)

W. SAMOA
(Fr.)

American Samoa (U.S.)

TONGA

Cook Is. (N.Z.)

French Polynesia (Fr.)

(U.K.)

Easter I. (Chile)

PERU

BOLIVIA

SOUTH AMERICA

BRAZIL

Ascension

St. Helena

Tropic of Capricorn

(U.K.)

PARA

Kermadec Is. (N.Z.)

CHILE

URU.

Tristan da Cunha

Chatham Is. (N.Z.)

PACIFIC OCEAN

ARGENTINA

ATLANTIC OCEAN

AN

Falkland Is. (U.K.)

South Georgia (U.K.)

South Sandwich Is.

Antarctic Circle

WEST INDIES

0 · · · 300 mi.
0 · · · 500 km

FLORIDA

Grand Bahama I.

Great Abaco I.

Miami

Nassau

Eleuthera

Andros I.

Cat I.

THE BAHAMAS

Havana

CUBA

Great Exuma I.

Long I.

Tropic of Cancer

Santiago-de-Cuba

Acklins I.

Mayaguana I.

Turks and Caicos (U.K.)

Great Inagua I.

Cayman Islands (U.K.)

JAMAICA

GREATER ANTILLES

Hispaniola

HAITI
DOMINICAN
REP.

Virgin (U.K.)
Is.

Anguilla
St. Martin (Fr.&Neth.)
Barbuda (ANT.)

Kingston

Port-au-Prince

Santo Domingo

San Juan

PUERTO RICO (U.S.)

St. CHRISTOPHER-NEVIS

Antigua (ANT.)
Guadeloupe (Fr.)

HONDURAS

CARIBBEAN SEA

DOMINICA

Montserrat (U.K.)

Martinique (Fr.)

ST. LUCIA

NETHERLANDS ANTILLES (Neth.)

Aruba Curaçao
Bonaire

BARBADOS

ST. VINCENT AND THE GRENADINES

NICARAGUA

LESSER ANTILLES

Port-of-Spain

GRENADA

Tobago

TRINIDAD AND TOBAGO

Trinidad

COSTA RICA

Barranquilla

Panama Canal

Panamá

Caracas

PANAMA

COLOMBIA

VENEZUELA

AFG.	—AFGHANISTAN	CAM.	—CAMEROON
ALB.	—ALBANIA	C.A.R.	—CENTRAL
ALG.	—ALGERIA		AFRICAN REP.
AND.	—ANDORRA	CZECH.	—CZECHOSLOVAKIA
ANT.	—ANTIGUA AND	DJI.	—DJIBOUTI
	BARBUDA	EL SAL.	—EL SALVADOR
AUST.	—AUSTRIA	EQ. GUI.	—EQUATORIAL GUINEA
BAN.	—BANGLADESH	GHA.	—GHANA
BEL.	—BELGIUM	GIB.	—GIBRALTAR (U.K.)
BHU.	—BHUTAN	HUN.	—HUNGARY
BOTS.	—BOTSWANA	KAM.	—KAMPUCHEA
BUR.	—BURUNDI	LEB.	—LEBANON
BURK.	—BURKINA	LIECH.	—LIECHTENSTEIN

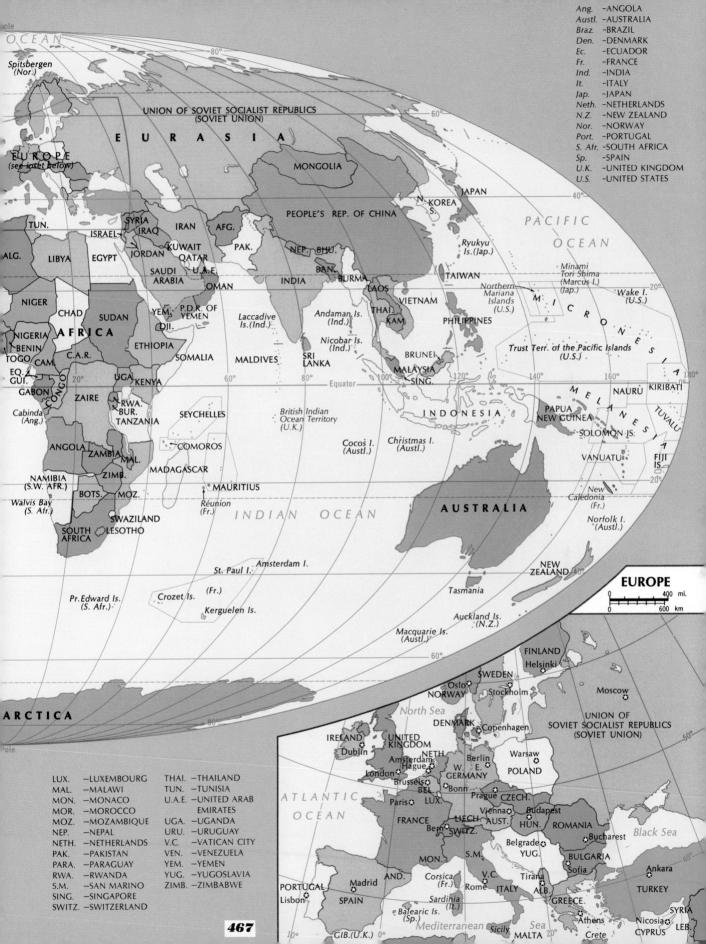

UNITED STATES OF AMERICA (Physical-Political)

CONN. —CONNECTICUT
D.C. —DISTRICT OF COLUMBIA
MASS. —MASSACHUSETTS
MD. —MARYLAND
N.H. —NEW HAMPSHIRE
R.I. —RHODE ISLAND
VT. —VERMONT
W.VA. —WEST VIRGINIA

C. —Cape
Mt. —Mountain
Pen. —Peninsula
Pk. —Peak

—— International boundaries
- - - State boundaries
⊛ National capitals
★ State capitals
● Other cities

Elevations

Feet		Meters
10,000		3,000
5,000		1,500
2,000		600
1,000		300
0		0

Miles 0 — 300
Kilometers 0 — 500

469

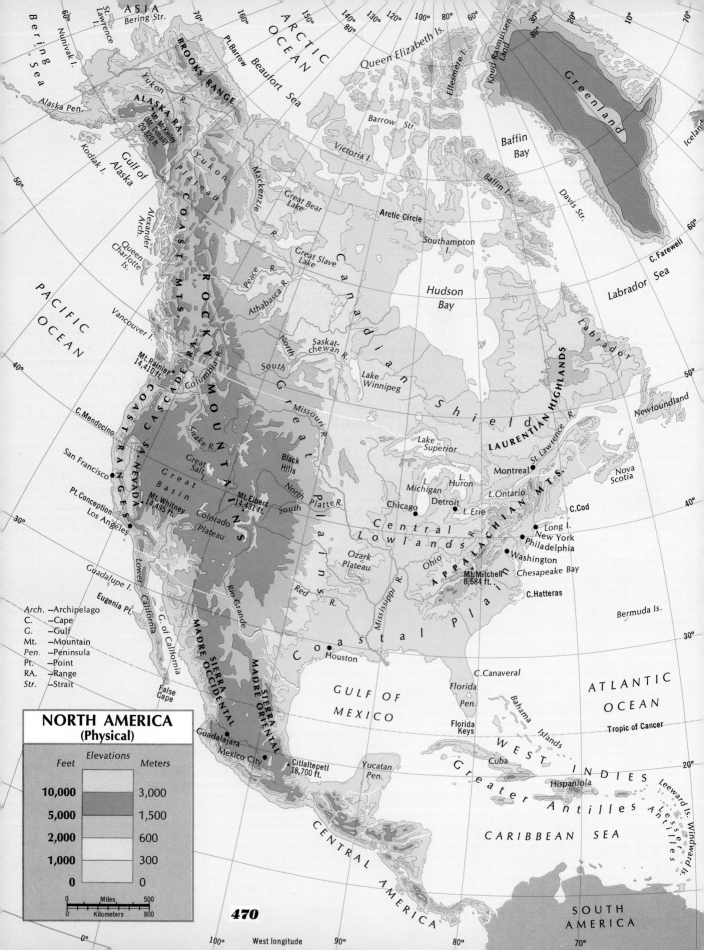

NORTH AMERICA
(Physical)

Feet	Elevations	Meters
10,000		**3,000**
5,000		**1,500**
2,000		**600**
1,000		**300**
0		**0**

Miles 500
Kilometers 800

Arch. —Archipelago
C. —Cape
G. —Gulf
Mt. —Mountain
Pen. —Peninsula
Pt. —Point
RA. —Range
Str. —Strait

ASIA
Bering Str.
St. Lawrence I.
Nunivak I.
Bering Sea
Alaska Pen.
Kodiak I.
Gulf of Alaska
ALASKA RA.
Mt. McKinley (Mt. Denali) 20,320 ft.
Yukon R.
Yukon Plateau
BROOKS RANGE
Pt. Barrow
Beaufort Sea
ARCTIC OCEAN
Alexander Arch.
Queen Charlotte Is.
Vancouver I.
Mackenzie R.
Peace R.
Athabasca R.
Great Bear Lake
Great Slave Lake
Victoria I.
Barrow Str.
Queen Elizabeth Is.
Ellesmere I.
Knud Rasmussen Land
Greenland
Iceland
C. Farewell
Davis Str.
Baffin Bay
Baffin I.
Southampton I.
Arctic Circle
Labrador Sea
Newfoundland
Nova Scotia
Labrador
Hudson Bay

PACIFIC OCEAN
C. Mendocino
San Francisco
Pt. Conception
Los Angeles
Mt. Rainier 14,410 ft.
Columbia R.
Snake R.
CASCADE RA.
COAST RANGES
COAST MTS.
ROCKY MOUNTAINS
SIERRA NEVADA
Mt. Whitney 14,495 ft.
Great Basin
Great Salt L.
North R.
Saskatchewan R.
South R.
Lake Winnipeg
Missouri R.
North Platte R.
South Platte R.
Colorado Plateau
Mt. Elbert 14,431 ft.
Black Hills
Red R.
Rio Grande
Ozark Plateau
Mississippi R.
Great Plains
Central Lowlands
Canadian Shield
Lake Superior
L. Michigan
L. Huron
L. Erie
L. Ontario
Chicago
Detroit
Montreal
St. Lawrence R.
LAURENTIAN HIGHLANDS
LAURENTIAN MTS.
APPALACHIAN MTS.
Mt. Mitchell 6,684 ft.
Ohio R.
Long I.
New York
Philadelphia
Washington
Chesapeake Bay
C. Cod
C. Hatteras
Coastal Plain
Bermuda Is.
ATLANTIC OCEAN

Guadalupe I.
Eugenia Pt.
False Cape
Lower California
G. of California
SIERRA MADRE OCCIDENTAL
SIERRA MADRE ORIENTAL
Guadalajara
Mexico City
Citlaltepetl 18,700 ft.
GULF OF MEXICO
Houston
C. Canaveral
Florida Pen.
Florida Keys
Yucatan Pen.
CENTRAL AMERICA
Bahama Islands
Cuba
Hispaniola
WEST INDIES
Greater Antilles
Lesser Antilles
Leeward Is.
Windward Is.
Tropic of Cancer
CARIBBEAN SEA
SOUTH AMERICA

West longitude

EURASIA (Physical)

Elevations		
Feet		Meters
10,000		3,000
5,000		1,500
2,000		600
1,000		300
0		0

Mt. —Mountain
Pen. —Peninsula
RA. —Range
Str. —Strait

Miles 800
Kilometers 1200

473

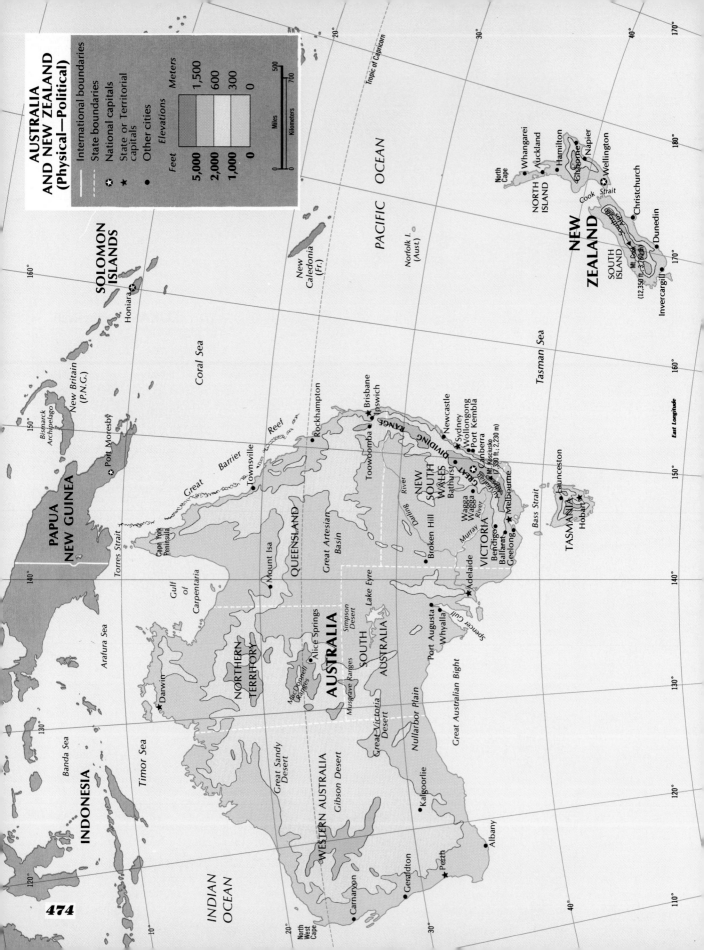

AUSTRALIA AND NEW ZEALAND (Physical—Political)

International boundaries
State boundaries
☆ National capitals
★ State or Territorial capitals
● Other cities

Elevations

Feet	Meters
5,000	1,500
2,000	600
1,000	300
0	0

Miles
Kilometers

INDONESIA

Banda Sea

Timor Sea

Arafura Sea

PAPUA NEW GUINEA

Bismarck Archipelago

New Britain (P.N.G.)

Port Moresby

Torres Strait

SOLOMON ISLANDS

☆ Honiara

Coral Sea

New Caledonia (Fr.)

PACIFIC OCEAN

Norfolk I. (Aust.)

Tropic of Capricorn

Cape York Peninsula

Gulf of Carpentaria

Great Barrier Reef

Rockhampton

Darwin ★

INDIAN OCEAN

North West Cape

Carnarvon

Geraldton

Perth ★

Albany

Kalgoorlie

Great Sandy Desert

Gibson Desert

WESTERN AUSTRALIA

Great Victoria Desert

Nullarbor Plain

Great Australian Bight

NORTHERN TERRITORY

Alice Springs

MacDonnell Ranges

Musgrave Ranges

Simpson Desert

SOUTH AUSTRALIA

Lake Eyre

AUSTRALIA

Mount Isa

QUEENSLAND

Great Artesian Basin

Townsville

Toowoomba

Brisbane ★
Ipswich

Darling River

NEW SOUTH WALES

Broken Hill

Bathurst

Newcastle

Sydney ★
Wollongong
Port Kembla

Canberra ☆

Wagga Wagga

Murray River

Mt. Kosciusko (7,330 ft; 2,230 m)

GREAT DIVIDING RANGE

Port Augusta

Whyalla

Spencer Gulf

Adelaide ★

VICTORIA

Bendigo

Ballarat

Geelong

Melbourne ★

Bass Strait

TASMANIA

Launceston

Hobart ★

Tasman Sea

NEW ZEALAND

North Cape

Whangarei

Auckland

Hamilton

NORTH ISLAND

Gisborne

Napier

Wellington ☆

Cook Strait

Christchurch

SOUTH ISLAND

Southern Alps

Mt. Cook (12,350 ft; 3,760 m)

Dunedin

Invercargill

PACIFIC OCEAN

East Longitude

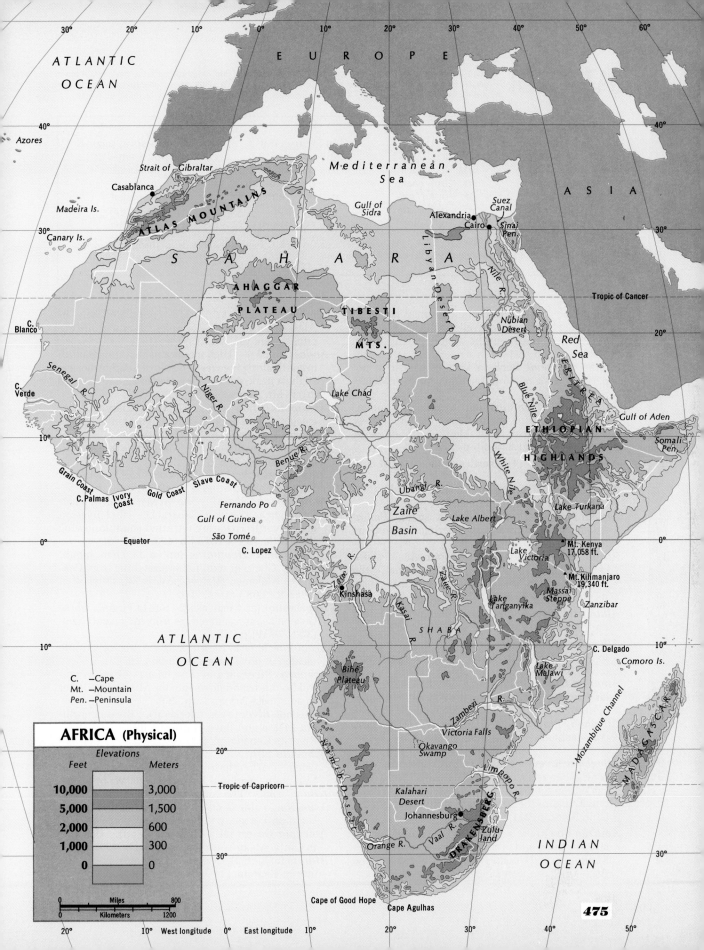

ATLANTIC
OCEAN

E U R O P E

Azores

30° 20° 10° 0° 10° 20° 30° 40° 50° 60°

*Mediterranean
Sea*

A S I A

40° 40°

Strait of Gibraltar

Casablanca

Madeira Is.

*Gulf of
Sidra*

Alexandria • Cairo •

*Suez
Canal*
*Sinai
Pen.*

30° 30°

Canary Is.

ATLAS MOUNTAINS

S A H A R A

Libyan Desert

Tropic of Cancer

C.
Blanco

AHAGGAR

PLATEAU TIBESTI

*Nubian
Desert*

*Red
Sea*

20°

MTS.

C.
Verde

Senegal R.

Niger R.

Lake Chad

E R I T R E A

Blue Nile

Gulf of Aden

10° 10°

Benue R.

ETHIOPIAN

HIGHLANDS

*Somali
Pen.*

Grain Coast
C. Palmas Ivory
Coast   Gold Coast Slave Coast

Fernando Po

Gulf of Guinea

São Tomé

Ubangi R.

*Zaïre
Basin*

Lake Albert

White Nile

Lake Turkana

Equator 0°

C. Lopez

Zaïre R.

*Lake
Victoria*

▲ Mt. Kenya
17,058 ft.

0°

Kinshasa •

Zaïre R.

Kasai R.

▲ Mt. Kilimanjaro
19,340 ft.

*Massai
Steppe*

Zanzibar

*Lake
Tanganyika*

SHABA

C. Delgado

10° ATLANTIC 10°

OCEAN

*Bihé
Plateau*

*Lake
Malawi*

Comoro Is.

C. —Cape
Mt. —Mountain
Pen. —Peninsula

R.

Zambezi R.

Mozambique Channel

M A D A G A S C A R

AFRICA (Physical)

Elevations

Feet		Meters
10,000		**3,000**
5,000		**1,500**
2,000		**600**
1,000		**300**
0		**0**

Tropic of Capricorn

Victoria Falls

*Okavango
Swamp*

Limpopo R.

20° 20°

*Kalahari
Desert*

Namib Desert

DRAKENSBERG

*Zulu-
land*

INDIAN

Johannesburg •

Vaal R.

Miles
0   800

Orange R.

30° OCEAN 30°

Kilometers
0   1200

Cape of Good Hope

Cape Agulhas

475

20° 10° 0° 10° 20° 30° 40° 50°
West longitude 0° East longitude

GAZETTEER

The Gazetteer is a geographical dictionary. It shows latitude and longitude for cities and certain other places. Latitude and longitude are shown in the form: 36°N/84°W. This means "36 degrees north latitude and 84 degrees west longitude." The page reference tells where each entry may be found on a map.

Abilene (ab′ ə lēn). Important railroad center at the end of the Chisholm Trail in the 1860s. Today, a city in Kansas on the Smokey Hill River. (39°N/97°W) p. 191.

Acadia National Park (ə kād′ ē ə nash′ ə nəl pärk). 116-acre (46-ha) national park in Maine. p. 309.

Adirondack Mountains (ad ə rän′ dak moun′ tənz). Mountains in northeast corner of New York. Highest peak is Mt. Marcy, with an elevation of 5,344 ft (1,629 m). p. 311.

Africa (af′ ri kə). The earth's second largest continent. p. 6.

Akron (ak′ rən). Large industrial city on the Cuyahoga River in Ohio. (41°N/82°W) p. 381.

Alaska Peninsula (ə las′ kə pə nin′ sə lə). Peninsula in Alaska separating the Bering Sea from the Pacific Ocean. p. 470.

Alaska Range (ə las′ kə rānj). Mountains in south central Alaska. Mt. McKinley (Mt. Denali), the highest peak in North America, is in this range. Its elevation is 20,320 ft (6,194 m). p. 403.

Albany (ôl′ bə nē). Capital of New York. Located on the Hudson River. (43°N/74°W) p. 324.

Albuquerque (al′ bə kėr kē). Most populated city in New Mexico. Located on the Rio Grande. (35°N/107°W) p. 397.

Aleutian Islands (ə lü′ shən ī′ lənz). Chain of islands extending west from the Alaska Peninsula. p. 468.

Allegheny Plateau (al ə gā′ nē pla tō′). Part of the Appalachian system west of the Blue Ridge. p. 329.

Allegheny River (al ə gā′ nē riv′ ər). River in north central Pennsylvania, flows northward into New York, then south back into Pennsylvania. At Pittsburgh, it joins the Monongahela River to form the Ohio River. p. 311.

Amazon River (am′ ə zän riv′ ər). Second longest river in the world. Tributaries rise in the Andes Mountains and Guiana Highlands. Flows into the Atlantic Ocean near Belém, Brazil. p. 439.

Anchorage (ang′ krij). Most populated city in Alaska. Located on Cook inlet, an arm of the Pacific Ocean. (61°N/150°W) p. 413.

Andes (an′ dēz). High mountains that stretch north to south along the western side of South America. Highest peak, with an elevation of 22,840 ft (6,690 m), is Mt. Aconcagua. p. 439.

Annapolis (ə nap′ ə ləs). Capital of Maryland. Located on Chesapeake Bay. Site of the United States Naval Academy. (39°N/77°W) p. 324.

Antarctica (ant ärk′ ti kə). The earth's third smallest continent. p. 6.

Antarctic Circle (ant ärk′ tik sėr′ kəl). A line of latitude located at 66½° south latitude. p. 9.

Antietam (an tēt′ əm). Site, in Maryland, of a battle fought as a result of General Lee's first invasion of the North. His army retreated south following this battle. (39°N/78°W) p. 175.

Appalachian Mountains (ap′ ə lā chən moun′ tənz). Chain of mountains stretching from Canada to Alabama. Highest peak is Mt. Mitchell at 6,684 ft (2,037 m). p. 263.

Appomattox (ap ə mat′ əks.). Site in Virginia where General Lee surrendered his army to General Grant. (37°N/79°W) p. 175.

Arctic Circle (ark′ tik sėr′ kəl). A line of latitude located at 66½° north latitude. p. 9.

Arkansas River (är kan′ zəs riv′ ər). Rises in central Colorado and flows into the Mississippi River in southeast Arkansas. p. 265.

Aroostook River (ə rüs′ tək riv′ ər). Rises in northern Maine and flows northeast into the St. John River in Canada. p. 287.

Asheville (ash′ vil). City in North Carolina. Located near eastern entrance to Great Smoky Mountains National Park. (36°N/83°W) p. 343.

Asia (ā′ zhə). The earth's largest continent. p. 6.

Asunción (ə sün sē ōn′). Capital of Paraguay. Located on Paraguay River. (25°S/58°W) p. 440.

Atacama Desert (ät ə käm′ ə dez′ ərt). Dry area in Chile. Major source of nitrates. p. 439.

Atlanta (ət lant′ ə). Capital of and most populated city in Georgia. (34°N/84°W) p. 343.

Atlantic Coastal Plain (ət lant′ ik kōs′ təl plān). Large plain located along the Atlantic coast from Maine to Florida. p. 263.

Atlantic Ocean (ət lant′ ik ō′ shən). Large body of water separating North and South America from Europe and Africa. p. 6.

Augusta (ô gəs′ tə). Capital of Maine. Located on the Kennebec River. (44°N/70°W) p. 306.

Austin (ôs′ tən). Capital of Texas. Located near the western edge of the Gulf Coastal Plain. (30°N/98°W) p. 362.

Australia (ô strāl′ yə). The earth's smallest continent. p. 6.

Bad Lands (bad′ lanz). Dry, rugged areas with little or no vegetation. Located in South Dakota, in North Dakota, and in Montana. p. 367.

Baja California (bô′ yô kal ə fôr′ nyə). A peninsula that separates the Pacific Ocean and the Gulf of California. Also called Lower California. p. 470.

Bakersfield (bā′ kərz fēld). City in southern California. Located at the southern end of the Central Valley. (35°N/119°W) p. 413.

Baltimore (bôl′ tə mōr). The most populated city in Maryland. Located on Chesapeake Bay. One of the busiest seaports in the nation. (39°N/77°W) p. 324.

Barrow (bar′ ō). Small town in northern Alaska. (71°N/157°W) p. 413.

Baton Rouge (bat ən rüzh′). Capital of Louisiana. Located on the Mississippi River. (30°N/91°W) p. 362.

Beaufort Sea (bō′fərt sē). Part of the Arctic Ocean northeast of Alaska. p. 403.

Belém (bə lem′). Seaport city on the Atlantic coast of Brazil. (1°S/48°W) p. 440.

Bering Sea (ber′ ing sē). Part of the North Pacific Ocean bounded on the east by mainland of Alaska and on the south and southeast by the Aleutian Islands. p. 468.

Bering Strait (ber′ ing strāt). Narrow body of water connecting the Arctic Ocean and Bering Sea. Separates Asia from North America. p. 470.

Berkshires (bərk′ shirz). Low mountains or hills in Massachusetts. They are part of the Appalachian system. Highest peak is Mt. Greylock, with an elevation of 3,491 ft (1,064 m). p. 287.

Birmingham (bər′ ming ham). Most populated city in Alabama. One of the nation's leading iron- and steel-producing centers. (34°N/87°W) p. 343.

Bismarck (biz′ märk). Capital of North Dakota. Located on the Missouri River. (47°N/101°W) p. 381.

Black Hills (blak hilz). Mountainous area with steep canyons. Located in South Dakota and Wyoming. Harney Peak, South Dakota, the highest peak in the North Central region, is in the Black Hills. Its elevation is 7,242 ft (2,209 m). p. 367.

Blue Ridge Mountains (blü rij moun′ tənz). Eastern part of the Appalachian system. They stretch from Pennsylvania to Georgia. p. 469.

Bogotá (bō gə tô′). Capital of Colombia. Located in the Andes Mountains. (5°N/74°W) p. 440.

Boise (boi′ sē). Capital of and most populated city in Idaho. (44°N/116°W) p. 397.

Boston (bô′ stən). Capital of and most populated city in Massachusetts. Located on Massachusetts Bay. (42°N/71°W) p. 306.

Brasilia (brə zil′ yə). Capital of Brazil. (16°S/48°W) p. 440.

Brazilian Highlands (brə zil′ yən hī′ lənz). Highland area located in southeast Brazil. p. 439.

Brooks Range (brüks′ rānj). Northernmost part of the Rocky Mountains. Located in northern Alaska. Mt. Michelson is the highest peak. Its elevation is 9,239 ft (2,816 m). p. 403.

Buenos Aires (bwā nə sar′ ēz). Capital of and most populated city in Argentina. Located on the Río de la Plata. (35°S/58°W) p. 440.

Buffalo (bəf′ ə lō). City in New York. Located on Lake Erie and the Niagara River. (43°N/79°W) p. 324.

Bull Run (bùl run). Stream that gave its name to the first big battle of the Civil War. Fought in Manassas, Virginia, the battle was won by the South. (39°N/77°W) p. 175.

Burlington (bər′ ling tən). Port city in Vermont located on Lake Champlain. (44°N/73°W) p. 306.

Cadillac Mountain (kad′ əl ak moun′ tən). Located on Mount Desert Island in Maine. It is the highest point on the Atlantic coast. It has an elevation of 1,530 ft (466 m). (44°N/68°W) p. 309.

Calgary (kal′ gə rē). City in Alberta, Canada. (51°N/114°W) p. 434.

Camden (kam′ dən). City in New Jersey. Located on the east side of the Delaware River, across from Philadelphia, Pennsylvania. (40°N/75°W) p. 324.

Canadian Shield (kə nād′ ē ən shēld). Upland region extending in a horseshoe shape from the Labrador coast to the Arctic Ocean west of Victoria Island. p. 427.

Cape Canaveral (kāp kə nav′ rəl). National Space Center. Site of launching for space flights. Located on the east coast of Florida. (28°N/81°W) p. 329.

Cape Cod (kāp käd′). Sandy peninsula in Massachusetts, known for its many beautiful beaches on the Atlantic Ocean. p. 287.

Caracas (kə rak′ əs). Capital of and most populated city in Venezuela. (11°N/67°W) p. 440.

Caribbean Sea (kar ə bē′ ən sē). Part of the Atlantic Ocean bounded by South America on the south, Central America on the west, and Cuba, Puerto Rico, and other islands on the north and east. p. 7.

Carson City (kärs′ ən sit′ ē). Capital of Nevada. Located near Lake Tahoe. (39°N/120°W) p. 397.

Cascade Range (ka skād′ rānj). Mountains that extend from northern California to Washington and into Canada. Highest peak, with an elevation of 14,408 ft (4,392 m), is Mt. Rainier. p. 468.

Cayenne (kī en'). Capital of French Guiana. (5°N/52°W) p. 440.

Central America (sen träl' ə mer ə kə). Made up of Guatemala, El Salvador, Honduras, Nicaragua, Costa Rica, Panama, and Belize. p. 7.

Central Lowlands (sen träl' lō' lənz). Large plain area located in the eastern part of the Central Plains. p. 263.

Central Plains (sen träl' plānz). Located in the middle of the United States. Largest plain in the nation. p. 263.

Central Valley (sen träl' val' ē). Located in California between the Sierra Nevada and the Coast Ranges. Made up of the Sacramento Valley in the north and the San Joaquin Valley in the south. p. 468.

Chaco (chäk' ō). Plains of the Paraná and Paraguay rivers. p. 439.

Charleston (chärl' stən). Port in South Carolina. Founded in 1670. (33°N/80°W) p. 343.

Charleston (chärl' stən). Capital of West Virginia. Located at point where the Elk and Kanawha rivers join. (38°N/82°W) p. 343.

Charlottetown (shär' lət toun). Capital of Prince Edward Island, Canada. (46°N/63°W) p. 434.

Chesapeake Bay (ches ə pēk' bā). Inlet of the Atlantic Ocean in Virginia and Maryland. It is about 190 miles (306 km) long. p. 311.

Cheyenne (shī an'). Capital of Wyoming. (41°N/105°W) p. 397.

Chicago (shə käg' ō). One of six cities in the United States with a population of more than 1,000,000. Located in Illinois, on the southern tip of Lake Michigan. (42°N/88°W) p. 381.

Cincinnati (sin sə nat' ē). Large city in Ohio. Located on the Ohio River. (39°N/85°W) p. 381.

Cleveland (klēv' lənd). Second most populated city in Ohio. Located on Lake Erie at the mouth of the Cuyahoga River. (42°N/82°W) p. 381.

Coast Ranges (kōst rānj' əz). Mountains along the Pacific coast of North America. They stretch from Alaska to California. p. 468.

Colorado Plateau (käl ə rad' ō pla tō'). Large, high area of land located in the southern part of the Mountain West. p. 263.

Colorado River (käl ə rad' ō riv' ər). Rises at the Continental Divide in Rocky Mountain National Park in northern Colorado and flows into the Gulf of California in Mexico. Very important source of irrigation water in southwest United States. p. 265.

Colorado Springs (käl ə rad' ō springz). City in Colorado. The United States Air Force Academy is located here. (39°N/105°W) p. 397.

Columbia (kə ləm' bē ə). City in Missouri. (39°N/92°W) p. 381.

Columbia (kə ləm' bē ə). Capital of South Carolina. Located on the Congaree River. (34°N/81°W) p. 343.

Columbia Plateau (kə ləm' bē ə pla tō'). High area of land located in the northern part of the Mountain West. p. 468.

Columbia River (kə ləm' bē ə riv' ər). Rises in Rocky Mountains in Canada, and flows into the Pacific Ocean along the Washington-Oregon boundary. p. 265.

Columbus (kə ləm' bəs). Capital of and most populated city in Ohio. Located on the Scioto River. (40°N/83°W) p. 381.

Concord (käng' kərd). Massachusetts town where the American patriots met the British redcoats in a skirmish at the beginning of the American Revolution. (42°N/71°W) p. 115.

Concord (käng' kərd). Capital of New Hampshire. Located on the Merrimack River. (43°N/72°W) p. 306.

Connecticut River (kə net' i kət riv' ər). Longest river in New England. Rises in northern New Hampshire and flows into Long Island Sound at Old Saybrook, Connecticut. p. 265.

Córdoba (kôrd' ə bə). Large city in Argentina. (31°S/64°W) p. 440.

Crater Lake (krāt' ər lāk). Located in Oregon in the Cascade Mountains. It is the deepest lake in the United States, with a depth of 1,932 ft (589 m). (43°N/122°W) p. 403.

Cumberland Plateau (kəm' bər lənd pla tō'). Part of the Appalachian system. Extends from West Virginia to Alabama. p. 329.

Cumberland River (kəm' bər lənd riv' ər). Starts in Kentucky, flows into Tennessee and then back into Kentucky, where it joins the Ohio River. p. 329.

Dallas (dal' əs). The second most populated city in Texas. Located on the Trinity River. (33°N/97°W) p. 362.

Deadwood (ded' wùd). City in Black Hills of South Dakota. Was a busy gold mining community in the late nineteenth century. (44°N/104°W) p. 191.

Death Valley (deth val' ē). Very low valley, located at the northern edge of the Mojave Desert. It is 282 ft (86 m) below sea level. p. 468.

Delaware Bay (del' ə wär bā). Arm of the Atlantic Ocean between New Jersey and Delaware. p. 311.

Delaware River (del' ə wär riv' ər). Rises in the Catskill Mountains in New York. Flows into the Atlantic Ocean at Delaware Bay. p. 265.

Delmarva Peninsula (del mär' və pə nin' sə lə). Located on the east coast of the United States. Parts of Delaware, Maryland, and Virginia are on this peninsula. p. 263.

Denver (den' vər). Capital of and most populated city in Colorado. Located at the base of the Rocky Mountains where they join the Great Plains. Has an elevation of 5,280 ft (1,609 m). (40°N/105°W) p. 397.

Des Moines (di moin'). Capital of Iowa. Located on Des Moines River. (42°N/94°W) p. 381.

Detroit (di troit′). One of six cities in the United States with a population of more than 1,000,000. Located on the Detroit River, in Michigan, near Lake Erie. (42°N/83°W) p. 381.

Dodge City (däj sit′ ē). City in Kansas on the Arkansas River. In 1860s it was an important railroad center on the Santa Fe Trail. (38°N/100°W) p. 191.

Dover (dō′ vər). Capital of Delaware. (39°N/75°W) p. 324.

Duluth (də lüth′). Port city in Minnesota. Located at the western end of Lake Superior. (47°N/92°W) p. 381.

Eastern Hemisphere (ēs′ tərn hem′ ə sfir). The half of the earth east of the Prime Meridian. p. 5.

Edmonton (ed′ mən tən). Capital of Alberta, Canada. Located on the North Saskatchewan River. (54°N/113°W) p. 434.

Equator (i kwā′ tər). A line drawn on maps that circles the earth halfway between the two poles. It is labeled 0° latitude. p. 5.

Erie (ir′ ē). Port city located on the south shore of Lake Erie in the northwest corner of Pennsylvania. (42°N/80°W) p. 324.

Erie Canal (ir′ ē kə nal′). Canal that connects Albany, New York, on the Hudson River, with Buffalo, New York, on Lake Erie. Original canal completed in 1825. p. 148.

Eurasia (yù rā′ zhə). The name often given to the total area covered by Europe and Asia. p. 472.

Europe (yùr′ əp). The earth's second smallest continent. p. 6.

Everglades, The (ev′ ər glādz). Large swamp located in southern Florida. p. 329.

Fairbanks (fār′ bangs). Town in central Alaska. Located on the Tanana River. (65°N/148°W) p. 413.

Falkland Islands (fô′ klənd ī′ lənz). Located in the South Atlantic Ocean, east of the southern tip of South America. p. 439.

Feather River (feᴛʜ′ ər riv′ ər). Located in California. Flows into the Sacramento River near Sacramento, California. p. 416.

Florida Keys (flôr′ əd ə kēz). Chain of islands about 150 miles (241 km) long. They stretch southwest around the tip of Florida from Virginia Key, near Miami, to Key West. p. 329.

Fortaleza (fôrt əl ā′ zə). Port city in northeast Brazil. (4°S/39°W) p. 440.

Fort McHenry (fôrt mək hen′ rē). Fort in Baltimore, which was attacked by British warships during the War of 1812. During the attack Francis Scott Key wrote the lyrics for the "Star-Spangled Banner." (39°N/77°W) p. 137.

Fort Sumter (fôrt səm′ tər). Fort on south side of the entrance to the harbor at Charleston, South Carolina. The first shots of the Civil War were fired here in 1861. (33°N/80°W) p. 175.

Fort Ticonderoga (fôrt tī kän dər ō′ gä). Fort on Lake Champlain. Captured in the first year of the American Revolution by Ethan Allen's soldiers but later retaken by the British. (44°N/73°W) p. 115.

Fort Worth (fôrt wərth′). City in Texas. Located on the Trinity River. (33°N/97°W) p. 362.

Frankfort (frangk′ fərt). Capital of Kentucky. Located on the Kentucky River. (38°N/85°W) p. 343.

Fraser River (frā′ zer riv′ ər). Rises in Canadian Rockies and flows into Pacific Ocean near Vancouver, British Columbia. p. 423.

Fredericton (fred′ rik tən). Capital of New Brunswick, Canada. (46°N/67°W) p. 434.

Gary (gar′ ē). City in Indiana on the southern end of Lake Michigan. One of the most important steelmaking centers in the United States. (42°N/87°W) p. 381.

Georgetown (jôrj′ toun). Capital and chief port of Guyana. (7°N/58°W) p. 440.

Gettysburg (get′ ēz bərg). Town in Pennsylvania. Site of a battle fought as a result of General Lee's second and last invasion of the North. His invasion was turned back. (40°N/77°W) p. 175.

Grand Banks (grand bangks). Rich fishing area in Atlantic Ocean south of Newfoundland. p. 423.

Grand Canyon (grand kan′ yən). Famous canyon in Arizona formed by the Colorado River. (36°N/113°W) p. 387.

Great Basin (grāt bā′ sən). Upland region. Located in the United States between the Rocky Mountains on the east and the Cascade Range and Sierra Nevada on the west. p. 468.

Greater Antilles (grā′ tər an til′ ēz). Group of islands in the West Indies. They include the islands of Cuba, Jamaica, Puerto Rico, and Hispaniola. p. 439.

Great Lakes (grāt lāks). Five large lakes located in North America mostly along the border between Canada and the United States. p. 265.

Great Plains (grāt plānz). Large plain area located in the western part of the Central Plains. p. 263.

Great Salt Lake (grāt sôlt lāk). Located in the Great Basin. An inland lake with no streams flowing out of it. (41°N/112°W) p. 387.

Great Slave Lake (grāt slāv lāk). The deepest lake in the Western Hemisphere. It is 2,105 ft (614 m) deep. It is in the Northwest Territories, Canada. (62°N/114°W) p. 423.

Great Smoky Mountains (grāt smō′ kē moun′ tənz). Part of the Appalachian system that extends along the North Carolina-Tennessee boundary. Highest peak is Clingmans Dome, with an elevation of 6,643 ft (2,024 m). p. 329.

Greenland (grēn′ lənd). Large island belonging to Denmark, off the coast of northeast North America. Excluding the continent of Australia, it is the largest island in the world. p. 470.

Green Mountains (grēn moun′ tənz). Located in Vermont. Part of the Appalachians. Highest point is Mt. Mansfield, with an elevation of 4,393 ft (1,339 m). p. 287.

Greenwich (gren' ich). A place in London, England, designated as 0° longitude. p. 11.

Groton (grät' ən). City in Connecticut. Located on Long Island Sound at the mouth of the Thames River. Site of large submarine shipbuilding base. (41°N/72°W) p. 306.

Guadalajara (gwäd ə lə här' ə). Second most populated city in Mexico. (21°N/103°W) p. 440.

Guadalupe Mountains (gwäd' əl üp moun' tənz). Located in New Mexico and Texas. Highest peak is Guadalupe Peak, with an elevation of 8,751 ft (2,667 m). p. 349.

Gulf Coastal Plain (gulf kōs' təl plān). Large plain located along the Gulf of Mexico from Florida to Texas. p. 263.

Gulf of Alaska (gulf ov ə las' kə). Part of the Pacific Ocean east of Kodiak Island. p. 468.

Gulf of Mexico (gulf ov mek' si kō). Body of water surrounded by the United States, Mexico, and Cuba. p. 265.

Guiana Highlands (gē an' ə hī' lənz). Located in northern South America from Venezuela through French Guiana. p. 439.

Halifax (hal' ə faks). Capital of Nova Scotia, Canada. Located on the Atlantic Ocean. (45°N/64°W) p. 434.

Hamilton (ham' əl tən). Industrial city in Ontario, Canada. (43°N/80°W) p. 434.

Hampton (ham' tən). City in Virginia. Located on Hampton Roads channel. (37°N/76°W) p. 343.

Harrisburg (har' əs bərg). Capital of Pennsylvania. Located on the Susquehanna River. (40°N/77°W) p. 324.

Hartford (härt' fərd). Capital of Connecticut. Located on the Connecticut River. (42°N/73°W) p. 306.

Havana (hə van' ə). Capital of Cuba and the most populated city in the West Indies. (23°N/82°W) p. 397.

Helena (hel' ə nə). Capital of Montana. (47°N/112°W) p. 397.

Hibbing (hib' ing). Town located in Mesabi Range in Minnesota. It is near the world's largest open-pit iron mine. (47°N/93°W) p. 381.

Hispaniola (his pən yō' lə). Second largest island in the West Indies. p. 470.

Honolulu (hän əl ü' lü). Capital of and most populated city in Hawaii. Located on the island of Oahu. (21°N/158°W) p. 413.

Hot Springs (hot springz). City in Arkansas located in the Ouachita Mountains. (35°N/93°W) p. 362.

Houston (hyü' stən). City near Galveston Bay in Texas. One of the six cities in the United States that has a population of more than 1,000,000. (30°N/95°W) p. 362.

Hudson Bay (həd' sən bā). Large body of water in Canada. Connected with Atlantic by Hudson Strait. p. 423.

Hudson River (həd' sən riv' ər). Rises in Adirondack Mountains and flows into New York harbor at New York City. p. 265.

Imperial Valley (im pir' ē əl val' ē). Located in southeastern California and Baja California. Mostly below sea level. The Salton Sea is in this valley. p. 403.

Indianapolis (in dē ə nap' ə ləs). Capital of and most populated city in Indiana. (40°N/86°W) p. 381.

International Falls (int ər nash' nəl fôlz). City in Minnesota on the Rainy River. (49°N/93°W) p. 381.

Jackson (jak' sən). Capital of Mississippi. Located on the Pearl River. (32°N/90°W) p. 343.

Jamestown (jām' stoun). First permanent English settlement in America. Founded in 1607. (37°N/77°W) p. 89.

Jefferson City (jef' ər sən sit' ē). Capital of Missouri. Located on the Missouri River. (39°N/92°W) p. 381.

Jersey City (jər' zē sit' ē). Second most populated city in New Jersey. Located on the Hudson River across from New York City. (41°N/74°W) p. 324.

Juneau (jü' nō). Capital of Alaska. Located on the Alaskan panhandle. (58°N/134°W) p. 413.

Ka Lae (kä lä'ā). A cape on the southern tip of the island of Hawaii. The most southern point in the United States. (19°N/156°W) p. 403.

Kansas City (kan' zes sit' ē). City in Kansas. Located where the Kansas and Missouri rivers meet. Separated from Kansas City, Missouri, by the state line. (39°N/95°W) p. 381.

Kansas City (kan' zes sit' ē). City in Missouri on the southern bank of the Missouri River. Across the state line from Kansas City, Kansas. (39°N/95°W) p. 381.

Kauai (kou' ī). Fourth largest of the Hawaiian Islands. p. 403.

Kennebec River (ken ə bek' riv' ər). River in Maine. Flows south from Moosehead Lake to Atlantic Ocean. p. 287.

Kingston (king' stən). Capital and chief seaport of Jamaica. (18°N/77°W) p. 444.

Knoxville (näks' vil). City in Tennessee. Located on the Tennessee River. (36°N/84°W) p. 343.

Lake Champlain (lāk sham plān'). Located between New York and Vermont. Named after its discoverer, Samuel de Champlain. p. 287.

Lake Erie (lāk ir' ē). Located along the border between Canada and the United States. Second smallest of the five Great Lakes. Has coastline in

Michigan, Ohio, Pennsylvania, and New York. p. 265.

Lake Huron (lāk hyür′ ən). Located along the boundary between Canada and the United States. Second largest of the five Great Lakes. United States portion of the lake is in Michigan. p. 265.

Lake Itasca (lāk ī tas′ kə). Source of Mississippi River. Located in Minnesota. p. 367.

Lake Maracaibo (lāk mar ə kī′ bō). An extension of the Caribbean Sea. Located in northwest Venezuela. Surrounded by rich oil fields. p. 439.

Lake Michigan (lāk mish′ i gən). Located in the United States. Third largest of the five Great Lakes. Has coastline in Michigan, Wisconsin, Illinois, and Indiana. p. 265.

Lake Okeechobee (lāk ō kə chō′ bē). Large lake in Florida. Located at northern edge of the Everglades. p. 329.

Lake Ontario (lāk än ter′ ē ō). Located along the border between Canada and the United States. Smallest of the five Great Lakes. United States portion of the lake is in New York. The only one of the Great Lakes that does not have a coastline in Michigan. p. 265.

Lake Pontchartrain (lāk pän′ chər trān). Lake near the southern end of the Mississippi River. p. 349.

Lake Superior (lāk sù pir′ ē ər). Located along the boundary between Canada and the United States. Largest of the five Great Lakes. Has coastline in Minnesota, Wisconsin. and Michigan. p. 265.

Lake Tahoe (lāk tä′ hō). Located on the border between California and Nevada. p. 403.

Lansing (lan′ sing). Capital of Michigan. Located on Grand River. (43°N/85°W) p. 381.

La Paz (lə paz′). Most populated city in Bolivia. The third highest city in the world. Its elevation is 11,736 ft (3,577 m). (17°S/68°W) p. 440.

Las Vegas (läs vā′ gəs). Resort city in Nevada. (36°N/115°W) p. 397.

Laurentian Highlands (lô ren′ chən hī′ lənz). Highland area in Quebec province, Canada, north of St. Lawrence River. Also called Laurentide Hills. p. 423.

Lead (lēd). City in South Dakota. Site of famous Homestake Mine, the largest gold mine in the United States. (44°N/104°W) p. 381.

Lesser Antilles (les′ ər an til′ ēz). Group of islands in the West Indies. Included in this island group are Virgin Is., Leeward Is., and Windward Is. p. 439.

Lexington (lek′ sing tən). Massachusetts town where, in April 1775, a group of minutemen (militia) resisted British troops in the first battle of the American Revolution. (43°N/71°W) p. 115.

Lima (lē′ mə). Capital of and most populated city in Peru. (12°S/77°W) p. 440.

Lincoln (ling′ kən). Capital of Nebraska. Located on a tributary of the Platte River. (41°N/97°W) p. 381.

Little Rock (lit′ əl räk). Capital of Arkansas. Located on the Arkansas River. (35°N/92°W) p. 362.

Llano Estacado (lan′ ō es tə käd′ ō). High plain in New Mexico, Oklahoma, and Texas. Also called the Staked Plains. p. 349.

Llanos (lan′ ōz). Large plain in northern South America. Drained by the Orinoco River. p. 439.

London (lən′ dən). Capital and most populated city in the United Kingdom. Located along the Thames River. (52°N/0° long.) p. 10.

Long Island Sound (lông ī′ lənd sound). Body of water between south shore of Connecticut and north shore of Long Island. p. 287.

Los Angeles (lô san′ jə ləs). City in southern California on the Pacific Ocean. One of six cities in the United States with a population of more than 1,000,000. (34°N/118°W) p. 413.

Louisville (lü′ i vil). Most populated city in Kentucky. Located on the Ohio River. (38°N/86°W) p. 343.

Lubbock (ləb′ ək). City in Texas. Located in the Llano Estacado. (34°N/102°W) p. 362.

Madison (mad′ ə sən). Capital of Wisconsin. Located on an isthmus between Lakes Monona and Mendota. (43°N/89°W) p. 381.

Manaus (mə nous′). City in rain forest of Brazil. Located on the Negro River, a branch of the Amazon River. (3°S/60°W) p. 440.

Maui (mou′ ē). Second largest of the Hawaiian Islands. p. 403.

Memphis (mem′ fəs). Large city in Tennessee. Located on the Mississippi River. (35°N/90°W) p. 343.

Merrimack River (mer′ ə mak riv′ ər). Begins at Franklin, New Hampshire, and flows into the Atlantic Ocean at Newburyport, Massachusetts. p. 287.

Mesabi Range (mə säb′ ē rānj). Range of low hills located in northeast Minnesota. Most important source of iron ore in the United States. p. 281.

Mexico City (mek′ si kō sit′ ē). Capital of Mexico. The most populated city in North America. (19°N/99°W) p. 440.

Miami (mī am′ ē). Large city in Florida. Located on Biscayne Bay. (26°N/80°W) p. 343.

Middle America (mid′ əl ə mer′ ə kə). The area from Mexico to Panama. It also includes the islands in the Caribbean. p. 7.

Milwaukee (mil wô′ kē). Most populated city in Wisconsin. Located on Lake Michigan. (43°N/88°W) p. 381.

Minneapolis (min ē ap′ ə ləs). Most populated city in Minnesota. Located on the Mississippi River. (45°N/93°W) p. 381.

Mississippi River (mis ə sip′ ē riv′ ər). Second largest river in the United States. Rises in northern Minnesota and flows into the Gulf of Mexico near New Orleans, Louisiana. p. 265.

Missouri River (mə zùr′ e riv′ ər). Longest river in the United States. Rises in western Montana and flows into Mississippi River near St. Louis, Missouri. p. 265.

Mohawk River (mō′ hôk riv′ ər).   Largest tributary of the Hudson River. Joins the Hudson near Troy, New York. Part of the New York State Barge Canal. p. 311.

Monongahela River (mə nän gə hē′ lə riv′ ər). Rises in West Virginia and flows into the Allegheny River at Pittsburgh to form the Ohio River. p. 311.

Monterrey (mänt ə rā′).   Industrial city in Mexico. (26°N/100°W) p. 440.

Montevideo (mänt ə və dā′ ō).   Capital of and most populated city in Uruguay. Located on the Río de la Plata. (35°S/56°W) p. 440.

Montgomery (mənt gəm′ rē).   Capital of Alabama. Located on the Alabama River. (32°N/86°W) p. 343.

Montpelier (mänt pēl′ yər).   Capital of Vermont. Located on the Winooski River. (44°N/73°W) p. 306.

Montreal (män trē ôl′).   Most populated city in Canada. Located on an island in the St. Lawrence River. (45°N/73°W) p. 434.

Mount Desert Island (mount də zərt′ ī′ lənd).   Located off the northeast coast of Maine. It is about 14 miles (23km) long and about 8 miles (13 km) wide. Part of Acadia National Park is on this island. p. 309.

Mount Elbert (mount el′ bərt).   Highest peak in the Rocky Mountains. Located in Colorado. It has an elevation of 14,433 ft (4,399 m). (39°N/106°W) p. 387.

Mount McKinley or Mt. Denali (mount mə kin′ lē or mount də näl′ ē).   Located in Alaska Range in Alaska. Highest mountain peak in North America. Its elevation is 20,320 ft (6,194 m). (64°N/150°W) p. 263.

Mount Mitchell (mount mich′ əl).   Has en elevation of 6,684 ft (2,073 m). Located in North Carolina. Highest peak in the Appalachians. (36°N/82°W) p. 329.

Mount Waialeale (mount wī āl ā äl′ ā).   Peak with an elevation of 5,080 ft (1,569 m). Located in Hawaii on the island of Kauai. One of the rainiest places in the world. (22°N/160°W) p. 403.

Mount Washington (mount wôsh′ ing tən).   Peak located in the White Mountains of New Hampshire. It is the highest point in New England. It has an elevation of 6,288 ft (1,917 m). It is also the windiest place in the United States. (44°N/71°W) p. 287.

Mystic (mis′ tik).   Town in Connecticut on Long Island Sound. Site of Mystic Seaport, a museum with a restored whaling port. (41°N/72°W) p. 306.

Nashville (nash′ vil).   Capital of Tennessee. Located on the Cumberland River. (36°N/87°W) p. 343.

Newark (nü′ ərk).   Most populated city in New Jersey. Located on the Passaic River and Newark Bay. (41°N/74°W) p. 324.

New Haven (nü hā′ vən).   Large city in Connecticut. Located on Long Island Sound. At one time it was one of two capitals of Connecticut. (41°N/73°W) p. 306.

New London (nü lən′ dən).   City in Connecticut. Located on Long Island Sound at the mouth of the Thames River. The United States Coast Guard Academy and a large United States Naval Submarine base are located here. (41°N/72°W) p. 306.

New Orleans (nü ôr′ lē ənz).   Most populated city in Louisiana. Located on the Mississippi River. One of the busiest ports in the United States. (30°N/90°W) p. 362.

Newport News (nü′ pôrt nüz).   City in Virginia. Located at entrance to Hampton Roads channel. (37°N/76°W) p. 343.

New York City (nü yôrk′ sit′ ē).   Most populated city in the United States. Located at mouth of the Hudson River in the state of New York. (41°N/74°W) p. 324.

Niagara River (nī ag′ rə riv′ ər).   Short river that flows north connecting Lake Erie on the south with Lake Ontario to the north. The river passes over the famous Niagara Falls. p. 311.

Norfolk (nôr′ fək).   City in Virginia. Located on Hampton Roads channel. (37°N/76°W) p. 343.

North America (nôrth ə mer′ ə kə).   The earth's third largest continent. p. 6.

Northern Hemisphere (nôr′ ᴛʜərn hem′ ə sfir). Half of the earth that is north of the Equator. p. 5.

North Pole (nôrth pōl).   Most northern place on the earth. p. 5.

North Slope (nôrth slōp).   Area of Alaska located between the Brooks Range and the Beaufort Sea. One of our nation's largest oil fields was discovered here in 1968. p. 403.

Ogden (ôg′ dən).   City in Utah. The transcontinental railroad was completed near here in 1869. (41°N/112°W) p. 191.

Ohio River (ō hī′ ō riv′ ər).   Formed at Pittsburgh, Pennsylvania by the joining of the Allegheny and Monongahela rivers. Flows into the Mississippi River at Cairo, Illinois. Forms part of the boundary of five states. p. 265.

Oklahoma City (ō klə hō′ mə sit′ ē).   Capital of Oklahoma. (35°N/98°W) p. 362.

Olympia (ō lim′ pē ə).   Capital of Washington. Located on Puget Sound. (47°N/123°W) p. 413.

Omaha (ō′ mə hô).   City in Nebraska. Located on the Missouri River. (41°N/96°W) p. 381.

Orinoco River (ōr ə nō′ kō riv′ ər).   Located in Venezuela. Rises in the Guiana Highlands and flows into the Atlantic Ocean near Trinidad and Tobago. p. 439.

Ottawa (ät′ ə wə).   Capital of Canada. (45°N/76°W) p. 434.

Ouachita Mountains (wäsh′ ə tô moun′ tənz).   Located in Arkansas and Oklahoma. Part of the Ozark Plateau. p. 349.

Outer Banks (ou′ tər bangks).   Group of islands located along the coast of North Carolina. p. 329.

Owens River (ō′ ənz riv′ ər). Located in California. Supplies water to Los Angeles through the Los Angeles Aqueduct. p. 416.

Ozark Plateau (ō′ zärk pla tō′). Elevated area extending from Missouri through Arkansas into Oklahoma. p. 349.

Pacific Ocean (pə sif′ ik ō′ shən). Large body of water stretching from the Arctic Circle to Antarctica and from the western coast of North America to the eastern coast of Asia. p. 6.

Padre Island (päd′ rē ī′ lənd). Sand reef off the coast of southern Texas in the Gulf of Mexico. A national seashore is located here. p. 349.

Paducah (pə dü′ kə). City in Kentucky. Located on Ohio river near the point where the Tennessee River joins the Ohio River. (37°N/89°W) p. 343.

Painted Desert (pānt′ əd dez′ ərt). Small desert located mostly in northeastern Arizona. p. 387.

Pampas (pam′ pəz). Fertile agricultural plains area in Argentina and Uruguay. p. 439.

Paraguay River (par′ ə gwī riv′ ər). Rises in Brazil and flows into the Paraná River at the southwest corner of Paraguay. p. 439.

Paramaribo (par ə mar′ ə bō). Seaport city and capital of Surinam. (6°N/55°W) p. 440.

Paraná River (par ə nä′ riv′ ər). Formed in Brazil; flows into the Río de la Plata. p. 439.

Pasadena (pas ə dē′ nə). City in southern California. Site of the annual Rose Bowl parade and football game. (34°N/118°W) p. 413.

Patagonia (pat ə gō′ nyə). Barren plains area in southern Argentina. p. 439.

Paterson (pat′ ər sən). City in New Jersey on the edge of the Atlantic Coastal Plain. (41°N/74°W) p. 324.

Pearl Harbor (pərl här′ bər). Inlet on the island of Oahu in Hawaii. Site of a U.S. naval base attacked by the Japanese on December 7, 1941. The next day, the United States declared war on Japan. (21°N/158°W) p. 403.

Penobscot Bay (pə näb′ skət bā). Inlet of the Atlantic Ocean. Located on the Maine coast. p. 287.

Penobscot River. (pə näb′ skət riv′ ər). River in Maine. Formed near Howland, Maine. Flows into Penobscot Bay. p. 287.

Philadelphia (fil ə del′ fē ə). City at the point where Delaware and Schuylkill rivers join. One of six cities in the United States with a population of more than 1,000,000. (40°N/75°W) p. 324.

Phoenix (fē′ niks). Capital of and most populated city in Arizona. Located on the Salt River. (33°N/112°W) p. 397.

Pierre (pir). Capital of South Dakota. Located on the Missouri River. (44°N/100°W) p. 381.

Pikes Peak (pīks pēk). Mountain peak in the Rocky Mountains. Has an elevation of 14,110 ft (4,304 m). (39°N/105°W) p. 191.

Pittsburgh (pits′ bərg). Second most populated city in Pennsylvania. Located at point where the Allegheny and Monongahela rivers join. (40°N/80°W) p. 324.

Point Barrow (point bar′ ō). Located in Alaska. The most northern place in the United States. (71°N/157°W) p. 403.

Port-au-Prince (pôrt′ ō prins). Capital of and chief seaport in Haiti. (19°N/72°W) p. 444.

Portland (pôrt′ lənd). Seaport city in southern Maine. Located on Casco Bay, which is part of the Atlantic Ocean. (44°N/70°W) p. 306.

Portland (pôrt′ lənd). Most populated city in Oregon. Located on the Willamette River near the point where it joins the Columbia River. (46°N/123°W) p. 413.

Pôrto Alegre (pôrt′ ü ə leg′ rə). Seaport city in southern Brazil on an inlet of the Pacific Ocean. (30°S/51°W) p. 440.

Portsmouth (pôrt′ sməth). City in Virginia. Located on Hampton Roads channel. (37°N/76°W) p. 343.

Potomac River (pə tō′ mək riv′ ər). Rises in West Virginia and flows into Chesapeake Bay. Washington, D.C., is located on this river. p. 311.

Prime Meridian (prīm mə rid′ ē ən). 0° line of longitude that passes through Greenwich, England. It divides the earth into Eastern and Western hemispheres. p. 11.

Promontory Point (präm′ ən tōr ē point). Place near Ogden, Utah, where tracks for the Central Pacific and the Union Pacific railroads were joined in 1869. (41°N/112°W) p. 191.

Providence (präv′ əd əns). Capital of Rhode Island. Located at the head of the Providence River. (42°N/71°W) p. 306.

Prudhoe Bay (prəd′ ō bā). Small bay on Beaufort Sea. Located in northern Alaska near the mouth of the Sagavanirktok River. p. 403.

Puget Sound (pyü′ jət sound). Inlet of the Pacific Ocean in Washington stretching from Juan de Fuca Strait to Olympia. p. 403.

Quebec (kwi bek′). City in Canada, on the north side of the St. Lawrence River. It was founded in 1608 by Samuel de Champlain. Today it is the capital of the province of Quebec. (47°N/71°W) p. 434.

Quincy (kwin′ sē). Shipbuilding city in eastern Massachusetts. Birthplace of John, and John Quincy, Adams, the second and the sixth Presidents of the United States. (42°N/71°W) p. 306.

Quito (kē′ tō). Capital of and most populated city in Ecuador. (0°lat./79°W) p. 440.

Raleigh (rô′ lē). Capital of North Carolina. (36°N/79°W) p. 343.

Recife (rə sē′ fə). Seaport city located on the Atlantic coast on the eastern bulge of Brazil. (8°S/35°W) p. 440.

Red River (red riv′ ər). Rises in New Mexico. Flows across the Texas panhandle and then forms boundary between Texas and Oklahoma. p. 349.

Regina (ri jī' nə). Capital of Saskatchewan, Canada. (50°N/105°W) p. 434.

Richelieu River (rish' ə lü riv' ər). Flows out of the northern end of Lake Champlain and into the St. Lawrence in Canada. p. 287.

Richmond (rich' mənd). Capital of Virginia. Located on the James River. (38°N/77°W) p. 343.

Rio de Janeiro (re' ō dā zhə ner' ō). The second most populated city in South America. Major port of Brazil. Located on the Atlantic coast. (23°S/43°W). p. 440.

Río de la Plata (rē ō də lə plät' ə). Body of water at the point where the Paraná and Uruguay rivers flow into the Atlantic Ocean. p. 439.

Rio Grande (re ō grän' dē). Rises in the Rocky Mountains in Colorado. It empties into the Gulf of Mexico near Brownsville, Texas. It forms the boundary between Texas and Mexico. p. 265.

Roanoke (rō' ə nōk). City in Virginia. Located on the Roanoke River. (37°N/80°W) p. 343.

Rocky Mountains (räk' ē moun' tənz). Longest mountain chain in the United States. Stretches from Alaska to Mexico. Highest peak is Mt. Elbert, with an elevation of 14,433 ft (4,399 m). p. 468.

Rosario (rō zär' ē ō). City in Argentina. Located on the Paraná River. (33°S/61°W) p. 440.

Sacramento (sak rə ment' ō). Capital of California. Located on the Sacramento River. (38°N/122°W) p. 413.

Sacramento River (sak rə ment' ō riv' ər). River in California that flows into San Francisco Bay. p. 416.

St. Augustine (sānt ô' gə stēn). City in Florida. Founded in 1565 by explorers from Spain. Oldest city in the United States. (30°N/81°W) p. 74.

St. John's (sānt jänz). Capital of Newfoundland, Canada. Located on southeast coast of Newfoundland Island. (48°N/53°W) p. 434.

St. Lawrence River (sānt lôr' əns riv' ər). Forms part of the boundary between Canada and the United States. Flows northeast from Lake Ontario to the Atlantic Ocean at the Gulf of St. Lawrence. p. 423.

St. Louis (sānt lü' əs). Most populated city in Missouri. Located on Mississippi River near the point where it is joined by the Missouri River. (39°N/90°W) p. 381.

St. Paul (sānt pôl). Capital of Minnesota. Located on the Mississippi River. (45°N/93°W) p. 381.

Salem (sāl' əm). Capital of Oregon. Located on the Willamette River. (45°N/123°W) p. 413.

Salt Lake City (sôlt lāk sit' ē). Capital of and most populated city in Utah. Located near Great Salt Lake. (41°N/112°W) p. 397.

Salton Sea (sôlt' ən sē). Salty, below-sea-level lake located in southern California. p. 403.

Salvador (sal' və dôr). Seaport city on east coast of Brazil. (13°S/39°W) p. 440.

San Antonio (san ən tō' nē ō). Large city in Texas. Located on the San Antonio River. Site of the Alamo. (30°N/98°W) p. 362.

San Diego (san dē ā' gō). First of 21 Spanish missions was built here. Today it is a large city located in southern California along the Pacific Ocean. (33°N/117°W) p. 413.

San Francisco (san frən sis' kō). Third most populated city in California. (38°N/122°W) p. 413.

San Joaquin River (san wä kēn' riv' ər). Located in California. Flows into the Sacramento River near San Francisco Bay. p. 416.

San Jose (san ə zā'). California city. One of the nation's 20 largest cities. (37°N/122°W) p. 413.

San Juan (san wän'). Capital of and most populated city in Puerto Rico. (18°N/66°W) p. 444.

San Salvador (san sal' və dôr). One of a group of islands called the Bahamas. Columbus landed on this island in 1492. p. 71.

Santa Fe (sant ə fā'). Spanish settlement started in 1609. Today the capital of New Mexico. (36°N/106°W) p. 397.

Santiago (sant ē äg' ō). Capital of and most populated city in Chile. (33°S/71°W) p. 440.

Santo Domingo (sant əd ə min' gō). Capital of and chief seaport of the Dominican Republic. (18°N/70°W) p. 444.

Santos (sant' əs). Seaport city on southeast coast of Brazil. (24°S/46°W) p. 440.

São Paulo (sou pou' lü). The most populated city in South America. Located in Brazil. (24°S/47°W) p. 440.

Saratoga (sar ə tō' gə). Revolutionary War battle site. Located in the present-day city of Schuylerville, New York. (43°N/74°W) p. 115.

Sault Ste. Marie (sü sānt' mə rē'). City in Michigan. Located at falls between Lakes Huron and Superior. (47°N/84°W) p. 381.

Savannah (sə van' ə). City in Georgia. Georgia colony was founded here in 1733 by a group led by James Oglethorpe. (32°N/81°W) p. 343.

Schefferville (shef' ər vil). Iron-mining town in Quebec. (55°N/67°W) p. 427.

Seattle (sē at' əl). Most populated city in Washington. Located on east shore of Puget Sound. (48°N/122°W) p. 397.

Sierra Madre Occidental (sē er' ə mäd' re äk sə den täl'). North-south mountain range in western Mexico. p. 439.

Sierra Madre Oriental (sē er' ə mäd' re ōr ē en täl'). North-south mountain range in eastern Mexico. p. 439.

Sierra Nevada (sē er' ə nə vad' ə). High mountain range located mostly in eastern California. Mount Whitney, with an elevation of 14,495 ft (4,418 m), is located in this range. It is the highest peak in the United States outside of Alaska. p. 263.

Snake River (snāk riv' ər). Rises in Yellowstone National Park in Wyoming. Flows into the Columbia River in Washington. p. 265.

South America (south ə mer' ə kə). The earth's fourth largest continent. p. 6.

Southern Hemisphere (suŦH′ ərn hem′ ə sfir). The half of the earth south of the Equator. p. 5.

South Pole (south pōl). The most southern place on the earth. p 5.

Springfield (spring′ fēld). Capital of Illinois. Located on the Sangamon River. (40°N/90°W) p. 381.

Springfield (spring′ fēld). Large city in central Massachusetts. (42°N/73°W) p. 306.

Sucre (sü′ krā). Capital of Bolivia. Located in the Andes Mountains. (19°S/65°W) p. 440.

Sudbury (səd′ ber ē). Nickel-mining town in Ontario, Canada. World's largest supply of nickel is in the area. (47°N/81°W) p. 427.

Superior (sù pir′ ē ər). City in Wisconsin. Located on Lake Superior. (47°N/92°W) p. 381.

Susquehanna River (səs kwə han′ ə riv′ ər). Rises in Otsego Lake in New York. Flows into northern end of Chesapeake Bay. p. 311.

Tallahassee (tal ə has′ ē). Capital of Florida. Located in northern Florida. (30°N/84°W) p. 343.

Tampa (tam′ pə). City in Florida. Located on Tampa Bay. (28°N/82°W) p. 343.

Tennessee River (ten ə sē′ riv′ ər). Formed near Knoxville, Tennessee, by the joining of the Holston and French Broad rivers. Flows into the Ohio River at Paducah, Kentucky. p. 265.

Toledo (tə lēd′ ō). City in Ohio. Located on Lake Erie. (42°N/84°W) p. 381.

Topeka (tə pē′ kə). Capital of Kansas. Located on the Kansas River. (39°N/96°W) p. 367.

Toronto (tə ränt′ ō). Capital of Ontario, Canada. Located on northeast end of Lake Ontario. (44°N/79°W) p. 434

Trenton (trent′ ən). Capital of New Jersey. Located on the Delaware River. (40°N/75°W) p. 324.

Tropic of Cancer (trop′ik ov kan′ sər). A line of latitude located at 23½° north. p. 9.

Tropic of Capricorn (trop′ik ov kap′rə kôrn). A line of latitude located at 23½° south. p. 9.

Tulsa (təl′ sə). Large city in Oklahoma. An important oil industry center. (36°N/96°W) p. 362.

Valdez (val dēz′). Port town in southern Alaska. Oil from Alaska's North Slope is transported by pipeline to Valdez. (61°N/146°W) p. 413.

Valparaíso (väl pä rä ē′ sō). Major seaport of Chile. Located on Pacific Ocean. (33°S/72°W) p. 339.

Vancouver (van kü′ vər). City in British Columbia, Canada. Located on an inlet of the Pacific Ocean. Canada's most important Pacific seaport. (49°N/123°W) p. 434.

Vicksburg (viks′ bərg). Civil War battle site on the Mississippi River. Grant's victory here split the South in two. (32°N/91°W) p. 175.

Victoria (vik tōr′ ē ə). Capital of British Columbia, Canada. Located on Vancouver Island. (48°N/123°W) p. 434.

Virginia City (vər jin′ yə sit′ ē). Once a booming mining town in Nevada. Today it is a very small village. (39°N/120°W) p. 191.

Washington, D.C. (wôsh′ ing tən D C). Capital of the United States. Located on the Potomac River. (39°N/77°W) p. 324.

Western Hemisphere (west′ tərn hem′ə sfir). The hemisphere in which all of South America and North America is located. The half of the earth west of the Prime Meridian. p.5.

West Indies (west in′dēz). Group of islands stretching about 2,500 mi (4,023 km) from near Florida to near Venezuela. p. 470.

White Butte (hwīt byüt). The highest peak in North Dakota. It has an elevation of 3,506 ft (1,069 m). (46°N/103°W) p. 367.

Whitehorse (hwīt′ hôrs). Capital of Yukon Territory, Canada. (61°N/135°W) p. 434.

White Mountains (hwīt moun′ tənz). Part of the Appalachian system. Located in New Hampshire. Highest peak is Mt. Washington, with an elevation of 6,288 ft (1,917 m). p. 287.

Wichita (wich′ ə tô). City in Kansas. Located on the Arkansas River. (38°N/97°W) p. 381.

Willamette River (wə lam′ ət riv′ ər). Located in Oregon. Flows into the Columbia River near Portland. p. 403.

Williamsburg (wil′ yəmz bərg). Colonial capital of Virginia. (37°N/77°W) p. 26.

Wilmington (wil′ ming tən). City in Delaware. Located on the Delaware River. (40°N/76°W) p. 324.

Winnipeg (win′ ə peg). Capital of Manitoba, Canada. Located on the Red River. (50°N/97°W) p. 434.

Yakima River (yak′ ə mô riv′ ər). Located in Washington. Flows into the Columbia River near Richland. p. 403.

Yellowknife (yel′ ə nīf). Capital of Northwest Territories, Canada. Located on Great Slave Lake at the mouth of Yellowknife River. (62°N/114°W) p. 434.

Yellowstone National Park (yel′ ə stōn nash′ ə nəl pärk). Oldest and largest national park in the United States. Most of it is in Wyoming. (45°N/110°W) p. 7.

Yonkers (yäng′ kərz). City in New York. Located on the Hudson River. (41°N/74°W) p. 324.

Yorktown (yôrk′ toun). The Americans won a decisive victory over the British here during the Revolutionary War. Following this loss the British were ready to make peace. (37°N/77°W) p. 115.

Yucatán Peninsula (yü kə tan′ pə nin′ sə lə). Located in Central America. Separates the Gulf of Mexico and the Caribbean Sea. p. 439.

Yukon River (yü′ kän riv′ ər). The third longest river in North America. Formed in Yukon Territory, Canada, and flows into the Bering Sea. p. 470.

Yuma (yü′ mə). City in southwest Arizona. Located where the Gila River joins the Colorado River. (33°N/115°W) p. 269.

GLOSSARY

The page references tell where each entry first appears in the text.

abolitionist (ab ə lish' ə nist). A person opposed to slavery and in favor of ending it. p. 142.

agricultural (ag rə kul' chər əl). Having to do with farming of crops or animals. p. 202.

Alamo (al' ə mō). An old Spanish mission in San Antonio. The *Alamo* was the scene of a famous battle between Texas and Mexico in 1836. p. 153.

Allies (al' īz). The name given to those countries supported by and later joined by the United States in World War I and World War II. p. 229.

altiplano (äl ti plä' nō). A very high plateau in the Andes of Bolivia. p. 452.

amendment (ə mend' mənt). A formal correction or change. p. 120.

annexation (an ək sā' shən). The taking of a country or other territory and making it a part of one's own nation. p. 224.

Antarctic Circle (ant ärk' tik sèr' kəl). A line of latitude that circles the earth at 66½° south latitude. p. 9.

anthem (an' thəm). A song in praise of one's country or religion. p. 136.

anthracite (an' thrə sīt). Hard coal. p. 279.

apprentice (ə pren' tis). A person learning a trade or craft. p. 93.

archaeologist (är kē ol' ə jist). A scientist who studies objects, ruins, and other evidence of human life in the past. p. 36.

architect (är' kə tekt). A person who designs and draws plans for buildings and makes sure the plans are carried out by the builders. p. 132.

architecture (är' kə tek chər). The designing of buildings. The style of buildings. p. 154.

Arctic Circle (ärk' tik sèr' kəl). A line of latitude that circles the earth at 66½° north latitude. p. 9.

armada (är mä' də). The Spanish word for a fleet of armed ships. p. 76.

armistice (är' mə stis). A halt to fighting by agreement between the warring nations. p. 230.

armory (är' mər ē). A place where firearms are manufactured or stored. p. 292.

arroyo (ə roi' ō). The name given to a dry streambed. p. 389.

Articles of Confederation (är' tə kəlz ov kən fed ə rā' shən). The document that listed the powers of the central government and the powers of the states in the period before the Constitution was written. p. 118.

artifact (är' tə fakt). An object left by people who lived long ago. p. 36.

assassination (ə sas ə nā' shən). The murdering of someone by secret or sudden attack. p. 246.

assembly line (ə sem' blē līn). A moving belt that carries a certain part of a product past workers who add pieces to the part. p. 243.

atomic energy (ə tom' ik en' ər jē). The power that is derived from making changes in atoms. Atoms are small bits of matter. p. 280.

aviation (ā vē ā' shən). The art or science of operating and navigating aircraft. Also, the designing, development, and manufacturing of aircraft. p. 243.

axis (ak' sis). An imaginary line that goes through the earth from the North Pole to the South Pole. p. 272.

Axis (ak' sis). The name given to Italy, Japan, and Germany, the countries that fought against the Allies in World War II. p. 231.

Bad Lands (bad landz). Areas in South Dakota, North Dakota, and Nebraska that are dry and rugged and have little or no vegetation. p. 366.

bank (bangk). A part of the ocean floor that rises above the rest of the surrounding ocean floor. p. 422.

barrier island (bar' ē ər ī' lənd). One of a group of islands that are just off the mainland and act as a protective obstruction, or barrier. p. 330.

bay (bā). A part of a lake or ocean extending into the land. p. 310.

bicentennial (bī sen ten' ē əl). A two-hundredth anniversary. p. 240.

Bill of Rights (bil ov rīts). The first ten amendments to the Constitution. p. 120.

bituminous (bə tü' mə nəs). Having to do with a type of coal. Bituminous coal is also called soft coal. p. 279.

blockade (blo kād'). To stop (block) a particular group from moving goods or people. During the Civil War, the North used its navy to blockade ports in the South. p. 173.

bluff (bluf). A high, steep bank or cliff. p. 368.

bog (bog). Wet, swampy land. p. 295.

bonanza (bə nan' zə). A mine producing rich ores. Something extremely profitable. p. 189.

Boston Tea Party (bôs' tən tē pär' tē). An incident staged by the Sons of Liberty to protest a tea tax imposed by Britain on the American colonies. On this occasion, 342 cases of tea, carried on British ships, were dumped into the Boston Harbor. p. 109.

boundary (boun' drē). The border of a state or country. p. 256.

boycott (boi' kot). An organized campaign in which people refuse to have any dealings with a particular group or business. p. 248.

bran (bran). The cracked outer coating of cereal grains separated from flour by sifting. Bran is used mostly in animal feed. It is high in fiber content. p. 372.

broadleaf (brôd′ lēf). Having a leaf that is broad (unlike a needle leaf). p. 300.

Bureau of Indian Affairs (byùr′ ō ov in′ dē ən ə fãrz′). A federal agency given the duties of controlling Native Americans and looking out for their interests. p. 198.

burgess (bèr′ jis). A representative in a branch of the legislature of colonial Virginia. p. 87.

butte (byüt). A small, flat-topped hill with steep sides. p. 368.

by-product (bī′ prod əkt). Something that is made or produced while the main product is being made. p. 376.

Cabinet (kab′ ə nit). A group of advisers to the President of the United States. p. 128.

cacao (kə kā′ ō). A South American plant whose seeds are used in the making of chocolate, cocoa, and cocoa butter. p. 444.

canal (kə nal′). A waterway made by people. *Canals* are dug to carry water for crops and people, for boats, and to drain swampy lands. p. 59.

canyon (kan′ yən). A very deep valley with steep sides. p. 366.

capital (kap′ ə təl). Money invested in factories, machines, or any other business. p. 206.

carpetbagger (kär′ pit bag ər). The name given to the Northern whites who moved to the South after the Civil War. p. 180.

cartographer (kär tog′ rə fər). A person who makes maps. p. 18.

cash crop (kash krop). A crop grown for sale rather than for the use of the farmer. p. 294.

causeway (kôz′ wā). A bridge made by building up earth in narrow strips until it is above the water. p. 58.

cede (sēd). To give up or surrender something to someone. p. 154.

census (sen′ səs). A government count of the number of people in a country. p. 121.

centimeter (sen′ tə mē tər). A measure of distance in the metric system. A centimeter (cm) is a little less than half an inch. p. 13.

Central Powers (sen′ trəl pou′ ərz). The name given to Germany, Austria-Hungary, and the Ottoman Empire (Turkey) during World War I. p. 229.

Chaco (chäk′ ō). The plains of the Paraná and Paraguay rivers. p. 448.

channel (chan′ əl). **1.** The path of a river. **2.** Another name for a canal. **3.** A strait, or narrow body of water, between two parts of land. p. 265.

Chief Justice (chēf jus′ tis). The leader of the Supreme Court. p. 128.

chronological order (kron ə loj′ ə kəl ôr′ dər). The listing or discussing of events in the order in which they took place. p. 30.

citizen (sit′ ə zən). A person who by birth or choice becomes a member of a country. p. 41.

citrus fruit (sit′ rəs früt). An edible fruit, with a firm thick skin and a pulpy flesh with a sweet-sour taste. Oranges, lemons, limes, and grapefruits are citrus fruits. p. 334.

civilization (siv ə lə zā′ shən). The stage of cultural development marked by the presence of cities, trade, government, art, writing, and science. p. 57.

climate (klī′ mit). The pattern of weather that a place has over a period of years. Temperature and precipitation are two important parts of *climate*. p. 268.

coastal plain (kōs′ təl plān). A wide area of flat or gently rolling land that is bordered by a large area of water. p. 262.

cold war (kōld wôr). A war of words that runs the risk of resulting in a real war. p. 234.

colony (kol′ ə nē). A place that is settled at a distance from the country that governs it. p. 70.

combine (kom′ bīn). A farm machine, developed in the late 1800s, that combines the work of the reaper, the harvester, and the thresher. p. 202.

commerce (kom′ ərs). The buying and selling of goods. p. 320.

commercial farmer (kə mèr′ shəl fär′ mər). A farmer who uses machinery to farm, and who raises crops and animals for sale. p. 204.

Committees of Correspondence (kə mit′ ēz ov kôr ə spon′ dəns). Colonial groups that maintained contact with and sent news to each other through letters. p. 108.

common (kom′ ən). The name given to the land in the center of most colonial New England towns. Such land belonged to everyone in the town. p. 92.

Commonwealth (kom′ ən welth). An association of countries that were once part of the British Empire. p. 424.

communicate (kə myü′ nə kāt). To exchange or give information in any way, such as by talking or writing. p. 207.

communism (kom′ yə niz əm). A social and economic system in which most property is owned by the government and shared by the governed. p. 234.

compass rose (kum′ pəs rōz). A small drawing on a map, used to show directions. p. 8.

competition (kom pə tish′ ən). The effort made by a business to gain a bigger share of the market for itself. p. 206.

conifer (kō′ nə fər). A cone-bearing, evergreen tree. p. 427.

conservation (kon sər vā′ shən). The management of natural resources in such a way as to prevent their waste or complete destruction. p. 242.

constitution (kon stə tü′ shən). A set of laws by which a country is governed. p. 118.

consulate (kon′ sə lit). The building or office in which a consul lives. A consul is an official sent to a foreign nation by his or her government to represent it. p. 339.

continent (kon′ tə nənt). A huge area of land. There are seven continents: North America, South

America, Europe, Africa, Asia, Australia, and Antarctica. p. 6.

Continental Congress (kon tə nen' təl kong' gris). The name given to the meeting of the group of representatives from the American colonies. p. 109.

Continental Divide (kon tə nen' təl də vīd'). A high ridge dividing rivers or streams that flow to opposite sides of a continent. In the United States, the Continental Divide is in the Rocky Mountains. p. 388.

coral (kôr' əl). A limestone-like hard substance made up of the skeletons of certain types of tiny sea animals. p. 330.

cotton gin (kot' ən jin). A machine used to separate cotton from its seeds. p. 150.

crop lien (krop lēn). A first claim on the profit of a crop. p. 178.

culture (kul' chər). The way of life of a group of people including their customs, traditions, and values. p. 50.

custom (kus' təm). A long-established way of doing things. p. 50.

debt (det). Something, usually money, that is owed to someone. p. 94.

deciduous (di sij' ù əs). Losing leaves at the end of a season. p. 295.

Declaration of Independence (dek lə rā' shən ov in di pen' dəns). The document that stated the reasons for the desire of the American colonies to be independent of British control. p. 112.

delta (del' tə). Land built up by silt deposits at the mouth of a river. p. 265.

democracy (di mok' rə sē). Rule or government of, for, and by the people. p. 92.

depression (di presh' ən). An economic condition in which busines is very bad and large numbers of people are unemployed. p. 244.

derrick (der' ik). A tall steel frame that is built over an oil well and that holds the equipment used for drilling and hoisting. p. 356.

descendant (di sen' dənt). One who comes from a specific ancestor. p. 46.

descent (di sent'). Ancestral background. p. 424.

desert (dez' ərt). A very dry place, with little rainfall and few plants. p. 55.

developed country (di vel' əpt kun' trē). A country that has a high level of industrialization and technology. p. 441.

developing country (di vel' əp ing kun' trē). A country that is trying to increase its level of industrialization and technology. p. 441.

dictatorship (dik tā' tər ship). Harsh rule by one person or group. p. 230.

diesel fuel (dē' zəl fyü' əl). A fuel used in trucks, buses, cars, and ships that have a specific type of engine. p. 357.

diplomat (dip' lə mat). One who represents his or her government in important dealings with other nations. p. 132.

District of Columbia (dis' trikt ov kə lum' bē ə). A part of the United States—not part of any state— set aside as the capital of the United States of America. p. 129.

dry farming (drī fär' ming). Farming techniques, used in areas of little rainfall and no irrigation, that are designed to keep moisture in the soil. p. 188.

Dust Bowl (dust bōl). The area in the Great Plains in which soil erosion caused by poor farming methods and a long period of little rainfall resulted in severe dust storms. p. 244.

earthquake (ėrth' kwāk). A shaking, or trembling, of the earth, often leaving cracks in the earth's surface, that is caused by the shifting of layers of the earth far beneath the surface. p. 405.

economic activity (ē kə nom' ik ak tiv' ə tē). Any activity that has to do with the production or selling of goods and services. p. 432.

electronics (i lek tron' iks). An area of scientific study from which television, radio, computers, and other electrical devices have developed. p. 358.

elevation (el ə vā' shən). The height of something. The *elevation* of land is its distance above or below sea level, usually measured in feet or meters. p. 286.

emancipate (i man' sə pāt). To set free. p. 174.

emigrate (em' ə grāt). To leave one's native land. p. 212.

empire (em' pīr). The territories and peoples under the control of a powerful nation. p. 58.

Equator (i kwā' tər). A line, drawn on maps and globes, that circles the earth exactly halfway between the North Pole and the South Pole. It is labeled 0° latitude. p. 4.

Era of Good Feelings (ir'ə ov gùd fē' lings). The period following the War of 1812 (during the presidency of James Monroe) when the United States experienced peace and unity. p. 139.

erode (i rōd'). To wear away the earth's surface. Wind and water can *erode* the earth. p. 338.

erosion (i rō' zhən). The wearing away of the earth's surface by wind, running water, waves, or ice. p. 353.

evaporate (i vap' ə rāt). To change from a liquid into gas (vapor). p. 370.

event (i vent'). An important happening. p. 27.

evergreen (ev' ər grēn). Having green leaves (either broadleaf or needle) all year round. p. 295.

executive branch (eg zek' yə tiv branch). The part of government responsible for carrying out the laws that Congress passes. The President is its head. p. 119.

expedition (eks pə dish' ən). A journey undertaken for a specific purpose, such as exploration. p. 72.

explore (ek splôr'). To search for new things and places. p. 64.

export (ek spôrt′). Something that is sent to another country, usually for sale there. Also, to send something to another country for sale. p. 341.

express (ek spres′). Traveling with very few or no stops between places. p. 24.

factory (fak′ tər ē). A building in which goods are made by machine. p. 33.

federal (fed′ ər əl). Having to do with a form of political organization in which power is divided between national government and the governments of the states. p. 119.

feedlot (fēd′ lot). A plot of land where livestock are fed and fattened for sale. p. 353.

fertile (fėr′ təl). Able to produce plentifully. p. 294.

fish hatchery (fish hach′ ər ē). A place where fish eggs are hatched and the young fish raised until they are old enough to be released in streams. p. 410.

fleet (flēt). A group of ships sailing together for a given purpose. p. 290.

foliage (fō′ lē ij). The leaves of trees. p. 300.

foothill (fút′ hil). A hill at the foot or near the bottom of mountains or higher hills. p. 312.

foreign policy (fôr′ ən pol′ ə sē). The way in which one country deals with another. p. 232.

fossil (fos′ əl). The hardened remains or traces of an ancient plant or animal. p. 393.

Freedman's Bureau (frēd′ mənz byûr′ ō). A governmental agency set up after the Civil War to help the freed slaves and others who were poor and homeless. p. 178.

free state (frē stāt). A state, before the Civil War, in which slavery was not permitted. p. 166.

frost-free (frôst frē). A term used to describe the period when the temperature is always above freezing. p. 332.

fuel (fyü′ əl). A substance burned to produce power or heat. p. 276.

garment (gär′ mənt). An article of clothing. p. 341.

gasohol (gas′ ə hôl). A fuel produced by mixing grain alcohol with gasoline. p. 373.

geologist (jē ol′ ə jist). A scientist who studies rocks and rock formations. p. 355.

ghetto (get′ ō). A neighborhood where people of similar ethnic, racial, or religious backgrounds live. p. 213.

glacier (glā′ shər). A large body of slowly moving ice. p. 368.

grain elevator (grān el′ ə vā tər). A large building for storing grain. p. 375.

grandfather clause (grand′ fä ᴛʜər klôz). Laws passed in the South in the 1890s that allowed only those persons to vote whose father or grandfather had voted on or before January 1867. p. 183.

Grange (grānj). The first major farmers group, organized to get better prices for farm products and as a social club. p. 205.

gristmill (grist′ mil). A place where grain is ground into flour. p. 302.

gulf (gulf). A part of the ocean that extends into the land. p. 348.

gully (gul′ ē). A ditch or small valley dug in the earth by running water. p. 366.

hail (hāl). Precipitation in the form of pieces of compacted ice and snow. p. 370.

harbor (här′ bər). A protected body of water, safe for ships and other vessels. p. 310.

hemisphere (hem′ ə sfir). The name given to any half of the earth. p. 2.

henequen (hen′ ə kin). The fiber of a plant grown mainly in Yucatán, used for making rope and other coarse materials. p. 443.

Hessian (hesh′ ən). A German soldier hired to fight for the British in the Revolutionary War. p. 115.

historian (his tôr′ ē ən). A person who studies the past and often writes about it. p. 37.

homestead (hōm′ sted). A house and the land surrounding it. Often, land given to a family or sold to them at a low rate to encourage settlement. p. 191.

House of Burgesses (hous ov bėr′ jis əs). The representative assembly in colonial Virginia. p. 87.

human rights (hyü′ mən rīts). The basic civil, economic, political, and social rights of all people. p. 247.

human sacrifice (hyü′ mən sak′ rə fīs). The killing of one or more people as offerings to a god. p. 58.

humid (hyü′ mid). Damp or wet. Humidity is measured by the amount of water vapor in the air at a given time. p. 333.

hurricane (hėr′ ə kān). A tropical storm with strong winds and heavy rains. p. 333.

hydroelectric power (hī drō i lek′ trik pou′ ər). Electricity produced from moving water. p. 267.

immigrant (im′ ə grənt). A person from one country who comes into another country to live there. p. 151.

impeach (im pēch′). To charge a public official with having done something illegal while in office. p. 180.

import (im pôrt′). To bring in goods from a foreign country, usually for the purpose of selling those goods. Also, the goods themselves. p. 293.

inauguration (in ô gya rā′ shən). A ceremony to put someone in office. p. 126.

income (in′ kum). Money earned. p. 244.

income tax (in′ kum taks). A tax based on the amount of money earned. p. 205.

indentured servant (in den′ chərd sėr′ vənt). A person who sold his or her services for a certain period of time in exchange for free passage to a foreign land. p. 86.

independence (in di pen′ dəns). Freedom from the control of another country or person. p. 106.

489

indigo (in′ də gō). A plant from which blue dye is made. p. 94.

Industrial Revolution (in dus′ trē əl rev ə lü′ shən). The period of great change in the way people worked and lived, brought about by the invention of power-driven machines. p. 149.

inflation (in flā′ shən). An economic condition in which the value of money decreases and the price of goods increases. p. 158.

initiative (i nish′ ē ə tiv). A procedure that allows voters to introduce a bill they would like to see become a law. p. 193.

inland sea (in′ lənd sē). A body of water, surrounded by land, that is too large to be considered a lake. p. 368.

interchangeable parts (in tər chān′ jə bəl pärts). Identical parts that can be used in place of each other in making a product. p. 150.

intermontane (in tər mon′ tān). Having to do with a land or region that lies between mountain ranges. p. 388.

irrigate (ir′ ə gāt). To bring water to crops, usually through canals, ditches, or pipes. p. 266.

island (ī′ lənd). A body of land completely surrounded by water. p. 264.

isolate (ī′ sə lāt). To set apart and alone from others. p. 237.

isthmus (is′ məs). A narrow strip of land joining two larger bodies of land. p. 73.

Jacksonian democracy (jak sō′ nē ən di mok′ rə sē). The increased participation in government by the people. Occurred during the presidency of Andrew Jackson. p. 141.

journal (jėr′ nəl). A diary-like record of events, experiences, and thoughts kept on a regular basis. p. 84.

judicial branch (jü dish′ əl branch). The part of government that is in charge of deciding the meaning of laws. p. 119.

key (kē). **1.** A device on a map used to tell what real things or places the symbols on the map stand for. p. 16. **2.** A small piece of land, barely above sea level, usually made of coral and limestone. For example, the Florida Keys. p. 330.

kilometer (kil′ ə mē tər). A measure of distance in the metric system. A *kilometer* (km) is a little more than half a mile. p. 13.

landform (land′ fôrm). A feature of the earth's surface created by nature. p. 261.

land grant (land grant). The distribution of land to settlers, railroads, and farming (agricultural) colleges by the government in the late 1800s. Also, the land so distributed. p. 191.

landlocked (land′ lokt). Having no coastline. A *landlocked* country is surrounded on all sides by other countries. p. 452.

landmark (land′ märk). An easily recognizable or famous object that marks or identifies an area. p. 301.

landscape (land′ skāp). The landforms of an area. p. 286.

latitude (lat′ ə tüd). Distance, measured in degrees, north and south of the equator. Lines of *latitude* are used to locate places on the earth. p. 9.

league (lēg). A group of people joined together for a common purpose. p. 53.

legislative branch (lej′ is lā tiv branch). The part of government responsible for making laws. p. 119.

levee (lev′ ē). A wide wall built with earth and used for flood control. p. 350.

livestock (līv′ stok). Farm animals raised for home use or profit. p. 294.

Llanos (lä′ nōs). A large plain in northern South America that is drained by the Orinoco River. *Llanos* is the Spanish word for "plains." p. 448.

lock (lok). An enclosed area on a canal, with gates on both ends, used for raising or lowering ships as they go from one water level to another. p. 428.

London Company (lun′ dən kum′ pə nē). A group formed for the purpose of establishing an English colony in Virginia. Members of the group were to share in the costs and the profits. p. 84.

Lone Star Republic (lōn stär ri pub′ lik). The independent nation of Texas (1836-1845), so called because its flag had only one star. p. 153.

longhouse (lông′ hous). A shelter built by Native Americans, especially the Iroquois. p. 52.

longitude (lon′ jə tüd). Distance, measured in degrees, east and west of the prime meridian. Lines of *longitude* are used to locate places on the earth. All *longitude* lines pass through the North Pole and the South Pole. p. 9.

Loyalist (loi′ ə list). A colonist who was a supporter of Great Britain and King George III. p. 114.

lubricant (lü′ brə kənt). A substance used to make a slippery coating between two surfaces to prevent wear on those surfaces. p. 357.

lumberjack (lum′ bər jak). One whose work involves cutting down trees for commercial use. p. 297.

Manufacturing Belt (man yə fak′ chər ing belt). The Middle Atlantic region, so called for its many factories and mills that manufacture a wide variety of goods. p. 316.

maritime (mar′ ə tīm). Having to do with the sea. p. 426.

market weight (mär′ kit wāt). The weight that an animal must reach before it is sent to be sold. p. 373.

marshland (märsh′ land). Soft, wet land that is usually soaked with water. p. 348.

massacre (mas′ ə kər). The killing of a large group of people who have little or no defense. p. 108.

mass production (mas prǝ duk′ shǝn). The making of goods in large quantities, usually by machine. p. 150.

mass transit (mas tran′ sit). A way of moving a great number of people from one place to another at the same time. Trains, subways, buses, and airplanes are types of *mass transit*. p. 23.

Mayflower Compact (mā′ flou ǝr kom′ pakt). A document signed by the Pilgrims by which they agreed to make laws as needed for the colony's good and to obey these laws. p. 88.

megalopolis (meg ǝ lop′ ǝ lis). A group of cities so close to one another that they seem to form a continuous urban area. p. 323.

meridian (mǝ rid′ ē ǝn). Another name for a line of longitude. p. 10.

mestizo (mes tē′ zō). A person of mixed European and Native American ancestry. p. 442.

metropolitan area (met rǝ pol′ ǝ tǝn ār′ ē ǝ). An area made up of a large city or several large cities and the surrounding towns, cities, and other communities. p. 302.

Middle Passage (mid′ ǝl pas′ ij). The name given to the trip from Africa to America on a slave ship. p. 96.

migratory bird (mī grǝ tôr′ ē bėrd). A type of bird that flies south (to a warmer area) for the winter. At the end of winter, *migratory birds* return to their northern homes. p. 335.

mileage chart (mī′ lij chärt). A table used to show the number of road miles between places. p. 22.

militia (mǝ lish′ ǝ). An organized military force usually called upon during emergencies. p. 114.

milling (mil′ ing). The grinding of grain into flour. Also, the processing of steel and other products. p. 282.

mineral (min′ ǝr ǝl). A substance, found in the earth, that is neither plant nor animal. p. 289.

mineral spring (min′ ǝr ǝl spring). Water, rising from the ground, that is thought to cure illness and relieve pain because of its high mineral content. Hot Springs, Arkansas, is famous for its *mineral springs*. p. 361.

Minuteman (min′ it man). A member of an army of citizens, at the time of the Revolutionary War, who claimed to be ready to fight the British at "a minute's notice." p. 110.

missionary (mish′ ǝ ner ē). A person sent to teach a religion to people of a different faith and to provide them with any help they might need. p. 78.

monopoly (mǝ nop′ ǝ lē). Sole control of an entire industry. p. 209.

monument (mon′ yǝ mǝnt). Something, such as a building, tower, or sculpture, built in remembrance of a person or an event. p. 380.

mound (mound). A pile of earth used as the platform for an important building or, by groups of Native Americans, as a burial site. p. 48.

mountain (moun′ tǝn). A part of the earth's surface that rises sharply from the land around it. A mountain has a broad base and narrows to a peak. p. 262.

mountain men (moun′ tǝn men). Fur trappers who played an important part in the expansion of the United States in the 1800s. p. 159.

mouth (mouth). A place where a stream or river enters a larger body of water. p. 265.

muckraker (muk′ rā kǝr). A person who writes about wrongdoing in business and politics. p. 242.

Native American (nā′ tiv ǝ mer′ ǝ kǝn). One of any group of American Indians; people whose ancestors came to America long before anyone else. p. 39.

NATO (nā′ tō). (Stands for North Atlantic Treaty Organization.) A military alliance between the United States and some countries in Europe. p. 235.

naturalist (nach′ ǝr ǝ list). A person who studies nature. p. 240.

naturalize (nach′ ǝr ǝ līz). To become a citizen of a country other than the one in which one was born. p. 212.

natural resource (nach′ ǝr ǝl ri sôrs′). Something that is provided by nature and is useful to people. p. 275.

naval stores (nā′ vǝl stôrz). Supplies made from pine trees, such as ships' masts, tar, and turpentine, produced and shipped by the Carolina settlers to England for use in England's navy. p. 94.

neutral (nü′ trǝl). Standing apart in an argument or fight and not taking sides. p. 228.

New Deal (nü dēl). A term used to describe policies put forward by President Franklin Roosevelt to fight the Great Depression. In the *New Deal*, the government created jobs and granted other types of aid to people. p. 245.

nitrate (nī′ trāt). A mineral used in the manufacture of fertilizers. p. 451.

North Pole (nôrth pōl). The most northern place in the world. The *North Pole* is located in the Arctic Ocean. p. 4.

Northwest Passage (nôrth west′ pas′ ij). A nonexistent water route, sought by early explorers, that would provide a shortcut from Europe to Asia and the East Indies via North America. p. 77.

nuclear energy (nü′ klē ǝr en′ ǝr jē). The power released from the nucleus, or core, of an atom. p. 280.

oasis (ō ā′ sis). A place in a desert where there is water; a fertile place in a dry area. p. 396.

oath (ōth). A solemn promise. p. 126.

ocean current (ō′ shǝn kėr′ ǝnt). A regular movement of the surface water of an ocean, caused mostly by winds and differences of water temperature. p. 405.

official language (ǝ fish′ ǝl lang′ gwij). The language authorized by a nation's government as the language of that nation, but not necessarily the language of the majority of the people. Government documents are written in the *official language*. Some countries have several *official languages*. p. 425.

oil shale (oil shāl). Rock containing a substance from which an oil-like product can be made. p. 391.

Old Ironsides (ōld ī′ ərn sīdz). The nickname given to the *Constitution*, a ship that became famous for its role in defeating the British in the War of 1812. p. 138.

open-pit mine (ō′ pən pit mīn). A mine in the form of a large hole dug in the earth's surface, rather than in the form of underground tunnels. p. 376.

open-range grazing (ō′ pən rānj grā′ zing). The unrestricted grazing of cattle. Such grazing ended with the use of barbed-wire fences by farmers in the late 1800s. p. 190.

oral history (ôr′ əl his′ tər ē). The history or tradition of a people handed down from one generation to another by word of mouth. p. 35.

ore (ôr). A material containing the mineral for which it is mined. Examples are iron *ore* and copper *ore*. p. 280.

Oregon Trail (ôr′ ə gon trāl). The route from Missouri to Oregon used by settlers moving to the northwest in the 1800s. p. 158.

overburden (ō′ vər bėr′ dən). The layers of earth that cover a bed of coal. In strip mining, the *overburden* is removed by machines, loaded into trucks, and dumped elsewhere. p. 338.

overgraze (ō vər grāz′). To allow animals to graze, or feed upon grass, for so long that the grass dies or is pulled up by the roots, allowing erosion to take place. p. 354.

Pampas (pam′ pəz). The name given to the large grasscovered plains of Uruguay and Argentina, in South America. p. 448.

panhandle (pan′ han dəl). A narrow strip of land. p. 352.

Parliament (pär′ lə mənt). The lawmaking body of England. Also, the lawmaking body of Canada. p. 106.

pasteurize (pas′ chə rīz). To heat a liquid to a high temperature and then rapidly chill it. This is a process used to kill harmful bacteria in liquids such as milk. p. 375.

Patagonia (pat ə gō′ nē ə). A barren plain in southern Argentina. p. 448.

patent (pat′ ənt). An official paper giving an inventor the right to be the only person to make or sell his or her invention for a certain time. p. 208.

patriot (pā′ trē ət). A person who loves and loyally supports his or her country. In the struggle against the British, a person who fought for the independence of the American colonies. p. 115.

Peace Corps (pēs kôr). A program started by President John F. Kennedy to help people in the developing world. p. 236.

peninsula (pə nin′ sə lə). A piece of land extending into the water from a larger body of land. p. 84.

permafrost (pėr′ mə frôst). A permanently frozen layer of the soil, sometimes extending to great depths below the earth's surface in very cold regions. p. 406.

persecution (pėr sə kyü′ shən). The harsh treatment of a person or group. p. 231.

petrochemical (pet rō kem′ə kəl). A chemical or synthetic material produced from petroleum or natural gas. p. 316.

petroleum (pə trō′ lē əm). The oily liquid, found in the earth, from which gasoline, kerosene, and many other things are made. p. 276.

physical map (fiz′ ə kəl map). A map that shows the kinds of land surfaces on the earth. p. 261.

pilgrim (pil′ grəm). A person who travels for religious reasons. p. 87.

pioneer (pī ə nir′). A person who does something first, preparing the way for others. The first settlers were *pioneers*. p. 159.

pitchblende (pich′ blend). The brownish black mineral that is the chief source of uranium. p. 430.

plain (plān). A wide area of flat or gently rolling land. p. 261.

plantation (plan tā′ shən). A large farm on which one main crop is grown. p. 95.

plateau (pla tō′). A large, high, rather level area that is raised above the surrounding land. p. 262.

political map (pə lit′ ə kəl map). A map that shows the different countries in the world or the different states in a country. p. 256.

poll tax (pōl taks). A tax a person had to pay in order to be allowed to vote. p. 183.

pollute (pə lüt′). To make the earth's soil, water, and air unclean by putting waste materials into them. p. 266.

population (pop yə lā′ shən). The number of people living in an area. p. 20.

population density (pop yə lā′ shən den′ sə tē). The average number of people per given unit of area (such as a square mile or square kilometer) in a state, country, or other area. p. 259.

Populist party (pop′ yə list pär′ tē). A political party that showed its greatest strength in the election of 1892. p. 205.

poultry (pōl′ trē). Chickens, turkeys, and other birds raised for eggs or meat. p. 315.

poverty (pov′ ər tē). The condition of being poor. p. 342.

preamble (prē′ am bəl). An introduction. p. 113.

precipitation (pri sip ə tā′ shən). Moisture that falls on the earth's surface in the form of rain, snow, sleet, hail, fog, or mist. p. 268.

presidio (pri sid′ ē ō). A Spanish word meaning "military fort." p. 155.

Prime Meridian (prīm mə rid′ē ən). A line of longitude that passes through the Royal Observatory in Greenwich, England. It is the 0° line of longitude, from which distances east and west are measured in degrees of longitude. p. 10.

privateer (prī və tir'). A privately owned, armed ship having the government's permission to attack enemy ships. In the Revolutionary War, *privateers* joined the United States in fighting the British. p. 116.

proclamation (prok lə mā' shən). An official announcement. p. 174.

promontory (prom' ən tôr ē). High rocky land that juts out into the sea along a coastline. p. 286.

protectorate (prə tek' tər it). A place or country under the protection of another country. p. 226.

province (prov' əns). A division of a country. In Canada, a *province* is similar to one of our states. p. 422.

public opinion (pub' lik ə pin' yən). The way most people feel about something. p. 225.

Puritan (pyùr' ə tən). A member of certain Protestant groups in sixteenth- and seventeenth-century England or New England. p. 90.

pyramid (pir' ə mid). A large building with a square base and triangular sides that are angled towards one another. p. 57.

Quaker (kwā' kər). A member of a religious group. *Quakers* also call themselves "Friends." p. 98.

quarry (kwôr' ē). A place from which materials such as marble, stone, slate, or limestone are cut, dug, or blasted. p. 289.

quota (kwō' tə). A fixed, and usually limited, number. p. 214.

radioactive (rā dē ō ak' tiv). Giving off harmful rays. p. 376.

rain shadow (rān shad' ō). The condition of dryness that occurs in places that are on the protected side of high mountains. p. 390.

ratify (rat' ə fī). To give formal approval to. p. 122.

ration (rash' ən). To put a limit on the amount of something that someone can buy or use. p. 233.

recall (ri kôl'). The removal, by the voters, of a person from elected office before the end of his or her term. p. 193.

Reconstruction (rē kən struk' shən). The name given to the period (1865–1877) following the Civil War. p. 177.

recycle (rē sī' kəl). To process used or discarded goods in order to create materials or goods that can be used again. p. 299.

reef (rēf). A chain of rocks or coral at or near the surface of the water. p. 330.

referendum (ref ə ren' dəm). A procedure that allows the people, rather than elected representatives, to vote on a law. p. 193.

refinery (ri fī' nər ē). A building with machines that change a natural resource to make it pure or to make different products from it. p. 356.

reform (ri fôrm'). To change with the hope of making better. p. 216.

refugee (ref yə jē'). A person who flees to another place for protection or safety. p. 178.

region (rē' jən). A part of the earth's surface that has common characteristics. p. 254.

relief map (ri lēf' map). A map that shows the elevation of land on the earth's surface. p. 261.

renewable resource (ri nü' ə bəl ri sôrs'). A resource that can be replaced by nature or by people. p. 296.

representative (rep ri zen' tə tiv). One who is elected to decide matters for others. A *representative* is usually in a lawmaking group. p. 87.

republic (ri pub' lik). The political system in which the people elect representatives to manage their country. p. 119.

reservation (rez ər vā' shən). A piece of public land set aside, or reserved, by the government for the use of a particular group of people. p. 198.

reserves (ri zėrvz'). Supplies of fuel or other things available or set aside for future use. p. 279.

resort (ri zôrt'). A place providing recreational and other facilities for people on vacation. p. 27.

revolution (rev ə lü' shən). 1. Complete, often violent, change in government. p. 106. 2. One complete turn of the earth around the sun. p. 273.

rodeo (rō' dē ō). A *rodeo* is a public show or contest in which those taking part may ride a bronco or a bull, rope a calf, or wrestle a steer. *Rodeo* is Spanish for "surround" or "round up." p. 354.

rotation (rō tā' shən). One complete turn of the earth on its axis. The earth takes 24 hours to complete one *rotation*. p. 273.

rural (rùr' əl). Having to do with the countryside; nonurban. p. 214.

sanitation (san ə tā' shən). The making of clean and healthful conditions, especially in terms of water supply, garbage, and sewage. p. 216.

savanna (sə van' ə). A treeless grassland, or a grassland with scattered trees and bushes, especially in tropical lands that have seasonal rains. p. 448.

saw timber (sô tim' bər). Lumber used for building. p. 297.

scalawag (skal' ə wag). A term used in the South after the Civil War to describe white Southerners who sided with the new state governments. p. 180.

scale (skāl). The relationship between real size and size used on a map or model. Also, the line, drawn on maps, that shows this relationship. p. 12.

schedule (skej' ùl). A printed timetable, such as a *schedule* listing the exact times of the coming and goings of trains, buses, and planes. Also, a timetable giving the days and times of events. p. 24.

seam (sēm). A layer of coal or other mineral. p. 338.

season (sē′ zən). A period of the year. There are four *seasons* in most areas of this country—spring, summer, autumn, and winter. p. 269.

secede (si sēd′). To withdraw from an organization or nation. p. 171.

secretary (sek′ rə ter ē). An officer of state who heads a government administrative department. p. 128.

secret ballot (sē′ krit bal′ ət). A term used to describe a way of voting in which only the voter knows how he or she has voted. p. 205.

sectionalism (sek′ shə nə liz əm). The attaching of great importance to the beliefs or interests of a region. p. 171.

semidesert (sem ē dez′ ərt). An area that has little rainfall or plant cover. A *semidesert* area is not quite as dry as a desert, nor does it have as much plant cover as a grassland. p. 389.

Seneca Falls convention (sen′ ə kə fôlz kən ven′ shən). A meeting in 1848 led by Elizabeth Stanton and Lucretia Mott to outline the goals of a women's rights movement. p. 143.

separation of powers (sep ə rā′ shən ov pou′ ərz). The division of governmental power into three parts, or branches: legislative, executive, and judiciary. p. 119.

Separatist (sep′ rət əst). **1.** A person wishing to separate from the Church of England; a Pilgrim. p. 87. **2.** One who wants political independence for a part of a country. p 425.

sharecropping (shār′ krop ing). Farming land for the owner in return for a share of the crops. p. 178.

shearing (shir′ ing). Cutting the wool off sheep or other animals. p. 391.

shoal (shōl). An underwater sandbar. *Shoals* make the water above them shallow. p. 330.

silt (silt). Very fine pieces of soil and ground stone carried by moving water. p. 348.

sit-in (sit′ in). A form of group protest in which the group sits in a public place for a long period of time. p. 248.

sleet (slēt). Frozen rain. p. 313.

smelting (smel′ ting). The process of separating metals from other materials in their ores. p. 280.

smog (smog). A mixture of smoke and fog. p. 416.

social work (sō′ shəl wėrk). A profession in which the worker helps people with their problems. p. 217.

solvent (sol′ vənt). A substance, usually in liquid form, that is capable of thinning or dissolving another substance. p. 357.

sorghum grain (sôr′ gəm grān). Grain from any of a group of tall grassy plants that look somewhat like corn plants. *Sorghum grain* is an important crop worldwide and is used in the making of syrup, as feed for livestock, and in the manufacture of brushes and brooms. p. 352.

sound (sound). A long, wide stretch of water connecting two larger bodies of water or separating a main body of land from an island. p. 288.

source (sôrs). The place where a stream or river begins. p. 265.

South Pole (south pōl). The most southern place in the world. The *South Pole* is located on the continent of Antarctica. p. 4.

spermaceti (spėr mə set′ ē). A waxlike substance obtained from the oil of the sperm whale. p. 291.

spiritual (spir′ ə chù əl). A type of religious song, originally composed and sung by slaves on Southern plantations. p. 98.

strait (strāt). A narrow body of water connecting two larger bodies of water. p. 46.

strip mining (strip mī′ ning). A type of mining in which large machines strip off the overlying material and dump it to one side to expose the mineral. *Strip mining* is often used when minerals are near the earth's surface. p. 338.

subsistence farmer (səb sis′ təns fär′ mər). A farmer who grows just enough crops to take care of his or her family's needs with little, if any, left over for sale. p. 202.

subtropical (sub trop′ ə kəl). Having to do with the regions bordering the tropics. p. 352.

suburb (sub′ ərb). A smaller community on the outskirts of a large city. p. 215.

subway (sub′ wā). An underground train used to transport a great number of people from one place to another, usually within a city. p. 23.

survey (sər vā′). To measure the size, shape, length, and width of a piece of land. p. 186.

swamp (swomp). Wet, spongy land. p. 34.

symbol (sim′ bəl). Something that stands for, or suggests, something else. p. 16.

synthetic (sin thet′ ik). Something that is not made directly from natural materials. Nylon is a *synthetic* that is made from chemicals produced from coal and other natural minerals. Also, artificial. p. 243.

telegraph (tel′ ə graf). A message sent electrically by wire. p. 150.

temperate (tem′ pər it). Not extreme. A *temperate* climate is neither extremely hot or cold nor extremely wet or dry. p. 328.

temperature (tem′ pər ə chər). The amount of heat or cold as measured on a given scale, such as the Fahrenheit scale or the Celsius scale. p. 268.

temperature extreme (tem′ pər ə chər ek strēm′). The highest or lowest recorded temperature. p. 288.

tenement (ten′ ə mənt). An apartment house with poor safety, sanitation, and comfort conditions. p. 215.

tepee (tē′ pē). The tentlike shelter used by certain tribes of native Americans. The *tepee* was made of buffalo skins stitched together, draped over poles, and secured to the ground. p. 54.

term (tėrm). The time during which an official may hold office. p. 129.

terraces (ter′ is əs). A series of flat, wide ledges cut into the side of a hill or mountain to make places where crops can be grown. p. 61.

textile (teks′ təl). Having to do with cloth. Also, woven fabric. p. 149.

tidal pools (tī′ dəl pülz). Pools of water left behind when the ocean changes from high tide to low tide. p. 358.

tidewater (tīd′ wôt ər). A low-lying coastal area often flooded by seawater. p. 328.

timberline (tim′ bər līn). The elevation above which trees, or timber, cannot grow. p. 386.

tornado (tôr nā′ dō). A violent, high-powered windstorm that can cause much destruction. A *tornado* is nicknamed "twister" because of the storm's swirling winds that form a cone-shaped cloud. p. 351.

tourism (tùr′ iz əm). The industry made up of the businesses that encourage tourists to come to an area and those that take care of tourists' needs once they have arrived. p. 299.

town meeting (toun mē′ ting). A meeting of the inhabitants of a town to discuss or vote on town affairs. p. 92.

tract (trakt). An area of land. p. 297.

Trail of Tears (trāl ov tirz). The name given by the Cherokees to their journey from Georgia to Oklahoma after they had been forced off their land by the United States government. p. 142.

transcontinental (trans kon tə nen′ təl). Going across a continent. p. 193.

transportation (trans pər tā′ shən). The moving of people and goods from one place to another. p. 33.

trawler (trô′ lər). A boat used for commercial fishing. p. 291.

tree farming (trē fär′ ming). The use of scientific methods to grow trees for the sale and commercial use of their lumber. p. 336.

tribe (trīb). A group held together by family and social ties, geography, or custom. p. 46.

tropical rain forest (trop′ ə kəl rān fôr′ ist). A very thick forest, usually of broad-leaved trees and vines, in an area where rainfall is very heavy and temperatures are warm all year long. p. 444.

Tropic of Cancer (trop′ ik ov kan′ sər). A line of latitude that circles the earth at 23½° north latitude. p. 9.

Tropic of Capricorn (trop′ ik ov kap′ rə kôrn). A line of latitude that circles the earth at 23½° south latitude. p. 9.

truck farm (truk färm). A farm on which large amounts of many types of vegetables are grown for sale. p. 315.

tundra (tun′ drə). A rolling or nearly level, treeless plain found in Arctic regions. p. 406.

tungsten (tung′ stən). A hard, heavy metal that is often mixed with steel to create a material hard enough to use in the making of machine tools. *Tungsten* is also used in electric light bulbs. p. 432.

turnpike (tèrn′ pīk). In early America, a toll road. Today, any high-speed highway. p. 146.

Underground Railroad (un dər ground′ rāl′ rōd). The secret routes by which abolitionists helped runaway slaves to escape to free states or to Canada where they could build new lives as free people. p. 169.

union (yün′ yən). **1.** A group of people or states, p. 129. **2.** In industry, a group formed for the purpose of protecting the interests of its members. p. 210.

upland (up′ lənd). High land. p. 286

urban (èr′ bən). Having to do with a town or city. p. 214.

valley (val′ ē). A long, low area, usually between hills or mountains or along a river. p. 312.

vitamin (vī′ tə min). Any of a group of substances, found in foods, that are needed for health and for the working of the body and its parts but that do not directly give energy or aid growth. p. 373.

volcano (vol kā′ nō). An opening in the earth, usually at the top of a cone-shaped hill, out of which gases, rock, ashes, and/or lava may pour from time to time. Also, the hill around such an opening. p. 405.

War Hawk (wôr hôk). A person, especially in Congress, who supported the War of 1812. In modern times, one who favors declaring war on another country. p. 137.

water cycle (wôt′ ər sī′ kəl). The process by which water evaporates from the earth's surface, forms clouds, condenses, and returns to the earth in the form of precipitation. p. 370.

water vapor (wôt′ ər vā′ pər). Water in its gaseous form. *Water vapor* is not visible. p. 352.

weather (weᴛʜ′ ər). The condition of the air at a certain time, in terms of precipitation, temperature, and other factors. p. 268.

wheat germ (hwēt jèrm). The innermost part of the wheat kernel. *Wheat germ* is high in vitamin content. p. 372.

White House (hwīt hous). The residence of the President of the United States. The *White House* is located in Washington, D.C., p. 131.

wholesale market (hōl′ sāl mär′ kit). A place where products are brought in large quantities and then sold in smaller quantities to businesses. p. 375.

yield (yēld). The total amount produced, p. 372.

zoning (zō′ ning). The division of a city into parts reserved for specific purposes. *Zoning* provides for residential, business, and other areas. p. 216.

INDEX

CREDITS

Unit openers: Gregory Hergert
Graphs and charts: Wendy Levenson
Maps: R. R. Donnelley Cartographic Services

State table art: Kathy Hendrickson
State flags: Reproduced by courtesy of Encyclopaedia Britannica, Inc. From *Compton's Encyclopedia* © 1980
Canadian and Latin American flags: The Flag Research Center

Chapter 1 3: © Earl Roberge/Photo Researchers, Inc. 4: Monroe Eisenberg. 16: Robert Lee II. 18: Doug Bates. 19: Silver Burdett, courtesy Northeast Airways. 20: © Barry Hennings/Photo Researchers, Inc. 23: © Tom McHugh/Photo Researchers, Inc. 24: W. McKinney/Shostal Associates. 25: Lakeland Bus Lines. 27: Peter Krempasky.

Chapter 2 31: © George Holton/Photo Researchers, Inc. 32: t. © 1984 William Hubbell/Woodfin Camp & Associates; b. Crazy Horse Foundation/Photo by Robb DeWall. 33: © Jack Spratt/Picture Group. 34: Culver Pictures. 35: Elizabeth Crews/Stock, Boston. 36: The Bettmann Archive. 37: William Franklin McMahon. 38: Wide World Photos. 39: Victoria Beller-Smith for Silver Burdett. 40: Harry T. Peters Collection, Museum of the City of New York. 41: Dan DeWilde for Silver Burdett.

Chapter 3 47: Natural History Museum of Los Angeles County. 48: Courtesy of the American Museum of Natural History. 49: © Georg Gerster/Photo Researchers, Inc. 50: E. R. Degginger. 51: Silver Burdett. 52: Kyuzo Tsugami. 53: J. R. Eyerman/Black Star. 54: James Jerome Hill Reference Library, St. Paul, Minnesota. 55: © 1984 Jeffrey Jay Foxx/Woodfin Camp & Associates. 56: Museum of the American Indian. 57: © George Holton/Photo Researchers, Inc. 59: © Robert Frerck. 61: Courtesy of the American Museum of Natural History.

Chapter 4 65: Courtesy of the U. S. Naval Academy Museum/Photo by M. E. Warren for Silver Burdett. 66: Ted Spiegel/Black Star. 67: Don Pulver. 69, 70, 73: The Bettmann Archive. 76: From the art collection of Business Men's Assurance Company, Kansas City, Missouri. 79: © 1979 Imagery. 80, 81: Culver Pictures.

Chapter 5 85: © Farrell Grehan/Photo Researchers, Inc. 87: Colonial Williamsburg. 88: Joseph LeMonnier/Craven Design Studio, Inc. 90: Culver Pictures. 91: The Bettmann Archive. 92: Greg Derr for Silver Burdett. 93: *Paul Revere*, by John Singleton Copley, Gift of Joseph W., William B., and Edward H. R. Revere, Courtesy, Museum of Fine Arts, Boston. 94: Enoch Pratt Free Library, Baltimore. 95: Taylor Oughton. 96: The Schomburg Center, The New York Public Library, Astor, Lenox and Tilden Foundations. 97: Kyuzo Tsugami. 99: Parker Galleries, London. 100: The Title Guarantee Company. 103: Culver Pictures.

Chapter 6 107: Selectmen's Room, Abbot Hall, Marblehead, Massachusetts. 109: The Bettmann Archive. 111: J. Clarence Davies Collection, Museum of the City of New York. 112: Architect of the Capitol. 114: The Valley Forge Historical Society. 116: The Granger Collection. 117: The Bettmann Archive. 119: Nebraska State Building Division. 123: Les Moore/UNIPHOTO.

Chapter 7 127: Private Collection of John and Lillian Harney. 130: White House Historical Association. 132: t. Eric Carle/Shostal Associates; b. © Lee Battaglia/Photo Researchers, Inc. 133: Port of New Orleans. 136: Les Moore/UNIPHOTO. 138: Courtesy of the U.S. Naval Academy Museum. 139: White House Historical Association. 140: Library of Congress. 142: United Press International. 143: The Bettmann Archive.

Chapter 8 147: t. C. R. Smith Collection, University of Texas, Austin, Texas; b. Prints Division, The New York Public Library, Stokes Collection. 149: Yale University Art Gallery, Mabel Brady Garvan Collection. 150: State Historical Society of Wisconsin. 152: Library of Congress. 153: San Jacinto Museum of History Association. 154: © 1979 Mical Heron. 155: Kyuzo Tsugami. 156: The Bettmann Archive. 158: The Schomburg Center, The New York Public Library, Astor, Lenox and Tilden Foundations. 160: Taylor Oughton. 161: Pat O'Hara/Visualeyes.

Chapter 9 167: U.S. Department of the Interior, National Park Service, Gettysburg National Military Park. 170: The Cincinnati Art Museum. 171: Culver Pictures. 173: The Bettmann Archive. 174: Harry T. Peters Collection, Museum of the City of New York. 175: Library of Congress. 177: U.S. Department of the Interior, National Park Service, Appomattox Court House National Historical Park. 178: Library of Congress. 180: The Bettmann Archive. 181: Library of Congress. 182: Culver Pictures.

Chapter 10 187: Harry T. Peters Collection, Museum of the City of New York. 188: The Nebraska State Historical Society. 189: California State Library. 193: Historical Pictures Service, Chicago. 194: Utah State Historical Society. 195: Manuscripts and Archives Department, Baker Library, Harvard University. 197: l. The Denver Public Library, Western History Department; r. National Archives. 199: Library of Congress.

Chapter 11 203: t. National Archives; b. © Harald Sund. 205: Library of Congress. 206: © M. E. Warren/Photo Researchers, Inc. 207, 209, 210: Culver Pictures. 211: The Bettmann Archive. 212: Culver Pictures. 213: Andrew Sacks/Black Star. 214: l. Phil Matt/Liaison; r. Jim Howard/Alpha. 216: Jacob Riis Collection, Museum of the City of New York. 217: l. Laurence R. Lowry; r. The Bettmann Archive. 219: The Des Moines Register.

Chapter 12 223: Courtesy of the U.S. Naval Academy Museum. 225: © Gemini Smith, Inc./Photo Researchers, Inc., from a lithograph in the Library of Congress. 226: Culver Pictures. 228: Brown Brothers. 229: U. S. Marine Corps Art Collection. 231: Culver Pictures. 232: t. Department of the Army; b. Culver Pictures. 234: National Archives. 237: Leon V. Kofod.

Chapter 13 241: Russell Bronson/Black Star; *inset*, Harry Benson/Gamma-Liaison. 243: © Dick Rowan/Photo Researchers, Inc. 244: Ford Archives/Henry Ford Museum, Dearborn, Michigan. 245: Culver Pictures. 246: © 1984 John Ficara/Woodfin Camp & Associates. 248: Wide World Photos. 249: Wide World Photos.

Chapter 14 255: Ed Malles/Southern Light. 260: Cary Wolinsky/Stock, Boston. 261: Dick Durrance II/Woodfin Camp & Associates. 262: © Kent and Donna Dannen/Photo Researchers, Inc. 264: Harald Sund. 266: Paul Cerny. 267: t. © 1984 Chuck O'Rear/Woodfin Camp & Associates; b. Hanson Carroll/Peter Arnold, Inc. 272: NASA 278: Bucyrus Erie. 282: © Harald Sund.

Chapter 15 287: Laurence R. Lowry. 290: Barre Granite Association. 291: Bohdan Hrynewych/Stock, Boston. 293: Laurence R. Lowry. 295: © Dick Hanley/Photo Researchers, Inc. 296: l. © 1978 Michael Philip Manheim; r. G. H. Coffman/Taurus Photos. 297: International Paper Company. 298: Ric Del Rossi. 300: © Robert Perron/Photo Researchers, Inc. 301: t. Clyde Smith/Peter Arnold, Inc.; b. © Farrell Grehan/Photo Researchers, Inc. 304: Ivan Massar/Black Star.

Chapter 16 311: E. R. Degginger. 313: Paul Pasquarello/Gamma-Liaison. 314: © Thomas D. W. Friedmann/Photo Researchers, Inc. 315: John Colwell/Grant Heilmann Photography. 317: Ric Del Rossi. 318: Jack Wolfe. 319: D. Brewster/Bruce Coleman. 321: Cary Wolinsky/Stock, Boston. 323: © Porterfield-Chickering/Photo Researchers, Inc.

Chapter 17 329: Laurence R. Lowry. 330: © Robert C. Hermes/Photo Researchers, Inc. 331: © Jerry Cooke/Photo Researchers, Inc. 333: Herman J. Kokojan/Black Star. 334: © Bruce Roberts/Photo Researchers, Inc. 335: © Russ Kinne/Photo Researchers, Inc. 336: E. R. Degginger. 337: © Steve Proehl/Photo Researchers, Inc. 338: © Farrell Grehan/Photo Researchers, Inc. 340: Gilles Vauclair/The Stock Shop. 341: © Van Bucher/Photo Researchers, Inc. 342: l. © 1984 Michal Heron/Woodfin Camp & Associates; r. West Virginia Department of Commerce/Photo by Gerald S. Ratliff.

Chapter 18 349: NASA. 350, 352: E. R. Degginger. 354: Silver Burdett. 356: Christopher Harris/Shostal Associates. 358: © 1984 Craig Aurness/Woodfin Camp & Associates. 359: © Dan Guravich/Photo Researchers, Inc. 360: C. Harris/Shostal Associates.

Chapter 19 367: © Harald Sund. 368: © Phil Degginger. 370, 371: Joseph LeMonnier/Craven Design Studio, Inc. 374: © Phil Degginger. 377: J. Fire/Shostal Associates. 378: Donald Dietz/Stock, Boston. 379: Robert Frerck/Odyssey Productions. 380: Robert Lee II.

Chapter 20 388: D. Dietrich/Shostal Associates. 390: Joseph LeMonnier/Craven Design Studio, Inc. 392: Adam Woolfitt/ Woodfin Camp & Associates. 393: Jeffrey Aaronson. 394: S. Voynick/Shostal Associates. 396: © Phil Degginger.

Chapter 21 404: © Harald Sund. 406: The Lens Unlimited, photography by Stu Rothman. 407: E. R. Degginger. 409: t. David Forbert/Shostal Associates. b. Ric Del Rossi. 411: Pro Pix/Monkmeyer Press. 414: Penelope Breese/Liaison. 415: Mitchell Barosh/Shostal Associates.

Chapter 22 423: G. Baer/Shostal Associates. 425: A. Williams/Shostal Associates. 429: Ted Hankey. 430: © G. R. Roberts/Photo Researchers, Inc. 431: t. Malek/Shostal Associates; b. Lillian N. Bolstad/Peter Arnold, Inc. 432: Eric Carle/Shostal Associates. 433: t. K. Sholz/Shostal Associates; b.l. Eric Carle/Shostal Associates; b.r. Eric Carle/Shostal Associates.

Chapter 23 443: Eric Carle/Shostal Associates. 445: © Gianni Tortoli/Photo Researchers, Inc. 447: G. Ziesler/Peter Arnold, Inc. 449: Joan Kramer & Associates. 451: R. Rosene/Shostal Associates. 453: G. Ricatto/Shostal Associates.

Epilogue 460, 462, 463, 464: Den Schofield.

8 9 — RRD — 99 98